PREPARING
Reading Professionals

SECOND EDITION

Rita M. Bean, Natalie Heisey, Cathy M. Roller

EDITORS

INTERNATIONAL
Reading Association
800 BARKSDALE ROAD, PO BOX 8139
NEWARK, DE 19714-8139, USA
www.reading.org

The International Reading Association attempts, through its publications, to provide a forum for a wide spectrum of opinions on reading. This policy permits divergent viewpoints without implying the endorsement of the Association.

Executive Editor, Books   Corinne M. Mooney
Developmental Editor   Charlene M. Nichols
Developmental Editor   Tori Mello Bachman
Developmental Editor   Stacey L. Reid
Editorial Production Manager   Shannon T. Fortner
Design and Composition Manager   Anette Schuetz

Project Editors   Charlene M. Nichols and Christina Terranova

Cover   Design, Adam Bohannon; Photographs (from left): © Veer Incorporated, © iStockphoto.com/kate_sept2004, © iStockphoto.com/ranplett

The publisher would appreciate notification where errors occur so that they may be corrected in subsequent printings and/or editions.

Library of Congress Cataloging-in-Publication Data
Preparing reading professionals / edited by Rita M. Bean, Natalie Heisey, and Cathy M. Roller. -- 2nd ed.
   p. cm.
 Includes bibliographical references.
 ISBN 978-0-87207-835-2
 1. Reading teachers--Training of--Standards--United States. I. Bean, Rita M. II. Heisey, Natalie. III. Roller, Cathy M. IV. International Reading Association.
 LB2844.1.R4P75 2010
 428.4'071--dc22

                                            2010025557

Suggested APA Reference
Bean, R.M., Heisey, N., & Roller, C.M. (Eds.). (2010). *Preparing reading professionals* (second edition). Newark, DE: International Reading Association.

Contents

Part 4: Diversity 203

Part 5: Literate Environment 263

Part 6: Professional Learning and Leadership 299

About the Editors

 **Rita M. Bean**, PhD, is Professor Emerita in the School of Education at the University of Pittsburgh, Pennsylvania, USA. Her newest book, *The Reading Specialist: Leadership for the Classroom, School, and Community* (2nd ed.), focuses on the role of the reading specialist, especially the leadership role. Prior to joining the University of Pittsburgh, Rita taught at the elementary level and also served as a reading supervisor for grades K–12. Rita has been an active member of the International Reading Association (IRA) at the local, state, and national levels. She served as a member of the IRA Board of Directors and as chair of several committees, including the Role of the Reading Specialist (1997–2000) and the Standards for the Preparation of Reading Professionals 2010.

Rita has published in many journals, monographs, and books on the topics of reading curriculum and instruction, professional development, and role of reading specialists/literacy coaches. Her current research focuses on the development and evaluation of early literacy reading programs and instruction for struggling readers. She has also studied the roles of the reading specialist and literacy coach in enhancing teacher practices and improving student achievement. A recent study about coaching, "Coaches and Coaching in Reading First Schools: A Reality Check," has been accepted for publication in *The Elementary School Journal*. Rita has received the Distinguished Teacher Award and the Chancellor's Distinguished Public Service Award from the University of Pittsburgh.

She is married to Tony Eichelberger, also a retired professor, and she has two stepchildren and three grandchildren. Tony and Rita enjoy their grandparenting responsibilities, reading, traveling, and golfing. Rita can be reached at ritabean@pitt.edu.

 **Natalie Heisey** is an assistant professor in the Department of Education at Geneva College in Beaver Falls, Pennsylvania, USA. Prior to this, she was a postdoctoral scholar and adjunct instructor in the Department of Instruction and Learning at the University of Pittsburgh, Pennsylvania, USA. She is working with Linda Kucan, also at the University of Pittsburgh, and Annemarie Palincsar, at the University of Michigan, on their Institute of Education Sciences–funded grant entitled "The Iterative Design of Modules to Support Reading Comprehension Instruction." Natalie is a member of the International Reading Association, Keystone State Reading Association, Literacy Research Association, Association of Literacy Educators and Researchers, and American Educational Research Association.

Natalie completed her doctoral degree in reading at the University of Pittsburgh in April 2009. As a graduate student, Natalie served as the supervisor of the Reading Center and was a member of the External Evaluation Team for Reading First in Pennsylvania with Rita Bean and Naomi Zigmond. Natalie holds a master's degree in curriculum and instruction and a bachelor's degree in elementary and special education. She was a classroom teacher for 11 years in first and second grades. She enjoyed teaching in self-contained classrooms but is most passionate about the power of effective instruction in teaching young children to read.

Her publications include "Introducing Science Concepts to Primary Students Through Read-Alouds: Interactions and Multiple Texts Make the Difference" in the May 2010 volume of *The Reading Teacher* and "Outcomes of On-line Professional Development in Pennsylvania" in the *Fifty-Sixth Annual Yearbook of the National Reading Conference*. She can be reached at ndh@zoominternet.net.

 **Cathy M. Roller** served as the International Reading Association's Director of Research and Policy from 1998 through 2009. She directed the Standards for Reading Professionals projects and has enjoyed working with three different committees to produce Standards for Reading Professionals, 1998, 2003, and 2010, and Preparing Reading Professionals in 2003 and 2010. During her tenure at IRA, she focused considerable attention on teacher preparation for reading instruction. A series of projects included the National Commission on Excellence in Elementary Teacher Preparation for Reading, the work of which resulted in more than 20 refereed publications. She also led a group that prepared a research review published in 2008 in *Reading Research Quarterly*. At the behest of the Board of Directors, she developed the Status of Reading Instruction Institute, which is currently completing the first description of reading instruction in grades 1 and 4 based on a nationally representative sample of classrooms.

Cathy began her career in 1970 as a 10th-grade English teacher in Brimfield, Ohio, USA, and worked as a reading specialist in Tulsa, Oklahoma, USA, and Great Falls, Montana, USA. She completed her PhD at the University of Minnesota, Minneapolis, USA, and began her university career at the University of Iowa, Iowa City, USA, in 1979. She was a professor at the University of Iowa until 1998 when she left to work for IRA. As a professor, she published frequently in IRA's journals and other prominent journals and published two books with IRA: *Variability Not Disability: Struggling Readers in a Workshop Classroom* and *So...What's a Tutor to Do?* While at the University of Iowa, she codirected the University's Summer Residential Program in Speech, Hearing, and Reading (SRP). Her two IRA books tell the story of the struggling readers who attended SRP.

Cathy is currently retired and spends her time between Anna Maria Island, Florida, and Omaha, Nebraska. She may be reached at rollercm@gmail.com.

Introduction

Rita M. Bean, Natalie Heisey, and Cathy M. Roller

Preparing Reading Professionals (second edition) is a compilation of previously published pieces from the journals, books, and online publications of the International Reading Association. This collection serves two purposes: (1) It provides in-depth information to support and extend the content of *Standards for Reading Professionals, Revised 2010* (henceforth known as Standards 2010), and (2) It provides a collection of knowledge about what reading professionals need to know and be able to do. Therefore, this publication can be used by individual readers or as a text in college courses or workshops to inform those interested in developing a deeper understanding of essential learning for reading professionals.

Preparing Reading Professionals was developed to accompany Standards 2010, which describe what reading professionals—education support personnel, pre-K and elementary classroom teachers, middle and high school content classroom teachers, middle school and high school classroom reading teachers, reading specialists/literacy coaches, teacher educators, and administrators—should know and be able to do when they complete their preparation programs. Community college, college, and university faculties use Standards 2010 for program planning and evaluation. Accrediting bodies such as the National Council for Accreditation of Teacher Education, Teacher Education Accreditation Council, and state departments of education certification personnel also use Standards 2010 to make decisions about accrediting preparation programs.

Standards, of necessity, are developed to provide a usable number of elements, stated succinctly; for example, in Standards 2010, there are six standards and 21 elements, 3–4 elements for each standard. However, given that succinctness, users of the Standards 2010 document may desire and benefit from additional information that can assist them in using the standards for developing or evaluating programs. This collection provides that information; it includes book chapters, journal articles, and news briefs as well as suggestions for further reading that elaborate on the content of the Standards 2010. Following the suggestions for further reading are lists of 3–4 questions that can be used for reflection and discussion.

In developing the Standards 2010, the Standards Committee used a format similar to that used in Standards 2003. Each of the six standards in Standards 2010 begins with a statement of the standard; for example, Standard 2 states the following: "Candidates use instructional approaches, materials, and an integrated, comprehensive, balanced curriculum to support student learning in reading and writing." A matrix lists the standard's elements in the left column and the professional categories across the top; Table 1 provides a sample matrix for Element 2.1 of Standard 2. Each cell provides examples of evidence that can be used in determining whether a candidate demonstrates

Table 1
Standard 2: Curriculum and Instruction

Element	Evidence that demonstrates competence may include, but is not limited to, the following:						
Candidates...	Education Support Personnel Candidates	Pre-K and Elementary Classroom Teacher Candidates	Middle and High School Content Classroom Teacher Candidates	Middle and High School Reading Classroom Teacher Candidates	Reading Specialist/Literacy Coach Candidates	Teacher Educator Candidates	Administrator Candidates
2.1: Use foundational knowledge to design or implement an integrated, comprehensive, and balanced curriculum.	• Implement lessons that are part of the reading and writing curriculum with teacher guidance and supervision.	• Explain how the reading and writing curriculum is related to local, state, national and professional standards. • Implement the curriculum based on students' prior knowledge, world experiences, and interests. • Evaluate the curriculum to ensure that instructional goals and objectives are met. • Plan with other teachers and support personnel in designing, adjusting, and modifying the curriculum to meet students' needs in traditional print, digital, and online contexts.	• Explain how reading and writing relate to their content areas and to local, state, national and professional standards. • Implement the curriculum based on students' prior knowledge, world experiences, and interests. • Evaluate the curriculum to ensure that instructional goals and objectives meet the reading and writing demands of the content areas. • Work with other teachers and support personnel to design, adjust, and modify the curriculum to meet students' literacy needs. • Support students as agents of their own learning and critical consumers of the discipline.	• Explain how reading and writing relates to their content area and the local, state, national, and professional standards. • Implement the curriculum based on students' prior knowledge, world experiences, and interests. • Evaluate the curriculum to ensure that instructional goals and objectives are met. • Work with the team or department to help ensure interdisciplinary connections in traditional print, digital, and online contexts.	• Demonstrate an understanding of the research and literature that undergirds the reading and writing curriculum and instruction for all pre-K–12 students. • Develop and implement the curriculum to meet the specific needs of students who struggle with reading. • Support teachers and other personnel in the design, implementation, and evaluation of the reading and writing curriculum for all students. • Work with teachers and other personnel in developing a literacy curriculum that has vertical and horizontal alignment across pre-K–12.	• Demonstrate knowledge of and evaluate the pre-K–12 reading and writing curriculum. • Convey knowledge and understanding of the curriculum to reading professionals. • Provide opportunities for reading professionals to develop an integrated, comprehensive, and balanced curriculum.	• Monitor instruction to determine that local, state, and national standards are met. • Provide opportunities for review and alignment of the curriculum with local, state, and national standards.

competency of a specific standard and element. For example, consider Element 2.1: Candidates use foundational knowledge to design or implement an integrated, comprehensive, and balanced curriculum. The cell under the Education Support Personnel column suggests that these candidates should be able to implement lessons that are part of the reading and writing curriculum under the supervision of the classroom teacher while the cell under the Pre-K and Elementary Classroom Teacher column suggests that candidates should be able to explain, implement, evaluate, and plan.

Although this format meets the need for succinctness and utility by standards users, the Standards 2010 Committee recognizes that the standards may not be specific enough to give an in-depth picture of each standard's demands. Thus, in the Standards 2010 document, the Standards Committee identified the major assumptions and a list of resources for each of the six standards; these are found in the document itself. This book, *Preparing Reading Professionals*, provides another resource for those working with Standards 2010. The content of this publication provides more depth and detail than was possible in the Standards 2010 document, includes pieces that exemplify the standards in action, and suggests additional resources that may be useful for an in-depth understanding of the standards.

The selected book chapters, journal articles, and news briefs address one or more standard elements. Although they provide readers with a much more detailed picture of what is meant by a specific standard element, these examples are not definitive. In most cases, the selected text represents one among many possible representations of the element. The examples are intended to help readers visualize the standard element and see how it might be instantiated within their own programs.

The collection is organized into six parts that correspond to the six standards.

1. Foundational Knowledge—Candidates understand the theoretical and evidence-based foundations of reading and writing processes and instruction.

2. Curriculum and Instruction—Candidates use instructional approaches, materials, and an integrated, comprehensive, balanced curriculum to support student learning in reading and writing.

3. Assessment and Evaluation—Candidates use a variety of assessment tools and practices to plan and evaluate effective reading and writing instruction.

4. Diversity—Candidates create and engage their students in literacy practices that develop awareness, understanding, respect, and a valuing of differences in our society.

5. Literate Environment—Candidates create a literate environment that fosters reading and writing by integrating foundational knowledge, instructional practices, approaches and methods, curriculum materials, and the appropriate use of assessments.

6. Professional Learning and Leadership—Candidates recognize the importance of, demonstrate, and facilitate professional learning and leadership as a career-long effort and responsibility.

Again, not only is this compilation valuable to those interested in Standards 2010, but also to those involved in studying, developing, or evaluating programs for improving student literacy learning, including the school-based practitioner, the teacher educator, and researcher.

Foundational Knowledge

The Foundational Knowledge Standard recognizes the need to prepare reading professionals who are in command of the knowledge that provides the foundation for understanding reading and reading instruction. The elements of Standard 1 focus on the kinds of knowledge reading professionals have and use as they carry out their daily responsibilities. Standard 1 and its elements follow:

Standard 1. Foundational Knowledge. Candidates understand the theoretical and evidence-based foundations of reading and writing processes and instruction. As a result, candidates

- **Element 1.1 Understand major theories and empirical research that describe the cognitive, linguistic, motivational, and sociocultural foundations of reading and writing development, processes, and components, including word recognition, language comprehension, strategic knowledge, and reading–writing connections.**

- **Element 1.2 Understand the historically shared knowledge of the profession and changes over time in the perceptions of reading and writing development, processes, and components.**

- **Element 1.3 Understand the role of professional judgment and practical knowledge for improving all students' reading development and achievement.**

Part 1 contains one book chapter and one journal article that may be helpful in understanding the substance of the standard and its elements. These pieces are described briefly here.

Pearson (2002) provides a summary of the historical knowledge base shared by reading professionals, which is particularly useful for understanding Element 1.1. This chapter notes the influences of other fields of research such as linguistic and sociocultural on reading research and reading professionals, and it summarizes recent history related to reading research and reading instruction.

Invernizzi and Hayes (2004) provide an overview of the development of the English language over time and relate that knowledge to the teaching and learning of reading and writing. It is an excellent historical summary that pertains directly to instructional issues and is particularly useful for understanding Element 1.2. By

Preparing Reading Professionals (second edition), edited by Rita M. Bean, Natalie Heisey, and Cathy M. Roller. © 2010 by the International Reading Association.

developing a framework of language knowledge that relates to historical development and reading and writing acquisition—alphabet, pattern, and meaning—the authors provide essential knowledge about writing and meaning systems that underlie reading and learning to read.

Invernizzi and Hayes (2004) also offer examples of how professional judgment and practical knowledge influence reading professionals, as addressed in Element 1.3. They challenge the idea that science has identified one right way to teach early reading. They describe their work with teachers who questioned the efficacy of teaching phonics to whole classes, helping these teachers learn how to use assessment evidence to determine which students knew what sounds and to develop a small-group approach to provide students with the specific lessons they needed.

Further Reading

Afflerbach, P., Pearson, P.D., & Paris, S.G. (2008). Clarifying differences between reading skills and reading strategies. *The Reading Teacher, 61*(5), 364–373. doi:10.1598/RT.61.5.1

Cowen, J.E. (2003). *A balanced approach to beginning reading instruction: A synthesis of six major U.S. research studies.* Newark, DE: International Reading Association.

Hoffman, J.V., & Goodman, Y.M. (Eds.). (2009). *Changing literacies for changing times: An historical perspective on the future of reading research, public policy, and classroom practices.* Newark, DE: International Reading Association.

Huey, E.B. (2009). *The psychology and pedagogy of reading* (Special ed.). Newark, DE: International Reading Association.

Questions for Reflection and Discussion

- Sometimes critics of educational research claim that reading is not a stand-alone field. Respond to this statement in light of the Pearson article.

- Why is it important for reading professionals to know the history of reading instruction and reading research?

- Why is it important to use professional judgment and practical knowledge in making instructional decisions?

American Reading Instruction Since 1967

P. David Pearson

This chapter is an account of reading instruction in the last third of the 20th century, from roughly the late 1960s onward.[1] In fact, I take the publication of Jeanne Chall's (1967) *Learning to Read: The Great Debate* as my starting point. It will end, as do most essays written at a century's turn, with predictions about the future. My hope is to provide an account of the past and present of reading instruction that will render predictions about the future transparent. I will end this piece with my speculations about pedagogical journeys that lie ahead in a new century and a new millennium.

Beginning at Mid-Century
Setting the Scene: Reading in the 1960s

The period that spans roughly 1935 to 1965 is best viewed as a time in which we engaged in fine-tuning and elaboration of instructional models that were born in the first third of the century. Most important, the look-say approach (start off with a corpus of high-frequency sight words practiced often in highly controlled stories and then teach phonics on the basis of already taught words), which had started its ascendancy at the turn of the century, gained increasing momentum throughout the middle third of the century until, as has been documented in survey research conducted in the 1960s, over 90% of the students in the country were taught to read using one commercial variation of this approach or another.[2] So common was this approach that Jeanne Chall (1967) felt comfortable describing the then prevailing

 Dick & Jane

approach as a set of principles, which can be roughly paraphrased as follows:[3]

- The goals of reading from the beginning of grade 1 should include comprehension, interpretation, and application, as well as word recognition.
- Instruction should begin with meaningful silent reading of stories that are grounded in children's experiences and interests.
- After a corpus of sight words is learned (between 50 and 100), analytic phonics instruction should begin. Phonics should be regarded as one of many cueing systems, including context and picture cues, available to children to unlock new words.
- Phonics instruction should be spread over several years rather than concentrated in the early grades.
- Phonics instruction should be contextualized rather than isolated from real words and texts. *Whole language*
- The words in the early texts (grades 1–3) should be carefully controlled for frequency of use and repeated often to ensure mastery.
- Children should get off to a slow and easy start, probably through a readiness program; those judged as not ready for formal reading instruction should experience an even longer readiness period.
- Children should be instructed in small groups.

Although a few elements in her list are new, such as the early emphasis on comprehension

Preparing Reading Professionals (second edition), edited by Rita M. Bean, Natalie Heisey, and Cathy M. Roller. © 2010 by the International Reading Association. Reprinted from Pearson, P.D. (2002). American reading instruction since 1967. In N.B. Smith, *American Reading Instruction* (Special ed., pp. 419–486). Newark, DE: International Reading Association.

and interpretation and the contextualization of phonics instruction, virtually all the elements introduced in the early part of the century were included in her description of the conventional wisdom of the 1960s. A few things are missing when one compares Chall's list of principles underlying the conventional wisdom with our earlier account of the key developments through 1935. One is the role of skills in commercial reading programs. Although skills did not make it onto Chall's (1967) list of principles, it is clear from several chapters (specifically, Chapters 7 and 8) that she was mindful of their importance and curricular ubiquity. By the 1960s, skills lessons in the teachers' manual, accompanied by workbooks allowing students to practice the skills, were much more elaborate than in the 1930s, 40s, or 50s. The other missing piece is the elaborate development of the teachers' manual. Earlier, I implied that the manuals got larger with each succeeding edition of a series. By the middle 1960s, the small teachers' guide section in the back of the children's book of the 1920s and 30s had expanded to the point where the number of pages devoted to the teachers' guide equaled the number of student text pages in the upper grades, and exceeded it in the primary grades.[4]

The materials of the 1960s continued traditions begun early in the century and documented in great detail in Nila Banton Smith's editions of *American Reading Instruction*.[5] Students read stories and practiced skills. Text difficulty was carefully controlled in the basal reading materials published between the 1930s and the 1960s. In the earliest readers (preprimer through first reader, at least), vocabulary was sequenced in order of decreasing frequency of word usage in everyday written and oral language. Because many of the most frequent words are not regularly spelled (*the, of, what, where*, etc.), this frequency principle provided a good fit with the whole-word or look-say emphasis characteristic of the words-to-reading approach so dominant during this period.

Students were still the recipients and teachers still the mediators of the received curriculum. Meaning and silent reading were more

important in the 1960s version of reading curriculum than in 1900 or 1935, as evidenced by a steady increase in the amount of time and teachers' manual space devoted to comprehension activities; but it was still not at the core of the look-say approach. When all is said and done, the underlying model of reading in the 1960s was still a pretty straightforward perceptual process; the simple view—that comprehension is the product of decoding and listening comprehension (RC = Dec* LC)—still prevailed. Readers still accomplished the reading task by translating graphic symbols (letters) on a printed page into an oral code (sounds corresponding to those letters), which was then treated by the brain as oral language. In both the look-say approach to learning sight vocabulary and its analytic approach to phonics, whether the unit of focus is a word or a letter, the basic task for the student is to translate from the written to the oral code. This view of reading was quite consistent with the prevailing instructional emphasis on skills. If sight words and phonics knowledge was what children needed to learn in order to perform the translation process, then decomposing phonics into separable bits of knowledge (letter-to-sound, or in the case of spelling, sound-to-letter, correspondences), each of which could be presented, practiced, and tested independently, was the route to helping them acquire that knowledge.

The Legacy of the Scholarship of the 1960s

In beginning reading, the decade of the 1960s was a period of fervent activity. In the early 1960s, in an effort to settle the debate about the best way to teach beginning reading once and for all (this time with the tools of empirical scholarship rather than rhetoric), the Cooperative Research Branch of the United States Office of Education funded an elaborate collection of "First-Grade Studies," loosely coupled forays into the highly charged arena of preferred approaches to beginning reading instruction.[6] Although each of the studies differed from one another in the particular emphasis, most of them involved a comparison of different methods of teaching beginning reading. They were published in a brand new journal, *Reading Research Quarterly*, in 1966. Jeanne Chall completed her magnum opus, *Learning to Read: The Great Debate*, in 1967. It, too, had been funded in order to put the debate behind, but Chall would use different scholarly tools to accomplish her goals. She would employ critical review procedures to examine our empirical research base, the content of our basal readers, and exemplary classroom practices. In 1965, Lyndon Johnson's Elementary and Secondary Education Act, one key plank in his Great Society platform, brought new resources for compensatory education to schools through a program dubbed Title I. And, Commissioner of Education James Allen would, at decade's end, establish the national Right to Read program as a way of guaranteeing that right to each child in the United States. The country was clearly focused on early reading, and many were optimistic that we would find answers to the questions about teaching reading that had vexed us for decades, even centuries.

Chall's book and the First-Grade Studies had an enormous impact on beginning reading instruction and indirectly on reading pedagogy more generally. One message of the First-Grade Studies was that just about any alternative, when compared to the business-as-usual basals (which served as a common control in each of 20+ separate quasi-experimental studies), elicited equal or greater performance on the part of first graders (and, as it turned out, second graders).[7] It did not seem to matter much what the alternative was—language experience, a highly synthetic phonics approach, a linguistic approach (control the text so that young readers are exposed early on only to easily decodable words grouped together in word families, such as the -*an* family, the -*at* family, the -*ig* family, etc.), a special alphabet (i.e., the Initial Teaching Alphabet), or even basals infused with a heavier-than-usual dose of phonics right up front—they were all the equal or the better of the ubiquitous basal. A second message, one that was both sent and received, was that

the racehorse mentality of studies that pits one method against another to see which would win had probably run its course. By accepting this message, the reading research community was free to turn its efforts to other, allegedly more fruitful, issues and questions—the importance of the teacher, quite irrespective of method, the significance of site, and the press of other aspects of the curriculum such as comprehension and writing.[8] With the notable exception of the Follow-Through Studies in the 1970s, which are only marginally related to reading, it would take another 25 years for large-scale experiments to return to center stage in reading.[9]

In spite of a host of other important recommendations, most of which had some short-term effect, the ultimate legacy of Chall's book reduces to just one—that early attention to the code in some way, shape, or form must be reinfused into early reading instruction. For the record, Chall recommended five broad changes, each of which will be discussed later:

(1) make a necessary change in method (to an early emphasis on phonics of some sort),

(2) reexamine current ideas about content (focus on the enduring themes in folktales),

(3) reevaluate grade levels (increase the challenge at every grade level),

(4) develop new tests (both single-component tests and absolute measures with scores that are independent of the population taking the test), and

(5) improve reading research (including its accessibility).

The look-say basals that had experienced virtually uninterrupted progress from 1930 to 1965 never quite recovered from the one-two punch delivered by Chall's book and the First-Grade Studies in 1967. Given the critical sacking they took from Chall and the empirical thrashing they took from the First-Grade Studies, one might have expected one of the pretenders to the early reading throne, documented so carefully in the First-Grade Studies, to assume the mantle of the new conventional wisdom in the years that followed. Ironically, it was the basals themselves, albeit in a radically altered form, that captured the marketplace of the 1970s and 1980s. This feat was accomplished by overhauling basals to adapt to a changing market shaped by these two important scholarly efforts. Basal programs that debuted in the five years after Chall's book appeared were radically different from their predecessors. Most notably, phonics, which had been relegated to a skill to be taught contextually after a hefty bank of sight words had been committed to memory, was back—from day one of grade 1—in the series that hit the market in the late 1960s and early 1970s. Surprisingly, it was not the highly synthetic alphabetic approach of the previous century or the remedial clinics of the 1930s (which one might have expected from reading Chall's book). It is better described as an intensification and repositioning (to grade 1) of the analytic phonics that had been taught in the latter part of grade 1, and in grades 2 to 4 in the look-say basals of the 1960s.[10] Equally significant, there was a change in content, at least in grade 1. Dick and Jane and all their assorted pairs of competing cousins—Tom and Susan, Alice and Jerry, Jack and Janet—were retired from the first-grade curriculum and replaced by a wider array of stories and characters; by the early 1970s, more of the selections were adaptations of children's literature rather than stories written to conform to a vocabulary restriction or a readability formula.

It is difficult to determine how seriously educators and publishers took Chall's other three recommendations. For example, in the basals that came out after Chall, the grade 1 books (the preprimers, primers, and readers) were considerably more challenging than their immediate predecessors, mainly by virtue of a much more challenging grade 1 vocabulary—more words introduced much earlier in the grade 1 program.[11] One series even divided its new vocabulary words into words that ought to be introduced explicitly as sight words, and those words, which they dubbed decodable, which should be recognized by the students by

applying the phonics skills they had been taught up to that point in the program.[12] Beyond grade 1, however, changes in difficulty were much less visible, and no appreciable increase in the readability scores of these later levels occurred.

In testing, a major change toward single-component tests did occur, although it is difficult to attribute this change solely to Chall's recommendation. Beginning in the early 1970s and continuing through at least the late 1980s, each successive edition of basal programs brought an increase in the number of single-component tests—tests for each phonics skill (all the beginning, middle, and final consonant sounds; vowel patterns; and syllabication), tests for each comprehension skill (main idea, finding details, drawing conclusions, and determining cause-effect relations) at every grade level, tests for alphabetical order and using the encyclopedia, and just about any other skill that comes to mind.

But, other events and movements of the period also pointed toward single-component tests. For one, owing to the intellectual contributions of Benjamin Bloom and John Carroll, the mastery learning movement[13] was gathering its own momentum during the late 1960s. According to proponents of mastery learning, if a complex domain could be decomposed into manageable subcomponents, each of which could be taught and learned to some predetermined level of mastery, then most, if not all, students should be able to master the knowledge and skills in the domain. Second, criterion-referenced tests were spawned during this same period.[14] The logic of criterion-referenced assessment was that some predetermined level of mastery (say 80% correct), not the average for a group of students in a given grade level, ought to be the reference point for determining how well a student was doing on a test. A third construct from this period, curriculum-embedded assessment,[15] held that students should be held accountable for precisely what was needed for them to march successfully through a particular curriculum—no less, no more. If one could specify the scope and sequence of knowledge and skills in the curriculum and develop assessments

more like current basal content

for each, then it should be possible to guide all students through the curriculum, even if some needed more practice and support than others. One can imagine a high degree of compatibility among all three of these powerful constructs—mastery learning, criterion-referenced assessment, and curriculum-embedded assessment. All three provide comfortable homes for single-component assessments of the sort Chall was advocating.

With powerful evidence from mastery learning's application to college students,[16] publishers of basal programs and some niche publishers began to create and implement what came to be called skills management systems.[17] In their most meticulous application, these systems became the reading program. Students took a battery of mastery tests, practiced those skills they had not mastered (usually by completing worksheets that looked remarkably like the tests), took tests again, and continued this cycle until they had mastered all the skills assigned to the grade level (or until the year ended). Unsurprisingly, the inclusion of these highly specific skill tests had the effect of increasing the salience of workbooks, worksheets, and other skill materials that students could practice on in anticipation of (and as a consequence of) mastery tests. Thus, the basals of this period were comprised of two parallel systems: (1) the graded series of anthologies filled with stories and short nonfiction pieces for oral and silent reading and discussion, and (2) an embedded skills management system to guide the development of phonics, comprehension, vocabulary, and study skills.

Chall's last recommendation was to improve reading research. Research had been too inaccessible (to the very audience of practitioners who most needed it), too narrow in scope, and too dismissive of its past. All that needed to change, she argued. As I will detail in the next section, reading research changed dramatically, but not necessarily in a direction Chall envisioned.

One other change in basal reading programs in this period worth noting was the technology that placed reduced facsimiles of student text pages onto pages surrounded by teaching suggestions and questions for guided reading. This was hailed as a major advance in the utility of manuals, because teachers did not have to turn back and forth from student text to the teachers' section in order to guide the reading of a story.

This was the scene, then, in the early 1970s, just as the reading field was about to embark on a new curricular trek that continues even today. If the middle third of the century was characterized by a steady, unwavering march toward the ever-increasing prominence of a particular philosophy and set of curricular practices encapsulated in ubiquitous basals that championed a look-say approach,[18] the early 1970s brought major challenges in philosophy and pedagogy—harder texts, more phonics, and a skill development program unlike anything seen before.[19]

But even with some alterations in the materials available and some new pedagogical twists, the pedagogy of the early 1970s revealed little fundamental change in the underlying assumptions about the role of the teacher and learner or the nature of reading and writing. Teachers, armed with their basal manuals, controlled the learning situation as never before, and students continued to play the role of passive recipient of the knowledge and skills mediated by the teacher. Most important, reading was still a fundamentally perceptual process of translating letters into sounds. If anything, the perceptual nature of reading was made more salient in the 1950s and 1960s by the return of phonics to center stage.

Developments in the Last Third of the Century

Reading as the Province of Other Scholarly Traditions[20]

Somewhere during this period (the exact point of departure is hard to fix), we began a journey that would take us through many new twists and turns on the way to different landscapes than we had visited before. Along the way, we confronted fundamental shifts in our views of reading and writing and began to create a variety of serious curricular alternatives to the conventional wisdom of the 1970s. Just beyond the horizon lay even more unfamiliar and rockier territory—the conceptual revolutions in cognition, sociolinguistics, and philosophy—which would have such far-reaching consequences for reading curriculum and pedagogy of the 1980s and 1990s.

Reading became an ecumenical scholarly commodity; it was embraced by scholars from many different fields of inquiry. The first to take reading under their wing were the linguists, who wanted to convince us that reading was a language process closely allied to the language processes of writing, speaking, and listening. Then came the psycholinguists and the cognitive psychologists, followed soon by the sociolinguists, the philosophers, the literary critics, and the critical theorists. It is not altogether clear why reading has attracted such interest from scholars in so many other fields. One explanation is that reading is considered by so many to be a key to success in other endeavors in and out of school; this is often revealed in comments such as, "Well if you don't learn to read, you can't learn other things for yourself." Another is that scholars in these other disciplines thought that the educationists had it all wrong, and it was time for another group to have their say. Whatever the reasons, the influence of these other scholarly traditions on reading pedagogy is significant; in fact, the pedagogy of the 1980s and 1990s cannot be understood without a firm grounding in the changes in world view that these perspectives spawned.

Linguistics. In 1962, Charles Fries wrote a book entitled *Linguistics and Reading*. In it, he outlined what he thought the teaching of reading would look like if it were viewed from the perspective of linguistics. In the same decade, several other important books and articles appeared, each carrying essentially the same message: The perspective of the modern science of linguistics, we were told, would privilege different models and methods of teaching reading. It would tell us, for example, that some

things do not need to be taught explicitly because the oral language takes care of them more or less automatically. For example, the three different pronunciations of -*ed*, (as in *nabbed, capped,* and *jaded*), need not be taught as a reading skill because our oral language conventions determine the pronunciation almost perfectly. English in its oral form demands the voiced alternative /d/ after a voiced consonant such as /b/. It demands the unvoiced alternative /t/ after an unvoiced consonant, such as /p/, and it requires the syllabic version /∂d/ after either /d/ or /t/. To teach these rules, which are very complex, would likely make things more confusing than simply allowing the oral language to do its work without fanfare.

Another linguistic insight came to us from the transformational generative grammars that replaced conventional structural linguistics as the dominant paradigm within the field during the 1960s and 70s. Noam Chomsky published two revolutionary treatises during this period: *Syntactic Structures* in 1957 and *Aspects of a Theory of Syntax* in 1965. With these books, Chomsky revolutionized the field of linguistics and paved the way, theoretically, for equally dramatic changes in the way that psychologists thought about and studied the processes of language comprehension and language acquisition.

Chomsky also provided the basis for a nativist view about language acquisition—a view that holds that humans come to the world "wired" to acquire the language of the community into which they are born. He and others drew this inference from two basic and contrasting facts about language: (a) language is incredibly complex, and (b) language is acquired quite easily and naturally by children living in an environment in which they are simply exposed to (rather than taught!) the language of their community well before they experience school. Only a view that children are equipped with some special cognitive apparatus for inferring complex rules could explain this remarkable feat.

Because our prevailing views of both reading comprehension and reading acquisition were derived from the same behavioristic assumptions that Chomsky and his peers had attacked, reading scholars began to wonder whether those assumptions would hold up when we applied similar perspectives and criticisms to analyses of written language comprehension and acquisition.[21]

Psycholinguistics. During the decade after the publication of *Syntactic Structures*, a new field of inquiry, psycholinguistics, evolved. In its first several years of existence, the field devoted itself to determining whether the views of linguistic competence and language acquisition that had been set forth by Chomsky and his colleagues could serve as psychological models of language performance. Although the effort to develop a simple mapping from Chomsky to models of language performance waned after a few unsatisfactory attempts, the field of psycholinguistics and the disposition of psychologists to study language with complex theoretical tools had been firmly established.

Particularly influential on our thinking about reading were scholars of language acquisition,[22] who established the rule-governed basis of language learning. In contrast to earlier views, these psycholinguists found that children did not imitate written language; rather, as members of a language community, they were participants in language and invented for themselves rules about how oral language worked. This insight allowed researchers to explain such constructions as "I eated my dinner" and "I gots two foots." Roger Brown and his colleagues showed conclusively that children were active learners who inferred rules and tested them out. Much as Kenneth Goodman would later show with written language, "mistakes," especially overgeneralizations, in oral language could be used to understand the rule systems that children were inventing for themselves.

The analogy with oral language development was too tempting for reading educators to resist. Several adopted something like a nativist framework in studying the acquisition of reading, asking what the teaching of reading and writing would look like if we assumed that

nativist view (Chomsky)

children can learn to read and write in much the same way as they learn to talk, that is, naturally. What would happen if we assumed that children were members of a community in which reading and writing are valued activities that serve important communication functions? What if we assumed that the most important factors in learning to read and write were having genuine reasons for communicating in these media and having access to a database in which there was so much print and talk about print that students could discover the patterns and regularities on their own, much as they do when they discover the patterns and regularities of oral language? Although the seminal work involved in putting these assumptions to empirical tests would wait for a couple of decades, the seeds of doubt about our perceptually based views of reading acquisition were firmly planted by the middle 1960s.

Two influential individuals, Kenneth Goodman and Frank Smith, led the reading field in addressing these kinds of questions. In 1965, Goodman demonstrated that the errors children made while reading orally were better viewed as windows into the inner workings of their comprehension processes than as mistakes to be corrected. He found that the mistakes that children made while reading in context revealed that they were trying to make sense of what they read. In another seminal piece, "Reading: A Psycholinguistic Guessing Game," Goodman (1967) laid out the elements of language that he thought readers employed as they constructed meaning for the texts they encountered. In reading, he conjectured, readers use three cue systems to make sense of text: syntactic cues, semantic cues, and graphophonemic cues. By attending to all these cue sources, Goodman contended, readers could reduce their uncertainty about unknown words or meanings, thus rendering both the word identification and comprehension processes more manageable.[23]

Smith's revolutionary ideas were first presented in 1971 in a book entitled, *Understanding Reading*.[24] In this seminal text, Smith argued that reading was not something one was taught, but rather something one learned to do. Smith believed that there were no special prerequisites to learning to read, indeed, that reading was simply making sense of one particular type of information in our environment. As such, reading was what one learned to do as a consequence of belonging to a literate society. One learned to read from reading. The implication, which Smith made explicit, was that the "function of teachers is not so much to teach reading as to help children read" (p. 3). This certainly challenged the notion of the teacher as the individual who meted out knowledge and skills to passively waiting students. For Smith, all knowing and all learning were constructive processes; individuals made sense of what they encountered based on what they already knew.[25] Even perception, he contended, was a decision-making, predictive process based on prior knowledge.

Smith also argued that reading was only incidentally visual. By that, Smith meant that being able to see was necessary but not sufficient to achieve understanding. He identified four sources of information: orthographic, syntactic, semantic, and visual, all of which he claimed were somewhat redundant. He argued that skilled readers made use of the three sources that were part of their prior knowledge (the orthographic, syntactic, and semantic) in order to minimize their reliance on visual information. In fact, the danger in relying too heavily on visual information is that readers might lose sight of meaning.

The psycholinguistic perspective had a number of influences on reading pedagogy. First, it valued literacy experiences that focused on making meaning. This meant that many classroom activities, particularly worksheets and games, which focused on enabling skills such as specific letter-sound correspondences, syllabication activities, structural analysis skills, specific comprehension activities, or study skills, were devalued. Second, it helped us to value texts for beginning readers (see Table 1, example 1) in which authors relied on natural language patterns, thus making it possible for emerging readers to use their knowledge of language to predict words and meanings. This meant that texts that relied on high-frequency words in short, choppy sentences (what we have come to call "basalese"; see Table 1, example 2) or those based on the systematic application of some phonics element (i.e., a decodable text; see Table 1, example 3) were correspondingly devalued.

Third, the psycholinguistic perspective helped us to understand the reading process and to appreciate children's efforts as readers. Errors were no longer things to be corrected; instead, they were windows into the workings of the child's mind, allowing both the teacher and the child to understand more about the reading process and reading strategies. Understanding miscues also helped educators focus on comprehension and appreciate risk-taking.

Fourth, psycholinguists gave us a means (miscue analysis) and a theory (reading as a constructive process) that was remarkably distinct from previous ideas about reading. The perspective made explicit links between oral and written language acquisition and helped us view reading as language rather than simply perception or behavior. In a sense, psycholinguistics continued the changes and traditions begun by the linguistic perspective; however, within the reading field, its influence was deeper and broader than its academic predecessor.

Table 1
Sample Texts for Beginning Reading

1. Red Fox, Red Fox, what do you see?
   I see a blue bird looking at me.
   Blue Bird, Blue Bird, what do you see?
   I see a green frog looking at me.
   Anon, anon.

2. Run, John, run.
   Run to Dad.
   Dad will run.
   Run, Dad.
   Run, John.
   See them run.

3. Nat can bat.
   Nat can bat with the fat bat.
   The cat has the fat bat.
   The rat has the fat bat.
   Nat has the fat bat.
   Bat the bat, Nat.

Most important, psycholinguistics affected our views of teaching and learning in a fundamental way. Reading scholars began to rethink ideas about what needed to be taught, as well as the relation between teaching and learning. So, instead of asking, "What can I teach this child so that she will eventually become a reader?" we began to ask, "What can I do to help this child as a reader so she will make the progress she deserves to make?" Some teachers began to welcome all children into what Smith referred to as "The Literacy Club" as an alternative to teaching children so-called prerequisite skills.[26]

Cognitive Psychology. If psycholinguistics enabled psychologists to reexamine their assumptions about language learning and understanding by placing greater emphasis on the active, intentional role of language users, cognitive psychology allowed psychologists to extend constructs such as human purpose, intention, and motivation to a greater range of psychological phenomena, including perception, attention, comprehension, learning, memory, and executive control of all cognitive process. All of these would have important consequences in reading pedagogy.

This was not tinkering around the edges; it was a genuine paradigm shift that occurred within those branches of psychology concerned with human intellectual processes. The previous half-century, from roughly the teens through the fifties, had been dominated by a behaviorist perspective in psychology that shunned speculation about the inner workings of the mind: Show the surface-level outcomes of the processes, as indexed by overt, observable behaviors and leave the speculation to the philosophers. That was the contextual background against which both psycholinguistics and cognitive psychology served as dialectical antagonists when they appeared on the scene in the late 1960s and early 1970s.

The most notable change within psychology was that it became fashionable for psychologists, perhaps for the first time since the early part of the century, to study reading.[27] And, in the decade of the 1970s, works by psychologists flooded the literature on basic processes in reading. One group focused on text comprehension by trying to figure out how it is that readers come to understand the underlying structure of texts. We were offered story grammars—structural accounts of the nature of narratives, complete with predictions about how those structures impede and enhance human story comprehension. Others chose to focus on the expository tradition in text.[28] Like their colleagues interested in story comprehension, they believed that structural accounts of the nature of expository (informational) texts would provide valid and useful models for human text comprehension. And, in a sense, both of these efforts worked. Story grammars did account for story comprehension. Analyses of the structural relations among ideas in an informational piece did account for text comprehension. But, what neither text-analysis tradition really tackled was the relationship between the knowledge of the world that readers bring to text and the comprehension of those texts. In other words, by focusing on structural rather than the ideational, or content, characteristics of texts, they failed to get to the heart of comprehension. That task, as it turned out, fell to one of the most popular and influential movements of the 1970s, schema theory.

Schema theory[29] is a theory about the structure of human knowledge as it is represented in memory. In our memory, schemata are like little containers into which we deposit particular experiences that we have. So, if we see a chair, we store that visual experience in our chair schema. If we go to a restaurant, we store that experience in our restaurant schema, if we attend a party, our party schema, and so on. Clearly schema theory is linked to Piaget's theories of development and his two types of learning: assimilation and accommodation. When we assimilate new information, we store it in an existing schema; when we accommodate new information, we modify the structure of our schemata to fit the new data. The modern iteration of schema theory also owes a debt to Frederic Bartlett, who, in the 1930s, used the construct of schema to explain culturally driven interpretations of stories. For Bartlett, cultural schemata for stories were so strong that they prevented listeners, whether European or native Alaskan in background, from adopting the story schema of the other culture to understand its stories. Bartlett's account predates the current constructivist models of cognition and learning by 60 years; and his view is as inherently constructive as those who have succeeded him. In essence, Bartlett was saying exactly what modern constructivists say, that readers and listeners actively construct meanings for texts they encounter rather than simply "receiving" meaning from the texts.[30]

Schema theory also provides a credible account of reading comprehension, which probably, more than any of its other features, accounted for its popularity within the reading field in the 1970s and 80s.[31] It is not difficult to see why schema theory was so appealing to theoreticians, researchers, and practitioners when it arrived on the scene in the 1970s. First, schema theory provides a rich and detailed theoretical account of the everyday intuition that we understand and learn what is new in terms of what we already know. Second, schema theory accounts for another everyday intuition about why we as humans so often disagree about our interpretation of an event, a story, an article, a movie, or a TV show: We disagree with one another because we approach the phenomenon with very different background experiences and knowledge. Third, schema theory accounts for an everyday intuition that might be called an "it's-all-Greek-to-me" experience: Sometimes we just don't have enough background knowledge to understand a new experience or text.

Although these insights may not sound earthshaking after the fact, for the field of reading, and for education more generally, they were daunting challenges to our conventional wisdom. Examined in light of existing practices in the 1970s, they continued the revolutionary spirit of the linguistic and psycholinguistic perspectives. Schema theory encouraged us to ask:

> What is it that my children already know? And, how can I use that to help them deal with these new ideas that I would like them to know? rather than, What

is it that they do not know? And how can I get that into their heads?

More specifically, with respect to reading comprehension, schema theory encouraged us to examine texts from the perspective of the knowledge and cultural backgrounds of our students in order to evaluate the likely connections that they would be able to make between ideas that are in the text and the schema that they would bring to the reading task. Schema theory, like the psycholinguistic perspective, also promoted a constructivist view of comprehension; all readers must, at every moment in the reading process, construct a coherent model of reading for the texts they read. The most important consequence of this constructivist perspective is that there is inherent ambiguity about where meaning resides. Does it reside in the text? In the author's mind as she sets pen to paper? In the mind of each reader as he or she builds a model of meaning unique to his or her experience and reading? In the interaction between reader and text?

Sociolinguistics. Sociolinguistics as a discipline developed in parallel with psycholinguistics. Beginning with the work of William Labov, and Joan Baratz and Roger Shuy, sociolinguists had important lessons for reading scholars.[32] Mainly, these lessons focused on issues of dialect and reading. Sociolinguists were finding that dialects were not ill- or half-formed variations of standard English. Instead, each dialect constituted a well-developed linguistic system in its own right, complete with rules for variations from standard English and a path of language development for its speakers. Speakers of dialects expressed linguistic differences, not linguistic deficits. The goal of schooling was not, and should not be, to eradicate the dialect in the process of making each individual a speaker of standard English. Instead, sociolinguists stressed the need to find ways to accommodate children's use of their dialect while they are learning to read and write. Several proposals for achieving this accommodation were tried and evaluated. The first was to write special readers for dialect speakers. In the early 1960s, several examples of black-dialect readers appeared and, almost as rapidly, disappeared from major urban districts. They failed primarily because African American parents did not want their children learning with "special" materials; they wanted their children to be exposed to mainstream materials used by other children.[33] The second equally unsuccessful strategy was to delay instruction in reading and writing until oral language became more standardized. Teachers who tried this technique soon found out just how resistant and persistent early language learning can be. The third and most successful approach to dialect accommodation involved nothing more than recognizing that a child who translates a standard English text into a dialect is performing a remarkable feat of translation rather than making reading errors. So, an African American child who says /pos/ when he sees *post* is simply applying a rule of black English, which requires a consonant cluster in ending position to be reduced to the sound of the first consonant. Unfortunately for children who speak a dialect, we, as a field, did not take the early lessons of the sociolinguists to heart. We continue to find schools in which children are scolded for using the oral language that they have spent their whole lives learning. We also continue to find children whose dialect translations are treated as if they were oral reading errors.

Prior to the advent of the sociolinguistic perspective, when educators talked about "context" in reading, they typically meant the print that surrounded particular words on a page. In the 1980s, and primarily because of the work of sociolinguists, the meaning of the word *context* expanded to include not only what was on the page, but what Bloome and Green referred to as the instructional, noninstructional, and home and community contexts of literacy.[34] From a sociolinguistic perspective, reading always occurred in a context, one that was shaped by the literacy event at the same time it shaped the event. The sociolinguistic versions of knowledge and language as socially and culturally constructed processes moved the constructivist metaphor to another plane, incorporating not only readers' prior knowledge in the form of schemata, but also the meanings constructed by peers and by one's cultural ancestors.

The most significant legacy of the sociolinguistic perspective was our heightened consciousness about language as a social and, therefore, cultural construction. Suddenly, reading was a part of a bigger and more complex world. Sociolinguists examined the role of language in school settings. For example, they pointed out that often success in reading was not so much an indication of reading "ability" per se, but of the success the individual experienced in learning how to use language appropriately in educational settings. Thus success, according to a sociolinguistic analysis, was more an index of how well children learned to "do school" than how well they could read. They contrasted the functions that language serves in school with the functions it serves outside of school and helped us rethink the role of language within the classroom. By studying the community outside of school, sociolinguists made us conscious of social, political, and cultural differences; as a result, we began to rethink our judgments of language and behavior. We saw that any judgment call we made, rather than reflecting the "right" way, simply reflected "our" way—the way we as teachers thought, talked, and behaved because of the cultural situation in which we lived, outside as well as inside school. By focusing on the role of community in learning, sociolinguists caused many educators to rethink the competitive atmosphere of classrooms and of school labels and recommended changes within schools so that children could learn from and with each other. With these contributions from sociolinguists, it was becoming more and more apparent that reading was not only not context-free, but that it was embedded in multiple contexts.

Literary Theory Perspective. One cannot understand the pedagogical changes in practice that occurred in the elementary reading curriculum in the 1980s without understanding the impact of literary theory, particularly reader-response theory. In our secondary schools, the various traditions of literary criticism have always had a voice in the curriculum, especially in guiding discussions of classic literary works. Until the middle 1980s, the "new criticism" that had emerged during the post–World War II era had dominated for several decades, and it had sent teachers and students on a search for the one "true" meaning in each text they encountered. With the emergence (some would argue the reemergence) of reader-response theories, all of which gave as much (if not more) authority to the reader than to either the text or the author, the picture, along with our practices, changed dramatically. Although there are many modern versions of reader response available, the work of Louise Rosenblatt has been most influential among elementary teachers and reading educators. In the 1980s, many educators reread (or more likely read for the first time) Rosenblatt's (1938) 1976 edition of *Literature as Exploration*, and *The Reader, the Text, the Poem*, which appeared in 1978. Rosenblatt argues that meaning is something that resides neither in the head of the reader (as some had previously argued) nor on the printed page (as others had argued).[35] Instead, Rosenblatt contends, meaning is created in the transaction between reader and document. This meaning, which she refers to as "the poem," resides above the reader-text interaction. Meaning is, therefore, neither subject nor object nor the interaction of the two. Instead, it is transaction, something new and different from any of its inputs and influences.[36]

The Pedagogical Correlates of New Perspectives

Although the post-Chall basal tradition continued well into the decade of the 1980s, new perspectives and practices began to appear in classrooms, journal articles, and basal lessons in the early 1980s.

Comprehension on Center Stage. Comprehension, especially as a workbook activity and a follow-up to story reading, was not a stranger to the reading classrooms of the 1930s through 1970s. As indicated earlier, it entered the curriculum as a story discussion tool and as a way of assessing reading competence in the first third of the 20th century.[37] Developments during mid-century were highlighted in an earlier National Study of School Evaluation yearbook devoted to reading;[38] by mid-century, the infrastructure of comprehension had been elaborated extensively and infused into the guided reading and workbook task. It was a staple of basal programs when Chall conducted her study of early reading, and had she emphasized reading instruction in the intermediate grades rather than grade 1, it undoubtedly would have been more prominent in her account.

During the late 1970s and through the decade of the 1980s, comprehension found its way to center stage in reading pedagogy. Just as a nationally sponsored set of research activities (i.e., the First-Grade Studies and Chall's book) focused energy on reforms in beginning reading in the late 1960s, it was the federally funded Center for the Study of Reading, initiated in 1976, which focused national attention on comprehension. Although the Center's legacy is undoubtedly bringing schema theory and the knowledge-comprehension relationship into our national conversation, it also supported much research on comprehension instruction,[39] including research that attempted to help students develop a repertoire of strategies for improving their comprehension.[40] This research was not limited to the Center; indeed many other scholars were equally involved in developing instructional strategies and routines during this period, including emphases on monitoring comprehension,[41] transactional strategies instruction,[42] K-W-L graphic organizers,[43] and, more recently, questioning the author.[44] Many of these new strategies found their way into the basals of the 1980s, which demonstrated substantially more emphasis on comprehension at all levels, including grade 1.[45]

Literature-Based Reading. Even though selections from both classical and contemporary children's literature have always been a staple of basal selections dating back to the 19th century (especially after grade 2 when the need for strict vocabulary control diminished), literature virtually exploded into the curriculum in the late 1980s. A short burst in literary content occurred after Chall's critical account of the type of selections and the challenge of basal content; more excerpts from authentic literature appeared, even in the grade 1 readers. But these selections had two characteristics that had always offended those who champion the use of genuine literature: excerpting and adaptation. Rarely were whole books included; instead, whole chapters or important slices were excerpted for inclusion. And, even when a whole chapter was included, it was usually adapted to (a) reduce vocabulary difficulty, (b) reduce the grammatical complexity of sentences, or (c) excise words (e.g., mild profanity) or themes that might offend important segments of the market.

Beyond basals, children's literature played an important supplementary role in the classrooms of teachers who believed that they must engage their students in a strong, parallel independent reading program. Often this took the form of each child selecting books to be read individually and later discussed with the teacher in a weekly one-on-one conference. And, even as far back as the 1960s, there were a few programs that turned this individualized reading component into the main reading program.[46]

But in the late 1980s, literature was dramatically repositioned. Several factors converged to pave the way for a groundswell in the role of literature in elementary reading. Surely, the resurgence of reader response theory as presented by Rosenblatt was important, as was the compatibility of the reader-response theory and its emphasis on interpretation, with the constructivism that characterized both cognitive and sociolinguistic perspectives. Research also played a role; in 1985, for example, in the watershed publication of the Center for the Study of Reading, *Becoming a Nation of Readers*, Richard Anderson and his colleagues documented the importance of "just plain reading" as a critical component of any and all elementary reading programs.[47] This period also witnessed an unprecedented expansion in the number of new children's books published annually. Finally, a few pieces of scholarship exerted enormous influence on teachers and teacher educators. Perhaps most influential was Nancie Atwell's (1987) *In the Middle: Writing, Reading, and Learning With Adolescents*, in which she told her story of how, as a middle school teacher, she invited readers, some of whom were quite reluctant, into a world of books and reading. The credibility of her experience and the power of her prose were persuasive in convincing thousands of classroom teachers that they could use existing literature and "reading workshops" to accomplish anything that a basal program could accomplish in skill development while gaining remarkable advantages in students' literary experience.[48]

In terms of policy and curriculum, the most significant event in promoting literature-based reading was the 1988 California Reading Framework. The framework called for reading materials that contained much more challenging texts at all levels. More important, it mandated the use of genuine literature, not the oversimplified adaptations and excerpts from children's literature that had been the staple of basal programs for decades. Publishers responded to the call of California's framework and produced a remarkably different product in the late 1980s and early 1990s than ever had appeared before on the basal market.[49] Gone were excerpts and adaptations and, with them, almost any traces of vocabulary control. Skills that had been front and center in the basals of the 1970s and 80s were relegated to appendix-like status. Comprehension questions were replaced by more interpretive, impressionistic response to literature activities. All this was done in the name of providing children with authentic literature and authentic activities to accompany it. The logic was that if we could provide students with real literature and real motivations for reading it, much of what is arduous about skill teaching and learning would take care of itself.

Book Clubs and literature circles are the most visible instantiations of the literature-based reading movement.[50] The underlying logic of Book Clubs is the need to engage children in the reading of literature in the same way as adults engage one another in voluntary reading circles. Such voluntary structures are likely to elicit greater participation, motivation, appreciation, and understanding on the part of students. Teachers are encouraged to establish a set of "cultural practices" (ways of interacting and supporting one another) in their classrooms to support students as they make their way into the world of children's literature. These cultural practices offer students both the opportunity to engage in literature and the skills to ensure that they can negotiate and avail themselves of that opportunity.

Process Writing. In the middle 1980s, writing achieved a stronghold in the elementary language arts curriculum that it had never before held. Exactly why and how it achieved that position of prominence is not altogether clear, but certain explanations are plausible. Key understandings from the scholarship of the 1970s and 80s paved the way. Functionality associated with the sociolinguistic perspective, process-writing approaches encouraged teachers to ask students to write for genuine audiences and purposes. The psycholinguistic notion of "error" as a window into children's thinking allowed us to worry less about perfect spelling and grammar and more about the quality of the thinking and problem solving children were producing. The general acceptance of constructivist epistemologies disposed us to embrace writing as the most transparently constructive of all pedagogical activities. All these constructs allowed us as a profession to take a different developmental view on writing, one consistent with the emergent literacy perspective that was gaining strength in early childhood literacy. We came to view all attempts to make sense by setting pen to paper, however deviant from adult models, as legitimate and

revealing in their own right if examined through the eyes of the child writer. Led by Donald Graves and Lucy Calkins, we revolutionized our views of early writing development.[51] Finally, we began to see reading and writing as inherently intertwined, each supporting the other.

Integrated Instruction. It is impossible to document the history of reading instruction in the 20th century without mentioning the ways in which we have attempted to integrate reading with other curricular phenomena. Two stances have dominated our thinking about how to integrate reading into other curricula: integration of reading with the other language arts (writing, speaking, and listening) and integration across subject matter boundaries (with mathematics, science, social studies, art, and music). Like literature-based reading, both senses of integration have long been a part of the thinking about elementary reading curriculum.[52] In fact, a look back to the progressivism of Dewey and other scholars in the first part of the century reveals substantial rhetoric about teaching and learning across curricular boundaries.[53] From that early spurt of energy until the late 1980s, however, integrations assumed a minor role in American reading instruction. In basal manuals, for example, integration was portrayed almost as an afterthought until the late 1980s; it appeared in the part of the lesson that follows the guided reading and skills instruction sections, signaling that these are things that a teacher can do "if time permits." Things changed in the late 1980s. For one, integrated curriculum fit the sociolinguistic emphasis on language in use: the idea that language, including reading, is best taught and learned when it is put to work in the service of other purposes, activities, and learning efforts. Similarly, with the increase in importance of writing, especially early writing of the sort discussed by Graves and his colleagues,[54] it was tempting to champion the idea of integrated language arts instruction. In fact, the constructivist metaphor is nowhere played out as vividly and transparently as in writing, leading many scholars to use writing as a model for the sort of constructive approach they wanted to promote in readers. The notion was that we needed to help students learn to "read like a writer."[55] Also influential in supporting the move toward integrated instruction was the work of Donald Holdaway, who, in concert with many teacher colleagues, had been implementing an integrated language arts approach in Australia for a few decades.[56]

Whole Language. Important as they are, comprehension, literature-based reading, process writing, and integrated instruction pale in comparison to the impact of whole language, which is regarded as the most significant movement in reading curriculum in the last 30 years.[57] In fact, one might plausibly argue that whole language co-opted all four of these allied phenomena—comprehension, literature-based reading, integrated instruction, and process writing—by incorporating them, problems along with strengths, into its fundamental set of principles and practices. Whole language is grounded in child-centered pedagogy reminiscent of the progressive education movement (the individual child is the most important curriculum informant).[58] Philosophically, it is biased toward radical constructivist epistemology (all readers must construct their own meanings for the texts they encounter). Curricularly, it is committed to authentic activity (real, not specially constructed, texts and tasks) and integration (both within the language arts and between the language arts and other subject matters). Politically, it is suspicious of all attempts to mandate and control curricular decisions beyond the classroom level; as such, it places great faith and hope in the wisdom of teachers to exercise professional prerogative in making decisions about the children in their care. Whole language owes its essential character and key principles to the insights of linguistics, psycholinguistics, cognitive psychology, sociolinguistics, and literary theory detailed earlier. It owes its remarkable, if brief, appearance in the national limelight of reading instruction to its committed leaders and a veritable army of committed teachers who instantiated it in their classrooms, each with his or her own unique signature.[59]

When whole language emerged as a movement in the 1980s, it challenged the conventional wisdom of basals and questioned the unqualified support for early code emphases that had grown between 1967 and the early 1980s.[60] One of the great ironies of whole language is that its ascendancy into curricular prominence is best documented by its influence on the one curricular tool it has most consistently and most vehemently opposed, the basal reader.[61] As suggested earlier, basals changed dramatically in the early 1990s, largely, I conjecture, in response to the groundswell of support within the teaching profession for whole language and its close curricular allies, literature-based reading and process writing.

Vocabulary control, already weakened during the 1970s in response to Chall's admonitions, was virtually abandoned in the early 1990s in deference to attempts to incorporate more literature, this time in unexpurgated form (i.e., without the practices of adaptation and excerpting that had characterized the basals of the 1970s and 80s) into the grade 1 program.[62] Phonics, along with other skills, was backgrounded, and literature moved to center stage.

Basal programs appropriated or, as some whole language advocates have argued, "basalized" the activities and tools of whole language. Thus, in the basals of the early 1990s, each unit might have a writing process component in which the rhetoric, if not the reality of some version of process writing, was presented to teachers and students. In the 1980s, comprehension questions, probably following a story line, might have sufficed for the guided reading section of the manual (the part that advises teachers on how to read and discuss the story), but in the 1990s, questions and tasks that supported deep probes into students' response to literature became more prevalent. Another concession to literature-based reading was the creation and marketing of classroom libraries—boxed sets of books, usually thematically related to each unit—that teachers could use to extend their lessons and units "horizontally" and enrich children's literary opportunities.

Basals also repositioned their "integrated language arts" and "integrated curriculum" strands. Dating back even to the 1920s and 1930s, basals had provided at least a "token" section in which teachers were encouraged to extend the themes or skills of the basal story into related writing (e.g., rewriting stories), oral language (e.g., transforming a story into a play and dramatizing it), or cross-curricular activities (e.g., conducting community surveys, tallying the results, and reporting them), but these forays were regarded as peripheral rather than core. In the basals of the early 1990s, as skills moved into the background,[63] these integrated language arts activities were featured more prominently as core lesson components.[64]

These changes can, I believe, be traced to the prominent position of whole language as a curricular force during this period.[65] Publishers of basals accomplished this feat of appropriation not by ridding their programs of the skills of previous eras, but by subtle repositioning—foregrounding one component while backgrounding another—and creating optional components or modules (e.g., an intensive phonics kit or a set of literature books) that could be added to give the program one or another spin. Unsurprisingly, this created bulkier teacher's manuals and more complex programs.

Acceptance of whole language was not universal. To the contrary, there was considerable resistance to whole language and literature-based reading throughout the country.[66] In many places, whole language never really gained a foothold. In others, what was implemented in the name of whole language was not consistent with the philosophical and curricular principles of the movement; California, whole language advocates would argue, is a case in point. Whole language got conflated with whole-class instruction and was interpreted to mean that all kids should get the same literature, even if teachers had to read it to them.[67]

Nor was there a single voice within the whole language movement. Whole language scholars and practitioners differed on a host of issues such as the role of skills, conventions, and strategies within a language arts program. Some said, if we can just be patient, skills will emerge from meaningful communication activities; others spurred things on by taking advantage of spontaneous opportunities for minilessons; still others were willing to spur spontaneity a bit.

Even so, it is fair to conclude that by the early 1990s, whole language had become the conventional wisdom, the standard against which all else was referenced. The rhetoric of professional articles belies this change. As late as the mid-1980s, articles were written with the presumption of a different conventional wisdom—a world filled with skills, contrived readers, and workbooks. By 1991–1992, they were written with the presumption that whole language reforms, while not fully ensconced in U.S. schools, were well on their way to implementation. The arguments in the 1990s were less about first principles of whole language and more about fine-tuning teaching repertoires. The meetings of the Whole Language Umbrella grew to be larger than most large state conventions and regional conferences of the International Reading Association. By 1995, whole language was no longer a series of assaults on skills and basals that characterized it through the mid-1980s. It had become the conventional wisdom in rhetoric, if not in reality.

Returning to the lenses outlined at the beginning of this chapter (range of materials and practices, role of teacher, role of learner, and the processes of reading and learning to read), in whole language, we finally encountered major shifts in emphasis in comparison to what we found at the beginning of the century. In whole language, teachers were facilitators not tellers. Teachers observed what children did, decided what they needed, and arranged conditions to allow students to discover those very insights about reading, writing, and learning for themselves. Because this was truly child-centered pedagogy, learners occupied center stage. As Jerome Harste puts it, the child was the primary curriculum informant. Students were decision makers involved in choices about the books they read and the stories they wrote. The materials of reading instruction were the materials of life and living—the books, magazines, newspapers, and other forms of print that children can encounter in everyday life are the materials they should encounter in the classroom—no less, no more. There was no need for the sort of contrived texts and tasks of the sort found in basal reading programs. Instructional practices focused not on presenting a diet of skills carefully sequenced to achieve mastery, but on creating activities and tasks that supported the learning students needed at a particular point in time. If skills and strategies were taught, they were taught in minilessons, highly focused forays into the infrastructure of a skill or strategy followed up by immediately recontextualizing the skill in a genuine reading or writing situation. In contrast to previous periods, reading was now regarded as a meaning-making, not a perceptual, process. The reader was an active participant in creating, not a passive recipient of, the message in a text. The process of acquiring reading was also markedly different from the "readiness" perspective so dominant in the first 80 years of the century. Emergent literacy, the alternative to traditional reading readiness views, did not specify a "prereading" period in which children are prepared for the task of reading. All readers, at all stages, were meaning makers, even those who can only scribble a message or "pretend" to read.[68] Thus, at century's end, reading pedagogy finally developed some viable alternatives to the conventional views of teacher, learner, and process that had dominated pedagogical practice for the entire century. As it turned out, the new directions were short-lived, or at least they appear to be so from the perspective of developments in the first few years of the 21st century.

The Demise of Whole Language

At century's end, just when it appeared as if whole language, supported by its intellectual cousins (process writing, literature-based reading, and integrated curriculum), was about to assume the position of conventional wisdom

for the field, the movement was challenged seriously, and the pendulum of the pedagogical debate began to swing back toward the skills end of the curriculum and instruction continuum. Several factors converged to make the challenge credible, among them (a) unintended curricular casualties of whole language; (b) questionable applications of whole language; (c) growing dissatisfaction with doctrinaire views of any sort; (d) a paradigm swing in the ideology of reading research; (e) increasing politicization of the reading research and policy agenda, and (f) increasing pressure for educators of all types, especially reading educators, to produce measurable results; and (g) a dramatic shift in the prevailing model of professional development.

Unintended Curricular Consequences. In #1 its ascendancy, whole language changed the face of reading instruction and, in the process, left behind some curricular casualties, few of which were intended by those who supported whole language. Those, myself included,[69] who supported practices that were discarded during the rise of whole language had difficulty supporting the whole language movement even though we might have been philosophically and curricularly sympathetic to many of its principles and practices. This lack of enthusiasm from curricular moderates meant that whole language failed to build a base of support that was broad enough to survive even modest curricular opposition, let alone the political onslaught that it would experience at century's turn.

There were four casualties: skills instruction, strategy instruction, emphasis on text structure, and reading in the content areas. Earlier, I suggested that one of the consequences of whole language was the relegation of skills to the "appendices" of instructional programs. In accepting whole language, we tacitly accepted the premise that skills are better "caught" in the act of reading and writing genuine texts for authentic purposes than "taught" directly and explicitly by teachers. The argument is the same for phonics, grammar, text conventions, and structural elements. These entities may be worthy of learning, but they are unworthy of teaching. This position presents us with a serious conundrum as a profession. Admit, for the sake of argument, that the skills instruction of the 1970s and earlier, with decontextualized lessons and practice on "textoids" in workbook pages, deserved the criticism accorded to it by whole language advocates (and scholars from other traditions). But, a retreat from most skills instruction into a world of "authentic opportunity" did not provide a satisfactory answer for teachers and scholars who understood the positive impact that instruction can have. Many young readers do not "catch" the alphabetic principle by sheer immersion in print or by listening to others read aloud. For some it seems to require careful planning and hard work by dedicated teachers who are willing to balance systematic skills instruction with authentic texts and activities.[70]

Strategy instruction was another casualty. This loss has been particularly difficult for scholars who spent the better part of the early 1980s convincing basal publishers and textbook authors that the thoughtful teaching of flexible strategies for making and monitoring meaning was a viable alternative to mindless skills instruction, where skills were taught as though they were only ever to be applied to workbook pages and end-of-unit tests. But the strategy lessons that filled our basals in the middle to late 1980s—direct advice from teachers about how to summarize what one has read, how to use text structure to infer relations among ideas, how to distinguish fact from opinion, how to determine the central thread of a story, how to use context to infer word meanings, and how to make and evaluate the accuracy of predictions—were virtually nonexistent in the basals of the early to middle 1990s. Although there is no inherent bias in whole language or literature-based reading against the learning and use of a whole range of cognitive strategies, there is, as with phonics and grammar, a serious question about whether direct, explicit instruction in how to use them will help. The advice is to let them emerge from attempts to solve real reading

problems and puzzles, the kind students meet in genuine encounters with authentic text. There may have been reason for concern about the strategy instruction of the 1980s. But revision rather than rejection of these strategies was not a part of the rhetoric of whole language.[71]

Structural emphasis was also suspect within whole language. This suspicion extended to formal grammars, story grammars, rhetorical structures, and genre features of texts. As with skills and strategies, whole language reformers do not claim that students should not learn and develop control over these structural tools; they simply claim that, like skills, they are best inferred from reading and writing authentic texts in the process of making meaning. So, the advocates are comfortable in adopting Frank Smith's[72] admonition to encourage kids to read like a writer (meaning to read the text with a kind of critical eye toward understanding the tools and tricks of the trade that the author uses to make her points and achieve her effects on readers), but they would likely reject a systematic set of lessons designed to teach and assess children's control of story grammar elements (such as plot, characterization, style, mood, or theme) or some system for dealing with basic patterns of expository text. As with skills and strategies, many of us see a compromise alternative to both the formulaic approach of the early 1980s and the "discovery" approach of the new reforms—dealing with these structural elements as they emanate from stories that a group is currently reading can provide some guidance and useful tools for students and teachers.

Content area reading also suffered during the ascendancy of whole language and literature-based reading. Content area texts—expository texts in general, but especially textbook-like entries—were not privileged in a world of literature-based reading. This is not an implicit criticism of the literature-based reading movement; rather it is a comment about the reallocation of curricular time and energy that occurs when a movement gains momentum. There is a certain irony in this development, for it is expository reading, not narrative reading, that most concerns middle and high school teachers. The cost here has been very dear. To enter middle school and high school classrooms in order to examine the role of expository text is to conclude that it has none. Occasionally, teachers assign expository texts for homework, but when students come to class the next day, clearly having avoided the assignment, teachers provide them with an oral version of what they would have gotten out of the text if they had bothered to read it. Most high school teachers have quite literally given up on the textbook for the communication of any important content. Although understandable, this approach is, of course, ultimately counterproductive. There comes a time in the lives of students— when they either go to college or enter the work world—when others expect them to read and understand informational texts on their own and in printed form rather than through oral or video transformation.[73]

Because whole language did not go out of its way to accommodate any of these curricular practices, those who were sympathetic with whole language but also champions of one or another approach were not available to help whole language respond to the criticism leveled at it in the late 1990s.

Questionable Applications of Whole Language. One dilemma faced by any curricular challenge is sustaining the integrity of the movement without imposing the very sorts of controls it is trying to eliminate. Whole language did not find and still has not found a satisfying way of managing this dilemma, and it has suffered as a consequence. Many schools, teachers, and institutions appropriated the whole language label without honoring its fundamental principles of authenticity, integration, and empowerment. Basal reader publishers made the most obvious and widespread appropriation, some even positioning their basal series as "whole language" programs. Earlier, I noted another misapplication in which whole language was confounded with whole-class instruction. Nowhere was this conflation more extreme than in the implementation of the California literature framework. The logic that

prevailed in many classrooms was that it was better to keep the entire class together at all costs. Implicit in this practice are two interesting assumptions: (1) that getting the content of the stories is the most important goal for reading instruction, and (2) that the skills and processes needed to read independently will emerge somehow from this environment in which many students are pulled through texts that far exceed the grasp of their current skills repertoire. Needless to say, whole language had enough on its hands dealing with its own assumptions and practices; these philosophical and curricular misapplications exposed the movement to a whole set of criticisms that derived from practices not of its own making.

One of the primary reasons for misapplication of whole language was, in my estimate, the lack of an explicit plan for professional development. Whole language gives teachers a wide berth for making curricular and instructional decisions, for whole classes and for individual children. It assumes that teachers who are empowered, sincere, and serious about their personal professional development will be able to tailor programs and activities to the needs and interests of individual children. Such an approach makes sense only when we can assume that teacher knowledge is widely and richly distributed in our profession. To offer these prerogatives in the face of narrow and shallow knowledge is to guarantee that misguided practices, perversions of the very intent of the movement, will be widespread. The puzzle, of course, is where to begin the reform: by ensuring that the knowledge precedes the prerogative, or by ceding the prerogative to teachers as a way of leveraging their motivation for greater knowledge.[74]

Growing Dissatisfaction With Extreme Positions. Although it has reached its peak in the last five years, concern about extreme positions, be they extremely child-centered (such as the more radical of whole language approaches) or extremely curriculum-centered (such as highly structured, unswerving phonics programs) is not new. Voices from the middle,

extolling balanced approaches or rationalizing the eclectic practices of teachers, began to be heard even in the earliest days of whole language's ascendancy.[75] Scholars and teachers raised a number of concerns about the assumptions and practices of the whole language movement. Most importantly, they expressed concern about the consequences of whole language outlined earlier in this chapter. They questioned the assumption that skills are best "caught" during the pursuit of authentic reading activity rather than "taught" directly and explicitly. They also questioned the insistence on authentic texts and the corollary ban on instructional texts written to permit the application of skills within the curriculum. They questioned the zeal and commitment of the movement *qua* movement, with its strong sense of insularity and exclusivity. Finally, they worried that the press toward the use of authentic literature and literature-based reading would eradicate, albeit unintentionally, what little progress had been made toward the use of informational texts and teaching reading in the content areas.[76]

Ironically, in the past few years, these voices from the middle have found themselves responding not to those who hold a radical whole language position, but to those who hold steadfastly to the phonics first position. Even so, the fact that those with centrist positions were not inclined to defend whole language when the political campaign against it began in the middle 1990s, they undoubtedly hastened the demise of whole language as the pretender to the title of conventional wisdom.

Changing Research Ideology. Prior to the 1980s, qualitative research in any form had little visibility within the reading research community. Among the array of qualitative efforts, only miscue analysis[77] and some early forays into sociolinguistic and anthropological accounts of literacy had achieved much in the way of archival status.[78] But all that changed in the 1980s and early 1990s. Qualitative research more generally, along with more specific lines of inquiry taking a critical perspective on literacy as a social and pedagogical phenomenon, became more widely accepted as part of the mainstream archival literature.[79] Treatises pointing out the shortcomings of traditional forms of quantitative inquiry, especially experimental research, appeared frequently in educational research journals.[80] In terms of curriculum and pedagogy, it is important to remind ourselves that much of the research that undergirds whole language comes from this more qualitative, more interpretive, more critical tradition. Thus the credibility of this type of research increased in concert with the influence of whole language as a curricular movement.

Somewhere in the mid-1990s, the discourse of literacy research began to take a new turn. Stimulated by research supported by the National Institute for Child Health and Human Development, a new brand of experimental work began to appear in the middle 1980s and gathered momentum that has reached a peak in the past year or two.[81] This is experimentalism reborn from the 1950s and 60s, with great emphasis placed on "reliable, replicable research," large samples, random assignment of treatments to teachers and/or schools, and tried and true outcome measures.[82] This work does not build on the qualitative tradition of the 1980s and early 1990s; instead it finds its aegis in the experimental rhetoric of science and medicine and in the laboratory research that has examined reading as a perceptual process.[83] Although not broadly accepted by the reading education community at the turn of the century, this work has found a very sympathetic ear in the public policy arena.[84]

The political positioning of this research is important, but so is its substance. Two themes from this work have been particularly important in shaping a new set of instructional practices: phonemic awareness and phonics instruction.

The absolutely critical role played by phonemic awareness (the ability to segment the speech stream of a spoken word, e.g., /cat/ into component phonemes /cuh + ah + tuh/ and/or to blend separately heard sounds, e.g., /cuh + ah + tuh/ into a normally spoken word /cat/) in the development of the ability to decode and to read for meaning was well documented in research studies spanning the last 25 years of the 20th century.[85] Irrespective of mode of instruction, the overwhelming evidence suggests that phonemic awareness is a necessary but not a sufficient condition for the development of decoding and reading. First, children who possess high degrees of phonemic awareness in kindergarten or early in first grade are very likely to be good readers throughout their elementary school careers.[86] Second, almost no children who are successful readers at the end of grade 1 exhibit a low level of mastery of phonemic awareness. On the other hand, a substantial proportion of unsuccessful end-of-grade-1 readers possess better than average phonemic awareness; this evidence is the critical piece in establishing that phonemic awareness is a necessary but not a sufficient condition for reading success. Although we can be confident of its critical role in learning to read, we are less sure about the optimal way to enhance its development. Many scholars have documented the efficacy of teaching it directly, but they also admit that it is highly likely to develop as a consequence of learning phonics, learning to read, or especially learning to write, especially when teachers encourage students to use invented spellings.[87] Research in whole language classrooms suggests that writing is the medium through which both phonemic awareness and phonics knowledge develop, the former because students have to segment the speech stream of spoken words in order to focus on a phoneme, and the latter because there is substantial transfer value from the focus on sound-symbol information in spelling to symbol-sound knowledge in reading.[88]

The second consistent thread in the new experimentalism of the 1990s is the simple but undeniable emphasis on the code in the early stages of learning to read.[89] Reminiscent of Chall's earlier conclusions, scholars in this tradition tend to advocate phonics—first, fast, and simple.[90] Less well documented, and surely less well agreed upon, is the optimal course of instruction to facilitate phonics development. Even Gough, a classic bottom-up theorist, while arguing that what distinguishes the good reader from the poor reader is swift and accurate word identification, suggests that an early insistence on reading for meaning may be the best way to develop such decoding proficiency. Both Philip Gough and Connie Juel are convinced that students can learn how to read when they have "cryptoanalytic intent" (a disposition to decipher the specific letter-to-sound codes), phonemic awareness, an appreciation of the alphabetic principle (i.e., regardless of the numerous exceptions, letters do stand for sounds), and data (some texts to read and someone to assist when the going gets tough).[91]

After reviewing available instructional evidence, two of the most respected scholars in this tradition, Marilyn Adams and Connie Juel, independently concluded that children can and should learn the "cipher" through a combination of explicit instruction in phonemic awareness and letter-sound correspondences, a steady insistence on invented spellings as the route to conventional spellings in writing activities, and many opportunities to read connected text (especially when the texts contain enough decodable words to allow students to apply the phonics information they are learning through explicit instruction). Both of these reviewers, known for their sympathies toward instruction in the code, are quick to add that rich experiences with language, environmental print, patterned stories, and Big Books should also be a staple of effective early reading instruction.[92]

Politicization of the Reading Research and Policy Agenda. From its beginnings, one of the great hopes of educational research (and those who conduct it) is that policymakers will take research seriously when they establish policy initiatives at a local, state, or national level. After all, the improvement of educational practice is the ultimate goal of educational research, and policy is our society's most transparent tool for educational improvement. Historically, however, research has been regarded as one among many information sources consulted in policy formation, including expert testimony from practitioners, information about school organization and finance, and evaluations of compelling cases. In the past half decade, research, at least selective bits of research, has never been taken more seriously. Several laws in California make direct references to research. For example, Assembly Bill 1086 (1998) prohibited the use of Goals 2000 money for professional developers who advocated the use of context clues over phonics or who supported the use of invented spellings in children's writing. The federally sponsored Reading Excellence Act of 1999, which allocated US$240,000,000 for staff development in reading, requires that both state and local applications for funding base their programs on research that meets scientifically rigorous standards. The "scientifically rigorous" phrase was a late entry; in all but the penultimate version of the bill, the phrase was "reliable, replicable research," which had been interpreted as a code word for experimental research. As of early 1999, "phonics bills" (bills mandating either the use of phonics materials or some sort of teacher training to acquaint teachers with knowledge of the English sound-symbol system and its use in teaching) had been passed or were pending in 36 states.[93] In the early days of the current Bush administration, the goal of "evidence-based practice" was made even more explicit, with the phrase "scientifically based reading research" appearing more than 110 times in the Reading First portion of the No Child Left Behind Act of 2001 reauthorizing Title I.[94]

Policymakers like to shroud mandates and initiatives in the rhetoric of science, and sometimes that practice results in very strained, if not indefensible, extrapolations from research. This has happened consistently in the current reading policy arena. Two examples make the point vividly. First, California Assembly Bill 1086, with its prohibition on context clues and invented spelling, represents an ironic application of research to policy. The irony stems from the fact that many of the advocates of a return to code emphasis, such as Marilyn Adams, read the research as supporting the use of invented spellings in the development of phonemic awareness and phonics.[95] Second, the mandate in several states calling for the use of decodable text (usually defined as text consisting of words that can be sounded out using a combination of the phonics rules taught up to that point in the program plus some instant recognition of a few highly frequent sight words) is based on the thinnest of research bases. The idea is that children will learn to use their phonics better, faster, and more efficiently if the texts they read permit facile application of the principles they are learning. Although it all sounds very logical, there is precious little research evidence to support the systematic and exclusive use of decodable text.[96] This lack of evidence, however, does not seem to have deterred advocates who, on the phonics issues, championed scientific evidence as the gold standard for policy implementation.

Professional groups have entered the policy fray in recent years. For example, the American Federation of Teachers (AFT) has endorsed a particular set of programs as scientifically validated to produce excellent results. Interestingly, each of the programs on their endorsed list is committed to early, systematic, explicit phonics instruction in a highly structured framework. The AFT influence is evident in some other professional movements, such as the Learning First Alliance.[97]

When research moves into the policy arena, one of two outcomes are most likely. If the research is widely accepted by members of the profession from which it comes, widespread acceptance and implementation usually follows. This often occurs in medical, pharmaceutical, or agricultural research. If widespread consensus on what the research says about practice is not reached, then research-based policy initiatives are likely to sharpen and deepen the schisms that already exist, and the entire enterprise is likely to be regarded as a war among factions within the field. The latter scenario appears to characterize the reading field.[98]

Interestingly, the debate, accompanied by its warlike metaphors, appears to have more life in the public and professional press than it does in our schools. Reporters and scholars revel in keeping the debate alive and well, portraying clearly divided sides and detailing a host of differences of a philosophical, political, and pedagogical nature.[99] Teachers, by contrast, often talk about, and more importantly enact, more balanced approaches. For example, several scholars, in documenting the practices of highly effective, highly regarded teachers, found that these exemplary teachers employed a wide array of practices, some of which appear decidedly whole language in character (e.g., process writing, literature groups, and contextualized skills practice) and some of which appear remarkably skills-oriented (explicit phonics lessons, sight-word practice, and comprehension strategy instruction).[100]

Producing Measurable Results.

Evaluation has always posed a conundrum for whole language supporters. First, some oppose the use of any sort of externally mandated or administered assessments as a matter of principle, holding that assessment is ultimately the responsibility of a teacher in collaboration with a student and his or her parents. Second, even those supporters who are open to external forms of accountability, or at least reporting outside the boundaries of the classroom or school, often claim that standardized tests, state assessments, and other external measures of student accomplishment do not provide sensitive indicators of the goals of curricula based on whole language principles. Most appealing would be assessments that are classroom-based and individualized in nature, with the option of aggregating these sorts of data at the classroom and school levels when accountability is required. During the 1990s, many felt that the increased emphasis on performance assessment and portfolios would fill this need.[101] In an age of high expectations, explicit standards, and school- and classroom-level accountability, none of these options is a good fit with the views and desires of policymakers and the public. Both of these constituents seem quite uneasy about the quality of our schools and our educational system, so uneasy that leaving assessment in the hands of our teachers seems an unlikely outcome. It is not at all clear to me

that the proponents of at least strong versions of whole language can, or will be willing to, hold themselves accountable to the sorts of measures that the public and policymakers find credible.

A Shift in the Prevailing Model of Professional Development.

Fast on the heels of the entry of scientifically based reading research into the professional discourse came a new vision of professional development. The models of teacher reflection and prerogative dominant in the early 1990s were replaced by training models that championed the development of the knowledge and skills required to implement scientifically based reading research. This led to implementation models that put a premium on monitoring for quality control and fidelity to programs touted as "scientific."[102] Earlier models emphasizing reflection and teacher inquiry shared a commitment to research as the basis for practice, but any similarity ends there. In the teacher inquiry models, research is used to inform practice, and practice is expected to vary from teacher to teacher and situation to situation. In the models emerging at the turn of the century, research is used to determine practice, and the expectation is that practice should vary minimally from teacher to teacher and situation to situation.

Who Holds the High Ground?

One other factor, both subtle and speculative (on my part) seems to be an undercurrent in the rhetoric of the field in the first years of the 21st century. Whole language has always privileged the role of the teacher as the primary curriculum decision maker. Teachers, the argument goes, are in the best position to serve this important role because of their vast knowledge of language and literacy development, their skills as diagnosticians (they are expert "kidwatchers"), and the materials and teaching strategies they have at their disposal. And, in the arguments against more structured approaches, this is exactly the approach whole language advocates have taken: "Don't make these decisions at the state, district, or even the school level. Arm teachers with the professional prerogative (and corollary levels of professional knowledge) they need in order to craft unique decisions for individual children." Although this may seem a reasonable, even admirable position, it has recently been turned into an apology for self-serving teacher ideology.[103] The counter argument suggests that the broad base of privilege accorded to teachers may come at the expense of students and their parents. Thus, those who advocate a strong phonics-first position often take the moral high ground: "We are doing this for America's children (and for YOUR child!), so that they have the right to read for themselves." Even if one opposes this rhetorical move, it is not difficult to appreciate the clever repositioning on the part of those who want to return to more phonics and skills.

Taken together, these factors created a policy environment in which whole language was unlikely to flourish as the mainstream approach to teaching reading and writing. In the final analysis, however, I believe that the reluctance to own up to the "measurable results" standards was the Achilles heel of whole language. If whole language advocates had been willing to play by the rules of external accountability, to assert that students who experience good instruction based on solid principles of progressive pedagogy will perform well on standardized tests and other standards of performance, they would have stood a better chance of gaining a sympathetic ear with the public and with policymakers. And, as long as the criteria for what counts as evidence for growth and accomplishment are vague or left to individual teachers, the public could question the movement and wonder whose interests were being served by an unwillingness to commit to common standards.

Looking Ahead: Will We Benefit From the Lessons of History?

So where has this journey taken us? And, where will it take us next? We are, as Regie Routman has suggested, at a crossroads.[104] Many recent developments suggest that we are retreating to a more familiar, more comfortable paradigm of basic skills, in which phonics, skills, and controlled text dominate our practices. Other developments suggest that we are on the verge of a new paradigm, a hybrid that weds some of the principles of whole language (integrated instruction and authentic texts and tasks) with some of the traditions of earlier eras (explicit attention to skills and strategies, some vocabulary control of early readers, and lots of early emphasis on the code) in an "ecologically balanced" approach to reading instruction.[105] The most cynical among us might even argue that we are just riding the natural swing of a pendulum that will, if we have the patience, take us back to whole language, or whatever its child-centered descendant turns out to be, in a decade or so. Before making a prediction about the direction the field will take, let me play out the first two scenarios, phonics first and balanced reading instruction.

One Alternative for the Future

If those who have advocated most strongly for a return to phonics and a heavy skills orientation have their way—if they are able to influence federal, state, and local policy as well as the educational publishing industry—we will experience moderate to substantial shifts on most, but not all, the criteria I have used to measure changes in reading pedagogy over the last 40 years (range of materials, range of pedagogical practices, role of teacher, role of student, and underlying theory of reading and reading acquisition). As I read their views about policy and practice, the greatest changes will occur at the very earliest stages of learning to read: kindergarten and grade 1. They suggest explicit instruction on phonemic awareness and phonics, with a strong preference for decodable texts in the early grades. When it comes to writing, literature, response, and comprehension, they seem quite content to cede curricular authority to the practices that emerged during the 1980s and early 1990s, those associated with whole language, literature-based reading, and process writing.[106] Thus, looking broadly at the entire elementary reading curriculum (the range of materials and the range of pedagogical practices), things might, on the surface, look similar to the early 1990s, with some retreat to the 1980s, especially in terms of skill and strategy instruction.

But, beneath that curricular surface, major changes would have occurred. For example, the role of the teacher and the learner would have reverted to what they have been throughout most of the 20th century. The role of the teacher would be to transmit the received knowledge of the field, as reflected in research-based curricular mandates, to students. Students would eventually be regarded as active meaning makers, but only after they had received the tools of decoding from their teachers. The greatest changes of all would have taken place in the underlying model of reading and reading acquisition. The simple view of reading (RC = Dec * LC) would have returned in full force, and the job of young readers would be to acquire the decoding knowledge they lack when they begin to learn to read.

A Second Alternative

If those who are pushing for ecological balance prevail, the field will experience less dramatic shifts. A balanced approach will privilege authentic texts and tasks, with a heavy emphasis on writing, literature, response, and comprehension, but it will also call for an ambitious program of explicit instruction for phonics, word identification, comprehension, spelling, and writing. A balanced approach is likely to look like some instantiations of whole language from the early 1990s, but recalibrated to redress the unintended curricular consequences outlined earlier in this chapter. Major differences between a balanced approach and the new phonics are likely to manifest themselves most vividly in kindergarten and grade 1, where a rich set of language and literacy experiences would provide the context from which teachers would carve out scaffolded instructional activities to spotlight necessary skills and strategies, for example, phonemic awareness, letter-sound knowledge, concepts of print, and conceptual development. Thus,

instruction, while focused and explicit, would also be highly contextualized.

Beneath the curricular surface, balanced approaches seem to share slightly more in common, at least on a philosophical plane, with whole language than with new phonics approaches. The teacher is both facilitator and instructor. The teacher facilitates learning by establishing authentic activities, intervening where necessary to provide the scaffolding and explicit instruction required to help students take the next step toward independence. The student is, as in whole language, an active meaning maker from day one of preschool. Reading is a process of constructing meaning in response to texts encountered in a specific context, and the emergent literacy metaphor, not the readiness metaphor, characterizes the acquisition process.

An Ecologically Balanced Approach

If my personal bias has not emerged, let me declare it unequivocally: I favor the conceptual map of the ecologically balanced approach. There are several reasons for favoring this stance. First, my reading of the research points to the balanced curricular position, not to the new phonics position, both at a theoretical and a pedagogical level. I do not see much support for the simple view of reading underlying the new phonics; readers do construct meaning, they do not find it simply lying there in the text. Regarding pedagogical research, my reading requires me to side with Chall's view that while some sort of early, focused, and systematic emphasis on the code is called for, no particular approach can be singled out. Even the recent report of the National Reading Panel took exactly that position. And, while I readily accept the findings of the phonemic awareness research, I do not read them as supporting drill and practice approaches to this important linguistic understanding; to the contrary, highly embedded approaches, such as invented spelling, are equally as strongly implicated in the research.[107]

Second, an ecologically balanced approach is more respectful of the entire range of research in our field. It does not have to exclude major research paradigms or methodological approaches to sustain its integrity.

Third, an ecologically balanced approach also respects the wisdom of practice. It is no accident that studies of exemplary teachers, those who are respected by their peers and nurture high student achievement, consistently find that they exhibit a balanced repertoire of instructional strategies. Teachers who are faced with the variations in achievement, experience, and aptitude found in today's classrooms apparently need and deserve a full tool box of pedagogical practices.

Finally, an ecologically balanced approach respects our professional history. It retains the practices that have proved useful from each era but transforms and extends them, rendering them more effective, more useful, and more supportive of teachers and students. And, it may represent our only alternative to the pendulum-swing view of our pedagogical history that seems to have plagued the field of reading for most of the 20th century. A transformative rather than a cyclical view of progress would be a nice start for a new century. It will be interesting to evaluate in another twenty years, with the lens of history at our disposal, which path we have followed.

Endnotes

[1] The work reported herein was supported in part under the Education Research and Development Centers Program PR/Award Number R305R70004, as administered by the Office of Educational Research and Improvement, U.S. Department of Education. However, the contents do not necessarily represent the positions or policies of the National Institute on Student Achievement, Curriculum, and Assessment or the National Institute on Early Childhood Development, or the U.S. Department of Education, and endorsement by the federal government should not be assumed. An earlier and more complete version of this essay, titled "Reading in the Twentieth Century," appeared in Good, Thomas (Ed.). (2000). *American education: Yesterday, today, and tomorrow* (Ninety-ninth yearbook of the National Society for the Study of Education, pp. 152–208). Chicago: University of Chicago Press. Adapted with permission.

[2] Austin, Mary C., & Morrison, Coleman. (1963). *The first R.* New York: Macmillan.

[3] This account is from Chall, J. (1967). *Learning to read: The great debate* (pp. 13–15). New York: McGraw Hill.

[4] Smith, N.B. (1986). *American reading instruction* (p. 276). Newark, DE: International Reading Association.

[5] Smith, N.B. (1986). *American reading instruction.*

[6] Bond, G.L., & Dykstra, R. (1997). The cooperative research program in first-grade reading instruction, *Reading Research Quarterly, 32*(4). Entire issue.

[7] The reporting of data for students through grade 2 did not receive the fanfare that the first-grade report did, an outcome which I find unfortunate because it was, in many ways, even more interesting. It showed stronger effects overall for code-based approaches, and it revealed the most provocative of all the findings in this entire enterprise—the project effect. The project effect was this: Using analysis of covariance to control incoming performance, students were better off being in the poorest performing approach in Project A than they were being in the best performing approach in Project B. This raises the whole issue of impact of contextual factors on reading achievement. See Dykstra, R. (1968). Summary of the second-grade phase of the cooperative research program in primary reading instruction. *Reading Research Quarterly, 4,* 49–70.

[8] If focus were on the impact of these studies on research rather than the practice, these issues would occupy more of our attention. In a sense, the First-Grade Studies created an opening for other research endeavors; indeed, the directions that reading research took in the mid-1970s—the nature of comprehension and the role of the teacher—suggest that there were groups of scholars ready to seize the opportunity.

[9] When large-scale experiments returned in the early 1990s, it was not the Department of Education, but the National Institute of Child Health and Human Development (NICHD), that led the renaissance. For accounts of the development of the NICHD effort, see Lyon, G.R. (1995). Research initiatives in learning disabilities: Contributions from scientists supported by the National Institute of Child Health and Human Development. *Journal of Child Neurology, 10,* 120–127; or Lyon, G.R., & Chhaba,V. (1996). The current state of science and the future of specific reading disability. *Mental Retardation and Developmental Disabilities Research Reviews, 2,* 2–9. It is also worth noting that one of the likely reasons for the demise of Method A vs. Method B experiments is that scholars in the 1960s were looking for main effects rather than interaction effects. Had they set out to find in this work that methods are uniquely suited to particular populations, they might not have rejected them so completely.

[10] The impact of Chall's book, particularly the phonics recommendation, was documented by Helen Popp (1975). Current practices in the teaching of beginning reading. In John B. Carroll and Jeanne S. Chall (Eds.), *Toward a literate society: The report of the Committee on Reading of the National Academy of Education.* New York: McGraw Hill.

[11] In an unpublished research study, researchers found two- and three-fold increases in the number of words introduced in the first-grade books for the popular series published by Scott Foresman and Ginn. Hansen, J., & Pearson, P.D. (1978). *Learning to read: A decade after Chall.* Unpublished manuscript, University of Minnesota.

[12] The teacher's manuals of the Ginn 360 program provide the most notable example of this new trend. See Clymer, T., et al. (1968). *Ginn 360.* Lexington, MA: Ginn.

13 Mastery learning can trace its intellectual roots to the works of Benjamin Bloom and John Carroll: Bloom, B. (1968). Learning for mastery. *Evaluation Comment, 1*; Carroll, J. (1963). A model of school learning. *Teachers College Record, 64*, 723–732.

14 For an account of criterion-referenced assessment as it emerged during this period, see Popham, J. (1978). *Criterion-referenced measurement*. Englewood Cliffs, NJ: Prentice-Hall.

15 Deno, S.L. (1985). Curriculum-based measurement: The emerging alternative. *Exceptional Children, 52*, 219–232.

16 Bloom, B. (1968). Learning for mastery.

17 During the 1970s, the most popular of these systems was the Wisconsin Design for Reading Skill Development, followed closely by Fountain Valley. Systems like these remained a staple in basal programs in the 1980s and 1990s and were still available as options in most commercial programs as late as 2002. For an account of the rationale behind these systems, see Otto, Wayne (1977). The Wisconsin Design, A reading program for individually guided education. In H.J. Klausmeier, R.A. Rossmiller, & M. Saily (Eds.), *Individually guided elementary education: Concepts and practices*. New York: Academic Press. For a critique of these programs during their ascendancy, see Johnson & Pearson, "Skills Management Systems."

18 This is not to say that there were no challengers to the conventional wisdom that emerged in the middle of the century. To the contrary, the alphabetic approach, now dubbed "synthetic phonics," survived as a force throughout the period, as did the language experience approach and a few assorted alternatives. See Chall, *Learning to Read*, and Mathews, *Teaching to Read*, for accounts of these programs.

19 It should be noted that a major child-centered reform movement, the open classroom, was creating quite a wave in educational circles and elementary schools throughout the United States in the early 1970s. It is hard, however, to find any direct impact of the open-classroom movement on reading instruction. However, one could make the argument that the open-classroom philosophy had a delayed impact in its influence on the whole language movement in the late 1980s.

20 Some portions of the text in this section were adapted in Pearson, P.D., & Stephens, D. (1993). Learning about literacy: A 30-year journey. In C.J. Gordon, G.D. Labercane, & W.R. McEachern (Eds.), *Elementary reading: Process and practice* (pp. 4–18). Boston: Ginn. (Sections adapted with the knowledge and permission of the coauthor and publisher.)

21 To assert that Chomsky laid the groundwork for an essential critique of behaviorism as an explanatory model for language processes is not to assert that he drove behaviorism out of psychology or education.

22 For an account of this view of language development, see Brown, R. (1970). *Psycholinguistics*. New York: Macmillan.

23 Goodman, K.G. (1965). A linguistic study of cues and miscues in reading. *Elementary English, 42*, 639–643; and Goodman, K.G. (1967). A psycholinguistic guessing game. *Journal of the Reading Specialist, 4*, 126–135.

24 Smith, F. (1971). *Understanding reading: A Psycholinguistic analysis of reading and learning to read*. New York: Holt, Rinehart, & Winston.

25 In all fairness, it must be admitted that this contribution was not exclusively Smith's. As we shall point out in later sections, many other scholars, most notably David Rumelhart and Richard Anderson, championed constructivist views of reading. It is fair, however, to say that Smith was the first scholar to bring this insight into the reading field. Rumelhart, D. (1980). Schemata: The building blocks of cognition. In R.J. Spiro, B.C. Bruce, & W.F. Brewer (Eds.), *Theoretical issues in reading comprehension*. Hillsdale, NJ: Erlbaum. Anderson, R.C. & Pearson, P.D. (1984). A schema-theoretic view of basic processes in reading comprehension. In P.D. Pearson, R. Barr, M.L. Kamil, & P. Mosenthal (Eds.), *Handbook of reading research*. New York: Longman.

26 Smith, F. (1983). Reading like a writer. *Language Arts, 60*, 558–567.

27 During this period, great homage was paid to intellectual ancestors such as Edmund Burke Huey, who as early as 1908 recognized the cognitive complexity of reading. Voices such as Huey's, unfortunately, were not heard during the period 1915 to 1965 when behaviorism dominated psychology and education.

28 Walter Kintsch and Bonnie Meyer wrote compelling accounts of the structure of exposition that were translated by others (e.g., Barbara Taylor and Richard Beach) into instructional strategies. See Kintsch, W. (1974). *The representation of meaning in memory*. Hillsdale, NJ: Erlbaum; Meyer, B.J.F. (1975). *The organization of prose and its effects on memory*. Amsterdam: North Holland Publishing; and Taylor, B.M., & Beach, R. (1984). The effects of text structure instruction on middle-grade students' comprehension and production of expository text. *Reading Research Quarterly, 19*, 134–146.

29 The most complete accounts of schema theory are provided by Rumelhart, D., (1980) "Schemata: The Building Blocks of Cognition," and Anderson & Pearson, (1984) "A Schema-Theoretic View of Basic Processes in Reading Comprehension."

30 Bartlett, F.C. (1932). *Remembering*. Cambridge, UK: Cambridge University Press.

31 It is not altogether clear that schema theory is dead, especially in contexts of practice. Its role in psychological theory is undoubtedly diminished due to attacks on its efficacy as a model of memory and cognition. See McNamara, T.P., Miller, D.L., & Bransford, J.D. (1991). Mental models and reading comprehension. In R. Barr, M.L. Kamil, P. Mosenthal, & P.D. Pearson (Eds.), *Handbook of reading research* (Vol. 2, pp. 490–511). New York: Longman.

32 For early accounts of this perspective, see Baratz, J., & Shuy, R. (1969). *Teaching black children to read*. Washington, DC: Center for Applied Linguistics; and Labov, W. (1972). *Language of the inner city*. Philadelphia: University of Pennsylvania Press.

33 Baratz & Shuy (1969). *Teaching black children to read*.

34 See Bloome, D., & Greene, J. (1969). Directions in the sociolinguistic study of reading. *Handbook of reading research* (Vol. 2, pp. 395–421).

35 Rosenblatt, L. (1936/1978). *Literature as exploration*. New York: Appleton Century Croft. Rosenblatt, L.

(1978). *Reader, text, and poem*. Carbondale, IL: Southern Illinois University Press.

[36] Rosenblatt (1938) credits the idea of transaction to John Dewey, who discussed it in many texts, including *Experience and Education*. New York: Kappa Delta Pi.

[37] A very interesting, even provocative attempt to understand comprehension processes appears in Thorndike, Edward L. (1917). Reading as reasoning: A study of mistakes in paragraph reading. *Journal of Educational Psychology, 8*, 323–332. The classic reference for using tests to reveal the psychological infrastructure of comprehension is the first published factor analysis of reading comprehension by Davis, F. (1944). Fundamental factors of reading comprehension. *Psychometrika, 9*, 185–197.

[38] Robinson, H.M. (Ed). (1968). *Innovation and change in reading instruction* (Sixty-seventh yearbook of the National Society for Study in Education, Part II). Chicago: University of Chicago Press.

[39] Dolores Durkin published a revealing study in 1978 documenting that what went on in the name of comprehension was essentially completing worksheets and answering questions during story discussions. She saw almost no instruction about how to engage in any sort of comprehension task—no modeling, no demonstration, no scaffolding. Durkin, D. (1978). What classroom observations reveal about reading instruction. *Reading Research Quarterly, 14* 481–533.

[40] Among the most notable efforts at the Center were the classic works on reciprocal teaching: Palincsar, A., & Brown, A.L. (1984). Reciprocal teaching of comprehension fostering and monitoring activities. *Cognition and Instruction, 1*, 117–175; Raphael, T.E., & Pearson, P.D. (1985). Increasing students' awareness of sources of information for answering questions. *American Educational Research Journal, 22*, 217–236; and explicit comprehension instruction as a general approach in Pearson, P.D., & Dole, J. (1988). Explicit comprehension instruction: A review of research and a new conceptualization of instruction. *Elementary School Journal, 88*, 151–165; Pearson, P.D. (1985). Changing the face of reading comprehension instruction. *The Reading Teacher, 38*, 724–738. This focus on comprehension and reasoning while reading continues today at the Center with the work of Anderson and his colleagues.

[41] The work of Scott Paris and his colleagues is exemplary in the area of metacognitive training and comprehension monitoring. Paris, S.G., Cross, D.R., & Lipson, M.Y. (1984). Informed strategies for learning: A program to improve children's reading awareness and comprehension. *Journal of Educational Psychology, 76*, 1239–1252.

[42] Michael Pressley, working in conjunction with a group of professionals in Montgomery County, Maryland, developed a set of powerful comprehension routines that, among other things, extended the four strategies of reciprocal teaching (questioning, summarizing, clarifying, and predicting) to include more aspects of literary response (e.g., personal response and author's craft). The best resource on this line of pedagogical research is a 1993 volume of *Elementary School Journal*, edited by Pressley, along with the following articles, one of which is from that volume: M. Pressley et al. Transactional instruction of comprehension strategies: The Montgomery County, Maryland, SAIL Program. *Reading and Writing Quarterly, 10*, 5–19; M. Pressley et al. Beyond direct explanation: Transactional instruction of reading comprehension strategies. *Elementary School Journal, 92*, 513–555.

[43] K-W-L, an acronym for a graphic organizer technique in which students chart before and after reading what they know, what they want to know, and what they learned, is an interesting phenomenon, because while it has attracted a great deal of curricular attention in basals, articles for practicners, and staff development materials, it is hard to find much research on its instructional efficacy. See Ogle, D. (1986). The K-W-L: A teaching model that develops active reading of expository text. *The Reading Teacher, 39*, 564–570.

[44] Isabel Beck and Margaret McKeown have spent several years in collaboration with a network of teachers perfecting this engaging practice, which focuses on how and why authors put text together the way they do. The net result of this routine is that students learn a great deal about how to read critically (What is the author trying to do to me as a reader?) and about author's craft (How do authors structure their ideas to achieve particular effects?). See Beck, I., McKeown, M., Hamilton, R.L., & Kucan, L. (1997). *Questioning the author: An approach for enhancing student engagement with text*. Newark, DE: International Reading Association.

[45] Chall, in the 1991 edition of *Learning to Read*, documented this important increase in basal comprehension activities.

[46] Chall devotes a section to individualized reading in her 1967 description of alternatives to the basal (pp. 41–42), but has little to say about it as a serious alternative to basal, phonics, or linguistic approaches. In that same period, it is, undoubtedly, Jeanette Veatch who served as the most vocal spokesperson for individualized reading. She published professional textbooks describing how to implement the program in the classroom, for example, *Individualizing your reading program* (1959). New York: G.P. Putnam. In the middle 1960s, Random House published a "series" of literature books that were accompanied (in a pocket on the inside cover) by a set of vocabulary and comprehension activities that look remarkably like basal workbook pages. The Random House materials remind one of the currently popular computer program, Accelerated Reader, which is similarly designed to manage some assessment and skill activity to accompany trade books that children read on their own.

[47] Anderson and his colleagues reported several studies documenting the impact of book reading on children's achievement gains: Anderson, R.C., Hiebert, E., Scott, J., & Wilkinson, I. (1984). *Becoming a nation of readers*. Champaign, IL: Center for the Study of Reading.

[48] Atwell, N. (1987). *In the middle: Writing, reading, and learning with adolescents*. Portsmouth, NH: Heinemann. While it is difficult to locate data to document these claims about Atwell's particular influence, the rise of literature in the middle school has been documented by changes in the teacher survey portion of the National Assessment of Educational Progress of Reading.

[49] James Hoffman and his colleagues painstakingly documented these sorts of changes in the basals of the

early 1990s. Hoffman, J.V., McCarthey, S.J., Abbott, J., Christian, C., Corman, L., Elliot, M.B., Matheme, D., & Stahle, D. (1994). So what's new in the "new" basals. *Journal of Reading Behavior, 26*, 47–73.

50 For a complete account of the Book Club movement, see McMahon, S.I., & Raphael, T. E., with Goatley, V., & Pardo, L. (1997). *The book club connection*. New York: Teachers College Press.

51 Two classic books by Donald Graves were influential in leading the process writing movement at the elementary level, as was Lucy Calkins' (1986) classic, *The Art of Teaching Writing*. Portsmouth, NH: Heinemann; Graves, D. (1983). *Writing: Teachers and students at work*. Portsmouth, NH: Heinemann; and Graves, D. (1984). *A researcher learns to write*. Portsmouth, NH: Heinemann.

52 Perhaps the most complete current reference on integrated curriculum is a new chapter in the third volume of the *Handbook of Reading Research*. Gavelek, J.R., Raphael, T.E., Biondo, S.M., and Wang, D. (in press). Integrated literacy instruction. In M.L. Kamil, P. Mosenthal, P.D. Pearson, & R. Barr (Eds.), *Handbook of Reading Research* (Vol. 3). Hillsdale, NJ: Erlbaum.

53 In Chapter 10 of Huey's 1908 book on reading, two such programs, one at Columbia and one at the University of Chicago, were described in rich detail. It is Dewey's insistence that pedagogy be grounded in the individual and collective experiences of learners that is typically cited when scholars invoke his name to support integrated curriculum. Huey, E.B. (1908). *The psychology and pedagogy of reading*. New York: Macmillan. (Revised 1912, 1915)

54 See Graves (1983) for an explication of his views on writing, and, for an account of how reading and writing support one another in an integrated language arts approach, see Hansen, J. (1987). *When readers write*. Portsmouth, NH: Heinemann.

55 Frank Smith and Robert Tierney and P. David Pearson carried this metaphor to the extreme. All three used the reading "like a writer" metaphor in titles to papers during this period: Smith, F. (1983). Reading like a writer. *Language Arts, 60*, 558–567; Tierney, R.J., & Pearson, P.D. (1983). Toward a composing model of reading. *Language Arts, 60*, 568–580; and Pearson, P.D., & Tierney, R.J. (1984). On becoming a thoughtful reader: Learning to read like a writer. In A. Purves & O. Niles (Eds.) *Reading in the secondary school* (Eighty-third yearbook of the National Society for the Study of Education, pp. 144–173). Chicago: National Society for the Study of Education.

56 Donald Holdaway's (1979) *The Foundations of Literacy*, summarizes this perspective and work.

57 The notion of significance here is intended to capture its impact, not its validity. Even those who question its validity would have difficulty discounting its influence on practice.

58 A rich account of the curricular antecedents of whole language and other progressive and critical pedagogies is found in Shannon, P. (1990). *The struggle to continue*. Portsmouth, NH: Heinemann. See also Goodman, Y. (1989). Roots of the wholelanguage movement. *Elementary School Journal, 90*, 113–127. The phrase, "the child as curriculum informant," comes from Harste, J., Burke, C., & Woodward, V. (1984). *Language stories and literacy lessons*. Portsmouth, NH: Heinemann.

59 One cannot possibly name all the important leaders of the whole language movement in the United States, but surely the list will be headed by Ken Goodman, Yetta Goodman, and Jerry Harste, all of whom wrote important works explicating whole language as a philosophical and curricular initiative.

60 In the third edition of *Learning to Read*, Chall makes the case that phonics instruction increased during the 1970s and began its decline in the middle 1980s, at the time comprehension became a dominant research and curricular issue. She also notes a further decline in phonics instruction in basals, based on the work of James Hoffman et al. (1994). So what's 'new' in the new basals. On this issue, one should also consult Goodman, K.G., Shannon, P., Freeman, Y., & Murphy, S. (1988). *Report card on basal readers*. Katonah, NY: Richard C. Owen.

61 My understanding of the primary focus of the opposition to basals is that whole language advocates regarded basals as a pernicious form of external control on teacher prerogative, one that would lead inevitably to the "de-skilling" of teachers. In 1988, several whole language advocates and supporters wrote a monograph documenting what they took to be these pernicious effects (Goodman, Freeman, Shannon, & Murphy, 1988).

62 See Hoffman et al. (1994). So what's 'new' in the new basals?"

63 Perhaps the most compelling sign of the background-ing of skills was their systematic removal from the pupil books. In the middle and even late 1980s, basal publishers featured skills lessons in the pupil books on the grounds that even teachers who chose not to use the workbooks would have to deal with skills that were right there in the student materials. By the early 1990s, as I noted earlier, they were removed from the student books.

64 One must keep in mind that I am discussing changes in published materials, not necessarily changes in classroom practice. Whether teachers changed their actual classroom practices in a matter consistent with, or at least proportional to, the basal practices is difficult to determine given our lack of broad-based data on classroom practices. One suspects that the pendulum swings of actual classroom practice are never quite as wide as the swings in the rhetoric of policy or even the suggestions in published materials.

65 Pearson, P.D. (1992). *RT* remembrance: The second 20 years. *The Reading Teacher, 45*, 378–385. This analysis documents the increasingly dominant force of whole language, literature-based reading, and process writing in the discourse of elementary reading and language arts instruction.

66 Perhaps the best documentation for the resistance to, or at least a more critical acceptance of, whole language practices comes from studies of exemplary teachers who, it appears, never bought into whole language lock, stock, and barrel, but instead chose judiciously those practices that helped them to develop rich, flexible, and balanced instructional portfolios. See Wharton-MacDonald, R., Pressley, M., & Hampton, J.M. (1998). Literacy instruction in nine first-grade classrooms: Teacher characteristics and student achievement. *The Elementary School Journal, 99*, 101–128.

[67] A recent analysis of the basals adopted in the early 1990s in California suggests that the vocabulary load of many of these basals was so great that most first graders could gain access to them only if they were read to them by a teacher: Martin, L.A., & Hiebert, E.H. (in press). *Little books and phonics texts: An analysis of the new alternatives to basals.* Ann Arbor, MI: Center for the Improvement of Early Reading Achievement, University of Michigan.

[68] In the late 1970s, Marie M. Clay coined the term *emergent literacy* to signal a break with traditional views of readiness in favor of a more gradual view of the shift from novice to expert reader. See Clay, M.M. (1966). *Emergent reading behavior.* Unpublished doctoral dissertation, University of Auckland, New Zealand.

[69] In my own case, it was the disdain that whole language seemed to spawn regarding the explicit teaching of skills and strategies, especially those that promoted the meaning-making goals of the movement: comprehension and metacognitive strategies.

[70] Hiebert, E.H., & Taylor, B.M. (Eds.). (1994). *Getting reading right from the start: Effective early literacy interventions.* Boston: Allyn & Bacon. The researchers describe several research-based interventions that balance skills instruction with authentic reading.

[71] Interestingly, a recent piece in *The Reading Teacher* makes exactly this point about the comprehension strategy instruction of the 1980s. See Dowhower, S.L. (1999). Supporting a strategic stance in the classroom: Comprehension framework for helping teachers help students to be strategic. *The Reading Teacher, 52,* 672–688.

[72] Smith, "Learning to Read like a Writer," makes just this point.

[73] For a compelling account of this "no text" phenomenon, see Schoenbach, R., Greenleaf, C., Cziko, C., & Hurwitz, L. (in press). *Reading for understanding in the middle and high school.* San Francisco: Jossey Bass. In this account, the staff developers and teachers of a middle school academic literacy course document the role of text in middle school as well as attempts to turn the tide.

[74] Similar arguments have been made for the reform movements in mathematics; for instance, that the reforms got ahead of the professional knowledge base. The results of the reform movement in mathematics have also been similar to the fate of the whole language movement. See Good, T., & Braden, J. (no date). *Reform in American education: A focus on vouchers and charters.* Hillsdale, NJ: Erlbaum.

[75] In 1989, a Special Interest Group with the apocryphal label, Balanced Reading Instruction, was organized at the International Reading Association. The group was started to counteract the unchecked acceptance of whole language as the approach to use with any and all students and to send the alternate message that there is no necessary conflict between authentic activity (usually considered the province of whole language) and explicit instruction of skills and strategies (usually considered the province of curriculum-centered approaches). For elaborate accounts of balanced literacy instruction, see McIntyre, E., & Pressley, M. (1996). *Balanced instruction: Strategies and skills in whole language.* Boston, MA: Christopher-Gordon; Gambrell, L.B., Morrow, L.M., Neuman, S.B., & Pressley, M. (1999). *Best practices in literacy instruction.* New York: Guilford; Pearson, P.D. (1996). Reclaiming the center. In M. Graves, P. van den Broek, & B.M. Taylor (Eds.), *The first R: Every child's right to read.* New York: Teachers College Press.

[76] Pearson details many of these concerns and arguments in "Reclaiming the Center."

[77] As early as 1965, Kenneth Goodman had popularized the use of miscues to gain insights into cognitive processes. The elaborate version of miscue analysis first appeared in Goodman, Y., & Burke, C. (1969). *Reading miscue inventory.* New York: Macmillan.

[78] For an index of the rising momentum of qualitative research in the early 1980s, see Guthrie, L.F., & Hall, W.S. (1984). Ethnographic approaches to reading research; and Bloome, D., & Greene, J. (1984). Directions in the sociolinguistic study of reading, in *Handbook of Reading Research.*

[79] As a way of documenting this change, examine *Handbook of Reading Research,* Vols. 1 (1984) and Vol. 2 (1991). Volume 1 contains only two chapters that could be construed as relying on some sort of interpretive inquiry. Volume 2 has at least eight such chapters. For an account of the historical patterns in nonquantitative inquiry, see Siegel, M., & Fernandez, S.L. (2000). Critical approaches. *Handbook of Reading Research* (Vol. 3).

[80] Beginning in the mid-1980s and continuing today, the pages of *Educational Researcher* began to publish accounts of the qualitative-quantitative divide. It is the best source to consult in understanding the terms of the debate.

[81] For an account of the evolution of this line of inquiry, consult Lyon, R. (1995). Research initiatives in learning disabilities: Contributions from scientists supported by the National Institute of Child Health and Human Development. *Journal of Child Neurology, 10,* 120–126; and Lyon, R., & Chhaba, V. (1996). The current state of science and the future of specific reading disability. *Mental Retardation and Developmental Disabilities Research Reviews, 2,* 2–9.

[82] The most highly touted pedagogical experiment supported by NICHD was published in 1998: Foorman, B.R., Francis, D.J., Fletcher, J.M., Schatschneider, C., & Mehta, P. (1998). The role of instruction in learning to read: Preventing reading failure in at-risk children. *Journal of Educational Psychology, 90,* 37–55. The NICHD work, in general, and the Foorman et al piece, in particular, have been cited as exemplary in method and as supportive of a much more direct code emphasis, even in the popular press (e.g., *Dallas Morning News,* May 12, 1998; *Houston Chronicle,* May 17, 1998; *Minneapolis Star Tribune,* August 5, 1998)

[83] Much, for example, is made in this new work of the inappropriateness of encouraging young readers to use context clues as a way of figuring out the pronunciations of unknown words. The data cited are eye-movement studies showing that adult readers appear to process each and every letter in the visual display on a page and, most likely, to then recode those visual symbols into a speech code prior to understanding.

[84] Allington, R., & Woodside-Jiron, H. (1998). Thirty years of research in reading: When is a research summary not a research summary? In K.S. Goodman (Ed.), *In defense*

of good teaching. York, ME: Stenhouse. These writers document the manner in which Bonnie Grossen's manuscript, which is an alleged summary of the research sponsored by NICHD, was used in several states as the basis for reading policy initiatives: Grossen, B. (1997). *30 years of research: What we now know about how children learn to read.* Santa Cruz, CA: The Center for the Future of Teaching and Learning. Web document: http://www.cftl.org/30years/30years

85 Classic references attesting to the importance of phonemic awareness are Juel, C. (1991). Beginning reading. In R. Barr, M. Kamil, P. Mosenthal, & P. David Pearson (Eds.), *Handbook of Reading Research* (Vol. 2, pp. 759–788). New York: Longman; and Adams, M. (1990). *Beginning to Read.* More recently, it has been documented in Snow, C., Burns, S.M., & Griffith, P. (1998). *Preventing reading difficulties in young children.* Washington, DC: National Academy Press.

86 See Juel, C. (1991). "Beginning Reading."

87 See Juel, C. (1991). "Beginning Reading"; and Adams, M., *Beginning to Read.*

88 The work of Linda K. Clarke (1988), "Invented versus traditional spelling in first graders' writings: Effects on learning to spell and read," *Research in the teaching of English*, 22(3), 281–309; and Pamela Winsor and P. David Pearson (1992). *Children at-risk: Their phonemic awareness development in holistic instruction* (Tech. Rep. No. 556). Urbana, IL: Center for the Study of Reading, University of Illinois, are most relevant on the issue of the various curricular routes to phonemic awareness development.

89 Nowhere is the rationale for the mandate of early, systematic phonics more clearly laid out than in the report of the National Reading Panel that appeared in April of 2000.

90 In Summer 1995, one entire issue of *American Educator*, 19(2), was devoted to the phonics revival. Authors of various pieces included those who would generally be regarded as leaders in moving phonics back to center stage—Marilyn Adams, Isabel Beck, Connie Juel, and Louisa Moats, among others. One piece by Marilyn J. Adams and Maggie Bruck (1995, Summer), "Resolving the Great Debate," *American Educator, 19*, 7, 10–20, is one of the clearest expositions of the modern phonics first position I can find. A second issue was also devoted entirely to reading (Spring/Summer, 1998, Vol. 22, No. 1 and 2).

91 See Connie Juel, "Beginning Reading"; and Gough & Hillinger (1980).

92 One of the reasons for the continuation of the debate is that few people seek common ground. Researchers who come from the whole language tradition, were they to read Adams and Juel openly, would find much to agree with about in the common privileging of Big Books, writing, invented spelling, and the like. They would not even disagree with them about the critical role that phonemic awareness or knowledge of the cipher plays in early reading success. They would, however, disagree adamantly about the most appropriate instructional route to achieving early success; phonics knowledge and phonemic awareness are better viewed, they would argue, as the consequence of, rather than the cause of, success in authentic reading experiences.

93 These and other reading policy matters have been well documented in a series of pieces in *Education Week* by Kathleen Manzo Kennedy (1997, 1998, 1999). See No. 99.

94 107th United States Congress (2002). Public Law 107-110. No Child Left Behind. Washington DC: Government Printing Office.

95 Marilyn Adams (see *Beginning to Read*, and Adams & Bruck, "Resolving the Great Debate") has consistently championed invented spelling.

96 Allington, R., & Woodside-Jiron, H. (1998, Spring). Decodable text in beginning reading: Are mandates and policy based on research? *ERS Spectrum*, 3–11. These researchers have conducted a thorough analysis of the genesis of this "research-based" policy and concluded that it all goes back to an incidental finding from a study by Juel and Roper-Schneider in 1983. They could find no direct experimental tests of the efficacy of decodable text.

97 Learning First Alliance (1998). *Every child reading.* Washington, DC: Author.

98 The war metaphor comes up time and again when the debate is portrayed in the public press. See, for example, Levine, A. (1994, December). The great debate revisited. *Atlantic Monthly.*

99 Manzo, Kathleen K. (1997, March 12). Study stresses role of early phonics instruction. *Education Week, 16*, pp. 1, 24–25; Manzo, Kathleen K. (1998, February 18). New national panel faulted before it's formed. *Education Week, 17*(23), p. 7; and Manzo, Kathleen K. (1998, March 25). NRC panel urges end to reading wars. *Education Week, 17*(28), pp. 1, 18.

100 Several studies are relevant here: First is the work of Wharton-McDonald and Pressley, cited earlier. Also important is the work of Pressley, M., & Allington, R. (1998); and Taylor, B.M., Pearson, P.D., Clark, K., & Walpole, S. (2000). Effective schools and accomplished teachers: Lessons about primary-grade reading instruction in low-income schools. *Elementary School Journal, 101*(2), 121–165.

101 See Pearson, DeStefano, & García (1998), for an account of the decrease in reliance on portfolio and performance assessment.

102 The clearest instantiation of this approach occurred in California where professional development-based on scientifically based reading research was transformed into law (AB 466). AB 466 required professional development funds from the state of California to be spent only on the state adopted materials, which were defined, prima facie, as based on scientific reading research. California State Legislature. (2001). Assembly Bill 466. The Mathematics and Reading Professional Development. Sacramento, CA: Author.

103 An interesting aside in all the political rhetoric has been the question, Who is de-skilling teachers? As early as the 1970s, whole language advocates were arguing that canned programs and basal reader manuals were de-skilling teachers by providing them with preprogrammed routines for teaching. Recently, whole language has been accused of de-skilling by denying teachers access to the technical knowledge needed to teach reading effectively; see McPike, E. (1995). Learning to read: The school's first mission. *American Educator, 19*, 4.

104 Written from a somewhat centrist whole language position, Regie Routman provides a compelling account of the political and pedagogical issues we confront in the current debates. Routman, R. (1996). *Literacy at the crossroads* Portsmouth, NH: Heinemann.

105 The *balance* label comes with excess baggage. I use it only because it has gained currency in the field. Balance works for me as long as the metaphor of ecological balance, as in the balance of nature, is emphasized, and the metaphor of the fulcrum balance beam, as in the scales of justice, is suppressed. The fulcrum, which achieves balance by equalizing the mass on each side of the scale, suggests a stand-off between skills and whole language—one for skills, one for whole language. By contrast, ecological balance suggests a symbiotic relationship among elements within a coordinated system. It is precisely this symbiotic potential of authentic activity and explicit instruction that I want to promote by using the term *balance*.

106 Adams and Bruck, "Resolving the Great Debate"; Adams, M. (1990). *Beginning to read: Thinking and learning about print*. Cambridge, MA: MIT Press; Fletcher, J., & Lyon, G.R. (1998). Reading: A research based approach. In W. Evers (Ed.), *What's gone wrong in America's classrooms?* Stanford, CA: Hoover Institution Press.

107 See the earlier cited studies by Clarke and Winsor and Pearson, as well as the review of phonemic awareness in Adams, M., *Beginning to Read*. See also the report of the National Reading Panel.

Developmental-Spelling Research: A Systematic Imperative

Marcia Invernizzi and Latisha Hayes

A team of first-grade teachers began to question their literacy/phonics program, which used a whole-class format for instruction. The teachers felt that teaching the whole class did not allow them to meet the diverse needs of all their students. One of the teachers introduced the rest of the team to developmental-spelling research (i.e., research on the development of spelling proficiency that builds on linguistic interpretations of students' unconventional spellings as they change over time) and, specifically, to an approach to phonics and spelling instruction called word study. By using developmental-spelling assessments, the teachers believed they could better meet their students' needs through differentiated word study in small groups.

The new school year began with qualitative spelling assessments and subsequent grouping plans. Many issues arose quickly. When teachers placed their students along a developmental continuum of spelling features, they saw that many students could bypass earlier features that, according to assessment results, they had already learned. The idea of having a group of students skip over easier features made them anxious about meeting the Reading First criteria for systematic phonics instruction. In their previous whole-class teaching, everyone started in the same place and proceeded systematically through the curriculum. Now the teachers were uncertain about choosing different spelling features for different groups. They found themselves spending more time preparing when they were used to depending upon an already prepared program. Management issues associated with differentiated groupings proved to be challenging. They wondered how teachers could take developmental-spelling research and make it practical for the classroom.

Developmental-spelling research has been at the fulcrum of several educational movements in the past few decades, two of them diametrically opposed to each other. On the one hand, discovery of rule-governed phonetic logic at work in children's invented spellings sparked a writing revolution in the primary classroom (Richgels, 2001). In Morris's (1989) words, "It is doubtful how far process-writing would have progressed in first and second grade classrooms had not teachers been given some kind of logical assurance that spelling is a developmental process" (pp. iii–iv). Some, unfortunately, took these assurances too far and eliminated spelling instruction entirely, a negligent immoderation to which plummeting National Assessment of Educational Progress (NAEP) scores have been repeatedly attributed ("Bad Spelling," 1995). Nevertheless, developmental-spelling research survived the reactionary restraints placed on invented spelling in school districts across the United States and is now coming into its own in the midst of a very different political arena. Word study, an approach

Preparing Reading Professionals (second edition), edited by Rita M. Bean, Natalie Heisey, and Cathy M. Roller. © 2010 by the International Reading Association. Reprinted from Invernizzi, M., & Hayes, L. (2004). Developmental-spelling research: A systematic imperative. *Reading Research Quarterly, 39*(2), 216–228. doi:10.1598/RRQ.39.2.4

to phonics and spelling instruction that has grown out of developmental-spelling research and theory, now appears in the phonics component of every major basal reading series, and developmental-spelling assessments are endorsed in policy-driven workshops across the United States (Moats, 2003). Virtually every teacher's manual in every major reading series at least nominally suggests word sorts, and even the Texas Reading First materials include word study as a best practice for one of the five pillars of evidence-based instruction (First Grade Teacher Reading Academies, 2002, see p. 89). Publishers of textbooks, instructional materials, computer programs, and other commercial ventures are capitalizing on word study as the panacea for the phonics and spelling mandate, a panacea that circumvents the boring, decontextualized nature of spelling books and the meaningless drill associated with the workbooks deplored in the past. The recent proliferation of educational books, curriculum guides, computer programs, and special themed issues of educational journals on spelling witness the advent of spelling as one of the most critical areas of interest and concern not only among reading and English language arts educators but also among other scholars and professionals (Templeton, 2003).

Despite these influences, the potential impact of developmental-spelling research for classroom instruction has yet to be realized. The fundamental idea that invented spellings provide a diagnostic cue to a student's current understanding of how written words work, and that instruction can be timed and targeted to this understanding, is still, for the most part, overlooked. Part of this oversight may be attributed to a lack of understanding about the English writing system itself—the orthography and the systematic way in which children acquire it. Equally culpable is the propagation of mixed messages from commercial publishers and from policymakers regarding the nature of systematic instruction.

To teach English orthography, teachers must sift through bits and pieces of information they hear and read regarding effective literacy instruction and separate the wheat from the chaff, especially now with the push for explicit, systematic phonics and spelling instruction. The National Reading Panel (National Institute of Child Health and Human Development, 2000), for example, reported advantages for synthetic phonics (i.e., explicit instruction about how to convert letters to sounds and then how to blend the sounds together) over analytic phonics approaches despite the fact that teachers almost always teach the sounding out strategy along with other word analysis strategies such as chunking word parts. According to Pressley (2002), teachers routinely complement synthetic phonics with the teaching of word families and other orthographic units, and this practice is supported by recent research that shows an advantage of combined approaches in improving spelling and word recognition over single approaches such as synthetic phonics (Berninger et al., 1998; Lovett, Lacerenza, Borden, Frijters, Steinbach, & De Palma, 2000). Furthermore, newer, alternative approaches, such as word sorting and make-a-word, have an increasingly promising research base (Hall, Cunningham, & Cunningham, 1995; Joseph, 2000; Weber & Henderson, 1989). So, how do teachers go about implementing systematic phonics and spelling instruction these days? How can developmental-spelling research help teachers decide what continuum of phonics and spelling features makes the most systematic curriculum? And how can they teach such a curriculum systematically and still meet diverse students' needs?

A System Within a System: The History of English Spelling Informs Teaching

A systematic curriculum for phonics and spelling must, first and foremost, reflect the structure of the writing system itself. For this reason, early research on spelling focused on chronicling English orthography from a historical perspective (Craigie, 1927; Scragg, 1974; Vallins, 1973). This early work by language historians described the evolution of English spelling from the first written artifacts found in seventh-century monasteries to modern English as we spell it today. The historical record of English orthography is central to a definition of *systematic* because the evolution of written English explains why our spelling system is the way it is—how it is organized and the key features within this organization. The historical record reveals a systematic layering of alphabet, pattern, and meaning as these elements were seamed together across time (Henderson & Templeton, 1986). Knowledge of this system better equips teachers to teach their students how English orthography works *systematically* to represent a balance of sound and meaning (Wolf & Kennedy, 2003).

The *alphabet tier* was established during the time of Old English, which spanned between the Germanic invasions of England in the sixth century to the conquest of England by William of Normandy in 1066. Old English was an inflected language whose written counterpart enjoyed a remarkable consistency in letter–sound correspondence. The long vowels in Old English were pronounced close to the way they are in modern French and German today. That is, long-*e* was pronounced like the modern long-*a*, long-*i* was pronounced like the modern long-*e*, and long-*a* was pronounced like the broad-*a* in *father*. A single vowel stood for both long- and short-vowel pairings. Nevertheless, Old English laid the foundation for the alphabet to systematically represent individual speech sounds. The simplicity and consistency of the grapheme–phoneme correspondence in Old English were such that, armed with a phonetic guide to letters and sounds, modern readers can still read Abbot Aelfric's *Lord's Prayer* similar to the way Aelfric himself may have recited it over a thousand years ago (Henderson, 1990).

Old English is relevant to teachers today because young children spell like little Saxons as they begin to read and write (Henderson, 1981). Armed with only a rudimentary knowledge of the alphabet and letter sounds, neophyte readers use their alphabetic knowledge quite literally. They rely on the sound embedded within the names of the letters to represent the sounds they are trying to represent (Read,

1971). This strategy works quite well for consonants when the names do in fact contain the corresponding speech sounds (Bee, Dee, eF, eS, etc.). It works less well for letters that have more than one sound (C, G), and it doesn't work at all for consonants with names that do not contain their corresponding speech sounds (W: double you; Y: why; H: aich, etc.). Short-vowel sounds are particularly problematic for novice readers because there is no single letter that "says" the short-vowel sound. As a result, beginning readers choose a vowel whose pronounced name is closest by place of articulation to the targeted short vowel sound (Beers & Henderson, 1977; Read). The result is similar to Old English, in which a single-vowel stood for two sounds. Today, a beginning reader may spell BED for *bad*, *band*, or *bead*. Rayner, Foorman, Perfetti, Pesetsky, and Seidenberg (2001) asserted that early spelling inventions such as these indicate a child's grasp of the alphabetic principle and presage the application of this principle in decoding (see p. 41).

The stability of Old English, however, was permanently altered by a massive influx of French words after the Norman Conquest in 1066. Because these words entered the existing language through bilingual Anglo-Norman speakers, some of the French pronunciations were adopted, too. Also, because the scribes who wrote the new words were biliterate, they used the French spelling for the new vocabulary and even applied French orthographic conventions to the spelling of some English words as well. Old English was thus overlaid with the vocabulary and spelling traditions of the ruling class, the Norman French. This complex interaction of pronunciation change on top of the intermingling of French and English spellings led to a proliferation of different vowel sounds represented by various vowel digraphs. The extensive repertoire of long-vowel patterns today is attributable to this period of history, which also accounts for the various pronunciations of the *ea* vowel pattern in words like *bread*, *thread*, *great*, *break*, *meat*, and *clean*. To be sure, this merging of oral and written traditions disrupted the relatively consistent relationship between letters and sounds that existed in Old English. However, in Middle English, a second tier of order was superimposed on the alphabetic foundation—a *pattern* tier in which letter combinations reflected roughly the language of origin.

During this time, somewhere around the 14th century, the pronunciation of long vowels gradually changed, and this change is known as the Great Vowel Shift. Although linguists do not know for sure what caused the Great Vowel Shift, it may have been the result of competing stress contours between English and French (Henderson, 1992). (English places stress most often on the first syllable, while in French secondary or tertiary stress is common—English speakers say ROBert while the French say RoBERT.) Regardless, the Great Vowel Shift is important in understanding the systematic pairing of long- and short-vowel sounds in Modern English and how children make sense of them as they learn to read and spell today. For example, beginning readers' short-vowel substitutions (e.g., *jet* spelled JAT; *bit* spelled BET) are explainable by the change in the pronunciation of vowels that occurred during the Great Vowel Shift.

During the Great Vowel Shift, each long vowel changed in pronunciation. The new pronunciations took the place of older pronunciations, forcing the older vowel into the next higher or lower articulatory position. For example, the old long-*a*, which had been pronounced as a broad-*a* as in *calm*, became the modern long-*a* whose sound we hear today in words like *wave*, *name*, or *take*. But in Old English, long-*e* had that spot; long-*e* was pronounced like a modern long-*a*—*mean* was pronounced *main*. This state of affairs forced the long-*e* to move to a different spot, so it appropriated the modern pronunciation of long-*e*. Unfortunately the old long-*i* used to be pronounced like the modern long-*e* (*hide* was pronounced *heed*) so it too had to change. The old sound of long-*i* thus dropped down to the space that *a* (formerly pronounced like a broad-*a*) had left, so the words *hide*, *fine*, or *five* became the modern diphthong sound we hear when we say these

words today: *hah-eed* (*hide*), *fah-een* (*fine*), and *fah-eev* (*five*). Although the pronunciation of the long vowels changed in this systematic way, the pronunciation of the short vowels remained the same. As a result, the long-*i* and the short-*i* today are pronounced as they are in the pair of words *ripe* and *rip*—whereas in Old English the single letter *i* represented the pair of vowel sounds heard in *read* and *rid* (Henderson, 1990).

It is uncanny that beginning readers must also make the "Great Vowel Shift" to make the transition from a purely linear, alphabetic stance to a more efficient use of patterns. As students' reading vocabularies expand sufficiently to sustain independent reading, their lexical store of known words leads them away from letter-name short-vowel substitutions to the correct spelling of short vowels and to find other ways of representing the long vowels. Students begin to take heed of additional silent vowels used to indicate a long-vowel sound and begin to "use but confuse" long-vowel patterns much like the Norman French (Invernizzi, Abouzeid, & Gill, 1994). Spellings like ROOTE BEER TAITS REELY SWETE (*root beer tastes really sweet*) look remarkably like Middle English.

The inclination to borrow words that started during England's long bilingual period foreshadowed a second era of massive word borrowing during the first half of the 16th century. At that time, classical vocabularies were acquired as educated men and women rediscovered the culture and knowledge of classical Greece and Rome. The Renaissance required a new, expanded vocabulary to accommodate the explosion in learning that occurred during this time. Classical roots and stems had the potential to meet this demand for meaning. Greek roots could be compounded (e.g., *autograph* and *autobiography*) and the meanings of Latin stems were recognizable despite derivational changes (*spectator*, *spectacular*, and *inspect*). So, to the orthographic record of English history was added a third layer of *meaning*, resulting in a complex but orderly system composed of alphabet, pattern, and meaning resulting in Modern English.

The spelling/meaning relations inherent in words brought into English during the Renaissance have important implications for vocabulary instruction today as students move through the intermediate grades and beyond (Templeton, 1991). As students explore how spelling visually preserves the semantic relationships among derivationally related words (e.g., *bomb* and *bombard*), vocabulary and spelling instruction become two sides of the same knowledge coin. Chomsky and Halle (1968) used the word *muscle* to show how the seemingly arbitrary spelling of some words is, in reality, central to understanding the meanings of related words (*muscle*, from the Latin *musculus*: *muscular, musculature*). The silent C in the word *muscle* represents a morphemic aspect of written English that preserves its etymological history.

The evolution of English orthography through tiers of alphabet, pattern, and meaning provides a historical structure through which to organize a systematic curriculum for phonics and spelling. It also provides an instructionally transparent, harmonious model for learning to read and write (Bear, Invernizzi, Templeton, & Johnston, 2003). Our spelling system is *alphabetic* because it represents the relationship between letters and sounds established by the Anglo-Saxon scribes. We can match letters—sometimes singly, sometimes in pairs—to speech sounds from left to right and create words. This is the goal of beginning readers and writers who must move from partial to full use of alphabetic cues to blend both letter sounds to decode and segment speech sounds to encode. The *pattern* layer overlays the alphabetic layer. When we look beyond single letter–sound matches and search for patterns that guide the groupings of letters, we find consistent categories of patterns that relate to categories of vowel sounds and the language of origin, largely Norman French (Bear, Invernizzi, et al.). The consolidation of letter patterns affords greater fluency in oral reading and writing, and this orthographic advancement heralds the onset of independent reading (Bear, 1992; Chall, 1983; Ehri & McCormick, 1998). In the third layer

of English orthography, the meaning layer, groups of letters (prefixes, suffixes, and Greek and Latin stems) represent meaning directly. Students operating within the meaning layer of English orthography have relatively automatic word recognition and encoding skills, and thus their minds are free to think as rapidly as they can read and write (Gough & Hillenger, 1980). Understanding the synchronous advances in reading, writing, and spelling development is crucial for balanced literacy instruction (Cramer, 1998).

Although most students are introduced to English spelling through the phonics component of a basal reading series, these programs may or may not conform to this general progression from sound to pattern to meaning in their phonics or spelling component. In the basal phonics lesson, the emphasis is usually on grapheme–phoneme correspondences as students learn how letters represent speech sounds. The presentation of vowel patterns and meaning elements (morphemes), the more advanced features in our orthographic history, is less deliberate. As Henry (1989) noted, "Rarely is this information organized for either teachers or their students" (p. 136).

Henry did organize this scope and sequence according to what she referred to as a historical structural perspective, and she examined the effectiveness of instruction in word features organized by the historical structures associated with the Anglo-Saxon, Romance, and Greek languages. Henry labeled these features letter–sound correspondences, syllable patterns, and morphemes, paralleling what Henderson and Templeton (1986) referred to as alphabet, pattern, and meaning. Henry (1989) found that third- and fifth-grade students who were explicitly taught historical structures and the specific features characteristic of those structures made greater gains in word recognition and spelling than did a control group. Not only did the curriculum follow a systematic progression of historical principles based on alphabet, pattern, and meaning, but also the content (orthographic features such as Latin stems like *tract*, *spect*, *dict*, etc.), structure (placement of features within words, such as *inspect* versus *spectator*), and process (teaching techniques, such as generating, reading, and spelling other examples) were presented in systematic routines. Henry wrote the following:

> In the *opening* teachers stated the purpose and goals for the lesson and introduced the new concept, pattern, and/or generalization. During the *middle* segment of the lesson, students discussed word features as they read words fitting a specific pattern, generated new words, and spelled numerous words fitting frequently used patterns. They often contrasted this pattern to other similar patterns and became aware of how word structure influences spelling. They spent little time in isolated drill and workbook practice. The lessons allowed the students to think of each concept and strategy as a problem solving activity.... To *close* the lesson, teachers and students summarized and reflected upon the lesson content, structural patterns, and procedures. *Follow-up* exercises promoted reinforcement of the concepts. For example, students looked for Greek words in their science texts...or looked for affixes in the evening newspaper. (p. 145)

In this example, historically derived orthographic structures, the organization of the content within each structure, and the consistency of the routines for teaching that content provide the *system*. Organizing the spelling curriculum according to historical orthographic structures also places the corpus of words to be studied in an evolutionary progression. Anglo-Saxon words, the oldest words in English, are among the easiest to read and the most familiar. Words like *sun*, *moon*, *day*, and *night* are high-frequency "earthy" words that populate easy reading material. Anglo-Saxon words most visibly survive in high-frequency prepositions, pronouns, conjunctions, and auxiliary verbs (e.g., *have*, *was*, *does*) where the pronunciation is now quite different from when English was an inflected language. More difficult Norman French words of one and two syllables—words like *chance*, *chamber*, *royal*, *feudal*, *guard*, and *conquer*—do not typically appear in beginning reading texts; they appear with greater frequency in books suitable for the upper elementary grades. English's most difficult words—words like *captive*, *circular*, *calculate*,

imitate, *maximum*, *cumulus*, *nucleus*, *hemisphere*, *hydraulic*, and *rhombus*—are of Latin and Greek origin and do not regularly appear in student reading selections until the middle grades and beyond. Thus, the history of English spelling explicates the frequency bands of written words as well as the appropriateness of certain kinds of words over others in relation to the learner. This historical structural perspective on word frequency has been borne out by more scientific accounts, from early computer studies of surface regularities in English spelling (Hanna, Hanna, Hodges, & Rudorf, 1966) to more recent taxonomies that considered frequency as well as predictability in the ordering of words along a continuum from easiest to more difficult (Venezky, 1995). Henderson (1990) added to our understanding of the role that frequency plays in learning to spell by considering the frequency of specific orthographic features, patterns, and morphemes as these relate to students' reading experience (Nelson, 1989). Programs that select words by frequency alone without also considering the frequency of specific orthographic patterns do not capture the consistency and predictability of English spelling.

Whereas the evolution of written English and a historical structural perspective may provide an overarching vision of a systematic spelling curriculum, the spelling development of individual students must be viewed in relation to the historic development of English spelling. By looking at individual spelling errors across an array of words organized by structures governing alphabet, pattern, and meaning, researchers have described an invariant order in which students acquire the features of English orthography (Ganske, 1999; Henderson, 1990; Invernizzi, 1992; Schlagal, 1982; Viise, 1994). The order is displayed in its simplest form under each tier of English orthography in Table 1. The different shadings represent the different stages or phases as described by developmental-spelling researchers. Note that some spelling features may be learned more or less simultaneously and that instruction can influence the order as well; an early emphasis on consonant digraphs

Table 1
The English Spelling System

Alphabet	Pattern	Meaning
1. Beginning consonants 2. Ending consonants 3. Short vowels 4. Consonant digraphs 5. Consonant blends 6. Preconsonantal nasals	7. Consonant-vowel-consonant-e (silent *e*) 8. Other common long-vowel patterns 9. Less common long-vowel patterns 10. Consonant-influenced vowels (*r, l, w*) 11. Complex consonant clusters 12. Diphthongs and other ambiguous vowels 13. Inflectional ending: Plural and past tense	17. Common prefixes 18. Common suffixes 19. Sounded-silent spelling/meaning connections
	14. Open- and closed-syllable patterns 15. Vowel patterns in accented syllables 16. Unaccented syllables	20. Consonant alternations in derivationally related pairs 21. Vowel alternations in derivationally related pairs 22. Greek roots 23. Latin stems 24. Predictable changes in derivationally related words 25. Advanced suffixes 26. Absorbed or assimilated prefixes

and blends, for example, may result in slightly earlier mastery. In addition, later features of one stage may overlap with some of the earlier features of the next stage, as can be seen with prefixes and suffixes at the top of the third column. Nevertheless, the general progressions within and across stages have been replicated in studies with many different groups of students from preschoolers (Templeton & Spivey, 1980) through adults (Bear, Truex, & Barone, 1989; Worthy & Viise, 1996), as well as across socioeconomic levels and dialects (Cantrell, 2001; Stever, 1980).

For bilingual learners the precise features of this progression are influenced by phonological and orthographical rules of their native language, but the general constructs within the stages appear similar across speakers of alphabetic languages (Gill, 1980; Temple, 1978). For example, research in the English spelling acquisition of Spanish bilingual learners shows that they sometimes use knowledge of their primary language to spell words in their second language (Fashola, Drum, Mayer, & Kang, 1996; Nathenson-Mejia, 1989; Zutell & Allen, 1988). By assessing the orthographic knowledge of Spanish and English, teachers can observe whether the children are applying Spanish rules of phonology and orthography to English or vice versa (Estes & Richards, 2002). Fashola et al. (1996) stressed

how important it is for teachers who work with limited-English-proficient Latino students to learn the phonological and orthographic rules of Spanish so they can differentiate rule-governed "transitioning" errors from random errors, and explicitly explain how a given English phonological or orthographic rule is different from the Spanish one (see p. 840). Spelling researchers have already identified which English consonant sounds are problematic for Spanish speakers, and they are currently working toward identifying additional areas that need explicit attention in other alphabetic languages (Bear, Templeton, Helman, & Baren, 2003). For example, Korean students may confuse the liquids /r/ and /l/ in English because in their native language /r/ and /l/ are an allophonic variation; that is, they are treated the same and are represented by the same letter in Hangul (M. Yang, personal communication, September 16, 2003).

Systematic Assessment and Systematic Instruction

Nothing has been more ubiquitous in U.S. schools than the spelling test on Friday despite the fact that most students do quite well on Friday only to misspell many of the same words on Monday. It is precisely this phenomenon that argues most convincingly against spelling skill as an outcome of rote memorization and suggests, instead, that learning to spell requires the understanding of the phoneme–grapheme regularities, vowel patterns, and morphological conventions that make up a spelling system. Although learning to spell does entail learning specific words, *general knowledge* is what is needed when students stumble upon words they have never seen before, or when they try to write words they don't know how to spell, or when they are not sure of the meaning of a specific word. For example, a student might invoke general knowledge of consonant blends and short vowels to read the word *blast* even if he or she has never seen the word before. Likewise, general knowledge that words with similar spellings are often related in meaning, such as *recite* and *recitation*, may help a student understand the meaning of *recital*, even if it is unfamiliar (Bear, Invernizzi, et al., 2003). To be sure, specific knowledge of individual words is absolutely necessary to learn to read and spell. Although the word *train* might be spelled *trane*, *train*, or *trayne* (all are orthographically and phonetically plausible), only specific knowledge will help us remember which one is correct. However, the relationship between specific knowledge and general knowledge of the system is reciprocal. The ability to remember specific words' spellings is influenced by general knowledge of the system. At the same time, general knowledge of the orthographic system evolves, in part, "from accumulated experiences with specific word spellings" (Ehri, 1992, p. 308). Short of this general understanding, students have no recourse but to use rote memorization for the test on Friday, and the words are easily forgotten by Monday.

Fortunately, spelling researchers have devised valid and reliable means of assessing students' general knowledge of the orthographic system as well as their specific knowledge of individual words and individual spelling features (cf. Bear, Invernizzi, et al., 2003; Ganske, 2000; Invernizzi, Meier, & Juel, 2003; Schlagal, 1989; Viise, 1994). Qualitative spelling inventories sample student spellings with words that have been carefully selected to reflect the taxonomy of written English. Students' spellings are typically scored by the presence or absence of specific spelling features in addition to whether the entire word is spelled rightly or wrongly. For example, in assessing student knowledge of consonant blends, *train* spelled TRANE would receive credit for the *tr* despite the fact that the whole word is not spelled correctly. Researchers have consistently demonstrated a relationship between "power scores" (number of total words correct) and quality of the spelling errors committed (Morris, Nelson, & Perney, 1986; Schlagal, 1989). Students who spell most words correctly tend to commit highly predictable errors of limited variability, while students who spell few words correctly frequently produce unexpected errors with a high degree of variability (Schlagal, 1986). Errors are most interpretable when students misspell neither too few nor too many words. Such a power score indicates students' instructional level in spelling or where they are in their general understanding of English orthography. The qualitative analyses of the actual spelling errors specify precisely which spelling features students have mastered and which ones must be learned next. Spanish inventories have been developed in a similar fashion for Spanish-speaking students, and these are especially informative when compared to English results for bilingual learners (Bear, Invernizzi, et al.; Estes & Richards, 2002). By methodically assessing students' orthographic development several times across the year, teachers can ensure that the instruction they plan fits the needs of the students they teach by differentiating spelling instruction in small groups (Bear, Invernizzi, et al.; Ganske, 2000).

Qualitative spelling inventories outline the general terrain of the orthographic system to be learned, and they itemize specific spelling features to be taught systematically in a developmental progression. Spelling researchers have provided evidence for the developmental progression of these features through Guttman scale analyses. A Guttman scale is a unidimensional and cumulative scale. For example, a word spelled correctly on a spelling inventory entails spelling less difficult words correctly as well; conversely, misspelling a word on an inventory entails misspelling more difficult words. Bear and Barone (1989), Ganske (1999), Viise (1994), and Invernizzi (1992) have all demonstrated Guttman coefficients of reproducibility and scalability well within acceptable ranges (reproducibility exceeds .90; scalability exceeds .60), suggesting that qualitative spelling inventories do in fact generate scales that are unidimensional and cumulative. The same cumulative progression has been documented through the use of these inventories with learning-disabled students (Worthy & Invernizzi, 1989), students identified as dyslexic (Sawyer, Wade, & Kim, 1999), and functionally literate adults (Worthy & Viise, 1996). Stage and Wagner (1992), providing additional evidence for the developmental nature of learning to spell, demonstrated the joint influences of phonology and orthography as these interact with working memory across the grades.

Morris explored the concept of a spelling instructional level in a series of studies stemming from a qualitative analysis of error types yielded in student spelling responses to a qualitative spelling inventory (Morris, Blanton, Blanton, Nowacek, & Perney, 1995; Morris, Blanton, Blanton, & Perney, 1995; Morris, Nelson, & Perney, 1986). In the first study, Morris et al. (1986) found positive correlations between overall spelling accuracy (total number of words correct) and the acquisition of specific orthographic features such as those displayed in Table 1. Next, Morris, Blanton, Blanton, and Perney (1995) followed students in four third-grade and two fifth-grade classrooms where all students received the same instruction at the same pace from the same grade-level spelling book regardless of their prior spelling accuracy. At the end of the year the students were tested on their mastery of curriculum-based words. The top third of each grade could spell most of the curriculum-based word list correctly. However, they found that undifferentiated, whole-group

instruction was ineffective for the low-achieving spellers. The bottom third could not spell even half of the words correctly. Finally, Morris, Blanton, Blanton, Nowacek, et al. examined the effects of teaching 48 low-achieving spellers in seven third-grade classrooms at their spelling instructional level instead of their grade level. Half of these low-achieving third-grade spellers were instructed in a second-grade speller (the intervention group) while the other half were instructed in the third-grade speller (control group). Not only did the intervention group score higher on the second-grade posttest, but also they scored nearly as well as the controls on the third-grade curriculum-based posttest, and even higher than the controls on the third-grade transfer test. Taken together, these three studies provide a rationale for establishing an instructional level for spelling instruction through qualitative spelling assessments and for differentiating instruction based on those assessed levels. These findings corroborate those of Schlagal (1982), who found a spread of at least three grade levels in spelling achievement in virtually every class in grades 1 through 6.

How do the basal programs stack up against this developmental evidence and the need for careful assessment to guide instruction? Ever since the National Reading Panel (NRP; National Institute of Child Health and Human Development, 2000) published its report on evidence-based implications for teaching children to read, publishers have beefed up their phonics and spelling instruction within the alphabetic tier to meet the systematic mandate. However, many of the commercial programs do not provide a theoretical or empirical rationale for the scope and sequence of letter–sound instruction (Purcell, 2002). Maslin (2003), in a meta-analysis of first-grade phonics and spelling instruction in five competing basal reading programs (2001–2003 editions), reported correlations ranging from .40 to .96 with the cumulative sequence of orthographic features within the alphabetic tier, as suggested by developmental-spelling research. However, the assessment procedures (mostly in multiple-choice format) did not relate to their instructional sequence. Although all the publishers reviewed paid lip service to using their assessments to differentiate instruction in phonics and spelling, "none of the programs advised starting students either in the kindergarten or the second-grade level program no matter what their strengths and weaknesses were on the assessments" (Maslin, 2003, p. 64). To the contrary, most of the programs suggested that students move through the lessons at the same pace, and suggestions for whole-class instruction were the norm. This is despite the fact that the NRP report clearly stated that "teachers should be able to assess the needs of individual students and tailor instruction to meet specific needs" (p. 11).

Systemizing the System: Translating Developmental-Spelling Research to Classroom Practice

Spelling research makes clear that the first step toward systemizing the teaching of phonics and spelling is for teachers, as Gentry and Henderson (1980) argued, "to respond appropriately to nonstandard spelling" (p. 116). Qualitative spelling assessments and feature analyses assist teachers in determining the instructional levels of their students, and this information allows knowledgeable teachers to place their students within a developmental continuum of systematic instruction. The second step charges educators to differentiate their phonics and spelling instruction according to their students' instructional spelling levels and, therefore, to implement small-group instruction in their classrooms.

The practice of teacher-directed small-group instruction for reading is not a new phenomenon in the elementary school arena and is supported by research of effective teachers (Taylor, Pearson, Clark, & Walpole, 2000). However, use of group configurations (e.g., circle, seat, center, or four blocks) to manage differentiated instruction in phonics and spelling appears to be slim to nil (Johnston, 2001). Moody, Schumm, Fischer, and Jean-Francois

(1999) investigated grouping plans suggested in commercial programs and found that grouping plans other than whole group (e.g., small groups, partner dyads, individualized) were suggested only as student-led extensions of an assignment previously taught in the whole group—not as teacher-directed lessons in small-group formats. This finding is similar to Maslin's (2003) discovery that the small-group instruction suggested in basal series was recommended only for the reteaching of English-language-learner (ELL) lessons that addressed previously taught skills from the whole-class work.

If we recognize the importance of differentiated instruction, it follows that teachers must adapt the programs that they may be using to reflect effective practice supported by research. Several recent studies emphasize the importance of pacing instruction to students' instructional levels and engaging them in a search for logical patterns. Juel and Minden-Cupp (2000) found that differentiated phonics instruction was especially beneficial for students with the lowest levels of entering literacy skill. Foorman and Torgesen (2001) also concluded that grouping students is one of the critical elements of instruction that promotes literacy success for at-risk students (see p. 209). Nevertheless, commercial programs directly influence daily teacher practice (Chall, 1996). Because of the ease of implementation, many teachers will want their students to continue through their grade-level program regardless of their instructional level. However, as Henderson (1990) cautioned, teachers must "recognize the absolute limit beyond which no such placement can be permitted" (p. 205).

Once qualitative spelling assessments and feature analyses are completed, teachers should place children in achievement-based groups based on their students' instructional levels and specific areas of need (Bear & Barone, 1989; Bear, Invernizzi, et al., 2003; Henderson, 1990). These groups are not the static groups of the past (i.e., tracking). Rather, these groups are flexible and dynamic. Teachers regroup as necessary to best meet the changing needs of the students. Effective classroom management, a characteristic of effective teachers, is crucial for grouping plans to be beneficial (Pressley et al., 2001).

Research in the area of professional development and teacher change provides some insight on the challenges related to implementing differentiated word study in the classroom. Johnston (2001) found that although teachers were largely dissatisfied with their students' spelling skill, they appeared to lack the knowledge and resources needed to teach spelling more effectively. Gill and Scharer (1996) provided a series of six professional development sessions for elementary school teachers attempting to implement developmental-spelling instruction in their school and found that the management of small groups was their overriding concern. In addition to general management concerns (e.g., group rotations), teachers were apprehensive about the meaningfulness of the independent work that students would be doing while not with a teacher-directed group. Some progress was made, however, as teachers learned about English orthography through facilitated discussions about their students' spelling errors on the qualitative spelling assessments, their change over time, and their response to differentiated word study instruction within a balanced reading and writing curriculum.

Vygotsky theorized that teachers must not only know the developmental level of their students but also work to understand the relationship between their students' development and the possibilities of instruction (Hedegaard, 1990). Thus, establishing consistent daily and weekly routines is also essential to establishing a systematic program for phonics and spelling instruction. Developmental-spelling researchers favor daily routines that involve sorting or categorizing words in isolation according to similarities and differences in sound, pattern, or meaning and then hunting for other words with similar properties in connected text (cf. Bear, Invernizzi, et al., 2003; Ganske, 2000). Word sorting and word hunting require students to examine the orthographic properties of words

in relation to the orthographic characteristics of other words they already know.

Advocates of word study claim that the process of comparing and contrasting orthographic features not only teaches the spelling of specific words but also encourages students to make generalizations about the spelling consistency of other words within a given category (Bear, Invernizzi, et al., 2003; Ganske, 2000). Through word sorting, students note specific letter–phoneme correspondence, patterns, or morphemes (depending on the instructional zone) that generalize across many English words. Although word study promotes an analytic approach to words that can serve students in encounters with unknown words, it is also synthetic in that teachers direct students to deconstruct their words by sound, pattern, or meaning in the process of sorting, depending on where students are on the developmental continuum.

Research on the effectiveness of word sorting is relatively new, but existing evidence indicates that this approach is at least as effective as creating word boxes (boxes for synthetic phoneme segmentation similar to Elkonin boxes) and more effective than more traditional approaches, at least in first grade (Joseph, 2000). Weber and Henderson (1989) studied the effects of computer-assisted word sorting using a random assignment, control group design. The word-sort condition yielded significantly greater gains in word recognition and contextual reading, and these gains transferred to a standardized spelling test. Hall et al. (1995) and Zutell (1998) provided additional evidence that word sorting is an effective approach to phonics and spelling instruction across the elementary grades. Henry (1989) used a compare-and-contrast approach in her historical–structural curriculum with intermediate students who compared targeted patterns with other similar patterns and reflected on how word structure influences spelling. These students made significant gains in spelling achievement as well as decoding, which Henry attributed to the shared orthography involved with both tasks.

Henderson (1981) devised the concept of word sorting because he was convinced that understanding how children learned to spell words could also provide insight on how they read them. He believed that children's growing word knowledge encompassed phonological, orthographic, and semantic information and that categorizing written words enabled them to sort out the relations among these linguistic sources. Henderson's instructional approaches (e.g., word sorts, word hunts, writing sorts) were shaped by his belief that both phonological and orthographic aspects of written words were critical facets in learning to read and write. His work, and the work of his colleagues and students, demonstrated that written word knowledge is developmental and advances progressively in relation to cognitive development, exposure to print, and instruction.

Henderson's intuitions have since been supported by a number of correlational and longitudinal studies that have consistently identified spelling as an independent contributor to reading acquisition (Cataldo & Ellis, 1988; Ehri & Wilce, 1987; Morris & Perney, 1984). Significant correlations between spelling and various measures of word identification and decoding have also been reported. For example, Ehri (2000) reviewed six correlational studies in which students of various ages (first grade through college) were asked to read and spell words and reported correlations ranging from .68 to .86. In other studies, spelling measures have accounted for as much as 40% to 60% of the variance in oral reading measures (Zutell, 1992; Zutell & Rasinski, 1989). In a two-year study following students from first through third grade, Ellis and Cataldo (1992) reported spelling to be the most consistent predictor of reading achievement. Even intervention studies exploring the added value of supplemental spelling instruction have repeatedly found that students who receive additional spelling instruction perform better on reading tasks such as oral reading, silent reading comprehension, and other reading-related measures in addition to spelling (Berninger et al., 1998; Goulandris, 1992; Graham, Harris, & Chorzempa, 2002; McCandliss, Beck, Sandak, & Perfetti, 2003).

In our statewide data, spelling scores generated from a qualitative spelling inventory administered to 68,817 first graders in the fall of first grade significantly correlated with reading achievement at the end of the year as measured by both word recognition in isolation and oral reading accuracy (Invernizzi, Landrum, Robey, & Moon, 2003). Correlations between spelling scores and reading levels obtained at the same point in time are even stronger, ranging from .79 (end of first grade) to .75 (end of second grade) to .69 (end of third grade). In addition, significant differences are obtained between reading levels, not only for overall spelling score but also for specific orthographic features mastered. For example, at the end of first grade there are significant differences in the inclusion of the silent-*e* to mark the long-vowel sound in words like *slide*, *brave*, or *shade*, across all reading levels assessed, preprimer through third grade, and these differences are reflected in the increase of the mean score for that particular feature across reading levels. These findings echo those of Stage and Wagner (1992), who found significant differences in phonetically acceptable spellings of nonwords by children in kindergarten through third grade. Results such as these make concrete the theoretical relationship between reading and spelling, underscore the necessity for differentiated instruction, and suggest implications for curriculum developers and publishers.

It takes time for students to develop spelling proficiency. First they must learn the alphabetic principle to generate phonetically plausible spellings. Ehri (1989) asserted that it is precisely this kind of alphabetic knowledge, knowledge of phoneme–grapheme relations, that allows students to make phonetic sense of words and remember them. As knowledge of the phoneme–grapheme relations expands, students begin to acquire many sight words, and they move into independent reading about the same time they begin to navigate through the pattern tier of English spelling. The more students read, write, and learn about the spelling system, the larger their vocabulary grows. Before they know it, students are learning and remembering so many words that their lexicons abound with words of more than one syllable, including, eventually, words of Greek and Latin derivation, words acquired in the meaning tier of written English.

Conclusion

The American Heritage Dictionary (www .yourdictionary.com/ahd) defines *systematic* as "of, characterized by, based on, or constituting a system; of or relating for classification or taxonomy; carried on using step-by step procedures; and, purposefully regular." In this review of how developmental-spelling research and theory inform classroom practice, we have described the three tiers of English spelling (alphabet, pattern, and meaning) as the system to guide teacher instruction. Further, we have described classroom procedures for implementing a systematic instructional program to include a qualitative assessment of student spellings, differentiated instruction through small-group instruction, and consistent, daily instructional routines. Last, we have provided evidence that students' knowledge of the orthography within these three tiers is a crucial component of their literacy achievement.

Knowing the system to be taught, devising a system to teach it, and situating word-level instruction within the larger context of comprehensive literacy instruction still leaves the efficacy of specific instructional approaches in question. Continued research investigating the effectiveness of the word study approach for phonics, spelling, and vocabulary instruction is needed. Building on past research, word sorting should be further investigated as an effective approach across the grades as well as an approach to be used in combination with other approaches, such as synthetic phonics. Drawing from and combining with the strengths of spelling approaches such as Orton-Gillingham and word sorting, teachers may better meet the needs of diverse learners. Educators need to know the degree of explicitness necessary to produce significant gains with all different types of learners (e.g., learning-disabled students, ELL

students, average-achieving students, gifted students) as well as students at different levels of literacy achievement (e.g., emergent readers, beginning readers, intermediate readers). Contrary to what commercial programs would have us believe, systematic, explicit instruction is not synonymous with everyone on the same page at the same time in the same workbook. Though we already know that whole-class instruction is ineffective, future research must demonstrate the feasibility of differentiating instruction through management plans that utilize small-group configurations. In addition, research is needed to support educators who strive to use teacher-driven techniques in their classroom word study instruction by demonstrating the effectiveness of professional development in developmental-spelling instruction and by providing evidence that knowledgeable teachers are the key to successful classrooms. Last, more research is needed to demonstrate the effectiveness of instructional materials other than those provided by basal reading companies where, more often than not, one size is force-fitted to all.

Although the full potential of alternative approaches to phonics and spelling instruction has yet to be realized, contemporary research will most certainly inform the definition and quality of balanced literacy instruction. The age-old complaint about the boring, decontextualized nature of phonics instruction will likely be supplanted by expressions of surprise and interest in the engaging, inquisitive nature of word study that, in turn, leads to more explicit understanding of English orthography.

References

Bad Spelling Now Viewed as Inventive Schools See Workbooks, Drills as Discouragements. (1995, July 10). *San Francisco Chronicle*, p. A1. Retrieved October 15, 2003, from Lexis/Nexis database.

Bear, D. (1992). The prosody of oral reading and stage or word knowledge. In S. Templeton & D.R. Bear (Eds.), *Development of orthographic knowledge and the foundations of literacy: A memorial festschrift for Edmund H. Henderson* (pp. 137–186). Hillsdale, NJ: Erlbaum.

Bear, D.R., & Barone, D. (1989). Using children's spellings to group for word study and directed reading in the primary classroom. *Reading Psychology, 10*, 275–292.

Bear, D.R., Invernizzi, M., Templeton, S., & Johnston, F. (2003). *Words their way: Word study for phonics, vocabulary, and spelling instruction* (3rd ed.). Upper Saddle River, NJ: Prentice-Hall.

Bear, D.R., Templeton, S., Helman, L., & Baren, T. (2003). Orthographic development and learning to read in different languages. In G.E. Garcia (Ed.), *English learners: Reaching the highest level of English literacy* (pp. 71–95). Newark, DE: International Reading Association.

Bear, D.R., Truex, P., & Barone, D. (1989). In search of meaningful diagnoses: Spelling-by-stage assessment of literacy proficiency. *Adult Literacy and Basic Education, 13,* 165–185.

Beers, J.W., & Henderson, E.H. (1977). A study of developing orthographic concepts among first grade children. *Research in the Teaching of English, 11,* 133–148.

Berninger, V.W., Vaughn, K., Abbott, R.D., Brooks, A., Abbott, S.P., Rogan, L., et al. (1998). Early intervention for spelling problems: Teaching functional spelling units of varying size with a multiple-connections framework. *Journal of Educational Psychology, 90,* 587–605.

Cantrell, R.J. (2001). Exploring the relationship between dialect and spelling for specific vocalic features in Appalachian first-grade children. *Linguistics and Education, 12,* 1–23.

Cataldo, S., & Ellis, N. (1988). Interactions in the development of spelling, reading, and phonological skills. *Journal of Research in Reading, 11,* 86–109.

Chall, J.S. (1983). *Stages of reading development.* New York: McGraw-Hill.

Chall, J.S. (1996). *Learning to read: The great debate* (3rd ed.). New York: McGraw-Hill.

Chomsky, N., & Halle, M. (1968). *The sound patterns of English.* New York: Harper Row.

Craigie, W.A. (1927). *English spelling: Its rules and reasons.* New York: FS Crofts.

Cramer, R.L. (1998). *The spelling connection: Integrating reading, writing, and spelling instruction.* New York: Guilford.

Ehri, L.C. (1989). The development of spelling knowledge and its role in reading acquisition and reading disability. *Journal of Learning Disabilities, 22,* 356–365.

Ehri, L.C. (1992). Review and commentary: Stages of spelling development. In S. Templeton & D.R. Bear (Eds.), *Development of orthographic knowledge and the foundations of literacy: A memorial festschrift for Edmund H. Henderson* (pp. 307–332). Hillsdale, NJ: Erlbaum.

Ehri, L.C. (2000). Learning to read and learning to spell: Two sides of a coin. *Topics in Language Disorders, 20,* 19–36.

Ehri, L.C., & McCormick, S. (1998). Phases of word learning: Implications for instruction with delayed and disabled readers. *Reading and Writing Quarterly: Overcoming Learning Difficulties, 14,* 135–164.

Ehri, L.C., & Wilce, L. (1987). Does learning to spell help beginners learn to read real words? *Reading Research Quarterly, 18,* 47–65.

Ellis, N., & Cataldo, S. (1992). Spelling is integral to learning to read. In C.M. Sterling & C. Robson (Eds.), *Psychology, spelling, and education* (pp. 122–142). Clevedon, UK: Multilingual Matters.

Estes, T., & Richards, H. (2002). Knowledge of orthographic features in Spanish among bilingual children. *Bilingual Research Journal, 26,* 295–307.

Fashola, O., Drum, P.A., Mayer, R.E., & Kang, S.J. (1996). A cognitive theory of orthographic transitioning: Predictable error in how Spanish-speaking children spell English words. *American Educational Research Journal, 33,* 825–843.

First Grade Teacher Reading Academies. (2002). Austin, TX: University of Texas System & Texas Education Agency.

Foorman, B.R., & Torgesen, J. (2001). Critical elements of classroom and small-group instruction promote reading success in all children. *Learning Disabilities Research & Practice, 16,* 203–212.

Ganske, K. (1999). The developmental spelling analysis: A measure of orthographic knowledge. *Educational Assessment, 6,* 41–70.

Ganske, K. (2000). *Word journeys: Assessment-guided phonics, spelling, and vocabulary instruction.* New York: Guilford.

Gentry, J.R., & Henderson, E.H. (1980). Three steps to teaching beginning readers to spell. In E.H. Henderson & J.W. Beers (Eds.), *Developmental and cognitive aspects in learning to spell* (pp. 112–119). Newark, DE: International Reading Association.

Gill, C.E. (1980). An analysis of spelling errors in French (Doctoral dissertation, University of Virginia, 1980). *Dissertation Abstracts International, 41*(09), 33924.

Gill, C.H., & Scharer, P.L. (1996). "Why do they get it on Friday and misspell it on Monday?" Teachers inquiring about their students as spellers. *Language Arts, 73,* 89–96.

Gough, P.B., & Hillenger, M.L. (1980). Learning to read: An unnatural act. *Bulletin of the Orton Society, 20,* 179–196.

Goulandris, N.K. (1992). Alphabetic spelling: Predicting eventual literacy attainment. In C.M. Sterling & C. Robson (Eds.), *Psychology, spelling, and education* (pp. 143–158). Clevedon, UK: Multilingual Matters.

Graham, S., Harris, K.R., & Chorzempa, B.F. (2002). Contribution of spelling instruction to the spelling, writing, and reading of poor spellers. *Journal of Educational Psychology, 94,* 669–686.

Hall, D.P., Cunningham, P.M., & Cunningham, J.W. (1995). Multilevel spelling instruction in third grade classrooms. In K.A. Hinchman, D.J. Leu, & C. Kinzer (Eds.), *Perspectives on literacy research and practice* (pp. 384–389). Chicago: National Reading Conference.

Hanna, P.R., Hanna, J.S., Hodges, R.E., & Rudorf, E.H. (1966). *Phoneme-grapheme correspondences as cues to spelling improvement.* Washington, DC: U.S. Government Printing Office, U.S. Office of Education.

Hedegaard, M. (1990). The zone of proximal development as basis for instruction. In L.C. Moll (Ed.), *Vygotsky and education: Instructional implications and applications of sociohistorical psychology* (pp. 349–371). Cambridge, UK: Cambridge University Press.

Henderson, E.H. (1981). *Learning to read and spell: The child's knowledge of words.* DeKalb, IL: Northern Illinois Press.

Henderson, E.H. (1990). *Teaching spelling* (2nd ed.). Boston: Houghton Mifflin.

Henderson, E.H. (1992). The interface of lexical competence and knowledge of written words. In S. Templeton & D.R. Bear (Eds.), *Development of orthographic knowledge and the foundations of literacy: A memorial festschrift for Edmund Henderson* (pp. 1–30). Hillsdale, NJ: Erlbaum.

Henderson, E.H., & Templeton, S. (1986). A developmental perspective of formal spelling instruction through alphabet, pattern, and meaning. *Elementary School Journal, 86,* 292–316.

Henry, M.K. (1989). Children's word structure knowledge: Implications for decoding and spelling instruction. *Reading and Writing, 1,* 135–152.

Invernizzi, M. (1992). The vowel and what follows: A phonological frame of orthographic analysis. In S. Templeton & D.R. Bear (Eds.), *Development of orthographic knowledge and the foundations of literacy: A memorial festschrift for Edmund H. Henderson* (pp. 106–136). Hillsdale, NJ: Erlbaum.

Invernizzi, M., Abouzeid, M., & Gill, J.T. (1994). Using students' invented spellings as a guide for spelling instruction that emphasizes word study. *The Elementary School Journal, 95,* 155–167.

Invernizzi, M., Landrum, T., Robey, R.R., & Moon, T. (2003). *Phonological Awareness Literacy Screening (PALS) 2002–2003: Description of sample, first-year results, task analyses, and revisions* (Technical Manual and report prepared for the Virginia Department of Education). Charlottesville, VA: University Printing Services.

Invernizzi, M., Meier, J., & Juel, C. (2003). *PALS 1–3: Phonological Awareness Literacy Screening* (4th ed.). Charlottesville, VA: University Printing Services.

Johnston, F. (2001). Exploring classroom teachers' spelling practices and beliefs. *Reading Research and Instruction, 40,* 143–156.

Joseph, L.M. (2000). Developing first graders' phonemic awareness, word identification and spelling: A comparison of two contemporary phonic instructional approaches. *Reading Research and Instruction, 39,* 160–169.

Juel, C., & Minden-Cupp, C. (2000). Learning to read words: Linguistic units and instructional strategies. *Reading Research Quarterly, 35,* 458–492.

Lovett, M.W., Lacerenza, L., Borden, S., Frijters, J.C., Steinbach, K.A., & De Palma, M. (2000). Components of effective remediation for developmental reading disabilities: Combining phonological and strategy-based instruction to improve outcomes. *Journal of Educational Psychology, 92,* 263–283.

Maslin, P. (2003). *A review of basal reading programs in first grade.* Unpublished doctoral dissertation, University of Virginia, Charlottesville.

McCandliss, B., Beck, I., Sandak, R., & Perfetti, C. (2003). Focusing attention on decoding for children with poor reading skills: Design and preliminary tests of the word building intervention. *Scientific Studies of Reading, 7,* 75–103.

Moats, L. (2003, February). *LETRS Institute.* Presentation at Sopris West, Boulder, CO.

Moody, S.W., Schumm, J.S., Fischer, M., & Jean-Francois, B. (1999). Grouping suggestions for the classroom: What do our basal reading series tell us? *Reading Research and Instruction, 38,* 319–331.

Morris, D. (1989). Editorial comment: Developmental spelling theory revisited. *Reading Psychology, 10,* iii–x.

Morris, D., Blanton, L., Blanton, W.E., Nowacek, J., & Perney, J. (1995). Teaching low achieving spellers at their "instructional level." *Elementary School Journal, 96,* 163–177.

Morris, D., Blanton, L., Blanton, W.E., & Perney, J. (1995). Spelling instruction and achievement in six classrooms. *Elementary School Journal, 92,* 145–162.

Morris, D., Nelson, L., & Perney, J. (1986). Exploring the concept of "spelling instruction level" through the analysis of error-types. *Elementary School Journal, 87,* 181–200.

Morris, D., & Perney, J. (1984). Developmental spelling as a predictor of first-grade reading achievement. *Elementary School Journal, 84,* 441–457.

Nathenson-Mejia, S. (1989). Writing in a second language: Negotiating meaning through invented spelling. *Language Arts, 66,* 516–526.

National Institute of Child Health and Human Development. (2000). *The report of the National Reading Panel. Teaching children to read: An evidence-based assessment of scientific research literature on reading and its implications for reading instruction.* Washington, DC: U.S. Government Printing Office.

Nelson, L. (1989). Something borrowed, something new: Teaching implications of developmental-spelling research. *Reading Psychology, 10,* 255–274.

Pressley, M. (2002). *Reading instruction that works: The case for balanced reading instruction* (2nd ed.). New York: Guilford.

Pressley, M., Wharton-McDonald, R., Allington, R., Block, C.C., Morrow, L., Tracey, D., et al. (2001). A study of effective first-grade literacy instruction. *Scientific Studies of Reading, 5,* 35–58.

Purcell, T.L. (2002). *Articulatory attributes of letter sounds: Considering manner, place, and voicing for kindergarten instruction.* Unpublished doctoral dissertation, University of Virginia, Charlottesville.

Rayner, K., Foorman, B.R., Perfetti, C.A., Pesetsky, D., & Seidenberg, M.S. (2001). How psychological science informs the teaching of reading. *Psychological Science in the Public Interest: A Journal of the American Psychological Society, 2,* 31–74.

Read, C. (1971). Pre-school children's knowledge of English phonology. *Harvard Educational Review, 41,* 1–34.

Richgels, D.J. (2001). Invented spelling, phonemic awareness, and reading and writing instruction. In S.B. Neuman & D.K. Dickinson (Eds.), *Handbook of early literacy research* (pp. 142–155). New York: Guilford.

Sawyer, D.J., Wade, S., & Kim, J.K. (1999). Spelling errors as a window on variations in phonological deficits among students with dyslexia. *Annals of Dyslexia, 49,* 137–159.

Schlagal, R. (1982). *A qualitative inventory of word knowledge: A developmental study of spelling grades one through six* (Doctoral dissertation, University of Virginia, 1982). *Dissertation Abstracts International, 47*(03), 915.

Schlagal, R. (1986). Informal and qualitative assessment of spelling. *Pointer, 30,* 37–41.

Schlagal, R. (1989). Constancy and change in spelling development. *Reading Psychology, 10,* 207–232.

Scragg, D. (1974). *A history of English spelling*. New York: Barnes & Noble Books, Manchester University Press.

Stage, S.A., & Wagner, R.K. (1992). Development of young children's phonological and orthographic knowledge as revealed by their spellings. *Developmental Psychology, 28*, 287–296.

Stever, E. (1980). Dialect and spelling. In E.H. Henderson & J.W. Beers (Eds.), *Developmental and cognitive aspects in learning to spell* (pp. 46–51). Newark, DE: International Reading Association.

Taylor, B.M., Pearson, P.D., Clark, K., & Walpole, S. (2000). Effective schools and accomplished teachers: Lessons about primary-grade reading instruction in low-income schools. *The Elementary School Journal, 101*, 121–165.

Temple, C.S. (1978). *An analysis of spelling errors in Spanish* (Doctoral dissertation, University of Virginia, 1978). *Dissertation Abstracts International, 40*(02), 721.

Templeton, S. (1991). Teaching and learning the English spelling system: Reconceptualizing method and purpose. *Elementary School Journal, 92*, 183–199.

Templeton, S. (2003). Spelling. In J. Flood, D. Lapp, J.R. Squire, & J.M. Jensen (Eds.), *Handbook of research on teaching the English language arts* (2nd ed., pp. 738–751). Mahwah, NJ: Erlbaum.

Templeton, S., & Spivey, E.M. (1980). The concept of "word" in young children as a function of level of cognitive development. *Research in the Teaching of English, 14*, 265–278.

Vallins, G.H. (1973). *Spelling*. London: Andre Deutsch.

Venezky, R.L. (1995). From orthography to psychology to reading. In V.W. Berninger (Ed.), *The varieties of orthographic knowledge: Relationships to phonology, reading, and writing* (pp. 23–46). Dordrecht, the Netherlands: Kluwer Academic Press.

Viise, N.M. (1994). *Feature word spelling list: A diagnosis of progressing word knowledge through an assessment of spelling errors*. Unpublished doctoral dissertation, University of Virginia, Charlottesville.

Weber, W.R., & Henderson, E.H. (1989). A computer-based program of word study: Effects on reading and spelling. *Reading Psychology, 10*, 157–171.

Wolf, M., & Kennedy, R. (2003). How the origins of written language instruct us to teach: A response to Steven Strauss. *Educational Researcher, 32*(1), 26–30.

Worthy, M.J., & Viise, N.M. (1996). Morphological, phonological, and orthographic differences in the spelling of basic literacy adults and achievement-level matched children. *Reading and Writing: An Interdisciplinary Journal, 18*, 139–159.

Worthy, M.J., & Invernizzi, M. (1989). Spelling errors of normal and disabled students on achievement levels one through four: Instructional implications. *Bulletin of the Orton Society, 40*, 138–149.

Zutell, J. (1992). An integrated view of word knowledge: Correlational studies of the relationships among spelling, reading, and conceptual development. In S. Templeton & D.R. Bear (Eds.), *Development of orthographic knowledge and the foundations of literacy: A memorial festschrift for Edmund H. Henderson* (pp. 213–230). Newark, DE: International Reading Association.

Zutell, J. (1998). Word sorting: A developmental spelling approach to word study for delayed readers. *Reading & Writing Quarterly: Overcoming Learning Difficulties, 14*, 219–238.

Zutell, J., & Allen, V. (1988). The English spelling strategies of Spanish-speaking bilingual children. *TESOL Quarterly, 22*, 333–340.

Zutell, J., & Rasinski, T. (1989). Reading and spelling connections in third and fifth grade students. *Reading Psychology, 10*, 137–155.

Curriculum and Instruction

The Curriculum and Instruction Standard recognizes the need to prepare educators who have a deep understanding of the elements of a balanced, integrated, and comprehensive literacy curriculum and have developed expertise in enacting that curriculum. The elements focus on the use of effective practices in a well-articulated curriculum, using both traditional print and online resources. Standard 2 and its elements follow:

> **Standard 2. Curriculum and Instruction. Candidates use instructional approaches, materials, and an integrated, comprehensive, balanced curriculum to support student learning in reading and writing. As a result, candidates**
>
> • **Element 2.1 Use foundational knowledge to design or implement an integrated, comprehensive, and balanced curriculum.**
>
> • **Element 2.2 Use appropriate and varied instructional approaches, including those that develop word recognition, language comprehension, strategic knowledge, and reading–writing connections.**
>
> • **Element 2.3 Use a wide range of texts (e.g., narrative, expository, and poetry) from traditional print, digital, and online resources.**

Part 2 includes six journal articles that may be helpful in understanding the substance of the standard and its elements. These pieces are described briefly here.

Mathes and colleagues (2005) investigate the effectiveness of combining enhanced classroom reading instruction with small-group reading intervention on first-grade students at risk for reading difficulties. This article compares two supplemental interventions grounded in two different theoretical perspectives. Results reveal that students who received either intervention performed better on multiple measures of reading than those students receiving only enhanced classroom instruction, suggesting that classroom instruction alone is inadequate in supporting readers who struggle. This article provides foundational knowledge useful for building a comprehensive literacy program (Element 2.1) and information about the theoretical underpinnings for instructional approaches (Element 2.2).

Manyak (2008) offers practical suggestions for engaging young students in phonemic awareness activities, and Rasinski, Rupley, and Nichols (2008) suggest a three-step sequence for implementing rhyming poetry in phonics and fluency instruction. These two articles aid in understanding the use of appropriate and varied instructional approaches with young students (Element 2.2).

Bromley (2007) discusses nine ideas that teachers in middle and high school should know about words and word learning to be effective teachers of vocabulary in their content areas. Suggestions are provided for practical implementation of each notion. This article contains information helpful in understanding the use of appropriate and varied instructional approaches with adolescents (Element 2.2).

Duke, Purcell-Gates, Hall, and Tower (2006) define two dimensions of authentic literacy activities, describe supporting research and theory, and give examples from their study. They identify strategies teachers can use to implement these authentic literacy activities in reading and writing. This article supports the understanding of planning and enacting effective literacy instruction (Element 2.2) and the use of informational text and procedural text with students (Element 2.3).

Castek, Bevans-Mangelson, and Goldstone (2006) define *new literacies* and emphasize the benefits of incorporating the Internet into the curriculum. They provide five practical ways of introducing the new literacies of the Internet through children's literature. This article encourages teachers to expose students to a variety of texts using online resources (Element 2.3).

Further Reading

Hicks, C.P. (2009). A lesson on reading fluency learned from *The Tortoise and the Hare*. *The Reading Teacher*, *63*(4), 319–323. doi:10.1598/RT.63.4.7

Lapp, D., Fisher, D., & Grant, M. (2008). "You can read this text—I'll show you how": Interactive comprehension instruction. *Journal of Adolescent & Adult Literacy*, *51*(5), 372–383. doi:10.1598/JAAL.51.5.1

McKeown, M.G., Beck, I.L., & Blake, R.G.K. (2009). Rethinking reading comprehension instruction: A comparison of instruction for strategies and content approaches. *Reading Research Quarterly*, *44*(3), 218–253. doi:10.1598/RRQ.44.3.1

Mesmer, H.A.E., & Griffith, P.L. (2005). Everybody's selling it—But just what is explicit, systematic phonics instruction? *The Reading Teacher*, *59*(4), 366–376. doi:10.1598/RT.59.4.6

Ross, D., & Frey, N. (2009). Learners need purposeful and systematic instruction. *Journal of Adolescent & Adult Literacy*, *53*(1), 75–78. doi:10.1598/JAAL.53.1.8

Schwanenflugel, P.J., Meisinger, E.B., Wisenbaker, J.M., Kuhn, M.R., Strauss, G.P., & Morris, R.D. (2006). Becoming a fluent and automatic reader in the early elementary school years. *Reading Research Quarterly*, *41*(4), 496–522. Medline doi:10.1598/RRQ.41.4.4

Yopp, H.K., & Yopp, R.H. (2000). Supporting phonemic awareness development in the classroom. *The Reading Teacher*, *54*(2), 130–143. doi:10.1598/RT.54.2.2

Questions for Reflection and Discussion

- What are some of the components of a balanced, comprehensive literacy curriculum? What factors should be considered in planning a balanced program?

- Think about what a balanced, comprehensive literacy curriculum looks like. How can teachers ensure that they are using the approaches and strategies needed by the students in their classrooms and that all areas of literacy are included?

- Reading professionals need to be "careful consumers" of research-based instructional practices. What are some factors that need to be considered when planning instruction that is appropriate for students? Why is it important to use various types of text (e.g., narrative, expository) and different forms of delivery (e.g., print, online) with students?

The Effects of Theoretically Different Instruction and Student Characteristics on the Skills of Struggling Readers

Patricia G. Mathes, Carolyn A. Denton, Jack M. Fletcher, Jason L. Anthony, David J. Francis, and Christopher Schatschneider

Perhaps the most important responsibility of educators in the primary grades is to ensure that all students become competent readers. The degree of success in becoming a competent reader typically is established in the early grades (Francis, Shaywitz, Stuebing, Shaywitz, & Fletcher, 1996; Juel, 1988; Torgesen & Burgess, 1998). Unless effective instructional practices are used in this critical period, the inequities that commonly divide our students are likely to continue (Snow, Burns, & Griffin, 1998).

During the previous 25 years there have been numerous studies focusing on the prevention of reading problems with young students. Converging evidence from these studies suggests that early instruction can be effective in preventing reading problems for many students (see Denton & Mathes, 2003; Snow et al., 1998) and that real schools and teachers can implement this instruction (e.g. Clay, 1993; Mathes & Torgesen, 1998). Further, it appears that without effective early instruction, which may require supplemental instruction, initial reading difficulties may eventually be compounded as students fall further and further behind their peers and habituate ineffective strategies for coping with reading failure (Clay, 1987; Stanovich, 1986). In other words, students may "learn to be learning disabled" (Clay, 1987, p. 155).

Pedagogical Framework

Beyond understanding the role that early intervention can play in reducing reading difficulties, we also have a greater understanding of the critical content for which struggling readers must gain ownership if they are to become competent readers. This content provides a framework to guide pedagogical decisions and includes provisions for teaching phonemic awareness, phonemic decoding skills, fluency in word recognition and text processing, construction of meaning, vocabulary, spelling, and writing (see Foorman & Torgesen, 2001; National Institute of Child Health and Human Development [NICHD], 2000; Pressley, 1998; Rayner, Foorman, Perfetti, Pesetsky, & Seidenberg, 2001; Snow et al., 1998). Likewise, it appears that instruction in these areas needs to be explicit. By explicit we mean that students are not required to infer new knowledge, but rather that new knowledge is shared directly. It also appears that for some students, instruction must be intensive in order to facilitate adequate reading development. By intensive instruction we mean that students are highly engaged in learning critical content and that the ratio of teachers to students is relatively small.

Preparing Reading Professionals (second edition), edited by Rita M. Bean, Natalie Heisey, and Cathy M. Roller. © 2010 by the International Reading Association. Reprinted from Mathes, P.G., Denton, C.A., Fletcher, J.M., Anthony, J.L., Francis, D.J., & Schatschneider, C. (2005). The effects of theoretically different instruction and student characteristics on the skills of struggling readers. *Reading Research Quarterly*, 40(2), 148–182. doi:10.1598/RRQ.40.2.2.

Unanswered Questions

What is less clear is exactly how much instruction must occur, how contextualized skills instruction needs to be, and the level of intensity at which it must occur in order for struggling readers to succeed. It is logical to assume that high-quality classroom instruction is a primary factor in determining success. The findings of several studies confirm that appropriate classroom-level instruction in the primary grades can dramatically reduce the prevalence of reading problems (Foorman, Francis, Fletcher, Schatschneider, & Mehta, 1998; Mathes, Howard, Allen, & Fuchs, 1998; Mathes, Torgesen, & Allor, 2001). However, even when classroom instruction is of high quality, approximately 5% to 7% of students do not meet benchmarks associated with reading proficiency in the early grades (Denton & Mathes, 2003; Mathes & Denton, 2002; Torgesen, 2000). For these students, it would appear that more intensive instruction is required.

There are many examples of successful individual and small-group intense interventions. For example, many struggling first-grade readers who receive one-on-one tutoring in the Reading Recovery program (Clay, 1993) routinely make substantial progress, enabling them to accurately read connected text at a level of difficulty similar to that of their more able peers (i.e., Gomez-Bellenge, Rogers, & Fullerton, 2003). Other interventions using a variety of methods show that individual and small-group tutorial programs effectively reduce the number of struggling readers (O'Connor, 2000; Simmons, Kame'enui, Stoolmiller, Coyne, & Harn, 2003; Torgesen et al., 1999; Torgesen, Rashotte, Alexander, Alexander, & MacPhee, 2003; Vellutino et al., 1996). While these interventions vary in how instruction is provided and in the amount of emphases placed on various content, each one generally reduces the number of struggling readers to 4.5% or less of the school population (Mathes & Denton, 2002; Torgesen et al., 2003).

What has not yet been investigated is the effect of providing high-quality classroom-level instruction in tandem with intense supplemental small-group interventions. Thus, while it is known that either enhanced classroom-level instruction or individual and small-group interventions significantly reduce the number of struggling readers, the effect of both practices together is not known. Further, while it is clear that many students at risk for reading failure need intense early reading instruction composed of content that research suggests is critical, it has yet to be determined whether individual characteristics of struggling readers can be identified that will assist practitioners in matching interventions to learner needs. To date, few researchers have entertained the idea that there may be an interaction between learner characteristics and the efficacy of specific approaches.

What is known is that individual students vary in their development of reading-related abilities. Thus, it is reasonable to speculate that students vary in which aspects of reading instruction are most critical. Generally speaking, some of the best validated predictors of later reading ability include letter knowledge (Simmons et al., 2003; Vellutino, Scanlon, & Jaccard, 2003), phonological awareness (Foorman et al., 1998; Torgesen et al., 1999; Vellutino et al., 2003), rapid naming of letters (Simmons et al., 2003; Vellutino et al., 2003), verbal memory (Vellutino et al., 2003), and oral language, including vocabulary (Storch & Whitehurst, 2002). To date, no researcher has changed the type of instruction provided to children with varying characteristics to determine if response to instruction is affected by children's individual characteristics.

In conducting the current research, we investigated the effectiveness of combining enhanced classroom instruction and intense supplemental intervention for struggling readers in first grade. Further, we explored the efficacy of two supplemental interventions derived from diverse theoretical foundations that we believe are widely embraced, at least implicitly, in today's schools, examining them in terms of interactions with child characteristics and academic outcomes.

Proactive Reading - behaviorist theory (scripted)
Responsive Reading - cognitive theory

One intervention, *Proactive Reading*, is derived from the model of Direct Instruction (Carnine, Silbert, Kame'enui, & Tarver, 2004; Engelmann, 1997; Engelmann & Carnine, 1982; Kame'enui & Simmons, 1990), which has its foundation in behavioral theory (Becker, 1973; Skinner, 1953) but goes beyond Skinnerian behaviorism to include teacher communications, student responses, and knowledge forms as elements for consideration when designing instruction (Engelmann & Carnine). The central characteristic of reading instruction based on behavioral theory is a focus on directly observable reading behaviors rather than on making inferences about the learner's cognitive processing (Pressley & McCormick, 1995). Behaviorism is a positive approach to learning in that the teacher supports the development of behaviors (such as the accurate and fluent application of reading skills) through positive reinforcement (such as praising and rewarding students for doing what is being taught). Skills instruction based on a behaviorist perspective is designed to be systematic; simpler skills are mastered before progressing to more complex skills. The role of the teacher in a behaviorist model is to teach content and model skills and then to provide practice and reinforcement for mastering those skills.

Proactive Reading includes these features but goes beyond Skinnerian behaviorism to include teacher communications, student responses, and knowledge forms as elements for consideration when designing instruction. In Proactive Reading, the tasks associated with fluent, meaningful reading were analyzed and systematically arranged into a scope and sequence intended to reduce student confusion and support successful learning. This was also intended to ensure that each child was gradually gaining cumulative knowledge and skills, resulting in ever-greater ability to read increasingly more complex text. From this scope and sequence daily lessons were derived. The result was that students learned phonetic elements in isolation before applying them strategically to words and practiced decoding words in isolation before reading decodable connected text and

applying comprehension strategies. Over time, the types of words read increased in complexity; stories became increasingly longer and story lines more complex. The teacher's job was to deliver this instruction as prescribed, following a daily lesson plan in which specific wording and expected student responses were provided. This wording was designed to communicate to children only critical attributes of new content without introducing possibly confusing information or overloading the student with too much information. Following a behavioral approach, lessons provided for frequent reinforcement on both an interval and intermittent schedule. This reinforcement included verbal praise provided as children performed tasks well, check marks on a mastery record, and stickers at the end of tasks and lessons. Likewise, when errors occurred, teachers retaught basic facts or scaffolded more complex content and then provided two to three additional practice opportunities for that fact or content.

The other supplemental intervention, *Responsive Reading*, is aligned with cognitive theory, following the model of cognitive strategy instruction (see Harris & Pressley, 1991), a form of cognitive apprenticeship (Brown, Collins, & Duguid, 1989; Rogoff, 1990; Rojewski & Schell, 1994). This model characterizes learning in terms of the acquisition of problem-solving strategies through a process of modeling, guided practice, coaching, scaffolding, and fading (Brown et al.; Rojewski & Schell). It is the role of the teacher to make his or her own knowledge explicit and to model strategies and then to coach and scaffold the learners as they apply these concepts and strategies in authentic activity. Ultimately, students are empowered to apply strategies independently. This model is also related to the theories of Vygotsky (1978), in that the social nature of learning is critical, and the teacher creates situations for learning that are sufficiently challenging to engage the learner in problem solving but not so challenging that the learner cannot achieve success (Rogoff). In their description of cognitive strategy instruction, Harris and Pressley discussed the development of preskills necessary for application of problem-solving strategies. Responsive Reading follows a pattern of explicit instruction in essential preskills and the modeling of strategies, which is then followed by application of these skills and strategies in reading and writing authentic text with teacher support and scaffolding. Responsive Reading is similar to the guided reading model (see Fountas & Pinnell, 1996) in its emphasis on modeling, prompting, and scaffolding within the learner's zone of proximal development (Vygotsky, 1978). It differs from that approach in terms of the explicit nature of instruction in essential preskills and the teaching of word identification to reflect current research findings in beginning reading (e.g., Snow et al., 1998).

The objectives of daily instruction within Responsive Reading were determined by the observed needs of students. Thus, there was no predetermined scope and sequence. The Responsive Reading teacher attended to behaviors that indicated the constructions each student was building up and responded contingently, providing scaffolds to help the student perform more effectively and promoting increasing independence over time. The Responsive Reading teacher had a dual role, providing explicit instruction in reading skills such as phonemic awareness and phonics but also serving as a coach to the student, directing the student's development of useful strategies while the student was engaged in reading and writing connected text. As students read stories chosen to reflect their ability and wrote words and sentences, their teacher observed what was easy for them and what types of errors were made, and he or she planned instruction accordingly. Thus, while both interventions were based on the same pedagogical content, the way instruction was delivered in the two approaches was distinctly different, reflecting the different theoretical orientations from which they were derived.

While different in their theoretical underpinnings, both interventions were comprehensive, integrated approaches to reading instruction that incorporated content deemed critical in recent reports to promote successful reading acquisition (NICHD, 2000; Pressley, 1998; Snow et al., 1998). Thus, the two approaches provided instruction in phonemic awareness, alphabetic knowledge and skills, and application of this knowledge to words and text, and they engaged students in making meaning from what they had read. However, they differed in the way this content was taught.

Research Hypotheses

In the current research, we asked two overarching questions. First, we asked if small-group supplemental intervention derived from either behavioral or cognitive theory provided in addition to research-based reading instruction was more effective than such instruction alone in promoting greater academic growth among struggling first-grade readers. Second, we asked if certain child characteristics known to be critically important for reading acquisition could differentially predict children's responses to the interventions, including phonological awareness, rapid naming of letters, and vocabulary. Specifically, we tested four hypotheses:

1. We hypothesized that small-group reading instruction, in the form of the Proactive or Responsive Reading intervention, provided in addition to the classroom reading program, would be, on average, more effective than high-quality classroom reading instruction alone for students at risk for reading failure. This prediction stems from the finding that interventions at different places on a direct instruction/cognitive apprenticeship continuum accelerated reading development. Therefore, adding intervention to classroom instruction should be more effective than classroom instruction alone.

2. Likewise, we predicted that despite differences in content emphasis and level of contextualization, the two supplemental interventions would be, on average, comparably effective because both incorpo-

rated instruction in critical components of learning to read.

3. We also hypothesized that because the interventions would accelerate development, the reading performance of struggling first-grade readers who received either supplemental intervention would approach the level of performance of their normally developing peers. We based this hypothesis on the fact that studies providing either enhanced core reading or individual or small-group reading intervention resulted in significantly greater numbers of children attaining normal reading levels (e.g., Denton & Mathes, 2003; Mathes & Denton, 2002). Thus, we speculated that coupling core and small-group reading instruction would result in even more children attaining normal reading levels.

4. Finally, based on the literature on predictors of response to intervention and reading outcomes, we hypothesized that initial phonological awareness, rapid automatic letter naming, and vocabulary would differentially predict individuals' responses to the two supplemental interventions. Based on differences in expected time devoted to different components of reading in the two interventions, we expected the Proactive approach to be more effective for children struggling with phonological processing and the Responsive approach to be more effective for children struggling with vocabulary development.

Method

Participants

Schools. This research was conducted in six U.S. schools in a large urban school district in Texas. We selected these schools because they had been designated as relatively high-performing schools in reading by the state's department of education and the school district, which we used as an indicator of a successful classroom reading program. One school was designated as *acceptable* (with high reading scores), two were identified as *recognized*, and three were designated as *exemplary* when the study began. Performance on a nationally normed, group-administered reading achievement test at the end of first grade indicated that the average reading performance in each of the six schools was above the national average. As we did not have the resources to provide extensive classroom-level intervention, selection of these schools helped ensure that we were examining the effect of quality classroom reading instruction with and without supplemental intervention. None of these schools were eligible for Title I (a federally funded program for at-risk students), and all served diverse student populations in terms of ethnicity and socioeconomic status.

Students. During each of two years, we identified within these schools a sample of first graders who showed significant risk for reading difficulties. In order to determine which students were at risk for reading difficulty, classroom teachers and our research team screened all students at the end of kindergarten within the six participating schools using the kindergarten screening portion of the Texas Primary Reading Inventory (TPRI). At the beginning of the first-grade year we screened any students entering the school for the first time with the first-grade TPRI screen.

The kindergarten screen of the TPRI was derived from a large longitudinal study of students in kindergarten through grade 2 (Schatschneider, Francis, Foorman, Fletcher, & Mehta, 1999). At kindergarten, it consists of a two-minute assessment of letter–sound knowledge and phonological awareness (blending sounds). However, this screen is designed to maximize the probability that students with risk characteristics would not be missed (i.e., false negative errors), resulting in overidentification of risk status (false positive errors). In order to accurately discriminate at-risk status, we followed the TPRI screening with the administration of the Woodcock–Johnson III

(W–J III) Word Identification subtest and the text reading subtest of the Observation Survey of Early Literacy Achievement, eliminating any student who could read five words or more on the Woodcock–Johnson or who could read texts designated as Level D or higher (Fountas & Pinnell, 1999) with at least 90% accuracy. Further, we collected a one-minute oral reading sample on an end-of-first-grade passage and only included children reading five or fewer words correctly per minute.

All students served in regular education classes were eligible for the study, including students who qualified for special education based on the identification of a learning disability, speech or language impairment, or "other health impairment." We excluded students with limited English proficiency who were served in bilingual classrooms and students served primarily in self-contained special education classes.

Once identified, all students designated as at risk *within* a school were randomly assigned to one of three conditions: enhanced classroom + Proactive Reading, enhanced classroom + Responsive Reading, or enhanced classroom only. In addition, we identified a sample of typically achieving readers by randomly selecting them from among all students in the same classrooms who evidenced no risk for reading problems. The purpose of this typically achieving group was to provide a benchmark of typical reading development in these classrooms.

To increase sample size, the study was conducted over two successive school years with two cohorts of students. In total, our sample included 92 students in the Proactive intervention group, 92 students in the Responsive intervention group, 114 students in the at-risk enhanced classroom condition, and 101 students who were typically achieving. After the effects of attrition, 78 Proactive Reading students, 83 Responsive Reading students, 91 at-risk students who received quality classroom instruction only, and 94 typically achieving students were assessed at posttest.

Table 1 summarizes the demographic information and educational status information for all participants because statistical analyses included all children. Given that the small number of Asian American children precluded treating them as a separate group in analyses and given that these children's language and literacy scores closely paralleled those of the Caucasian children, the Asian American and Caucasian groups were combined for analyses that sought to evaluate ethnicity effects prior to the main hypothesis testing. Most notably, no statistically significant differences among the at-risk groups were detected for any of the demographic or educational status variables.

Intervention Teachers. We employed six certified teachers to provide the intensive supplemental instruction. Three of the teachers taught Proactive Reading and three taught Responsive Reading. Each teacher taught at two different schools during each school day, enabling us to place both a Proactive and a Responsive teacher in each school so that school effects and intervention teacher effects were not confounded. Four of the six teachers held master's degrees, and several had teaching certifications in multiple areas. Five were certified in elementary general education, two in special education, three in English as a second language, one in early childhood education, and two as reading specialists. Two of the teachers also held certificates in educational administration. The mean years of teaching experience for the six teachers prior to the onset of the study was nine years, with a range from 3 to 22 years. All six teachers were experienced at teaching primary-grade students. The same six teachers delivered the Proactive and Responsive interventions during the two years of the study.

Classroom Teachers. Thirty first-grade classroom reading teachers from the six schools participated in this research across two years. Sixteen of these teachers participated in both years of the study. All teachers used one of two basal reading series adopted by the district and selected by their respective schools. Both of these basal programs provided guidance for delivering a comprehensive reading curriculum

Table 1
Student Demographic Information by Group

	Proactive			Responsive			Enhanced Classroom			Typically Achieving		
	n	%	M (SD)	n	%	M (SD)	n	%	M (SD)	n	%	M (SD)
Age in months	92	—	78 (4.9)	92	—	78 (4.2)	114	—	78 (4.8)	101	—	79 (4.8)
Ethnicity												
Caucasian and Asian	29	31		30	32		34	30		36	36	
African American	40	44		41	45		52	45		41	40	
Latino/Hispanic	23	25		21	23		27	24		24	24	
Native American	0	0		0	0		1	1		0	0	
Gender												
Male	52	57		53	58		68	60		63	62	
Female	40	43		29	32		46	40		38	38	
Special services												
Special education	3	3		2	2		3	3		1	1	
Speech therapy	6	7		3	3		8	7		2	2	
ESL	0	0		4	5		6	5		4	4	

Note. No contrasts were significantly different.

and included the previously discussed critical content. Observations of the classroom reading instruction indicated that teachers' implementation of their adopted basal programs was highly varied and that almost all teachers included other resources and methods to supplement or replace activities in the basal. Also, there was considerable variation in the classroom management styles observed, but all classroom teachers had routines and behavioral expectations that were known to the students.

Enhanced Classroom Instruction

The local district had implemented its own reading initiative for several years prior to the onset of this research, and teachers had received considerable professional development and coaching in providing comprehensive balanced literacy instruction. To build on the district's extensive professional development program, our research team worked with classroom teachers to further enhance classroom

instruction in several ways. First, we provided each teacher and principal access to several types of assessment data that were collected as part of the study. We initially shared our more comprehensive screening data, identifying for each teacher those students within the classroom who were at risk for reading difficulties and thus required greater teacher attention. For all participating students, we provided classroom teachers and intervention teachers with ongoing progress monitoring data reflective of reading growth every three weeks. These data were provided in the form of graphs of passage reading fluency for each child who participated in the study. Research has demonstrated that such ongoing progress monitoring data can enhance teacher decision making and instructional planning, improve student awareness of learning, and promote greater student achievement (e.g., Fuchs, Fuchs, Hamlett, & Stecker, 1991). Graphs of student progress in fluency of reading connected text were likewise provided to school principals and to the parents of participating students three times during the school year.

In order to enhance teachers' use of available assessment data, we provided classroom teachers with a one-day professional development session focusing on the use of assessment data to plan and deliver differentiated instruction in the general education classroom. During the first year, this inservice focused on providing differentiated instruction based on data from the TPRI, which had been administered by first-grade teachers in each of the schools, and our one-minute passage reading fluency data. During the second year of the study, we again provided classroom teachers with a one-day inservice focused on providing differentiated instruction. In year 2, we shifted our content to focus on peer tutoring as an effective and feasible tool for accommodating academic diversity (e.g., Mathes & Fuchs, 1994; Shanahan, 1998). The final component for ensuring enhanced classroom instruction was offering the classroom teachers our services as consultants for any concerns they might have related to literacy instruction or to instructional needs of specific students. During the two years of the study, teachers often accessed the expertise of the Proactive Reading and Responsive Reading teachers who worked in their schools.

We observed the 30 teachers in the enhanced classroom condition during their language arts time three times during each year of the study, for a total of 90 observations. These observations provided information about the nature of instruction provided to students in this condition. During these observations, the observers recoded whether or not specific strategies occurred. These observers reported that the classroom was stimulating and motivating for 72.62% of the observations and that children were encouraged to express their ideas verbally in 90.27% of the observations. In terms of instructional content, instruction was provided in phonemic awareness during 34.65% of the observations, letter–sound correspondences in isolation during 72.72% of the observations, practice in reading words by sounding out

during 82.36% of the observations, and decoding words using visual memory or context in 40.53% of the observations. Comprehension strategies instruction occurred in only 15.09% of the observations, vocabulary was presented in 83.75% of the observations, spelling was taught in 70.48% of the observations, and writing was included in 54.76% of the observations. While little comprehension instruction was provided, teachers frequently assessed students' comprehension of text, asking literal questions in 83.53% of the observations and inferential questions in 61.60% of the observations.

Small-Group Intervention

Students in both supplemental intervention conditions met in small groups of three students for 40 minutes a day, five days a week, from October through May. Our decision to deliver instruction in groups of three was based on syntheses of recent research that do not identify differences in outcomes from 1:3 vs. 1:1 tutoring (Elbaum, Vaughn, Hughes, & Moody, 2000; Vaughn & Linan-Thompson, 2003). Instruction was provided at a time during the day that did not conflict with the core reading lessons offered in the regular classroom. Thus, the small-group instruction was provided in addition to enhanced classroom instruction.

The six intervention teachers who delivered this small-group instruction received 42 hours of professional development training from the authors of each intervention prior to the onset of the research. During the second year, an additional 12 hours of professional development was provided. Across both years of the study, intervention teachers also participated in monthly half-day inservice meetings. During these meetings, which were conducted separately for teachers in the two interventions, teachers (a) viewed videotaped lessons with discussion and feedback, (b) discussed issues regarding implementation of the interventions, and (c) collaborated in problem solving to plan for accelerating the growth of specific students. These teachers also received frequent onsite coaching from the intervention developers.

Proactive Reading

The objective in the design of Proactive Reading was to arrange the instructional environment to reduce the occurrence of errors and facilitate ownership and integration of skills and strategies that build cumulatively over time, and to assist students in becoming competent readers who read both fluently and with comprehension. The tasks associated with fluent, meaningful reading were analyzed and elements sequenced into a cumulatively building and carefully integrated scope and sequence. From this scope and sequence, daily lesson plans were developed. These lessons were fully specified and provided exact wording to ensure teacher language was clear and kept to a minimum. Following these prescribed lesson plans, teachers delivered explicit instruction designed to assist students in the integrated and fluent use of alphabetic knowledge and comprehension strategies. These lessons were constructed so that various content strands (i.e., phonemic awareness, word recognition, comprehension strategies) were carefully woven together.

A Typical Lesson. A primary focus of Proactive Reading was teaching efficient word identification. Thus, a large portion of each lesson was spent learning and reviewing letter–sound correspondences, sounding out and reading words rapidly, or spelling words in isolation. In a typical Proactive Reading lesson, students played word games designed to promote phonemic awareness, practiced letter–sound correspondences for previously taught letters or letter combinations, practiced writing these letters, and learned the sound of a new letter or letter combination. Students also practiced sounding out and reading words composed of previously taught letter–sound correspondences and various syllable types, spelled words from dictation based on their sound–symbol correspondences, practiced automatic recognition of words that do not conform to alphabetic rules, read and reread decodable connected text, and applied comprehension strategies to this text.

Over time, the nature of these lessons changed. In the beginning, the bulk of each lesson was devoted to learning to use the alphabetic principle quickly and efficiently, with less focus on connected text and reading for meaning. As students progressed, lessons changed in nature to focus on decoding multisyllabic and irregular words, fluency building of connected text, and applying comprehension strategies. In later lessons, students engaged in timed readings and partner reading of narrative stories, and they engaged in retelling, with emphasis on sequencing and identifying story grammar elements.

Text Characteristics. Beginning on the seventh day of instruction, students read connected text daily. This text was fully decodable, meaning that all phonetic elements and all irregular sight words appearing in the text had been taught previously and that students had already demonstrated mastery of those elements and words. In the beginning, this text was stilted and unnatural sounding. However, as students acquired greater mastery of more and more elements, as well as the ability to decode more difficult words, this text became more and more natural.

Lesson Format. A primary feature of Proactive Reading was that it maximized academic engagement (Brophy & Good, 1986; Rosenshine & Stevens, 1986). Instruction was delivered to small homogeneous groups of students who sat in a semicircle around the instructor and was delivered in a rapid-fire manner in which there was constant interchange between the instructor and students. In a typical activity, the teacher asked all students to respond to letters, words, or text in unison, followed by individual turns when each child was able to demonstrate his or her personal ownership of the content. Moreover, the instructor moved quickly from activity to activity within each lesson. Within a typical lesson there were 7 to 10 short activities that encompassed multiple strands of content.

An overarching teaching routine repeated throughout the entire curriculum comprised the teacher modeling new content, providing guided practice for students, and implementing independent practice for every activity. Instructors were required to consistently monitor students' responses, provide positive praise for correct responses, and provide immediate corrective feedback if an error occurred. Instructors had to make on-the-spot judgments about why an error occurred and to focus on that aspect of the task when corrective feedback was provided.

To facilitate student enthusiasm for learning, instructors provided immediate positive feedback about each activity as students demonstrated mastery. Because the curriculum was designed to gradually and cumulatively become more complex, the majority of each lesson was composed of review and generalization work. Thus, each lesson contained very little new content. The expectation was that students would enter each new activity each day able to achieve at least 80% accuracy on their first try, with 100% accuracy being achieved after error corrections and scaffolding had occurred.

Responsive Reading

Responsive Reading also provided for explicit instruction in phonemic awareness and phonemic decoding, but it dedicated relatively less time to the practice of these skills in isolation than did the Proactive approach. Students in the Responsive intervention spent about one fourth of their daily 40-minute lesson in isolated skills instruction and practice. During the balance of the lesson, students in Responsive Reading were prompted to apply literacy skills and strategies in the context of extensive reading and writing practice.

A Typical Lesson. In contrast to Proactive Reading, Responsive Reading did not include a predetermined scope and sequence. Responsive teachers used data from student assessments and daily anecdotal records to identify student needs and strengths, and they planned their instruction based on this analysis, attempting to provide instruction and support within students' zone of proximal development (Vygotsky, 1978)—the level of difficulty

at which students could be successful with the support of the teacher. Teachers individualized instruction by focusing their daily lesson planning and text selection on an individual student within each group, alternating between the three students each day. Thus, every three days, each child in the group received this concentrated attention from the teacher. Each day, the teacher sat beside the focus child and directed instructional scaffolding, prompting predominantly to that child while including the others in the lesson activities.

Responsive Reading teachers adhered to a lesson cycle that demarcated how time was used across each 40-minute lesson. This cycle had five components: fluency building, assessment, letter and word work, supported reading, and supported writing. Teachers were required to choose activities from a menu of options for each part of the lessons based on the observed needs of their students. The nature of these activities, as well as the texts the students read in the lessons, became more complex over time.

During the first two components, fluency building and assessment, which lasted 8 to 10 minutes, students engaged in repeated reading with teacher modeling and prompting to support passage reading fluency. The teacher modeled fluent and expressive reading, explicitly taught the meaning and oral interpretation of punctuation marks, and prompted students to read smoothly and in phrases. The instruction and modeling were directed to the daily focus student, while the other two students in the group engaged in partner reading. Following the fluency activities, the teacher observed one student reading a book that had been introduced on the previous day, using running record procedures (see Clay, 2002). The teacher individually assessed the reading strengths and needs of each student in the group one to two times per week.

During the third component, letter and word work, students received 10 to 12 minutes of explicit instruction and practice related to phonemic awareness, letter–sound relationships, word reading, or spelling. Teachers explicitly taught phonological awareness skills, letter–sound correspondences, and how to sound out words, and students reviewed and practiced these skills daily. Students were taught to manipulate onsets and rimes to arrive at new words through analogy with known words, but they were also asked to segment the phonemes within each onset and rime before applying these larger units to read words. Students practiced decoding and encoding skills in several formats, including blending and sounding out words presented by the teacher and segmenting and writing dictated words.

The fourth component, supported reading, lasted 10 to 12 minutes. During this time, students read a text they had not previously read. Each day, the focus student read a portion of the book alone, while the teacher coached, scaffolded, and prompted the student to apply skills and strategies. Next the entire group read the same book, either chorally or individually. Prior to the reading of a new book, teachers pre-taught potentially difficult vocabulary words, discussed potentially confusing subject matter, and encouraged students to make predictions to link the book's subject matter to prior knowledge and to establish a purpose for reading. During and after reading, teachers frequently asked questions referring to the text meaning and asked students to retell or summarize portions of the story. Teachers provided feedback and supported students as they discussed the meaning of text.

The final lesson component, supported writing, consisted of 8 to 10 minutes of sentence writing with the teacher providing coaching and scaffolding in the application of the strategy of sound analysis for the spelling of unknown words. During supported writing, teachers assisted students in writing sentences about the new story in journals. Teachers sometimes provided explicit instruction in word patterns, modeled the segmenting of words in order to record their phonemes, or used Elkonin sound boxes (Elkonin, 1973) as a framework to assist students in the application of the alphabetic principle.

Word Identification Strategies. As students practiced reading words in isolation

and reading connected text, there was a clear emphasis on teaching efficient word recognition. The following was the primary word recognition strategy taught in Responsive Reading: (a) look for parts you know (i.e., identify known letter combinations), (b) say the word slowly and blend the sounds (i.e., sound it out), and (c) reread the sentence with the word in it and decide whether it makes sense (i.e., check the word within context). Students were also taught to decode unknown words using analogy to known words. Students were taught to access semantic and syntactic information primarily to self-monitor their reading. Contextual information was used to support decoding only occasionally, always in conjunction with the primary strategy of phonemic decoding. Likewise, students were taught to segment words and apply letter–sound associations as a strategy for spelling unknown words.

Text Characteristics. In our study, the Responsive teachers selected books ranked for difficulty in 16 different levels for use in guided reading instruction (Fountas & Pinnell, 1999). These books were leveled for difficulty but were not intended to be phonetically decodable. They progress in complexity of word types and syntax as well as aspects of print size and page layout (see Peterson, 1991).

Comparison of the Two Interventions

Key distinctions between the Proactive and Responsive interventions can be categorized into four main differences. First, Proactive Reading provided a detailed scope and sequence with fully specified daily lessons. In contrast, Responsive Reading relied on the teacher to plan instruction based on observed student needs and strengths. Second, the type of text students read in each intervention was different. Proactive Reading exclusively relied on decodable text, which in the beginning was not particularly natural sounding but became more natural and engaging over time. Responsive Reading made use of leveled text that was not phonetically decodable, but was

1) planning
2) type of text used
3) writing component
4) time of skill in isolation

more natural sounding and arguably more engaging even from the beginning. Third, these two interventions differed in the amount of time focused on learning skills in isolation versus in context. Students in Proactive Reading spent substantial time practicing skills and words in isolation, contrasted with the time Responsive Reading students spent applying strategies and skills with teacher support while they engaged in reading and writing connected text. Finally, the interventions differed in the incorporation of a writing component. Writing in Proactive Reading was limited primarily to spelling words in isolation, while students in Responsive Reading spent about nine minutes of each lesson learning to record their thoughts in complete sentences, while also receiving instruction in the application of the alphabetic principle in spelling words.

Intervention Fidelity

In order to ensure that each intervention was conducted as described, the first and second authors observed intervention teachers and students during an entire instructional session every eight weeks for a total of four observations of each teacher. A 3-point rating scale was used to evaluate the fidelity of implementation of each activity or section of a lesson across four categories: (a) appropriate pacing, (b) implementation of prescribed procedures, (c) error correction with appropriate scaffolding, and (d) student engagement and attentiveness. A score of 3 indicated that the teacher implemented the category in exactly the way it was intended. A score of 2 indicated that the category was implemented in an acceptable manner, but with some error. A score of 1 indicated the category was poorly represented. Likewise, we included a global checklist for readiness of instructional materials, appropriate student seating arrangement, and instructor warmth and enthusiasm. On average, both sets of intervention teachers conducted their respective interventions with high levels of fidelity.

Proactive teachers were rated as having materials ready, having students seated appropriately, and having a warm and enthusiastic manner 100% of the time. Likewise, they were rated as having good instructional pacing ($M = 2.75$, $SD = .53$), following procedures by presenting the lesson as prescribed ($M = 2.64$, $SD = .65$), correcting errors and scaffolding appropriately ($M = 2.71$, $SD = .57$), and maintaining student attentiveness ($M = 2.84$, $SD = .44$).

In a similar manner, Responsive teachers were rated as having materials ready 96% of the time, having students seated appropriately 96% of the time, and being warm and enthusiastic 100% of the time. They were rated as having appropriate pacing ($M = 2.48$, $SD = .73$), following procedures for each section of the lesson routine ($M = 2.59$, $SD = .62$), scaffolding student responses appropriately ($M = 2.67$, $SD = .54$), and maintaining student attentiveness ($M = 2.74$, $SD = .55$). No statistically significant differences were detected in levels of fidelity between the Proactive and Responsive groups, with the exception of pacing, in which the Proactive intervention was rated slightly, but reliably better, $t (252) = 3.69$, $p < .001$.

Measures

Rationale. Proficiency in reading requires, at a minimum, that children be able to read words and text accurately and fluently and understand the meaning of the text. These outcomes are consistent with the content of the reading interventions. Thus, to address the first research question, which concerned the effectiveness of the reading interventions, the measures included assessments of word reading, fluency, and reading comprehension. Given the differences in the amount of time devoted to these different reading domains, we predicted that the Proactive intervention might have more impact on word reading, while Responsive might have more impact on fluency and comprehension. Assessments were done throughout the year to assess the impact of the interventions on growth in word reading and fluency. Assessments of word reading, fluency, and comprehension using norm-referenced tests were conducted at the end of the school year to determine the effects of the interventions on practically important outcomes. This approach permits multiple measures of these constructs as a way of increasing reliability for the assessment outcomes, which is important in ensuring that the results are not dependent on how the outcome was measured. In addition, we did not want the results to be dependent on a particular form of assessment. Thus, fluency was assessed for words and text, and comprehension was assessed with a cloze procedure in which the child filled in missing words from a passage and answered comprehension questions about longer passages. Because the two interventions addressed word recognition instruction differently, separate assessments of accuracy and fluency of real word reading and pseudoword reading were conducted. Phonological awareness was also assessed during the year as both programs explicitly taught phonological awareness. Our approach to assessment of outcomes for the first research question was thus consistent with reading theory and with the instructional content of the two programs.

Some of these measures, in combination with a measure of rapid serial naming of letters, could also be used to address the second research question, whether specific child characteristics predicted response to different types of intervention. Phonological awareness is most strongly linked to word recognition, rapid naming to fluency, and vocabulary to comprehension. Thus, we predicted that children who were weaker in phonological awareness might make more progress with the Proactive intervention, while children weaker in speed of phonological retrieval and vocabulary might do better with Responsive.

Description of Growth Assessments. The assessments of growth were administered four times during the school year at two-month intervals beginning in October, and they included phonological awareness, rapid automatized naming of letters (RAN letters), untimed word reading, word reading fluency, nonword reading fluency, and passage reading fluency (done every three weeks). Phonological awareness was measured using the First Sound

Comparison, Blending Onset-Rime, Blending Words, Blending Nonwords, and Phoneme Elision subtests from the Comprehensive Test of Phonological Processes (CTOPP). Children's scores on the various phonological awareness measures were placed on a single scale based on item response theory (IRT) work (Schatschneider et al., 1999) so that individuals could be assigned a single score of overall phonological awareness ability. This phonological awareness score, reported as a theta score, is much more reliable than individual subtest scores or a typical composite score and is thereby more sensitive and more appropriate for monitoring growth. The final subtest from the CTOPP administered in this research was the RAN Letters subtest, which measures a child's efficiency of phonological access. In this subtest, students are timed as they provide the names of a set of known letters for 60 seconds. The range of reliabilities (internal consistency) on the CTOPP subtests for this age group range from .70 to .91, all acceptable or better.

Untimed word reading entailed reading words from an IRT-based list of increasingly more difficult words developed by our research team. This list has been found to be very sensitive to short-term growth in word recognition ability (see Foorman et al., 1998). The words on the list were selected according to frequency and diversity of linguistic and orthographic features represented in early primary texts. The internal consistency of this measure is .90 (O'Malley, Francis, Foorman, Fletcher, & Swank, 2002).

Word reading fluency and nonword reading fluency were measured using the Sight Word Efficiency and Phonemic Decoding Efficiency subtests from the Test of Word Reading Efficiency (TOWRE). In these subtests, students read as many words as they could in 45 seconds or decoded as many pseudowords as they could in 45 seconds. Each list of words and nonwords was arranged so that items increased in difficulty. We included both words and nonwords to ensure that we measured both phonological decoding ability and sight recognition of familiar or partially familiar words. Internal consistency exceeds .95 for both subtests.

Passage reading fluency was measured as words read correctly per minute (WCPM) on timed one-minute oral reading samples of end-of-first-grade-level passages that had been developed for Teachers Continuous Assessment for Reading Excellence software (TCARE; Mathes, Torgesen, & Heron, 2004). The passages used to evaluate oral reading fluency were subjected to substantial field-testing to determine equivalence of difficulty.

Description of End-of-Year Assessments. Measures that were administered only at the end of the school year (i.e., posttest only) included the WJ-III, the Comprehensive Assessment of Reading Battery Revised for First-Grade (CRAB-R; see Mathes et al., 1998), and the Vocabulary subtest of the Wechsler Abbreviated Scale of Intelligence (WASI). From the WJ-III, the Word Attack, Word Identification, Passage Comprehension, Reading Fluency, Spelling, and Calculations subtests were administered. Reliability ranges from .87 to .97. The Word Attack subtest is a measure of accurate decoding of nonwords, whereas Word Identification is a measure of the ability to read sight words in lists. Reading Fluency measures how quickly students read sentences and determine if they are true or false. Passage Comprehension is measured through a cloze procedure, where students read a sentence or brief passage in which certain words have been taken out and students are required to produce the missing words or acceptable substitutions for them. Spelling requires students to spell words of increasing complexity. The test of Mathematical Calculation was included to determine whether students made generalized academic progress or gains specific to reading acquisition. The CRAB-R yields fluency and comprehension scores with test–retest reliability of .92 to .96 for different indexes. For this test, students read two stories orally for three minutes each and answered 10 questions about each story. The CRAB-R was not administered

to students who had a raw score of 4 or less on WJ-III Passage Comprehension.

Results

Analytic Approach

Multilevel modeling techniques represented the primary data analysis procedures. Research on students in schools represented nested levels of analysis because each student was embedded in a classroom, which in turn was embedded in a school. Although our research questions focused on the student level of analysis, outcomes were affected by classroom-level differences (e.g., curriculum, classroom teacher styles) and school-level differences (e.g., variations in the number of high-poverty students at a school). If growth was assessed, this represented another level in the design (i.e., time) that was nested within students. Thus, multilevel modeling permitted us to address the primary research questions while controlling for sources of variability that could produce potentially unexplained sources of differences in the outcomes. When time was included in the analysis, as was the case for the growth measures, this approach allowed us to estimate growth curves for each student relative to the entire samples' growth pattern. With growth curves, we could (a) estimate the average rate of change for the entire sample, represented by the slope parameter; (b) estimate the extent to which individual growth rates differed from this average rate of change; (c) estimate the average level of performance at the final time point in April for the entire sample, represented by the intercept parameter; (d) estimate the extent to which individuals differed from this average April performance; and (e) evaluate correlates of change while controlling for classroom effects. The same multilevel modeling approach was used with the norm-referenced, end-of-year data, except that time was not included in the model and rates of growth were therefore not computed. Analyses that addressed hypotheses 1, 2, and 3 focused on the intervention group, as it predicted the intercept or slope parameters, as the correlate of change. Analyses that addressed hypothesis 4 examined student characteristics as correlates of change that may have interacted with intervention.

Prior to predicting individual students' growth patterns, it was necessary to accurately characterize the overall growth pattern of the sample for each outcome. Accurate descriptions of the sample's general growth patterns were achieved through a process called building the *unconditional models*. Growth can be linear, characterized by a slope that is a straight line. It can also be nonlinear, which is common in grade 1 (see Foorman et al., 1998). Thus, it was necessary to test models with linear and curvilinear growth.

Building accurate unconditional models of the sample's growth patterns also required that we examine whether there was significant variability among individual children's growth patterns. Examination of individuals' variability from the average growth pattern involved testing whether the change parameters (e.g., intercept and slope) should be fixed or freely estimated. Fixed parameters have the same values for all children. Random parameters are freely estimated across children and quantify the degree of individual variability.

Characterizing the present sample's growth patterns involved sequentially testing a series of models that increased in complexity by one change parameter per model to determine which model best characterized the sample's growth. The order of the five models that could have potentially been examined were as follows: (a) straight line growth with random intercept and fixed slope; (b) straight line growth with random intercept and random slope; (c) curvilinear growth with random intercept, fixed slope, and fixed quadratic; (d) curvilinear growth with random intercept, random slope, and fixed quadratic; and (e) curvilinear growth with random intercept, random slope, and random quadratic. If the mean value of the target change parameter in a given model was significantly different from 0 using a criterion alpha level of .05, then that parameter was kept and model building continued in the order above. If

the new parameter being tested was not significant, then that parameter was dropped from the model and model building ceased.

Identifying parameters that should or should not be in the unconditional model is not the same as testing for significant differences between groups, even though a *t* statistic is reported for both. It is possible that the number of tests of significance of parameters could lead to Type I errors in some instances, falsely identifying a parameter as important, but such errors are less critical than failure to identify a potentially significant parameter. Setting alpha at .05 provided an appropriate balance for Type I and II errors. We centered growth trajectories at the final wave of assessment so that intercepts represented expected levels of achievement in April. This approach is standard practice for growth curve modeling and is necessary to develop unconditional models that accurately, parsimoniously, and understandably characterize change within the sample.

Once the best unconditional models were determined, change parameters were correlated with relevant predictors of growth, such as intervention group or children's initial status on reading-related skills. These *conditional models* directly tested the effectiveness of the interventions and whether specific child characteristics differentially predicted change associated with an intervention. We tested each outcome separately because a univariate approach is consistent with our interest in replicating findings across measures of the same construct that vary in assessment method, thus avoiding method dependence of the findings.

Magnitude and Reliability of Effects

Hypotheses 1, 2, and 3 involved follow-up comparisons of intervention-group effects. Hypothesis 4 involved a few follow-up comparisons of intervention group by child characteristic interaction effects. All of these comparisons were conducted using a critical alpha level of .05. A Bonferroni adjusted alpha of .01 was not used because it was judged too conservative and would inflate the Type II error rate. Instead, our use of a .05 criterion was consistent with our goal of using the current sample and being able to detect practically important and educationally significant effects of at least moderate effect size. The tables indicate statistical significance at multiple criterion alpha levels so that readers can independently judge the contrasts if they desire to do so. The second way we evaluated our interventions did not rely on an arbitrarily determined criterion but instead involved examining effect sizes. This helped us quantify the magnitude of group differences on the intercept (i.e., scores in April or May) and slope (i.e., growth rates) of the two supplemental intervention groups relative to the intercept and slope of the enhanced classroom group. Effect sizes were calculated for the intercept and slope terms by subtracting the estimates of the enhanced classroom group from the estimates of the intervention groups and dividing by the square root of the residual.

Analyses to Identify Confounding Variables

Prior to addressing our two primary research questions, it was necessary to consider the influence of differences among the groups that might influence the outcomes. First we examined differences in initial status. Differences in initial levels of literacy development between the typically achieving and at-risk groups were expected. However, we did not expect the three at-risk groups to differ in these characteristics. Second, we examined other student-level variables that would represent potential covariates in the analyses. These included gender, ethnicity, classroom, and cohort. Cohort had to be considered because we conducted the study over two consecutive years to increase the sample size. Covariate effects are reported for each analysis in which they were significant. There were no instances where any covariate interacted with intervention.

Analyses of Baseline Differences in October

Multilevel modeling was used to control for classroom effects and test for group differences in initial status on the following baseline measures: TPRI letter names and sounds (used to identify students' risk status), untimed word reading, TOWRE word reading fluency, TOWRE nonword reading fluency, TCARE passage reading fluency, CTOPP phonological awareness IRT-based theta score, and WASI Vocabulary subtest. There were significant overall group differences on all of these baseline variables, $Fs(3, 330-356) = 8.2$ to 94.7, $ps < .001$. As expected, the typically achieving group had higher language and literacy scores than the three at-risk groups. Generally, the three at-risk groups had comparable baseline language and literacy scores. The only exception was that students in the Responsive group had higher baseline scores on letter names than students in the enhanced classroom group. Baseline scores for each group are presented in Table 2.

Hypotheses 1, 2, and 3: Effectiveness of the Interventions

We examined effectiveness of the interventions relative to quality classroom instruction for at-risk students, relative to quality classroom instruction for typically achieving students, and relative to each other in terms of rate of growth (slope) and April levels of performance (intercept) for each growth measure. These three contrasts were also used to examine the effectiveness of the interventions on end-of-year (May) outcomes.

Analyses of Growth

Table 3 reports comparisons of the slope, intercept, and, when appropriate, quadratic values for all growth measures among the four groups.

Phonological Awareness. The sample's growth in phonological awareness was best described by a model that included random intercept, random slope, and random quadratic terms. In other words, the unconditional model

Table 2
Baseline Scores by Group

| | Observed Scores by Group | | | | | | | |
| Measure | Enhanced Classroom (n = 114) | | Proactive (n = 92) | | Responsive (n = 92) | | Typically Achieving (n = 101) | |
	M	(SD)	M	(SD)	M	(SD)	M	(SD)
Word reading[a]	−1.25	(.65)	−1.30	(.64)	−1.22	(.61)	.29	(1.1)
CTOPP								
Phonological Awareness[a]	−.77	(.62)	−.87	(.67)	−.79	(.64)	−.02	(.57)
RAN Letters[b]	.84	(.28)	.81	(.25)	.80	(.22)	1.13	(.25)
Nonword Repetition[c]	9.5	(4.2)	9.2	(3.8)	9.5	(3.5)	11.6	(4.2)
TPRI								
Letter Names[c]	9.2	(1.4)	9.2	(1.5)	9.5	(1.0)	9.9	(.50)
Letter Sounds[c]	6.1	(2.9)	6.1	(3.1)	6.4	(2.7)	9.0	(1.3)
TOWRE								
Word Reading Efficiency[d]	86.2	(8.3)	86.2	(9.0)	86.8	(7.4)	95.9	(12.2)
Nonword Reading Efficiency[d]	93.0	(8.2)	93.4	(7.7)	93.1	(6.7)	100.8	(10.4)

[a]IRT-based theta scores; [b]Letters per minute; [c]Raw scores; [d]Standard scores.

indicated that there were reliable individual differences in the rates of growth, the degree of curvilinearity in that growth, and April scores. The unconditional model also included a random intercept term at the classroom level that modeled reliable classroom differences on April phonological awareness scores. Examination of potential covariates found significant effects of ethnicity only on individuals' expected phonological scores in April, $F(2, 50) = 11.27$, $p < .001$. Subsequent analyses of growth in phonological awareness controlled for effects of ethnicity and classroom.

The overall impact of intervention group was significant on the intercept, $F(3, 85) = 15.71$, $p < .001$, and slope $F(3, 1431) = 29.25$, $p < .001$. Follow-up comparisons of the groups' slope values (see first column of Table 3) indicated that the Proactive and Responsive groups demonstrated significantly more rapid development of phonological awareness than the enhanced classroom and typically achieving

groups. In addition, the Proactive group demonstrated more rapid growth than the Responsive group. Growth patterns for each group are illustrated in Figure 1.

Follow-up comparisons of the groups' intercept values, which represent predicted April scores, indicated that the Proactive and Responsive intervention groups had higher April scores than the enhanced classroom group (see Table 4 and Figure 1). However, the two intervention groups continued to have April scores that were lower than those of the typically achieving group. Finally, the Proactive and Responsive groups had comparable phonological awareness scores in April.

Untimed Word Reading. The sample's growth in untimed word reading ability was best described by an unconditional model including random intercept, random slope, and fixed quadratic terms, indicating that there were significant amounts of individual variation in

Table 3
Group Differences in Growth Patterns of Literacy Skills

Contrasts	Phonological Awareness diff.	(SE)	df	t	Untimed Word Reading diff.	(SE)	df	t	Word Reading Fluency diff.	(SE)	df	t	Nonword Reading Fluency diff.	(SE)	df	t	Passage Reading Fluency (Cohort 1) diff.	(SE)	df	t	Passage Reading Fluency (Cohort 2) diff.	(SE)	df	t
Slope																								
P vs. EC	0.16	(.02)	1431	6.72***	0.17	(.04)	1428	4.26***	3.90	(1.18)	1428	3.28**	0.95	(.41)	1436	2.30	0.27	(.53)	1935	0.51	2.23	(.80)	2370	2.77**
R vs. EC	0.08	(.02)	1431	3.22**	0.11	(.04)	1428	2.73**	2.06	(1.18)	1428	1.75+	0.34	(.41)	1436	0.83	0.77	(.53)	1935	1.47	2.04	(.79)	2370	2.57*
P vs. R	0.08	(.02)	1431	3.40***	0.06	(.04)	1428	1.49	1.83	(1.21)	1428	1.51	0.61	(.41)	1436	1.44	0.50	(.55)	1935	0.92	0.19	(.82)	2370	0.23
P vs. TA	0.21	(.02)	1431	8.76***	0.46	(.04)	1428	11.50***	3.55	(1.18)	1428	3.01**	0.88	(.41)	1436	2.11*	1.83	(.51)	1935	-2.97**	2.26	(.80)	2370	2.82**
R vs. TA	0.12	(.02)	1431	5.27***	0.39	(.04)	1428	10.01***	1.71	(1.17)	1428	1.47	0.27	(.41)	1436	0.65	1.56	(.53)	1935	-2.06*	2.08	(.79)	2370	2.63**
Intercept																								
P vs. EC	0.34	(.08)	85	4.34***	0.37	(.08)	85	4.75***	4.57	(2.10)	85	2.17*	2.43	(1.37)	85	-1.78	1.12	(5.59)	56	-0.20	10.91	(5.54)	53	1.97+
R vs. EC	0.19	(.08)	85	2.45*	0.31	(.08)	85	4.03***	4.83	(2.08)	85	2.33*	1.08	(1.36)	85	-0.80	7.79	(5.56)	56	-1.40	12.23	(5.52)	53	2.22*
P vs. R	0.15	(.08)	85	1.84+	0.05	(.08)	85	0.74	0.26	(2.16)	85	0.12	1.36	(1.41)	85	0.95	6.67	(5.79)	56	-1.15	1.32	(5.70)	53	0.23
P vs. TA	-0.16	(.08)	85	-2.05	-0.18	(.08)	85	2.38*	-15.50	(2.13)	85	-7.28***	-6.58	(1.39)	85	-4.74***	-30.35	(5.57)	56	-5.45***	-25.85	(5.85)	53	-4.63***
R vs. TA	-0.31	(.08)	85	-3.97***	-0.24	(.08)	85	-3.17**	-15.24	(2.10)	85	-7.27****	-7.93	(1.34)	85	-5.81***	-23.68	(5.43)	56	-4.36*	-24.54	(5.56)	53	-4.41***
Quadratic																								
P vs. EC									0.75	(.30)	1428	2.54*									0.11	(.05)	2370	2.40*
R vs. EC									0.29	(.30)	1428	0.96									0.81	(.05)	2370	1.82+
P vs. R									0.47	(.31)	1428	1.52									0.03	(.05)	2370	0.59
P vs. TA									0.89	(.30)	1428	3.00**									0.26	(.05)	2370	-5.80
R vs. TA									0.42	(.30)	1428	1.41									0.23	(.05)	2370	5.26***

Note. P = Proactive; R = Responsive; EC = enhanced classroom; TA = typically achieving; diff = difference between the estimates; *df* = degrees of freedom.
+*p* < .10; * *p* < .05; ** *p* < .01; *** *p* < .001.

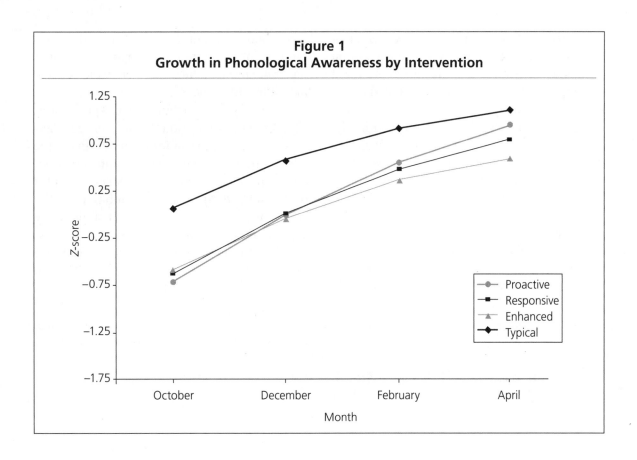

Figure 1
Growth in Phonological Awareness by Intervention

Legend:
- Proactive
- Responsive
- Enhanced
- Typical

Y-axis: Z-score
X-axis: Month (October, December, February, April)

Table 4
Intervention Effect Sizes Compared to Enhanced Classroom Instruction on Slope and Intercept Terms

Measure	Proactive		Responsive	
	Slope	Intercept	Slope	Intercept
Phonological awareness	.81	1.76	.39	.99
Untimed word reading TOWRE	.47	1.03	.30	.87
Nonword reading fluency	.21	.52	.07	.23
Word reading fluency Passage reading fluency	1.13	1.33	.60	1.41
Cohort 1	.04	.15	.11	1.06
Cohort 2	.33	1.62	.30	1.81

Note. Slope represents growth and intercept represents April scores.

rates of growth and April scores. The unconditional model also included a random intercept term at the classroom level. This parameter indicated there were reliable classroom differences in April scores. There were no effects of cohort, gender, or ethnicity that needed to be covaried.

The overall effect of group was significant on the slope, $F(3, 1428) = 53.22$, $p < .001$, and intercept, $F(3, 85) = 18.70$, $p < .001$. Follow-up comparisons of the groups' slopes indicated that both the Proactive and Responsive intervention groups demonstrated significantly more rapid development than that of the enhanced classroom and typically achieving groups (see second column of Table 3 and Figure 2). Finally, rates of growth in untimed word reading among the two intervention groups were comparable.

Comparisons of the groups' intercepts revealed that both intervention groups had April scores in untimed word reading that were significantly higher than those of the enhanced classroom group (see Table 3). Both intervention groups had April scores that continued to be lower than those of the typically achieving group. Finally, the two intervention groups had comparable scores on untimed word reading in April.

Word Reading Fluency. The sample's growth in TOWRE Word Reading Fluency was best described by an unconditional model with random intercept, random slope, and random quadratic terms, indicating there were reliable individual differences in rates of growth, curvilinearity of growth patterns, and April scores. The unconditional model also included random intercept and random slope terms at the classroom level. These later parameters modeled reliable classroom differences in rates of growth and April scores. Among potential covariates, there was a small but statistically significant effect of cohort on individuals' degree of curvilinearity of growth in word reading fluency, $F(1, 437) = 4.33, p < .05$, such that the second cohort had slower initial growth but similar April scores.

There were significant differences in growth patterns in word reading fluency between the four groups, controlling for classroom and cohort, as illustrated in Figure 3. The overall effect of intervention group was significant on

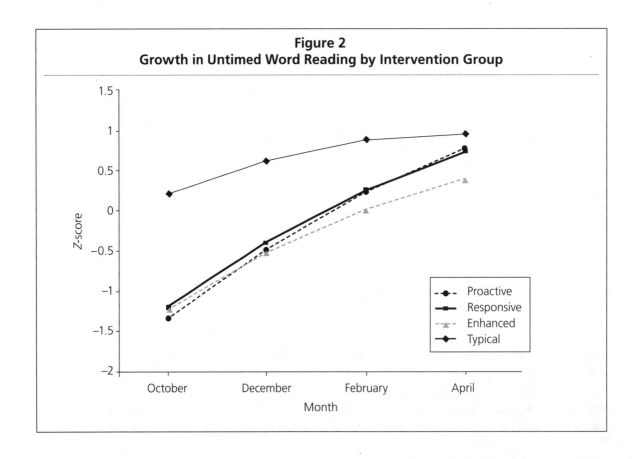

Figure 2
Growth in Untimed Word Reading by Intervention Group

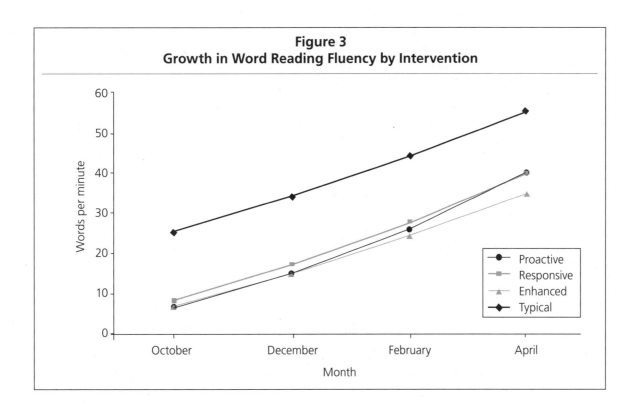

Figure 3
Growth in Word Reading Fluency by Intervention

Legend:
- Proactive
- Responsive
- Enhanced
- Typical

Y-axis: Words per minute
X-axis: Month (October, December, February, April)

the intercept, $F(3, 85) = 36.08$, $p < .001$; slope, $F(3, 1428) = 4.53$, $p < .01$; and quadratic terms, $F(3, 1428) = 3.46$, $p < .05$. The Proactive group demonstrated more rapid development than the typically achieving and enhanced classroom groups (see comparisons of slope terms in third column of Table 3). The Proactive group also showed significantly more acceleration in their rate of growth relative to the typically achieving and enhanced classroom groups (see comparisons of quadratic terms in Table 3 or increasingly steeper slope of the Proactive group in Figure 3). The Responsive group failed to demonstrate a growth rate or acceleration pattern that was significantly different from the typically achieving or enhanced classroom groups. Finally, there were no statistically significant differences between the growth rates and acceleration patterns of the two intervention groups.

Comparisons of the intercept values found that both of the intervention groups had word reading fluency scores in April that were higher than those of the enhanced classroom group.

The intervention groups continued to have lower April scores than the typically achieving group, and they were comparable to one another.

Nonword Reading Fluency. The sample's growth in TOWRE nonword reading fluency was best described by a model including random intercept and random slope terms, indicating there were reliable individual differences in linear rates of growth and April scores. The unconditional model also included random intercept and random slope terms at the classroom level, indicating there were reliable classroom differences in rates of growth and April scores. There were no effects of cohort, gender, or ethnicity. There were significant group differences in students' growth in nonword reading fluency, controlling for classroom. The overall effect of group was significant on the intercept, $F(3, 85) = 18.11$, $p < .001$, but not the slope, $F(3, 1436) = 2.14$, $p = .09$ (see Table 3). Only the Proactive group demonstrated a statistically significant quicker growth rate than the enhanced classroom group or the typically achieving group. The intervention groups had comparable growth rates. All three at-risk groups had comparable April scores on nonword reading fluency, and all three at-risk groups had lower April scores than the typically achieving group.

Passage Reading Fluency. We examined cohorts separately on passage reading fluency because we collected a different number of one-minute oral reading samples in year 1 and year 2 and because the same stories were administered at different time points during those years.

Cohort 1. The unconditional model that best described the sample's improved ability to fluently read connected text during the first year of the study was a model with random intercept, random slope, random quadratic, and fixed cubic terms. In other words, there were reliable

individual differences in rates of growth, curvilinearity of growth patterns, and April scores. The unconditional model also included random intercept and random slope terms at the classroom level, reflecting reliable classroom differences in growth rates and April passage reading fluency scores.

There were significant group differences in growth of passage reading fluency, controlling for classroom (see Figure 4). The overall effect of group was significant on the intercept, $F(3, 56) = 14.58$, $p < .001$, and slope, $F(3, 1935) = 5.03$, $p < .01$. The typically achieving group demonstrated significantly more rapid development (slope) than the Proactive, Responsive, and enhanced classroom groups. Both intervention groups demonstrated growth rates comparable to those of the enhanced classroom group and to each other. Accordingly, the typically achieving group had higher April scores (intercept) than all three at-risk groups, and the three at-risk groups had comparable April scores.

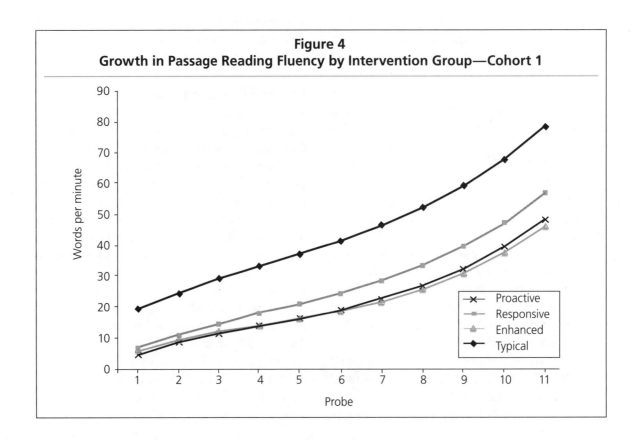

Figure 4
Growth in Passage Reading Fluency by Intervention Group—Cohort 1

Cohort 2. Growth in ability to read connected text in year 2 was best described by a model including random intercept, random slope, and random quadratic terms. There were reliable individual differences in rates of growth, curvilinearity of growth patterns, and April scores. The unconditional model also included a random intercept term at the classroom level, reflecting reliable classroom differences in April passage reading fluency scores. Among potential covariates, there was a significant effect of gender on the intercept, $F(1, 17) = 9.94$, $p < .01$; slope, $F(1, 2379) = 6.64$, $p = .01$; and quadratic, $F(1, 2379) = 3.57$, $p = .05$. Specifically, the passage reading fluency of girls started off higher and increased more rapidly than for boys.

There were significant group differences in growth in reading connected text, controlling for classroom and gender. The overall effect of group was significant on the intercept, $F(3, 53) = 16.45$, $p < .001$; slope; and quadratic terms,

Fs$(3, 2370) = 4.86$ and 13.98, ps $< .01$, respectively. The three at-risk groups demonstrated more accelerated rates of growth relative to the typically achieving group, such that the at-risk groups showed slower initial growth followed by accelerated growth during the last two thirds of the year (see Figure 5). Most important was that the two intervention groups demonstrated quicker growth rates than the enhanced classroom group and the typically achieving group as evidenced by steeper slopes (see last column of Table 3).

Effect Sizes. We also examined the effects of our interventions in terms of effect sizes on the intercept and slope terms centered at the final wave of growth assessments. This helped us quantify the magnitude of differences on the intercept (i.e., April scores) and slope (i.e., growth rates) of the two supplemental intervention groups relative to the intercept and slope of the enhanced classroom group. Table

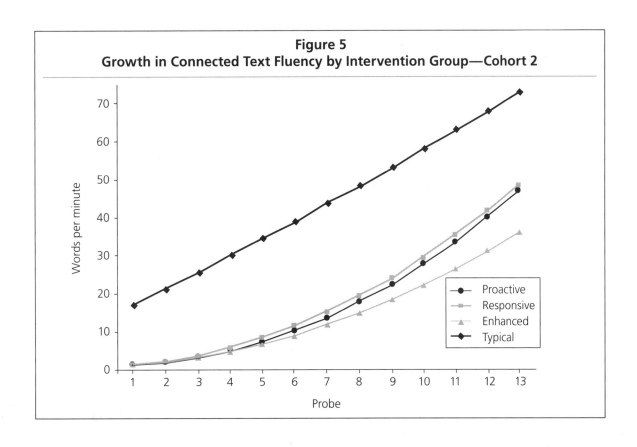

Figure 5
Growth in Connected Text Fluency by Intervention Group—Cohort 2

The Effects of Theoretically Different Instruction and Student Characteristics   79

4 shows that effect sizes for the intercept, or April scores, tended to be large for both interventions and for untimed word reading, word reading fluency, and phonological awareness. Effect sizes on phonological awareness and untimed word reading were somewhat larger for the Proactive than for the Responsive intervention, while effect sizes for April scores in word reading fluency were slightly larger for the Responsive intervention. For April scores in passage reading fluency (cohort 1) effects were small for the Proactive group and large for the Responsive Group. For the second cohort, effect sizes were large for both groups, but they were somewhat larger for the Responsive group. The effects of Proactive intervention on April scores in nonword reading fluency were moderate, whereas the effects of Responsive intervention on this outcome were small.

The effect sizes for the Proactive intervention for growth (slope) in phonological awareness and word reading fluency were large, while effects on growth in untimed word reading were moderate and effects on growth in nonword reading fluency and passage reading fluency were small. The Responsive intervention demonstrated moderate effects on growth in word reading fluency and smaller effects on growth on all other measures. The overall pattern of effect sizes is consistent with the different instructional emphases of the two programs.

Analyses of End-of-Year Achievement

Multilevel modeling was used to control for classroom effects and examine intervention-group differences on end-of-year (May) literacy scores. WJ-III achievement was analyzed using W-scores rather than age-based or grade-based standard scores because we were interested in examining group differences in absolute abilities rather than relative abilities as a norm-referenced score would produce. Examination of potential covariates found significant classroom effects on WJ-III Spelling, WJ-III Calculations, and CRAB-R Fluency, zs = 1.71, 2.33, 1.81, $ps < .05$; significant main effects of ethnicity on WJ-III Word Attack, $F(2, 303) = 5.80, p < .01$; and significant main

effects of gender on CRAB-R Fluency, $F(1, 296) = 5.96, p < .05$. After controlling for classroom, ethnicity, and gender when appropriate, we found significant overall group differences on all end-of-year literacy scores, $Fs(3, 262–305) = 13.45$ to $23.26, ps < .001$, and end-of-year WJ-III Calculation scores, $F(3, 304) = 9.15, p < .001$.

Follow-up contrasts examined the effectiveness of the interventions in terms of effects on end-of-year achievement scores (see Table 5). These contrasts demonstrated that the two intervention groups obtained significantly higher scores than the enhanced classroom group on end-of-year WJ-III Word Identification and Spelling. Only the Proactive group demonstrated significantly higher differences than the enhanced classroom group on WJ-III Word Attack. Neither of the interventions demonstrated significant effects on WJ-III Calculations, WJ-III Reading Fluency, WJ-III Passage Comprehension, CRAB-R Fluency, or CRAB-R Comprehension. Table 6 presents W-scores and grade-based standard scores on the WJ-III outcomes or raw scores on the CRAB-R outcomes for each group, as well as relevant effect sizes.

Analyses of the WJ-III Reading Fluency and both CRAB-R subtests included only children who read well enough to be administered these tests. There were 43 children who were administered the end-of-year assessment battery but who did not read well enough to be administered the WJ-III Reading Fluency test. Moreover, the four groups differed in terms of the proportion of children who could or could not be administered WJ-III Reading Fluency at the end of the year, $x2 (3) = 19.14, p < .001$. Specifically, 2 of the 43 children were in the typically achieving group, 7 children were in the Proactive intervention group, 14 children were in the Responsive intervention group, and 20 children were in the enhanced classroom group. The difference in proportions of children who were testable between the Proactive and enhanced classroom groups was significant, $x2 (1) = 5.29, p = .02$. Similarly, there were eight children who were administered the

Table 5
Group Differences in End of the Year Achievement

Contrasts	WJ-III Word Attack W-Score				WJ-III Word Identification W-Score				WJ-III Passage Comprehension W-Score				WJ-III Reading Fluency W-Score			
	diff.	(SE)	df	t	diff.	(SE)	df	t	diff.	(SE)	df	t	diff.	(SE)	df	t
P vs. EC	11.00	(2.74)	303	4.01***	10.81	(3.26)	305	3.31***	3.19	(2.35)	305	1.36	0.01	(2.57)	262	0.00
R vs. EC	4.11	(2.70)	303	1.53	7.58	(3.21)	305	2.36*	4.50	(2.31)	305	1.95+	3.35	(2.59)	262	1.29
P vs. R	6.88	(2.80)	303	2.45*	3.23	(3.33)	305	0.97	-1.31	(2.40)	305	-0.54	-3.34	(2.59)	262	-1.29
P vs. TA	4.35	(2.76)	303	1.59	-13.92	(3.24)	305	-4.30***	-12.77	(2.33)	305	-5.47***	-14.03	(2.42)	262	-5.79***
R vs. TA	-11.20	(2.67)	303	-4.20***	-17.15	(3.18)	305	-5.39***	-11.46	(2.29)	305	-5.00***	-10.68	(2.44)	262	-4.38***

Contrasts	WJ-III Spelling W-Score				WJ-III Calculations W-Score				CRAB-R Fluency W-Score				CRAB-R Comprehension W-Score			
	diff.	(SE)	df	t	diff.	(SE)	df	t	diff.	(SE)	df	t	diff.	(SE)	df	t
P vs. EC	8.13	(2.37)	305	3.42***	1.00	(1.83)	304	0.55	6.49	(3.92)	269	1.66+	0.45	(.57)	304	0.79
R vs. EC	8.22	(2.33)	305	3.45***	2.00	(1.80)	304	1.11	6.83	(3.88)	269	1.76+	0.91	(.56)	304	1.62
P vs. R	-0.09	(2.42)	305	-0.04	1.00	(1.87)	304	0.54	-0.34	(3.97)	269	-0.09	-0.46	(.58)	304	-0.79
P vs. TA	-8.37	(2.36)	305	-3.54***	7.38	(1.82)	304	4.05***	-19.02	(3.86)	269	-4.93***	-3.49	(.57)	304	-6.15***
R vs. TA	-8.28	(2.31)	305	-3.58***	8.38	(1.78)	304	4.07***	-18.67	(3.79)	269	-4.93***	-3.02	(.56)	304	-5.46***

Note. P = Proactive; R = Responsive; EC = enhanced classroom; TA = typically achieving; diff = difference between the estimates; df = degrees of freedom.
+p < .10; * p < .05; **p < .01; ***p < .001.

Table 6
End-of-Year Outcome Measure by Group

Measure	Proactive			Responsive			Enhanced Classroom			Typically Achieving			ES Proactive vs. EC	ES Responsive vs. EC
	W	(SE)	M	W	(SE)	M	W	(SE)	M	W	(SE)	M		
WJ-III[a]														
Word Attack	480.80	(2.16)	109	473.92	(2.10)	105	469.81	(2.03)	103	485.12	(1.99)	111	0.76	0.28
Word Identification	446.75	(2.43)	107	443.50	(2.36)	106	435.94	(2.26)	102	460.67	(2.22)	113	0.51	0.36
Passage Comprehension	456.80	(1.82)	95	485.11	(1.76)	97	453.61	(1.70)	94	469.57	(1.66)	103	0.21	0.30
Spelling	461.64	(1.94)	102	461.73	(1.88)	103	453.51	(1.83)	97	470.01	(1.78)	109	0.54	0.55
Calculations	463.02	(1.61)	104	462.02	(1.57)	103	464.02	(1.53)	105	470.40	(1.49)	111	0.09	0.17
Reading Fluency[b]	441.85	(1.91)	98	445.20	(1.93)	100	441.85	(1.90)	98	445.88	(1.69)	107		
CRAB-R[c]														
Fluency		(3.60)	44		(3.60)	44		(3.50)	37		(3.40)	63		
Comprehension		(0.47)	4.3		(0.46)	4.7		(0.45)	3.8		(7.70)	7.7		

Note. M = WJ-III age-based standard score or CRAB-R raw scores.
CRAB-R and WJ-III Reading Fluency effect sizes are not reported because of the inability of some students to take these subtests resulted in biasing outcomes in favor of the enhanced classroom condition.
Sample Size:

[a] Proactive n = 80	Responsive n = 83	Enhanced classroom n = 82	Typically achieving n = 98
[b] Proactive n = 73	Responsive n = 69	Enhanced classroom n = 62	Typically achieving n = 96
[c] Proactive n = 80	Responsive n = 80	Enhanced classroom n = 77	Typically achieving n = 98

end-of-year assessment battery but who could not be administered either of the CRAB-R subtests. Of these children, three participated in the Responsive intervention, and five participated in the enhanced classroom condition.

The two intervention groups had comparable scores on all but one end-of-year outcome measure. Specifically, the Proactive group had higher scores than the Responsive group on end-of-year WJ-III Word Attack skills. The Proactive intervention effect on word attack was also the only exception to the general finding that children in the intervention groups continued to have lower end-of-year scores than children in the typically achieving group.

Effect sizes for the intervention groups relative to the enhanced classroom group were calculated in the same manner as for the growth analyses, except that effect sizes were only calculated for the intercept because there was no slope term. It should also be noted that the scores on the norm-referenced tasks are largely in the average range. Effect sizes are in the small to moderate range (see Table 6). Effects sizes are largely comparable in the two intervention groups except for word attack, where effects for Proactive were larger.

Hypothesis 4: Child Characteristics Predicting Response to Intervention

We examined hypothesis 4 by asking if children's initial status on relevant reading-related skills interacted with group when predicting either growth rates or April scores of growth outcomes or end-of-year standardized achievement. The interaction terms that specifically addressed hypothesis 4 were sequentially dropped if found nonsignificant so that any main effects of initial reading skills on literacy acquisition would be apparent.

Growth Outcomes

Phonological Awareness. Students' phonological awareness at the beginning of the year was significantly and positively related to all fluency scores across the school year (see main effects of phonological awareness on intercepts for TOWRE word reading fluency, TOWRE nonword reading fluency, and TCARE passage reading fluency in Table 7). Initial phonological awareness scores were positively associated with growth in all fluency scores, such that higher initial phonological awareness scores were associated with steeper growth in fluency and lower initial phonological awareness scores were associated with slower growth in fluency (see main effects of phonological awareness on slopes in Table 7). The positive relations of initial phonological awareness with growth in fluency and with fluency scores throughout the year were most pronounced in the typically achieving group and were less pronounced in the three at-risk groups, which accounted for the significant group by phonological awareness interaction effects in Table 7. No significant interactions were apparent among the at-risk groups.

The relationship of initial phonological awareness with growth in untimed word reading was very different than the relationship of initial phonological awareness with growth in fluency. Initial phonological awareness was still positively related with untimed word reading scores at all time points; however, initial phonological awareness was *negatively* related to growth in untimed word reading in the typically achieving group. The negative relationship of initial phonological awareness with growth among the typically achieving students, along with the relative lack of association between initial phonological awareness and growth in the at-risk groups, accounted for the significant group by phonological awareness interaction on the slope term of the untimed word reading model in Table 7.

Efficiency of Phonological Access. Letter naming efficiency on RAN at the beginning of the year was significantly and positively related to fluency scores across the school year (see main effects of RAN on intercepts for word reading fluency, nonword reading fluency, and passage reading fluency in Table 8).

Table 7
Effects of Initial Phonological Awareness on Growth in Reading and Response to Intervention

	Intercept		Slope		Quadratic	
	df	F	df	F	df	F
Word reading fluency						
Group	3, 85	19.05***	3, 1423	5.47***	3, 1423	3.45*
PA	1, 1423	46.35***	1, 1423	6.58***	1, 1419	1.34[a]
Group X PA	3, 1423	6.15***	3, 1420	2.34[a]	3, 1416	1.19[a]
Nonword reading fluency						
Group	3, 85	7.56***	3, 1431	4.06**	—	—
PA	1, 1431	62.32***	1, 1431	10.11**	—	—
Group X PA	3, 1431	13.61***	3, 1428	0.65[a]	—	—
Passage reading fluency (cohort 1)						
Group	3, 56	4.55**	3, 1924	2.68*	3, 1924	1.58[a]
PA	1, 1924	15.21***	1, 1924	9.12**	1, 1923	0.37[a]
Group X PA	3, 1924	0.89	3, 1924	2.66*	3, 1920	0.58[a]
Passage reading fluency (cohort 2)						
Group	3, 53	7.32***	3, 2365	6.62***	3, 2365	13.92***
PA	1, 2365	28.33***	1, 2365	10.47***	1, 2361	0.04[a]
Group X PA	3, 2365	10.88***	3, 2362	0.28[a]	3, 2358	1.14[a]
Untimed word reading						
Group	3, 85	5.07**	3, 1420	37.17***	—	—
PA	1, 1420	44.33***	1, 1420	19.53***	—	—
Group X PA	3, 1420	2.51	3, 1420	10.69***	—	—

Note. df = degrees of freedom; PA = phonological awareness. Models of growth in untimed word reading and nonword reading fluency did not include quadratic terms.
[a]Nonsignificant terms that were dropped from the model, resulting in an increase in degrees of freedom.
*p < .05; **p < .01; ***p < .001.

In addition, initial RAN scores were positively associated with growth in all fluency scores. Higher initial RAN scores were associated with steeper growth in fluency, and lower initial RAN scores were associated with slower growth in fluency (see main effects of RAN on fluency slopes in Table 8). Moreover, initial RAN scores significantly interacted with group when predicting growth patterns in fluency (see Table 8). Specifically, initial RAN scores were more strongly related to fluency scores at all testing periods in the typically achieving group than in the three at-risk groups, where no interactions were apparent.

The relationship of initial RAN with untimed word reading was similar to that of initial phonological awareness with word reading. Initial RAN was positively related to untimed word reading scores at all time points; however, initial RAN was *negatively* related to growth rates in the typically achieving group, accounting for the significant group by RAN interaction on the slope term of the untimed word reading model in Table 8. Again, there were no interactions apparent among the at-risk groups.

Vocabulary. Table 9 shows that WASI Vocabulary scores were unrelated to growth

Table 8
Effects of Initial RAN on Growth in Reading and Response to Intervention

	Intercept		Slope		Quadratic	
	df	F	df	F	df	F
Word reading fluency						
Group	3, 85	3.57*	3, 1419	6.12***	3, 1419	3.39*
RAN	1, 1419	89.65***	1, 1419	18.91***	1, 1415	0.25[a]
Group X RAN	3, 1419	10.96***	3, 1416	2.59[a]	3, 1412	0.33[a]
Nonword reading fluency						
Group	3, 85	8.76***	3, 1427	5.04**	—	—
RAN	1, 1427	58.01***	1, 1427	19.36***	—	—
Group X RAN	3, 1427	16.25***	3, 1424	0.20[a]	—	—
Passage reading fluency (cohort 1)						
Group	3, 56	0.48	3, 1930	1.82	3, 1927	1.51[a]
RAN	1, 1930	30.17***	1, 1930	18.24***	1, 1923	0.18[a]
Group X RAN	3, 1930	2.65*	3, 1924	0.04[a]	3, 1920	0.11[a]
Passage reading fluency (cohort 2)						
Group	3, 53	0.82	3, 2349	1.44	3, 2349	14.04***
RAN	1, 2349	42.39***	1, 2349	14.62***	1, 2348	2.74[a]
Group X RAN	3, 2349	1.47	3, 2349	3.73**	3, 2345	0.[a]
Untimed word reading						
Group	3, 85	4.14**	3, 1416	2.03	—	—
RAN	1, 1416	32.99***	1, 1416	17.00***	—	—
Group X RAN	3, 1416	1.41	3, 1416	4.40**	—	—

Note. df = degrees of freedom; RAN = rapid letter naming. Models of growth in untimed word reading and nonword reading fluency did not include quadratic terms.
[a]Nonsignificant terms that were dropped from the model, resulting in an increase in degrees of freedom.
*p < .05; **p < .01; ***p < .001.

patterns in word reading fluency, nonword reading fluency, and passage reading fluency in the second cohort. However, WASI Vocabulary was positively related to growth rates on passage reading fluency among children in the Proactive and typically achieving groups who were in the first cohort. In other words, children in these two groups with higher vocabularies improved their passage reading fluency faster than children in the same groups with smaller vocabularies. WASI Vocabulary scores were unrelated to growth rates on the Passage Reading Fluency subtest among children in the Responsive or enhanced classroom groups. The significant group by vocabulary interaction described above indicated that children's vocabularies played a greater role in passage reading fluency growth if children were in the typically achieving or Proactive groups than if children were in the Responsive or enhanced classroom groups. In terms of vocabulary effects on growth in untimed word reading, there were only main effects of vocabulary such that children with higher vocabulary scores generally scored higher on untimed word reading across the year regardless of which group they were in.

Table 9
Effects of Initial WASI Scores on Growth in Reading and Response to Intervention

	Intercept		Slope		Quadratic	
	df	F	df	F	df	F
Word reading fluency						
Group	3, 85	36.08***	3, 1428	4.53**	3, 1428	3.46*
WASI	1, 1284	0.76[a]	1, 1280	0.00[a]	1, 1276	0.38[a]
Group X WASI	3, 1281	0.84[a]	3, 1277	0.04[a]	3, 1273	0.41[a]
Nonword reading fluency						
Group	3, 85	18.11***	3, 1436	2.14	—	—
WASI	1, 1292	2.08[a]	1, 1288	0.68[a]	—	—
Group X WASI	3, 1289	0.58[a]	3, 1285	0.24[a]	—	—
Passage reading fluency (cohort 1)						
Group	3, 55	0.87	3, 1862	1.66	3, 1862	3.07*
WASI	1, 1862	1.68	1, 1862	1.76	1, 1862	1.25
Group X WASI	3, 1862	0.76	3, 1862	2.25	3, 1862	3.32*
Passage reading fluency (cohort 2)						
Group	3, 53	16.45***	3, 2370	4.86**	3, 2370	13.98***
WASI	1, 2015	0.17[a]	1, 2011	0.36[a]	1, 2007	2.31[a]
Group X WASI	3, 2012	1.80[a]	3, 2008	2.03[a]	3, 2004	2.28[a]
Untimed word reading						
Group	3, 79	11.37***	3, 1286	44.16***	—	—
WASI	1, 1286	6.49**	1, 1285	1.53[a]	—	—
Group X WASI	3, 1282	0.03[a]	3, 1279	2.32[a]	—	—

Note. df = degrees of freedom; WASI = Vocabulary subtest of the Wechsler Abbreviated Scale of Intelligence. Models of growth in untimed word reading and nonword reading fluency did not include quadratic terms.
[a]Nonsignificant terms that were dropped from the model, resulting in an increase in degrees of freedom.
*$p < .05$; **$p < .01$; ***$p < .001$.

End-of-Year Outcomes

In terms of norm-referenced end-of-year outcomes, analyses of group by child characteristic interactions found that initial phonological awareness was differentially important for children in the various intervention groups when predicting end-of-year word attack skills (see Table 10). Specifically, initial phonological awareness scores were less closely related to end-of-year word attack scores in the Proactive group relative to all other groups. For all other end-of-year outcomes, initial phonological awareness scores only had significant main effects, such that children with higher phonological awareness scores in October had higher literacy scores in May. Initial RAN scores only demonstrated significant main effects (see Table 11), such that higher RAN scores in October were associated with higher literacy scores in May. In a similar manner, there were only main effects of vocabulary scores (see Table 12), such that higher vocabulary scores were associated with higher end-of-year literacy scores.

Discussion

The purpose of this study was to address the effectiveness of combining enhanced

Table 10
Effects of Initial Phonological Awareness on End-of-Year Outcomes and Responses to Intervention

	WJ-III Word Attack		WJ-III Word Identification		WJ-III Passage Comprehension		WJ-III Reading Fluency	
	df	F	df	F	df	F	df	F
Group	3, 299	2.30	3, 304	10.22***	3, 304	6.87***	3, 261	5.16***
PA	1, 299	50.70***	1, 304	56.70***	1, 304	42.80***	1, 261	31.72***
Group X PA	3, 299	2.72*	3, 301	0.86[a]	3, 301	0.79[a]	3, 258	1.02[a]

	WJ-III Spelling		WJ-III Calculations		CRAB-R Fluency		CRAB-R Comprehension	
	df	F	df	F	df	F	df	F
Group	3, 302	10.62***	3, 303	1.22	3, 295	8.55***	3, 303	7.65***
PA	1, 304	23.72***	1, 303	49.09***	1, 295	15.85***	1, 303	42.29***
Group X PA	3, 301	0.31[a]	3, 300	1.24[a]	3, 292	0.42[a]	3, 300	1.79[a]

Note. WJ-III = Woodcock–Johnson-III; CRAB-R = Comprehensive Assessment of Reading Battery—Revised; PA = phonological awareness; df = degrees of freedom.
[a]Nonsignificant terms that were dropped from the model, resulting in an increase in degrees of freedom.
*p < .05; **p < .01; ***p < .001.

Table 11
Effects of Initial RAN on End-of-Year Outcomes and Responses to Intervention

	WJ-III Word Attack		WJ-III Word Identification		WJ-III Passage Comprehension		WJ-III Reading Fluency	
	df	F	df	F	df	F	df	F
Group	3, 301	7.52***	3, 303	8.85***	3, 304	6.91***	3, 261	5.00**
RAN	1, 301	14.97***	1, 303	38.02***	1, 304	25.52***	1, 261	30.11***
Group X RAN	3, 298	0.93[a]	3, 300	2.44[a]	3, 301	1.89[a]	3, 258	0.83[a]

	WJ-III Spelling		WJ-III Calculations		CRAB-R Fluency		CRAB-R Comprehension	
	df	F	df	F	df	F	df	F
Group	3, 303	7.94***	3, 302	2.34	3, 294	4.33**	3, 302	5.84***
RAN	1, 303	38.25***	1, 302	19.26***	1, 294	58.65***	1, 302	48.34***
Group X RAN	3, 300	1.40[a]	3, 299	1.98[a]	3, 291	2.45[a]	3, 299	0.65[a]

Note. WJ-III = Woodcock–Johnson-III; CRAB-R = Comprehensive Assessment of Reading Battery—Revised; RAN = rapid automatic naming of letter names; df = degrees of freedom.
[a]Nonsignificant terms that were dropped from the model, resulting in an increase in degrees of freedom.
*p < .05; **p < .01; ***p < .001.

classroom reading instruction with small-group supplemental reading instruction derived from either behavioral or cognitive theory for first-grade students at risk for reading difficulties. Specifically, we hypothesized (a) that small-group reading instruction, in the form of the Responsive and Proactive interventions, provided in addition to the classroom reading program, would be more effective than high-quality classroom reading instruction alone

Table 12
Effects of Initial Vocabulary on End-of-Year Outcomes and Responses to Intervention

	WJ-III Word Attack		WJ-III Word Identification		WJ-III Passage Comprehension		WJ-III Reading Fluency	
	df	F	df	F	df	F	df	F
Group	3, 274	9.04***	3, 276	14.98***	3, 276	12.57***	3, 237	9.35***
WASI	1, 274	14.82***	1, 276	6.94**	1, 276	12.11***	1, 237	16.30***
Group X WASI	3, 271	0.96[a]	3, 273	0.31[a]	3, 273	0.30[a]	3, 234	0.18[a]

	WJ-III Spelling		WJ-III Calculations		CRAB-R Fluency		CRAB-R Comprehension	
	df	F	df	F	df	F	df	F
Group	3, 276	14.12***	3, 275	6.65***	3, 295	15.03***	3, 303	19.11***
WASI	1, 276	4.12*	1, 275	10.13***	1, 295	116.20***	1, 303	94.65***
Group X WASI	3, 273	0.69[a]	3, 272	0.75[a]	3, 292	0.56[a]	3, 300	0.55[a]

Note. WJ-III = Woodcock–Johnson-III; WASI = WASI vocabulary; CRAB-R = Comprehensive Assessment of Reading Battery—Revised; *df* = degrees of freedom.
[a]Nonsignificant terms that were dropped from the model, resulting in an increase in degrees of freedom.
*p < .05; **p < .01; ***p < .001.

for students at risk for reading failure; (b) that these two interventions would be comparably effective; (c) that the reading performance of at-risk students who received this additional intervention would approach the level of performance of their normally developing peers; and (d) that specific child characteristics would differentially predict individual responses to these two interventions, which were provided in different formats and emphasized different aspects of the reading process.

Our results revealed that struggling first-grade readers who received one of the two interventions did, on average, perform better on multiple measures of reading after participating in either Responsive or Proactive interventions than children who received only enhanced classroom instruction (hypothesis 1). These gains were true both in terms of rate of growth (slope) and in terms of end-of-year status (intercept). Specifically, the students who received either form of supplemental intervention were better able to (a) read words in both timed and untimed formats, (b) spell words, (c) read connected text accurately and fluently, and (d) demonstrate phonological awareness than were the at-risk readers who did not receive

intervention. Further, consistent with hypothesis 2, the outcomes achieved by each intervention were largely comparable as evidenced by similar overall average effect sizes (Proactive ES = .84 and Responsive ES = .78). In terms of hypothesis 3, these outcomes reflect the more rapid growth of Proactive and Responsive students relative to the enhanced classroom group and, in some cases, the typically achieving group. Even so, struggling readers who participated in our interventions did not attain academic levels commensurate with their normally achieving peers in the same classrooms receiving the same core reading instruction, with the one exception of word attack ability of children in the Proactive condition. However, the majority of children at risk for reading failure who participated in intervention did reach average achievement levels on many normative measures. In terms of hypothesis 4, there was little evidence for interactions between child characteristics and intervention programs.

Hypothesis 1: Added Value of Small-Group Supplemental Intervention

To fully appreciate the impact of the interventions, it is important to first consider the effectiveness of the enhanced classroom condition, which promoted high levels of reading growth for many children at risk for reading failure. Although we cannot separate the efficacy attributable to the districts' professional program and our assessment and consultation additions to classroom programs, only 16% of at-risk readers in our sample who received enhanced classroom instruction alone remained below average performance levels on basic reading skills at the end of first grade. Extrapolating to the total school population, this figure translates to only 3% of all children. In other studies of classroom-level instruction, inadequate responder rates have only been reduced to 5% to 7% (e.g., Denton & Mathes, 2003; Mathes & Denton, 2002). Likewise, at-risk readers in the enhanced classroom group achieved, on average, standard scores that placed them consistently in the average range on multiple measures by the end of first grade. Thus, it is fair to say that the enhanced classroom condition served as a rigorous comparison group for the two interventions.

Even so, regardless of the nature of the small-group intervention, children who received supplemental small-group intervention performed significantly better than their at-risk peers who received only enhanced classroom instruction on tests of phonological awareness, timed and untimed word reading, passage reading fluency, and spelling. These findings are educationally significant, given the close association of phonological awareness (Wagner, 1988) and accurate and fluent word reading (Lyon, 1995) with successful reading acquisition and development in later grades (Torgesen & Burgess, 1998) and the close association of fluent text reading with reading comprehension (Fuchs, Fuchs, Hosp, & Jenkins, 2001).

Further, students in both Proactive and Responsive groups had significantly faster rates of learning than those of the typically achieving comparison group in phonological awareness, word reading, and passage reading fluency of first-grade text (cohort 2). These results indicate that both interventions promoted a "closing of the gap" for students who began the year

significantly behind their normally developing peers. In both interventions, not only were students developing key skills in phonological awareness and word identification more quickly than children without reading difficulties, but also this development of key reading subskills was manifested in a concurrent growth in the ability to read end-of-year connected text smoothly and accurately. In fact, the average end point of the students in both interventions of approximately 55 words read correctly per minute places them firmly within average parameters for passage reading fluency (Good, Wallin, Simmons, Kame'enui, & Kaminski, 2002). Beyond the issue of statistical significance, the magnitude of the differences between intervention groups and the enhanced classroom condition on most measures was moderate to large, and thus educationally relevant and meaningful. These effect sizes are relative to the gains of the enhanced classroom group, representing the magnitude of the *value-added* impact of the interventions, rather than effect sizes comparing intervention to a no-intervention control.

Perhaps the most compelling evidence of the value-added impact of the two reading interventions comes from simple counts of the number of children reading below the average range. We adopted a cut point used in many early intervention studies (Torgesen, 2000; Torgesen et al., 2003), namely performance below the 30th percentile on the Woodcock–Johnson III Basic Reading Skills cluster. The 30th percentile is an arbitrary designation, representing the lower end of the average range. If we define *average* conventionally as all children with one standard deviation of the mean, the range on the WJ-III would be 92.5–107.5. Developing a confidence interval that takes into account the standard error of measurement (4 points) would yield a range of 92 (30th percentile) to 108. Obviously we can compute these outcomes using other measures, but the results are similar across domains. Using the Basic Reading cut point, 16% (15 of 92 students) in the enhanced classroom instruction condition, 7% (6 of 83 students) in the Responsive intervention, and 1% (1 of 80 students) in the

Proactive group were reading below the average range at the end of the intervention period. Extrapolating these figures to the total population, based on the fact that the TPRI identifies the lowest 20% of readers, enhanced classroom instruction reduced the number of poor readers to about 3%, Responsive and Proactive to below 1%. Thus, all three instructional conditions significantly reduced the number of at-risk children, but they had increased benefit from the supplemental interventions. Given that 6% of students across the nation receive special education services for a learning disability (over 90% with reading problems; Kavale & Reese, 1992), and that many more students struggle in becoming readers, these reductions are educationally significant. Students in the at-risk groups were predominantly minority, economically disadvantaged students, and hardly restricted to those at risk for special education placement.

Hypothesis 2: Comparison of the Two Interventions

Although both interventions were associated with better outcomes than enhanced classroom instruction, there was little reliable evidence that the two interventions were differentially effective. Overall average effect sizes also illustrate that these interventions were comparable in their impact.

At the same time, intervention specificity was apparent when examining outcomes in terms of both statistical significance and effect size. For example, students who received Proactive intervention improved their word reading fluency and nonword reading fluency more quickly than students who received only classroom instruction, whereas students who received Responsive intervention improved their word reading fluency and nonword reading fluency at the same rate as students who received only enhanced classroom instruction. In a similar manner, students in the Proactive intervention also had better word attack skills at the end of the year than students who received only enhanced classroom instruction. Students

in the Responsive intervention had end-of-year word attack skills that were comparable to those of students who received only enhanced classroom instruction. In contrast, effect sizes for oral reading fluency were higher for the Responsive intervention than for Proactive, congruent with the relatively higher percentage of time Responsive reading students spent engaged in reading connected text. These findings lend credibility to the idea that students learn what they are taught (Allington, 1983), and they support the validity of the differences in the two interventions, as the Proactive intervention placed greater emphasis on phonological awareness, sounding out words in isolation, and reading words in lists, and students in the Responsive intervention spent relatively more of their lesson time reading connected text. Even so, to put these differences into perspective, the two interventions yielded comparable scores on seven of eight end-of-year outcomes. Furthermore, the average performance of students in both interventions was in the average range in terms of standard scores.

Hypothesis 3: Closing the Achievement Gap

Students who participated in either Proactive or Responsive interventions had steeper slopes than typically achieving students on several measures, including untimed word reading, phonological awareness, and passage reading fluency (cohort 2). Further, students who received the Proactive intervention had steeper slopes on word reading fluency and nonword reading fluency than typically achieving students. These findings suggest that intervention students were learning more rapidly than their typically developing peers, thereby progressively closing the achievement gap. However, there was only one instance in which the achievement gap was fully closed. This was achieved in May by the Proactive group on word attack skills. Of course, it should also be recognized that the typically achieving students in this sample scored in the high average range on all but one posttest measure (see Table 6).

Thus, despite scores in the average or better range, it is not surprising that our at-risk students did not achieve statistical equivalence with their higher performing peers given their high performance, another testament to the quality of instruction in the six schools.

Hypothesis 4: The Interaction of Child Characteristics With Responsiveness to Intervention

Contrary to our predictions, we found that, in general, at-risk readers who started the year with low levels of phonological awareness, less efficient letter-naming ability, or lower vocabulary knowledge were equally likely to make progress regardless of their assignment to the Proactive or Responsive groups. The only exceptions to our findings were that initial phonological awareness had less impact on WJ-III Word Attack scores for students who received the Proactive intervention and that initial vocabulary scores were less important to Passage Reading Fluency outcomes for cohort 1. While consistent with our hypotheses, it should be noted that these findings were not replicated on other measures testing similar constructs and, in the case of the Passage Reading Fluency subtest, were not replicated with cohort 2. Further, the interactions were not wide reaching, with no interaction being detected for any other measures regardless of initial status scores. Thus, it is fair to say that, while initial status on phonological awareness, phonological access, and vocabulary predicted outcomes, interactions with the efficacy of the interventions were not apparent.

This finding has important implications for educators who must select from multiple research-supported early reading interventions. It appears that different interventions can be effective for a wide variety of students as long as they include key components addressing phonological awareness, phonological decoding, fluency in reading words in isolation and in text, and comprehension of text. Further, the way in which the key components are taught to students can differ. It is important to remember that the teachers in this research were selected because they possessed personal philosophies aligning them to either Proactive or Responsive methods. Having this initial "buy in" ensured that these teachers believed in the approach to which they were assigned and worked hard to deliver daily instruction to the best of their ability. Had we taken a one-method approach, we speculate that some of our teachers would have felt alienated, and less willing to deliver daily instruction in accordance with our research protocol. In short, the results of this research suggest that, at the very least, there is room for choice in selecting an approach for providing supplemental intervention.

Nonsignificant Findings

Outcomes for which statistically significant differences were not detected between interventions groups and the enhanced classroom group included TOWRE Nonword Reading Efficiency, WJ-III Reading Fluency, WJ-III Passage Comprehension, WJ-III Calculations, CRAB-R Fluency, and CRAB-R Comprehension. We suspect that the lack of significant differences between at-risk groups on the TOWRE Nonword Reading Efficiency subtest is related to speed of phonological access. Because the TOWRE is a timed test, students had to quickly access their knowledge of letter–sound correspondences and quickly string the sounds together to form words, a task requiring both phonological access and adequate working memory. The lack of statistical differences likely reflects problems with phonological access because on a similar but untimed measure (i.e., WJ-III Word Attack) a significant difference was detected for the Proactive intervention group. Alphabetic knowledge and working memory demands were identical on these two tasks; however, speeded phonological access demands were substantially higher on the TOWRE.

The WJ-III subtests for which the year-end analysis indicated a lack of statistically significant differences favoring the intervention groups were reading fluency, passage comprehension, and mathematical calculations. When examining the results of the WJ-III Reading Fluency subtest and the CRAB-R Fluency and Comprehension subtests, it is important to keep in mind that children who could not complete the sample items were excluded from this subtest, resulting in removal of the lowest performers and increasing mean scores. Because more children in the enhanced classroom group were excluded from this subtest, mean scores were biased in favor of the enhanced classroom group, making them appear to be more similar to the intervention groups. The fact that significantly more students in the Proactive intervention were actually able to be administered this subtest demonstrated the advantage of this intervention. It is important to keep in mind that growth in passage reading fluency on first-grade text, which had a lower floor, did yield significant differences favoring the two intervention groups (cohort 2), thus corroborating the advantage of the interventions on fluency development.

In terms of calculations, we did not expect to find differences because we did not intervene in the domain of mathematics. If students in the intervention groups were exhibiting generalized growth rather than development specific to reading acquisition, they might be expected to differ from other at-risk students in their ability to perform mathematical calculations. This was not the case, indicating that growth was specific to the domain in which they received intervention.

Implications for Practice

This research affirms the value of providing early reading intervention to struggling readers. Students who participated in one of the two interventions, on average, finished first grade better prepared for second grade than students who received only enhanced classroom instruction. Further, this research lends support to our hypothesis that intervention instruction should be provided in tandem with quality classroom instruction. In other studies with similar types of interventions that were not provided in conjunction with quality classroom instruction, the results, while positive, have not reduced the

levels of struggling readers to levels demonstrated in the current research. Likewise, this research clearly demonstrates that enhanced classroom instruction alone is inadequate for a small number of students who require instruction of higher intensity.

Perhaps the most important finding of this research is that supplemental intervention approaches derived from different theoretical perspectives were both effective. These findings suggest to us that there is likely not "one best approach" and not one right philosophy or theory for how to best meet the needs of struggling readers. Nor did we find evidence that one approach was better for some at-risk children than another. Thus, the outcomes of this research led us to surmise that schools and teachers can be granted some latitude in choosing an approach to providing supplemental instruction for struggling readers. We hypothesize that if schools are allowed to choose from among effective choices an approach that best aligns to personal philosophy and theory, then there is likely to be less resistance, higher quality implementation, as well as sustainability over the long term.

At the same time it is critical that our outcomes *not* be interpreted as saying that the content included in supplemental instruction for struggling readers does not matter. It is clearly not the case that "anything goes." Both the Proactive and Responsive Reading interventions included elements that have been identified as critical for instruction of students who struggle to acquire the ability to read well (see Foorman & Torgesen, 2001; NICHD, 2000; Rayner et al., 2001; Snow et al., 1998). Both interventions provided for instruction in key reading skills, balanced with opportunities to apply reading and writing skills in connected text, and they both provided students with explicit instruction and practice in skills related to phonemic awareness, decoding, fluent word recognition and text processing, and spelling. Likewise, both approaches provided instruction in comprehension strategies applied to connected text. Thus, the interventions were comprehensive, integrated approaches to reading instruction.

This research also indicates that it is possible to provide effective early reading instruction to students at risk for reading difficulties using text that is not phonetically decodable and without following a detailed scope and sequence. Teachers in the Responsive Reading intervention in our study had extensive training on topics such as the order in which phonic elements should be introduced (i.e., more useful elements introduced earlier, separating potentially confusing elements such as *b* and *d*), the most frequently occurring words that should be taught at sight, and interpreting the results of assessments and anecdotal observations to plan instruction. In addition, these teachers did not create teaching activities and strategies but rather selected activities from a menu provided to them in the Responsive Reading handbook (Denton & Hocker, 2004). Finally, as described above, students in the Responsive Reading intervention were provided with explicit instruction and practice in phonemic decoding and were taught to rely primarily on graphophonemic information rather than text or picture contexts to identify words. Adding such components to other programs developed from a similar theoretical background may well enhance outcomes with children who have poorer development of prereading skills and in a more cost-effective manner because of implementation in small-group rather than individual instruction.

Study Limitations and Future Directions

In interpreting this research it is important to consider limitations that may reduce the generalizability of our findings. The most significant question involves the provision of 40 minutes of additional reading instruction to students in the supplemental instructional groups. As the first step in our research was to determine whether supplemental instruction had a value-added impact, we did not control for the additional structured reading time. It seems unlikely that simply reading for an additional 40 minutes daily or even extending the language arts block to two hours would produce similar gains, especially as other studies that have controlled this factor have also shown better gains in small-group instruction relative to classroom instruction alone (Simmons et al., 2003; Torgesen et al., 1999). But the issue of controlling for time spent in reading activities is a next step for this type of research in which supplemental instruction is added to classroom instruction. Second, while conducted in public schools, the interventions were delivered under highly controlled conditions. Even though the intervention teachers were employees of the public schools, they were selected for this research because of their demonstrated expertise as reading teachers. Likewise, we were able to assign teachers to provide the intervention that was most aligned with their personal philosophy and prior teaching experiences. While working with highly knowledgeable and motivated teachers facilitated our ability to test our hypotheses fairly, it is likely that these intervention teachers are not representative of all teachers teaching reading in U.S. schools. Thus, it is not clear if similar results would be achieved with less knowledgeable teachers. Likewise, we conducted this research in relatively high-functioning schools providing solid, core reading instruction. Further research is necessary to determine if similar results would be achieved in schools facing greater challenges.

The authors of the interventions provided considerable coaching and support to the intervention teachers. It is unlikely that similar levels of coaching and support typically would be available to teachers implementing or sustaining these interventions in the "real world." Thus, it remains to be seen if the results of this research would be replicated under less controlled conditions. Currently, little is known about how best to provide staff development and support to teachers as they work to implement new innovations. Even less is known about maintaining and sustaining innovations (Denton & Fletcher, 2003).

Another area needing further research relates to group size. While group size was held constant at three students per group between the two interventions in this research, future work needs to be done to determine if other grouping formats, such as one-on-one tutoring, would result in even stronger outcomes, or conversely, if the outcomes can be replicated with larger group sizes. Because group size largely dictates the cost of providing supplemental reading instruction in schools, and because financial considerations can either facilitate or deter implementation of new innovations within schools, the group size issue cannot be ignored.

Conclusion

This study reinforced the added value of supplemental intervention provided to first-grade students who demonstrate risk factors for reading difficulty. Likewise, the results of the study indicate that interventions originating from different theoretical viewpoints, but both of which emphasize word recognition strategies and contain elements previously identified as essential in early reading instruction, can be effective for at-risk first-grade readers. In fact, no reliable interactions were detected between child characteristics and success in one type of intervention or the other.

We propose that these findings lend support to the argument that it is time to stop debating the "best" method for providing early reading intervention. Time is better devoted to determining how to overcome the great challenges that exist in getting effective interventions placed into schools. Likewise, our findings support the idea that schools can be allowed to choose from among good choices those interventions that best fit personal philosophies and personnel talents.

References

Allington, R.L. (1983). The reading instruction provided readers of differing reading abilities. *Elementary School Journal, 83,* 548–559.

Becker, W.C. (1973). Applications of behavior principles in typical classrooms. In C.A. Thorensen (Ed.), *Behavior modification in education* (72nd yearbook of the National Society for the Study of Education, part 1, pp. 77–106). Chicago: National Society of the Study of Education.

Brophy, J., & Good, T. (1986). Teacher-effects results. In M.C. Wittrock (Ed.), *Handbook of research on teaching* (3rd ed., pp. 328–375). New York: Macmillan.

Brown, J.S., Collins, A., & Duguid, P. (1989). Situated cognition and the culture of learning. *Educational Researcher, 18,* 32–42.

Carnine, D.W., Silbert, J., Kame'enui, E.J., & Tarver, S.G. (2004). *Direct instruction reading* (4th ed.). Upper Saddle River, NJ: Merrill-Prentice Hall.

Clay, M.M. (1987). Learning to be learning disabled. *New Zealand Journal of Educational Studies, 22,* 155–173.

Clay, M.M. (1993). *Reading Recovery: A guidebook for teachers in training.* Portsmouth, NH: Heinemann.

Clay, M.M. (2002). *An observation survey of early literacy achievement* (2nd ed.). Portsmouth, NH: Heinemann.

Denton, C.A., & Fletcher, J.M. (2003). Scaling reading interventions. In B.R. Foorman (Ed.), *Preventing and remediating reading difficulties: Bringing science to scale* (pp. 445–463). Timonium, MD: York Press.

Denton, C.A., & Hocker, J. (2004). *Responsive reading instruction: Teacher handbook.* Unpublished manuscript.

Denton, C.A., & Mathes, P.G. (2003). Intervention for struggling readers: Possibilities and challenges. In B.R. Foorman (Ed.), *Preventing and remediating reading difficulties: Bringing science to scale* (pp. 229–251). Timonium, MD: York Press.

Elbaum, B., Vaughn, S., Hughes, M.T., & Moody, S.W. (2000). How effective are one-to-one tutoring programs in reading for elementary students at risk for reading failure? A meta-analysis of the intervention research. *Journal of Educational Psychology, 92,* 605–619.

Elkonin, D.B. (1973). USSR. In J.A. Downing (Ed.), *Comparative reading: Cross-national studies of behavior and processes in reading and writing* (2nd ed., pp. 551–579). New York: Macmillan.

Engelmann, S. (1997). *Preventing failure in the primary grades.* Eugene, OR: Association for Direct Instruction.

Engelmann, S., & Carnine, D. (1982). *Theory of instruction: Principles and applications.* New York: Irvington.

Foorman, B.R., Francis, D.J., Fletcher, J.M., Schatschneider, C., & Mehta, P. (1998). The role of instruction in learning to read: Preventing reading disabilities in at-risk children. *Journal of Educational Psychology, 90,* 37–55.

Foorman, B.R., & Torgesen, J. (2001). Critical elements of classroom and small-group instruction promote reading success in all children. *Learning Disabilities Research and Practice, 16,* 203–212.

Fountas, I.C., & Pinnell, G.S. (1996). *Guided reading.* Portsmouth, NH: Heinemann.

Fountas, I.C., & Pinnell, G.S. (1999). *Matching books to readers: Using leveled books in guided reading K–3.* Portsmouth, NH: Heinemann.

Francis, D.J., Shaywitz, S.E., Stuebing, K.K., Shaywitz, B.A., & Fletcher, J.M. (1996). Developmental lag versus deficit models of reading disability: A longitudinal individual growth curves analysis. *Journal of Educational Psychology, 88,* 3–17.

Fuchs, L.S., Fuchs, D., Hamlett, C.L., & Stecker, P.M. (1991). Effects of curriculum-based measurement and consultation on teacher planning and student achievement in mathematics operations. *American Educational Research Journal, 28,* 617–641.

Fuchs, L.S., Fuchs, D., Hosp, M.K., & Jenkins, J. (2001). Oral reading fluency as an indicator of reading competence: A theoretical, empirical, and historical analysis. *Scientific Studies of Reading*, 3, 239–256.

Gomez-Bellenge, F.X., Rogers, E., & Fullerton, S.K. (2003). *Reading Recovery and Descubriendo la Lectura national report 2001–2002*. Columbus: Ohio State University, Reading Recovery National Data Evaluation Center.

Good, R.H., Wallin, J., Simmons, D.C., Kame'enui, E.J., & Kaminski, R.A. (2002). *System-wide percentile ranks for DIBELS Benchmark Assessment* (Tech. Rep. 9). Eugene: University of Oregon.

Harris, K.R., & Pressley, M. (1991). The nature of cognitive strategy instruction: Interactive strategy construction. *Exceptional Children*, 57, 392–404.

Juel, C. (1988). Learning to read and write: A longitudinal study of children in first and second grade. *Journal of Educational Psychology*, 80, 437–447.

Kame'enui, E.J., & Simmons, D.C. (1990). *Designing instructional strategies: Prevention of academic learning problems*. Columbus, OH: Merrill.

Kavale, K.A., & Reese, J.H. (1992). The character of learning disabilities: An Iowa profile. *Learning Disability Quarterly*, 15, 74–94.

Lyon, R.G. (1995). Toward a definition of dyslexia. *Annals of Dyslexia*, 45, 2–37.

Mathes, P.G., & Denton, C.A. (2002). The prevention and identification of reading disability. *Seminars in Pediatric Neurology*, 9, 185–191.

Mathes, P.G., & Fuchs, L.S. (1994). The efficacy of peer tutoring in reading for students with mild disabilities: A best-evidence synthesis. *School Psychology Review*, 23, 55–76.

Mathes, P.G., Howard, J.K, Allen, S., & Fuchs, D. (1998). Peer-assisted learning strategies for first-grade readers: Making early reading instruction more responsive to the needs of diverse learners. *Reading Research Quarterly*, 33, 62–94. doi:10.1598/RRQ.33.1.4

Mathes, P.G., & Torgesen, J.K. (1998). All children can learn to read: Critical care for students with special needs. *Peabody Journal of Education*, 73, 317–340.

Mathes, P.G., Torgesen, J.K., & Allor, J.H. (2001). The effects of peer assisted learning strategies for first-grade learners with and without additional computer assisted instruction in phonological awareness. *American Educational Research Journal*, 38, 371–410.

Mathes. P.G., Torgessen, J.K., & Heron, J. (2004). Teachers computerized assessment for reading excellence [Computer software]. San Rafael, CA: Talking-Fingers.

National Institute of Child Health and Human Development. (2000). *Report of the National Reading Panel: Teaching children to read: An evidence-based assessment of the scientific research literature on reading and its implications for reading instruction* (NIH Publication No. 00-4769). Washington, DC: U.S. Government Printing Office.

O'Connor, R. (2000). Increasing the intensity of intervention in kindergarten and first grade. *Learning Disabilities Research & Practice*, 15, 43–54.

O'Malley, K.J., Francis, D.J., Foorman, B.R., Fletcher, J.M., & SWANK, P.R. (2002). Growth in precursor reading skills: Do low-achieving and IQ-discrepant readers develop differently? *Learning Disability Research and Practice*, 17, 19–34.

Peterson, B. (1991). Selecting books for beginning readers. In D.E. DeFord, C.A. Lyons, & G.S. Pinnell (Eds.), *Bridges to literacy: Learning from Reading Recovery* (pp. 119–147). Portsmouth, NH: Heinemann.

Pressley, M.P. (1998). *Elementary reading instruction that works*. New York: Guilford.

Pressley, M.P., & McCormick, C.M. (1995). *Cognition, teaching, and assessment*. New York: HarperCollins.

Rayner, K., Foorman, B.R., Perfetti, C.A., Pesetsky, D., & Seidenberg, M.S. (2001). How psychological science informs the teaching of reading. *Psychological Science in the Public Interest*, 2, 31–74.

Rogoff, B. (1990). *Apprenticeship in thinking: Cognitive development in social context*. New York: Oxford University Press.

Rojewski, J.W., & Schell, J.W. (1994). Cognitive apprenticeship for learners with special needs. *Remedial and Special Education*, 15, 234–243.

Rosenshine, B., & Stevens, R. (1986). Teaching functions. In M.C. Wittrock (Ed.), *The handbook of research on teaching* (3rd ed., pp. 376–391). New York: Macmillan.

Schatschneider, C., Francis, D.J., Foorman, B.R., Fletcher, J.M., & Mehta, P. (1999). The dimensionality of phonological awareness: An application of item response theory. *Journal of Educational Psychology*, 91, 439–449.

Shanahan, T. (1998). On the effectiveness and limitations of tutoring in reading. *Review of Research in Education*, 23, 217–234.

Simmons, D.C., Kame'enui, E.J., Stoolmiller, M., Coyne, M.D., & Harn, B. (2003). Accelerating growth and maintaining proficiency: A two-year intervention study of kindergarten and first-grade children at-risk for reading difficulties. In B.R. Foorman (Ed.), *Preventing and remediating reading difficulties: Bringing science to scale* (pp. 197–228). Baltimore: York Press.

Skinner, B.F. (1953). *Science and human behavior*. New York: Macmillan.

Snow, C.E., Burns, M.S., & Griffin, P. (Eds.). (1998). *Preventing reading difficulties in young children*. Washington, DC: National Academy Press.

Stanovich, K.E. (1986). Matthew effects in reading: Some consequences of individual differences in the acquisition of literacy. *Reading Research Quarterly*, 21, 360–397. doi:10.1598/RRQ.21.4.1

Storch, S.A., & Whitehurst, G.J. (2002). Oral language and code-related precursors to reading: Evidence from a longitudinal structural model. *Developmental Psychology*, 38, 934–947.

Torgesen, J.K. (2000). Individual responses in response to early interventions in reading: The lingering problem of treatment resisters. *Learning Disabilities Research & Practice*, 15, 55–64.

Torgesen, J.K., & Burgess, S.R. (1998). Consistency of reading-related phonological processes throughout early childhood: Evidence from longitudinal-correlational and instructional studies. In J. Metsala & L. Ehri (Eds.), *Word recognition in beginning reading* (pp. 161–188). Hillsdale, NJ: Erlbaum.

Torgesen, J.K., Rashotte, C., Alexander, A., Alexander, J., & MacPhee, K. (2003). Progress toward understanding the instructional conditions necessary for remediating reading difficulties in older children. In B.R. Foorman (Ed.), *Preventing and remediating reading difficulties:*

Bringing science to scale (pp. 275–298). Baltimore: York Press.

Torgesen, J.K., WAgner, R.K., Rashotte, C.A., Rose, E., Lindamood, P., Conway, T., et al. (1999). Preventing reading failure in your children with phonological processing disabilities: Group and individual responses to instruction. *Journal of Educational Psychology, 91*, 579–593.

Vaughn, S., & Linan-Thompson, S. (2003). Group size and time allotted to intervention: Effects for students with reading disabilities. In B.R. Foorman (Ed.), *Preventing and remediating reading difficulties: Bringing science to scale* (pp. 299–324). Baltimore: York Press.

Vellutino, F.R., Scanlon, D.M., & Jaccard, J. (2003). Toward distinguishing between cognitive and experiential deficits as primary sources of difficulty in learning to read: A two year follow-up to difficult to remediate and readily remediated poor readers. In B.R. Foorman (Ed.), *Preventing and remediating reading difficulties: Bringing science to scale* (pp. 73–120). Baltimore: York Press.

Vellutino, F.R., Scanlon, D.M., Sipay, E.R., Small, S.G., Pratt, A., Chen, R., et al. (1996). Cognitive profiles of difficult-to-remediate and readily remediated poor readers: Early intervention as a vehicle for distinguishing between cognitive and experiential deficits as basic causes of specific reading disability. *Journal of Educational Psychology, 88*, 601–638.

Vygotsky, L.S. (1978). *Mind in society: The development of higher psychological processes* (M. Cole, V. John-Steiner, S. Scribner, & E. Souberman, Eds. & Trans.). Cambridge, MA: Harvard University Press.

Wagner, R.K. (1988). Causal relations between the development of phonological processing abilities and the acquisition of reading skills: A meta-analysis. *Merrill-Palmer Quarterly, 34*, 261–279.

Authors' Note

The work presented in this article was supported by Grant # NSF 9979968; Early Development of Reading Skills: A Cognitive Neuroscience Approach from the Interagency Educational Research Initiative, with conjoint funding from the National Science Foundation, National Institute of Child Health and Human Development, and U.S. Department of Education. We thank the Houston Independent School District in Houston, Texas, for allowing us to conduct this research and the principals, teachers, and students in the participating schools. Requests for information should be addressed to Patricia G. Mathes.

Conflict of interest statement: Both interventions presented in this research are under contract for publication. The Proactive intervention will be published under a different name. Neither intervention was under contract at the time this research was conducted or during the review process.

Phonemes in Use: Multiple Activities for a Critical Process

Patrick C. Manyak

Several decades of research have established the critical role of phonemic awareness in the development of beginning reading. Phonemic awareness contributes centrally to children's acquisition of the alphabetic principle—the understanding that the letters of the alphabet represent phonemes in speech. This understanding makes early phonics instruction useful for children and facilitates children's ability to blend letter sounds while decoding words, to learn sight words reliably, and to spell phonetically. Given this importance, it is vital that teachers understand phonemic awareness and can teach it effectively.

Phonemic awareness is often referred to as the ability to recognize and manipulate phonemes—the individual sounds in words in oral language. While this is a practical way to talk about phonemic awareness, scholars often point out that phonemes commingle with one another in speech and that the "individual sounds in words" are more of a hypothetical notion than a linguistic reality (Liberman, 1998). This commingling of phonemes suggests why it can be difficult for children to acquire phonemic awareness. Recent research suggests that instruction that helps children to attend to vocal gestures (the particular ways that we position our mouths as we produce phonemes) is effective in developing phonemic awareness and has a positive effect on the students' word reading (Castiglioni-Spalten & Ehri, 2003). This type of explicit attention to vocal gestures

can be helpful at the beginning of phonemic awareness instruction. A second key finding in phonemic awareness research is that instruction involving segmenting and blending phonemes combined with a focus on the letters that represent those phonemes contributes greatly to success in beginning reading and spelling (National Reading Panel, 2000). This is the type of phonemic awareness instruction that I address in this article.

For several years I have helped teachers in Wyoming meet the needs of students who enter kindergarten or first grade with little phonemic awareness or decoding ability. We have learned that after having received some basic instruction in phonemic awareness and letter–sound relationships, students benefit greatly from a variety of activities combining phoneme segmenting and blending with letter–sound instruction. As a result, we have borrowed, adapted, and invented in order to create a small set of activities focusing on what we call "phonemes in use." These activities all involve segmenting and blending phonemes within the context of reading and writing words, but each one does so in a slightly different way. This variety allows children to develop a robust ability to apply phonemic awareness to tasks of reading and writing and supports students who may struggle with this critical process. Here, I offer brief descriptions of our five phonemes-in-use activities and practical ideas for implementing them in the classroom.

Preparing Reading Professionals (second edition), edited by Rita M. Bean, Natalie Heisey, and Cathy M. Roller. © 2010 by the International Reading Association. Reprinted from Manyak, P.C. (2008). Phonemes in use: Multiple activities for a critical process. *The Reading Teacher*, *61*(8), 659–662. doi:10.1598/RT.61.8.8.

Beginning-Middle-End

We borrowed the Beginning-Middle-End activity from *Words Their Way* (Bear, Invernizzi, Templeton, & Johnston, 2003). The activity involves three steps. First, the teacher places the letters of a three- or four-letter word face down in a pocket chart so that the students cannot see them and tells the students the word (e.g., *man*). Second, the teacher and students sing the following brief song to the tune of "Are You Sleeping, Brother John?": "Beginning, middle, end; beginning, middle, end / Where is the sound? Where is the sound? / Where's the *mmm* in man? Where's the *mmm* in man? / Let's find out. Let's find out." After the song, one student comes forward, picks the position (beginning, middle, or end) that he or she believes the sound is in, and turns around the letter card. If the child reveals the letter *m* the teacher asks the class, "Does this letter make the *mmm* sound?" and confirms, "Yes, it does, doesn't it? We hear the *mmm* sound at the beginning of man." The class then repeats this process for the other two phonemes. Of course, the game is more engaging if the teacher does not ask for the phonemes in sequence. Beginning-Middle-End is useful as an extremely brief, whole-class activity. I recommend that teachers use Beginning-Middle-End one or two times each day during kindergarten and early first grade, selecting words that reinforce the letters that students are studying.

Say-It-And-Move-It

Say-It-And-Move-It was the cornerstone of the extremely effective phonemic awareness intervention researched by Ball and Blachman (1991) and made available to teachers in the manual *Road to the Code* (Blachman, Ball, Black, & Tangel, 2000). Say-It-And-Move-It involves moving tiles one at a time from the top of a piece of paper down to a line at the bottom, saying each corresponding phoneme while doing so (/m/, /a/, /n/) and then running a finger under the tiles while blending the phonemes to make the word (*man*). I like teachers to introduce Say-It-And-Move-It at the same time that they begin letter–sound instruction and to use the activity to reinforce the letters being taught. Students are given a couple of blank tiles and tiles with the letters that they are currently learning (e.g., the letters *m* and *b*). The teacher then announces a two- or three-phoneme word that begins with one of those letters (e.g., *my*) and asks the students to find the tile with the letter that makes the phoneme they hear at the beginning of the word. The students put the *m* tile together with a blank tile at the top of their paper and then move the tiles down while saying each phoneme, using the m tile to represent /m/ and the blank tile to represent /long i/. Then they run their fingers under the letters while saying the word *my*.

At this point, the students place the tiles back at the top of the page. The teacher and students repeat this sequence with other words that either begin or end with the letters being practiced. For instance, for a session focusing on *m* and *b*, the teacher might give the following words: *my*, *man*, *ram*, *him*, *mat*, *be*, *bat*, *tub*, *bow* (using only two tiles because there are only two phonemes), and *rub*. For each of these words, the students use the *m* or *b* letter tiles to represent the /m/ and /b/ phonemes and the blank tiles for all other phonemes. It is important that the children practice hearing the target phonemes at the beginning and end of the words. The teachers that I work with like to do Say-It-And-Move-It daily in small groups as a part of a series of fast-paced letter–sound activities.

Scaffolded Spelling

As children carefully stretch out words and attempt to represent the sounds through invented spelling, they develop phonemic awareness (Richgels, 2001). Motivated by this insight, we developed the brief activity of Scaffolded Spelling as a way to increase phonemic awareness and reinforce letter–sound knowledge in the context of writing words. In simple terms, Scaffolded Spelling engages students in carefully stretching out the phonemes in simple words, writing the letters that correspond to those phonemes, and reading the words that they have written. The teacher begins by choosing three to five words that include letters that the children have or are currently learning. For instance, if a kindergarten class has just studied the phonemes represented by *m*, *b*, *s*, and *t*, the teacher might choose the following words: *man*, *sat*, *bat*, and *tab*. The teacher introduces the first word and asks the students to stretch it out and listen for the phonemes. During this step, the students put their hands to their lips and "stretch the word like bubble gum," slowly pulling their hand away from their lips while carefully articulating each phoneme in the word. The teacher then tells the students to stretch the word again, to stop after "the first sound of the stretch," and to think about what letter makes that sound.

The students then write the letter on a white board or half sheet of paper. Next, the teacher directs the students to stretch the word again and listen for the second sound in the stretch. They then write the letter that makes that sound. The students repeat this process for the last sound in the stretch and thus complete their spelling of the word. The group repeats this process with two or three more words and then the teacher and children read the list of words that they have written two times. As children learn more letter sounds, the teacher can begin to incorporate words featuring consonant digraphs and clusters. Typically, it takes only a few minutes to write three to five words. Yet in those few minutes the children have listened for the individual phonemes in words, reinforced their knowledge of the letters that represent those phonemes, and practiced a deliberate process for invented spelling that they can use while writing independently. As with Say-It-And-Move-It, many teachers that I work with incorporate Scaffolding Spelling into a daily set of fast-paced word study activities.

Word Mapping

Efficient and reliable sight-word learning occurs when children completely map the letters in a word's spelling to the phonemes in its pronunciation, thus producing lasting bonds in memory between a word's spelling, pronunciation, and meaning (Ehri, 1998). Inspired by this principle, I developed a visual letter–phoneme mapping activity to use with high-frequency words. Word Mapping borrows a portion of Gaskins, Ehri, Cress, O'Hara, and Donnelly's (1996/1997) Word Analysis Chart. The teachers that I work with use a large laminated version of this chart (shown in Figure 1) for daily word mapping.

The teacher begins Word Mapping by announcing the high-frequency word to be mapped. The teacher and students segment

---

Figure 1
Word Mapping Chart

The word is _____ . Map:

It has _____ sounds.

It has _____ letters...

Spelling: l i k e

Sounds: l i k

because _____ .

---

the word together, counting the phonemes on their fingers. The teacher then writes the number of phonemes on the chart. Next, the teacher writes the word, asks the students to count the letters, and adds the number to the chart. The teacher maps the letters to the phonemes before filling in the "because" line. First, the teacher writes the word. Then the teacher segments the word orally, asking students what letter or letters best represent each phoneme and writing those letters below the spelling. (We continually remind the students that the proper spelling is on top and that the letters below stand for the sounds we hear in the word.) The teacher then returns to the beginning of the word, asks the students what letter or letters make each sound, and draws arrows connecting the letters to the sounds they make. When there is a consonant digraph or vowel pair in which two letters make one phoneme, we make a Y-shaped arrow to map this relationship. Silent letters have no arrow connecting them to phonemes. Finally, the teacher asks the students to use this visual map to explain any discrepancy between the number of sounds and letters (e.g., "The *th* makes one sound" or "The *e* is silent") and summarizes their explanation on the chart. If the sounds and letters are the same, then the students simply respond, "Each letter makes a sound." While the teachers use Word Mapping to introduce nearly all high-frequency words,

they do not do so with a few words that contain multiple irregularities or highly unpredictable letter–sound relationships (such as *one*) that might prove to be confusing. I suggest that teachers use Word Mapping in a whole-class setting for each new high-frequency word that they introduce (one to two per day).

Word Wall Boxes

The last activity, Word Wall Boxes, provides children with a daily review of three previously introduced high-frequency words while continuing to build their phonemic awareness. The Word Wall Boxes activity uses a sheet featuring Elkonin boxes (Figure 2). Popularized by Reading Recovery, Elkonin boxes provide another way for students to map the letters of a word to its phonemes. The teacher begins the high-frequency word review by asking a student to choose a word from the word wall. The teacher directs the students to the first line of boxes on their sheet and asks them to cross out any boxes beyond those required for the phonemes in the word (e.g., "How many sounds does *the* have? Two? OK, count two boxes and cross out the rest"). Then, the teacher asks the class to stretch out the word carefully and write the letter or letters that represent each phoneme in the corresponding boxes ([*th*] [*e*]). Many teachers work along with students on the overhead. Then the students write the word on the line beside the boxes and repeat this process with two additional words. Finally, the children read the three words written on the lines chorally and independently. As when using the word analysis chart, the teachers that I work with do not use the Elkonin boxes with a few words containing multiple irregularities or highly unpredictable letter–sound relationships. If a student chooses one of those words during the word wall review, I recommend that teachers simply review the word by talking through its irregularities with the students.

Each of the activities that I have described prompts students to use phonemic awareness within the context of reading and writing words. Used together as part of a fast-paced

---

Figure 2
Word Wall Boxes Sheet

Word Wall Word Boxes

word study block or sprinkled throughout the day, they offer children multiple opportunities to develop and solidify this critical process in beginning reading.

References

Ball, E., & Blachman, B. (1991). Does phoneme awareness training in kindergarten make a difference in early word recognition and developmental spelling? *Reading Research Quarterly, 26*(1), 49–66.

Bear, D., Invernizzi, M., Templeton, S., & Johnston, F. (2003). *Words their way: Word study for phonics, vocabulary, and spelling instruction* (3rd ed.). Upper Saddle River, NJ: Pearson.

Blachman, B., Ball, E., Black, R., & Tangel, D. (2000). *Road to the code: A phonological awareness program for young children.* Baltimore: Paul Brookes.

Castiglioni-Spalten, M.L., & Ehri, L.C. (2003). Phonemic awareness instruction: Contribution of articulatory segmentation to novice beginners' reading and spelling. *Scientific Studies of Reading, 7*(1), 25–52.

Ehri, L. (1998). Grapheme–phoneme knowledge is essential for learning to read words in English. In J. Metsala & L. Ehri (Eds.), *Word recognition in beginning literacy* (pp. 3–40). Mahwah, NJ: Erlbaum.

Gaskins, I., Ehri, L., Cress, C., O'Hara, C., & Donnelly, K. (1996/1997). Procedures for word learning: Making discoveries about words. *The Reading Teacher, 50*(4), 312–327.

Liberman, A. (1998). Why is speech so much easier than reading? In C. Hulme & J. Joshi (Eds.), *Reading and spelling: Development and disorders* (pp. 5–17). Mahwah, NJ: Erlbaum.

National Institute of Child Health and Human Development. (2000). *Report of the National Reading Panel. Teaching children to read: An evidence-based assessment of the scientific research literature on reading and its implications for reading instruction* (NIH Publication No. 00-4769). Washington, DC: U.S. Government Printing Office.

Richgels, D. (2001). Invented spelling, phonemic awareness, and reading and writing instruction. In S. Neuman & D. Dickinson (Eds.), *Handbook of early literacy research* (pp. 142–155). New York: Guilford.

Two Essential Ingredients: Phonics and Fluency Getting to Know Each Other

Timothy Rasinski, William H. Rupley, and William Dee Nichols

Phonics and fluency are two main ingredients in the teaching of reading and in children's reading development (National Institute of Child Health and Human Development [NICHD], 2000). They can be thought of as essential spices in reading: Alone neither adds much to the process of reading, but together they blend into a fine and enjoyable outcome—reading for pleasure and learning at a level commensurate to a reader's background knowledge. Just as leaving out essential ingredients in a recipe can result in a less than desirable culinary product, readers who have difficulties in word decoding and fluency will experience problems in reading comprehension and overall reading achievement (Duke, Pressley, & Hilden, 2004). Both phonics and fluency need to be taught, practiced, and nurtured in the earliest stages of reading instruction. The crucial question is not, Are phonics and fluency of great consequence in learning to read? but, rather, How should they be taught in ways that are natural, authentic, synergistic, effective, and engaging?

In most reading curricula, phonics and fluency are thought of as distinct instructional elements—that they should be taught separately. Indeed, Chall's (1996) own model of reading development proposes that they be developed sequentially—first, mastery in decoding, then fluency. However, as with our earlier comparison to spices in a recipe, sometimes it is the mixing of the spices that results in a special ingredient that adds more to a culinary delight than what each could contribute individually. One such special ingredient able to promote and develop the meaningful integration of word recognition, accuracy, fluency, and expressiveness is rhyming poetry.

How Does Rhyming Poetry Become the Special Ingredient?

Certain and relatively common spelling patterns have consistent pronunciations. Perhaps the most useful spelling patterns for beginning readers are rimes, also known as word families or common phonograms. A rime is simply the part of a syllable that begins with the sounded vowel and contains any consonants that follow the vowel. For example, the *-at* in *hat* and *cat* is a rime or a word family, as is the *-ight* in *light* or *sight*. Readers who can perceive a rime in one word they decode can then apply that knowledge to other words with the identical spelling pattern.

The idea, then, is to teach beginning readers word families so that they can use their knowledge of these spelling patterns in other words they encounter in their reading. This approach to phonics instruction has been recognized and supported by many of the foremost scholars in reading (Adams, 1990; Cunningham, 2005; Ehri, 2005; Gaskins, Ehri, Cress, O'Hara, & Donnelly, 1996/1997; Gunning, 1995; Snow, Burns, & Griffin, 1998).

There are several hundred word families that readers should know, and students who can

Preparing Reading Professionals (second edition), edited by Rita M. Bean, Natalie Heisey, and Cathy M. Roller. © 2010 by the International Reading Association. Reprinted from Rasinski, T., Rupley, W.H., & Nichols, W.D. (2008). Two essential ingredients: Phonics and fluency getting to know each other. *The Reading Teacher, 62*(3), 257–260. doi:10.1598/RT.62.3.7.

recognize these word families in one-syllable and multisyllabic words have the ability to process such words accurately and efficiently. Edward Fry (1998) demonstrated the utility of word families in his "most common phonograms."

According to Fry, knowledge of the word families listed in Table 1 gives a reader the ability to decode and spell over 600 one-syllable words simply by adding a consonant, consonant blend, or consonant digraph to the beginning of the word family. In addition to one-syllable words, knowledge of these word families can help readers partially decode thousands of words in which these word families regularly appear. For example, the rime -am can help a reader with words like *ham, Sam, slam,* and *jam.* The same word family can also help a reader with more challenging words such as *Abraham, Amsterdam, bedlam, camera, hamster, grammar, telegram,* and many more.

For some students, simply seeing and practicing word families, on a word wall for example, may be enough for them to generalize other identical spelling patterns and grow in their ability to decode words. For others, however, more teacher-guided and supervised practice is needed. These students especially need the opportunity to read words with these spelling patterns in meaningful texts. What kinds of texts feature such words with sufficient frequency to draw attention to the targeted word family? Rhyming poetry fills that bill.

The following rhymes, for example, work well for teaching, practicing, and enjoying the -ot and -old word families.

> Peas porridge hot
> Peas porridge cold
> Peas porridge in the pot
> Five days old.

In the same way that Trachtenburg (1990) advocated the use of children's literature for teaching phonics, we feel that rhyming poetry is ideal for teaching phonics through word families.

Table 1
Fry's Most Common Phonograms

-ab	-ew	-ock
-ack	-ed	-ore
-ag	-eed	-ot
-ail	-ick	-out
-ain	-ing	-ow (how, chow)
-am	-ink	-ow (low, throw)
-an	-ip	-op
-ank	-ight	-uck
-ap	-ill	-ug
-at	-im	-um
-ay	-in	-unk
-ell	-ine	-y
-est	-ob	

Why Rhyming Poetry for Fluency?

Both repeated oral reading of texts (rehearsal) and teachers modeling fluent reading—and supporting students while reading orally by reading with them—have been identified as key methods for teaching reading fluency (Kuhn & Stahl, 2000; NICHD, 2000; Rasinski, 2003; Rasinski & Hoffman, 2003). In repeated oral readings, students read text several times until they can read with a degree of automaticity and expression. An abundance of evidence has shown that students engaged in repeated readings are more accurate in their word recognition, read more rapidly with expression and comprehension, and are more confident as readers (Dowhower, 1987, 1994; Rasinski & Hoffman, 2003; Samuels, 1979).

What kinds of activities are best suited for engaging students in purposeful reasons to participate eagerly in repeated readings or rehearsal? One answer is to perform for an audience. If oral performance is a natural outcome or goal of repeated reading, then what sorts of texts or genre are meant to be performed for an audience?

Speeches, songs, scripts, and especially poetry exist for performance. Poetry is a natural text choice for performance and practice: Most poems for young children are relatively short, making them easy to read more than once and helping students gain a sense of accomplishment by reading the poems fluently.

Using Rhyming Poetry to Teach Phonics and Fluency

So how might a teacher use rhyming poetry to spice up both phonics and reading fluency instruction? We'd like to suggest a simple three-step sequence of instruction.

Step 1: Identifying the Word Family

A teacher identifies a target word family, demonstrates its spelling and sound, and then brainstorms with students words that belong to that word family. For example, if the word family being taught is -ay, the teacher and students brainstorm words such as *day*, *say*, *may*, *jay*, *pay*, *play*, *stay*, and *pray*, as well as some multisyllabic words such as *daylight* and *playmate*. Then, over the course of the next few days, the teacher and the students revisit the list of words (perhaps written on a phonogram word wall) that they brainstormed, talk about the words, and add other words that belong to that word family.

Step 2: Working With the Word Family

Step 2 moves word family instruction from words in isolation to words in the context of rhyming poetry. For example, after reading the -ay word list from a phonogram word wall, the teacher can put the following rhyme on chart paper and read it with students several times throughout the day and encourage students to read it on their own as well.

> Rain, rain go away
> Come again another day
> Little Johnny wants to play

The teacher points to the words as they are read, drawing the children's visual attention to the words themselves. When the rhyme is essentially memorized, the teacher takes individual words from the poem (this includes -ay words as well as other interesting words such as *little* and *again*). If an appropriate poem to share with students cannot be found for a particular rhyme, then one can be easily written. Here is one that Tim (first author) wrote when working with students on the -est word family.

> My best friend Chester is a real pest
> He pesters his sister and his sister's guest
> He thinks he's a jester, never gives them any rest
> Oh my friend Chester is a real pest

This brief text contains nine instances of the -est word family—four in multisyllabic words. The students loved to read that rhyme throughout the day and requested their own copy to take home and share with their parents.

Step 3: Follow-Up Activities for Word Mastery

After having read and reread the poem in a variety of ways (e.g., whole-group choral, antiphonal choral, echo reading, with a partner together, with a partner alternating lines, reading into a recorder, solo oral reading, solo silent reading, etc.), the teacher guides students in selecting interesting words from the poem. This of course includes any of the word family words but should also include other words of interest from the poem. The words are written on a sheet of chart paper, put on display in the classroom, read, and reread.

Then various follow-up activities such as word sorting (Bear, Invernizzi, Templeton, & Johnston, 2008) can draw students' attention to the words and structural features within the words. For example, students can sort the words by the presence or absence of a rime, by words that do and do not rhyme, words that have one or more than one syllable, words that contain the *s* sound and words that don't, words that represent things and words that do not, words that contain a word within them and words that do not, and so on. Each time students sort the words, they are practicing the words again, but with each sort, they are examining the words from a different perspective that requires a deep analysis of the words and leads to developing mastery over the words.

Blending Spices in the Classroom

Elementary teachers have always found a place for rhyming poetry in their classrooms—mainly to allow children to experience the sheer delight that comes from reading rhythmical and rhyming words aloud. We have found that the use of rhyming poetry in this three-step sequence serves other important literacy purposes. It allows students to develop mastery of the word families both in and out of context, and it promotes fluency through repeated and assisted readings. Moreover, research has begun to show that the use of rhyming poetry on a regular basis, whether in school or at home, can have a significant and positive impact on students' word recognition and reading fluency (Padak & Rasinski, 2004; Rasinski, Padak, Linek, & Sturtevant, 1994; Rasinski & Stevenson, 2005; Wilfong, 2008). Just as two or more spices when blended together often result in a taste much more enjoyable than either spice could produce by itself, such is the synergy that comes from this blending of phonics and fluency. Phonics and fluency can blend together authentically and delightfully in the reading of rhyming poetry to help students develop mastery of each—two key goals of the elementary reading program.

References

Adams, M.J. (1990). *Beginning to read: Thinking and learning about print.* Cambridge, MA: MIT Press.

Bear, D.R., Invernizzi, M., Templeton, S., & Johnston, F. (2008). *Words their way: Word study for phonics, vocabulary, and spelling instruction* (4th ed.). New York: Prentice Hall.

Chall, J.S. (1996). *Stages of reading development* (2nd ed.). Fort Worth, TX: Harcourt Brace.

Cunningham, P.M. (2005). *Phonics they use: Words for reading and writing* (4th ed.). New York: Allyn & Bacon.

Dowhower, S.L. (1987). Effects of repeated reading on second-grade transitional readers' fluency and comprehension. *Reading Research Quarterly, 22*(4), 389–407. doi:10.2307/747699

Dowhower, S.L. (1994). Repeated reading revisited: Research into practice. *Reading & Writing Quarterly, 10*(4), 343–358. doi:10.1080/1057356940100406

Duke, N.K., Pressley, M., & Hilden, K. (2004). Difficulties in reading comprehension. In C.A. Stone, E.R. Silliman, B.J. Ehren, & K. Apel (Eds.), *Handbook of language and literacy: Development and disorders* (pp. 501–520). New York: Guilford.

Ediger, M. (1998). Reading poetry in the language arts. In *Teaching Reading Successfully in the Elementary School* (pp. 147–156). Kirksville, MO: Simpson Publishing Company.

Ehri, L.C. (2005). Learning to read words: Theory, findings, and issues. *Scientific Studies of Reading, 9*(2), 167–188. doi:10.1207/s1532799xssr0902_4

Fry, E. (1998). The most common phonograms. *The Reading Teacher, 51*(7), 284–289.

Gaskins, I.W., Ehri, L.C., Cress, C.O., O'Hara, C., & Donnelly, K. (1996/1997). Procedures for word learning: Making discoveries about words. *The Reading Teacher, 50*(4), 312–327.

Gunning, T. (1995). Word building: A strategic approach to the teaching of phonics. *The Reading Teacher, 48*(6), 484–488.

Kuhn, M.R., & Stahl, S.A. (2000). *Fluency: A review of developmental and remedial practices* (CIERA Rep. No. 2-008). Ann Arbor, MI: Center for the Improvement of Early Reading Achievement.

National Institute of Child Health and Human Development. (2000). *Report of the National Reading Panel. Teaching children to read: an evidence-based assessment of the scientific research literature on reading and its implications for reading instruction: Reports of the subgroups* (NIH Publication No. 00-4754). Washington, DC: U.S. Government Printing Office.

Padak, N., & Rasinski, T. (2004). Fast Start: Successful literacy instruction that connects schools and homes. In J.A.R. Dugan, P. Linder, M.B. Sampson, B.A. Brancato, & L. Elish-Piper (Eds.), *Celebrating the power of literacy* (26th yearbook of the College Reading Association, pp. 11–23). Commerce, TX: College Reading Association.

Rasinski, T.V. (2003). *The fluent reader: Oral reading strategies for building word recognition, fluency, and comprehension.* New York: Scholastic.

Rasinski, T.V., & Hoffman, J.V. (2003). Theory and research into practice: Oral reading in the school literacy curriculum. *Reading Research Quarterly, 38*(4), 510–522. doi:10.1598/RRQ.38.4.5

Rasinski, T.V., Padak, N.D., Linek, W.L., & Sturtevant, E. (1994). Effects of fluency development on urban second-grade readers. *The Journal of Educational Research, 87*(3), 158–165.

Rasinski, T.V., & Stevenson, B. (2005). The effects of Fast Start reading: A fluency based home involvement reading program, on the reading achievement of beginning readers. *Reading Psychology, 26*(2), 109–125.

Samuels, S.J. (1979). The method of repeated readings. *The Reading Teacher, 32*(4), 403–408.

Snow, C.E., Burns, M.S., & Griffin, P. (Eds.). (1998). *Preventing reading difficulties in young children.* Washington, DC: National Academy Press.

Trachtenburg, P. (1990). Using children's literature to enhance phonics instruction. *The Reading Teacher, 43*(9), 648–654.

Wilfong, L.G. (2008). Building fluency, word recognition ability, and confidence in struggling readers: The Poetry Academy. *The Reading Teacher, 62*(1), 4–13.

Nine Things Every Teacher Should Know About Words and Vocabulary Instruction

Karen Bromley

"There is a great divide between what we know about vocabulary instruction and what we (often, still) do" (Greenwood, 2004, p. 28). Many teachers know they need to do a better job teaching vocabulary to students who find reading difficult (Tompkins & Blanchfield, 2004). Teachers also know that one of the challenges of struggling middle school readers is their limited vocabulary and knowledge of the world (Broaddus & Ivey, 2002). While teaching vocabulary well in every curriculum area is only one aspect of developing engaged and successful readers, it is a key aspect.

Traditional vocabulary instruction for many teachers involves having students look words up in the dictionary, write definitions, and use words in sentences (Basurto, 2004). Word lists, teacher explanation, discussion, memorization, vocabulary books, and quizzes often are used in an effort to help students learn new words. But these methods ignore what research and theory tell us about word learning and sound vocabulary instruction.

Vocabulary is a principle contributor to comprehension, fluency, and achievement. Vocabulary development is both an outcome of comprehension and a precursor to it, with word meanings making up as much as 70–80% of comprehension (Davis, 1972; Nagy & Scott, 2000; Pressley, 2002). Fluent readers recognize and understand many words, and they read more quickly and easily than those with smaller vocabularies (Allington, 2006; Samuels, 2002). Students with large vocabularies understand text better and score higher on achievement tests than students with small vocabularies (Stahl & Fairbanks, 1986).

What should middle and high school teachers understand about word learning? This article discusses nine things teachers may have forgotten (or have never known) but need to remember about words and word learning to be effective teachers of vocabulary and their content area. Suggestions for classroom practice related to each idea are provided.

1. English Is a Huge and Unique Collection of Words.
English is three times larger in total number of words than German and six times larger than French. Three out of every four words in the dictionary are foreign born. Many words are pronounced the same in both languages (Lederer, 1991), including *camel* (Hebrew), *zoo* (Greek), *shampoo* (Hindi), and *opera* (Italian). English grows and changes daily with neologisms (new words) from science, technology, and our culture. Things to do:

- Teach students words recently added to the Merriam-Webster's Collegiate Dictionary (2005; www.m-w.com/info/new_words.htm), such as *cybrarian* (noun)—a person who finds, collects, and manages information from the World Wide Web.

- Invite students to create their own lists of words and the definitions they think will soon be added to the dictionary. Have them find these words in our spoken

Preparing Reading Professionals (second edition), edited by Rita M. Bean, Natalie Heisey, and Cathy M. Roller. © 2010 by the International Reading Association. Reprinted from Bromley, K. (2007). Nine things every teacher should know about words and vocabulary instruction. *Journal of Adolescent & Adult Literacy, 50*(7), 528–537. doi:10.1598/JAAL.50.7.2.

- Have students work together to write "paired sentences" as a way to develop their concept and word knowledge. For example, give students two terms and ask them to talk first and then write about how they are similar and how they are different.

4. Words Are Learned Because of Associations That Connect the New With the Known.
When students store new information by linking it to their existing schema, or network of organized information, there is a better chance the new word will be remembered later (Rupley, Logan, & Nichols, 1999). Also, information about words is "dual-coded" as it is stored in memory (Paivio, 1990). It is processed in linguistic form that includes print and meaning and nonlinguistic form that includes visual and sensory images. Learning a word's linguistic elements is enhanced by storing a nonlinguistic form or sensory image along with the linguistic image. Things to do:

- Engage students' prior knowledge and related experiences before teaching new words to introduce a chapter or content area selection. For example, before reading a selection on Communication Cyberspace, teach the word *blog*, define it (an online journal), provide the word's derivation (blog comes from web log), and show a picture of someone seated at a computer composing an essay or report to post on their personal website. Then, show students an actual blog, (e.g., Jessamyn West's www.librarian.net/).

- Use the K–W–L strategy (know, want to know, and learned; Ogle, 1986) when you introduce a new word. First, list what students already know about the word and what they want to know about it. After you've taught the word or students have read it, make a list of what they learned about the word.

- Depending on students' abilities, either individually or in pairs, have them create three-dimensional words (Bromley,

2002). On paper (see Figure 1), have students include a definition, sentence, drawing, and real object to represent the word. Then have students peer teach their words to one another in small groups or to the whole class and post their work on a bulletin board for review and reference.

5. Seventy Percent of the Most Frequently Used Words Have Multiple Meanings.
Students need to remember this fact (Lederer, 1991). It is especially important for struggling readers and English-language learners to understand this and learn to use context to help derive appropriate meanings for words. For example, *hand* can have many meanings (e.g., to give someone something, applause, a way of measuring a horse's height, cards dealt to someone playing a card game, or the part of the anatomy at the end of the wrist). Words such as *foot*, *ball*, and *java* also possess multiple meanings. Context often helps unlock the meaning of words, but when it doesn't help, students have a purpose for using the glossary, dictionary, or thesaurus. Using these references can expand vocabularies and encourage curiosity about words. Things to do:

- Use a fiction or nonfiction selection to teach students how context can give clues to a word's meaning in several ways. Show students that many words have multiple meanings and explicitly teach them how to use context and references to help unlock appropriate meanings.

- Show students how to use context to figure out new words by reading to the end of a sentence or paragraph, reading a caption, analyzing a picture or graphic, or looking at a footnote. Teach students to use a picture, a phrase that defines a word, a synonym or antonym, or the position of the unknown word in a series of other words. For example, *commodity* can have several meanings (e.g., merchandise, goods, article, asset, belonging, chattel). But, the context of the following sentence suggests *merchandise* or *goods* as possible

Figure 1
A Three-Dimensional Word

definition- exactly alike or equal

sentence- The identical twins were dressed just like each other.

meanings and rules out *belonging* or *chattel*: Our product combines intermarket analysis and predicted moving averages to generate consistently accurate commodity forecasts.

• Challenge students to make as many words as they can from a key content term like *evaporation*, *ecosystem*, or *geography* (99 smaller words can be made from the word *planets*). Then teach them the multiple meanings of some of the smaller words they have created.

6. Meanings of 60% of Multisyllabic Words Can Be Inferred by Analyzing Word Parts. Students also need a mindset to alert them to this (Nagy & Scott, 2000). Knowing the meaning of a root, prefix, or suffix often gives clues to what a word means. Because

much of the English language comes from Greek and Latin, we would do well to teach students the common derivatives. This is especially true in science because it contains many multisyllabic terms. Knowing just a few roots makes it much easier to figure out several other words that contain these roots. There are many dictionaries of Greek and Latin roots to help students infer meanings of difficult, multisyllabic terms. Things to do:

• Print a short dictionary of Greek and Latin roots for each of your students like the Dictionary of Greek and Latin Roots found at http://english.glendale.cc.ca.us/ roots.dict.html or have them bookmark it on their computers. Encourage students to use the list as a quick way to unlock science terms like *neophyte* (little plant— *neo* means *new* and *-phyte* means *plant*) and *teleconference* (talking from far away—*tele* means *far away* and *confer* means *to talk*). This dictionary helps with meanings of everyday words, too, like Florida, which traces its origins to *flora* (*flower*) and helps unlock the meanings of *florid* (*gaudy*) and *floriferous* (*flowery* or *showy*).

- Help students use this type of dictionary to learn derivations of words they already know. For example, *Arctic* comes from the Greek *arktos*, which means *bear*, and Antarctica means the converse or opposite, no bears.

- Encourage students to create word trees of often-used roots (see Figure 2) to involve them in using dictionaries to find related multisyllabic words. In this case, print a prefix on each branch, and students can add appropriate words to each one as they find them in a dictionary or glossary, on the Web, or hear them used in the media.

7. **Direct Instruction in Vocabulary Influences Comprehension More Than Any Other Factor.** Although wide reading can build word knowledge, students need thoughtful and systematic instruction in key vocabulary as well (Blachowicz & Fisher, 2004; Graves & Watts-Taffe, 2002; Nagy, 1988). Instruction that engages students in the meanings of new words and their letter, sound, and spelling patterns promotes more effective word learning than just analyzing context (Juel & Deffes, 2004). As students learn new words, they can use them to learn other new words and build independent word learning strategies (Baumann & Kame'enui, 1991; Nagy). Things to do:

- Explicitly teach students new vocabulary focusing on both meaning and word structure. Make connections with other words whenever possible because it helps build from the known to the new. For example, when you teach the word *counterrevolutionary*, relate it to *revolt*, *revolution*, *act*, and *counteract* to build on what students may already know.

Selected Professional Resources on Vocabulary Teaching

Allen, J. (1999). *Words, words, words: Teaching vocabulary in grades 4–12.* Portland, ME: Stenhouse.

Beck, I.L., McKeown, M.G., Kucan, L. (2002). *Bringing words to life: Robust vocabulary instruction.* New York: Guilford.

Blachowicz, C., & Fisher, P.J. (2002). *Teaching vocabulary in all classrooms* (2nd ed.). Upper Saddle River, NJ: Merrill.

Brand, M. (2005). *A day of words: Integrating word work in the intermediate grades* (VHS or DVD). Portland, ME: Stenhouse.

Brand, M. (2004). *Word savvy: Integrating vocabulary, spelling, & word study, grades 3–6.* Portland, ME: Stenhouse.

Bromley, K. (2002). *Stretching students' vocabulary, grades 3–8.* New York: Scholastic.

Ganske, K. (2000). *Word journeys: Assessment guided phonics, spelling, and vocabulary instruction.* New York: Guilford.

Literacy study group: Vocabulary module. (2002). Discussion guide, articles, and books on vocabulary. Newark, DE: International Reading Association.

Murray, M. (2004). *Teaching mathematics vocabulary in context.* Portsmouth, ME: Heinemann.

Nagy, W.E. (1988). *Teaching vocabulary to improve reading comprehension.* Urbana, IL: National Council of Teachers of English; Newark, DE: International Reading Association.

- Have students keep vocabulary notebooks in which they illustrate a new word, write a paraphrased definition, and use it in a sentence. The vocabulary notebook provides a record for review before a test and a source for the correct spelling of content terms.

- Teach students to "chunk" multisyllabic words like *prestidigitation* (sleight of hand, trickery) to help them develop the habit of unlocking new words independently.

- Analyze a classroom test with students (or the practice version of a standardized test they have taken recently or will soon take). Highlight or make a list of key vocabulary from the directions and

Figure 2
A Word Tree

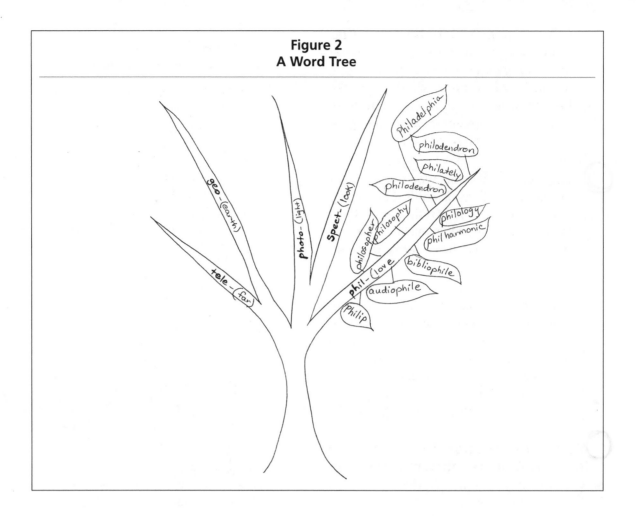

from the reading selections that students must know to answer questions. Look at specific questions that pertain directly to vocabulary knowledge and show students how to locate the word in the selection to determine its meaning in context.

- Have students creatively peer teach new words to one another in small groups before they begin a chapter or unit and encourage them to present their words in several ways (visually and verbally).

8. Teaching Fewer Words Well Is More Effective Than Teaching Several Words in a Cursory Way. Science, math, and social studies material contain many conceptually dense terms, and most students need instruction in this technical vocabulary (Vacca et al., 2005). While it may be tempting to introduce the entire list of new vocabulary from a chapter in a content text, it is more effective to teach fewer words well rather than several words less well (Robb, 2000). Few teachers realize that they can occasionally teach vocabulary during or at the end of a lesson (Watts, 1995). Things to do:

- Teach struggling students and English-language learners no more than three to five new words at a time because they might have difficulty retaining more than that. Teach words students will need to know in the future and teach only words related to the main idea of new material.

- Call attention to important terms that appear in bold or italicized print. Show students that the meaning often follows the term or appears in the glossary at the back of the text.

- Teach most new words before reading to enhance students' comprehension. Occasionally teach new words after reading to allow students to use their own word-attack skills independently or to let you know which words they had trouble with so you can teach these words.

9. Effective Teachers Display an Attitude of Excitement and Interest in Words and Language. Teachers who are curious and passionate about words inadvertently share their enthusiasm with students, and it becomes contagious. These teachers possess word consciousness (Graves & Watts-Taffe, 2002). They appreciate out-of-the-ordinary, powerful, and appealing word use. They are excited about words and language. They model, encourage, and engage students in wordplay, adept diction, and independent investigations into words to build students' word consciousness. Things to do:

- Reflect on your vocabulary teaching. Are you excited about language and teaching or using new words? How do you most often teach new words? Are there other, more effective ways?

- Educate yourself about best practice vocabulary teaching. Talk with colleagues about how they teach vocabulary and what works for them. Read articles and books for new ways to teach vocabulary.

- Share your excitement with students about the fascinating nature of words and language by providing students with a Word of the Day. Find these at Wordsmith (www.wordsmith.org/awad/index.html), which introduces a word a day (around a weekly theme) with definition, pronunciation, etymology, usage, and a quotation. (Students can subscribe and receive it automatically.)

- Word walls aren't just for the elementary grades. Add several new content terms each week to a word wall of science, math, or social studies to provide standard spellings for student writing. As terms are used in class discussions, visually reinforce each word by pointing it out on the word wall.

Final Thoughts

"The good intentions of conscientious teachers concerning traditional vocabulary instruction have often had pernicious side effects..." (Greenwood, 2004, p. 34). Overuse of dictionary hunting, definition writing, or teacher explanation can turn students off learning new words and does not necessarily result in better comprehension or learning. Word learning is a complicated process. It requires giving students a variety of opportunities to connect new words to related words, analyze word structure, understand multiple meanings, and use words actively in authentic ways. The goal of vocabulary instruction should be to build students' independent word learning strategies that can empower them for lifelong learning. This requires teachers who are passionate about words and language, who immerse their students in language, and who provide direct instruction that is thoughtful, intentional, and varied.

References

Allington, R. (2006). *What really matters for struggling readers: Designing research-based programs* (2nd ed.). Boston: Allyn & Bacon.

Basurto, I. (2004). Teaching vocabulary creatively. In G.E. Tompkins & C.L. Blanchfield (Eds.), *Teaching vocabulary: 50 creative strategies, grades K–12* (pp. 1–4). Upper Saddle River, NJ: Pearson Education.

Baumann, J.F., & Kame'enui, E.J. (1991). Research on vocabulary instruction: Ode to Voltaire. In J. Flood, J.M. Jensen, D. Lapp, & J.R. Squire (Eds.), *Handbook of research on teaching the language arts* (pp. 602–632). New York: Macmillan.

Blachowicz, C., & Fisher, P. (2004). Vocabulary lessons. *Educational Leadership, 61*(6), 66–69.

Broaddus, K., & Ivey, G. (2002). Taking away the struggle to read in the middle grades. *Middle School Journal, 34*(2), 5–11.

Bromley, K. (2002). *Stretching students' vocabulary, grades 3–8.* New York: Scholastic.

Davis, F.B. (1972). Psychometric research on comprehension in reading. R*eading Research Quarterly, 7,* 628–678.

Graves, M.F., & Watts-Taffe, S.M. (2002). The place of word-consciousness in a research-based vocabulary program. In A.E. Farstrup & S.J. Samuels (Eds.), *What research has to say about reading instruction* (3rd ed., pp. 140–165). Newark, DE: International Reading Association.

Greenwood, S. (2004). Content matters: Building vocabulary and conceptual understanding in the subject areas. *Middle School Journal, 35*(3), 27–34.

Hahn, M.L. (2002). *Reconsidering read-aloud.* Portland, ME: Stenhouse.

Juel, C., & Deffes, R. (2004). Making words stick. *Educational Leadership, 61*(6), 30–34.

Lederer, R. (1991). *The miracle of language.* New York: Pocket Books.

Merriam-Webster's collegiate dictionary (11th ed.). (2005). Retrieved November 7, 2005, from http://www.m-w.com/info/new_words.htm

Moats, L.C. (2005/2006). How spelling supports reading: And why it is more regular and predictable than you think. *American Educator, 29*(4), 12–22, 42–43.

Nagy, W.E. (1988). *Teaching vocabulary to improve reading comprehension.* Urbana, IL: National Council of Teachers of English; Newark, DE: International Reading Association.

Nagy, W., & Scott, J. (2000). Vocabulary processes. In M.L. Kamil, P.B. Mosenthal, P.D. Pearson, & R. Barr (Eds.), *Handbook of reading research* (Vol. 3, pp. 269–284). Mahwah, NJ: Erlbaum.

Ogle, D. (1986). K–W–L: A teaching model that develops active reading of expository text. *The Reading Teacher, 39*, 564–570.

Paivio, A. (1990). *Mental representations: A dual coding approach.* New York: Oxford University Press.

Pressley, M. (2002). Comprehension instruction: What makes sense now, what might make sense soon. *Reading Online, 5*(2), Retrieved November 7, 2005, from http://www.readingonline.org/articles/art_index.asp?HREF=/articles/handbook/pressley/index.html

Robb, L. (2000). *Teaching reading in middle school.* New York: Scholastic.

Rupley, W.H., Logan, J.W., & Nichols, W.D. (1999). Vocabulary instruction in a balanced reading program. *The Reading Teacher, 52*, 336–346.

Samuels, S.J. (2002). Reading fluency: Its development and assessment. In A.E. Farstrup & S.J. Samuels (Eds.), *What research has to say about reading instruction* (3rd ed., pp. 166–183). Newark, DE: International Reading Association.

Stahl, S.A., & Fairbanks, M.M. (1986). The effects of vocabulary instruction: A model-based meta-analysis. *Review of Educational Research, 56*(1), 72–110.

Tompkins, G., & Blanchfield, C.L. (Eds.). (2004). *Teaching vocabulary: 50 creative strategies, grades K–12.* Upper Saddle River, NJ: Pearson.

Trelease, J. (2001). *The read-aloud handbook* (5th ed.). New York: Penguin.

Vacca, J.L., Vacca, R.T., Gove, M.K., Burkey, L., Lenhart, L.A., & McKeon, C. (2005). *Reading and learning to read* (6th ed.). Boston: Allyn & Bacon.

Watts, S. (1995). Vocabulary instruction during reading lessons in six classrooms. *Journal of Reading Behavior, 27*, 399–424.

1. English keeps growing
2. English is a fairly simple language in comparison to others
3. Listening/Speaking vocab translate to reading/writing vocab
4. Connect to prior knowledge
5. Multiple Meaning Words
6. Teach word parts to help decipher multisyllabic words
7. DI in vocab influences comprehension the most
8. Less is more
9. Teacher attitude

Authentic Literacy Activities for Developing Comprehension and Writing

Nell K. Duke, Victoria Purcell-Gates, Leigh A. Hall, and Cathy Tower

Ms. Jones (all names are pseudonyms) hushed her excited second graders. She began to read aloud a letter from the director of the local nature center. All of the students recalled their recent trip to the pond as part of their science unit on pond life.

> Dear Boys and Girls,
> I hope you enjoyed your visit to our pond. I enjoyed answering your many good questions about what lives in ponds. After you left, I thought about all of the other children who visit us and who also have many of the same questions. I thought it might be a good idea to have a brochure for them with answers to some of their questions. I am writing to ask if you would prepare a brochure like this. It could be called something like "Questions and Answers About Pond Life." You could include some of your questions that you had before you visited us. If you write this, I will have many copies printed that we can put in the main office. That way, people can pick one up when they come or as they are leaving. I hope you can do this for us.
>
> Sincerely, Mr. Hernandez

After a quick vote of approval, the students went to work. They studied similar brochures collected from museums and other sites of natural science. They worked in groups to brainstorm questions for the brochure, after which they researched answers by reading from a variety of science texts. Finally, they wrote drafts of their text until they were satisfied it would serve as a useful information brochure for the public. Their final draft was published as a brochure and displayed in a stand in the front office of the nature center, where many visitors appreciated its availability.

Authentic Literacy

The second graders in Ms. Jones's science class were actively involved in what we consider to be authentic literacy. We documented this incident, and many others, over the course of a two-year experimental research study of genre learning in second- and third-grade science classes. In this article, we provide a brief introduction to authentic literacy and to the research study. We then discuss theory and research behind authentic literacy. Finally, we share lessons from teachers about setting up authentic literacy activities in their classrooms. We hope to provide teachers with many ideas for their own practice.

The terms *authentic literacy* and *authentic reading and writing* are familiar to many teachers. We are encouraged to include authentic literacy activities in our instruction. Students, we believe, need to read authentic literature and to engage in authentic writing. But what *is* authentic literacy? In many ways, the term is a pedagogical one. People who are not involved with issues of instruction do not use it. Yet to many teachers, authentic literacy means reading and writing that is unlike the kind done in school.

In the research literature, authentic reading has primarily been defined in terms of children's literature (Hiebert, 1994). Authentic writing is often defined as writing on topics

Preparing Reading Professionals (second edition), edited by Rita M. Bean, Natalie Heisey, and Cathy M. Roller. © 2010 by the International Reading Association. Reprinted from Duke, N.K., Purcell-Gates, V., Hall, L.A., & Tower, C. (2006). Authentic literacy activities for developing comprehension and writing. *The Reading Teacher, 60*(4), 344–355. doi:10.1598/RT.60.4.4.

of one's choice, which can take the form of a personal narrative or story. When asked to define authentic literacy, the vast majority of preservice and inservice teachers respond with notions of "interesting or motivating," "relevant topics," "fun," or "classical and contemporary children's literature." Returning to the scenario of Ms. Jones's second graders and their response to a request for a pond-life brochure, these definitions seem incomplete. They also are not consistent or specific enough to be sufficiently useful for teachers or researchers.

We confronted these problems of defining *authenticity* when conducting a study that involved engaging students in authentic literacy activities. We needed a definition of authentic literacy that would help teachers in our study create authentic literacy activities and that would help us recognize these activities when we saw them—we needed an operational definition. We give this definition, and many more examples of authentic literacy activities, later in this article.

The Study

Our two-year study involved 26 second- and third-grade teachers and their students from school districts serving families of low and middle socioeconomic status (see Purcell-Gates, Duke, & Martineau, 2007). Our interest was in the development of students' ability to comprehend and compose informational and procedural texts in science (definitions of informational and procedural texts are provided later). All of the teachers in our study worked with us to introduce authentic literacy activities with informational and procedural texts in science and to understand the construct of authentic literacy.

Authenticity Theory

Why were we so committed to including authenticity in all the classrooms in this study? Why do we believe that authentic literacy activities should be part of any instructional model designed to teach comprehension or writing? We believe in theories of situated learning—that learning happens in particular contexts (Brown, Collins, & Duguid, 1989), that these contexts make a big difference to learning, and that it is difficult to transfer learning to new contexts. Language is best acquired within functional contexts (Gee, 1992; Hymes, 1974). Students learn language not in abstract, decontextualized terms but in application, in a context that language is really for. For students, language learning occurs best when the learning context matches the real functional context. Scholars from a range of theoretical and pedagogical orientations agree that authentic experience is essential to genre and discourse learning (Delpit, 1992; Lemke, 1994; New London Group, 1996; Reid, 1987). However, there is little agreement, or clarity, on the conceptualization of authentic literacy.

Authenticity Research

The extent of the research base for authenticity depends a lot on how authenticity is defined. Given the definition we propose, and focusing on literacy only, the research base is not large. However, in a nationwide U.S. study of adult learners, researchers found that adults in programs with more authentic literacy activities reported (a) reading and writing more often in their out-of-school lives, and (b) reading and writing more complex texts (Purcell-Gates, Degener, Jacobson, & Soler, 2002). And the longer the students remained in these programs, the more this was true.

In our study we, too, found support for authentic literacy activities (Purcell-Gates & Duke, 2004). We monitored the authenticity of literacy activities with informational and procedural texts in science weekly. Two or three times each year we also assessed students' ability to comprehend and to write (compose) informational and procedural texts in science. We found that those teachers who included more authentic literacy activities more of the time had students who showed higher growth in both comprehension and writing.

Other effective approaches to literacy education include activities we would classify as authentic, although they may not use the term *authenticity*. For example, Concept-Oriented Reading Instruction, or CORI (Guthrie, Wigfield, & Perencevich, 2004), involves students reading and writing trade books and other authentic texts for the purpose of learning about something of interest to them and communicating what they have learned to others. Other approaches, and certainly many individual classroom teachers, involve students in activities we would characterize as authentic.

An Operational Definition

We conceptualize authentic literacy activities in the classroom as those that replicate or reflect reading and writing activities that occur in the lives of people outside of a learning-to-read-and-write context and purpose. Each authentic literacy activity has a writer and a reader—a writer who is writing to a real reader and a reader who is reading what the writer wrote.

To judge the authenticity of a literacy activity, we look at two dimensions: *purpose or function* and *text*. Authentic purpose or function means that the activity serves a true communicative purpose—for example, reading informational text to inform oneself or to answer one's own questions, or writing to provide information for someone who wants or needs it—in addition to teaching and learning particular skills or content. To be authentic, a text (written or read) must be like texts that are used by readers and writers outside of a learning-to-read-or-write context (i.e., to serve communicative purposes or functions). For example, a newspaper read in class must be either a newspaper brought in from outside the classroom or a newspaper specially written for the classroom that is close to identical in form, language, and so on to one from outside the classroom.

These authentic texts and purposes are contrasted, within our frame, with those texts written primarily to teach reading and writing skills for the purposes of learning to read and write or to develop literacy skills, strategies, values,

and attitudes—literacy activity we term "school only." Prototypical school-only texts include worksheets, spelling lists, short passages with comprehension questions, flashcards, and lists of sentences to be punctuated. School-only purposes for reading these texts are to learn or improve reading and writing skills. School-only purposes for writing these texts would be to assist in the teaching and learning of literacy skills.

Authentic texts can be read or written with school-only purposes, rendering the literacy activity less authentic (i.e., more school only). For example, novels can be read in preparation for an exam on comprehension and interpretive skills, news articles can be read to identify new vocabulary words, or fliers can be composed to complete a history unit with an innovative assignment designed to link to art and language arts. Each of these examples includes an authentic text read for a school-only purpose. To be considered highly authentic, a literacy activity must include an authentic text read or written for an authentic purpose. Authentic literacy activity in the classroom is always accompanied by school-only (or literacy teaching and learning) purposes, simply because that is the overall purpose of school—teaching and learning. However, literacy activities can become authentic for students if teachers attend to those aspects we have just discussed: text types and purposes for reading and writing them.

In our study, the focus was on authentic literacy activities with informational and procedural text in science. We defined the purpose of informational text as being to convey information about the natural or social world, with the text typically written by someone presumed to be more knowledgeable on the subject for someone presumed to be less so. We defined the purpose of procedural text as being to tell how to do something, with the text typically written by someone who knows how to perform that action for someone who does not. Authentic uses had to include these purposes for reading and writing informational and procedural texts in addition to the instructional purposes held by the teachers.

We used a 3-point scale to rate the degree to which the purpose of an informational text being written or read in the classroom mirrors the actual purpose of an informational text (e.g., to learn something that you want to know about a topic). We also rated the degree of authenticity of text on a 3-point scale. For literacy activities involving writing we did not rate the authenticity of the text. In order for the activity to be rated (i.e., for it to be classified as informational or procedural) it had to involve actual and therefore authentic informational or procedural text.

Our rating categories for purpose and text are described on the authenticity rating sheet (see Figure 1).

Examples of literacy activities and how they would be rated are provided in Table 1. As you can see, highly authentic reading and writing of informational text involves *seeking and acquiring information* (for reading) and *providing information* (for writing). Authentic reading and writing of procedural text involves *doing procedures* (for reading) and *enabling the doing of procedures* (for writing).

Figure 1
Authenticity Rating Sheet

Brief description of activity, including (a) text students are reading, writing, or listening to, and (b) purpose of students' reading, writing, or listening:

_____

_____

_____

_____

Authenticity of purpose

Rating: 3   2   1

3 = This reading, writing, or listening-to-text purpose exists in the lives of people outside a classroom, or it is as authentic as the use of that genre for that purpose can be.

2 = This reading, writing, or listening-to-text purpose exists in the lives of people outside a classroom, but it differs in that for reading the impetus is less personal and for writing the audience is less compelling.

1 = This reading, writing, or listening-to-text purpose is identified by its absence of any purpose beyond school work. This takes different forms depending on the genre and process (reading or writing).

Authenticity of text

Rating: 3   2   1

3 = This text type occurs naturally in the lives of people outside a classroom. You can find it in bookstores or order it for home delivery. This category also includes texts that are written primarily for instructional purposes but that closely mimic the naturally occurring texts—the only difference being the publisher's audience.

2 = This text is written primarily for use in schools and, although it mimics to an extent the genre style, form, and purpose of those texts that do occur naturally outside school, it includes enough school "stuff" to be recognizable. This type would include texts that have comprehension questions, special vocabulary sections, and perhaps even "Checking What You Have Learned" sections. These texts are hybrid forms reflecting school and authentic genres in different combinations and emphases.

1 = This text would not occur anywhere except in a school or other teaching and learning contexts. It is written to teach skills and is used only for learning and practicing skills. You may be able to purchase these texts in stores but they reflect a skills-learning purpose.

Total authenticity rating: _____

Table 1
Examples of Activities With Differing Levels of Authenticity of Purpose

Activites and Text Type	Rating 3	Rating 2	Rating 1
Reading activities, informational text	Following an activity using owl pellets, students were asked to generate questions about owls and their habits. These questions were listed on chart paper and grouped. Small groups of students were assigned to read informational texts to find answers to the questions, which were then shared with the class as a whole.	The teacher suggested that the kindergartners would like to have information books on reptiles. She asked for topics and divided the class into small groups. Each group read to find information to put in the books for the kindergartners.	In the science unit "weather," the teacher chose five topics or concepts related to weather and created five centers, each focusing on one concept. At each center, the teacher placed informational texts on these topics, accompanied by reading guides that the students used to find out the designated information from the texts. Students rotated through the centers.
	The day following the eruption of a volcano in Mexico, a discussion arose about volcanoes and how they happen. Students disagreed about where the lava comes from and how hot it is. The teacher put together a group of information books about volcanoes. She distilled the questions and assigned students to work in pairs to read for the answers to the questions.	The class went outside to collect rocks from the playground. When they returned, the teacher suggested writing an information pamphlet about the rocks at the school for parents who might not know about them. The students read informational text about rocks and prepared the pamphlets to take home to their parents.	The teacher demonstrated how to find answers to questions that students had been assigned to answer and she talked through her thinking as she looked for the answer in an information book, located the information, and read the answer to the class.
	A student brought in a snake skin to class. Several questions arose from the group about why snakes shed their skin and how long it takes to grow new skin. The teacher found an information book about snakes, located the answers, and read those sections to the class.		Students were assigned an information book about where insects live. They were to find all the highlighted vocabulary, write out the words, and write the definition of each word or word phrase as provided by the book.
			Students were given an informational text on tornadoes. The teacher led them through a lesson where each heading was read aloud and the students were then asked to predict what the section following the heading would be about. They read to confirm their hypotheses.
			While the students watched and listened, the teacher did a lesson on indexes. She put five words on the chalkboard and demonstrated how to look in the index of an information book, find a word, and locate the page number where the word appears.

(continued)

Table 1 (Continued)
Examples of Activities With Differing Levels of Authenticity of Purpose

Activites and Text Type	Rating 3	Rating 2	Rating 1
Writing activities, informational text	In pairs, students researched a topic that they believed would be of interest to children in Mrs. X's class. Mrs. X's class generated questions and sent them to the students to guide them. The students' ultimate purpose was to write and publish information books on each topic and present them to Mrs. X for her class library. The kindergarten class requested picture books about animal babies. In groups of three, students created the books. They either drew or used cut-out pictures, and they wrote accompanying labels, captions, or sentences. They laminated each page and bound the books, which were presented to the kindergarten class and read aloud by the students who created them. Students contributed text to an informational brochure to be printed and left for visitors to a local nature center. This project was prompted by the guide at the center after the students had visited there. He wrote a letter to the class requesting the brochure.	The teacher led the class in composing an information pamphlet about what was discovered in the dirt in the playground. She elicited "text" from the students and wrote it on chart paper. The pamphlet was to be sent home to parents, for display and also to provide information about the school playground. Students contributed as a group to an information pamphlet that was posted as a class project in the hallway on Back-to-School Night. The topic was assigned as part of the district-mandated curriculum on force and motion. The teacher did the actual writing. The teacher suggested writing information books for the kindergartners. She elicited questions from the class on what they thought kindergartners would like to know. She assigned groups to read to find the answers to the questions and then to write an informational text for the kindergarten library.	The teacher told the class to imagine that an alien lands in the playground and sees a pine tree there. This alien asks one of the students what the tree is. The assignment was to write an information book about trees for the alien. The teacher told the class that each student was to pretend to have a pen pal in another country. The students wrote an information book about the plants that grow in their backyards to inform pen pals who have never been to the United States. Students answered questions referring to sample procedures such as these: How many materials are required? What are you supposed to do after you have poured the water into the glass?
Reading activities, procedural text	Students were given a procedural text about a concept related to force and motion. They were asked to read and follow the procedures individually. The class then reconvened to discuss the concept, or "point," of the demonstration. As part of a unit on insects, students decided to build and stock their own ant farm. They found instructions on the Internet and divided into groups to build a farm and to stock it.	Students were tested on their ability to follow a procedure. Teachers read to students or students read a prepared procedure. Students were evaluated on their ability to follow the directions. In a lesson on force and motion, the culminating activity was a demonstration procedure. Each student pair was given the procedural handout and told to follow it. The point was to get the procedure to come out right and to enjoy a hands-on activity at the end of	Students read through procedures for demonstrating that fire will not burn in the absence of oxygen. They were told not to try this themselves.

(continued)

Activities and Text Type	Rating 3	Rating 2	Rating 1
Reading activities, procedural text	The teacher read from a procedural text and demonstrated procedures while the whole class listened and watched. The focus afterward was on the science concept demonstrated or tested.	a lesson. As students finished, there was a lot of laughter, pats on the back, cleaning up, and a sense of ending the day or week. But there was no more "science" talk around the concept of force and motion.	
Writing activities, procedural text	Students were assigned different tasks related to growing corn inside their classroom. As spring break approached, they composed—in their task-related groups—a list of instructions for the aide who had volunteered to take care of the plants while the students were away. Students created a procedures book that will be passed on to the class next year. They worked in pairs to create procedures for demonstrations for key science concepts. Each pair picked a different one from a list generated by the teacher. As part of this, they had to "field test" their demonstration by doing it according to their written procedures. The teacher fully expected the students to use the procedures to help learn the concepts. The teacher led the class in composing a procedural text. She elicited text from the students and wrote it on the board. The students then copied the text to be included in their individual procedures book that they will eventually take home and use.	Following a lesson on planting seeds, the teacher assigned students to write a procedure for doing so. They were to use all that they had learned about planting seeds. They took turns following one another's procedures to see how well they were written. Many had to do rewrites. After a unit on underwater plants, students were assigned to create a procedural pamphlet telling readers how to prepare and care for an underwater plant aquarium. They worked with the teacher to compose it, and the teacher saved the finished products for next year's students.	Students were told to pretend that an alien arrived at their school and wanted to know how to take care of baby chickens. The teacher assigned students to work in groups of three and prepare a "how-to" pamphlet for the alien. The teacher led these groups in composing this procedural text. She wrote it on chart paper or on the chalkboard. Students watched and answered questions while the teacher wrote parts of a procedure on the chalkboard in a lesson on "writing procedures." Teacher questions were of this type: Now, what do I call the section that lists the things you need? Materials, that's right. I'll write that right here.

Classroom Activities: Lessons From Teachers

The remainder of this article focuses on how teachers in our study established conditions for authentic reading and writing of informational and procedural texts in science. These portraits are based on our analysis of literacy activities rated 3 (highly authentic) for both purpose and text. The teachers participated in summer workshops devoted to building an understanding of authentic literacy, and each teacher was coached once a week for the entire year she or he was part of the study.

Over time, the teachers developed many different strategies for establishing authentic literacy events in science. We identified and categorized them in order to share these strategies with other teachers.

Authentic Reading of Informational Text in Science

To establish authentic contexts and purposes for the reading and writing of informational text, the teachers looked for different ways to generate the need to seek information that the student readers required or wanted to know. Teachers often generated student questions prior to the reading of informational text. These types of set-ups fell into several categories.

Hands-On Demonstrations. Teachers conducted demonstrations to generate questions as well as general interest in a science topic the class was about to study. For example, one teacher created a model volcano and, by pouring a solution of baking soda and vinegar into the top, caused a reaction that looked like a lava eruption. Another teacher brought in caterpillars for the students to observe and handle. Questions that arose naturally or in response to the teacher's elicitation were used to inspire and guide informational reading. Teachers recorded questions on a clipboard as they circulated, and wrote them on chart paper during a group discussion. This integration of hands-on, or first-hand, investigations with text-based, or second-hand, investigations is supported by a number of research studies (e.g., Anderson & Guthrie, 1999; Palincsar & Magnusson, 2001; Romance & Vitale, 2001).

Teachable Moments. Teachers responded to unexpected events in ways that connected with their science instruction. For example, a second grader appeared in class one day with her arm in a cast. Her teacher, realizing that she could use this unfortunate accident for her unit on the skeletal system, centered the class discussion on the student's broken arm. Questions like "How did you break it?" "Does it hurt?" "Which bone is broken?" were asked. Students read many informational texts on bones that day. Another teacher proceeded in a similar manner when a student brought in an unusual and interesting rock, in response to a unit on rocks.

Topic Announcements. K–W–Ls (Ogle, 1986) were often used by teachers for eliciting questions about topics. These activities followed the K–W–L template for the most part (K = what we *know*; W = what do we *want* to know; L = what we have *learned*). The teachers first elicited what the students knew—for example, about sound. Then they elicited questions the students had about the topic—what they wanted to know—structuring their reading of informational text about sound. In a similar approach, teachers announced a new science topic, read aloud from a text about it, and then asked students if they had any questions on that topic. These questions guided future reading.

Discrepant Events. Finally, teachers set up situations involving *discrepant events* to generate questions about science content. A discrepant event reflects a reality that conflicts with what students might expect to see. For a study unit on light, one teacher set up a prism on the overhead while her class was out of the room. This caused rainbows to appear on the ceiling. When the students returned there were many "oohs" and "ahs" and a rush of questions about how the rainbow effects occurred. Capturing these questions, the teacher led the class in finding informational text on light to help them understand the phenomenon.

Authentic Reading and Writing of Procedural Texts in Science

Given our operational definition of authentic reading and writing of procedural texts—

reading in order to do a procedure and writing to instruct someone how to do one—the set-ups for these authentic literacy activities were fairly straightforward. Highly authentic reading of procedural text occurred when teachers let students in their science units read and conduct procedures that were an integral part of the content being learned (e.g., investigations intended to demonstrate science concepts). For the most part, students wrote procedural text for the authentic purpose of providing the requisite instruction to someone who would be reading the text when conducting the procedures. These could be procedures for conducting investigations, caring for plants and animals in or outside the classroom, and so on.

Authentic Writing and Reading

All of the teachers gave evidence of conceiving authenticity as a literacy construct—that is, as including writing, reading, and other language processes much of the time. This meant that teachers often used the communicative purposes of writing informational and procedural text as a rationale for reading. Although we can look at these data on integrated reading and writing activities in several ways, we use three lenses: literacy in response to community need, literacy as part of problem solving, and audience as integral to authentic writing.

Literacy in Response to Community Need.
Our opening vignette is an example of this sort of set-up. Over the course of two years, several teachers arranged ways to involve their students in authentic reading and writing in response to community needs.

The teacher in our opening vignette, Ms. Jones, arranged this activity by asking the director of information at the nature center to write the letter to her class requesting the brochure. She posted an enlarged copy of the letter in the room for students to consult as they worked in groups to answer questions of "What kinds of things would other visitors want to know about?" The students were writing a text type that exists in the world outside of school (a brochure) to a real and appropriate audience for the purpose of providing information to their readers' questions—all prerequisites of authentic informational writing. And it is worth noting that, although the teacher initiated the request for the brochure, the final text was published and made available to visitors to the pond at the nature center.

In another school, a teacher arranged for the principal to visit the class and ask students to take responsibility for the school garden that year. This task would serve as the culminating activity for the class's study unit on plants and would involve reading about different flowers and vegetables and how to grow them (including soil, water, and light requirements). The students wrote informational text for the seed packets typically posted in gardens at the ends of rows and wrote procedural texts for other school and community members who would be responsible for caring for the growing plants over the summer.

Literacy as Part of Problem Solving. A
number of the teachers presented their students with real-life problems that required science knowledge to solve. The teachers wove authentic purposes for reading and writing into these problem-solving activities. At various times, students were faced with such problems as dying tadpoles and wilting plants, setting up class aquariums, helping their teacher's father move from one home to another, and arranging for the removal of a large file cabinet that appeared inexplicably in the middle of their classroom one morning.

This last activity was the brainstorm of one of the second-grade teachers in our project. Her students were studying simple machines, and it occurred to her that an authentic purpose for learning about simple machines was to actually have to move an object from one place to another. She arranged with the custodian to deposit a large, heavy file cabinet in the middle of her classroom after school hours. When the students arrived the next morning, they and she were nonplussed: How did that object get there? And how to get it out?

She called the principal from the classroom as the class looked on and listened. The principal sent the custodian to the room and he explained that the delivery was a mistake but that he did not have time to move the cabinet. The teacher then convinced the class to take on the removal of the cabinet as a project for which they could use what they were learning about simple machines (levers, pulleys, etc.). Students worked in groups to read about ways that simple machines could help. They then wrote up their ideas and tried them out. As a culminating event, they wrote procedural texts for those who found themselves in a similar predicament and placed these texts in their classroom library under the topic of science.

Audience as Integral to Authentic Writing.
Audience is generally agreed to be a critical aspect of writing process and product. The construct of audience played a major role in our conceptualization of authentic writing as we thought about authenticity in the light of real-life writing practices. Outside an instructional context, literate people almost always write only if there is a reader for their writing, even if (in the case of journal or personal memo writing) the reader is the writer. One challenge for the teachers in our study (and, we suspect, for teachers in general) was the establishment of real audiences—or real readers—for the students' writing. By *real* here, we mean a reader who will read the written text for its communicative purpose and not solely for evaluation, as so often happens to writing done in instructional contexts. The teachers rose to this challenge in admirable and inventive ways.

Teachers established real audiences and readers at different distances from their student writers. Many texts were written to be read by readers outside the school setting, such as the brochure written for visitors at the nature center. Others were directed toward readers within the school but outside the students' classrooms. And many were composed for classmates, resulting in texts that reflected shared background knowledge.

Purposes for Writing to a More Distant Reader. Many teachers in the study proved to be inventive in establishing purposes for writing informational and procedural scientific texts for real readers outside their schools and, in some cases, outside their communities and countries. They called on personal and professional friends to act as readers and audiences. They took advantage of e-mail, the Internet, and other technological venues. And they worked with local community members to establish authentic contexts for authentic writing, as our example of the pond brochure illustrates.

One Michigan teacher arranged for a friend who teaches third grade in Costa Rica to request via e-mail some information books on Michigan's climate for her students. While reading and writing in response to this request, the Michigan students also learned about the climate of Costa Rica so they could better explain their weather through compare-and-contrast techniques. Other distant, authentic, teacher-arranged audiences included students who requested information on living things, light, and sound; visitors to the local library whose librarian requested information books on coral reefs; museum-goers whose director requested information sheets about light; and readers of the ZOOM website (http://pbskids .org/zoom/), which solicited science-related procedures from children.

Arranging Within-School Audiences. As teachers searched for authentic audiences for their student writers, they also found them within their school communities. These readers provided the distance that is pragmatically required for much writing but were more immediately accessible than those outside school. Students wrote information books on a variety of science topics for their school libraries, for "next year's class," "for the kindergartners" (who were often willing listeners), and for numerous other classes in their schools. For each of these writing events, which always required background reading, the teachers made sure that the students knew there was a real audience and that the texts would be read by that audience.

Informational texts other than books were also written for authentic audiences within school communities, always in response to a demonstrated need or request for such texts. Answers providing information about science topics were written as a result of a question jar placed in school libraries. Students were encouraged to write questions to put in the jar. Bookmarks with information on dinosaurs were written for students and made available in a central place. Posters like those found in natural history museums were placed in school hallways. Factoids on weather were written to be read over the public address system for the daily weather report. Video scripts about water were written and then produced for the morning announcement event in a school that featured television monitors in each classroom.

Authentic writing for within-school audiences also took place with procedural text. For example, teachers arranged with colleagues to request procedures for experiments that their classes could conduct. Or one class would serve as an audience for another in reading student-written text on how to grow lima beans.

Classroom Community as Audience.

Finally, teachers would often turn to their own classrooms to provide purposes and audiences for the informational and procedural reading and writing. All of these activities, rated 3, could and do occur naturally in the world outside the learning-to-read-and-write context. For example, sometimes students would read about mammals with the purpose of sharing orally with class members interesting facts they discovered. Or students would write informational books on a variety of science topics for their class library, to be read by class members during the year.

Because procedural texts specific to the classrooms' science topics and curricula and appropriate for students of this age were hard to find, the rationale for writing procedures to demonstrate concepts under study was very natural and obvious. In these cases, students would often write different procedures in groups and then share them with classmates in other groups who would then conduct the procedures. One interesting example of this was the class that wrote procedures for creating different musical instruments (as part of a study of sound) and then exchanged them with other students who tried to build the instruments and play them.

A final example of writing for classmates is the production of informational posters on different science topics that were posted around the room for study and perusal. The actual reading of these posters took different forms—from special events akin to science fairs to more casual reading when opportunities arose, much like environmental print for the room. They were all written, however, to provide information for a reader who wanted or needed it, not simply as displays of products.

Learning to Read and Write While Reading and Writing

We offer these ideas and strategies, gleaned from teachers, for bringing authentic reading and writing into the classroom in the spirit of collaboration. As teachers struggle to make learning and learning to read and write meaningful and authentic, we believe it helps to share ideas and experiences. We also believe that although the strategies in this report came from second- and third-grade science teachers, they are generally applicable to different content and in higher grades. For example, taking advantage of current events, either in the lives of the students or in the life of the community, to engender authentic reading for information is a natural activity for a social studies class. Authentic writing of historical text for real readers can also be incorporated into studies of history.

Furthermore, we encourage teachers to think beyond the specific genres we used for our study. The two dimensions of authentic literacy activities discussed—text type and purpose—can be applied to many different genres that occur in the daily lives of literate people. Some examples of such genres, along with

Table 2
Sample Genres and Purposes For Reading and Writing Them

Genre	Purpose for Reading	Purpose for Writing
Informational text	To obtain information about the natural or social world	To provide information about the natural or social world to someone who wants or needs it
Procedural text	To make something or do something according to procedures	To guide the making or doing of something for someone who wants or needs it
Fictional narrative text	To relax; for entertainment broadly defined; to discuss	To provide relaxation; to entertain, broadly defined; to foster discussion
Personal letter	To maintain a relationship; to learn about personal events; to share emotions	To maintain a relationship; to inform about personal events; to express emotions
List	To be informed about a related group of items	To record a related group of items
Biography	To learn about a person's life	To convey information about a person's life
Book review	To learn about a book and someone's opinion of and responses to it	To convey information about a book and one's opinion of and responses to it

various real-life purposes for reading and writing them, are included in Table 2.

Many teachers attested to the power of authentic literacy activities. They reported that students came alive when they realized they were writing to real people for real reasons or reading real-life texts for their own purposes. Beyond this, the results of our research provide teachers with evidence that more authentic literacy activities are related to greater growth in the ability to read and write new genres (Purcell-Gates & Duke, 2004). With this additional motivation to involve students in authentic literacy activities, we believe that the strategies and scenarios offered here will be particularly helpful as teachers attempt to create opportunities to bring authentic literacy into their classrooms.

Note

This article is based upon work supported by the National Science Foundation under Grant No. 9979904.

References

Anderson, E., & Guthrie, J.T. (1999, April). *Motivating children to gain conceptual knowledge from text: The combination of science observation and interesting texts.* Paper presented at the annual meeting of the American Educational Research Association, Montreal, QC.

Brown, J.S., Collins, A., & Duguid, P. (1989). Situated cognition and the culture of learning. *Educational Researcher, 18,* 32–42.

Delpit, L.D. (1992). Acquisition of literate discourse: Bowing before the master? *Theory Into Practice, 31,* 296–302.

Gee, J.P. (1992). *The social mind.* Westport, CT: Bergin & Garvey.

Guthrie, J.T., Wigfield, A., & Perencevich, K.C. (2004). *Motivating reading comprehension: Concept-Oriented Reading Instruction.* Mahwah, NJ: Erlbaum.

Hiebert, E.H. (1994). Becoming literate through authentic tasks: Evidence and adaptations. In R.B. Ruddell, M.R. Ruddell, & H. Singer (Eds.), *Theoretical models and processes of reading* (4th ed., pp. 391–413). Newark, DE: International Reading Association.

Hymes, D. (1974). *Foundations in sociolinguistics: An ethnographic approach.* Philadelphia: University of Pennsylvania Press.

Lemke, J.L. (1994, November). *Genre as a strategic resource.* Paper presented at the annual meeting of the National Council of Teachers of English, Orlando, FL.

New London Group. (1996). A pedagogy of multiliteracies: Designing social futures. *Harvard Educational Review, 66,* 60–92.

Ogle, D.S. (1986). K–W–L group instructional strategy. In A.S. Palincsar, D.S. Ogle, B.F. Jones, & E.G. Carr (Eds.), *Teaching reading as thinking* (pp. 11–17). Alexandria, VA: Association for Supervision and Curriculum Development.

Palincsar, A., & Magnusson, S. (2001). The interplay of first-hand and text-based investigations to model and support the development of scientific knowledge and reasoning. In S. Carver & D. Klahr (Eds.), *Cognition and instruction: Twenty-five years of progress* (pp. 151–193). Mahwah, NJ: Erlbaum.

Purcell-Gates, V., Degener, S.C., Jacobson, E., & Soler, M. (2002). Impact of authentic adult literacy instruction on adult literacy practices. *Reading Research Quarterly, 37,* 70–92.

Purcell-Gates, V., & Duke, N.K. (2004). *Learning to read and write genre-specific text: The roles of authentic experience and explicit teaching.* Unpublished manuscript, University of British Columbia, Vancouver. Purcell-Gates, V., Duke, N.K., & Martineau,

J.A. (2007). Learning to read and write genre-specific text: Roles of authenitic experience and explicit teaching. *Reading Research Quarterly, 42*(1).

Reid, I. (Ed.). (1987). *The place of genre in learning: Current debates.* Melbourne, VIC, Australia: Deakin University, Centre for Studies in Literary Education.

Romance, N.R., & Vitale, M.R. (2001). Implementing an in-depth expanded science model in elementary schools: Multi-year findings, research issues, and policy implications. *International Journal of Science Education, 23,* 373–404.

Reading Adventures Online: Five Ways to Introduce the New Literacies of the Internet Through Children's Literature

Jill Castek, Jessica Bevans-Mangelson, and Bette Goldstone

Young people of all ages are turning to the Internet to expand their reading experiences. Deion (pseudonym), a fifth grader, visits a virtual book club website during literacy center time to find out what kids around the world are reading. Here, students discuss their favorite books and recommend new titles to explore. Deion navigates to the discussion board where he sees that *Harry Potter and the Half-Blood Prince* (Rowling, 2005, Scholastic) has three new posts. Rebecca, Oliver, and Mark offer their impressions of the latest in this popular series.

> Subject: Harry Potter & the Half-Blood Prince, New Zealand
>
> Hi,
>
> I just got done reading the latest Harry Potter book this afternoon and came on here. I was surprised to find that no one else had posted anything about it yet! I think the other Harry Potter stories had more suspense and better plots, but this book is much funnier!
>
> What's your opinion?
>
> Rebecca

> Subject: Re: Harry Potter & the Half-Blood Prince, Canada
>
> Hey,
>
> Wow, I thought I was the only one who thought that! I totally agree with you. I didn't enjoy this book as much as I liked the other ones. But I do like how Harry and everyone else are growing up and learning more magic.

> I think Harry has to go back to school. All the adventures happen at Hogwarts and if he doesn't go back, how will he learn everything he needs to know? I can't wait until the next book comes out.
>
> Send a reply,
> Oliver

> Subject: Re: Harry Potter & the Half-Blood Prince, USA
>
> I was a little disappointed that I figured out who the Half Blood Prince was. As soon as you knew where Harry read the name, it was easy to guess. Now we have to wait two years until the next adventure.
>
> Impatiently counting the days,
> Mark

Many exciting literacy adventures await our students online. Deion's teacher understands that providing opportunities for students to use the Internet at school helps them develop literacy skills that are important for their future participation in a digital world. She also recognizes that using computers increases students' motivation to read, write, and learn (Becker, 2000). Deion navigates the discussion board as his teacher observes. She is amazed by the critical thinking skills students use as they participate in online exchanges. Providing Internet activities as part of your classroom literature program helps students acquire important new skills and strategies required to take advantage of today's information and communica-

Preparing Reading Professionals (second edition), edited by Rita M. Bean, Natalie Heisey, and Cathy M. Roller. © 2010 by the International Reading Association. Reprinted from Castek, J., Bevans-Mangelson, J., & Goldstone, B. (2006). Reading adventures online: Five ways to introduce new literacies of the Internet through children's literature. *The Reading Teacher, 59*(7), 714–728. doi:10.1598/RT.59.7.12.

tion technologies (ICTs) (Leu, Castek, Henry, Coiro, & McMullan, 2004).

In this column, we explore links between the Internet and children's literature. We begin by defining the term *new literacies* and sharing the important benefits students gain when we make the Internet part of the classroom curriculum. In our discussion of new literacies, we highlight the importance of developing positive dispositions toward using the Internet. We then share five exciting ways to introduce the new literacies of the Internet through children's literature. We are also pleased to present within this column Bette Goldstone's Children's Books That Mirror Techno Text, a discussion of high-quality books that weave together multiple story lines and involve students in applying high-level comprehension strategies online and offline.

What Are New Literacies?

The term *new literacies* has many meanings (Gee, 2000; Lankshear & Knobel, 2003; Leu, Kinzer, Coiro, & Cammack, 2004, Street, 2003). We use the term here to describe the new skills, strategies, and dispositions that are required to successfully identify important questions, locate information, engage in critical evaluation, synthesize information, and communicate on the Internet (Leu, Kinzer, et al., 2004). New literacies are required for participation in a digital world (International Reading Association, 2001). Although they are not included in the assessments used to measure student growth as a result of the No Child Left Behind Act of 2001 (2002), they are nevertheless vitally important to our students' futures (International ICT Literacy Panel, 2003; Partnership for 21st Century Skills, 2004).

When we use the Internet in our classrooms for teaching and learning, we extend opportunities for all students to acquire these skills and strategies. New literacies build upon the foundational literacies we have always taught in schools. However, new literacies include the new reading, writing, viewing, navigating, and communication skills required by the many ICTs that continually appear in our lives (Leu, Castek, et al., 2004). New literacies are required to search for information on the Internet (Henry, 2006). Navigating within and between websites, anticipating what information might be connected to a hyperlink on any given site, synthesizing information found at different locations, and critically evaluating online resources also require new skills and strategies (Coiro, 2003a, 2003b, 2005). To take full advantage of the Internet's information potential, readers must acquire the new literacies that are needed to use them effectively (Leu, 2002). Fortunately, there are many excellent resources available that encourage, motivate, and support readers as they acquire these new literacies. Visit the resources on the New Literacies page (http://ctell.uconn.edu/cases/ newliteracies.htm) for practical ideas that are fun and easy to implement.

Developing Positive Dispositions Toward the Internet

As educators, we aim to engage students in experiences that will inspire a lifelong love of learning. We play a central role in developing and sustaining positive student dispositions toward the Internet and other ICTs. Dispositions are "habits of mind or tendencies to approach and respond to situations in certain ways" (Katz, 1988, p. 30). They are learned through observation, modeling, and exposure (Noyes, 2004).

Dispositions are influenced by support, enjoyment, and engagement. Students with limited experiences on the Internet have more difficulty developing positive dispositions. Like most of us, they may avoid investing time in the things they do not do well. As a result of negative dispositions toward reading online, students may lose out on opportunities to take full advantage of the rich informational resources available on the Internet. In contrast, the development of positive dispositions toward the Internet and other ICTs is the first step toward acquiring expert Internet skills that can be used to further learning. Students who have acquired positive dispositions are collaborative, constructive, and active in problem solving (Guthrie & Wigfield, 2000). They enjoy reading on the Internet and seek out opportunities to use it to fulfill their learning aims (International ICT Literacy Panel, 2003; Organisation for Economic Co-operation and Development, 2005).

While many students are finding the Internet to be an exciting world (Rainee & Hilton, 2005), some teachers continue to be reluctant to embrace new technologies. We hope to encourage you to more fully integrate these new literacies into your classroom by exploring the teaching and learning opportunities in children's literature. It is indeed possible to support students in developing positive dispositions toward the Internet. Fun, engaging, and meaningful online experiences in the classroom help shape positive attitudes and a strong desire to learn to use technology well.

Why Is Teaching With the Internet Important?

Some scholars believe that the Internet is this generation's defining technology for literacy and learning (Hartman et al., 2005). Roughly 73% of young people ages 12 through 17 in the United States use the Internet regularly to gather information, exchange ideas, and share opinions (Lenhart, Madden, & Hitlin, 2005). Compared with responses collected in 2001, the use of the Internet among today's teens has intensified and broadened (Lenhart et al.). A similar survey reported that 66% of regular Internet users and 49% of nonusers in the United States believe new communication technologies, including the Internet, have made the world a better place (Lebo, 2004). Also in that survey, 67% of Internet users said they consider the Internet to be an important or extremely important source of information for them (Lebo).

The Internet has become a widespread communication tool used extensively in the workplace. As a result, we are seeing profound changes in the nature of reading and writing taking place there. In just one year (August 2000 to September 2001), use of the Internet at work among employed U.S. adults age 25 and older increased by nearly 60%, from 26.1% of the workforce to 41.7% (U.S. Department of Commerce, 2002). A national survey (Lebo, 2004) reported that 42% of U.S. workers use e-mail every day to gather information and collaborate with others. This growing dependency on networked information makes it a necessity that all students acquire the new literacies that are central to the world of work.

Nations around the world see Internet use as important to their curricular goals. Great Britain's National Grid for Learning www.ngfl.gov.uk, The Education Network of Australia (EdNA) www.edna.edu.au/edna/page1.html, and Canada's SchoolNet www.schoolnet.ca/home/e/ict.asp are national efforts aimed at helping teachers make information and communication technologies an integral part of their school curriculum. Take a look at these international sites to gather resources to support your own curriculum changes. In order to compete with students around the world for the jobs of the future, we will need to ensure that students possess the new literacies of Internet technologies and can use them skillfully and effectively. With the growing number of Internet-connected computers available in schools across the United States, our classrooms are the best places for students to acquire the new literacy skills they will need for participation in the workplaces of the 21st century. As teachers, we have a responsibility to provide students with a wide range of literacy experiences that demonstrate the ways we read and write in our daily lives. Approximately 13% of U.S. students do not have access to the Internet at home (Lenhart et al., 2005). The classroom is the only place these children will learn the skills and strategies required to take full advantage of the Internet. It is up to us to provide these experiences so that all students are given the tools to succeed in the careers that will define the 21st century.

Five Exciting Ways to Use the Internet to Teach Literature

The new literacies for reading, writing, and communicating online can be introduced to students by using the Internet across the curriculum, particularly with children's literature. In this column, we address five exciting ways to bring the Internet into your literature program:

1. *Explore stories on the Web.* Online stories are engaging and interactive literacy tools that motivate readers to explore the world of books while using online tools.

2. *Invite students to become authors on the Web.* Publishing student work on the Internet helps students become more invested in producing quality products they are proud to share.

3. *Participate in virtual book clubs.* Online forums provide a worldwide audience for book discussions that enrich comprehension while exposing students to new perspectives.

4. *Collaborate on Internet projects.* Internet projects get students working collaboratively with others to explore topics of common interest.

5. *Add informational websites to your study of literature.* Informational sites extend content themes found in literature, promote inquiry, and encourage in-depth topic exploration.

The resources and instructional strategies included here are designed to promote the enjoyment of literature while developing the important skills, strategies, and dispositions required for success on the Internet. In the following sections, we explore useful online resources, share our own ideas, and showcase how exceptional teachers use the Internet in their classroom literacy programs.

Explore Stories on the Web

Reading is an adventure that extends the imagination and makes learning fun. Literature exposes children to new worlds filled with heroes, villains, new friends, and new possibilities. McEwan and Egan (1995) explained how stories provide opportunities to embark on explorations of experience from various perspectives. Great books offer opportunities for higher level thinking, character analysis, and rich discussions of the author's message. Stories on the Web build students' understanding of story structures and introduce new opportunities to develop online navigational skills. Connecting stories on the Web with opportunities to explore the Internet is a first step in developing positive dispositions toward technology.

Online Read-Alouds

Your students can enjoy exciting works of literature read aloud by actors such as Amanda Bynes, Lou Diamond Phillips, Tia and Tamera Mowery, and Melissa Gilbert in a project by the Screen Actors Guild Foundation. Visit BookPALS Storyline www.storylineonline.net, an online series of streaming videos where children of all ages can find and appreciate these wonderful stories. This site celebrates classic picture books such as *Knots on a Counting Rope* (Martin & Archambault, 1997), *Thank You, Mr. Falker* (Polacco, 1998), *The Polar Express* (Van Allsburg, 1985), and many others.

Children of all ages enjoy hearing stories read aloud. Books entertain, arouse curiosity, inform, and inspire new interests. Reading aloud to children has additional benefits, which include building listening skills, creating background knowledge, introducing new vocabulary, and making connections between text and life. Not only is reading aloud important for literacy development and learning, but also sharing a book is a bonding experience during which the reader serves as a reading role model for the listener (Trelease, 2001). The Screen Actors Guild Foundation recognizes this influence and capitalizes on it in the creation of the Storyline website (See Figure 1). This site makes read-aloud experiences accessible to students during the school day and also

Figure 1
Screen Shot of BookPALS Storyline Online

Note. **www.storylineonline.net.** Used with permission

at home. Storyline offers an open invitation to enjoy good books again and again as they are read and performed.

Interactive Read-Along Stories

The TumbleBook Library is an online collection of animated, talking picture books that kids really love. This collection of interactive, electronic texts can be accessed through participating public library sites such as the branch in Sunnyvale, California, http://sunnyvale.ca.gov/

Departments/Library/ebooks.htm or from the TumbleBook Library's main page at www .tumblebooks.com (see Figure 2). Don't miss out on these entertaining interactive stories.

Electronic texts such as these provide opportunities for learners to become familiar with stories in a new format. The Internet has made it possible to transform traditional oral and print stories by adding graphics, sound, animation, and video to create interactive texts. In Matthew's 1996 study (as cited in Chen,

Figure 2
**Screen Shot of *Coming Home: A Story of Josh Gibson* by Nanette Mellage,
From the TumbleBook Library's Collection**

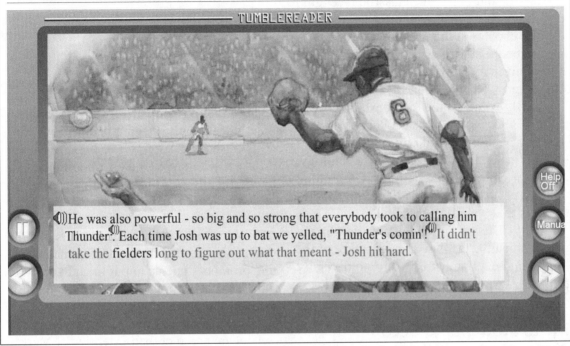

Note. Visit TumbleBooks at www.tumblebooks.com or the Sunnyvale Public Library site (http://sunnyvale.ca.gov/Departments/Library/ebook.htm) and follow the link to Tumblebook Library. Used with permission.

Ferdig, & Wood, 2003), electronic storybooks yielded higher reading comprehension for pairs of children who used them compared to those who read traditional print versions of the same story. Animated illustrations and high-quality voice-overs make stories on the Web not only engaging but also beneficial to emerging and struggling readers.

TumbleBooks offer digital features that foster strategies for decoding, fluency, and comprehension. For example, students can read along with the text's electronic voice to practice proper phrasing and fluency. As the voice reads, the text automatically changes color, helping the reader to track the words. The word-helper feature allows students to click on specific words to have them sounded out or spoken. All texts are available in three languages (English,

Spanish, and Chinese) for students who are acquiring English or building biliteracy skills.

The animated graphics and quality narratives at Mythic Journeys (http://mythicjourneys.org/bigmyth/index.htm) will engage your intermediate-grade students in online story adventures. Those in the primary grades will appreciate the Storybook Web www.ltscotland.org.uk/storybook and the read-along songs and stories on the RIF Reading Planet website at www.rif.org/readingplanet/content/read_aloud_stories.mspx. At these sites, students can listen to stories read aloud, play games, and learn about an author's writing process. These sites make great classroom center activities. By taking advantage of the wealth and variety of books available on the Internet, kids will never run out of stories to enjoy.

Storybooks on the Web

At a time when book budgets are limited, the Internet offers a wide variety of free texts to students in and out of the classroom. Digital texts encourage reading by offering a variety of book choices at the click of a button. The International Children's Digital Library (ICDL) at the University of Maryland (www.icdlbooks.org) offers 820 books online in nine languages. The ICDL examines the relationship between children's access to a digital collection of multicultural materials and children's attitudes toward books, libraries, reading, technology, and other countries and cultures. Combining the Internet with children's literature enables students to develop a richer understanding of the many different cultural experiences in the world, preparing them to take advantage of the important benefits that exposure to diversity provides (Leu, Castek, et al., 2004).

2. Invite Students to Become Authors on the Web

Digital Storytelling

A new literature experience is emerging on the Internet—the genre of the digital story. Some schools in Kentucky have found an innovative way for students to become online authors while learning 21st-century communication skills. Through digital storytelling, learners of all ages have proudly published their personal stories on the Web. The creation of personal narratives teaches students the writing process while instilling a sense of pride in their accomplishments. To create a digital story, students begin by writing. Once the narrative is constructed, illustrations are created, voice recordings are added, and digital photos are incorporated. The final product is published as a QuickTime movie that can be posted on the Internet. Digital storytelling turns each student into an instant biographer and published author. The Scott County Student Digital Storytelling site at www.scott.k12.ky.us/technology/digital storytelling/studentstories.html will provide you with many new ideas for bringing new literacies into your classroom. In addition to sparking interest in writing, this site is a great place for students to read and enjoy new online book forms. The digital storytelling site at http://electronicportfolios.com/digistory will guide you in learning how to begin teaching this unique literary genre.

Publishing Student Work

One of the most powerful ways of encouraging student involvement in Internet activities is to publish their responses to literature online. Many teachers have taken advantage of this powerful strategy to increase engagement in writing. Works such as poetry and art can be easily showcased on the Internet and made available to a wide audience of peers, families, and readers around the world. Internet publishing prompts students to put thought and effort into their assignments. Revising and editing become more palatable.

Third graders at one Kentucky elementary school are proud of their extension of Margaret Wise Brown's *The Important Book* (1990, Harper Trophy). They used this popular text as a model for their online story *The Important Book of Simple Machines* at www.montgomery.k12.ky.us/Camargo/Projects/simplemachines/simplemachines.htm. The various linked pages not only explain how simple machines work but also feature digital pictures of students demonstrating them. View the links on the left to learn about levers, inclined planes, wedges, screws, pulleys, and more. These third graders also collected follow-up activities and science labs to offer more opportunities for readers to explore simple machines. Publishing student work online encourages the writing process and provides a way for students to receive comments from readers other than their teacher.

Additional Resources

Scholastic's Writing With Writers http://teacher.scholastic.com/writewit and Children's Story Online www.childrenstory.com/stories/index.htm are useful resources students will enjoy. Both sites get them thinking and working with other student authors around the world. Through participation, students learn to make connections between reading and writing that deepen their appreciation of the author's craft. As students share their stories and other writings on the Internet, they are bound to develop increasingly positive dispositions for contributing to the body of information the Web contains.

Participate in Virtual Book Clubs

Virtual book clubs are forums set up for students to exchange ideas on discussion boards. Here, students write to a wide audience about the books that are important to them. Keeping in touch with others near and far through e-mail exchanges encourages new literacy opportunities and introduces students to today's ICTs. Sending messages around the world helps students develop reading, writing, and communication skills that are an important part of their daily lives. Such communication also enriches cultural understanding by teaching students to appreciate diverse points of view.

E-mail Discussion Boards

The ePals Book Club (www.epals.com/projects/book_club) provides a discussion forum for students to post comments, questions, and perspectives on their favorite books. Some teachers shy away from class e-mails because they do not have "control" of what is being said and sent. ePals addresses that concern by offering free accounts that can be easily monitored by the teacher. Discussion posts can be exchanged class to class or student to student. (See the ePals teacher project site for directions on how to pair up with a partner class.)

Book Raps (http://rite.ed.qut.edu.au/old_oz-teachernet/projects/book-rap/index1.html), based in Australia, is a do-not-miss site for those looking to participate in online book discussions conducted via e-mail. Individuals or groups of students from across Australia and around the world are invited to discuss the scheduled books offered on this site.

The Spaghetti Book Club at www.spaghettibookclub.com is a discussion forum set up like a clubhouse. Here, students or classes can post book reviews, comment on what they are reading, and exchange ideas about their favorite books. Provocative questions raised in posts spark ideas that promote text analysis and encourage students to think critically.

Online Book Reviews

The Germantown Academy Super Readers at www.germantownacademy.net/Library/InfoManage/Guide.asp?FolderID=2835 have posted over 1,000 book reviews online. Their student-friendly site aims to help children everywhere make great reading choices. Here, your students can find honest appraisals of books, written *by* kids *for* kids. This amazing online collection speaks to the power of what can be accomplished when a community of highly engaged readers and writers uses the Internet to encourage an appreciation of literature.

Scholastic's Share What You're Reading site (http://teacher.scholastic.com/activities/swyar) makes crafting book reviews fun. Organized by genre and grade level, the site provides easy-to-use tools for students to find books of interest to them. Students can also go to the "write a review" part of the site to tell others about a book they liked. Those who need writing support can follow the link for tips on how to write quality book reviews. For additional reading suggestions, take a look at the link to today's popular books and authors.

Literature Extension Projects

Literature extension projects are a great place to gather new ideas. Visit www.redmond.k12.or.us/patrick/renz/bookprojects.htm to see some examples. These literature extensions offer excellent alternatives to book reports. Heather Renz designed the extension projects and posted student examples that demonstrate the many ways children can creatively appreciate literature. An extension project friendly to readers in primary grades can be found at

First Grade, First Grade What Do You See? (www.district87.org/oakland/brownbear). This site highlights the reading enthusiasm experienced with Bill Martin, Jr.'s book *Brown Bear, Brown Bear, What Do You See?* (1992, Holt, Rinehart and Winston). The excitement can hardly be contained on these webpages.

Teaching students how to read and write on the Internet helps strengthen traditional literacy skills while also introducing new elements that are unique to online communication (Castek, 2004a). Writing succinctly in the rapid back-and-forth manner common to online exchanges can be difficult for even the most proficient writer, yet these skills are essential for success in today's collaborative workplaces. Reading and writing e-mail, for example, increases the speed at which ideas can be shared and widely disseminated. Teaching students how to communicate online exposes them to language constructs and etiquette common to the Web (Castek, 2004b).

4 Collaborate on Internet Projects

Internet projects are partnerships between classes in different locations formed to solve a common problem or explore a common topic. Participating in Internet projects helps children acquire the collaborative problem-solving, information, and communication skills they will use when they enter the world of work (Leu, 2001; Leu, Leu, & Coiro, 2004).

Preservice Teacher/Student Collaborations

Many successful Internet projects have taken place around the celebration of great books. A Series of Unfortunate Collaborations at http://comsewogue.org/~ssilverman/snicket paired graduate and middle school students to exchange ideas about Lemony Snicket's *The Bad Beginning* (1999, HarperCollins). Visit the online resources for activities that extend the first book in the Series of Unfortunate Events collection.

Class-to-Class Collaborations

First- and second-grade classes used *The Important Book* (Brown, 1990, HarperTrophy) as a model for their My Town Is Important project www.mrsmcgowan.com/town/about2003.htm. Participating classes around the world described what was important about their town by researching facts on the Internet. Visit the student showcase link and click on the individual states and counties to see the variety of ways students extended Brown's classic text. Locating projects and classes to collaborate with is as easy as checking out the following three links.

1. Kidlink—Hooked on books http://65.42.153.210/kidspace/start.cfm?HoldNode=898

2. Internet projects—Student-to-student and class-to-class exchanges www.schoolworld.asn.au/projects.html

3. E-pals Internet projects www.epals.com/resources/online/internet_projects.tpl

5 Incorporate Informational Websites With Your Study of Literature

The Internet transports readers to new places to investigate firsthand accounts, primary source documents, and other resources. Informational websites do a great job of extending themes found in literature and help readers make connections to new content. Many sites for children not only offer text but also feature images, videos, animations, and sound files. Depending on the content being investigated, the possibilities are infinite.

Pairing Texts With Informational Websites

Texts and Internet companion pieces connect information resources that enhance the entire reading experience. Take, for example, the How I Spent My Summer Vacation site at www.montgomery.k12.ky.us/Camargo/students/reading/series/vacation.htm. This resource helps students learn Wild West vocabulary introduced in Mark Teague's imaginative story *How I Spent My Summer Vacation* (1997, Dragonfly Books). Designed with a third-grade reader in mind, this site features informational links to cowboy and rodeo history as well as facts about buckaroos and the geography of the plains of the western United States. As Wallace, the main character in the text, describes being captured by cowboys who teach him all their tricks, we picture ourselves being transported, through sound and photo displays accessed from this website, to a ranch where cowboys wrangle their herds. The Internet offers new resources that help us to capitalize on the rich content connections that can be made with this book while also inviting further reading. Links to the National Cowboy & Western Heritage Museum site at www.nationalcowboymuseum .org and the America's Story Buckaroo site at www.americaslibrary.gov/cgi-bin/page.cgi/sh/ cowboy inspire students to question, inquire, and explore.

Explore the website Midnight Rider: A Paul Revere Virtual Museum at www.cvesd.k12 .ca.us/finney/paulvm/_welcomepv.html before reading *The Midnight Ride of Paul Revere* (Longfellow, 2001, Handprint Books). This book (see Figure 3) celebrates Henry Wadsworth Longfellow's epic poem with engravings and original paintings by Christopher Bing. The text is factual, explaining what is correct and

---

Figure 3
Book Cover, *The Midnight Ride of Paul Revere* by Henry Wadsworth Longfellow,
Engraved and Illustrated by Christopher Bing

Note. Used with permission.

incorrect about the classic poem. Its visual display of artifacts and illustrations makes it a standout among children's literature favorites. The text incorporates letters recounting the midnight ride, and the other artifacts help readers imagine life in Paul Revere's time. After exploring, readers walk away with a better understanding of the events as they happened. While the Internet site provides the historical context of this important period in U.S. history, the text provides opportunities for teaching a critical stance.

Bringing literature to life in the classroom inspires further independent reading and information gathering. To this end, the Internet is the perfect place to turn. By pairing Internet and text reading, students are invited to make connections between topics. For more examples of these kinds of connections, see Table 1.

A sixth-grade teacher in Duluth, Minnesota, used the comprehensive instructional resources on Web Inquiry Projects by San Diego State University (http://edweb.sdsu.edu/wip) to help students design their own Western Immigration inquiries (http://edweb.sdsu.edu/wip/examples/westward/index.htm). She paired this project with *Children of the Dust Bowl: The True Story of the School at Weedpatch Camp* by Jerry Stanley (1992, Knopf Books for Young Readers). This book tells of the formidable hardships of the "Okies" as they worked their way to California during the 1930s. Through moving descriptions and firsthand accounts, readers feel the desperation the Okies faced in the Midwest. Hardships continued as they journeyed westward toward the promise of work in California, where eventually their hopes were dashed. The sixth-grade teacher uses the Dust Bowl Days resource guide at http://edsitement .neh.gov/view_lesson_plan.asp?id=300, a portal developed by the MarcoPolo Foundation, to bring to life primary source documents such as photographs, song lyrics, and firsthand accounts. Using these incredible resources, students can extend their personal inquiries in a new direction.

Scholastic's Flashlight Readers page at http://teacher.scholastic.com/activities/flashlight readers/flashT_landingPage.asp contains a Great Depression Historical Journal companion for *Esperanza Rising* by Pam Muñoz-Ryan (2002, Blue Sky Press). This book describes a Mexican girl's fall from riches and her immigration to California in the 1930s. The Flashlight Readers website provides interactive features

---

Table 1
A Listing of Children's Literature Books That Can Form Units in Conjunction With the Titles Listed in the Article

Good Books for a Unit on the Depression
Booth, D. (1997). *The dust bowl.* Toronto, ON: Kids Can Press. ISBN 1550742957.
Koller, J.F. (1991). *Nothing to fear.* New York: Gulliver. ISBN 0152575820.
Peck, R. (2000). *A year down yonder.* New York: Dial. ISBN 0803725183.
Ray, D. (2003). *Ghost girl: A Blue Ridge mountain story.* New York: Clarion. ISBN 0618333770.
Stewart, S. (1997). *The gardener.* New York: Farrar Straus Giroux. ISBN 0374325170.
Taylor, M. (1991). *Roll of thunder, hear my cry.* New York: Puffin. ISBN 014034893X.
Turner, A. (1995). *Dust for dinner.* New York: HarperCollins. ISBN 0060233761.

Good Books for a Unit on Summer Vacation
Brashares, A. (2001). *The sisterhood of the traveling pants.* New York: Delacorte Books for Young Readers. ISBN 0385730586.
Martinez, A. (2004). *Poe Park.* New York: Holiday House. ISBN 0823418340.
Paulsen, G. (1994). *Harris and me: A summer remembered.* Orlando, FL: Harcourt. ISBN 0152928774.
Rawls, W. (1976). *Summer of the monkeys.* New York: Yearling. ISBN 0440415802.
Rylant, C. (1985). *The relatives came.* New York: Aladdin. ISBN 0689717385.

Good Books for a Unit on the Wild West
Davis, K.C. (2003). *Don't know much about the pioneers.* New York: HarperCollins. ISBN 0060286172.
Freedman, R. (1983). *Children of the Wild West.* Clarion Books. ISBN 0395547857.
Hopkins, B. (2000). *My America: A poetry atlas of the United States.* New York: Simon & Schuster. ISBN 0689812477.
Pinkney, A.D. (1996). *Bill Pickett: Rodeo-ridin' cowboy.* Orlando, FL: Voyager Books. ISBN 0152021035.

that connect readers to valuable resources that extend students' background knowledge.

Online Encyclopedias

The Internet offers quick access to large amounts of new information. *E-encyclopedia* (2003, Dorling Kindersley) is a powerful resource for teaching students how to search for information on the Internet. This book, together with the companion website www.dke -encyc.com, capitalizes on the features of a traditional encyclopedia while also offering access to animations, videos, sound buttons, virtual tours, interactive quizzes, data-bases, timelines, and real-time reports. Created in partnership with Google (www.google.com), the e-encyclopedia teaches students how to avoid the pitfalls of inaccurate information. By being guided to the most appropriate sites, students gain easy access to the best information resources the Web has to offer. Grouped thematically in nine subject areas, topics of interest are easy for students to locate.

Articles in the book explain key facts and also display a keyword to input on the companion website. What results are a handful of student-friendly sites that provide additional information on a topic. For example, inputting the keyword *space* from page 10 in the book yields the following results:

- How big is space,
- A history of space exploration,
- Satellite photographs of stars, planets, and galaxies,
- An astronomy timeline and related links you might find useful.

The site also has a sidebar that provides search tips for using Google.

The book and companion site offer exciting new resources for finding information while supporting the development of searching skills. Teachers can use these resources to help students more easily navigate the best sites on the Web and in the process learn how search engines work. This great resource has many pluses, but it also has one drawback: Students can only use keywords printed in the book to search on the website for the specially selected links. Nevertheless, the broad topic areas on the site link students to many topics to explore. This type of supportive e-encyclopedia is a useful resource for students and teachers alike.

Continuing the Adventure

Deion, the fifth grader introduced at the beginning of this column, composes his message and considers the worldwide audience that it will reach. He applies the e-mail writing strategies his teacher has taught in class to craft a concise message that conveys his ideas clearly. He carefully reads and reorganizes his thoughts before posting them on the discussion board. As his teacher observes Deion composing his response, she thinks about how interdependent the processes of reading and writing are on the Internet. As readers and writers exchange information, they are simultaneously reading and writing as their online conversations unfold. She takes a few notes in preparation for a think-aloud lesson she'll introduce tomorrow and marks several posts on the ePals Book Club website www.epals.com/tools/forum/ forum.e?bo=53 to point to as examples of effective online communication.

> Subject: Re:Harry Potter & the Half-Blood Prince, USA
>
> Greetings Harry Potter Fans,
> I'm eagerly waiting for the next book in the series, for which I have many expectations. In the next adventure, I believe Professor Minerva McGonagall will become headmistress of Hogwarts School, if it opens again.
> Hope to hear back from anyone else with views on this message,
>
> Deion

Like Deion, you will discover new tools and learn important new skills and strategies as you journey through the Internet. Building the Internet into your classroom literacy program makes learning enjoyable. Create opportunities for students to explore stories on the Web, participate in virtual book clubs, collaborate on

Children's Books That Mirror Techno Texts

Bette Goldstone

"Think left and think right/and think low and think high," wrote Dr. Seuss in *Oh, The THINKS You Can Think* (first published in 1975). This is very wise advice for comprehending digital text and images, for traditional book comprehension skills are only a part of the skills repertoire today's students need. Literacy in hyperspace also requires understanding nonlinear text structure, taking on responsibilities of coauthoring—deciding what will be read, and in what order, and visually understanding the multiple screens (or spatial planes) and their interconnections. These literacy characteristics are not, however, solely relegated to screen-based texts. A form of children's book that has been emerging since the 1970s also uses these patterns. Sometimes called "postmodern," these books—which are becoming more prevalent each day—are nonlinear, require involved coauthoring on the part of the reader, and may have multiple spatial planes in the illustrations. Our students have to approach "technology text" and "postmodern text" thinking and viewing from high and low, right and left. They need to use skills that make them adept at being active coauthors and at maneuvering nonlinear texts and multiple spatial planes.

Explicit teaching, however, must occur. Every student is not necessarily comfortable or initially capable of using the latitude nonlinear texts offer. Deciding what to read on the page or screen, and in what sequence, and how to comprehend the seemingly disparate elements can be very confusing. Postmodern books can become a teaching tool to make transparent the needed thinking skills. Reading aloud a storybook quickly creates a shared experience and sense of community—computer use can be isolating. Books don't evaporate in cyberspace like some hyperlinks or websites—they are concrete, so they can easily be referred to again and again. Reading aloud books and investigating pictures as a group takes time—book time is slower than computer time and is thus easier to think about and reflect upon. These books also provide another venue for students to reshape, extrapolate, and apply important comprehension skills. Practicing skills in multiple contexts enhances and intensifies the learning experience.

Books with multiple story lines (told through words or illustrations) are excellent for understanding nonlinearity. The following are examples of such books:

- Burningham, J. (1978). *Time to get out of the bath, Shirley*. Ill. by the author. New York: Crowell.
- Browne, A. (1992). Zoo. Ill. by the author. New York: Knopf.
- Cherry, L. (1996). *The armadillo from Amarillo*. Ill. by the author. San Diego, CA: Harcourt Brace.
- Martin, J.B. (1999). *Snowflake Bentley*. Ill. M. Azarian. New York: Scholastic.
- Oppenheim, J. (1994). *Floratorium*. Ill. S. Schindler. New York: Bantam.
- Macauley, D. (1999). *Shortcut*. Ill. by the author. New York: Houghton Mifflin.
- Pullman, P. (1989). *Spring-heeled Jack*. Ill. D. Mostyn. New York: Knopf.
- Sís, P. (1996). *Starry messenger*. Ill. by the author. New York: HarperCollins.

Books that contain multiple voices, like multiple story lines, also provide greater insights and sensitivity to nonlinear texts. These also require coauthoring from the reader because connections are not explicitly apparent. The following are examples of these:

- Atkin, S.B. (2001). *Voices from the fields: Children of migrant farmworkers tell their stories*. Ill. with photos. New York: Scholastic.
- Avi. (1993). *Nothing but the truth: A documentary novel*. New York: Morrow/Avon.
- Browne, A. (1998). *Voices in the park*. Ill. by the author. New York: Dorling Kindersley.
- Creech, S. (2000). *The wanderer*. New York: Scholastic.
- Danzinger, P., & Martin, A.H. (2000). *Snail mail no more*. New York: Scholastic.
- Goldschmidt, J. (2005). *The secret blog of Raisin Rodriguez*. New York: Penguin.
- Hesse, K. (2001). *Witness*. New York: Scholastic.
- Konigsburg, E.L. (1999). The view from Saturday. New York: Scholastic.
- Sís, P. (2000). *Madlenka*. Ill. by the author. New York: Frances Foster.

Modern illustrators have been playing with multiple spatial plans, which make intriguing images and allow for interesting explorations of space and time. The following are examples of these:

- Banyai, I. (1995). *Zoom*. Ill. by the author. New York: Viking.
- Lehman, B. (2004). *The red book*. Ill. by the author. Boston: Houghton Mifflin.
- Lyon, G.E. (1996). *A day at Damp Camp*. Ill. P. Catalanotto. New York: Orchard.
- Raschka, C. (1997). *Mysterious Thelonious*. Ill. by the author. New York. Orchard.
- Rathmann, P. (1995). *Officer Buckle and Gloria*. Ill. by the author. New York: Putman.
- Sneed, B. (2002). *Picture a letter*. Ill. by the author. New York: Fogelman.
- Wiesner, D. (2001). *The three pigs*. Ill. by the author. New York: Scholastic.
- Yorinks, A. (1986). *Hey, Al*. Ill. R. Egielski. New York: Farrar Straus Giroux.

Nontraditional postmodern children's books allow students to practice necessary comprehension skills. More important, they offer exciting new investigations into literary formats that resemble technology text but are unique unto themselves. They demonstrate that story structure is flexible and dynamic and that, similar to digital text, it will continue to be reconfigured and reimagined in the future.

Internet projects, design responses to literature, and learn from informational websites. When students are involved in Internet use for learning in class, they have special opportunities to acquire other new literacies as well. While traditional literacy skills continue to be a necessary foundation for students, the new literacies required for Internet use must also be taught if we intend to teach students to read, write, and communicate online effectively (Garner & Gillingham, 1996; Leu, Leu, & Coiro, 2004; Tao & Reinking, 2000). As students take advantage of these online opportunities, positive dispositions will develop toward technology, fostering motivation, engagement, and a lifelong love of reading. As we begin to use the Internet for teaching and learning, we open the door for students to acquire new literacies for reading, writing, communicating, and collaborating online. These skills increase opportunities for all students to participate in a growing high-tech workforce. We are instrumental in helping our students to develop the new skills and strategies that are important to learning now and essential for participation in an information-centered world. At the same time, we make great strides in helping *all* students become fully literate.

References

Becker, H.J. (2000). Pedagogical motivations for student computer use that lead to student engagement. *Educational Technology, 40*(5), 5–17. Retrieved October 2, 2005, from http://www.crito.uci.edu/tlc/findings/spec_rpt_pedagogical/ped_mot_pdf.pdf

Castek, J. (2004, October). *Writing across time and space: New literacies and online communication.* Iowa Technology and Education Connection Conference, Des Moines, IA.

Castek, J. (2004, November). *Internet applications for writing: Composing, communicating, and publishing in online contexts.* Connecticut Reading Association Conference, Cromwell, CT.

Chen, M., Ferdig, R., & Wood, A. (2003). Understanding technology-enhanced storybooks and their roles in teaching and learning: An investigation of electronic storybooks in education. *The Journal of Literacy and Technology, 3.* Retrieved September 28, 2005, from http://www.literacyandtechnology.org/v3n1/chenferdigwood.htm

Coiro, J. (2003a). Rethinking comprehension strategies to better prepare students for critically evaluating content on the Internet. *The NERA Journal, 39*(2), 29–34.

Coiro, J. (2003b). Reading comprehension on the Internet: Expanding our understanding of reading comprehension to encompass new literacies [Exploring Literacy on the Internet department]. *The Reading Teacher, 56,* 458–464. Retrieved November 1, 2005, from http://www.readingonline.org/electronic/elec_index.asp?HREF=/electronic/rt/2-03_Column/index.html

Coiro, J. (2005). Making sense of online text. *Educational Leadership, 63*(2), 30–35.

Garner, R., & Gillingham, M.G. (1996). *Internet communication in six classrooms: Conversations across time, space and culture.* Mahwah, NJ: Erlbaum.

Gee, J.P. (2000). Teenagers in new times: A new literacy studies perspective. *Journal of Adolescent & Adult Literacy, 43,* 412–420.

Guthrie, J.T., & Wigfield, A. (2000). Engagement and motivation in reading. In M.L. Kamil, P.B. Mosenthal, P.D. Pearson, & R. Barr (Eds.), *Handbook of reading research* (Vol. 3, pp. 403–422). Mahwah, NJ: Erlbaum.

Hartman, D., Fogarty, E., Coiro, J., Leu, D.J., Jr., Castek, J., & Henry, L.A. (2005, December). *New literacies for learning.* Symposium presented at the 55th annual meeting of the National Reading Conference, Miami, FL.

Henry, L.A. (2006). SEARCHing for an answer: The critical role of new literacies while reading on the Internet. *The Reading Teacher, 59.*

International ICT Literacy Panel. (2003). *Digital transformation: A framework for ICT literacy.* Princeton, NJ: Educational Testing Service. Retrieved December 15, 2004, from http://www.ets.org/Media/Research/pdf/ICTREPORT.pdf

International Reading Association. (2001). *Integrating literacy and technology in the curriculum* (Position statement). Retrieved December 12, 2005, from http://www.reading.org/downloads/positions/ps1048_technology.pdf

Katz, L.G. (1988, Summer). What should young children be doing? *American Educator,* 28–45.

Lankshear, C., & Knobel, M. (2003). *New literacies: Changing knowledge in the classroom.* Buckingham, England: Open University Press.

Lebo, H. (2004). *Surveying the digital future, year four: Ten years ten trends.* Los Angeles: UCLA Center for Communication Policy. Retrieved November 1, 2005, from http://www.digitalcenter.org/downloads/DigitalFutureReport-Year4-2004.pdf

Lenhart, A., Madden, M., & Hitlin, P. (2005). *Teens and technology.* Washington, DC: Pew Internet and American Life Project. Retrieved November 2, 2005, from http://www.pewinternet.org/pdfs/PIP_Teens_Tech_July2005web.pdf

Leu, D.J., Jr. (2001). Internet project: Preparing students for new literacies in a global village. *The Reading Teacher, 54,* 568–585. Retrieved November 2, 2005, from http://www.readingonline.org/electronic/elec_index.asp?HREF=/electronic/RT/3-01_Column/index.html

Leu, D.J., Jr. (2002). The new literacies: Research on reading instruction with the Internet. In A.E. Farstrup & S.J. Samuels (Eds.), *What research has to say about reading instruction* (3rd. ed., pp. 310–336). Newark, DE: International Reading Association.

Leu, D.J., Jr., Castek, J., Henry, L., Coiro, J., & McMullan, M. (2004). The lessons that children teach us: Integrating children's literature and the new literacies of the Internet. *The Reading Teacher, 57,* 496–503.

Leu, D.J., Jr., Kinzer, C.K., Coiro, J., & Cammack, D. (2004). Toward a theory of new literacies emerging from the Internet and other information and communication technologies. In R.B. Ruddell & N. Unrau (Eds.), *Theoretical models and processes of reading,* (5th ed., 1570–1613). Newark, DE: International Reading Association. Retrieved November 2, 2005, from http://www.readingonline.org/newliteracies/lit_index .asp?HREF=/newliteracies/leu

Leu, D.J. Jr., Leu, D.D., Coiro, J. (2004). *Teaching with the Internet: New literacies for new times* (4th ed.) Norwood, MA: Christopher Gordon.

McEwan, H., & Egan, K. (Eds.). (1995). *Narrative in teaching, learning, and research.* New York: Teachers College Press.

No Child Left Behind Act of 2001, Pub. L. No. 107-110, 115 Stat 1425 (2002). Retrieved October 1, 2005, from http:// www.ed.gov/nclb/overview/intro/index.html

Noyes, D. (2004). Developing the disposition to be a reader: The educator's role. In D. Rothenburg (Ed.), *Issues in early childhood education: Curriculum, teacher education and the dissemination of information.* Proceedings of the Lillian Katz Symposium, November 5–7, 2000 (pp. 313–317). Retrieved October 2, 2005, from http:// ceep.crc.uiuc.edu/pubs/katzsym/noyes.html

Organisation for Economic Co-operation and Development. (2005). *Learning a living: First results of the adult literacy and life skills survey.* Ottawa, ON: Statistics Canada; Paris: Author.

Partnership for 21st Century Skills. (2004). *Learning for the 21st century.* Washington, DC: Author. Retrieved December 12, 2005, from www.21stcenturyskills.org/ reports/learning.asp

Rainee, L., & Hilton, P. (2005). *The Internet at school.* Washington, DC: Pew Internet & American Life Project. Retrieved September 15, 2005, from http://www.pew internet.org/pdfs/PIP_Internet_and_schools_05.pdf

Street, B. (2003). What's "new" in New Literacy Studies? Critical approaches to literacy in theory and practice. *Current Issues in Comparative Education, 5*(2). Retrieved October 2, 2005, from http://www .tc.columbia.edu/cice/articles/bs152.htm

Tao, L., & Reinking, D. (2000). Issues in technology: E-mail and literacy education. *Reading and Writing Quarterly, 16,* 169–174.

Trelease, J. (2001). *The read-aloud handbook* (5th ed.). New York: Penguin.

U.S. Department of Commerce, Economics and Statistics Administration, National Telecommunications and Information Administration. (2002). *A nation online: How Americans are expanding their use of the Internet.* Washington, DC: Authors. Retrieved November 3, 2005, from http://www.ntia.doc.gov/ntiahome/dn/anation online2.pdf

Children's Books Cited

Brown, M.W. (1990). *The important book.* Ill. L. Weisgard. New York: HarperTrophy. ISBN 0064432270.

E-encyclopedia (2003). New York: Dorling Kindersley. ISBN 0789498693.

Longfellow, H.W. (2001). *The midnight ride of Paul Revere.* Ill. C. Bing. New York: Handprint. ISBN 1929766130.

Martin, B., Jr. (1992). *Brown bear, brown bear, what do you see?* Ill. E. Carle. New York: Holt, Rinehart and Winston. ISBN 0805017445.

Martin, B., Jr, & Archambault, J. (1997). *Knots on a counting rope.* Ill. T. Rand. New York: Henry Holt. ISBN 0805054790.

Muñoz-Ryan, P. (2002). *Esperanza rising.* New York: Blue Sky Press. ISBN 043912042X.

Polacco, P. (1998). *Thank you, Mr. Falker.* New York: Philomel. ISBN 0399231668.

Rowling, J.K. (2005). *Harry Potter and the Half-Blood Prince.* New York: Scholastic. ISBN 0439784549.

Snicket, L. (1999). *The bad beginning.* New York: HarperCollins. ISBN 0064407667.

Stanley, J. (1993). *Children of the dust bowl: The true story of the school at Weedpatch Camp.* New York: Knopf Books for Young Readers. ISBN 0517880946.

Teague, M. (1997). *How I spent my summer vacation.* New York: Dragonfly Books. ISBN 0517885565.

Van Allsburg, C. (1985). *The Polar Express.* New York: Houghton Mifflin. ISBN 0395389496.

Assessment and Evaluation

The Assessment and Evaluation Standard recognizes the need to prepare teachers to use a variety of assessment tools and practices for planning and evaluating effective reading and writing instruction. The elements featured in the Assessment and Evaluation Standard relate to the systematic monitoring of student performance at individual, classroom, school, and systemwide levels. Teacher educators who specialize in literacy play a critical role in preparing teachers for multifaceted assessment responsibilities. Standard 3 and its elements follow:

> **Standard 3. Assessment and Evaluation. Candidates use a variety of assessment tools and practices to plan and evaluate effective reading and writing instruction. As a result, candidates**
>
> • **Element 3.1 Understand types of assessments and their purposes, strengths, and limitations.**
>
> • **Element 3.2 Select, develop, administer, and interpret assessments, both traditional print and online, for specific purposes.**
>
> • **Element 3.3 Use assessment information to plan and evaluate instruction.**
>
> • **Element 3.4 Communicate assessment results and implications to a variety of audiences.**

Part 3 includes five journal articles that may be helpful in understanding the substance of the standard and its elements. These pieces are briefly described here.

Applegate, Applegate, McGeehan, Pinto, and Kong (2009) address the discrepancy between the results of National Assessment of Educational Progress (NAEP) reading assessments and the widely reported state assessments. Specifically, they compare assessment approaches in NAEP to the approaches in a sample of state tests. The results of this study suggest that not all tests of reading are created equal. More important, their findings suggest that NAEP is more congruent with the widely accepted definition of mature reading comprehension and, therefore, is likely to distinguish among advanced, proficient, and basic readers far more effectively than the state tests in their sample. Johnston and Costello (2005) offer a framework for understanding literacy assessment that incorporates the relational aspects of assessment. They argue that assessment is a social practice and indicate that considering only *what*

Preparing Reading Professionals (second edition), edited by Rita M. Bean, Natalie Heisey, and Cathy M. Roller. © 2010 by the International Reading Association.

gets assessed is not enough—*how* it gets assessed has implications for student learning. This notion has important implications for assessment practices in schools. Both of these articles provide useful information about assessment, its purposes, strengths and limitations; further they contribute to the scholarly dialogue about assessment (Element 3.1).

Valencia and Buly (2005) describe performance patterns of students who failed a typical fourth-grade state reading test. Drawing on results from an empirical study conducted by the authors, this article provide profiles of six prototypical readers and suggestions for appropriate instruction to meet students' needs. This article is helpful in understanding how to interpret assessment results and use that information to plan instruction (Elements 3.2 and 3.3).

Lenski, Ehlers-Zavala, Daniel, and Sun-Irminger (2006) provide practical suggestions for assessing English-language learners (ELLs) in the classroom context. They describe the importance of recognizing the varied groups of students identified as ELLs. The authors also discuss setting a purpose for assessment and making decisions of how to assess this growing population of students. This article aids in recognizing fair and equitable assessment procedures as outlined in Element 3.2. In addition, this article elaborates on the need to learn how to communicate assessment results, specifically by collaborating with students (Element 3.4).

Mokhtari, Rosemary, and Edwards (2007) propose a Data Analysis Framework for Instructional Decision Making as a practical tool for schoolwide implementation. They suggest applying the framework in pre-K–12 settings, using a team approach in making sense of assessment data. Their ideas are useful in understanding assessment data and using it to plan instruction (Element 3.3) and in recognizing the importance of communicating assessment data within the school community (Element 3.4).

Further Reading

Afflerbach, P. (2007). *Understanding and using reading assessment, K–12*. Newark, DE: International Reading Association.

Edwards, P.A., Turner, J.D., & Mokhtari, K. (2008). Balancing the assessment *of* learning and *for* learning in support of student literacy achievement. *The Reading Teacher, 61*(8), 682–684. doi:10.1598/RT.61.8.12

McKenna, M.C., & Walpole, S. (2005). How well does assessment inform our reading instruction? *The Reading Teacher, 59*(1), 84–86. doi:10.1598/RT.59.1.9

Pearson, P.D., Hiebert, E.H., & Kamil, M.L. (2007). Vocabulary assessment: What we know and what we need to learn. *Reading Research Quarterly, 42*(2), 282–296. doi:10.1598/RRQ.42.2.4

Questions for Reflection and Discussion

- What are some of the purposes for assessing students? What defines an authentic assessment? What are some potential limitations to assessments that warrant caution?

- What considerations need to be made when determining what type of assessment best meets the intended purpose? How does the type of assessment and the manner in which it was administered affect the interpretation of its results?

- In what ways can assessment data inform instructional decisions? Which types of assessment data are more useful for planning instruction?

- What factors need to be considered in sharing assessment data? How does the target audience affect the way reading professionals communicate these results?

The Assessment of Thoughtful Literacy in NAEP: Why the States Aren't Measuring Up

Anthony J. Applegate, Mary DeKonty Applegate, Catherine M. McGeehan,
Catherine M. Pinto, and Ailing Kong

The widespread publicity in the United States surrounding the "reading wars" that date back to the 1960s served to obscure one clear fact: When it comes to a definition of the nature of mature reading (the ultimate goal of all reading instruction), there is a remarkable level of agreement. This agreement exists among proponents of opposing philosophical camps; among reading theorists from the 19th, 20th, and 21st centuries; and among assessment specialists charged with measuring reading achievement at state, national, and international levels. The essence of the agreement is this: Mature reading involves thoughtful literacy—an ability to link the text with one's existing knowledge to arrive at a considered and logical response.

When Thorndike (1917) issued his oft-quoted comparison of reading to the act of human thinking, he had already been preceded in that line of reasoning by Huey (1908). Anderson (1984) cautioned his readers not to imagine that there is a simple, literal level of comprehension that does not require the reader to access a schema from world experience. When Goodman, Watson, and Burke (1996) described reading as an intellectually active process of creating meaning based on one's own experiences, Chall (1996) concurred, claiming that at all stages of development, reading depends upon full engagement with the text—its content, ideas, and values (p. 12). Even the National Reading Panel (National Institute of Child Health and Human Development, 2000) weighed in with their claim that comprehension requires that readers use knowledge of the world to make meaning of the text. In short, nowhere in the literature could we find a theorist or practitioner who would define mature reading as the ability to reproduce the message encoded in the text without also responding thoughtfully to it.

Our examination of all 50 U.S. state instructional frameworks and the specifications upon which the state assessments are based was equally unanimous and unequivocal. Specifications ranged from the "deep discussion and questioning" required in Alabama (Alabama Reading Initiative, 2001) to the ability "to use comprehension strategies to enhance understanding, to make predictions, and to respond to literature" in Tennessee (Tennessee Department of Education, 2007). No state defined reading solely as the ability to extract information from text. All state assessments expect at least some level of thoughtful response on the part of the reader.

It should come as no surprise that the National Assessment of Educational Progress (NAEP) Framework focuses on similar dimensions of reading. The 2007 NAEP Framework defined reading as including the ability

Preparing Reading Professionals (second edition), edited by Rita M. Bean, Natalie Heisey, and Cathy M. Roller. © 2010 by the International Reading Association. Reprinted from Applegate, A.J., Applegate, M.D., McGeehan, C.M., Pinto, C.M., & Kong, A. (2009). The assessment of thoughtful literacy in NAEP: Why the states aren't measuring up. *The Reading Teacher, 62*(5), 372–381. doi:10.1598/RT.62.5.1.

to develop a more complete understanding of what is read, to connect information in the text with knowledge and experience, and to examine content by critically evaluating, comparing and contrasting, and understanding the effect of such features as irony, humor, and organization. (National Assessment Governing Board, 2006)

At the international level, the Progress in International Reading Literacy Study (PIRLS) assesses the ability to make inferences about ideas not explicitly stated, to interpret and integrate ideas, and to examine and evaluate content, language, and textual elements (Mullis, Kennedy, Martin, & Sainsbury, 2006).

The Ideal and the Real

The scope and unanimity of this agreement on the nature of mature reading offers reading educators an unprecedented opportunity to gear our instruction to the achievement of these goals. But a wide variety of researchers have found anything but a united front on how we approach the development of thoughtful literacy. For the most part they have observed classrooms that do not engage readers in thinking and responding to a text, but rather in memorizing and reciting its details (Allington, 2001; Brown, 1991; Elmore, Peterson, & McCarthey, 1996; Knapp, 1995; Tharp & Gallimore, 1989). What these researchers have observed seems at first glance to be nothing more than an instance of the educational community saying one thing and doing something completely different—a thorough disconnect between the ideal and the real.

One possible explanation for this seeming disconnect in the nation's literacy classrooms was put forth by Black and Wiliam (1998), who suggested that many teachers emphasize literal recall because they assume that they are preparing their students to perform well on accountability measures. This is an intriguing hypothesis and in fact state reading test results seem to support the thinking of the teachers. Well-publicized reports of assessment data suggest that a large proportion of students in a great number of states have achieved reading proficiency. The problem is that results from NAEP are not following suit. The state–NAEP comparisons for 2005 reveal that states reported a level of proficiency at a startling average rate of 40% higher than that found on NAEP (Wallis & Steptoe, 2007). In the face of what appear to be inflated levels of achievement on state tests, it is tempting to simply conclude that the state tests have "lowered the bar" in the face of demands stemming from the No Child Left Behind Act (Thomas B. Fordham Foundation, 2005).

We wondered whether the differences between state tests and NAEP ran deeper. The assumption that reading tests are roughly equivalent because they ask a reader to respond to questions about text is one that deserves closer examination. Furthermore, the issue of NAEP–state test equivalency has profound implications for the way that the U.S. educational community interprets its sometimes conflicting assessment data and uses those data as guides for future instruction. We set out to see if there were qualitative differences between state tests and NAEP in the assessment of thoughtful response.

Methods

We began by obtaining a sample of state achievement tests in reading comprehension. We elected to focus on fourth-grade assessments because NAEP is administered to both fourth- and eighth-grade samples. We obtained sample reading comprehension tests from the NAEP website and from the 20 most heavily populated states in the United States. We used the following four criteria to guide our state test selection process:

1. Fourth-grade sample tests were available online and included enough items to allow for reliable analysis.
2. These tests were specifically offered as samples designed to familiarize educators with the format and item types used to measure comprehension.
3. Items were accompanied by the passages upon which they were based.

4. Items were accompanied by designations of the level of thinking the items were intended to assess.

Sample tests from the following states met our screening criteria: California, Florida, Wisconsin, Illinois, New York, North Carolina, Pennsylvania, and Texas. Sources for the sample tests are found in Table 1. The average difference between results on the selected state assessments and NAEP was 40 points, exactly the average for all 50 states.

Analysis of Test Items

We set out to classify each item in our sample of tests according to three criteria, which we selected because they might serve as possible explanations of the state–NAEP discrepancy:

1. Item type—Did the test item use an open-ended or multiple-choice format?

2. Item objective—Was the item intended to assess vocabulary knowledge, familiarity with genre, text organization, characterization, or text detail? The rubric we used for this classification is included in Figure 1.

3. Item purpose and cognitive demand— Did the item require the reader to understand the content of the text (text emphasis), or did the item require the reader to interpret the meaning of the text (higher order)?

Using several tests not included in the final sample, we met and discussed our classifications until we had achieved a solid level of confidence in our command of classification criteria. Each of us then independently classified each item in each sample test. The majority opinion was regarded as the final classification and we agreed on 96.1% of the Item objective and 94.7% of the Cognitive demand classifications, suggesting that the criteria we had developed could be used with a high level of confidence. The Item type criterion is self-explanatory (multiple choice or open ended), but Item objective and Item purpose/cognitive demand will require some elucidation.

Item Objective

Vocabulary Knowledge. To assess vocabulary, the test identifies a word or phrase (either underlining it in the text and referring the reader to its location, or quoting the sentence in which it appears). The intended objective for the test taker is to use the context clues available in the text to determine the meaning of the word or

---

Table 1
Sample Test Items Retrieved From Websites

Test and Date	Website
California (2007)	www.cde.ca.gov/ta/tg/sr/documents/RTqGr4ela.pdf
Florida (2001, 2007)	FCAT.fldoe.org/pdf/sample/0607/reading/FL07_STM_G4R_TB_cwf001.pdf fcat.fldoe.org/pdf/fc4rib0a.pdf
Illinois (2008)	www.isbe.state.il.us/assessment/htmls/sample_books.htm
National Assessment of Educational Progress (2007)	nces.ed.gov/nationsreportcard/ITMRLS/Startsearch.asp
New York (2007)	www.nysedregents.org/testing/elaei/07exams/home.htm
North Carolina (2005)	www.ncpublicschools.org/accountability/testing/eog/sampleitems/reading
Pennsylvania (2006–2007)	www.pde.state.pa.us/a_and_t/lib/a_and_t/2006-2007gr4ReadingItemSampler.pdf
Texas (2006)	www.tea.state.tx.us/student.assessment/resources/release/taks/2006/gr4taks.pdf
Wisconsin (2005)	dpi.state.wi.us/oea/readingptri.html

Figure 1
Item Objective Classification Guidelines

Vocabulary items
• The reader must identify a word's meaning, presumably based on context clues provided in the text.
• The reader must identify the meaning of a phrase or figure of speech.

Genre items
• The reader must apply the definition of a genre type to identify the genre in which a piece of text is written.
• The reader is asked to identify a specific convention of writing, such as
  • A metaphor or simile
  • A fact or opinion
  • The difference between fantasy and reality
  • Writing techniques such as onomatopoeia, italics, parentheses, etc.

Organization items
• The reader is asked to
  • Detect the writer's purpose for writing a piece of text
  • Create or select an alternate title for a piece of text
  • Predict what is likely to happen, based on events that have already occurred
  • Identify an idea or ideas that are most important in the passage
  • Select or create a statement of the main idea or main event of a passage
  • Describe the way that the author choose or order the events or information in a passage
  • Describe an alternative ending for a story
  • Identify appropriate items that would fit into a schema map of text

Characterization items
• The reader must identify personality characteristics that are supported or developed in the text.
• The reader is asked to
  • Choose a word that best describes a character
  • Choose a word that best describes a character's feelings
  • Identify factors that may have motivated a character to act or to arrive at a set of beliefs
  • Identify characteristics that can be compared or contrasted to those of another character
  • Predict the action that a character would be likely to take based on what the reader has found out about that character
  • Identify a change in a character's behavior or attitude

Detail items
• The reader must recognize elements of the text that are stated verbatim in text or paraphrased.
• The reader must identify similarities or differences between selections or characters based on clearly stated elements of the text.

phrase and to select the best synonym or definition from among the choices presented.

Familiarity With Genre. These items may ask the reader to identify the particular genre in which a text selection is written. An effective genre item challenges readers to call to mind an entire range of ideas surrounding a particular kind of writing and to use those ideas to construct a framework in which the details in the text will unfold. This knowledge of the overall framework of the story can establish a set of expectations that will aid in an active response to text and a deeper level of comprehension. A more limited type of item asks readers to identify a specific convention of writing, such as a metaphor or simile, or to label a statement as fact or opinion.

Text Organization. Comprehension assessment items require readers to recognize the ways in which writers organize text or present their ideas. They may challenge readers to consider a writer's intent, distinguish between main and subordinate ideas, devise appropriate titles that do justice to the content of text, or to consider ways in which writers have framed arguments. Good text organization items assess a reader's appreciation for the variety of ways in which events and arguments can unfold and the levels of effectiveness associated with that variety.

Characterization. These items ask the reader to identify personality characteristics that are supported or developed in the text. They may require the reader to select a word that best describes a character or a character's feelings. They may ask that the reader identify a character's motivation or predict the actions that a character may take, based on what the reader has already learned about that character. Characterization items are not limited to narrative text; expository text also includes people whose characters are developed in the text. Effective characterization items call for a thoughtful analysis of human nature.

Detail. Detail items are geared toward the recognition of information stated directly, or nearly so, in text. They may involve comparison or contrast based on factual information. They may also involve recognition of the same information after it has undergone slight, extensive, or subtle paraphrasing. Effective detail items force the reader to turn attention to significant text elements related to the central message of the text. However, weak items may direct a reader's attention to obscure facts and can, over time, distort a child's view of the nature of reading by encouraging memorization of less salient information.

Item Purpose and Cognitive Demand

Text Emphasis Items. We have defined text emphasis items as those with answers stated verbatim in the text or so nearly so that they require only translation from one set of words to another (Applegate, Quinn, & Applegate, 2002). Pure verbatim items at the fourth-grade level are relatively rare. After all, the objective

of test items is to discriminate between capable and less capable readers, and items that require readers to simply look up answers in the target text are unlikely to deliver that level of discrimination. Items that require the student to recognize the same message in a different linguistic form are far more likely to distinguish between capable and less capable readers, even if they require little thoughtful response.

But there are other variations of text emphasis items to be considered in any analysis of assessments. We viewed as text emphasis any item that used distractors so improbable that recognition of the correct answer required only a very low level of understanding of text. In a similar vein, we classified as text emphasis those items that could be answered on the basis of test-taking skills without the need to thoughtfully respond to the author's message.

Higher Order Interpretation Items. This category of items is most reflective of and congruent with the definitions of mature reading comprehension discussed at the beginning of this article. These items require readers to draw logical conclusions based upon their understanding of the text and their own, often unique, related personal experiences. They may call upon readers to take and defend a stand, using elements from both text and personal experience. Higher order questions are often characterized by challenges to readers to compare or contrast characters, situations, conclusions, or even elements of personal experience that might be related to their understanding of text. These items constitute what we have referred to as *thoughtful literacy*, a response to text that reflects the ability of readers to use their life experiences to flesh out and make sense of the stories and information in text. Throughout our analysis, we took the position that even if a single distractor required readers to engage in a thoughtful interpretation of the text, it was enough to mark that item as requiring higher order thinking.

Results

Item Types and Item Objectives

The first point of comparison we examined between state tests and NAEP was the proportion of items that assessed comprehension in an open-ended as opposed to a multiple choice format (see Table 2). Our sample of comprehension items from NAEP included 57.0% open-ended items as opposed to an average of only 7.0% from our sample of state assessments. Among the state tests that we examined, only Florida made significant use of open-ended questions, but even so, their sample included less than half of the proportion of

open-ended items that we observed in NAEP. Thus it appears that NAEP places a great deal more emphasis upon a reader's ability to construct and explain a response to text, whereas the state tests place a higher premium upon a reader's ability to recognize a response and distinguish it from other less adequate responses.

The results of our analysis of item objectives are presented in Table 3. Vocabulary items were seldom used in NAEP; only 1 of a sample of 62 items assessed vocabulary. In our state sample, however, two tests (California and Wisconsin) allocated more than 25.0% of their comprehension items to the assessment of vocabulary. On the whole, the state sample averaged over 17.0%

Table 2
Percentages of Items in Item Type Categories on NAEP and Selected State Tests

Test	Multiple-Choice	Open-Ended
NAEP (N = 62)	43.0	57.0
California STAR (N = 36)	100.0	0.0
Florida FCAT (N = 32)	73.0	27.0
Illinois ISAT (N = 19)	95.0	5.0
Wisconsin WKSE (N = 21)	95.0	5.0
New York (N = 35)	88.0	12.0
North Carolina (N = 31)	100.0	0.0
Pennsylvania PSSA (N = 26)	92.0	8.0
Texas TAKS (N = 40)	100.0	0.0
State average	93.0	7.0

Table 3
Percentages of Items in Item Objective Categories on NAEP and Selected State Tests

Test	Vocabulary	Genre	Organization	Characterization	Detail
NAEP	1.6	3.2	25.0	46.0	24.0
California STAR	28.0	17.0	25.0	11.0	19.0
Florida FCAT	13.0	13.0	13.0	25.0	36.0
Illinois ISAT	16.0	16.0	32.0	32.0	4.0
Wisconsin WKCE	28.0	5.0	38.0	10.0	19.0
New York	14.0	9.0	31.0	26.0	20.0
North Carolina	20.0	16.0	10.0	35.0	19.0
Pennsylvania PSSA	15.0	12.0	35.0	23.0	15.0
Texas TAKS	18.0	0.0	35.0	33.0	14.0
State average	17.1	11.0	27.4	24.4	18.3

vocabulary items. Our examination of vocabulary items in the state tests revealed one major difficulty—the inability of the test constructors to ensure that the target word is unknown to the reader. If the word is already known, the need to use context clues is short-circuited and the reader need only find the synonym from among the listed choices. Under those circumstances, the reader need not even to have read the passage, let alone comprehended it. In any case, it appears that NAEP de-emphasizes vocabulary items and our sample of state tests uses them regularly in comprehension assessment.

Genre items accounted for only 2 of 62 items on our NAEP sample in contrast to the state tests that on average allocated 11% of their items to the ability to identify elements of genre. The proportion of genre items in Texas and Wisconsin was very similar to NAEP's but California, Illinois, and North Carolina used more than 15.0% of their items to assess knowledge of genre. Weak genre items ask only that the reader apply a rote definition of a genre element to a piece of text or identify a convention of writing. Consequently, they can frequently be answered without reference to the text itself. For example, an item that presents readers with four sentences and asks them to identify which is an opinion is simply asking them to apply a definition and identify the sentence that cannot be proven. When we examined the 25 genre items that were included in our state test sample, we found that 88.0% called for rote recall of definitions of textual elements.

Elements of text organization accounted for 25.0% of NAEP's items, and the state average was very similar. States that emphasized text structure and organization significantly less included Florida and North Carolina. Several of the states devoted more than a third of their items to this objective. Effective text organization items require readers to use text information to predict events or to hypothesize about alternative endings. However, some weaker items ask only that the reader identify the event that happened first or last in the text.

NAEP devoted a significantly higher proportion of its items to characterization (46%) than did the average state in our sample (24.3%) with California and Wisconsin weighing in with the fewest items devoted to analysis of characters. Even the state test with the highest proportion of characterization items (North Carolina) trailed NAEP by 11.0%.

Detail items accounted for 24.0% of the questions in the NAEP sample as compared with an average of 18.3% in the state sample. However, Illinois devoted significantly fewer items to detail than did NAEP; Florida devoted significantly more. The weakest of detail items call for the reader to exercise test-taking skills and eliminate distractors that are highly unlikely.

Recognition vs. Interpretation

We set out to determine whether state test developers primarily intended to measure the reader's ability to recognize information or to interpret that information. The item designations proposed by the state tests and NAEP are presented in Table 4 under the columns labeled Intended. We then assessed what we judged as the actual cognitive demands of those same items, and those results are summarized in the adjoining columns under the label Actual.

The data in Table 4 suggest that the state and NAEP test developers place a great deal of emphasis upon the interpretation of the text. With the exception of California and Texas, each of the state tests, as well as NAEP, report that more than half of their comprehension test items assess the reader's ability to think about text and to draw conclusions that go beyond mere memory for details. This proportion of items suggests that the intent of nearly all of the tests is congruent with the universally accepted definition of the mature reader we discussed earlier.

But an examination of our actual item demand classifications reveals that NAEP called for higher order interpretation more than twice as frequently as the highest ranked state test (Texas), more than three times as frequently as the average state test, and more than eight times as frequently as the lowest ranked state test (California). A breakdown of various item

Table 4
Comparison of Percentages of Items in Intended and Actual Cognitive Demand
Categories on NAEP and Selected State Tests

Test	Text Emphasis		Higher Order	
	Intended	Actual	Intended	Actual
NAEP	6.5	32.2	93.5	67.8
California STAR	55.6	91.7	44.4	8.3
Florida FCAT	40.6	84.4	59.4	15.6
Illinois ISAT	45.5	78.9	54.5	21.1
Wisconsin WKCE	40.0	85.7	60.0	14.3
New York	40.6	71.4	59.4	28.6
North Carolina	35.5	71.0	64.5	29.0
Pennsylvania	32.5	69.2	67.5	30.8
Texas TAKS	50.0	67.5	50.0	32.5
State average	42.5	77.5	57.5	22.5

objectives can shed some further light on the differences between our sample of state tests and NAEP.

Text organization items and characterization items were much more challenging on state tests, weighing in at 43.0% and 40.0% higher order, respectively. Thus it seems that these two item classes have the greatest potential to elicit thoughtful responses from readers. However, NAEP organization items were 93% higher order and characterization items were ranked at 79% higher order. In both cases, the challenge to think on NAEP was roughly double that on our sample of state tests.

Open-ended items seem to have a great deal more potential to assess reading as a linking of text with an individual's unique experiences than forced choice items. What we found surprising was that fully one half of the open-ended items on our state sample fell into the Text-emphasis category; only 15% of NAEP's open-ended items assessed pure recognition of text elements.

The Analysis of Cognitive Demand

We found that test developers tended to classify multiple-choice items based on the question stem, often without regard to the quality of the distractors. It is the nature of a multiple-choice item, however, to require the reader to select the best choice and eliminate the incorrect ones. For example, one state test included a story about a captured sparrow kept in a rattan cage and sold as a pet to several different characters. Each time he changes hands, the sparrow begs his new owner to set him free but he cannot be understood. Finally a worker buys the sparrow and takes him home to cheer his daughter who is confined to bed with an illness. The girl immediately understands the sparrow's predicament and sets him loose, asking him to fly in freedom for both of them.

One multiple-choice test item asks the reader to determine how the bird and the little girl are alike, an item stem that cuts directly to the heart of the story and one that is clearly intended to assess thoughtful response. The correct response is that they both know what it is like to be trapped inside. The incorrect responses are that both the girl and the bird are very sick (directly contradicts passage content), both like rattan cages (illogical), and both are free to travel wherever they want (directly contradicts passage content). The nature of these distractors is such that only a reader who has understood very little of the gist of the story could possibly choose one of them. Thus a question that should require a great deal of thoughtful consideration requires in the final analysis only an understanding of the barest facts of the story.

Similarly, the consistent use of a particular type of distractor may convert even very thought-provoking items into exercises in test-taking skills that have little to do with actual comprehension. In many instances, test constructors overused a form of distractor labeled a Quiz Contestant response (Applegate, Quinn, & Applegate, 2006), in which the distractor provides a logical or sensible answer, but one that is drawn from pure experience without reference to the text. For example, a test item based on the passage described above asked why the characters could not understand what the bird was saying. One of the distractors was that they were not used to hearing bird sounds. If it were true, that fact would logically account for the inability of the characters to understand the bird, but there is no indication in the text that this was the case. If students are taught to identify and eliminate such distractors, they may circumvent any intended demands for thoughtful response. Consequently, we classified such items as text emphasis.

We must emphasize that multiple-choice test items do indeed have the potential to elicit thoughtful responses from readers; it is the content of the items that determines cognitive demand. A question that asks a reader to select which event fits in a sequence of events taken directly from the text differs significantly from an item that asks the reader to predict what is likely to happen next, based on the events in a story. By the same token, asking a reader what motivated a character to behave in a particular way when that motivation is stated directly in the passage is in no way equivalent to asking the reader to identify which character in the story would be most likely to agree with a statement.

Conclusions, Cautions, and Recommendations

While our sample of state tests was limited to eight, our study supports the conclusion that not all tests labeled *reading comprehension* are measuring the same objectives. Our analysis suggests that there are qualitative differences between NAEP and our sample of state tests that may have contributed to the state–NAEP achievement gap. To assume that the state tests are simply an easier version of the same assessment seems to us to be a serious oversimplification.

In summary, we found that NAEP uses far more open-ended items in its assessment of reading, uses far fewer vocabulary and genre items, and demands far more thoughtful response than any of the state tests in our sample. Our analysis showed that just under one third of the items in NAEP centered on Text-emphasis reading and more that three quarters of the items in our state test sample fell into that category. Thus NAEP is far more congruent with the widely accepted definition of mature reading comprehension as a dynamic process of thinking about what we read and how it fits in with our experiences and values. NAEP is also much more closely aligned with the frameworks published by a vast majority of the states, frameworks that unanimously call for thoughtful responses to text. It is difficult to avoid the conclusion that the state tests are not particularly well aligned with their own testing frameworks. If that is the case, they may not be effective assessments of the results of their own curricula.

A significant advantage of NAEP is related to the complaint voiced by many educators—that assessment is driving curriculum, and teachers are being pressured to teach to the test rather than toward the achievement of a set of clearly articulated goals. But if that assessment tool is NAEP, a measure that seems to us to be effectively assessing widely agreed upon goals, then teaching to a test that assesses thoughtful response may actually work to the advantage of a great many of our children. If, on the other hand, we simply assume that all tests are equal determinants of achievement, that assumption may lead us to a national educational disaster.

What may be called for at this point is a national dialogue about the nature of our goals for reading instruction, and the means we must select to assess them. NAEP expects readers to be able to read, understand, and respond to text, but much of our instruction and assessment seems geared toward recognizing the literal content of the text (Durkin, 1978; Pressley et al., 2001). There is little doubt that U.S. students are better able to perform on tests that require remembering than on tests that require a thoughtful response to text (Donahue, Voelkl, Campbell, & Mazzeo, 1999). And once we recognize that fact, we need to decide if we as a nation are satisfied with that state of affairs. Our results suggest strongly that not all tests are created equal and that state–NAEP comparisons suggest that all is not well. To assume that the state test results are showing us that a sizeable majority of our children are on the road to mature reading is a potentially serious error, one that may have critical educational repercussions.

The state tests that we examined represented a string of missed opportunities to assess thoughtful response. For example, one test included a narrative about a pair of twin turtles who decide to play a trick on a hippopotamus by having one twin challenge the hippo to a swimming race. The hippo knows that he is much faster but when he arrives at the river bank, there is the other twin waiting for him. Rematches bring about the same result, and the hippo is forced to admit that the turtle is the faster swimmer. This is a simple narrative but it has multiple layers of meaning. The assessment of comprehension for this passage consists of four questions: two vocabulary items, an item that asks the reader to identify a hyperbole, and an item that asks the reader to select a word (tricky, lazy, brave, or stingy) to describe the turtles. In the case of the last item, it is difficult to avoid the conclusion that only a reader who had failed to understand the basic gist of the text could select one of the distractors.

It is important to note that if a test includes a sufficient number of such distractor items, it does not lose its value entirely. In most cases, it can serve as a discriminator between below basic readers on the one hand, and a combination of basic, proficient, and advanced readers on the other. However, when it is asked to discriminate among basic, proficient, and advanced readers, it simply does not include enough thought-provoking questions to accomplish the task. Among the tests that we analyzed, only NAEP required enough of a variety of thinking tasks to discriminate among these groups. This observation alone may account for a great deal of the discrepancy between state and NAEP scores.

Finally, let us return to the hypothesis of Black and Wiliam (1998) who suggested that many teachers emphasize literal recall in their classrooms under the mistaken assumption that their students will perform well on accountability measures. Our analysis suggests that such literal-minded teachers may not be so mistaken after all, if we stay the course and continue to assess comprehension as if it consisted primarily of literal recall. But we run the risk of creating a growing number of students who perform well on state tests, yet continue to view reading as an exercise in literal recall of information, an exercise that does not require a spontaneous thoughtful response.

Our analysis of the content of state tests and NAEP suggests that teachers who encourage their students to engage thoughtfully with text and attend to the ways that details support thoughtful conclusions will prepare them to do well on both state and national accountability assessments. But as literacy professionals, we must call upon our state accountability tests to do much more to assess higher order interpretation of text if more of our children are ever to achieve the vision of mature reading that stands at the very core of the field of reading and literacy instruction.

References

Alabama Reading Initiative. (2001). *Comprehension strategies, grades K–1.* Retrieved November 30, 2007, from ftp://ftp.alsde.edu/documents/50/K-1_COMPREHENSION_2001.doc

Allington, R.L. (2001). *What really matters for struggling readers: Designing research-based programs.* New York: Addison-Wesley Higher Education.

Anderson, R.C. (1984). Role of the reader's schema in comprehension, learning and memory. In R.C. Anderson,

J. Osborn, & R.J. Tierney (Eds.), *Learning to read in American schools: Basal readers and content texts* (pp. 243–257). Hillsdale, NJ: Erlbaum.

Applegate, M.D., Quinn, K.B., & Applegate, A.J. (2002). Levels of thinking required by comprehension questions in informal reading inventories. *The Reading Teacher, 56*(2), 174–180.

Applegate, M.D., Quinn, K.B., & Applegate, A.J. (2006). Profiles in comprehension. *The Reading Teacher, 60*(1), 48–57. doi:10.1598/RT.60.1.5

Black, P., & Wiliam, D. (1998). Assessment and classroom learning. *Assessment in Education, 5*(1), 7–74.

Brown, R.G. (1991). *Schools of thought: How the politics of literacy shape thinking in the classroom.* San Francisco: Jossey-Bass.

Chall, J.S. (1996). *Stages of reading development* (2nd ed.). Fort Worth, TX: Harcourt Brace.

Donahue, P.L., Voelkl, K.E., Campbell, J.R., & Mazzeo, J. (1999). *The NAEP 1998 reading report card for the nation and the states.* Washington, DC: National Center for Education Statistics.

Durkin, D. (1978). What classroom observations reveal about reading comprehension instruction. *Reading Research Quarterly, 14*(4), 481–533.

Elmore, R.F., Peterson, P.L., & McCarthey, S.J. (1996). *Restructuring in the classroom: Teaching, learning, and school organization.* San Francisco: Jossey-Bass.

Goodman, Y.M., Watson, D.J., & Burke, C.L. (1996). *Reading strategies: Focus on comprehension* (2nd ed.). Katonah, NY: Richard C. Owens.

Huey, E.B. (1908). *The psychology and pedagogy of reading.* New York: Macmillan.

Knapp, M.S. (1995). *Teaching for meaning in high-poverty classrooms.* New York: Teachers College Press.

Mullis, I.V.S., Kennedy, A.M., Martin, M.O., & Sainsbury, M. (2006). *PIRLS 2006 assessment framework and specifications* (2nd ed.). Chestnut Hill, MA: Boston College, International Study Center.

National Assessment Governing Board. (2006). *Reading framework for the 2007 National Assessment of Educational Progress.* Retrieved December 18, 2007, from www.nagb.org/frameworks/reading_07.pdf

National Institute of Child Health and Human Development. (2000). *Report of the National Reading Panel. Teaching children to read: An evidence-based assessment of the scientific research literature on reading and its implications for reading instruction* (NIH Publication No. 00-4769). Washington, DC: U.S. Government Printing Office.

Pressley, M., Wharton-McDonald, R., Allington, R.L., Block, C.C., Morrow, L., Tracey, D., et al. (2001). A study of effective first-grade literacy instruction. *Scientific Studies of Reading, 5*(1), 35–58. doi:10.1207/S1532799XSSR0501_2

Tennessee Department of Education. (2007). *Academic standards.* Retrieved November 30, 2007, from www.state.tn.us/education/ci/english/grade_4.shtm/

Tharp, R.G., & Gallimore, R. (1989). Rousing schools to life. *American Educator, 13*(2), 20–25, 46–52.

Thomas B. Fordham Foundation. (2005, October 19). *Gains on state reading tests evaporate on 2005 NAEP* (Press release). Retrieved October 4, 2007, from www.edexcellence.net/detail/news.cfm?news_id=404&id=

Thorndike, E.L. (1917). Reading as reasoning: A study of mistakes in paragraph reading. *Journal of Educational Psychology, 8*(6), 323–332. doi:10.1037/h0075325

Wallis, C., & Steptoe, S. (2007, June 4). How to fix No Child Left Behind. *TIME, 169,* 34–41.

Principles for Literacy Assessment

Peter Johnston and Paula Costello

In a "learning society" everyone will need to become, and remain, committed to learning. If assessment potentially represents the key to achieving this, it also currently represents the biggest single stumbling block. (Broadfoot, 2002, p. 6)

"What gets assessed is what gets taught" is a common assertion whose meaning is often underestimated. It is not just *what* gets assessed, but *how* it is assessed that has implications for what is learned. When a child who is asked the meaning of his report card grades responds, "If I knew that I'd be the teacher" he is saying something about the relationships of authority learned in the process of assessment. When a teacher wishes out loud that her faculty "could discuss retention and realistic expectations for grade levels without the nastiness and accusations," she is also reporting on the relational aspect of assessment practices (Johnston, 2003, p. 90). Our goal in this article is to offer a framework for understanding literacy assessment that incorporates these dimensions and reminds us of the broader picture of literacy assessment of which we often lose sight.

Literacy Is a Complex Construct

Although we often think of literacy as a set of all-purpose skills and strategies to be learned, it is more complex, more local, more personal, and more social than that. Becoming literate involves developing identities, relationships, dispositions, and values as much as acquiring strategies for working with print (Brandt, 2001; Collins & Blot, 2003; Gee, 2000). Children

becoming literate are being apprenticed into ways of living with people as much as with symbols. Consequently, literacy assessment must be grounded in current understandings of literacy and society (Johnson & Kress, 2003; Johnston, 1999). We have to consider what kind of literacy might benefit individuals, what kind of literate society we aspire to, and what assessment might best serve those ends.

For example, what kind of literacy assessment will enable children to live in and contribute to an increasingly democratic society? Democracy has to do with "the way persons attend to one another, care for one another, and interact with one another...[and] the capacity to look at things as though they could be otherwise" (Greene, 1985, p. 3), and citizens who "have the convictions and enthusiasms of their own responses, yet...are willing to keep an open mind about alternate points of view, and... to negotiate meanings and actions that respect both individual diversity and community needs" (Pradl, 1996, pp. 11–12). In other words, our literacy assessment practices must foster a literate disposition towards *reciprocity* (Carr & Claxton, 2002); that is, "a willingness to engage in joint learning tasks, to express uncertainties and ask questions, to take a variety of roles in joint learning enterprises and to take others' purposes and perspectives into account" (p. 16).

What might such assessment look like? The National Educational Monitoring Project (NEMP) in New Zealand is charged with taking stock of the nation's progress in educating a literate society. To this end, the NEMP includes items such as providing a group of children

Preparing Reading Professionals (second edition), edited by Rita M. Bean, Natalie Heisey, and Cathy M. Roller. © 2010 by the International Reading Association. Reprinted from Johnston, P., & Costello, P. (2005). Principles for literacy assessment. *Reading Research Quarterly, 40*(2), 256–267. doi:10.1598/RRQ.40.2.6.

with a set of books from which they, as a class library committee, must make their best selection. Students individually justify their choices to the group before the group negotiates and justifies the final selection. The negotiation has a time limit and is videotaped for analysis of reading and literate interactions (Flockton & Crooks, 1996). This item requires children to evaluate the qualities of texts, take a stance, make persuasive arguments, actively listen, and negotiate a collective position—all independent and interdependent literate practices central to democratic classroom and society. The item reflects and encourages an individual and mutual disposition toward reciprocity, a foundation for a democratic literacy.

Literacy has complications that assessment must deal with. Not only is literacy complex and social but also the literate demands of the world keep changing with exponential acceleration. The apparent boundaries between spoken and written words and their conventions have been obliterated by instant messaging, book tapes, cell-phone text messaging, speech translation software, interactive hypertext, and the facility with which text and image (moving or still) are fused. Literate demands are changing so rapidly that we can't predict with certainty what kindergartners will face in adulthood. We do know however, that they will need to be resilient learners (Carr & Claxton, 2002) to maintain their literate development in the face of the increasingly rapid transformations of literacy in their communities.

Because "what is assessed is taught," literacy assessment should reflect and encourage resilience—a disposition to focus on learning when the going gets tough, to quickly recover from setbacks, and to adapt. Its opposite is brittleness—the disposition to avoid challenging tasks and to shift into ego-defensive behaviors when learning is difficult. A brittle learner believes that having difficulty with a literate task reveals a lack of "ability." A brittle disposition in children prior to first grade negatively predicts word recognition in grades 1 and 2, and is a better predictor than assessments of phonological awareness (Niemi & Poskiparta, 2002).

This negative effect on learning is amplified by the pressures of competitive and overly difficult situations, particularly where ability is the primary emphasis. These are exactly the contexts produced by current testing practices.

Resilience can be assessed. For example, teachers can collect specific examples of resilience with quotes and artifacts to produce documented narratives (Carr & Claxton, 2002) for later review with the student and other stakeholders (see also Himley & Carini, 2000). In fact, the process of generating such assessment narratives will foster a resilient literate disposition (Johnston, 2004).

We begin with these uncommon examples of literacy assessment to suggest that, although assessing literacy in its complexity can be challenging, it is possible. It is also important. Failure to keep our attention on the bigger picture might not be a problem except that, intended or not, literacy assessment instruments define literacy within the assessment activity and, particularly when the stakes are high, within instruction (Smith, 1991). The higher the stakes, the more necessary it is that assessments reflect the breadth of literacy. Alas, most assessment practices, particularly testing practices, oversample narrow aspects of literacy, such as sound-symbol knowledge (Stallman & Pearson, 1991), and undersample other aspects such as writing, any media beyond print on paper, and ways of framing texts and literacy, such as the critical literacies necessary for managing the coercive pressures of literacy.

The more an assessment focuses on a narrow sample of literate behavior, as happens in individual tests, the more undersampling occurs. Literacy assessments distorted in this way affect instruction in many subtle ways. For example, the extensive use of pencil-and-paper state tests has forced many teachers to decrease instructional use of computers, particularly for writing. This problem is most damaging in urban and poor-performing schools (Russell & Abrams, 2004). The tests simultaneously risk underestimating the writing competence of students used to writing on computers, while reducing the likelihood of students not familiar with computer writing to ever become so.

Assessment Is a Social Practice

Assessment is a social practice that involves noticing, representing, and responding to children's literate behaviors, rendering them meaningful for particular purposes and audiences (Johnston & Rogers, 2001). Teacher feedback to students on their literate behavior is assessment just as much as is grading students' work, classifying students as handicapped, certifying students as being "above grade level," or establishing a school as "in need of improvement" (Black & Wiliam, 1998a; Johnston, 1993). *Testing* is a subset of assessment practices in which children's literate behavior is elicited in more controlled conditions.

Although assessment often is viewed as a technical matter of developing accurate measuring instruments, it is more centrally a set of social practices in which various tools are used for various purposes. For example, leveled books can be used as part of teaching in order to monitor children's early reading growth without the use of tests. Some books can even be kept aside specifically for assessment. The same procedure could also be used as part of holding teachers accountable for children's progress (Paris, 2002). However, this is a very different social practice and would invite greater concern about the measurement precision of the "levels" and different social action. For example, teachers would be more likely to use the assessment books for instruction and to focus the curriculum on the accuracy of word reading.

Although the instrument is the same, it has different meaning in the different social practice. In the accountability context, we worry more about the measurement qualities of the instrument in order to be fair. Fairness in the teaching context is more about ensuring that children are developing adequately, focusing instruction, and ensuring that the discourse of "levels" does not dominate the children's interactions and self-assessments. Paradoxically, though we worry more about the psychometric properties of an instrument in the accountability context, the social properties of the *use* of the instrument, such as the defensiveness it might induce, or the constriction of the curriculum, can be of far more significance.

With the realization that assessments are social practices has come the awareness that the validity of an assessment instrument cannot be established outside of its consequences in use (Messick, 1994; Moss, 1998). Literacy assessment practices affect the constructs used to organize teaching practice and to represent children (Johnston, 1997; Moss). This is especially powerful when tests are used for purposes that attach high stakes such as teacher salaries, student retention, graduation, or classification.

Although there are occasional studies claiming that high-stakes testing has no negative effects, or even some positive effects on children's learning, there are many more studies showing the opposite and with greater specificity. For example, high-stakes accountability testing has consistently been demonstrated to undermine teaching and learning (Allington & McGill-Franzen, 1995; Morrison & Joan, 2002; Rex & Nelson, 2004; Smith, 1991; Smith & Rottenberg, 1991) particularly for lower achieving students (Harlen & Crick, 2003). It restricts the literacy curriculum, thus defeating the original intention to improve literacy learning. Teachers under threat drop from the curriculum complex literacy practices involving, for example, multimedia, research, and role-play, and at the same time their learning community is disrupted (Rex & Nelson). Increasing accountability pressure on teachers is counterproductive, especially when teachers already have an internal accountability system. It results instead in "escalating teacher outrage, diminishing moral [sic], and the exiting of committed teachers... from teaching" (Rex & Nelson, p. 1324).

The dictum "first do no harm" has become part of validity in theory, though rarely in assessment practice. Indeed, although high-stakes testing has lately been supported by arguments that it will reduce literacy achievement differences associated with race and poverty, there is evidence that the long-term effect of such testing is to create a curriculum that extends stratification rather than reducing it (Darling-Hammond, 2004; McNeil, 2000).

Individual and Institutional Learning

Literacy assessment is part of a larger project to educate children both for their immediate and long-term benefit and for the evolution of society. The implication of this is that literacy assessment must be grounded in current understandings of individual and institutional learning. There are two general kinds of assessment—summative and formative. Summative assessments are the backward-looking assessments *of* learning, the tests we most commonly think of that summarize or judge performance as in educational monitoring, teacher and student accountability testing, and certification (Black & Wiliam, 1998a). These have not been overtly associated with current understandings of individual or institutional learning.

Indeed, the theories of learning underlying psychometric practices have largely been implicit, individualistic, and behavioristic (Shepard, 1991). For example, current accountability testing, driven by psychometrics, is based on rewarding and punishing students, teachers, and school systems. The evidence so far is that, rather than accomplishing the intended learning, these practices shift participants' goals toward avoidance of punishment, which thwarts the goal of improving the quality of literacy learning for all students and particularly for historically low-achieving students (McNeil, 2000).

Formative assessment, or assessment *for* learning, is the forward-looking assessment that occurs in the process of learning, the feedback the teacher provides to the student, and the nature of the feedback matters (Crooks, 1988). For example, rather than praise or grades, comments improve performance, though praise keeps students thinking they are doing well (Black & Wiliam, 1998a). Feedback that focuses attention on traits such as ability, smartness, or goodness, undermines resilience (Dweck, 1999).

But the *process* of formative assessment is also critical. For example, the most common assessment practices associated with comprehension involve asking for retellings or asking questions to which teachers already know the answers. These interactional patterns teach children about how literacy is done and how authority is organized (Johnston, Jiron, & Day, 2001; Nystrand, Gamoran, Kachur, & Prendergast, 1997). Arranging for children to ask the questions and selectively discuss them can provide more interesting information regarding children's understanding, while simultaneously socializing them into productive literacy practices and identities (Comeyras, 1995).

Formative assessment is specifically directed toward affecting learning. Its validity depends on its ability to do so (Crooks, 2001). This means that the validity of formative assessment rests on factors not normally considered in discussions of validity, such as trust and sensitivity, the social supports, and motivations of the classroom. Task factors will be important, such as the nature and difficulty of the task, its personal and external relevance, the articulation of task features, and performance criteria. Each of these will affect the development of self-assessment. The nature and timing of feedback will be important. But because human interactions are structured around who the participants think they are and what they think they are doing, teachers' understanding of such things as literate practice, how children learn, and cultural difference will also be important, as will their social imagination and insight on conceptual confusions.

While this is true of formative assessments, summative assessment practices affect learning too. Some, such as accountability testing, do so deliberately. Consequently, to be valid, *all* assessment practices should be grounded in current and consistent understandings of learning, including the above factors. Both summative and formative assessments participate in socializing children's and teachers' self-assessments, with implications for control of learning and the management of self-assessment to serve learning goals.

Basing assessment on current understandings about learning does not simply negate principles of psychometrics. For example, neo-Piagetian theories of learning view the process of confronting and resolving discrepancies as a primary vehicle for learning (Schaffer, 1996; Tudge & Rogoff, 1989). A self-extending literacy learning system requires children to attend to discrepancies between cue systems, for example (Clay, 1991). In a similar way, learning communities require disjunctures, such as between minority and mainstream performance, to stimulate learning. However, as with formative assessment, the independent sources of information providing the conflict must be trusted, and measurement principles can help provide the grounds for this. The context in which such discrepancies are presented affects what is learned. The assessment activity must enable productive *engagement* of the disjunctures and foster productive use of data.

Thinking about assessment in terms of individual and institutional learning can change the way we value technical characteristics of assessment. For example, consider the role of consistent agreement among examiners (reliability). Complex authentic assessment items such as those used in the NEMP often reduce reliability (Shavelson, Baxter, & Pine, 1992). Weighty assessment practices like sorting and certifying students demand practices that ensure agreement—the higher the stakes, the more important this agreement.

Disagreements in this context are viewed as "measurement error," which leads to a reduction of complex authentic items. By contrast, in low-stakes and more formative assessment, disagreement among teachers about the meaning of particular documentation, such as portfolios, can open an important learning space by inviting discussions that lead to improvements in instruction and assessment itself. Indeed, this negotiation of values, qualities, and purposes is the most productive part of standards-based or performance-based assessments (Falk, 2001; Johnston, 1989; Moss & Schutz, 2001; Sadler,

1987). Complex and problematic examples provoke the most productive teaching-learning conversations. In other words, when the stakes are low, the less reliable the assessment is—to a point—the more likely it is to produce new learning and innovation in teaching. Because the validity of an assessment rests partly upon its consequences, improving teaching increases the validity of the assessment. In this context, imperfect reliability, contrary to psychometric theory, can increase validity.

As a concrete example, consider the NEMP test item mentioned at the beginning of this article in which children evaluate books individually and collaboratively as a library committee. The item and instrument are possible because NEMP uses a light matrix sample. Different children take a different selection of items; nationally, only a sample of children takes any items at all. The sampling system is possible because the emphasis is on the performance of the system, not of individual schools, teachers, or children. The instrument provides system information without raising individual or organizational defenses (Argyris, 1990).

Aggregate performance is published and analyzed by kind and size of school, minority percentage, community size, socioeconomic status, ethnicity, and gender, but direct institutional comparisons cannot be made. Test items are also published to reduce emphasis on abstracted numerical comparisons. The four-year assessment cycle allows time for both the construction of complex assessments and productive institutional and societal responses. At the same time, each administration of the assessment requires training a group of teachers to reliably administer the assessment. Teachers involved in the training report that it is an exceptional form of professional development that influences their own assessment and teaching competence, and that they pass this competence on to others (Gilmore, 2002).

Minds in Society

Children's thinking evolves from the discourses in which they are immersed. So, for example, the ways children assess themselves as literate individuals will reflect the discourse of classroom assessment practices. Consider Henry (all names are pseudonyms), for example, a fourth-grade student who describes himself as a writer (Johnston et al., 2001). Though he says writing takes him a little longer than some, he notes that he has a journal with lots of entries and can borrow ideas from other authors, among whom he includes peers whose feedback and suggestions he values. He talks about their writing in terms of the ways they can affect him as a reader. He enjoys reading, and if he wanted to learn about another person as a reader, he would ask about favorite and current books and authors.

Indeed, he describes peers first in terms of their reading interests (topic, author, genre, difficulty) and then, matter-of-factly, their reading speed. He is confident that he makes important contributions to book discussions, but he also feels he benefits from hearing other students' experiences and interpretations. He has learned to manage these discussions to maximize this learning. In his research efforts he has encountered disagreements among authors, which he ascribes to one of them not "doing his homework," and he resolves them by consulting more sources (print, personal, and electronic). Henry has a strong sense of agency and uniqueness in his literate practice, which is an important part of who he feels he is. He recognizes a range of sources of authority and that none is beyond critique. When his teacher describes Henry's literate development, it is in terms of details of his interests and engagements, what he has accomplished, how he approaches literate activities, and what he is beginning to do collaboratively or with assistance.

Henry's self-assessment, his interpretation and representation of himself as a literate person, reflects the literate practices and values of his classroom. In a different discourse community, his and his teachers' assessments could have focused more centrally on his decoding skills, what he is *un*able to do, or on his normative standing. The test used by his school district does provide a numerical quantity to represent the amount of his literacy and places him in the lower quarter of his class. But this particular teacher in this particular school and district finds that representation of little significance, and it does not enter the discourse of the classroom. Another teacher in another discursive community in which the pressures and goals are different would likely represent the child's literacy development differently.

Indeed, teachers in districts more concerned with accountability pressures tend to describe children's literacy development with less detail, with less attention to the child's interests, and with more distancing language (Johnston, Afflerbach, & Weiss, 1993). In a similar manner, the pressures of standards assessment change not only the representations but also the relationships among teacher and students, making them more authoritarian (Deci, Siegel, Ryan, Koestner, & Kauffman, 1982), a relationship that is part of the literacy that is acquired.

A corollary of the "mind in society" principle is that literate development is constructed. Mandy, for example, in the same grade in another school district, feels that she is a good writer because she "writes fast" and feels that she will get an "excellent" on her report card for writing with a comment that she "has behaved and she is nice to other classmates." She feels that the good readers are recognizable because they "are quiet and they just listen...and they get chapter books." However, she does not think that conversations between writers are good because they would result in other writers taking ideas and having the same stories and because feelings might get hurt.

Mandy's conception of literacy foregrounds convention, conformity, speed, and individualism (Johnston et al., 2001). Rather than acquiring similar amounts of literacy, as their test scores might suggest, Henry and Mandy have acquired different literacies. Literate development is not a matter of acquiring a series of stepping stones in a particular order. First graders are quite capable of acquiring knowledge of letters and sounds and other print conventions as part of developing a critical literacy. The conventions, however, will mean something different when acquired as part of different literacies. The fact that there are predictable sequences of development is as much a feature of our assessment and curricular imperatives as it is a feature of a natural sequence of literate subskills, or of biological or other potentials and limitations.

Representation and Interpretation

Assessment practices are always representational and interpretive. A teacher, an administrator, and a parent are likely to make different sense of a child's literate behavior both because they bring different histories to the assessment and because they often have different goals as part of different, if overlapping, social practices. Even a test score (a particular choice of representation) will mean different things to them. Each assessment practice is associated with distinct ways of using language that influence the interpretations made (Fairclough, 1992; Gee, 1996). A school psychologist or a speech therapist can tilt the representational language of a committee on the handicapped toward "learning disabled" or "language delayed" on the basis of the same evidence (Rueda & Mercer, 1985). A single teacher can bring different discourses to representing different children depending on the way the child has been categorized, and these representations have consequences for children's understandings of literacy, themselves, and one another as literate individuals (Arya, 2003; Johnston et al., 2001).

Representational practices in assessment perpetuate the wider cultural discourses. If our discourse offers a category called "reading disabled," then we will find assessment tools to identify members of the category and an appealing narrative of "services" and "support" (McDermott, 1993). The representational language of trait and deficit (Johnston, 1993; Mehan, 1993) within which learning narratives are set offers children, teachers, parents, and other community members problematic identities and dispositions. Once "identified," children remain caught in the problematic

discursive web, partly because the problem is represented as a trait of the child rather than as in the instructional environment, partly because the identification process groups children together who share common identifications, and partly because the child is moved to a system that specializes in children's problems that often emphasizes different understandings about literacy learning (Allington & McGill-Franzen, 1989).

Although we might worry about the nature of the categories, which are surely important, the practice is about more than that. As Yalom (1989) pointed out, "If we relate to people believing that we can categorize them, we will neither identify nor nurture...the vital parts of the other that transcend category" (cited in Greenberg & Williams, 2002, p. 107). This is evident in casual transformations such as "He's a two, borderline three, right now and we hope that this enrichment program will put him over the edge" (Baudanza, 2001, p. 8).

Primacy of Teachers' Assessment Practices

No instrument or assessment practice can overcome the fact that the teacher is the primary agent of assessment (International Reading Association and National Council of Teachers of English Joint Task Force on Assessment, 1994). The bulk of literacy assessment occurs moment by moment as part of the activity of teaching (Black & Wiliam, 1998b; Crooks, 1988; Johnston, 1989). Consider an example. A teacher was observed introducing to a student a predictable book with the pattern "Grandpa is [verb—e.g., sitting]." The last page was "Grandpa is snoring," at which the child laughed and said that his grandpa snores too. However, when he read the book he read that page as "Grandpa is so funny." The teacher prompted the child to recall what his grandpa does and then prompted a rereading. The child reread, hesitated before *snoring*, and read it correctly.

But why *that* prompt or teaching strategy? Why not ask the child to read with his finger to emphasize the mismatch between the number of words spoken and in print? Because the teacher hypothesizes, based on her ongoing assessment of the child, that he thinks *so funny* is one word. Pointing would not prompt rethinking because he would still have a one-to-one match and an initial letter match. Why not simply provide accuracy feedback? Because, she hypothesizes, that the process through which the child solves the problem himself will help build a sense of literate agency. Her feedback is based on a theory of learning more than a notion of performance.

The essence of formative assessment is noticing details of literate behavior, imagining what they mean from the child's perspective, knowing what the child knows and can do, and knowing how to arrange for that knowledge and competence to be displayed, engaged, and extended. This requires a "sensitive observer" (Clay, 1993) or "kidwatcher" (Goodman, 1978), a teacher who is "present" in the classroom—focused and receptive to noticing the children's literate behavior (Rodgers, 2002). A child's acquisition of a "reading disabled" classification (and identity) begins with the teacher's assessment, and teachers who notice less about children's literacy development refer more children to be classified than do those who notice more (Broikou, 1992). The more detailed teachers' knowledge of children's literate development, the more agency they appear to feel with respect to solving literacy learning problems.

Formative assessment requires not only noticing and making productive sense of the literate behaviors that occur but also arranging classroom literacy practices that encourage children to act in literate ways and that make their literate learning visible and audible. A child explaining how she figured out a word is not only providing this information for the teacher but also spinning an agentive narrative of her own literate competence. She is building a productive self-assessment and literate identity (Johnston, 2004).

If a classroom is arranged so that children routinely engage in literate activities that provide manageable challenges and talk about the process and experience of their literate practice, assessment information is available to the teacher and, simultaneously, strategic information is available for the students. *Play* is a particularly rich context for the display of young children's understanding of how literate practices work (Roskos & Neuman, 1993; Teale, 1991). In a similar way, *collaboration* demands an externalization of shared thinking, which also provides an excellent source of information.

To the extent that formative assessment is a technical matter, the "instrument" is the teacher and his or her mind and its social and textual supports. Improving performance on summative assessments requires improving formative assessment. There is research that suggests how to do this, but it also suggests that change will be slow because the practices assume active involvement on the part of students as well as changes in the ways teachers understand students, themselves, and what they are trying to accomplish (Black & Wiliam, 1998b). These changes are strongly resisted by societal assessment discourses and their sedimentation in teachers' own subjectivities, as we discuss presently.

Literacy Assessment and Context

Literacy is somewhat local in that people engage in literate practices differently in different contexts. Different tools and social contexts invoke different strategies and ways of thinking. Common assessment practices do not recognize this fact; instead they assume that performance on a particular task in a testing context is representative of all literate contexts. But children perform differently, for example, in more meaningful or authentic activities. The Primary Language Record (PLR) (Barrs, Ellis, Hester, & Thomas, 1989), an early literacy assessment instrument, requires the assessment community (teachers, families, administrators, and students) to recognize (and document) performance in different contexts including "collaborative reading and writing activities," "play," "dramatic play," and "drama and storying" across different social groups that include "pair," "small group," and "child with adult" (p. 38). It draws attention to what a child can do independently and with different kinds of support.

Assessing children's literate learning requires attending not only to what they know and do but also at least as much to the context in which they know and do. Indeed, as the PLR manual notes, "progress or lack of progress should always be seen in relation to the adequacy of the context" (p. 18). When a child appears to be unsuccessful at literate endeavors, we want to know the circumstances in which this happens. Such circumstances include the extent to which literate practices and the logic of participation are made visible in the classroom and valued as purposeful social activities, the extent to which materials are relevant and accessible, and the extent to which classroom discourse is supportive, specific, reflective, nonjudgmental, and values problem solving (Allington & Johnston, 2002; Johnston & Rogers, 2001; Pressley, Allington, Wharton-MacDonald, Collins-Block, & Morrow, 2001).

Shifting the focus of assessment away from the isolated mind to the mind in a social context has begun to be recognized in the assessment of reading disabilities. For example, Clay (1987) proposed that labeling a child as reading disabled is premature without first eliminating the possibility that the child's progress is a result of poorly configured instruction. The assessment strategy of providing the best instructional intervention we can muster has proven effective in eliminating the need to classify most children (Scanlon, Vellutino, Small, & Fanuele, 2000). However, because this strategy remains in a discourse that expects individual disabilities, the handful of children who remain unsuccessful become viewed as bona fide "disabled," or "treatment resisters" (Torgeson, 2000). This need not happen. Indeed, Smith and her colleagues (Smith, 1997) rejected that discourse. Instead of locating the problem in the child, they entertained the possibility that their intervention might still be insufficiently responsive. Through collaborative self-assessment using videotapes, they refined their intervention and produced the desired acceleration in literate learning, removing the need to classify even these students. This concept of attending to the child in the learning context might be applied to large-scale assessments too. Teachers and schools do not operate in a vacuum.

Assessment Discourses Distribute Power

Assessment discourses distribute and sustain power relationships. For example, formative assessments, while grounded in current understandings of learning, are not taken seriously as a form of assessment (Black & Wiliam, 1998a). They are referred to as "informal," as opposed to the more authoritative "formal" assessments. There are probably many reasons for their lack of institutional power aside from the fact that they don't always involve a textual record or artifact such as running records, documented events, or writing samples. They are the purview of teachers, mostly women, and they are normally not in the language of mathematics. When brought to a Committee on Special Education meeting, these assessments are easily trumped by the tests of the school psychologist.

Rogers (2003) showed how a mother, vehemently committed to protecting her daughter from assignment to special education, is reduced to passive acceptance by an assessment discourse that invokes subjectivities from her own unsuccessful history in schooled literacy. Rogers also showed how the discursive context induces this passivity just as well in those with highly successful histories of schooled literacy. The normative discourse of testing provides a powerful tool for asserting symbolic domination and intimidation of students, teachers, and parents (Bourdieu, 1991; Fennimore, 2000; Rogers, 2002). When an adult basic education student at the end of a reading lesson asks timidly, "Did I read this good?" (Rogers, 2002), she demonstrates the internalization of an oppressive assessment discourse.

It is possible to design assessment practices to alter these power arrangements. To return to the PLR, the manual describes specific ways for reducing power differences in assessment conferences with children and families. The form of the assessment also insists that members of the learning community focus attention on the child's assets and their instructional context. Because it directs attention toward differences in performance in a range of contexts and on a range of dimensions, it resists narrow and debilitating ability interpretations. At the same time it provides a language that represents literacy as centrally involving identity and engagement in practice, describing a child's development as a reader and a language user and implying a dimension of agency.

However, breaking free of more limiting assessment discourses is increasingly difficult as these discourses saturate a wider array of media. Constant reminders in the newspaper and reports from school are now supplemented through the Internet. Parents going to the Web are encouraged to obtain reading tests that they can use with their child. Like any advertising, these tests create a need and then direct parents to purchase the remedial instruction on the basis of the normative assessment and the "latest brain research" (Learning, 2002) to fulfill the need. At the same site, parents learn of the routinely massive company growth rate, its even better prospects following federal No Child Left Behind regulations (2002), and how they can profit through investment (Johnston & Rogers, 2001). By both reflecting and enforcing traditions of literate practice (including who gets to participate in what ways and in which media), assessment practices stabilize the literate society, limiting social change and adaptability.

Clashes in Practices

Literacy assessment consumes resources, so there is a constant search for multipurpose assessments. However, each new function often has different demands, requiring difficult trade-offs and bringing different discourses. Recall the NEMP assessment described earlier. Many of the features of the NEMP

were once part of the National Assessment of Educational Progress (NAEP in the United States). However, political pressures have changed the timing of the NAEP to a two-year cycle, increasing pressure for simpler computerized responses. The sampling structure has changed to enable state-by-state comparisons, and state performance has become pegged to federal funding through the No Child Left Behind legislation (2002), thus increasing the assessment stakes. These changes add up to a change in the nature of the assessment activity from educational monitoring for productive curricular conversations to instrumental control of literacy teaching and learning. This is a different assessment practice, grounded in different views of learning and literacy.

The clash of these different discourses is common in school systems as formative and summative functions are forced together, often catching teachers in the middle (Delandshere, 2001; Hill, 2004). As with the earlier example of using leveled books for accountability practices, the higher stakes assessment will generally subvert the lower stakes practice. However, it is possible to have consistency among school literacy curriculum and assessment practices.

The PLR, described earlier, was developed in London for literacy assessment in multicultural/multilingual inner-city communities. It represents a complex, contextual, and social view of literacy learning and assessment practice that involves teacher, student, and parent in collaboratively documenting the child's literacy development over time. It was deliberately designed to inform and support teaching, students, and family literacies through clear documentation and the *process* of that documentation—the assessment *activity*. Although it is a "record," its developers took seriously the educative, communicative, and relational dimensions of assessment practice. In systematic interviews, parents describe the child's home literacy and must agree on what is recorded. Because interview topics include "opportunities that might be possible for writing at home and whether the child chooses to write" (Barrs, Ellis, Hester, & Thomas, 1989,

p. 16), parents simultaneously learn about possible ways to expand family literacy practices.

The representation of the child is centrally focused on documentation of what the child does and how the child does it and understands it. In context, though, it also includes numerical ratings for aggregation at the institution level and to complement the descriptive detail. Serious professional development is required for a complex assessment system like the PLR. But that has not prevented its successful adoption (Falk, 1998; Falk & Darling-Hammond, 1993). Implementation is not expected to occur overnight, and it is recommended that teachers begin by selecting a small group of students to document, expanding the group as expertise develops.

However, much of the professional development is built into the process of the assessment. In order to obtain reliable ratings, participants in the assessment community (teachers, administrators, parent representatives) regularly gather to compare their analyses of one another's assessments. The discussion around cases of disagreement is productive in clarifying the need for recording detail and the bases for judgment. The public nature of these discussions keeps teachers responsible for their assessments and requires a measure of courage. Because the assessment requires a range of literacy learning contexts and particular kinds of evidence, it helps teachers to structure their classroom practice.

We provide this example to show that more common approaches to assessment should not be thought of as "givens" that merely need tweaking. This assessment holds very different assumptions from the more standard views and has very different consequences. For example, the assumption behind current accountability testing is that schools as organizations, and the individuals within them, are not only unable to monitor their own performance but also are unlikely to provide the best instruction they can unless forced to do so annually through rewards and punishments. The successful use of the PLR suggests that this assumption, at least in some contexts, is not tenable. Instead, we might sensibly ask, "Under what circumstances can organizations and individuals productively monitor their teaching and learning as part of improving literacy learning?"

Darling-Hammond (2004), examining successful examples of assessment-driven reforms, provided some answers, concluding that consistency in assessment and curricular imperatives across the institutional learning community is essential. Other critical properties that the system provides, in a timely way, included sophisticated information that is consistent with current understandings of learning and relevant for teaching individual students. Successful assessment systems also provide information about the qualities of students' learning opportunities (the context of learning), develop productive teacher-student relationships, and are able to "leverage continuous change and improvement" through a focus on teacher quality and learning (p. 1078). She noted that relatively low stakes and consistency among the assessment and curricular imperatives are important and that institutional size is not trivial. Although Darling-Hammond focused on the testing context privileged in the United States, these emphases are exactly the design features of the PLR. This is a description of the PLR.

Final Comment

Assessment always (a) is representational and interpretive; (b) is a dynamic part of ongoing, goal-directed social activities and societal discourses; (c) reflects and imposes particular values, beliefs, relationships, and ways of being literate; and thus (d) has consequences for individuals' and communities' understandings of themselves and one another, as well as for the kinds of individuals and communities they will become. If the accelerating shifts in society will require everyone "to become, and remain, committed to learning," (Broadfoot, 2002, p. 6) and to acquire literacies that are more flexible and open, more resilient and self-directed, and more collaborative in a culturally and linguistically diverse context (Kalantzis, Cope, & Harvey, 2003), they will need to be socialized into a literacy that makes this possible, and our assessment systems are part of that socialization.

This means that learning must form the basis of our assessment practice. Current understandings show that the ability to guide and monitor one's own learning is essential to this project (Crooks, 2001). Focusing on learning in this way might incidentally accomplish other shorter term goals. For example, creating classrooms in which assessment practices socialize children into self-regulated literacy learning not only serves students' development as learners but also develops their literate achievement (Harlen & Crick, 2003; McDonald & Boud, 2003). The same principles almost certainly apply to teachers as individuals and as institutional communities. Indeed, if we are to have consistency among assessment and curricular imperatives within schools, the consistency should apply to the processes as well as the content. If literacy assessment is to serve literacy learners and society, then it has to be grounded in processes that reflect current understandings of learning, literacy, and society. It also has to remain open to evolution in both literacy and assessment, which at the very least means encouraging some diversity in assessment practice.

Nearly a decade ago, Shepard and her colleagues interviewed officials from state departments across the United States and concluded that more complex and authentic forms of literacy assessment were developing and that the previous excesses and problems of assessing children, particularly young children, for high-stakes purposes like accountability and retention were largely gone (Shepard, Taylor, & Kagan, 1996). The opposite is now true, a development that has everything to do with politics and relatively little to do with research (Allington, 2002; Allington & Woodside-Jiron, 1999; Johnson & Kress, 2003; Wixson & Pearson, 1998).

Indeed, the United States has currently reached the highest volume of testing and the highest stakes testing in its history. We are reminded of a definition of fanaticism as the act of redoubling one's efforts while having forgotten what one is fighting for (de Toqueville, cited in Claxton, 1999, p. 281). Although this article is in the service of "theory and research into practice," we must not pretend that literacy assessment can be improved by simple application of either. At the very least our theory in practice has to include the fact that changing assessment practices is about changing societal discourses regarding children, literacy, and education, with all the values, relationships, identities, and resources that entails.

References

Allington, R.L. (Ed.). (2002). *Big brother and the national reading curriculum: How ideology trumped evidence.* Portsmouth, NH: Heinemann.

Allington, R.L., & Johnston, P.H. (Eds.). (2002). *Reading to learn: Lessons from exemplary fourth-grade classrooms.* New York: Guilford.

Allington, R.L., & McGill-Franzen, A. (1989). Different programs, indifferent instruction. In A. Gartner & D. Lipsky (Eds.), *Beyond separate education* (pp. 75–98). Baltimore: Brookes.

Allington, R.L., & McGill-Franzen, A. (1995). Flunking: Throwing good money after the bad. In R.L. Allington & S.A. Walmsley (Eds.), *No quick fix: Rethinking literacy programs in America's elementary schools* (pp. 45–60). New York: Teachers College Press.

Allington, R.L., & Woodside-Jiron, H. (1999). The politics of literacy teaching: How "research" shaped educational policy. *Educational Researcher, 28*(8), 4–13.

Argyris, C. (1990). *Overcoming organizational defenses: Facilitating organizational learning.* Boston: Allyn & Bacon.

Arya, P. (2003). Influences of reading group experiences on second graders' perceptions of themselves as readers. *Literacy Teaching and Learning, 8*(1), 1–18.

Barrs, M., Ellis, S., Hester, H., & Thomas, A. (1989). *The primary language record: Handbook for teachers.* London: Inner London Education Authority/Centre for Language in Primary Education.

Baudanza, L. (2001). *Disabilities of a child or disabilities of the system?* Unpublished manuscript, University at Albany, Albany, NY.

Black, P., & Wiliam, D. (1998a). Assessment and classroom learning. *Assessment in Education: Principles, Policy & Practice, 5*(1), 7–74.

Black, P., & Wiliam, D. (1998b, October). Inside the black box: Raising standards through classroom assessment. *Phi Delta Kappa International,* pp. 139–148.

Bourdieu, P. (1991). *Language and symbolic power* (J.B.Thompson, Ed.; G. Raymond & M. Adamson, Trans.). Cambridge, MA: Harvard University Press.

Brandt, D. (2001). *Literacy in American lives.* Cambridge, UK: Cambridge University Press.

Broadfoot, P. (2002). Editorial. Assessment for lifelong learning: Challenges and choices. *Assessment in Education*, 9(1), 5–7.

Broikou, K. (1992). *Understanding primary grade classroom teachers' special education referral practices*. Unpublished doctoral dissertation, State University of New York at Albany, Albany, NY.

Carr, M., & Claxton, G. (2002). Tracking the development of learning dispositions. *Assessment in Education*, 9(1), 9–37.

Claxton, G. (1999). *Wise up: The challenge of lifelong learning*. New York: Bloomsbury.

Clay, M.M. (1987). Learning to be learning disabled. *New Zealand Journal of Educational Studies*, 22, 155–173.

Clay, M. (1991). *Becoming literate: The construction of inner control*. Portsmouth, NH: Heinemann.

Clay, M.M. (1993). *An observation survey of early literacy achievement*. Portsmouth, NH: Heinemann.

Collins, J., & Blot, R.K. (2003). *Literacy and literacies: Texts, power, and identity*. New York: Cambridge University Press.

Comeyras, M. (1995). What can we learn from students' questions? *Theory Into Practice*, 34, 101–106.

Crooks, T. (2001, September). *The validity of formative assessments*. Paper presented at the annual meeting of the British Educational Research Association, Leeds, UK.

Crooks, T.J. (1988). The impact of classroom evaluation practices on students. *Review of Educational Research*, 58, 438–481.

Darling-Hammond, L. (2004). Standards, accountability, and school reform. *Teachers College Record*, 106, 1047–1085.

Deci, E.L., Siegel, N.H., Ryan, R.M., Koestner, R., & Kauffman, M. (1982). Effects of performance standards on teaching styles: Behavior of controlling teachers. *Journal of Educational Psychology*, 74, 852–859.

Delandshere, G. (2001). Implicit theories, unexamined assumptions and the status quo of educational assessment. *Assessment in Education*, 8, 113–133.

Dweck, C.S. (1999). *Self-theories: Their role in motivation, personality, and development*. Philadelphia: Psychology Press.

Fairclough, N. (1992). *Discourse and social change*. London: Longman.

Falk, B. (1998). Using direct evidence to assess student progress: How the Primary Language Record supports teaching and learning. In C. Harrison & T. Salinger (Eds.), *Assessing reading 1: Theory and practice: International perspectives on reading assessment* (pp. 152–165). London: Routledge.

Falk, B. (2001). Professional learning through assessment. In A. Lieberman & L. Miller (Eds.), *Teachers caught in the action: Professional development that matters* (pp. 118–140). New York: Teachers College Press.

Falk, B., & Darling-Hammond, L. (1993). *The Primary Language Record at P.S. 261: How assessment transforms teaching and learning*. New York: The National Center for Restructuring Education, Schools, and Teaching, Teachers College, Columbia University.

Fennimore, B.S. (2000). *Talk matters: Refocusing the language of public school*. New York: Teachers College Press.

Flockton, L., & Crooks, T. (1996). *National Education Monitoring Project: Reading and speaking: Assessment results: 1996* (No. 6). Dunedin, New Zealand: Educational Assessment Research Unit.

Gee, J.P. (1996). *Social linguistics and literacies: Ideology in discourses* (2nd ed.). London: Falmer.

Gee, J.P. (2000). Discourse and sociocultural studies in reading. In M.L. Kamil, P.B. Mosenthal, P.D. Pearson, & R. Barr (Eds.), *Handbook of reading research* (Vol. III, pp. 195–207). Mahwah, NJ: Erlbaum.

Gilmore, A. (2002). Large-scale assessment and teachers' assessment capacity: Learning opportunities for teachers in the National Education Monitoring Project in New Zealand. *Assessment in Education*, 9, 343–361.

Goodman, Y. (1978). Kidwatching: Observing children in the classroom. In A. Jagger & M.T. Smith-Burke (Eds.), *Observing the language learner* (pp. 9–18). Newark, DE: International Reading Association.

Greenberg, K.H., & Williams, L. (2002). Reciprocity and mutuality in dynamic assessment: Asking uncomfortable questions. In G.M. v. d. Aalsvoort, W.C.M. Resing, & A.J.J.M. Ruijssenaars (Eds.), *Learning potential assessment and cognitive training* (Vol. 7, pp. 91–110). Amsterdam: JAI.

Greene, M. (1985). The role of education in democracy. *Educational Horizons*, 63, 3–9.

Harlen, W., & Crick, R.D. (2003). Testing and motivation for learning. *Assessment in Education: Principles, Policy & Practice*, 10(2), 169–207.

Hill, C. (2004). Failing to meet the standards: The English language arts test for fourth graders in New York State. *Teachers College Record*, 106, 1086–1123.

Himley, M., & Carini, P.F. (Eds.). (2000). *From another angle: Children's strengths and school standards: The Prospect Center's descriptive review of the child*. New York: Teachers College Press.

International Reading Association and National Council of Teachers of English Joint Task Force on Assessment. (1994). *Standards for the assessment of reading and writing*. Newark, DE: International Reading Association.

Johnson, D., & Kress, G. (2003). Globalisation, literacy and society: Redesigning pedagogy and assessment. *Assessment in Education*, 10(1), 5–14.

Johnston, P.H. (1989). Constructive evaluation and the improvement of teaching and learning. *Teachers College Record*, 90, 509–528.

Johnston, P.H. (1993). Assessment as social practice. In D. Leu & C. Kinzer (Eds.), *42nd yearbook of the National Reading Conference* (pp. 11–23). Chicago: National Reading Conference.

Johnston, P.H. (1997). *Knowing literacy: Constructive literacy assessment*. York, ME: Stenhouse.

Johnston, P.H. (1999). Unpacking literate achievement. In J. Gaffney & B. Askew (Eds.), *Stirring the waters: A tribute to Marie Clay* (pp. 17–25). Portsmouth, NH: Heinemann.

Johnston, P.H. (2003). Assessment conversations. *The Reading Teacher*, 57, 90–92.

Johnston, P.H. (2004). *Choice words: How our language affects children's learning*. York, ME: Stenhouse.

Johnston, P.H., Afflerbach, P., & Weiss, P. (1993). Teachers' evaluation of teaching and learning of literacy. *Educational Assessment*, 1(2), 91–117.

Johnston, P.H., Jiron, H.W., & Day, J.P. (2001). Teaching and learning literate epistemologies. *Journal of Educational Psychology, 93*(1), 223–233.

Johnston, P.H., & Rogers, R. (2001). Early literacy assessment. In S.B. Neuman & D.K. Dickenson (Eds.), *Handbook of early literacy research* (pp. 377–389). New York: Guilford.

Kalantzis, M., Cope, B., & Harvey, A. (2003). Assessing multiliteracies and the new basics. *Assessment in Education: Principles, Policy & Practice, 10*, 15–26.

Learning, S. (2002). *FastForWord*. Retrieved August 3, 2002, from http://www.scilearn.com.

Mcdermott, R.P. (1993). The acquisition of a child by a learning disability. In S. Chaiklin & J. Lave (Eds.), *Understanding practice: Perspectives on activity and context* (pp. 269–305). Cambridge, UK: Cambridge University Press.

McDonald, B., & Boud, D. (2003). The impact of self-assessment on achievement: The effects of self-assessment training on performance in external examinations. *Assessment in education: Principles, Policy & Practice, 10*(2), 209–220.

McNeil, L.M. (2000). *Contradictions of school reform: Education costs of standardized tests.* New York: Routledge.

Mehan, H. (1993). Beneath the skin and between the ears: A case study in the politics of representation. In S. Chaiklin & J. Lave (Eds.), *Understanding practice: Perspectives on activity and context* (pp. 241–268). Cambridge, UK: Cambridge University Press.

Messick, S. (1994). The interplay of evidence and consequences in the validation of performance assessments. *Educational Researcher, 23*(2), 13–23.

Morrison, K., & Joan, T.F.H. (2002). Testing to destruction: A problem in a small state. *Assessment in Education, 9*, 289–317.

Moss, P., & Schutz, A. (2001). Educational standards, assessment and the search for consensus. *American Educational Research Journal, 38*(1), 37–70.

Moss, P.A. (1998). The role of consequences in validity theory. *Educational Measurement: Issues and Practice, 17*(2), 6–12.

Niemi, P., & Poskiparta, E. (2002). Shadows over phonological awareness training: Resistant learners and dissipating gains. In E. Hjelmquist & C.V. Euler (Eds.), *Dyslexia and literacy* (pp. 84–99). London, UK: Whurr.

No Child Left Behind Act of 2001, Pub. L. No. 107-110, 115 Stat. 1425 (2002).

Nystrand, M., Gamoran, A., Kachur, R., & Prendergast, C. (1997). *Opening dialogue: Understanding the dynamics of language and learning in the English classroom.* New York: Teachers College Press.

Paris, S.G. (2002). Measuring children's reading development using leveled texts. *The Reading Teacher, 55*, 168–170.

Pradl, G.M. (1996). Reading and democracy: The enduring influence of Louise Rosenblatt. *The New Advocate, 9*(1), 9–22.

Pressley, M., Allington, R.L., Wharton-MacDonald, R., Collins-Block, C., & Morrow, L. (2001). *Learning to read: Lessons from exemplary first-grade classrooms.* New York: Guilford.

Rex, L.A., & Nelson, M.C. (2004). How teachers' professional identities position high-stakes test preparation in their classrooms. *Teachers College Record, 106*, 1288–1331.

Rodgers, C. (2002). Defining reflection: Another look at John Dewey and reflective thinking. *Teachers College Record, 104*(4), 842–866.

Rogers, R. (2002). Between contexts: A critical analysis of family literacy, discursive practices, and literate subjectivities. *Reading Research Quarterly, 37*, 248–277.

Rogers, R. (2003). *A critical discourse analysis of family literacy practices: Power in and out of print.* Mahwah, NJ: Erlbaum.

Roskos, K., & Neuman, S.B. (1993). Descriptive observations of adults' facilitation of literacy in young children's play. *Early Childhood Research Quarterly, 8*, 77–97.

Rueda, R., & Mercer, J. (1985, June). *Predictive analysis of decision-making practices with limited English proficient handicapped students.* Paper presented at the Third Annual Symposium: Exceptional Hispanic Children and Youth. Monograph series, Denver, CO.

Russell, M., & Abrams, L. (2004). Instructional uses of computers for writing: The effect of state testing programs. *Teachers College Record, 106*, 1332–1357.

Sadler, R.R. (1987). Specifying and promulgating achievement standards. *Oxford Review of Education, 13*, 191–209.

Scanlon, D.M., Vellutino, F.R., Small, S.G., & Fanuele, D.P. (2000, April). *Severe reading difficulties—can they be prevented? A comparison of prevention and intervention approaches.* Paper presented at the American Educational Research Association, New Orleans, LA.

Schaffer, H.R. (1996). Joint involvement episodes as context for development. In H. Daniels (Ed.), *An introduction to Vygotsky* (pp. 251–280). London: Routledge.

Shavelson, R.J., Baxter, G.P., & Pine, J. (1992). Performance assessments: Political rhetoric and measurement reality. *Educational Researcher, 21*(4), 22–27.

Shepard, L.A. (1991). Psychometricians' beliefs about learning. *Educational Researcher, 20*(7), 2–16.

Shepard, L.A., Taylor, G.A., & Kagan, S.L. (1996). *Trends in early childhood assessment policies and practices.* Washington, DC: Office of Educational Research & Improvement.

Smith, M.L. (1991). Put to the test: The effects of external testing on teachers. *Educational Researcher, 20*(5), 8–11.

Smith, M.L., & Rottenberg, C. (1991). Unintended consequences of external testing in elementary schools. *Educational Measurement: Issues and Practice, 10*(4), 7–11.

Smith, P. (1997). *A third chance to learn: The development and evaluation of specialized interventions for young children experiencing difficulty with learning to read* (No. 13227). Wellington, New Zealand: National Council for Educational Research.

Stallman, A.C., & Pearson, P.D. (1991). Formal measures of early literacy. In L.M. Morrow & J.K. Smith (Eds.), *Assessment for instruction in early literacy* (pp. 7–44). Englewood Cliffs, NJ: Prentice Hall.

Teale, W. (1991). The promise and the challenge of informal assessment in early literacy. In L.M. Morrow & J.K.

Smith (Eds.), *Assessment for instruction in early literacy* (pp. 45–61). Englewood Cliffs, NJ: Prentice Hall.

Torgeson, J.K. (2000). Individual differences in response to early interventions in reading: The lingering problem of treatment resisters. *Learning Disabilities Research and Practice, 15*(1), 55–64.

Tudge, J., & Rogoff, B. (1989). Peer influences on cognitive development: Piagetian-Vygotskian perspectives. In M.H. Bornstein & J.S. Bruner (Eds.), *Interactions in human development* (pp. 17–40). Hillsdale, NJ: Erlbaum.

Wixson, K.K., & Pearson, P.D. (1998). Policy and assessment strategies to support literacy instruction for a new century. *Peabody Journal of Education, 74*, 202–227.

Yalom, I.D. (1989). *Love's executioner and other tales of psychotherapy.* New York: Basic Books.

Behind Test Scores:
What Struggling Readers *Really* Need

Sheila W. Valencia and Marsha Riddle Buly

Every year thousands of U.S. students take standardized tests and state reading tests, and every year thousands fail them. With the implementation of the No Child Left Behind legislation (www.ed.gov/nclb/landing.jhtml), which mandates testing all children from grades 3 to 8 every year, these numbers will grow exponentially, and alarming numbers of schools and students will be targeted for "improvement." Whether you believe this increased focus on testing is good news or bad, if you are an educator, you are undoubtedly concerned about the children who struggle every day with reading and the implications of their test failure.

Although legislators, administrators, parents, and educators have been warned repeatedly not to rely on a single measure to make important instructional decisions (Elmore, 2002; Linn, n.d.; Shepard, 2000), scores from state tests still seem to drive the search for programs and approaches that will help students learn and meet state standards. The popular press, educational publications, teacher workshops, and state and school district policies are filled with attempts to find solutions for poor test performance. For example, some schools have eliminated sustained silent reading in favor of more time for explicit instruction (Edmondson & Shannon, 2002; Riddle Buly & Valencia, 2002), others are buying special programs or mandating specific interventions (Goodnough, 2001; Helfand, 2002), and some states and districts are requiring teachers to have particular instructional emphases

(McNeil, 2000; Paterson, 2000; Riddle Buly & Valencia, 2002). Furthermore, it is common to find teachers spending enormous amounts of time preparing students for these high-stakes tests (Olson, 2001), even though a narrow focus on preparing students for specific tests does not translate into real learning (Klein, Hamilton, McCaffrey, & Stecher, 2000; Linn, 2000). But, if we are really going to help students, we need to understand the underlying reasons for their test failure. Simply knowing which children have failed state tests is a bit like knowing that you have a fever when you are feeling ill but having no idea of the cause or cure. A test score, like a fever, is a symptom that demands more specific analysis of the problem. In this case, what is required is a more in-depth analysis of the strengths and needs of students who fail to meet standards and instructional plans that will meet their needs.

In this article, we draw from the results of an empirical study of students who failed a typical fourth-grade state reading assessment (see Riddle Buly & Valencia, 2002, for a full description of the study). Specifically, we describe the patterns of performance that distinguish different groups of students who failed to meet standards. We also provide suggestions for what classroom teachers need to know and how they might help these children succeed.

Study Context

Our research was conducted in a typical northwestern U.S. school district of 18,000

Preparing Reading Professionals (second edition), edited by Rita M. Bean, Natalie Heisey, and Cathy M. Roller. © 2010 by the International Reading Association. Reprinted from Valencia, S.W., & Buly, M.R. (2004). Behind test scores: What struggling readers *really* need. *The Reading Teacher, 57*(6), 520–531.

students located adjacent to the largest urban district in the state. At the time of our study, 43% were students of color and 47% received free or reduced-price lunch. Over the past several years, approximately 50% of students had failed the state fourth-grade reading test that, like many other standards-based state assessments, consisted of several extended narrative and expository reading selections accompanied by a combination of multiple-choice and open-ended comprehension questions. For the purposes of this study, during September of fifth grade we randomly selected 108 students who had scored below standard on the state test given at the end of fourth grade. These 108 students constituted approximately 10% of failing students in the district. None of them was receiving supplemental special education or English as a Second Language (ESL) services. We wanted to understand the "garden variety" (Stanovich, 1988) test failure—those students typically found in the regular classroom who are experiencing reading difficulty but have not been identified as needing special services or intensive interventions. Classroom teachers, not reading specialists or special education teachers, are solely responsible for the reading instruction of these children and, ultimately, for their achievement.

Data Collection and Assessment Tools

Our approach was to conduct individual reading assessments, working one-on-one with the children for approximately two hours over several days to gather information about their reading abilities. We administered a series of assessments that targeted key components of reading ability identified by experts: word identification, meaning (comprehension and vocabulary), and fluency (rate and expression) (Lipson & Wixson, 2003; National Institute of Child Health and Human Development, 2000; Snow, Burns, & Griffin, 1998). Table 1 presents the measures we used and the areas in which each provided information.

To measure word identification, we used two tests from the 1989 Woodcock-Johnson Psycho-Educational Battery–Revised (WJ–R) that assessed students' reading of single and

Table 1
Diagnostic Assessments

Assessment	Word Identification	Meaning	Fluency
Woodcock-Johnson–Revised			
Letter-word identification	X		
Word attack	X		
Qualitative Reading Inventory–II			
Reading accuracy	X		
Reading acceptability	X		
Rate			X
Expression			X
Comprehension		X	
Peabody Picture Vocabulary Test–Revised			
Vocabulary meaning		X	
State fourth-grade passages			
Reading accuracy	X		
Reading acceptability	X		
Rate			X
Expression			X

multisyllabic words, both real and pseudowords. We also scored oral reading errors students made on narrative and expository graded passages from the 1995 Qualitative Reading Inventory–II (QRI–II) and from the state test. We calculated total accuracy (percentage of words read correctly) and acceptability (counting only those errors that changed the meaning of the text). Students also responded orally to comprehension questions that accompanied the QRI–II passages, providing a measure of their comprehension that was not confounded by writing ability. To assess receptive vocabulary, we used the 1981 Peabody Picture Vocabulary Test–Revised (PPVT–R), which requires students to listen and point to a picture that corresponds to a word (scores of 85 or higher are judged to be average or above average). As with the comprehension questions, the vocabulary measure does not confound understanding with students' ability to write responses. Finally, in the area of fluency, we assessed rate of reading and expression (Samuels, 2002). We timed the readings of all passages (i.e., QRI–II and state test selections) to get a reading rate and used a 4-point rubric developed for the Oral Reading Study of the fourth-grade National Assessment of Educational Progress (NAEP) (Pinnell, Pikulski, Wixson, Campbell, Gough, & Beatty, 1995) to assess phrasing and expression (1–2 is judged to be nonfluent; 3–4 is judged to be fluent).

Findings

Scores from all the assessments for each student fell into three statistically distinct and educationally familiar categories: word identification (word reading in isolation and context), meaning (comprehension and vocabulary), and fluency (rate and expression). When we examined the average scores for all 108 students in the sample, students appeared to be substantially below grade level in all three areas. However, when we analyzed the data using a cluster analysis (Aldenderfer & Blashfield, 1984), looking for groups of students who had similar patterns across all three factors, we found six distinct profiles of students who failed the test. Most striking is that the majority of students were not weak in all three areas; they were actually strong in some and weak in others. Table 2 indicates the percentage of students in each group and their relative strength (+) or weakness (–) in word identification, meaning, and fluency.

The Profiles

We illuminate each profile by describing a prototypical student from each cluster (see Figure) and specific suggested instructional targets for each (all names are pseudonyms). Although the instructional strategies we recommend have not been implemented with these particular children, we base our recommendations on

Table 2 **Cluster Analysis**						
Cluster	Sample Percentage	English Language Learner Percentage	Low Socio-economic Status Percentage	Word Identification	Meaning	Fluency
1—Automatic word caller	18	63	89	+ +	–	+ +
2—Struggling word caller	15	56	81	–	–	+ +
3—Word stumblers	17	16	42	–	+	–
4—Slow comprehenders	24	19	54	+	+ +	–
5—Slow word caller	17	56	67	+	–	–
6—Disabled readers	9	20	80	– –	– –	– –

Prototypical Students From Each Cluster

Cluster 1—Automatic Word Callers (18%)

Word Identification	Meaning	Fluency
+ +	−	+ +

Tomas

Word identification = ninth grade (WJ–R)
> fourth grade (QRI–II)
= 98% (state passages)
Comprehension = second/third grade
Vocabulary = 108
Expression = 3
Rate = 155 words per minute
Writing = proficient

Cluster 2—Struggling Word Callers (15%)

Word Identification	Meaning	Fluency
−	−	+ +

Makara

Word identification = fourth grade (WJ–R)
< second grade (QRI–II)
= 75% (state passages)
Comprehension = < second grade
Vocabulary = 58
Expression = 2.5
Rate = 117 words per minute
Writing = below proficient

Cluster 3—Word Stumblers (17%)

Word Identification	Meaning	Fluency
−	+	−

Sandy

Word identification = second grade (WJ–R)
= second-grade accuracy/third-grade
acceptability (QRI–II)
= 80% accuracy/99% acceptability
(state passages)
Comprehension = fourth grade
Vocabulary = 135
Expression = 1.5
Rate = 77 words per minute
Writing = proficient

Cluster 4—Slow Comprehenders (24%)

Word Identification	Meaning	Fluency
+	+ +	−

Martin

Word identification = sixth grade (WJ–R)
> fourth grade (QRI–II)
= 100% (state passages)
Comprehension = > fourth grade
Vocabulary = 103
Expression = 2.5
Rate = 61 words per minute
Writing = proficient

Cluster 5—Slow Word Callers (17%)

Word Identification	Meaning	Fluency
+	−	−

Andrew

Word identification = seventh grade (WJ–R)
> fourth grade (QRI–II)
= 98% (state passages)
Comprehension = second grade
Vocabulary = 74
Expression = 1.5
Rate = 62 words per minute
Writing = not proficient

Cluster 6—Disabled Readers (9%)

Word Identification	Meaning	Fluency
− −	− −	− −

Jesse

Word identification = first grade (WJ–R)
< first grade (QRI–II)
< 50% (state passages)
Comprehension = < first grade
Vocabulary = 105
Writing = not proficient

our review of research-based practices (e.g., Allington, 2001; Allington & Johnston, 2001; Lipson & Wixson, 2003; National Institute of Child Health and Human Development, 2000), our interpretation of the profiles, and our experiences teaching struggling readers. We conclude with several general implications for school and classroom instruction.

Cluster 1—Automatic Word Callers

[handwritten: Kacey, Karen, Aisha]
[handwritten: ELL who no longer receive services]

We call these students Automatic Word Callers because they can decode words quickly and accurately, but they fail to read for meaning. The majority of students in this cluster qualify for free or reduced-price lunch, and they are English-language learners who no longer receive special support. Tomas is a typical student in this cluster.

Tomas has excellent word identification skills. He scored at ninth-grade level when reading real words and pseudowords (i.e., phonetically regular nonsense words such as *fot*) on the WJ–R tests, and at the independent level for word identification on the QRI–II and state fourth-grade passages. However, when asked about what he read, Tomas had difficulty, placing his comprehension at the second-grade level. Although Tomas's first language is not English, his score of 108 on the PPVT–R suggests that his comprehension difficulties are more complex than individual word meanings. Tomas's "proficient" score on the state writing assessment also suggests that his difficulty is in understanding rather than in writing answers to comprehension questions. This student's rate of reading, which was quite high compared with rates of fourth-grade students on the Oral Reading Study of NAEP (Pinnell et al., 1995) and other research (Harris & Sipay, 1990), suggests that his decoding is automatic and unlikely to be contributing to his comprehension difficulty. His score in expression is also consistent with students who were rated as "fluent" according to the NAEP rubric, although this seems unusual for a student who is demonstrating difficulty with comprehension.

The evidence suggests that Tomas needs additional instruction in comprehension and most likely would benefit from explicit instruction, teacher modeling, and think-alouds of key reading strategies (e.g., summarizing, self-monitoring, creating visual representations, evaluating), using a variety of types of material at the fourth- or fifth-grade level (Block & Pressley, 2002; Duke & Pearson, 2002). His comprehension performance on the QRI–II suggests that his literal comprehension is quite strong but that he has difficulty with more inferential and critical aspects of understanding. Although Tomas has strong scores in the fluency category, both in expression and rate, he may be reading too fast to attend to meaning, especially deeper meaning of the ideas in the text. Tomas's teacher should help him understand that the purpose for reading is to understand and that rate varies depending on the type of text and the purpose for reading. Then, the teacher should suggest that he slow down to focus on meaning. Self-monitoring strategies would also help Tomas check for understanding and encourage him to think about the ideas while he is reading. These and other such strategies may help him learn to adjust his rate to meet the demands of the text.

Tomas would also likely benefit from additional support in acquiring academic language, which takes many years for English-language learners to develop (Cummins, 1991). Reading activities such as building background; developing understanding of new words, concepts, and figurative language in his "to-be-read" texts; and acquiring familiarity with genre structures found in longer, more complex texts like those found at fourth grade and above would provide important opportunities for his language and conceptual development (Antunez, 2002; Hiebert, Pearson, Taylor, Richardson, & Paris, 1998). Classroom read-alouds and discussions as well as lots of additional independent reading would also help Tomas in building language and attention to understanding.

Cluster 2—Struggling Word Callers

[handwritten: Chris]

The students in this cluster not only struggle with meaning, like the Automatic Word Callers in Cluster 1, but they also struggle with word identification. Makara, a student from Cambodia, is one of these students. Like Tomas, Makara struggled with comprehension. But unlike Tomas, he had substantial difficulty applying word identification skills when reading connected text (QRI–II and state passages), even though his reading of isolated words on the WJ–R was at a fourth-grade level. Such word identification difficulties would likely contribute to comprehension problems. However, Makara's performance on the PPVT–R, which placed him below the 1st percentile compared with other students his age, and his poor performance on the state writing assessment suggest that language may contribute to his comprehension difficulties as well—not surprising for a student acquiring a second language. These language-related results need to be viewed with caution, however, because the version of the PPVT–R available for use in this study may underestimate the language abilities of students from culturally and linguistically diverse backgrounds, and written language takes longer than oral language to develop. Despite difficulty with meaning, Makara read quickly—117 words per minute. At first glance, this may seem unusual given his difficulty with both decoding and comprehension. Closer investigation of his performance, however, revealed that Makara read words quickly whether he was reading them correctly or incorrectly and didn't stop to monitor or self-correct. In addition, although Makara was fast, his expression and phrasing were uneven and consistent with comprehension difficulties.

Makara likely needs instruction and practice in oral and written language, as well as in constructing meaning in reading and writing, self-monitoring, and decoding while reading connected text. All this needs to be done in rich, meaningful contexts, taking into account his background knowledge and interests. Like Tomas, Makara would benefit from teacher or peer read-alouds, lots of experience with independent reading at his level, small-group instruction, and the kinds of activities aimed at building academic language that we described earlier, as well as a more foundational emphasis on word meanings. Makara also needs instruction in self-monitoring and fix-up strategies to improve his comprehension and awareness of reading for understanding. Decoding instruction is also important for him, although his teacher would need to gather more information using tools such as miscue analysis or tests of decoding to determine his specific decoding needs and how they interact with his knowledge of word meanings. Makara clearly cannot be instructed in fourth-grade material; most likely, his teacher would need to begin with second-grade material that is familiar and interesting to him and a good deal of interactive background building. At the same time, however, Makara needs exposure to the content and vocabulary of grade-level texts through activities such as teacher read-alouds, tapes, and partner reading so that his conceptual understanding continues to grow.

Cluster 3—Word Stumblers Isaac

Students in this cluster have substantial difficulty with word identification, but they still have surprisingly strong comprehension. How does that happen? Sandy, a native English speaker from a middle class home, is a good example of this type of student. Sandy stumbled on so many words initially that it seemed unlikely that she would comprehend what she had read, yet she did. Her word identification scores were at second-grade level, and she read the state fourth-grade passages at frustration level. However, a clue to her strong comprehension is evident from the difference between her immediate word recognition accuracy score and her acceptability score, which takes into account self-corrections or errors that do not change the meaning. In other words, Sandy was so focused on reading for meaning that she spontaneously self-corrected many of her decoding miscues or substituted words that preserved the meaning. She attempted to read every word in the reading selections, working until she could figure out some part of each word and then using context clues to help her get the entire word. She seemed to over-rely on context because her decoding skills were so weak (Stanovich, 1994). Remarkably, she was eventually able to read the words on the state fourth-grade reading passages at an independent level. But, as we might predict, Sandy's rate was very slow, and her initial attempts to read were choppy and lacked flow—she spent an enormous amount of time self-correcting and rereading. After she finally self-corrected or figured out unknown words, however, Sandy reread phrases with good expression and flow to fit with the meaning. Although Sandy's overall fluency score was low, her primary difficulty does not appear in the area of either rate or expression; rather, her low performance in fluency seems to be a result of her difficulty with decoding.

With such a strong quest for meaning, Sandy was able to comprehend fourth-grade material even when her decoding was at frustration level. No doubt her strong language and vocabulary abilities (i.e., 99th percentile) were assets. As we might predict, Sandy was more than proficient at expressing her ideas when writing about her experiences. She understands that reading and writing should make sense, and she has the self-monitoring strategies, perseverance, and language background to make that happen.

Sandy needs systematic instruction in word identification and opportunities to practice when reading connected text at her reading level. She is clearly beyond the early stages of reading and decoding, but her teacher will need to determine through a more in-depth analysis precisely which decoding skills should be the focus of her instruction. At the same time, Sandy needs supported experiences with texts that will continue to feed and challenge her drive for meaning. For students like Sandy, it is critical not to sacrifice intellectual engagement with text while they are receiving decoding instruction and practice in below-grade-level material. Furthermore, Sandy needs to develop automaticity with word identification, and to do that she would benefit from assisted reading (i.e., reading along with others, monitored reading with a tape, or partner reading) as well as unassisted reading practice (i.e., repeated reading,

reading to younger students) with materials at her instructional level (Kuhn & Stahl, 2000).

Cluster 4—Slow Comprehenders

Almost one fourth of the students in this sample were Slow Comprehenders. Like other students in this cluster, Martin is a native English speaker and a relatively strong decoder, scoring above fourth-grade level on all measures of decoding. His comprehension was at the instructional level on the fourth-grade QRI–II selections, and his vocabulary and writing ability were average for his age. On the surface, this information is puzzling because Martin failed the fourth-grade state test.

Insight about Martin's reading performance comes from several sources. First, Martin was within two points of passing the state assessment, so he doesn't seem to have a serious reading problem. Second, although his reading rate is quite slow and this often interferes with comprehension (Adams, 1990), results of the QRI–II suggest that Martin's comprehension is quite strong, in spite of his slow rate. This is most likely because Martin has good word knowledge and understands that reading should make sense, and neither the QRI–II nor the state test has time limits. His strong score in expression confirms that Martin did, indeed, attend to meaning while reading. Third, a close examination of his reading behaviors while reading words from the WJ–R tests, QRI–II, and state reading selections revealed that he had some difficulty reading multisyllabic words; although, with time, he was able to read enough words to score at grade level or above. It appears that Martin has the decoding skills to attack multisyllabic words, but they are not yet automatic.

The outstanding characteristic of Martin's profile is his extremely slow rate combined with his relatively strong word identification abilities and comprehension. Our work with him suggests that, even if Martin were to get the additional two points needed to pass the state test, he would still have a significant problem with rate and some difficulty with automatic decoding of multisyllabic words, both of which could hamper his future reading success. Furthermore, with such a lack of automaticity and a slow rate, it is unlikely that Martin enjoys or spends much time reading. As a result, he is likely to fall further and further behind his peers (Stanovich, 1986), especially as he enters middle school where the amount of reading increases dramatically. Martin needs fluency-building activities such as guided repeated oral reading, partner reading, and Readers Theatre (Allington, 2001; Kuhn & Stahl, 2000; Lipson & Wixson, 2003). Given his word identification and comprehension abilities, he most likely could get that practice using fourth-grade material where he will also encounter multisyllabic words. It is important to find reading material that is interesting to Martin and that, initially, can be completed in a relatively short time. Martin needs to develop stamina as well as fluency, and to do that he will need to spend time reading short and extended texts. In addition, Martin might benefit from instruction and practice in strategies for identifying multisyllabic words so that he is more prepared to deal with them automatically while reading.

Cluster 5—Slow Word Callers

The students in this cluster are similar to Tomas, the Automatic Word Caller in Cluster 1. The difference is that Tomas is an automatic, fluent word caller, whereas the students in this cluster are slow. This group is a fairly even mix of English-language learners and native English speakers who have difficulty in comprehension and fluency. Andrew is an example of such a student. He has well-developed decoding skills, scoring at the seventh-grade level when reading words in isolation and at the independent level when reading connected text. Even with such strong decoding abilities, Andrew had difficulty with comprehension. We had to drop down to the second-grade QRI–II passage for Andrew to score at the instructional level for comprehension, and, even at that level, his retelling was minimal. Andrew's score on the PPVT–R, corresponding to first grade (the 4th percentile for his age), adds to the comprehension picture as well. It suggests that Andrew

may be experiencing difficulty with both individual word meanings and text-based understanding when reading paragraphs and longer selections. Like Martin, Andrew's reading rate was substantially below rates expected for fourth-grade students (Harris & Sipay, 1990; Pinnell et al., 1995), averaging 62 words per minute when reading narrative and expository selections. In practical terms, this means he read just one word per second. As we might anticipate from his slow rate and his comprehension difficulty, Andrew did not read with expression or meaningful phrasing.

The relationship between meaning and fluency is unclear in Andrew's case. On the one hand, students who realize they don't understand would be wise to slow down and monitor meaning. On the other hand, Andrew's lack of automaticity and slow rate may interfere with comprehension. To disentangle these factors, his teacher would need to experiment with reading materials about which Andrew has a good deal of background knowledge to eliminate difficulty with individual word meanings and overall comprehension. If his reading rate and expression improve under such conditions, a primary focus for instruction would be meaning. That is, his slow rate of reading and lack of prosody would seem to be a response to lack of understanding rather than contributing to it. In contrast, if Andrew's rate and expression are still low when the material and vocabulary are familiar, instruction should focus on both fluency and meaning. In either case, Andrew would certainly benefit from attention to vocabulary building, both indirect building through extensive independent reading and teacher read-alouds as well as more explicit instruction in word learning strategies and new words he will encounter when reading specific texts (Nagy, 1988; Stahl & Kapinus, 2001).

It is interesting that 50% of the students in this cluster scored at Level 1 on the state test, the lowest level possible. State guidelines characterize these students as lacking prerequisite knowledge and skills that are fundamental for meeting the standard. Given such a definition, a logical assumption would be that these students lack basic, early reading skills such as decoding. However, as the evidence here suggests, we cannot assume that students who score at the lowest level on the test need decoding instruction. Andrew, like others in this cluster, needs instruction in meaning and fluency.

Cluster 6—Disabled Readers Noah

We call this group Disabled Readers because they are experiencing severe difficulty in all three areas—word identification, meaning, and fluency. This is the smallest group (9%), yet, ironically, this is the profile that most likely comes to mind when we think of children who fail state reading tests. This group also includes one of the lowest numbers of second-language learners. The most telling characteristic of students in this cluster, like Jesse, is their very limited word identification abilities. Jesse had few decoding skills beyond initial consonants, basic consonant-vowel-consonant patterns (e.g., *hat*, *box*), and high-frequency sight words. However, his knowledge of word meanings was average, like most of the students in this cluster, which suggests that receptive language was not a major problem and that he does not likely have limited learning ability. With decoding ability at the first-grade level and below, it is not surprising that Jesse's comprehension and fluency were also low. He simply could not read enough words at the first-grade level to get any meaning.

As we might anticipate, the majority of students in this cluster were not proficient in writing and scored at the lowest level, Level 1, on the state fourth-grade reading test. It is important to remember, however, that children who were receiving special education intervention were not included in our sample. So, the children in this cluster, like Jesse, are receiving all of their instruction, or the majority of it (some may be getting supplemental help), from their regular classroom teachers.

Jesse clearly needs intensive, systematic word identification instruction targeted at beginning reading along with access to lots of reading material at first-grade level and below. This will be a challenge for Jesse's fifth-grade teacher. Pedagogically, Jesse needs explicit instruction in basic word identification. Yet few intermediate-grade teachers include this as a part of their instruction, and most do not have an adequate supply of easy materials for instruction or fluency building. In addition, the majority of texts in other subject areas such as social studies and science are written at levels that will be inaccessible to students like Jesse, so alternative materials and strategies will be needed. On the social-emotional front, it will be a challenge to keep Jesse engaged in learning and to provide opportunities for him to succeed in the classroom, even if he is referred for additional reading support. Without that engagement and desire to learn, it is unlikely he will be motivated to put forth the effort it will take for him to make progress. Jesse needs a great deal of support from his regular classroom teacher and from a reading specialist, working together to build a comprehensive instructional program in school and support at home that will help him develop the skill and will to progress.

Conclusions and Implications

Our brief descriptions of the six prototypical children and the instructional focus each one needs is a testimony to individual differences. As we have heard a thousand times before, and as our data support, one-size instruction will not fit all children. The evidence here clearly demonstrates that students fail state reading tests for a variety of reasons and that, if we are to help these students, we will need to provide appropriate instruction to meet their varying needs. For example, placing all struggling students in a phonics or word identification program would be inappropriate for nearly 58% of the students in this sample who had adequate or strong word identification skills. In a similar manner, an instructional approach that did not address fluency and building reading stamina for longer, more complex text or that did not provide sufficient reading material at a range of levels would miss almost 70% of the students who demonstrated difficulty with fluency. In addition to these important cautions about

WIN time ↓

overgeneralizing students' needs, we believe there are several strategies aimed at assessment, classroom organization and materials, and school structures that could help teachers meet their students' needs.

First and most obvious, teachers need to go beneath the scores on state tests by conducting additional diagnostic assessments that will help them identify students' needs. The data here demonstrate quite clearly that, without more in-depth and individual student assessment, distinctive and instructionally important patterns of students' abilities are masked. We believe that informal reading inventories, oral reading records, and other individually tailored assessments provide useful information about all students. At the same time, we realize that many teachers do not have the time to do complete diagnostic evaluations, such as those we did, with every student. At a minimum, we suggest a kind of layered approach to assessment in which teachers first work diagnostically with students who have demonstrated difficulty on broad measures of reading. Then, they can work with other students as the need arises.

However, we caution that simply administering more and more assessments and recording the scores will miss the point. The value of in-depth classroom assessment comes from teachers having a deep understanding of reading processes and instruction, thinking diagnostically, and using the information on an ongoing basis to inform instruction (Black & Wiliam, 1998; Place, 2002; Shepard, 2000). Requiring teachers to administer grade-level classroom assessments to all their students regardless of individual student needs would not yield useful information or help teachers make effective instructional decisions. For example, administering a fourth-grade reading selection to Jesse, who is reading at first-grade level, would not provide useful information. However, using a fourth- or even fifth-grade selection for Tomas would. Similarly, assessing Jesse's word identification abilities should probably include assessments of basic sound/symbol correspondences or even phonemic awareness, but assessing decoding of multisyllabic words would

be more appropriate for Martin. This kind of matching of assessment to students' needs is precisely what we hope would happen when teachers have the knowledge, the assessment tools, and the flexibility to assess and teach children according to their ongoing analysis. Both long-term professional development and time are critical if teachers are to implement the kind of sophisticated classroom assessment that struggling readers need.

Second, the evidence points to the need for multilevel, flexible, small-group instruction (Allington & Johnston, 2001; Cunningham & Allington, 1999; Opitz, 1998). Imagine, if you will, teaching just the six students we have described, who could easily be in the same class. These students not only need support in different aspects of reading, but they also need materials that differ in difficulty, topic, and familiarity. For example, Tomas, Makara, and Andrew all need instruction in comprehension. However, Tomas and Andrew likely can receive that instruction using grade-level material, but Makara would need to use easier material. Both Makara and Andrew need work in vocabulary, whereas Tomas is fairly strong in word meanings. As second-language learners, Tomas and Makara likely need more background building and exposure to topics, concepts, and academic vocabulary as well as the structure of English texts than Andrew, who is a native English speaker. Furthermore, the teacher likely needs to experiment with having Tomas and Makara slow down when they read to get them to attend to meaning, whereas Andrew needs to increase his fluency through practice in below-grade-level text.

So, although these three students might be able to participate in whole-class instruction in which the teacher models and explicitly teaches comprehension strategies, they clearly need guided practice to apply the strategies to different types and levels of material, and they each need attention to other aspects of reading as well. This means the teacher must have strong classroom management and organizational skills to provide small-group instruction. Furthermore, he or she must have access to a wide range of books and reading materials that are intellectually challenging yet accessible to students reading substantially below grade level. At the same time, these struggling readers need access to grade-level material through a variety of scaffolded experiences (i.e., partner reading, guided reading, read-alouds) so that they are exposed to grade-level ideas, text structures, and vocabulary (Cunningham & Allington, 1999). Some of these students and their teachers would benefit from collaboration with other professionals in their schools, such as speech and language and second-language specialists, who could suggest classroom-based strategies targeted to the students' specific needs.

The six clusters and the three strands within each one (word identification, meaning, fluency) clearly provide more in-depth analysis of students' reading abilities than general test scores. Nevertheless, we caution that there is still more to be learned about individual students in each cluster, beyond what we describe here, that would help teachers plan for instruction. Two examples make this point. The first example comes from Cluster 1, Automatic Word Callers. Tomas had substantial difficulty with comprehension, but his scores on the vocabulary measure suggested that word meanings were likely not a problem for him. However, other students in this cluster, such as Maria, *did* have difficulty with word meanings and would need not only comprehension instruction like Tomas but also many more language-building activities and exposure to oral and written English. The second example that highlights the importance of looking beyond the cluster profile is Andrew, our Slow Word Caller from Cluster 5. Although we know that in-depth assessment revealed that Andrew had difficulty with comprehension and fluency, we argue above that the teacher must do more work with Andrew to determine how much fluency is contributing to comprehension and how much it is a result of Andrew's effort to self-monitor. Our point here is that even the clusters do not tell the entire story.

Finally, from a school or district perspective, we are concerned about the disproportionate number of second-language students who failed the test. In our study, 11% of the students in the school district were identified as second-language learners and were receiving additional instructional support. However, in our sample of students who failed the test, 43% were second-language learners who were *not* receiving additional support. Tomas and Makara are typical of many English-language learners in our schools. Their reading abilities are sufficient, according to school guidelines, to allow them to exit supplemental ESL programs, yet they are failing state tests and struggling in the classroom. In this district, as in others across the state, students exit supplemental programs when they score at the 35th percentile or above on a norm-referenced reading test— hardly sufficient to thrive, or even survive, in a mainstream classroom without additional help. States, school districts, and schools need to rethink the support they offer English-language learners both in terms of providing more sustained instructional support over time and of scaffolding their integration into the regular classroom. In addition, there must be a concerted effort to foster academically and intellectually rigorous learning of subject matter for these students (e.g., science, social studies) while they are developing their English-language abilities. Without such a focus, either in their first language or in English, these students will be denied access to important school learning, will fall further behind in other school subjects, and become increasingly disengaged from school and learning (Echevarria, Vogt, & Short, 2000).

Our findings and recommendations may, on one level, seem obvious. Indeed, good teachers have always acknowledged differences among the students in their classes, and they have always tried to meet individual needs. But, in the current environment of high-stakes testing and accountability, it has become more of a challenge to keep an eye on individual children, and more difficult to stay focused on the complex nature of reading performance and reading instruction. This study serves as a reminder of these cornerstones of good teaching. We owe it to our students, their parents, and ourselves to provide struggling readers with the instruction they *really* need.

References

Adams, M.J. (1990). *Beginning to read: Thinking and learning about print*. Cambridge, MA: MIT Press.

Aldenderfer, M., & Blashfield, R. (1984). *Cluster analysis*. Beverly Hills, CA: Sage.

Allington, R.L. (2001). *What really matters for struggling readers*. New York: Longman.

Allington, R.L., & Johnston, P.H. (2001). What do we know about effective fourth-grade teachers and their classrooms? In C.M. Roller (Ed.), *Learning to teach reading: Setting the research agenda* (pp. 150–165). Newark, DE: International Reading Association.

Antunez, B. (2002, Spring). Implementing reading first with English language learners. *Directions in Language and Education, 15*. Retrieved October 15, 2003, from http://www.ncela.gwu.edu/ncbepubs/directions

Black, P., & Wiliam, D. (1998). Assessment and classroom learning. *Assessment in Education, 5*(1), 7–74.

Block, C.C., & Pressley, M. (2002). *Comprehension instruction: Research-based best practices*. New York: Guilford.

Cummins, J. (1991). The development of bilingual proficiency from home to school: A longitudinal study of Portuguese-speaking children. *Journal of Education, 173*, 85–98.

Cunningham, P.M., & Allington, R.L. (1999). *Classrooms that work* (2nd ed.). New York: Longman.

Duke, N.K., & Pearson, P.D. (2002). Effective practices for developing reading comprehension. In A.E. Farstrup & S.J. Samuels (Eds.), *What research has to say about reading instruction* (pp. 9–129). Newark, DE: International Reading Association.

Echevarria, J., Vogt, M.E., & Short, D. (2000). *Making content comprehensible for English language learners: The SIOP model*. Boston: Allyn & Bacon.

Edmondson, J., & Shannon, P. (2002). The will of the people. *The Reading Teacher, 55*, 452–454.

Elmore, R.F. (2002, Spring) Unwarranted intrusion. *Education Next*. Retrieved March 21, 2003, from http://www.educationnext.org

Goodnough, A. (2001, May 23). Teaching by the book, no asides allowed. *The New York Times*. Retrieved March 21, 2003, from http://www.nytimes.com

Harris, A.J., & Sipay, E.R. (1990). *How to increase reading ability* (9th ed.). New York: Longman.

Helfand, D. (2002, July 21). Teens get a second chance at literacy. *Los Angeles Times*. Retrieved March 21, 2003, from http://www.latimes.com

Hiebert, E.H., Pearson, P.D., Taylor, B.M., Richardson, V., & Paris, S.G. (1998). *Every child a reader: Applying reading research to the classroom*. Ann Arbor, MI: Center for the Improvement of Early Reading Achievement, University of Michigan School of Education. Retrieved March 21, 2003, from http://www.ciera.org

Klein, S.P., Hamilton, L.S., McCaffrey, D.F., & Stecher, B.M. (2000). What do test scores in Texas tell us? *Education Policy Analysis Archives, 8*(49). Retrieved March 21, 2003, from http://epaa.asu.edu/epaa/v8n49

Kuhn, M.R., & Stahl, S.A. (2000). *Fluency: A review of developmental and remedial practices* (CIERA Rep. No. 2-008). Ann Arbor, MI: Center for the Improvement of Early Reading Achievement, University of Michigan School of Education. Retrieved March 21, 2003, from http://www.ciera.org

Linn, R.L. (2000). Assessments and accountability. *Educational Researcher, 29*(2), 4–16.

Linn, R.L. (n.d.). *Standards-based accountability: Ten suggestions*. CRESST Policy Brief. 1. Retrieved March 21, 2003, from http://www.cse.ucla.edu

Lipson, M.Y., & Wixson, K.K. (2003). *Assessment and instruction of reading and writing difficulty: An interactive approach* (3rd ed.). Boston: Allyn & Bacon.

McNeil, L.M. (2000). *Contradictions of school reform: Educational costs of standardized testing*. New York: Routledge.

Nagy, W.E. (1988). *Teaching vocabulary to improve reading comprehension*. Urbana, IL: ERIC Clearinghouse on Reading and Communication Skills and the National Council of Teachers of English.

National Institute of Child Health and Human Development. (2000). *Report of the National Reading Panel. Teaching children to read: An evidence-based assessment of the scientific research literature on reading and its implications for reading instruction* (NIH Publication No. 004 769). Washington, DC: U.S. Government Printing Office. Retrieved March 21, 2003, from http://www.nationalreadingpanel.org

Olson, L. (2001). Overboard on testing. *Education Week, 20*(17), 23–30.

Opitz, M.F. (1998). *Flexible grouping in reading*. New York: Scholastic.

Paterson, F.R.A. (2000). The politics of phonics. *Journal of Curriculum and Supervision, 15*, 179–211.

Pinnell, G.S., Pikulski, J.J., Wixson, K.K., Campbell, J.R., Gough, P.B., & Beatty, A.S. (1995). *Listening to children read aloud*. Washington, DC: U.S. Department of Education.

Place, N.A. (2002). Policy in action: The influence of mandated early reading assessment on teachers' thinking and practice. In D.L. Schallert, C.M. Fairbanks, J. Worthy, B. Malock, & J.V. Hoffman (Eds.), *Fiftieth yearbook of the National Reading Conference* (pp. 45–58). Oak Creek, WI: National Reading Conference.

Riddle Buly, M., & Valencia, S.W. (2002). Below the bar: Profiles of students who fail state reading tests. *Educational Evaluation and Policy Analysis, 24*, 219–239.

Samuels, S.J. (2002). Reading fluency: Its development and assessment. In A. Farstrup & S.J. Samuels (Eds.), *What research has to say about reading instruction* (pp. 166–183). Newark, DE: International Reading Association.

Shepard, L.A. (2000). The role of assessment in a learning culture. *Educational Researcher, 29*, 4–14.

Snow, C.E., Burns, M.S., & Griffin, P. (Eds.). (1998). *Preventing reading difficulties in young children*. Washington, DC: National Academy Press.

Stahl, S.A., & Kapinus, B.A. (2001). *Word power: What every educator needs to know about vocabulary*. Washington, DC: National Education Association Professional Library.

Stanovich, K.E. (1986). Matthew effects in reading: Some consequences of individual differences in the acquisition of literacy. *Reading Research Quarterly, 21*, 360–407.

Stanovich, K.E. (1988). Explaining the difference between the dyslexic and garden-variety poor reader: The phonological-core variable-difference model. *Journal of Learning Disabilities, 21*, 590–612.

Stanovich, K.E. (1994). Romance and reality. *The Reading Teacher, 47*, 280–290.

Assessing English-Language Learners in Mainstream Classrooms

*Susan Davis Lenski, Fabiola Ehlers-Zavala, Mayra C. Daniel,
and Xiaoqin Sun-Irminger*

A great many classroom teachers in the United States find themselves teaching English-language learners (ELLs). The total number of ELLs in the public schools is more than 4.5 million students, or 9.6% of the total school population (National Center for Education Statistics, 2002). This number continues to rise because more than a million new U.S. immigrants arrive annually (Martin & Midgely, 1999). Not all communities have large populations of ELLs, but many do, and others will experience changes in the diversity of their populations, especially schools in the inner suburbs of metropolitan centers (Hodgkinson, 2000/2001).

Because assessment is a critical part of effective literacy instruction, it is important for classroom teachers to know how to evaluate ELLs' literacy development. Nevertheless, many teachers are unprepared for the special needs and complexities of fairly and appropriately assessing ELLs. To complicate the matter further, the U.S. federal No Child Left Behind Act (NCLB) of 2001 has established assessment mandates that all teachers must follow. Title I of NCLB requires that ELLs attending public schools at levels K–12 should be assessed in the various language domains (i.e., listening, speaking, reading, and writing). According to NCLB, ELLs must be included in statewide standardized testing. The results of the tests are reported in a segregated data format that highlights the achievement of each subgroup of students. As with all subgroups under NCLB, ELLs must make Adequate Yearly Progress (AYP) for the schools to meet state requirements (Abedi, 2004).

Over the years, ELLs have historically lagged behind their native–English-speaking counterparts, and this achievement gap is not likely to close in the near future (Strickland & Alvermann, 2004). ELLs come to public schools in large numbers, and they have unique learning and assessment needs. ELLs bring a wide range of educational experiences and academic backgrounds to school. They represent a variety of socioeconomic, cultural, linguistic, and ethnic backgrounds. In school, ELLs need to simultaneously develop English competence and acquire content knowledge. An overwhelming majority of assessment tools are in English only, presenting a potential threat to the usefulness of assessments when ELLs' lack of English prevents them from understanding test items.

Whether ELLs are newcomers to the United States or from generations of heritage language speakers, they are disadvantaged if assessment, evaluation, and the curriculum do not make allowances for their distinctive differences (Gay, 2001; Gitlin, Buendía, Crossland, & Doumbia, 2003; Greenfield, 1997). This article provides recommendations for literacy assessment practices for teachers of ELLs that will inform their instruction.

Preparing Reading Professionals (second edition), edited by Rita M. Bean, Natalie Heisey, and Cathy M. Roller. © 2010 by the International Reading Association. Reprinted from Lenski, S.D., Ehlers-Zavala, F., Daniel, M.C., & Sun-Irminger, X. (2006). Assessing English-language learners in mainstream classrooms. *The Reading Teacher, 60*(1), 24–34. doi:10.1598/RT.60.1.3.

Toward Appropriate Assessment of ELLs

The assessment of ELLs is a "process of collecting and documenting evidence of student learning and progress to make informed instructional, placement, programmatic, and/or evaluative decisions to enhance student learning, as is the case of assessment of the monolingual or mainstream learner" (Ehlers-Zavala, 2002, pp. 8–9). Assessments of ELLs, however, are more critical. Many teachers have little experience with ELLs and may not understand the challenges faced by students in the process of acquiring English. Because assessment practices pave the way to making instructional and evaluative decisions, teachers need to consider all educational stakeholders (i.e., the students themselves, parents, administrators, and other teachers) as they plan to assess students from different cultural backgrounds.

Hurley and Blake (2000) provided guiding principles that teachers should consider when assessing ELLs:

- Assessment activities should help teachers make instructional decisions.

- Assessment strategies should help teachers find out what students know and can do...not what they cannot do.

- The holistic context for learning should be considered and assessed.

- Assessment activities should grow out of authentic learning activities.

- Best assessments of student learning are longitudinal...they take place over time.

- Each assessment activity should have a specific objective-linked purpose. (pp. 91–92)

Furthermore, because the NCLB legislation drives state standards, teachers should consider those standards as they assess ELLs. Standards can assist teachers in planning effectively linked instruction and assessment practices for ELLs at all levels of instruction and across the curriculum. In the absence of district or state standards, teachers can consult the standards that professional organizations, such as Teachers of English to Speakers of Other Languages (TESOL; 1997) have prepared (see www.tesol.org/s_tesol/seccss.asp?CUD=95&DID=1565). They may also consult the work other professionals have developed (Lenski & Ehlers-Zavala, 2004).

Assessing English-Language Learners

Teachers who assess ELLs must ask themselves a number of basic questions such as these: Who am I going to assess? How am I going to assess them? Why am I going to assess them? What specific aspects of literacy am I going to assess? When am I going to administer the assessment? Can I evaluate my students in my own classroom? In order to answer these questions, teachers should investigate their students' prior schooling before assessment.

Learn About ELLs' Literacy Backgrounds

English-language learners come to public schools with vastly different backgrounds. Teachers should never assume that students who share the same language will observe the same cultural practices or understand the same types of texts. Even speakers of the same language exhibit differences in their lexicon, in the grammar that they use, and in the formality and informality of expression that is acceptable in their everyday lives (Chern, 2002). ELL teachers should, therefore, become aware of their students' backgrounds before assessment takes place.

According to Freeman and Freeman (2004), ELLs fall into four categories that help teachers understand their background: newly arrived students with adequate formal schooling, newly arrived students with limited formal schooling, students exposed to two languages simultaneously, and long-term English-language learners. (See Table 1 for a complete description of these categories.) Knowing which category best

Table 1
Categories of English-Language Learners

Newly Arrived Students With Adequate Formal Schooling
- Have been in the country for fewer than five years,
- Have had an adequate degree of schooling in their native country,
- Perform in reading and writing at grade level,
- Find it relatively easy to catch up with their native–English-speaking peers,
- Have difficulty with standardized tests,
- Have parents who are educated speakers of their L1 (native language),
- Developed a strong foundation in their L1,
- Demonstrate the potential to make fast progress in English, and
- Have found it easy to acquire a second or third language.

Newly Arrived Students With Limited Formal Schooling
- Have recently arrived in an English-speaking school (fewer than five years),
- Have experienced interrupted schooling,
- Have limited native-language and literacy skills,
- Perform poorly on achievement tasks,
- May not have had previous schooling,
- May experience feelings of loss of emotional and social networks,
- Have parents who have low literacy levels, and
- Could have difficulty learning English.

Students Exposed to Two Languages Simultaneously
- Were born in the United States but have grown up in households where a language other than English is spoken,
- Live in communities of speakers who primarily communicate in their L1 or go back and forth between languages,
- Have grown up being exposed to two languages simultaneously,
- May have not developed academic literacy in either L1 or L2 (second language),
- Often engage in extensive code-switching, thus making use of both linguistic systems to communicate, and
- Have acquired oral proficiency in a language other than English first but may not have learned to read or write in that language.

Long-Term English-Language Learners
- Have already spent more than five years in an English-speaking school,
- Have literacy skills that are below grade level,
- Have had some English as a second language classes or bilingual support, and
- Require substantial and ongoing language and literacy support.

Note. Adapted from Freeman and Freeman (2003).

describes an ELL can help teachers begin to learn about their students.

Understanding that ELLs come from different types of literacy backgrounds can help teachers as they develop appropriate assessments. Students' needs are mediated by who the students are, which includes their type of literacy background. Oftentimes, an understanding of students is fogged by the use of acronyms such as "ELLs," which, on the surface, seem to point at group homogeneity rather than heterogeneity. Differences are blurred in the use of such acronyms; consequently, there is always the potential to forget how diverse ELLs truly are. Understanding each ELL's background will

help a teacher to choose the most appropriate assessment and instruction.

Predictability Log. An ELL's knowledge base might include traditional and nontraditional literacies. Teachers can understand the types of literacies ELLs bring to the classroom by completing a predictability log (PL). A PL helps teachers understand their students' prior literacy experiences and the factors that helped shape them. (See Table 2 for an example.) According to Snyder (2003), assessing students' abilities to predict can assist teachers in creating a learning environment that is rich in predictable printed language. To use a PL, teachers should target the questions that are most relevant for the students' situations. Teachers can gather data for a PL from a variety of sources: by interviewing the students, talking with the students' parents, observing the students in a classroom context, and talking with others who know the students (e.g., family members, other teachers, community members). A bilingual specialist or someone who is fluent in the students' native language can also be of assistance in completion of the log. Whether the teacher or another adult gathers the data, the information can provide the teacher with a deeper grasp of the students' literacy backgrounds.

Using Predictability Logs. Information from PLs can help teachers understand that students who have been exposed to effective literacy practices in other contexts, such as their countries of origin, may be further along in their literacy development. Furthermore, in understanding that ELLs differ in the literacy practices of their native language (L1), teachers may be in a better position to determine whether those literacy practices are facilitating or interfering with the development of literacy in English—the learners' second language. This situation is contingent upon the degree of similarity or difference between English and the native language of the students. An example of this would be the knowledge students bring to the learning process regarding concepts of print. An ELL who is a native speaker of Spanish may benefit from having been exposed to concepts about print in Spanish because they are similar to those a native speaker of English would know (i.e., reading from left to right). Conversely, an ELL who is a native speaker of Arabic may display a different understanding of concepts about print learned in Arabic (i.e., reading from right to left).

Decide on the Purposes for Assessment

Once teachers know about a student's literacy background and knowledge base, they need to think about the reasons for further assessment.

Table 2
Predictability Log Questions

Language Use
- What languages does the student know and use?
- What types of alphabets does the student know?
- What language and literacy experiences interest the student?

Knowledge
- What is the student's cultural background?
- What does the student enjoy doing out of school?
- In what areas or ways has the student helped classmates?
- What has the student said or what stories has the student told?

Events or Experiences That Matter to the Student
- What has happened to the student recently that has been important?
- Have any major events occurred, especially recently, that have been of great interest to the student?

Narrative
- What kinds of stories does the student enjoy?
- What specific stories does the student know well?
- Can the student tell a story about a relative or a good friend?
- What activities is the student involved in?

Relationship
- What is the student's family situation?
- Who are the key family members in the student's life?
- Has the student left anyone behind in his or her home country?
- Who are the student's best friends?
- Is there anyone whom the student talks about frequently?
- Whom might you contact to follow up on one of the student's interests or needs?

Aesthetics and Ethics
- What personal belongings does the student bring to class or wear?
- What objects or ideas appeal to the student?
- What values has the student expressed through actions or stories?

Note. Adapted from Snyder (2003).

The purposes for assessment can be quite diverse; they can range from student placement to instructional decisions and from program development to program evaluation. It is critical that teachers identify the purposes for assessing their students before choosing the assessment instrument to be used.

As teachers consider the purposes for assessment, they should ask, "Does my assessment connect to the language and content standards and goals?" Teachers should also think about whether their assessment practices are consistent with their own instructional objectives and goals. When teachers think about the purposes for assessment beforehand, they can make better decisions about what information they should gather about their students.

Teachers can use language and content standards as the basis for what ELLs ought to know, and these standards then provide the purposes for assessment. For example, one of the TESOL standards is "Students will use learning strategies to extend their communicative competence" (TESOL, 1997, p. 39). Teachers can use this statement to develop an instrument to assess how well students are satisfying the standard. Figure 1 provides an example of an assessment that Ehlers-Zavala (second author) developed based on the standard.

Decide How to Assess Students

Teachers of ELLs should conduct multiple forms of evaluation, using a variety of authentic assessment tools (e.g., anecdotal records, checklists, rating scales, portfolios) to fairly assess the placement and progress of their students and to plan instruction. Authentic assessment tools will provide direct insights on the students' literacy development and showcase students' progress and accomplishments. Assessments also serve as mechanisms that reveal what instruction needs to be modified to help the students reach the necessary standards and goals.

Adopt a Multidimensional Approach Including Alternative Assessments (AAs). Reading is a complex interactive process. According to O'Malley and Valdez Pierce (1996), the term *interaction* refers not only to the interactions between the reader, the text, and a given context but also to the interactions

---

Figure 1
Sample Checklist for Reading (Grades Pre-K–3)

Student:

Date:

ESL Goal, ESL Standard: Goal 1, Standard 3
"To use English to communicate in social settings: Students will use learning strategies to extend their communicative competence" (TESOL, 1997, p. 39).

Progress indicator	Student performed task independently (✔)	Student performed task with help (✔)	Student was unable to perform the task (✔)
Understands new vocabulary			
Recites poems			
Retells stories			
Uses new vocabulary in story retelling			
Formulates hypothesis about events in a story			

among the mental processes involved in comprehension. These range from the decoding of words on the printed page to making use of prior knowledge and "making inferences and evaluating what is read" (p. 94). Indeed,

> the assessment of reading ability does not end with the measurement of comprehension. Strategic pathways to full understanding are often important factors to include in assessing students, especially in the case of most classroom assessments that are formative in nature. (Brown, 2004, p. 185)

For this reason, it is important that teachers consider AAs to document ELLs' performance and growth in reading.

Alternative assessments provide teachers with a more complete picture of what students can or cannot do as they encounter reading materials. Through the use of AAs, teachers gain a direct view of the students' reading development in a variety of contexts and under different circumstances. AAs go beyond traditional testing, which provides a very narrow and discrete view of the students' capabilities when confronted with a reading task. They also evolve naturally from regular classroom activities and allow students the opportunity to show growth in literacy as they learn and practice.

Alternative assessment tasks are a more appropriate and fair way to measure ELLs' progress (Gottlieb, 1995; O'Malley & Valdez Pierce, 1996; Smolen, Newman, Wathen, & Lee, 1995). They provide teachers with the opportunity to identify what students need regarding reading instruction and literacy support. From information gathered as a result of AAs, teachers can devise a plan to instruct students in more meaningful ways because they have direct insights on the needs of each one. Finally, through AAs teachers can assess ELLs' literacy in more naturally occurring situations and thus document students' progress more thoroughly and progressively (Ehlers-Zavala, 2002).

As teachers attempt to put into practice multiple AAs, they may want to approach this task incrementally and consider the following practical suggestions:

- Learn what constitutes alternative or authentic assessment of ELLs. Examples of AAs generally include observations (i.e., anecdotal records, rating scales, checklists), journals (i.e., buddy journals, dialogue journals, reader response), conferring, questionnaires, portfolios, and self-assessments.

- Develop a philosophy of second-language acquisition that will assist you in the evaluation of ELLs.

- Know your district's curriculum of the program before planning assessments. The curriculum (specifically the reading curriculum) in any given school program must be sensitive to the students' needs, the institutional expectations, and the availability of resources. Because these will vary from setting to setting, it is nearly impossible to attempt to prescribe any guidelines or universal curriculum for all instructional settings (Grabe, 2004); thus, teachers must know the reality of their own localities.

- Implement the assessments once you have understood the features of the tools available and have determined the appropriateness of implementation at any given time.

- Plan assessments that yield data that can be used for evaluative and instructional purposes.

- Ensure that students understand how to use self-assessments (i.e., logs, journals).

- Use the results of your assessments to modify instruction.

- Communicate assessment results to the respective stakeholders (i.e., students, parents, administrators, community) in clear and meaningful ways.

The key to successful alternative assessment is thorough planning and organization (O'Malley & Valdez Pierce, 1996). As teachers plan, they should identify the purpose of the assessment, plan the assessment itself, involve students in self- and peer assessment, develop rubrics or scoring procedures, set standards, select assessment activities, and record teacher observations. For a helpful reminder of effective assessment practices, Figure 2 offers a teacher's bookmark on alternative assessment practices that Ehlers-Zavala developed.

Assess in Nontraditional Ways. Teachers should keep in mind that all assessments in

---

**Figure 2
A Teacher's Bookmark on Alternative Assessment Practices**

Know your curriculum and collaborate with other teachers when possible.

Determine what, who, why, how, and when to assess.

Ensure that your students understand your assessments.

Reflect on the results of your assessments.

Modify instruction in a meaningful way informed by your assessments.

Communicate the results of your assessments to stakeholders.

Use technology to facilitate your assessment practices.

English are also assessments *of* English. Because ELLs are in the process of acquiring language as they acquire content, teachers need to ensure that their assessment addresses the linguistic component of the learning continuum. Therefore, teachers should provide ELLs with opportunities to demonstrate knowledge in nontraditional ways (O'Malley & Valdez Pierce, 1996). Specifically, teachers might consider some of the following suggestions when assessing ELLs:

- Involve students in performance assessment tasks.
- Offer students opportunities to show and practice knowledge in nonlanguage-dependent ways through Venn diagrams, charts, drawings, mind maps, or PowerPoint slides.
- Promote participation in nonthreatening situations that encourage experimentation with the target language of study. Assess language learning in the participation activities.
- Before assessing students, teachers can help ELLs develop reading strategies that in themselves could constitute alternative forms of literacy assessment (Lenski, Daniel, Ehlers-Zavala, & Alvayero, 2004).
- Use the Language Experience Approach as assessment rather than just for instructional purposes (Lenski & Nierstheimer, 2004). As students read their language-experience stories, informally assess their oral reading fluency.

Modify Traditional Assessments. There will be times when teachers have to give ELLs traditional assessments. Some tests should not be modified because their results are based on standardized procedures. If in doubt, teachers should contact an administrator or bilingual teacher about which tests should or should not be modified. A rule of thumb, however, is that teacher-written tests can be modified for ELLs, but achievement tests should not be modified. When teachers modify traditional tests for ELLs, they learn what students know about the content without the barrier of language knowledge, and the assessment more accurately reflects what ELLs know and can do.

Teachers may consider the following assessment modifications appropriate for newcomers and ELLs who are in the process of acquiring English:

- Permit students to answer orally rather than in writing.
- Allow a qualified bilingual professional to assist with the assessment.
- Consider offering ELLs the possibility to demonstrate reading progress and growth through group assessments.
- Allow students to provide responses in multiple formats.
- Accept a response in the students' native language if translation support systems exist in the school or community.
- Allow ELLs to use a bilingual dictionary in the beginning stages of their language-learning experience in English (United States Department of Education, Office for Civil Rights, 2000).

Teachers who are developing ELLs' literacy but still need modifications for accurate assessment information might consider the following suggestions:

- Have an aide record students' answers.
- Divide assessment time into small chunks.
- Use visuals.
- Add glossaries in English or the first language.
- Simplify vocabulary.
- Begin the assessment with several examples.
- Simplify assessment directions.
- Write questions in the affirmative rather than the negative and also teach sentence structures so that students are familiar with the language of testing.
- Give students breaks during assessments.

- Give directions in students' native languages.

Assessment Materials, Activities, and Language Issues

Assessment should be conducted through the use of authentic reading materials that connect to the students' real-life experiences in their personal and academic contexts. "Literacy is intimately bound up with their lives outside the classroom in numerous and complex cultural, social, and personal ways that affect their L1 and L2 identities" (Burns, 2003, p. 22). For ELLs, literacy in English can be an extension of their identity both in school and at home.

Assessment materials should also be adjusted to the student's English proficiency level because a text that is not comprehensible will only measure the vocabulary that a student does not know. A valid look at an ELL's literacy can only be accomplished through pragmatic integrative assessment. When teachers use purposeful communication and authentic material, the results of the assessment are more useful.

Clearly, materials used to informally assess ELLs may be different from those that a teacher would choose to assess the literacy level of mainstream students.

A book that fosters an emotional link between the student and the written word is an authentic text for that particular reader, even if it is not what would ordinarily be appropriate for a grade level. Such a book may not be an academic text. Instead, for a young reader, it could be a comic book about Spider-Man or another superhero. For an adolescent female of Cuban American descent, it might be the chronicle of a young teenager's immigration, *Flight to Freedom* (Veciana-Suarez, 2002). When students determine whether a text is authentic, they use many important thinking processes. As teachers talk with students about why books are authentic to them, they can learn a great deal of information about students' literacy interests (Carrell & Eisterhold, 1983; Davidman & Davidman, 2001).

Engage Students in Collaborative Assessment Activities. Collaborative work helps ELLs feel safe, work comfortably at a level where incoming stimuli are kept at a minimum, and demonstrate literacy to teachers in informal ways (Kagan & Kagan, 1998; Krashen, 1993, 2003). Because conversations between students can scaffold learning (Vygotsky, 1934/1978), collaborative assessment activities provide a powerful lens through which to view ELLs' literacy.

Collaboration permits students to showcase their talents and work in a manner that is a good fit with their individual learning styles and intelligence (Kagan & Kagan, 1998). As students collaborate, they should be free to code-switch without being penalized. Code-switching is moving between the native language and English during an activity and helps ELLs keep conversations moving. It is a natural occurrence among bilinguals, and there are many purposes behind its practice; for example, to stress a point in communication, to express a concept for which there is no equivalent in the other language, to indicate friendship, to relate a conversation, or to substitute a word in another language (Baker, 2001). Teachers should bear in mind that when code-switching compensates for lack of knowledge (e.g., of a word or a grammatical structure), ELLs should be helped to acquire the linguistic knowledge they lack. This type of instructional support should be given in a friendly manner to ensure that students do not feel they are being punished for using their native languages (Freeman & Freeman, 2003).

Teachers can also add an important collaborative component to the instruction and assessment of ELLs when they invite families and community members to participate in literacy projects (Moll & Gonzalez, 1994; Young & Helvie, 1996). For example, parents who are fluent in the native language and also know English can assist teachers in some informal assessment measures. Parents can talk with students in both languages and can alert teachers to difficulties that students face. Parents can also help students record lists of books that they have read. If parents do not know how to write in English, they can keep tape-recorded logs, or simply speak to teachers in the native language. Teachers who are unable to find bilingual parents can seek assistance from bilingual paraprofessionals or from local and state resource centers.

Use the Students' Native Languages as an Assessment Resource. Students should be allowed to use their language abilities to complete literacy tasks (Brisk, 2002) and to express their knowledge in the language they know best when being assessed. Oftentimes, knowledge of the first language means that students possess linguistic skills that can assist them in mastering literacy tasks in the second language (Cummins, 1981). One of these tasks may relate to understanding the meaning of words. Sometimes students may think of what words mean in their first language and successfully guess the meaning of the equivalents in the second language. For example, a word like *compensation* may be understood by native speakers of Spanish if they know the Spanish term *compensación*. In this case, students may use a combination of letter–sound correspondence knowledge and pronunciation to figure out the meaning of the word. During assessment, ELLs may demonstrate their knowledge more accurately if teachers allow them to use their native languages to process their answers.

Encourage Self-Assessment

Self-assessments convey the message that students are in control of their own learning and the assessment of that learning. As students engage in self-assessment practices, they learn how their past learning is shaping their new learning. This type of assessment practice helps students understand that they can direct their learning, which paves the way to teaching students to become independent readers and learners.

As teachers use self-assessment with ELLs, they should keep in mind that ELLs vary in their linguistic ability and, by definition, are in the process of learning a language. Thus, teachers should be aware that ELLs might experience difficulties at first with self-assessments. In order to assist ELLs, teachers should provide them with support through substantial scaffolding activities. Teachers should model responses to self-assessment tasks and then provide students with group, peer, and finally independent practice. For example, a teacher might want to assess students' prior knowledge of a topic for a book students are going to read. Teachers might want to have students engage in self-assessment practices, but prior to asking students to do so, teachers need to model how to engage in a self-assessment activity. An example of a strategy that could be used for student self-assessment is a Connections chart (Lenski & Ehlers-Zavala, 2004). This strategy encourages students to read a story; stop at given points; and make connections to other books, past learning, and themselves. (See Figure 3 for an example of a Connections chart.) When students are engaged in this type of reflective activity, they learn how to use an important literacy strategy and provide teachers with information that could be used for making instructional decisions.

Effective Teaching Means Effective Assessments

English-language learners are not a homogeneous group; they can range from students who are emergent literacy learners in their first language to those who are proficient readers. Literacy in the first language mediates literacy in the second language (Odlin, 1989). Thus, literacy experiences that students may have had in their first language will influence their ability to acquire literacy in English. Because the range of literacy proficiencies may be quite vast in any classroom with ELLs, traditional testing formats are inadequate for the evaluation of the English literacy of the nonnative English speaker.

The most effective types of assessments teachers can use to make instructional decisions for ELLs are authentic performance-based assessments such as observations, journals,

Figure 3
Connections Chart

Story Title	Author
Connections to other books	
Connections to school learning	
Connections to self	

portfolios, and self-assessments. Performance assessment tasks allow teachers to simultaneously instruct and assess. When students undertake the process of completing an authentic performance assessment, the students plan, self-monitor, and evaluate progress continually, while creating a product. Throughout this process, the teacher is able to engage in ongoing informal assessment of the student's progress. No professionally prepared protocol will result in student learning if only a single test result is used to inform the development of the curricula. When authentic, performance-based assessments are administered throughout the year, they can provide not only a much more accurate picture of students' literacy development but also documented formative data that chart the students' literacy development.

Effective teaching, above all, is the key to the sustained achievement of all students, especially ELLs who struggle with reading. With effective teaching comes the teacher's ability to meet the needs of all students at all points in the educational continuum. Teachers must develop the ability to tailor instruction that helps all ELLs achieve English literacy. However, without a thorough understanding of students' background and current literacy levels, teachers will have difficulty providing effective instruction to meet the unique needs of ELL students.

Although instruction is the key to student learning, authentic assessment can help teachers understand the needs of their struggling readers who are English-language learners. Teachers can use assessment results to evaluate student progress and plan the direction classroom instruction and learning will take. Only when measurement, assessment, evaluation, and excellent teaching are present in classrooms will ELLs make real progress toward literacy.

References

Abedi, J. (2004). The No Child Left Behind Act and English language learners: Assessment and accountability issues. *Educational Researcher, 33*, 4–14.

Baker, C. (2001). *Foundations of bilingual education and bilingualism* (3rd ed.). Buffalo, NY: Multilingual Matters.

Brisk, M. (2002). *Literacy and bilingualism.* Mahwah, NJ: Erlbaum.

Brown, D.H. (2004). *Language assessment: Principles and classroom practices.* White Plains, NY: Pearson/ Longman.

Burns, A. (2003). Reading practices: From outside to inside the classroom. *TESOL Journal, 12*(3), 18–23.

Carrell, P.L., & Eisterhold, J.C. (1983). Schema theory and ESL reading pedagogy. *TESOL Quarterly, 17*, 553–573.

Chern, C.-I. (2002, July). *Orthographic issues and multiple language literacies.* Paper presented at the IRA Multilingual Literacy Symposium, Edinburgh, Scotland. Retrieved February 16, 2006, from http://www .readingonline.org/international/inter_index.asp? HREF=Edinburgh/chern/index.html

Cummins, J. (1981). *Schooling and language minority students: A theoretical framework.* Los Angeles: California State University.

Davidman, L., & Davidman, P. (2001). *Teaching with a multicultural perspective: A practical guide* (3rd ed.). New York: Longman.

Ehlers-Zavala, F. (2002). *Assessment of the English-language learner: An ESL training module.* Chicago: Board of Education of the City of Chicago.

Freeman, D., & Freeman, Y. (2004). *Essential linguistics: What you need to know to teach reading, ESL, spelling, phonics, and grammar.* Portsmouth, NH: Heinemann.

Freeman, Y., & Freeman, D. (2003). Struggling English language learners: Keys for academic success. *TESOL Journal, 12*(3), 18–23.

Gay, G. (2001). Preparing for culturally responsive teaching. *Journal of Teacher Education, 53*, 106–115.

Gitlin, A., Buendía, E., Crossland, K., & Doumbia, F. (2003). The production of margin and center: Welcoming-unwelcoming of immigrant students. *American Educational Research Journal, 40*, 91–122.

Gottlieb, M. (1995). Nurturing students' learning through portfolios. *TESOL Journal, 5*(1), 12–14.

Grabe, W. (2004). Research on teaching reading. *Annual Review of Applied Linguistics, 24*, 44–69.

Greenfield, P.M. (1997). You can't take it with you: Why ability assessments don't cross cultures. *American Psychologist, 52*, 1115–1124.

Hodgkinson, H. (2000/2001). Education demographics: What teachers should know. *Educational Leadership, 57*, 6–11.

Hurley, S.R., & Blake, S. (2000). Assessment in the content areas for students acquiring English. In S.R. Hurley & J.V. Tinajero (Eds.), *Literacy assessment of second language learners* (pp. 84–103). Boston: Allyn & Bacon.

Kagan, S., & Kagan, M. (1998). *Multiple intelligences: The complete MI book.* San Clemente, CA: Kagan Cooperative Learning.

Krashen, S. (1993). *The power of reading.* Englewood, CO: Libraries Unlimited.

Krashen, S. (2003). *Explorations in language acquisition and use.* Portsmouth, NH: Heinemann.

Lenski, S.D., Daniel, M., Ehlers-Zavala, F., & Alvayero, M. (2004). Assessing struggling English-language learners. *Illinois Reading Council Journal, 32*(1), 21–30.

Lenski, S.D., & Ehlers-Zavala, F. (2004). *Reading strategies for Spanish speakers.* Dubuque, IA: Kendall/Hunt.

Lenski, S.D., & Nierstheimer, S.L. (2004). *Becoming a teacher of reading: A developmental approach.* Columbus, OH: Merrill Prentice Hall.

Martin, P., & Midgley, E. (1999). Immigration to the United States. *Population Bulletin, 54*, 1–44.

Moll, L.C., & Gonzalez, N. (1994). Critical issues: Lessons from research with language-minority children. *Journal of Reading Behavior, 26*, 439–456.

National Center for Education Statistics. (2002). *Public school student, staff, and graduate counts by state: School year 2000–01* (NCES Pub. 2003-348). Washington, DC: Author.

Odlin, T. (1989). *Language transfer: Cross-linguistic influence in language learning.* New York: Cambridge University Press.

O'Malley, J.M., & Valdez Pierce, L. (1996). *Authentic assessment for English language learners: Practical approaches for teachers.* Reading, MA: Addison-Wesley.

Smolen, L., Newman, C., Wathen, T., & Lee, D. (1995). Developing student self-assessment strategies. *TESOL Journal, 5*(1), 22–27.

Snyder, S.C. (2003). Foundations of predictability in L2 literacy learning. *TESOL Journal, 12*(3), 24–28.

Strickland, D.S., & Alvermann, D.E. (Eds.). (2004). *Bridging the literacy achievement gap grades 4–12.* New York: Teachers College Press.

Teachers of English to Speakers of Other Languages. (1997). *ESL standards for Pre-K–12 students.* Alexandria, VA: Author.

United States Department of Education, Office for Civil Rights. (2000). *The use of tests as part of high-stakes decision-making for students.* Washington, DC: Author.

Veciana-Suarez, A. (2002). *Flight to freedom.* New York: Orchard.

Vygotsky, L.S. (1978). *Mind in society: The development of higher psychological processes* (M. Cole, V. John-Steiner, S. Scribner, & E. Souberman, Eds. & Trans.). Cambridge, MA: Harvard University Press. (Original work published 1934)

Young, M.W., & Helvie, S.R. (1996). Parent power: A positive link to school success. *Journal of Educational Issues of Language Minority Students, 16,* 68–74.

Making Instructional Decisions Based on Data: What, How, and Why

Kouider Mokhtari, Catherine A. Rosemary, and Patricia A. Edwards

One of my weaknesses has always been documenting a student's progress, because I always found it such an overwhelming task. I would assess students, hand in the scores to an administrator, and then file them away. I literally would assess here and there, never use the results, and concentrate on whole-group instruction. Individual needs based on assessment were never taken into consideration. (Calderon [a kindergarten teacher], cited in Reilly, 2007, p. 770)

If you can relate to Calderon's sense of disenchantment with respect to documenting students' progress in your classroom or school and then not using the information, you are not alone. In our teaching experiences over more than two decades, we have often heard comments such as these from many of the PreK–12 teachers, literacy specialists, and principals in classroom and school settings with whom we have worked. We often found and continue to find that, although these educators spend significant amounts of time collecting assessment data, they do not take time or perhaps know how to organize and use data consistently and efficiently in instructional decision making. When asked, most teachers often admit, like Calderon, that documentation of student literacy progress is one of their weaknesses because it can be an overwhelming and time-consuming task. Other teachers say that they simply lack the knowledge and skills to develop a system for assessing and documenting students' progress.

The challenges that go along with data-based decision making are even more apparent in the current context of increased accountability as seen in local, state, and federal policies. At a time when teachers and administrators are pressed to demonstrate students' literacy growth, collecting, organizing, analyzing, and using data for instructional and curriculum improvement is a new way of working for many educators. How should assessment data be examined to improve instruction and curriculum and thereby advance students' reading and writing performance? In this column, we offer a promising framework that can support school teams (i.e., teachers, literacy coaches, data managers, and principals) in making sense of various types of data for instructional planning. Instruction that is data based and goal driven sets the stage for continuous reading and writing improvement.

Research on the Intersection of Literacy Assessment and Instruction

Literature on the influence of literacy assessment on instruction focuses on the relationship between assessment and instruction rather than on whether one does or should drive the other. In one extensive study aimed at determining how assessment influences instruction within four particular schools, Stephens and her colleagues (Stephens et al., 1995) found that "the salient relationship was not between assessment and instruction per se. Granted, the two were related, but their relationship was moderated by the decision-making model of the

Preparing Reading Professionals (second edition), edited by Rita M. Bean, Natalie Heisey, and Cathy M. Roller. © 2010 by the International Reading Association. Reprinted from Mokhtari, K., Rosemary, C.A., & Edwards, P.A. (2007). Making instructional decisions based on data: What, how, and why. *The Reading Teacher, 61*(4), 354–359. doi:10.1598/RT.61.4.10.

district" (p. 494). The implication here is that assessment and instruction issues are embedded within broader power structures within particular schools and that both are influenced greatly by the decision-making model operating within those schools.

Shea, Murray, and Harlin (2005) noted that school-wide committees or teams typically have a wide-angle view of student achievement: The information they examine often comes from various sources and diverse perspectives. They suggested that schoolwide teams analyze aggregated or disaggregated assessment data focused on curriculum and instruction for whole classrooms, small groups, or individual learners. After reporting students' current level of achievement, they then can make recommendations pertaining to schoolwide, grade-level, or individualized instruction. However, it is important to keep in mind that "as important as these recommendations are, they should not mark the end of a committee's work. At future meetings, members must review progress made as a result of their recommendations and modify them when appropriate" (p. 148). In other words, the systematic use of data to make instructional decisions requires leadership, training, and the development of a culture of data-driven decision making and accountability.

The analytical framework described in the following section was inspired by the *Standards for the Assessment of Reading and Writing* developed and published collaboratively by The National Council of Teachers of English and the International Reading Association Joint Task Force on Assessment (1994). This valuable report provides a set of 11 standards aimed at guiding the decisions schools make about assessing the teaching of reading and writing. These standards express the conviction Joint Task Force members had that involving the entire school community is essential if assessment is truly to foster student and teacher learning. The report offers guidelines for assessment strategies that reflect the complex interactions among teachers, learners, and communities; that ensure fair and equitable treatment of all students; and that foster thoughtful literacy learning and teaching.

Introducing the Data Analysis Framework for Instructional Decision Making

The Data Analysis Framework for Instructional Decision Making is a practical tool that provides school teams with a structure and process for organizing, analyzing, and using multiple sources and types of data for instructional decision making. Three major categories of data that are considered for improving reading and writing instruction include (1) professional development data, (2) classroom data, and (3) reading performance data.

1. Professional development data may consist of evaluation or feedback surveys and coaches' logs of how they spend their time and the types of activities they engage in to assist classroom teachers.

2. Classroom data may consist of teacher surveys of instructional practices, such as U.S. Elementary Reading Instruction (Bauman, Hoffman, Duffy-Hester, & Moon Ro, 2000), and The Language Arts Curriculum Survey (Center for Policy Research, n.d.), which surveys teachers on the time they spend on reading components and the cognitive demand of learning tasks. Informal data on reading instruction may consist of teachers' daily lesson plans or weekly schedules that include instructional time frames, content taught, and organizational grouping (i.e., individual, small-group, or whole-group instruction). Working together, literacy coaches and teachers may use observational data collected from tools such as the Early Language and Literacy Classroom Observation Toolkit (Smith & Dickinson, 2004) and Classroom Environment Profile (Wolfersberger, Reutzel, Sudweeks, & Fawson, 2004). Coaches' documentation of informal observations conducted systematically and regularly (e.g., Bean, 2004, pp. 106–111) may also provide valuable sources of classroom data.

3. Reading performance data, arguably the most important aspect of instructional decision making, may include standardized tests, criterion-referenced tests, informal classroom assessments, and student-work samples.

Taken together, these sources provide a rich data set for school teams to use in setting goals and devising action steps to improve literacy instruction within classrooms, across grade levels, and throughout schools.

Using the Framework

The Data Analysis Framework for Instructional Decision Making consists of guiding questions to assist school literacy team members in analyzing data, discussing the patterns and relationships within those data, and constructing interpretations that they can then translate into goals and action steps to improve reading and writing achievement (see Figure 1).

General procedures that may guide implementation of the Data Analysis Framework for Instructional Decision Making consist of the following five steps:

1. Organize the data set so that members of the literacy team can partner in analyzing different portions of the data set. Partnering allows for more than one set of eyes on the same data and provokes substantive discussion of individual observations.

Figure 1
Worksheet for School Teams Using Data Analysis Framework
for Instructional Decision Making

Professional Development Data
1. What patterns do you observe in the professional development data?
2. How do you explain the patterns you see in the data?

Classroom Data
1. What are some instructional strengths?
2. What aspects of instruction show a need for improvement?
3. What content and strategies are emphasized in the instruction?
4. What content and strategies are not emphasized?
5. How do you explain the patterns you see in the data?

Student Data
1. What patterns do you observe in the student data at the school level, grade level, and classroom level?
    a. Where is growth demonstrated?
    b. Is the growth equal across grades?
    c. Is the growth equal for all students?
    d. What are specific areas of strength?
    e. What are specific areas that need improvement?
2. How do you explain the patterns you see in the data?

Put It All Together
1. What connections can you make between professional development data, classroom data, and student data?
2. What are the strengths and needs?
3. What do the patterns mean for you in your role (e.g., literacy coach, principal, data manager, teacher)?
4. What are the implications for change as you see them in your role?
5. Overall, based on the analysis and findings, what are the professional development and school improvement goals?
6. What action steps will you take to meet the goals?
7. How will you communicate the improvement plan to other school personnel and stakeholders?

---

2. Select a recorder for the team. The recorder takes notes on the team's discussion of the observations during step 4.

3. Partners analyze their data and each person jots down observations on his or her worksheet.

4. After sufficient time for partners to carefully analyze their data, the team "puts it all together" in a discussion of their findings (patterns in data) and interpretations (what the patterns show in terms of strengths and needs) and then devises professional development and school improvement goals and action steps.

5. The team plans when and how they will communicate the formative plan to other school personnel and stakeholders and monitors the implementation of their plan.

The example provided in Figure 2 illustrates the results of a school literacy team's use of the Data Analysis Framework for Instructional Decision Making. The school team example of a Put It All Together is a composite created from authentic samples of a literacy team's work. The literacy team members included the school-based literacy coach, principal, data manager, and grade-level teacher representatives in an elementary school.

Figure 2
Example of a School Literacy Team's "Put It All Together" From the Data Analysis Framework for Instructional Decision Making

---

Put It All Together

What connections can you make between professional development data, classroom data, and student data?

Our data overall show that the professional development has helped to improve classroom instructional practices, and the student data shows stronger achievement. Coaching logs showed that the coaches' are spending a large amount of time providing professional development in five areas (fluency, phonics, phonemic awareness, comprehension, and vocabulary) and not as much time on individual coaching. The teacher surveys showed strong use of research-based strategies presented at professional development, which may be related to higher Early Language and Literacy Classroom Observation (ELLCO) scores in approaches to curriculum integration, reading instruction, and presence of books. ELLCO scores for oral language facilitation are lower than other areas, and students scoring at or above grade level are not making good gains. This suggests a need for differentiated instruction. Our student data showed improvement over two years, and TerraNova results showed growth in two of three grade levels.

What are the strengths and needs?
Strengths:
Better alignment of curriculum to state indicators (based on Language Arts Curriculum Survey). The disaggregated data show growth for students scoring in the at-risk and some-risk categories. Teachers are using data.

Needs:
Improve instruction for students scoring at or above grade level. First-grade scores dropped at third benchmark so we need to look more closely at first-grade instruction.

What do the patterns mean for you in your role (e.g., literacy coach, principal, teacher, data manager)?
Literacy coach:
Based on my coaching log data, I need to spend more time in classrooms, work more with teachers on differentiating instruction, and follow up with teachers after progress monitoring.

Principal:
I need to more frequently observe classroom instruction and provide feedback.

(continued)

Figure 2 (Continued)
Example of a School Literacy Team's "Put It All Together" From the Data Analysis Framework for Instructional Decision Making

First-grade teacher:
I should identify specific areas of need for students reading below grade-level expectations and work with the coach to differentiate instruction in areas of need.

Data manager:
I need to stress progress monitoring for students reading at or above grade level more often.

What are the implications for change as you see them in your role?
We need to utilize our data to better plan instruction. We need to streamline interventions and make sure to address needs of students reading at or above grade level. Coaches need to spend more time in classrooms and conduct teaching demonstrations.

Overall, based on the analysis and findings, what are the professional development and school improvement goals?
   Professional development goals:

   1. Continue to analyze and use data
      • include data at beginning of professional development
      • take time to analyze data
   2. Increase differentiated instruction
      • work with teachers to plan for small groups and target needs for instruction
      • continue to examine the content of reading instruction using data and identify specifics within the five areas to target—what we want students to know and be able to do
      • assist teachers with ways to monitor student performance and analyze student work

   School goals:

   1. Improve data use at classroom and school levels
      • schedule grade-level meetings for teachers to analyze data regularly
      • principal follows up with literacy coach on classroom instructional needs
      • principal schedules regular observations of instruction and provides feedback to teachers
   2. Align curriculum, instructional resources, and instruction with student needs
      • use intervention specialists more with first grade
      • examine what's working in our intervention model and make changes as needed
      • examine the core reading program to see how it addresses what we need to teach more effectively

How will you communicate the plan to other school personnel and stakeholders?
At the opening-of-school meeting—principal, literacy coaches, and teachers share in a presentation of findings from the data analysis and communicate broad, school goals. Teachers on the school literacy team meet with grade-level colleagues to refine goals and develop two action steps. The grade-level facilitator records specific goals and action steps.

At the follow-up meeting of the school literacy team, the grade-level facilitators share plans and post them in the professional development classroom. All teachers post respective grade-level goals in classrooms in student-centered language. At regular meetings throughout the year, the school literacy team assesses progress in meeting the goals and monitors or adjusts the action steps accordingly.

Applications

The Data Analysis Framework for Instructional Decision Making may be applied in a variety of preK–12 educational settings. It can be easily modified to include other types of data collected outside of literacy including mathematics, science, or other subject areas. Its team approach allows for different educator groups to collaborate—teachers within and across grade levels and district-wide school improvement teams. The Data Analysis Framework for Instructional Decision Making is easily adapted to small or large teams who may modify the questions to suit local purposes and contexts. As with other collaborative processes, the utility of the framework is best judged by those who use it for its intended purpose—to support a systematic and thorough analysis of multiple sources of data to improve student learning and achievement.

References

Baumann, J.F., Hoffman, J.V., Duffy-Hester, A.M., & Ro, J.M. (2000). The First R yesterday and today: U.S. elementary reading instruction practices reported by teachers and administrators. *Reading Research Quarterly, 35*, 338–377.

Bean, R. (2004). *The reading specialist: Leadership for the classroom, school, and community.* New York: Guilford.

Center for Policy Research. (n.d.). *The language arts curriculum survey* (Unpublished document). Madison, WI: University of Wisconsin.

International Reading Association & National Council of Teachers of English. (1994). *Standards for the assessment of reading and writing.* Newark, DE; Urbana, IL: Authors.

Reilly, M.A. (2007). Choice of action: Using data to make instructional decisions in kindergarten. *The Reading Teacher, 60*, 770–776.

Shea, M., Murray, R., & Harlin, R. (2005). *Drowning in data? How to collect, organize, and document student performance.* Portsmouth, NH: Heinemann.

Smith, M., & Dickinson, D. (2002). *Early language and literacy classroom observation toolkit.* Baltimore: Brookes.

Stephens, D., Pearson, P.D., Gilrane, C., Roe, M., Stallman, A., Shelton, J., et al. (1995). Assessment and decision making in schools: A cross-site analysis. *Reading Research Quarterly, 30*, 478–499.

Wolfersberger, M.E., Reutzel, D.R., Sudweeks, R., & Fawson, P.C. (2004). Developing and validating the classroom literacy environment profile (CLEP): A tool for examining the "print richness" of early childhood and elementary classrooms. *Journal of Literacy Research, 36*, 211–272.

PART 4

Diversity

The Diversity Standard focuses on the need to prepare teachers to build and engage their students in a curriculum that places value on the diversity that exists in society. The elements featured in this standard relate to race, ethnicity, class, gender, religion, and language. This standard is grounded in a set of principles and understandings that reflect a vision for a democratic and just society. Standard 4 and its elements follow:

Standard 4. Diversity. Candidates create and engage their students in literacy practices that develop awareness, understanding, respect, and a valuing of differences in our society. As a result, candidates

- **Element 4.1 Recognize, understand, and value the forms of diversity that exist in society and their importance in learning to read and write.**

- **Element 4.2 Use a literacy curriculum and engage in instructional practices that positively impact students' knowledge, beliefs, and engagement with the features of diversity.**

- **Element 4.3 Develop and implement strategies to advocate for equity.**

Part 4 includes five journal articles that may be helpful in understanding the substance of the standard and its elements. These pieces are briefly described here.

Black (2009) describes the literature on language, literacy studies, and 21st-century skills to discuss how English-language learners, through their engagement with digital technologies and popular media, are developing proficiencies that have been identified as critical to success in society today. Sanford (2005) reports research about how out-of-school literacies can influence present and future learning of adolescents, suggesting that there are differences in the ways in which girls and boys engage in literacy. Both of these studies address forms of diversity and what we know about how that diversity influences literacy learning; they are especially important for understanding Elements 4.1 and 4.3.

Landt (2006) speaks to the importance of using quality young adult literature to expose students to viewpoints and experience that can broaden their visions of self and the world while Tatum (2004) provides important guidelines for reading professionals, especially reading specialists, working in schools with large numbers of students of

Preparing Reading Professionals (second edition), edited by Rita M. Bean, Natalie Heisey, and Cathy M. Roller. © 2010 by the International Reading Association.

diversity. Although both of these articles are especially relevant to Element 4.2, they also provide important information for addressing Elements 4.1 and 4.3.

Finally, Hill (2009) provides a thoughtful piece chronicling her work with a teacher and two African American students. In this article, she discusses the way in which the teacher provides nonthreatening spaces for negotiating and applying nonstandard and Standard English. This final article assists readers in thinking about Element 4.3 and also addresses Elements 4.1 and 4.2.

Further Reading

Au, K.H., & Raphael, T.E. (2000). Equity and literacy in the next millennium. *Reading Research Quarterly*, *35*(1), 170–188. doi:10.1598/RRQ.35.1.12

Coppola, J., & Primas, E.V. (Eds.). (2009). *One classroom, many learners: Best literacy practices for today's multilingual classrooms*. Newark, DE: International Reading Association.

Jiménez, R.T., & Pang, V.P. (Eds.). (2006). *Race, ethnicity, and education: Vol. 2: Language and literacy in schools*. Westport, CT: Praeger.

Rogers, R., & Mosley, M. (2006). Racial literacy in a second-grade classroom: Critical race theory, whiteness studies, and literacy research. *Reading Research Quarterly*, *41*(4), 462–495. doi:10.1598/RRQ.41.4.3

Questions for Reflection and Discussion

• Compare and contrast the various notions described in these articles about selecting and using materials and strategies that would have a positive impact on students' knowledge, beliefs, and engagement with the features of diversity. Think about the concept of "new literacies" and its impact on the way we teach and how students learn.

• What are the key ideas in the Black article about the ways in which digital technologies can enhance the learning of ELLs? What possibilities exist for using technology in the classrooms as a means of helping students understand, respect, and value diversity in society?

• After reading these articles, identify the major points that might be included in a professional development program for teachers who want to know more about how they can develop and implement a curriculum that reflects the diversity in their classrooms. What rationale can be shared with them for such a curriculum and what practical ideas could be offered?

English-Language Learners, Fan Communities, and 21st-Century Skills

Rebecca W. Black

Globalization is a term often used to describe the increasing flow of people, ideas, goods, and capital across national borders (Appadurai, 1996; Suárez-Orozco & Qin-Hilliard, 2004). In many ways, globalization has been facilitated by and tied to new tools and technologies. For example, new technologies have played a significant role in expediting transportation and communication across physical space, which in turn has made it easier for people to live, communicate, and conduct business across national borders. As technology and such cross-border forms of social and economic practice become increasingly prevalent, it stands to reason that there also may be a concomitant shift in the sort of skills and abilities that individuals will need for effective participation in modern work, academic, and leisure environments. In recognition of such a shift, partnerships among businesses, schools, and researchers have been working toward a common understanding of the sort of so-called 21st-century skills that students should be developing as they prepare for their futures.

This article draws from literature on 21st-century skills as a framework for exploring the forms of literacy and learning that many adolescents are engaging with in out of school spaces. In particular, this article is a theoretical exploration of themes that emerged during a longitudinal ethnographic study of adolescent English-language learners' (ELLs') literate and social activities surrounding online fan fiction. Fan fictions are texts written about media and popular culture by fans. In these texts, fan

fiction authors take up the characters and plotlines of the original media and creatively rework them by developing new relationships between characters, extending plot and timelines, creating new settings, and exploring novel themes. By considering how such practices relate to 21st-century skills, this article aims to provide insight on youth-led, technology-mediated learning and literacy practices and to stimulate thinking about how our understandings of 21st-century skills in out-of-school spaces might inform pedagogical approaches in the teaching of language and literacy in more formal learning environments.

Literacy and Learning in the 21st Century

21st-Century Skills

Rapid technological advances and ongoing processes of globalization have given rise to serious consideration of the goals and responsibilities for institutions of formal learning in the 21st century. The 21st Century Workforce Commission (2000) suggested that "the current and future health of America's 21st century economy depends directly on how broadly and deeply Americans reach a new level of literacy—'21st-Century Literacy'" (p. 4). Organizations such as the International Reading Association (2001) and the North Central Regional Educational Laboratory (NCREL; 2003) are developing educational frameworks for 21st-century literacy and

Preparing Reading Professionals (second edition), edited by Rita M. Bean, Natalie Heisey, and Cathy M. Roller. © 2010 by the International Reading Association. Reprinted from Black, R.W. (2009). English-language learners, fan communities, and 21st-century skills. *Journal of Adolescent & Adult Literacy, 52*(8), 688–697. doi:10.1598/JAAL.52.8.4.

skills. Also, members of research, education, and business communities have formed partnerships to create such frameworks, working together to identify proficiencies that currently are or will be extremely valuable in future work and academic environments. These consortiums aim to strengthen the U.S. education system (Partnership for 21st Century Skills, 2004, n.p.) and to ensure the United States' competitiveness in a global, technology-mediated market.

The NCREL (2003) described the need for digital literacy skills on their enGauge 21st Century Skills Website, emphasizing the notion that traditional literacy skills are now only a starting point for engaging in other forms of literate interaction:

> As society changes, the skills needed to negotiate the complexities of life also change. In the early 1900s, a person who had acquired simple reading, writing, and calculating skills was considered literate. Only in recent years has the public education system expected all students to build on those basics, developing a broader range of literacies. (International ICT Literacy Panel, 2002, as cited in NCREL, 2003, n.p.)

The digital literacy skills identified by various 21st-century consortiums include proficiencies such as basic print literacy, scientific, economic, technological, visual, information, and multicultural literacies as well as global awareness (NCREL, 2003). It is important to note that developing such proficiencies can pose an extra challenge for certain populations of students, such as ELLs, if they are relegated to classroom contexts where the primary focus is mastery of traditional forms of print-based literacy. Clearly it is crucial that ELLs receive quality instruction in and access to standard, academic forms of language. However, as discussion in this article will demonstrate, activities based on popular culture as well as new technologies and ICTs can offer opportunities for the development of standard language proficiency in tandem with the development of digital literacy and 21st-century skills.

Literacy in Online Contexts

In public discourse, literacy is often narrowly construed as a skill set related to the decoding and encoding of print-based texts. However, this article draws from a sociocultural approach to literacy known as the New Literacy Studies (NLS) that provides a basis for more broadly conceptualizing writing and reading as communicative practices that are rooted within certain social, historical, and political contexts of use (Gee, 1999; Hull & Schultz, 2002; Lankshear & Knobel, 2006; Street, 1984). In recent decades, work within the NLS has attempted to "extend the idea and scope of literacy pedagogy to account for the context of our culturally and linguistically diverse and increasingly globalized societies" and to "account for the burgeoning variety of text forms associated with information and multimedia technologies" (New London Group, 1996, n.p.). Such an approach is helpful for understanding the many shifts taking place as a great deal of contemporary communicative and meaning-making practices move to online, globally networked contexts. Moreover, it is particularly helpful to this article for understanding how many adolescent ELLs are developing language, literacy, and social skills across national borders, as they use new technological tools and semiotic forms to communicate, share information, and negotiate meaning with youths located in many different countries.

As many adolescents socialize and spend a great deal of time in such online, global social settings—the process of relocation for many immigrant youths also takes place at least partially in technology-mediated environments such as online discussion boards, social networking sites, fan communities, and video gaming environments. Thus, it is important to consider how youths' literacy, learning, and identity practices are both shaped by and shape the interactions they have in online spaces (Jensen, 2003). In addition, such research can help us to understand how youths take on and negotiate social roles that may have implications for learning in both on- and offline spaces.

Related Research

Digital literacy and 21st-century skills resonate with research across disciplines exploring the potential impact of technological advances (Gee, 2004; Lankshear & Knobel, 2006), global connectedness (Suárez-Orozco & Qin-Hilliard, 2004), and participatory culture (Jenkins, 1992) on youths' learning and literacy practices. For instance, research on adolescents' extracurricular engagement with technology has described an array of sophisticated literate and social practices that include but are not limited to traditional print and standard forms of English. These studies include explorations of how youths use technologies such as instant messaging to create or maintain on and offline social networks (Lewis & Fabos, 2005), or chatting to author social identities (Lam, 2004). Other studies have described multimodal practices such as digital storytelling (Hull, 2003), online journaling (Guzzetti & Gamboa, 2005), remixing (Lankshear & Knobel, 2006) or redesigning (Chandler-Olcott & Mahar, 2003a, 2003b) media texts. Through such multimodal activities, youths engage in creative manipulation of popular cultural and textual artifacts, drawing from a mixture of text, image, color, and sound as a means of representing themselves and communicating in online spaces.

The aforementioned work has provided much-needed insight on adolescents' extracurricular, technology-mediated activities. However, there has been little exploration of how youths, particularly ELLs, are developing proficiencies that are aligned with many 21st-century skills through voluntary participation in online spaces. This article addresses this gap through an explicit focus on literacy and 21st-century proficiencies in relation the following research questions:

- What sort of 21st-century skills are youths developing through participation in online fan-related contexts?
- What is the relationship between traditional, print-based and 21st-century literacy skills in online fan fiction spaces?

- What sorts of social roles or identities are associated with 21st-century proficiencies and literacy practices?

It is important to note that while this article is based on data from case studies of adolescent ELLs literacy and social practices in online environments, the purpose of the analysis is not to present detailed ethnographic accounts of these individual learners' experiences. Instead, the purpose is to provoke a broader discussion of fan-based literacy and learning practices in relation to 21st-century skills.

Study Context and Methods

The primary context for the larger study, Fanfiction.net (FFN), is the largest online fan fiction archive, housing over a million fan fiction texts, with over 300,000 texts in the Harry Potter section alone. FFN has servers in North America, Asia, and Europe and attracts fan authors from across the globe. Fans on the site compose and publicly post texts based on their favorite media canons—including books, music, movies, Japanese animation (anime), and video games—and then the audience has the option of reading and publicly posting feedback or *reviews* of the texts. Participation on the site extends beyond posting texts for entertainment, as fans engage in activities such as peer reviewing, collaborative writing, and exploring certain genres of writing. Participation also includes substantive discussion around composition as well as discussion of the themes and topics addressed in many of the fan fiction texts (Black, 2005, 2008). Ethnographic (Geertz, 1973) and discourse analytic (Gee, 1999) methods were used to gain a rich sense of the FFN community, as I spent three years as a participant observer on the site. Primary data sources were adolescent ELL focal participants' fan fiction texts, reader reviews of these texts, and interviews with focal participants. The purpose of the larger study was to explore how this informal, online writing space might provide ELLs with access to literacy learning and how the virtual environment might promote affiliation with composing and interacting in English.

Data discussed in this article are drawn primarily from case studies of three ELL focal participants, Grace, Nanako, and Cherry-chan (all names are pseudonyms). Although Grace, Nanako, and Cherry-chan are all ELLs, these young women differ greatly in terms of experiences with and exposure not only to English but also to other languages. Grace is a popular fan fiction authoress from the Philippines who has written many multichapter stories on FFN since 2001. She grew up speaking Kapangpangan, which she considers her first language, and she began learning Filipino (a standardized version of Tagalog) at an early age and used Filipino for most academic activities in early grade school. At around age 7, Grace also began learning English in school. Much of her productive experience with English has been in written rather than spoken format, as she primarily has used English for her academic activities, online communications, and fan fiction compositions.

Nanako is a generation 1.5 Chinese immigrant who moved from Shanghai to Canada with her parents and began learning English when she was 11. Nanako's family speaks Mandarin Chinese at home, and Nanako was fully literate in Chinese when she immigrated to North America. Cherry-chan, on the other hand, is a second generation immigrant whose family moved to Canada from Taiwan before she was born. Of the three focal participants, Cherry-chan is the only one who grew up speaking languages that she is not fully literate in. In an interview, she explains that she grew up speaking Mandarin Chinese and Taiwanese, but she learned to write in English and never learned what she calls "the true basics" of writing in Chinese.

These participants were chosen for this article because they have had notably different experiences with English-language learning and exhibit proficiency with similar 21st-century skills in their online activities. Analyses from the larger study primarily focus on how Grace, Nanako, and Cherry-chan engaged in activities that were aligned with or differed from

school-based literacy practices. The following analysis extends that discussion by describing Grace, Nanako, and Cherry-chan's engagement with traditional print literacy, as well as with a range of 21st century skills including multimodal, technological, and information literacy.

Analysis: Digital Age Literacy

Print Literacy

Digital Age Literacy is a category of 21st-century skills that includes but is not limited to basic proficiency with print-based text. Other Digital Age forms of literacy include the ability to read visual and multimodal texts, as well as technological and information literacy (NCREL, 2003). In terms of basic print literacy, it is worth noting that through their fan-related activities, all three focal participants were able to practice and improve their English-language and composition skills. For example, each of these young women was able to find and work with a β-reader when producing some of their texts. According to FFN, "A beta reader (or betareader, or beta) is a person who reads a work of fiction with a critical eye, with the aim of improving grammar, spelling, characterization, and general style of a story prior to its release to the general public" (Fanfiction.net, 2008, n.p.). Working with beta readers gave Grace, Nanako, and Cherry-chan opportunities to receive explicit feedback on their writing and rhetorical skills.

Additionally, FFN, like many fan fiction sites, has a built-in mechanism to encourage audience feedback. Specifically, each text has an option for readers to submit feedback or a "review" of the fiction. Grace and Nanako, who are dedicated fan fiction authors, have received approximately 7,600 and 9,400 reviews respectively. Cherry-chan, who infrequently updates her stories and leaves many of her fan texts unfinished, has received 650 reviews. It is important to note that most of these reader reviews are what, in a chapter exploring fan readers' feedback (Black, 2008), I have called "OMG Standards." These are a common type of review that begins with common Internet parlance of the acronym for *Oh My God!* and "consists of enthusiastic statements of appreciation for the fiction such as, 'OMG! I love this chapter!'" (Black, 2008, p. 107). These reviews provide authors with hearty encouragement to continue writing and can be a crucial element for helping ELLs feel comfortable composing in this space.

In addition to the short and sweet support of OMG Standards, other reviews are aimed at providing explicit feedback on grammar and spelling, as well as story elements such as plot, characterization, and adherence to genre. These reviews come in many different forms. For example, some readers pull out sentence-level excerpts of the author's texts and explicitly discuss the errors in each sentence. Other readers will examine entire paragraphs, recasting the writing to make it more grammatically sound (see Black, 2008 for examples). Thus, the FFN community provides ELL youths with support for the development of traditional print literacy by encouraging interactions between writers and readers, promoting confidence, and helping authors to explicitly focus on different aspects of language and composition.

These basic literacy skills are building blocks of communication that are crucial to effective participation in online environments. However, it is worth noting that focal participants' fan-related compositions, while text-based, did not rigidly adhere to the standards and conventions of print-based English. For example, as mentioned previously, the ELL focal participants often had grammatical and spelling errors in their texts. Additionally, all three focal participants incorporated languages other than English into their prose, often using Japanese or Chinese to convey certain information or for effect.

Notwithstanding errors, within the fan community, focal participants were treated as legitimate participants and interlocutors in their own right. Moreover, their multilingual texts and diverse perspectives were viewed as meaningful contributions to the "fanon" or collective body of fan knowledge (Black, 2005). As ELLs, this acceptance was important to focal participants' literacy and language socialization for several reasons. First, it provided them with a sense of belonging in a community that was important to them. Second, this acceptance of their writing and attempts to communicate using English, notwithstanding errors, provided inspiration and confidence for attempting additional and more complex written and communicative endeavors. Finally, the sense of acceptance and belonging enabled these ELL authors to develop identities as accomplished creators and users of English text.

Multimodal and Technological Literacy

Multimodal and technological proficiencies also fall under the realm of Digital Age Literacy and are an integral part of successful participation in fan communities. As Kress (2000) aptly pointed out, multimodality, or conveyance of meaning through multiple modes of representation, is hardly a new phenomenon, as human communication in various forms is inherently multimodal. However, the increasing prevalence of computer-mediated forms of communication has made the simultaneous integration of multiple modes of meaning a salient feature of online texts and environments.

As technological advances make new communication tools and participatory spaces available on what seems like a daily basis, the skills needed for successful online interactions are constantly in flux. For example, the interface and conventions for conveying information via work-based e-mail and instant messaging; school-based wikis, blogs, and websites; and out-of-school social networking sites (e.g., Facebook, MySpace), LiveJournals, and Massively Multiplayer Online Role-playing Games all differ significantly. Thus, learning to effectively use and adapt to such technological innovations is a skill that will serve youths well in the 21st century. Moreover, for ELLs, using multiple modes of representation to convey meaning can be an integral part of communicating effectively and taking on meaningful social roles in online environments where much of the print-based text is in English.

It is worth noting that neither Grace, Cherry-chan, nor Nanako was particularly tech-savvy when first participating on FFN. For example, Grace initially penned her fictions on paper and then paid to upload them at a local Internet café in the Philippines. Cherry-chan had virtually no Web presence and made it clear that she had very little access to the computer she shared with her family. Of the three, Nanako had the greatest computer access, although she also complained of intermittent Internet availability at times when her mother had the service disconnected. In spite of this intermittent access to the Web, Nanako did create an anime fan website during her early years of participation on FFN. However, the site still had many technical difficulties such as images that failed to load, links that were often broken, and pull-down menus that did not work, thus marking Nanako as an inexperienced Web technology user.

Over time and through participation in various fan websites Grace, Cherry-chan, and Nanako all developed a notable measure of multimodal and technological proficiency. For example, all three participants now have personal websites, LiveJournal accounts, or online forums. Multiple modes of meaning-making, such as space, color, image, movement, and sound are all integral components of how these young women design their webpages to convey their identities and affiliations with certain social and cultural groups. They also use these forms of expression to augment the content of traditional print messages and fan fiction texts. To effectively use such modes of expression, youths must have at least some measure of visual literacy and an understanding of how these multimodal elements can be combined to create meaning.

Through their participation in online spaces, all three focal participants have also developed what is known as technological literacy, or the ability to choose appropriate technology for specific activities and use it in the most effective ways (NCREL, 2003). To be more specific, these young women all alternate between communicating ideas in public writing forums, through e-mail, or via instant messenger depending on the content and goal of their messages. For example, Grace used the public nature of online fan forums to garner widespread support from other fans when the site administrators on FFN banned some of her fictions for violating the terms of service. However, she chose e-mail as the means of contacting site administrators and effectively presenting her arguments for why her fictions were not in violation of the site rules, which ultimately led to the reinstatement of her FFN account. Through these different activities and mediums, Grace presented herself in very different social roles—in the online forums, she was a powerful self-advocate defending her right to freedom of speech; whereas in the e-mails with site administrators, she was a courteous and principled fan who would attempt to balance her own desire for creative expression with the rules of the site.

Also, as discussed previously, all three focal participants maintain several Web spaces. Maintaining these spaces requires at least some measure of proficiency with different user-interfaces, programming languages, and video and image-editing software, as well as the conventions for designing materials and conveying information in each of these contexts (i.e., conventions for communication in a LiveJournal community are quite different from those of an online anime forum). Thus, through participation in fan spaces, all three focal participants have developed skills in designing webpages; using various software programs; creating videos; and manipulating online, multimodal texts to effectively communicate and convey information.

Information Literacy

In this study, the development of focal participants' technological literacy also was closely related to another 21st-century proficiency known as information literacy. Information literacy refers to the ability to seek out and critically evaluate information across a range of media. This includes recognizing when information is needed and then using technology, such as communication networks and electronic resources, to locate, evaluate, synthesize, and put this information to use (NCREL, 2003). One of Nanako's sources of computer-related knowledge was the computer classes she was taking in school. However, the emphasis in school-based computer classes is often on basic or mechanical aspects of computer use or computer-based reproductions of print-based activities. Thus, the skills from her computer classes did not all readily transfer to her extracurricular computer-based activities. In fact, the primary way that Grace, Nanako, and Cherry-chan developed their technological literacy was by accessing online sources of information and tapping into networks of people who were skilled at using these technologies.

This finding is akin to the findings of Chandler-Olcott and Mahar's (2003b) study investigating adolescent girls' technology-mediated literacy practices. In this article, the authors focused on two focal participants, Rhiannon and Eileen, who created and designed multimodal texts within the anime fan community. According to the authors, "both girls received a good deal of mentorship related to their technology use and their composing processes from other members of their online communities" (p. 366). The authors also emphasize the point that these young women did not receive mentorship for their technology use in schools. Instead, they relied on related print resources or went online to seek out examples of and explicit instructions for how to design tech-savvy texts.

Grace, Nanako, and Cherry-chan also engaged in such self-directed forms of learning. For example, Nanako would sometimes publicly post questions or rants about technological challenges that she was having on her webpages as a means of eliciting feedback and help from the audience. Also, all three youths visited online help sites and forums to find information about how to create and maintain their various webpages, forums, and LiveJournal accounts. In so doing, they continued to develop their information literacy skills, as they sought out information, decided which materials

were relevant to the tasks they were trying to accomplish, and then applied this information to complete their online projects and activities.

Discussion

In thinking about 21st-century proficiencies and how they might relate to classroom instruction, it is important to recognize that technology alone is not the defining characteristic of such skills. As Lankshear and Knobel (2007) aptly pointed out, technology can be used to search for information, construct essays, and communicate in ways that differ very little from traditional, print-based enactments of such practices. What makes skills and literacies "new" is how "they mobilize very different kinds of values and priorities and sensibilities than the literacies we are familiar with" (2007, p. 7). These new sensibilities allow for a flexible range of expertise in which all participants are able to take up the roles of both teacher and learner (Black, 2008; Gee, 2004; Lankshear & Knobel, 2007). For example, within the fan community, an ELL who has not yet mastered the conventions of print-based writing can still take up the role of an expert webpage designer or popular cultural expert and achieve social status and solidarity with online peers (Lam, 2000).

Such new sensibilities also place value on collaborative practices and forms of knowledge in which authorship, teaching, and learning is distributed across community members (Black, 2008; Gee, 2004; Lankshear & Knobel, 2007). One such example is the collaborative authoring of online fan texts (Black, 2008; Thomas, 2005; Yi, 2008) in which youths are able to coconstruct knowledge around a particular media text while at the same time exchanging ideas and receiving feedback on their rhetorical and composition skills. Another example is the informal mentoring and apprenticeship that the young women from this and the Chandler-Olcott and Mahar (2003a, 2003b) study received through participation in online fan communities, and how such scaffolding enabled them to develop more sophisticated technological skills. These skills and sensibilities are often associated with the ethos of Web 2.0, in which technology users actively contribute to the content of online spaces (Lankshear & Knobel, 2007). Such skills also are related to effective instructional approaches for ELLs that involve peer-to-peer cooperative learning as well as teacher, parent, and community scaffolding. These approaches are empowering because they take an additive rather than subtractive approach to the resources that ELL learners bring to the classroom. They also support collaborative creation of classroom knowledge, and students are able to "participate competently in instruction as a result of having developed a secure sense of identity and the knowledge that their voices will be heard and respected within the classroom" (Cummins, 1996, p. 16).

Even in classrooms where technological access and resources are scarce, there are opportunities to develop lessons and activities that incorporate many of the proficiencies, sensibilities, and values associated with effective participation in the 21st century. As the National Council of Teachers of English (NCTE) points out,

> Although technology is important to literacy in the new century, other dimensions of learning are essential. Studies of workforce readiness show that employers rate written and oral communication skills very highly, and collaboration, work ethic, critical thinking, and leadership all rank higher than proficiency in information technology. The Partnership for 21st-Century Skills advocates for core academic subjects, learning and innovation skill, and life and career skills, along with technology skills. (2007, n.p.)

Along these lines, Warschauer (2007) pointed out that the shift to online and technology-mediated contexts is making traditional print-based literacy skills perhaps more crucial than they have been at any other time in history. Thus, lessons that are grounded in a 21st-century mindset would necessarily involve a synthesis of traditional and new proficiencies.

Interestingly enough, online activities related to fandom encompass many of the proficiencies outlined in the NCTE excerpt. What

is more, these elements are not dependent on or wholly tied to technology. For instance, in addition to the traditional, print-based literacy skills that fan authors develop through composing texts, they are also developing effective collaboration and communication skills as they read, revise, discuss, and critique each other's work. Many youths also take on leadership roles within various fan communities as they design, deploy, and maintain the content of popular websites and forums that are frequented by youths from around the world. These roles also require good communication skills as well as 21st-century and new literacy proficiencies such as diplomacy and communicating across linguistic and cultural barriers, as the fan-administrators of such sites are called upon to define appropriate content and conduct, and to mediate and resolve disputes between site members.

Fan authors, artists, β-readers, and webmasters are also developing a strong work ethic as they engage in self-motivated and self-monitored forms of content creation and set their own learning goals and standards in relation to their textual products. Collectively, these activities are all illustrative of the sort of "learning and innovation...and life and career skills" (NCTE, 2007, n.p.) that are valued in the 21st century and can be developed either in tandem with or independently of new technologies. Such activities also illustrate that ELLs, in spite of language barriers, are fully capable of using technology and multimodal forms of representation to learn and generate knowledge through participation in linguistically sophisticated and cognitively demanding tasks.

As this paper deals with literacy and literate practices, it is not surprising that an underlying theme running through the discussion is that of identity. Many adolescents spend time communicating and creating content online largely as a means of forging social connections and representing themselves and their perspectives to their peers. As adolescents develop new literacy, technology, and 21st-century proficiencies, they are also taking on the values, mindsets (Lankshear & Knobel, 2007), and ways of being in the world (Gee, 1992) associated with such practices and digital media spaces. In terms of literacy education then, it might be useful to begin thinking about how activities in such spaces recruit identities and literacy practices and mindsets that are valuable for learning. For example, the appeal of many online communities or affinity spaces (Gee, 2004) is that they allow youths to adopt a variety of social roles including peer, mentor, learner, collaborator, technology-expert, webmaster, author, reader, and consultant. Also in these sites, youths take on leadership roles, set their own goals for participation, and engage in self-directed forms of learning.

These kinds of identities and ways of being in the world also have the potential to serve students well in schools. As Cummins (1996) pointed out, "[t]here is a reciprocal relationship between cognitive engagement and identity investment" (p. 126). Specifically, the more that ELL students can take on powerful roles as learners and experience success with learning, "the more their academic self-concept grows, and the more academically engaged they become" (1996, p. 126). However, nonmainstream students more often receive the message that their cultural and linguistic backgrounds and prior knowledge and experiences are irrelevant to classroom activities, thus giving them little to build on as learners.

The challenge then, is thinking of ways to make our classrooms more open to what Lankshear and Knobel (2007) referred to as the "ethos stuff" of new literacies (p. 9). This might involve creating classroom environments that emphasize inquiry-based, participatory forms of learning in which students are encouraged to explore alternative interpretations of literature and classroom materials, much as they explore alternative interpretations of media through their fanfiction texts. Activities would, of course, require expert guidance by teachers; however, in keeping with the ethos of new literacies and 21st-century proficiencies, they also would involve a great deal of collaborative

learning among students and would stress the importance of accessing, evaluating, and integrating knowledge across available on- and offline sources. Such an approach presents an alternative to the "teacher as authority" model and allows students to build on their existing competencies, consider the validity of multiple perspectives, and enact powerful identities as both teachers and learners.

ELLs Can Benefit From Online Activity

While it might be tempting to dismiss youths' online activities as leisure-time pursuits that have little relation to academic endeavors, as discussion from this article demonstrates, popular media and new technologies can provide a basis for ELL youths to develop valuable print literacy as well as 21st-century skills. As pointed out in Thorne and Black (2007), the Internet should not be viewed merely as "a proxy environment for the development of conventional L2 learning objectives such as face-to-face communication and nondigital writing" (p. 149). Instead, it is important to recognize that "Internet-mediated communication is now a high-stakes environment that pervades work, education, interpersonal communication, and, not least, intimate relationship building and maintenance" (p. 149).

As globalization and technology continue to fuel changes in modern communicative contexts, it is crucial to ensure that ELL students are not relegated to remedial language drills or positioned as passive recipients of cultural and linguistic materials presented through textbooks and lectures. Lessons based on popular culture or technology and grounded in a productive ethos have the potential to benefit ELL students in many ways. Building on activities and literacy practices that many youths are accustomed to engaging with in their leisure time can help ELL students draw from prior knowledge to contextualize and develop understandings of new language forms and content. Using new technologies for collaborative inquiry and content-creation activities also provide options for ELLs to use language and other modes of representation for authentic communication with peers, teachers, and other experts that they may encounter in their research and explorations (e.g., community members, parents, online mentors), thus extending learning outside of the classroom walls. Such activities can provide a forum for the development of new literacies and 21st-century skills for youths who do not have ready access to computers or do not engage in such activities at home and can support ELL youths in developing identities as powerful learners, language users, and as active producers of their own social, cultural, and ideological materials.

References

Appadurai, A. (1996). *Modernity at large: Cultural dimensions of globalization.* Minneapolis: University of Minnesota Press.

Black, R.W. (2005). Access and affiliation: The literacy and composition practices of English-language learners in an online fanfiction community. *Journal of Adolescent & Adult Literacy, 49*(2), 118–128. doi:10.1598/JAAL.49.2.4

Black, R.W. (2008). *Adolescents and online fanfiction.* New York: Peter Lang.

Chandler-Olcott, K., & Mahar, D. (2003a). Adolescents' anime-inspired "fanfictions": An exploration of multiliteracies. *Journal of Adolescent & Adult Literacy, 46*(7), 556–566.

Chandler-Olcott, K., & Mahar, D. (2003b). Tech-savviness meets multiliteracies: Exploring adolescent girls' technology-mediated literacy practices. *Reading Research Quarterly, 38*(3), 356–385. doi:10.1598/RRQ.38.3.3

Cummins, J. (1996). *Negotiating identities: Education for empowerment in a diverse society.* Los Angeles: California Association for Bilingual Education.

Fanfiction.net. (2008). *Beta Readers.* Retrieved February 15, 2009, from www.fanfiction.net/betareaders

Gee, J.P. (1992). *The social mind: Language, ideology, and social practice.* New York: Bergin & Garvey.

Gee, J.P. (1999). *An introduction to discourse analysis: Theory and method.* New York: Routledge.

Gee, J.P. (2004). *Situated language and learning: A critique of traditional schooling.* New York: Routledge.

Geertz, C. (1973). *The interpretation of cultures.* New York: Basic.

Guzzetti, B.J., & Gamboa, M. (2005). Online journaling: The informal writings of two adolescent girls. *Research in the Teaching of English, 40*(2), 168–206.

Hull, G. (2003). Youth culture and digital media: New literacies for new times. *Research in the Teaching of English, 38*(2), 229–233.

Hull, G., & Schultz, K. (2002). *School's out! Bridging out-of-school literacies with classroom practice.* New York: Teachers College Press.

International Reading Association. (2001). *Integrating literacy and technology in the curriculum: A position statement of the International Reading Association.* Retrieved January 12, 2008, from www.reading.org/downloads/positions/ps1048_technology.pdf

Jenkins, H. (1992). *Textual poachers: Television, fans, and participatory culture.* New York: Routledge.

Jensen, L.A. (2003). Coming of age in a multicultural world: Globalization and adolescent cultural identity formation. *Applied Developmental Science, 7*(3), 189–196. doi:10.1207/S1532480XADS0703_10

Kress, G. (2000). Multimodality. In B. Cope & M. Kalantzis (Eds.), *Multiliteracies: Literacy learning and the design of social futures* (pp. 182–202). London: Routledge.

Lam, W.S.E. (2000). L2 literacy and the design of the self: A case study of a teenager writing on the Internet. *TESOL Quarterly, 34*(3), 457–482. doi:10.2307/3587739

Lam, W.S.E. (2004). Second language socialization in a bilingual chat room: Global and local considerations. *Language Learning and Technology, 8*(3), 44–65. Retrieved August 16, 2006, from llt.msu.edu/vol8num3/lam/default.html

Lankshear, C., & Knobel, M. (2006). *New literacies: Changing knowledge and classroom learning* (2nd ed.). Philadelphia: Open University Press.

Lankshear, C., & Knobel, M. (2007). Sampling "the new" in new literacies. In M. Knobel & C. Lankshear (Eds.), *A new literacies sampler* (pp. 1–24). New York: Peter Lang.

Lewis, C., & Fabos, B. (2005). Instant messaging, literacies, and social identities. *Reading Research Quarterly, 40*(4), 470–501. doi:10.1598/RRQ.40.4.5

National Council of Teachers of English. (2007). 21st century literacies. *AdLit.org.* Washington, DC: WETA. Retrieved March 15, 2007, from www.adlit.org/article/20832

New London Group. (1996). A pedagogy of multiliteracies: Designing social futures. *Harvard Educational Review, 66*(1), 60–92.

North Central Regional Educational Laboratory. (2003). *21st century skills: Literacy in the digital age.* Retrieved February 15, 2009, from web.archive.org/web/20070205041546/www.ncrel.org/engauge/skills/agelit.htm

Partnership for 21st Century Skills. (2004). *Framework for 21st Century Learning.* Retrieved September 30, 2007, from www.21stcenturyskills.org/index.php?option=com_content&task=view&id=254 &It emid=120

Street, B.V. (1984). *Literacy in theory and practice.* Cambridge, MA: Cambridge University Press.

Suárez-Orozco, M., & Qin-Hilliard, D.B. (Eds.). (2004). *Globalization: Culture and education in the new millennium.* Berkeley: University of California Press.

Thomas, A. (2005). *Positioning the reader: The affordances of digital fiction.* In J. Clark (Ed.) *Reading the past, writing the future: Measuring progress.* Proceedings of the 2005 Queensland Council for Adult Literacy Conference (pp. 24–33). Brisbane, Queensland Council for Adult Literacy.

Thorne, S.L., & Black, R. (2007). Language and literacy development in computer mediated contexts and communities. *Annual Review of Applied Linguistics, 27,* 133–160.

21st Century Workforce Commission. (2000, June). *A nation of opportunity: Building America's 21st century workforce.* Retrieved January 12, 2008, from digitalcommons .ilr.cornell.edu/cgi/viewcontent.cgi?article=1003& context=key_workplace

Warschauer, M. (2007). The paradoxical future of digital learning. *Learning Inquiry, 1*(1), 41–49. doi:10.1007/ s11519-007-0001-5

Yi, Y. (2008). Relay writing in an adolescent online community. *Journal of Adolescent & Adult Literacy, 51*(8), 670–680. doi:10.1598/JAAL.51.8.6

Gendered Literacy Experiences: The Effects of Expectation and Opportunity for Boys' and Girls' Learning

Kathy Sanford

There has been considerable concern expressed in the past decade for the literacy—or lack of literacy—of boys in the western world. Popular media, school administrators, and government ministries of education have taken up the banner for boys, demanding that something be done to fix the problem and to place attention where it belongs—on better education for boys. And while the literacy of boys is of great concern to me as an educator, I am struck by the ease and speed with which girls are again made invisible in concerns of education, ignored in the general call for improved literacy skills. My increased discomfort with the framing of current gender-based discussions of literacy with concerns for boys led me to conduct a yearlong research project in a Canadian middle school examining literacy practices of boys *and* girls. The intent of the research was to develop an understanding of how students' out-of-school literacies can influence their present and future learning. There is evidence to suggest that boys are becoming literate in many ways through out-of-school activities (Blair & Sanford, 2004), but girls are not engaging in these same activities. Although girls appear more successful throughout school, are the literacy skills they learn there supplying sustained opportunities to acquire lifelong skills?

Throughout a school year I made regular visits to two classrooms in a suburban middle school. I was supported by two teachers, Mr. M and Ms. F, who were in the first few years of their teaching careers. I observed regularly in each of the classes throughout the year, conducted formal and informal interviews with the teachers, surveyed the students in the two classes regarding their perceptions of literacy and gender, and interviewed six boys and six girls. I also participated in three meetings of the school's "Gender Committee" in hopes of understanding, in this particular context, issues of literacy for girls as well as for boys. The comments and ideas of the students and teachers are reported in this article. (All names are pseudonyms.)

The school administration and the teachers involved in the committee were very helpful in supporting this research but were mostly concerned with issues of boys in the school—their lack of success on large-scale examinations of reading and writing, their lack of interest in school leadership positions, and the higher percentage of behavior problems among boys. They were of the opinion, as Osler and Vincent (2003) suggested, that girls never had problems related to literacy and no longer had problems relating to any important aspects of education. Osler and Vincent commented,

> At first glance, girls seem to have benefited most from developments in education over recent years. They appear to be out-performing boys in school-leaving examinations in a range of international

Preparing Reading Professionals (second edition), edited by Rita M. Bean, Natalie Heisey, and Cathy M. Roller. © 2010 by the International Reading Association. Reprinted from Sanford, K. (2005). Gendered literacy experiences: The effects of expectation and opportunity for boys' and girls' learning. *Journal of Adolescent & Adult Literacy, 49*(4), 302–315. doi:10.1598/JAAL.49.4.4.

contexts, and are now more likely than boys to enter higher education in many countries. Educators, politicians and journalists have all focused their attention on boys, who are commonly assumed to be underachieving. But concern about boys' "underachievement" hides some real problems facing many girls and young women. The rhetoric about boys' "failure" and girls' "success" masks a reality where there are vast differences in educational experiences and opportunities among girls, as there are among boys. (2003, p.1)

However, evidence of educational success is still largely determined by test scores, and by this measure girls no longer are a concern. "Boys' needs," Osler and Vincent pointed out, "have been prioritised over those of girls and the links between educational exclusion and crime have contributed to a moral panic about boys' social and educational exclusion" (2003, p. 5).

Newspaper headlines in Canada, Great Britain, and the United States, such as "Schools Size Up Gender Achievement Gap" (2003), "Boys and Literacy" (1999), and "The Trouble with Boys" (2000), suggest that "as a whole, boys are being eclipsed academically by girls in almost every subject and grade level" ("Schools Size Up," 2003, p. 17A). Such stories have provoked a general alarm that girls have become overly successful in school and have improved their scores in mathematics and science, while continuing to maintain their standing in the humanities, and increasingly attend postsecondary institutions and join the ranks of professionals. Moreover, girls are often blamed for the troubles boys experience developing literacy skills because they are said to siphon off the resources and attention that boys should have.

Girls' academic achievements are turned on their head. Instead of being seen as a cause for satisfaction, they are presented in the media and in popular discourse as a widespread problem of failure among boys, about which the educational community in general, and teachers in particular, should concern themselves. (Crozier & Anstiss, 1995, p. 36)

It is boys who are almost invariably referred for counseling or remedial support for "underachievement, reluctance to work, uncooperative and rude behaviour, bullying (victim or bully), fighting and criminal activity" (Osler & Vincent, 2003, p. 15). When girls are deemed to need remediation, it is for concerns such as

absence from school, health problems (particularly eating problems), victim of bullying, appearance (hair, dress, length of nails, jewellry), problems at home and relationships with boyfriends. It appears that boys are described in terms of their behaviour and academic performance, while girls are described in terms of their appearance and sexuality. (Osler & Vincent, 2003, p. 15)

These gendered perspectives of students affect not only their developing self-identity but also the expectations placed on them and their opportunities to engage in various literacy activities.

It is critical that we not lose sight of the educational gains for girls—regarding access to traditionally male areas of study, success in higher education, and inclusion in a wider range of work and leisure pursuits—while we work toward broadening boys' opportunities for success. It is also critical to recognize that there are still many opportunities *not* available to girls and that there is considerable work to be done to ensure equity of opportunity and access for all students. We need to ask where the success in school leads for boys and for girls. Are girls more successful when they leave school? How is *success* understood and measured other than by school exam scores?

In this article, I examine issues of school-based and out-of-school literacy as they relate to girls as well as boys, recognizing that gender is a construct that shapes literacy experiences for adolescents in school. Gender-based expectations of teachers, administrators, and parents offer different—in quality and quantity—opportunities for boys and girls in school. I will examine the sites of intersection between gender and modern literacy practices. In order to discuss these intersections, however, it is important to first define my use of terms.

Literacy and Gender: Intersecting Complexities of Schooling

The term *literacy* today means something very different than in the 1960s and 1970s when it "was used generally in relation to non-formal educational settings and, in particular, in relation to adults who were deemed to be illiterate" (Lankshear & Knobel, 2003, p. 3). "Within formal educational settings, *reading and writing* [emphasis added] were seen as essential tools for learning to occur, and as vehicles for accessing and communicating meaning via printed text" (p. 4). Kress (2003), however, suggested that "[i]t is no longer possible to think about literacy in isolation from a vast array of social, technological and economic factors" (p. 1). He saw a "move from the...dominance of writing to the new dominance of the image and...from the dominance of the medium of the book to the dominance of the medium of the screen" (p. 1). Literacy now relates to a much broader set of texts including visual, multimodal, and digital texts that appear in many forms all around us. Because of their many powerful uses, these texts are accessible to everyone. Billboards, magazines, the Internet, text messaging, video—all are instantly available in multiple modes to people of all ages, cultures, and classes. These texts have much more appeal, connection, and power than traditional school texts and much more significance in students' lives. School texts—informational textbooks, novels, educational films—cannot compete with all the diverse texts available today.

I also need to define my use of the term *gender*. Rather than the biological definition, de Lauretis (1987) suggested a much more complex understanding and has defined *gender* as "not a property of bodies or something originally existent in human beings...it is the product and process of various social technologies, institutional discourses, epistemologies, and critical practices, as well as practices of daily life" (p. 3). Gender as a social construct affects learning in and out of school, dictating what is and can be learned and what is out of bounds. As such, then, there are many intersections between *literacy* and *gender*; some are developed and exploited, while others are entirely overlooked. If students are to become capable, functioning members of today's society, it is important to examine the intersections of these two powerful constructs critically and explicitly.

Schools and curricula have generally not embraced literacy as it has been broadly defined here and have given little notice to pedagogical issues of gender. At best, digital, screen, visual, and multimodal literacies are viewed as "alternative" and still remain on the extreme fringes of school-based learning experiences. Classroom activities center largely on print-text literacy (i.e., reading and writing in its traditional forms). This is not surprising given the gaps between teachers' experiences and those of their students. As Lankshear and Knobel (2003) pointed out, "teachers' cultural identities and experiences are often very different from those of their students. This makes it difficult for them to connect learning as closely as possible to students' varied cultural identities and experiences" (p. 179). In addition, "low levels of technical and cultural knowledge on the part of teachers often result in culture-mediated learning activities being ineffective, inefficacious, or mystifying" (p. 179). Teachers are often required to call upon student/insider "savvy" to help at the technical operational level of implementing alternative literacies. This lack of confidence and competence discourages teachers from engaging with alternative types of texts.

There is, then, an increasing gap between the types of literacy activities being practiced in school and out of school. Beyond the classroom walls, out-of-school activities involving texts such as the Internet, e-mail, text messaging, video or computer games, and digital video are being rapidly taken up by more and more students at younger ages. However, there is a marked gender difference in the engagement with new technologies and the willingness to explore, read, or write using these alternative texts. What are the implications for boys' *and* for girls' literacy development and school success in an era when the "moral panic" of boys' lack of literacy success on large-scale exams is becoming widely noted and reported in public media, where girls are seen as "doing better" at school from inception to postsecondary?

Research examining issues of literacy for boys (Blair & Sanford, 2004; Epstein, Elwood, Hey, & Maw, 1998; Gilbert & Gilbert, 1998; Millard, 1997; Smith & Wilhelm, 2002) has revealed lacks, but it tends not to have revealed what might be more gaping omissions for girls. Educational theorists and educators express concern for boys' lack of success using traditional literacies but fail to recognize their competence and skill in navigating alternative digital literacies. Girls, on the other hand, are continuing to develop skill in school-based literacy activities, reading and writing competently and effectively. They are gaining the skills required for admission to postsecondary education, but as they "gain" on the boys in formal educational success (identified through grades and awards) they lose ground in other ways, particularly development of skills in alternative and computer-based literacies.

The comments of Mr. M demonstrate one way these differences between girls' and boys' behaviors can be interpreted:

> We did some math this morning on reviewing metric conversion, and there was a three-sentence blurb of instruction on how to check your answer. It was the boys who kept asking how to get the answer, and I said, "Well, read it," and some of them would read it and ask me again. But I don't think a single girl asked me, which means they read it and they understood the instructions.

Although the teacher's interpretation of this event shows girls as successful literacy learners, there are other possible interpretations (e.g., they were not noticed, they did not have the confidence to ask the teacher, they would rather not point out their difficulties). None of these possibilities were mentioned by the teacher.

Throughout the 1990s, a "growing and compelling body of research has documented the dramatic decline in self-esteem, body image, and academic performance experienced by girls" (Mazzarella & Pecora, 2002, p. 2). Issues of identity and body image are foregrounded in such a way that a girl's identity is intricately linked to her physical appearance and compliant behavior. Mainstream culture, found in messages in school as well as out-of-school contexts, "instructs" girls on the "approved" ways to become women. Pipher (1994) referred to a "girl-poisoning culture" (p. 20) and demonstrated that girls seem to lose themselves in adolescence, and they know it. Sadker and Sadker (1995) presented a compelling argument that schooling disadvantages female students, and Gilbert and Gilbert (1998) claimed that schools have contributed significantly to gender differentiation and sex-role socialization that privileges males. If an alternative reality is out there for girls, they probably will not find it in schools as we now know them.

However, as discussed earlier, there are increasing alternatives for girls in terms of involvement in science and technology, sports, and careers outside the home. If girls experience alternatives and see themselves as part of the greater world, they will more readily see themselves belonging to and creating an alternative world. Alternative opportunities are most often created for children before they begin school and, once they have entered school, in their experiences beyond the school walls. Opportunities arise for children as they engage with parents and relatives doing interesting things. Several students in the grade 7 class I worked with provided examples of opportunities they had been offered at home. Christie was able to play hockey on a boys' team because her parents encouraged her to do so; Alice learned to play soccer and video games because she had five older brothers, and that was the world she knew. Paul became interested in building motorcycles because he had an uncle who used to make bikes and took Paul for rides. Shaun wants to be one of the Snowbirds who fly planes because his dad works at a control tower and owns three planes. These unique opportunities that shape students' lives are not always acknowledged in school. School expectations tend to draw on (often stereotypical) generalizations about the interests of boys and girls and how they learn. These unexamined stereotypes shape teachers' expectations of the students in their classes, limiting opportunities for them to explore and define alternative realities.

Messages of Expectation

Popular culture (and much "high" culture disseminated in school) "continues to present to girls stereotyped and potentially dangerous messages about a femaleness we hope to move beyond" (Mazzarella & Pecora, 2002, p. 7). However, it is not only popular culture that sends and perpetuates stereotyped messages about gender. The expectations of teachers, as noted in their comments, also suggest gendered stereotypes. Ms. F commented that girls are more interested in reading, noting that "a much larger percentage of girls in my class will pick up a book and read or be really focused" and that boys "read less by choice—although there are a handful of boys who are just as strong and involved in their reading." She also believes that girls have a better attitude toward school, saying "girls seem more keen to read something out of the textbook, but girls are more keen to do a lot of things than boys tend to be." However, she sees girls as not being risk-takers, commenting that "girls won't do anything without asking me"; boys, on the other hand, "are more eager to take the chances; they figure things out by doing it."

Mr. M suggested that girls are less naturally talented than boys, saying, "It's more uniform with the girls; there are fewer exceptional students with the girls," and that (even though girls are generally seen to have stronger literacy skills) boys "write some of the best poetry, and one is a major hockey player, too." While these two teachers generally saw girls as capable and interested students, both were continually defending the boys for their uniqueness, initiative, and willingness to challenge the rules. These mixed, tacit expectations influence the types of encouragement given to students, the types of work accepted, and the application of school rules.

Working with diverse groups of students is a complex and challenging task. Teachers rely on categorization and routine to make sense of hectic classroom lives. As they struggle with new or alternative literacies that have exponentially increased and surrounded us outside of school, teachers often give their students mixed messages. On one level they express the desire for students to critically examine texts, but on a less conscious level they often maintain gendered expectations of their students and subtly pass them along, thus reinforcing societal perceptions of gendered difference. At the same time, teachers are attempting to understand the increasing complexities of gender and the intersections of gender and literacy as they are juxtaposed. However, given limited time and resources to make sense of these two highly complex social constructs, teachers' practices are often shaped through behaviors they observe. In classroom interactions and through their own personal experiences, they attempt to make sense of changes to reading and literacy, to society, and to perceptions of gender.

Teachers' understanding of learning and their different expectations for boys and girls have a powerful impact on engagement in class activities and students' attitudes toward these activities. Literacy continues to be discussed in terms of print-based text, and girls are recognized as navigating print text better than boys. Ms. F described her literacy instruction by saying,

> I try to do a variety of things that involve reading, get them reading newspapers and different types of reading and writing. We'll read and write some radio plays, different forms, different lengths and purposes, and looking at reading in lab procedures.

These texts, while diverse, represent the types of materials society recognizes as forms of literacy and do not diverge from these.

Mr. M commented about a student's reading ability: "He can read, he's one of those that is capable of being a better reader, but he just doesn't practice." These comments reflect a traditional understanding of reading and literacy as centered around print materials. Regarding social change, as it relates to teachers' workplace realities, Ms. F and Mr. M saw themselves as constrained by institutional structure, commenting that "teachers try and provide different opportunities, but we're limited in what we can do" and that "the structure of the school limits what we can do, the way we run things." These constraints apply to their teaching activities and inhibit consideration of alternative texts and views.

In relation to gender, the teachers frame their understanding of success and opportunity on the basis of their personal and professional beliefs and values. Ms. F commented,

> Boys are more successful at certain things, but in very few cases are the boys generally more successful than the girls, and I don't think it's because they're not capable, but they're not appearing to work as hard. A lot of it is work ethic in my class.

Mr. M said,

> I think girls know they can be anything they want—we pushed that for a long time—astronauts or nurses, but boys still can't say they want to be nurses. But there's no realm for them, like even a soldier now is open to everybody, so there's no place in a sense.

These comments mirror the views and values offered regularly in public media, which are then accepted, unchallenged by teachers.

Gendered Literacy Expectations: Assignments

Many of the assignments given by their teachers offered multiple ways for the students to express "anything they want," yet this opportunity was neither encouraged nor reinforced by the teachers. A poster assignment given to one class early in the year involved the students creating an acrostic from their first name, identifying their most important characteristics using descriptive words, phrases, and visual images. Although there was a range of descriptors, there were obvious gendered differences in the words and the images. For example, the girls' posters displayed words and phrases such as *happy, excited, likes elephants, puppy lover, horse fan, has a cat, nice, neat, lots of friends*, and *adorable*. Their selected images showed male rock stars; numerous domestic

and farmyard animals (often baby animals); and pictures of themselves standing, sitting with family, or with a pet. While there were references to other constructions such as *intelligent* and *terrific*, these were isolated and in the minority.

The words and phrases offered by the boys included *hyper, impeccable, radical, definitely cool, ordinary—NOT!, brilliant, hungry, chocolate mousse, potato salad, mountain bikes, skateboarding, martial arts*, and *Dungeons and Dragons*. Images showed money, dragons, cartoon characters, hot cars, skateboarders, snowboarders, weapons, and themselves engaged in activities such as soccer and snowboarding. There were references made to tap dancing and playing the keyboard, but again, these were a small minority of the descriptors.

While this poster activity offered great scope for the students, there was no explicit encouragement to go beyond superficial and gendered constructions of their identity. The posters were accepted without critique and displayed on the classroom wall for the entire year. The gendered differences were strikingly clear to me as an outside observer, showing a proliferation of relatively limited and stereotypical characteristics. However, at no time were the students required to reflect upon the descriptions they had created of themselves, encouraged to recognize the predominance of similar images on the posters, or asked to look at differences (gender, culture, race) demonstrated on the posters.

Other assignments I observed throughout the year also offered considerable scope for students to explore their ideas in unique and individual ways: writing and videotaping a commercial, presenting one-minute stories orally, mapping their community, studying "classic" films, cartooning, creating magazines, researching global art forms. Nevertheless, students repeatedly selected gender-appropriate topics and modes of presenting, not thinking or being encouraged to consider different possibilities. For example, most of the girls chose to write stories or poems about friends and family, going shopping, comparing fashion ideas. Pets and other animals figured largely in the girls' writing. Most of the boys chose to write about adventures, activities, and humorous incidents (generally involving some type of accident and embarrassment). Vehicles, machines, and weapons figured largely in the boys' representations.

Gendered Literacy Expectations: Computer Room

The computer room at the school was used frequently for class instruction. Students were assigned research projects and activities intended to use knowledge gained from the Internet. Generally these activities were very similar in structure to the activities done in the classroom with more traditional tools, and the gendered responses remained consistent—girls completed their work and boys had difficulties remaining focused long enough to finish. During recess and lunch breaks, however, students (mostly boys) filled the room to play computer and Internet games. At this time, students' attention and interest shifted—their focus was intense, and their enthusiasm as they played and commented to their friends was of a very different level of concentration than during class time.

There were rules posted on the wall about using the computer room, suggesting adult-imposed limitations (Lankshear & Knobel, 2003) as described earlier in this article. (See Table 1.) On first look, these rules seem reasonable. They are intended to ensure students'

safety and maintain an academic focus. However, the rules suggest the significant gaps between the teachers' and students' experiences and understandings of alternative literacies, as discussed by Lankshear and Knobel (2003), limiting the potential uses of digital literacies and the potential·participants. First, the poster was titled "Recess & Lunch Computer Games"; this is a recreational site of choice for many students (almost exclusively boys) during their school breaks and not a homework class. The tone of the list of rules, however, suggests that this is not a site of fun and excitement.

Second, from repeated observations of the computer lab and its 35 computers, I noticed that there were no more than one or two girls in the room at any time. The activity centered around game play and was done either independently or with partners. It would be an intimidating experience indeed for a student intent on using a word processor for schoolwork to enter this male-dominated space to request that a game player vacate the station.

My observations in computer rooms are not unique to the classrooms I visited but are similarly "gendered" across western society. Boys dominate technological spaces; they explore new sites, try new strategies, and demonstrate their knowledge to friends. Unlike when they are using computers for school-based activities, their discussion is animated and their focus is intense when they are playing games. As I suggest in the following section, students' out-of-school activities show similar gender differentiations.

Table 1
Recess & Lunch Computer Games

1. Schoolwork gets first priority on the computers.
2. Games may be played from CD only (no online or downloads from the Internet).
3. Each CD must be signed out by the person using it.
4. There are no reservations of computers or CDs for games.
5. Anyone ignoring these rules will lose the privilege of being in this room.

Activities Beyond the Classroom

In the sample of 50 students I surveyed, there are some predictable yet thought-provoking trends. When asked what they liked to do in their spare time, the students responded in the ways shown in Table 2. Although gendered responses appear for all of the categories and support the expectations we have constructed for girls and boys, I focus in this article on the last four columns, those dealing with literacy practices as I defined them earlier: watching

	Play Sports	Build Models	Ride Bikes	Collect Things	Talk to Friends	Cook	Watch Television	Read	Write	Play Video or Computer Games
Table 2 Students' Survey Responses										
Grade 7 Boys	71%	50%	71%	35%	64%	28%	71%	21%	7%	78%
Grade 6 Boys	72%	46%	81%	54%	63%	37%	81%	72%	18%	81%
Grade 7 Girls	46%	13%	46%	20%	73%	66%	80%	66%	40%	53%
Grade 6 Girls	84%	7%	38%	15%	92%	84%	92%	69%	46%	61%

television, reading, writing, and playing video or computer games.

There is a great range of television viewing interests reported by girls and boys. Sitcoms lead the way, and cartoon sitcoms are frequently mentioned. Reality shows, sports entertainment, and music videos also figure in their viewing. Although there is evidence of considerable television consumption by these adolescents, their comments suggest that they watched what was on when they turned on the television rather than specifically selecting favorite programs.

Clearly, students do not see writing as a viable activity for their spare time. This is not surprising, but it is of some concern. The only writing activity reported by boys was for Starcraft (a computer game), which requires some writing. Girls variously reported writing biographies, stories, songs, notes to pass to friends, and instant text messages. The reading selections that students reported complemented the writing that they did for class projects—girls liked to write about their friends, pets, and family; boys tended to write about fantasy or adventure. However, what the students did not report was the types of consumption and production of texts that are outside the scope of school texts, such as magazines, environmental texts, e-mail and instant messages, chatrooms, and video or computer games. Their responses tended to correspond with the way they had been taught to consider "reading" and "writing" more traditionally.

The students' reports on playing video or computer games suggest considerable use by both girls and boys. However, when I more closely examine the types of games they report, there is a clear distinction between their choices. Boys' choices include racing, war, and fantasy role-playing games. The girls' choices include adventure role-playing games and games of skill. Furthermore, boys reported using computers to create games and download them from the Internet and to play online hockey; girls reported using computers to type paragraphs and homework, do word processing, create collages, and watch movie trailers. The type and amount of use of new technologies reported by boys and girls often corresponded with opportunity (generally out of school) and expectations of parents and teachers regarding uses of alternative literacies and technologies. Although statistics regarding various literacy engagements give us some insights, it is the nature of these literacies that adds depth to our understanding of the gendered differences.

Adolescents Creating Opportunity

The participants in this study provided surprising and significant insights regarding gendered literacy differences. In the interviews, students struggled to articulate their thoughts and observations regarding gender and difference. As Hubbard, Barbieri, and Power (1998) pointed out, it's difficult when dealing with adolescents to face what's hard to confront within ourselves—"the patterns of language, power, and hidden agendas can be almost impossible for us to see clearly, let alone change" (p. 2). These adolescents initially struggled to articulate any difference between boys and girls and resisted those notions of difference. Sharla commented, "If you like reading, then you read more than people who don't, but I think boys and girls are exactly the same." Jessica agreed, saying,

> I think it's more the person. In general, some boys can be really accurate and work faster, but just sometimes it tends that the girls learn faster; I don't think there's a huge difference. We can both like sports, but a boy wouldn't so much like a dance class like a girl would. Some people want to, but they just won't because nobody else is, and maybe just because they're not like that themselves; they like sports more.

However, as Mark spoke he began to identify some superficial differences: "Boys and girls don't learn differently, it depends on how fast a learner the person is...girls like different colors than boys do, and they like different shows, and they buy different toys than we do." And Brianne suggested, "Some people like horses and some people don't, but last year there were lots of boys who liked horses; they like different things from me, because they like car-racing movies, and I like Shrek."

Opportunities Supported by Family

Other students identified differences but did not see themselves as possessing typically male or female characteristics. Some of the students identified family influences as shaping their practices and interests. Susan commented,

> I think boys' learning styles and girls' are the same. Boys are into sports more, and some girls are, too, but most of them don't really like it. And lots of my sister's friends don't like sports; they like to sit on the computer and talk to their friends, but my sister likes sports. She plays the same sports I do, soccer and baseball.

Alice described how she has grown up in a family with five older brothers and has always been included in their activities. Her interests and skills developed as a result of doing whatever her brothers did, and she didn't really

know if or how girls were any different. She suggested,

> I probably don't learn any different [from boys]... because I never saw how girls acted...my brother didn't get his girlfriend until about two years ago. So I didn't really have a sister until she came in, and she was, like, really nice, so I probably learn the same as my brother.

Carly reported that she loves to play hockey, and although her older brother is good at hockey, she sees herself as the athletic one in the family, like her Dad. She also loves to dance, take voice lessons, and write in her journal but defines herself in relation to similarities with her father. She commented,

> I think I have different interests than most girls. I think the girls generally, I think I'm the exception, kind of want to be quieter and not want to take things as funky as guys, like guys will always want to go fast on their skates or fast in a car, or they'll want to be really bad. And I think the girls are more in between, and when they go in a car they go at a pace like a normal driver...guys want to be more extreme.

These girls have had opportunities to engage in activities that have traditionally been exclusive to boys; their gender does not create a barrier for them as they choose what they want to do.

Some of the students identified differences between boys and girls by way of attitude toward school and interest in being successful. Matt noted,

> Boys don't seem to try as hard as most girls; some of them that are smart, actually try to do their work, and some of them just fool around and don't really do it. Girls try a little harder, in my opinion.

Paul commented,

> I'm not saying that boys are dumber; I mean there's a lot of smart boys, but there's just a lot of girls in our class that if they want to do [something] they'll do it—like they put their mind to it, they'll do it— they're more focused.

Shaun attempted to shape a theory to support boys' lack of focus by saying,

> Boys are sort of distracted easily, I think, maybe because they use the computer a lot more, so a lot

more stuff gets into their minds. So they sort of think about a lot more stuff and not just their schoolwork. And they get agitated and don't think about their school work, they think about what is in their mind.

He continued,

Girls don't use the computers as much, I don't know why, it's just sort of like a thing that boys do more I guess. Like, they don't play as many computer games; some boys don't really care what they get in school, they'll just goof off and they're sort of out of the category. They just want to get the attention so everyone will be, like, "oh, there he goes," but then there's some boys and girls that are the same, and like they all sort of stay on their school-work and everything. I care about schoolwork quite a bit; I have a little bit of trouble getting my home-work done because there are too many things. Like, we're just living in a cul-de-sac where there are a whole bunch of houses being built, so I like to go outside and watch the machines dig and stuff, so I find myself out there a lot instead of doing my homework.

Boys tend to occupy public and outside spaces, as suggested by their activities (bike riding, playing sports, building models), whereas girls occupy private and inside spaces (cooking and writing stories and notes to friends). As the students explored the concept of difference between boys and girls, they raised the notion of opportunity rather than "difference." For example, Alice was able to learn like her brothers because of opportunities she had around them; Susan was more inclined to play soccer and baseball because her sister did, rather than to sit around with friends. Paul commented that boys are "more interested in things that make loud noises, like chargers, cars, or street bikes"; his interest and knowledge stemmed from an uncle who introduced him to the world of motorcycles. All students knew more about their fathers' work and activities than their mothers'. Carly remembered, "My mom and I always make supper...my dad will take me on errands and we'll talk." The students were often more attracted to activities in the public spaces of the "male" world than in the private spaces of the traditionally "female" world. They reported their fathers working as pilots, coaches, and air-traffic controllers. Comments

about their mothers tended to be memories of earlier childhood days, of their mothers helping them learn to read, singing songs to them, and of their baking together. The literacy aspects of these activities were generally not recognized as such and were not valued as important elements of future literacy successes in diverse workplace opportunities.

Examining Expectations, Creating New Opportunities

Although feminists have put much work into changing the hegemonic patriarchal culture in the world, a lot of work remains to be done so that a progressive stand does not automatically generate feelings of "otherness." We cannot neglect the needs of one group to support the needs of another. As Valdivia and Bettivia (2002) suggested, "We have paid very little attention to girls' consumption and production of popular culture. Indeed we have paid very little attention to girls in general" (p. 160).

Girls' school time is filled with interactions and representations that are gendered masculine. Research shows that "girls are nearly erased as subjects within the schooling experience, whether it be in terms of how teachers and administrators pay attention to them or in terms of their representation in instructional materials" (Valdivia & Bettivia, 2002, p. 161) such as textbooks and other classroom aids (Sanford, 2002). Their cultural activities occur in the "safe" spaces of home and school.

Bruce (2003) suggested that

teachers may now certainly be more aware than I was a decade ago of the gender distinctions among boys' and girls' experiences during adolescence and the ways that schooling disadvantages the young women we teach. Yet we still have too few instructional tools available to us to respond equitably in the classroom. (p. 6)

We still select classroom activities based on the perceived needs and interests of boys and praise boys for succeeding in literacy activities that girls regularly complete successfully. "Successful" girls are described in terms of masculine activities and values (competitive sports, aggression, independence). As Mr. M's following comment suggests, those who are aware of gender distinctions have been inclined to frame the disadvantages from boys' perspectives rather than girls'.

> I think we've forgotten about the boys; I think school has become "feminized" in terms of what the boys aren't allowed to do.... I think we can talk about boys for a long time without doing any harm to girls, because I think we've done enormous good for girls over the last 20 years in terms of the opportunities they have—and look at how well they're doing—and I think that will stay where it is...what might have happened is we picked up the girls and forgot about the boys.

He went on to say,

> I don't know the history of education enough to know why it is that we didn't see that boys were having trouble succeeding. And maybe it's just that girls are so much better than boys, and we've just been holding them back for so many years—*but I don't think so.*

The disadvantages of girls are virtually invisible to the teachers working with them, whereas the plight of the "poor boys" is increasingly reinforced through media representations and the boys' own responses to school-based literacy activities. Schooling as it is organized now does not work in disrupting gendered patterns of learning and being in the world—girls continue to comply and boys continue to resist.

Were the Girls "Picked Up" and the Boys Forgotten?

Clearly there are complex interactions among opportunity and access, expectations, and individual interests and abilities. Students engage in a much wider range of literacy learning activities not fitting traditional gender expectations than we see at first glance (Blair & Sanford, 2004). Students are thinking differently about gender roles, doing things because they have been encouraged by caring adults, because it is simply an unspoken expectation, or because of personal interests (often linked to what parents and older siblings do). Family

plays a significant role in setting the stage regarding opportunities and expectations, and gender expectations and opportunities at school are often more reinforcing of societal values. Families can support and encourage equity of opportunity for their children, regardless of gender, but they can also reinforce the more limiting accepted societal roles, as seen in the toys and activities they provide and their children's reactions to them (Murphy & Elwood, 1998). Parents, like teachers, "are not a homogeneous group nor are children passive in this process" (p. 163). Media and market pressure also exert influence on children's interests and developing abilities.

Paechter (2003) suggested that children learn gendered discourses through participating in what Lave and Wenger (1991) termed "communities of practice," groups that share particular discourses. These groups initially draw on families and then are formed in schools, with friends in classrooms. Children, like apprentices, watch and learn (often unconsciously) in a group in order to develop full "membership" in that particular community, whether it relates to school literacies, social practices, or peer friendships. Gender lines are often drawn in these communities, albeit unconsciously, limiting the opportunities for girls and boys because of unexamined gender expectations. Millard (1997) has provided evidence that boys and girls like to read and write about different things, have different attitudes toward schooled literacy, and do different things with their literacy skills outside school. According to Marsh (2003), any analysis of gendered literacy issues

> should also identify ways in which girls' literacy is also often limited by their propensity to conform to traditional conceptions of literacy propagated by schools, when success in employment is increasingly predicated on wider notions of literacy (embedded within the technological developments since the 1980s). (p. 61)

Children outside school engage in a wide variety of literacy activities that are embedded within media, new technologies, and popular culture (e.g., sending text messages via cell phones, getting information from the Internet, using e-mail, downloading music and digital videos, and creating websites). However, as Marsh (2003) stated, girls

> are known to conform more readily to schooled literacy practices and therefore, the *disadvantages* [emphasis added] may appear on the surface to be less marked for them, as we have seen to be the case with the recent focus on the increasing disengagement with literacy that many boys exhibit. Nevertheless, the disadvantages girls face in engaging compliantly with dated conceptions of literacy in school are just as pressing. (p. 67)

Hegemonic constructions of masculinity and femininity need to be analyzed and children helped to question how they shape, and are shaped by, these discourses.

> Popular culture, media and new technologies offer a myriad of opportunities for deconstructing these representations of gender and developing critical literacy skills, skills that are essential in order to challenge the stereotypes which perpetuate literacy myths, including those relating to underachievement. (Marsh, 2003, p. 67)

Marsh continued,

> Isolated strategies and projects which focus on the needs of one gender at the expense of the other will not do...ensuring that a wide gulf does not exist between schooled literacy practices and children's out-of-school interests will not only motivate boys, it will ensure that girls are engaged in a wider range of literacy activities than may often be the case for them. (p. 75)

The ever-increasing emphasis on results of high-stakes testing serves to provide only simplistic evidence that feeds the moral panic highlighted in popular media. High-stakes testing limits the potential to develop connections between traditional literacy practices and those of (mostly male) adolescents today.

Teachers need to examine hidden and deep-rooted gendered assumptions and expectations as they engage with students, so that they consciously provide a wide range of explicit opportunities for all students to develop their identities more fully but not be limited by gender. We need to take more than a passing glance at the gendered issues in classrooms and ensure that surface measures of success do not mask inconsistencies in education where girls are again being left behind. Issues of gendered literacy, relating to new and alternative technological, digital, and visual literacies, need to be examined with an eye to preparing all students for the ongoing changes of the 21st century.

Boys are engaging in the world differently, using alternative literacies for their present and future benefit. In the long run, in many societal structures boys will still benefit by being male, and girls will still lose out by being female. However, as boys continue to increase their confident engagement with technology, it is possible that they will decrease their engagement with the people in their lives, that the virtual world will further remove them from caring for the real world around them. Teachers, as representatives of society, cannot always assume that the traditionally masculine world and values are best. They need to begin to see and value the collaboration and caring that girls have the courage to offer as they engage in the world differently.

References

Blair, H., & Sanford, K. (2004). Morphing literacy: Boys reshaping their school-based literacy practices. *Language Arts, 81*, 452–460.

Boys and literacy. We can do better. (1999, March 18). *Globe and Mail*, p. A14.

Bruce, H. (2003). *Literacies, lies, & silences: Girls writing lives in the classroom.* New York: Peter Lang.

Crozier, J., & Anstiss, J. (1995). Out of the spotlight: Girls' experience of disruption. In M. Lloyd-Smith & J.D. Davies (Eds.), *On the margins: The educational experiences of "problem" pupils* (pp. 31–47). Stoke, England: Trentham.

de Lauretis, T. (1987). *Technologies of gender: Essays on theory, film, and fiction.* Bloomington: Indiana University Press.

Epstein, D., Elwood, J., Hey, V., & Maw, J. (Eds.). (1998). *Failing boys? Issues in gender and achievement.* Buckingham, England: Open University Press.

Gilbert, R., & Gilbert, P. (1998). *Masculinity goes to school.* London: Routledge.

Hubbard, R., Barbieri, M., & Power, B. (1998). *"We want to be known": Learning from adolescent girls.* York, ME: Stenhouse.

Kress, G. (2003). *Literacy in the new media age.* London: Routledge.

Lankshear, C., & Knobel, M. (2003). *New literacies: Changing knowledge and classroom learning.* Buckingham, England: Open University Press.

Lave, J., & Wenger, E. (1991). *Situated learning: Legitimate peripheral participation*. New York: Cambridge University Press.

Marsh, J. (2003). Superhero stories: Literacy, gender and popular culture. In C. Skelton & B. Francis (Eds.), *Boys and girls in the primary classroom* (pp. 59–79). Buckingham, England: Open University Press.

Mazzarella, S.R., & Pecora, N.O. (2002). Introduction. In S.R. Mazzarella & N.O. Pecora (Eds.), *Growing up girls: Popular culture and the construction of identity* (pp. 1–10). New York: Peter Lang.

Millard, E. (1997). Differently literate: Gender identity in the construction of the developing reader. *Gender and Education*, *9*(1), 31–48.

Murphy, P., & Elwood, J. (1998). Gendered learning outside and inside school: Influences on achievement. In D. Epstein, J. Elwood, V. Hey, & J. Maw (Eds.), *Failing boys? Issues in gender and achievement* (pp. 162–181). Buckingham, England: Open University Press.

Osler, A., & Vincent, K. (2003). *Girls and exclusion: Rethinking the agenda*. London: Routledge Falmer.

Paechter, C. (2003). Masculinities and femininities as communities of practice. *Women's Studies International Forum*, *26*(1), 69–77.

Pipher, M. (1994). *Reviving Ophelia: Saving the selves of adolescent girls*. New York: Ballantine Books.

Sadker, M., & Sadker, D. (1995). *Failing at fairness: How America's schools cheat girls*. Toronto, ON: Maxwell Macmillan International.

Sanford, K. (2002). Social studies classrooms and curricula—Potential sites for inclusionary practices. *Canadian Social Studies*, *36*(3). Retrieved September 5, 2005, from www.quasar.ualberta.ca/css.

Schools size up gender achievement gap. (2003, December 15). *Tennessean*, p. 17A.

Smith, M., & Wilhelm, J. (2002). *"Reading don't fix no Chevys": Literacy in the lives of young men*. Portsmouth, NH: Heinemann.

The trouble with boys. (2000, August 21). *The Guardian*. Retrieved September 6, 2005, from http://www.guardian.co.uk/leaders/story/0,,356622,00.html.

Valdivia, A., & Bettivia, R. (2002). A guided tour through one adolescent girl's culture. In S.R. Mazzarella & N.O. Pecora (Eds.), *Growing up girls: Popular culture and the construction of identity* (pp. 159–174). New York: Peter Lang.

Multicultural Literature and Young Adolescents: A Kaleidoscope of Opportunity

Susan M. Landt

> Literature has the capacity to enter our lives, to interact with what we already know and believe, and perhaps even to change us. (Salvner, 2001, p. 9)

As a child, I was fascinated by the magic of the kaleidoscope. By holding it to my eye, I could view a wondrous scene; tap it a bit, and everything changed. The vision was never ending—always a delight to my eyes. For me, literature served a similar purpose; each book offered a new delight for my mind. Whether I followed individuals through numerous adventures or encountered assorted characters in various volumes, the effect was the same; each reading brought new ideas and different perspectives—a kaleidoscope of dreams.

Because I was living in an isolated rural neighborhood in the days before television arrived, reading was my window to the world. The stories guided my dreams; the characters populated my imaginings. I learned of love, fear, triumph, and hope. I put myself in the lives of the characters and imagined possibilities beyond my reality. It was through literature that a small girl running barefoot in the summer and picking beans to earn money for the county fair discovered a world full of possibility and promise.

It is these memories that reinforce my belief in the power of literature to open doors in our minds. However, the kaleidoscopic visions I experienced, while beautiful and astounding to my mind, now seem to have been small, white, and constrained. It would take years for the world of color and diversity to be open for me, and more years for it to cease to be foreign and exotic. All characters in the books I read were renditions of one another—merely older, richer, smarter, and more experienced versions of myself.

Today, I devour literature written for middle school students and young adults, marveling at the range of material available for current readers. While young adult literature remains primarily Eurocentric, there are marvelous books available that provide readers with a diverse array of perspectives. Quality offerings about nonmainstream cultures are slowly appearing at bookstores and libraries. The challenge is to bring these to the attention of young readers. One way to accomplish this is through educators. Providing teachers with information on quality multicultural literature and strategies for including it in the curriculum will encourage them to use this vital resource for their students' development.

A kaleidoscope does not offer one true picture; it morphs and changes at every move, proffering a multifaceted, prismatic perspective. That is what I propose we offer to the developing minds of our students: not a static, narrow vision, but a spectrum of perceptions and possibilities. My goal is to facilitate awareness and

Preparing Reading Professionals (second edition), edited by Rita M. Bean, Natalie Heisey, and Cathy M. Roller. © 2010 by the International Reading Association. Reprinted from Landt, S.M. (2006). Multicultural literature and young adolescents: A kaleidoscope of opportunity. *Journal of Adolescent & Adult Literacy, 49*(8), 690–697. doi:10.1598/JAAL.49.8.5.

availability of quality literature that can provide young minds with a richer, clearer, and more accurate window through which to gaze.

Although there are wonderful selections of multicultural books available for readers of all ages, this article focuses on literature appropriate for adolescents and young adults. I chose this mid-age range partly because, as Zitlow and Stover (1998) noted, "The opportunity and ability to see how others experience life is especially important for young adults who are in the process of becoming independent participants in a world much larger than their own school and community" (Introduction section, para. 6). Providing a multitude of perspectives through literature at this point in students' development is an effective way to help facilitate their engagement in self and social understanding (Ford, Tyson, Howard, & Harris, 2000).

Multicultural literature encompasses a wide range of perspectives "of groups that have been marginalized because of race, gender, ethnicity, language, ability, age, social class, religion/spirituality, and/or sexual orientation" (Muse, 1997, p. 1). All of the above deserve and require consideration when searching for literature to share with students. The examples within this article, however, are delimited to the relatively narrow constructs of race and ethnicity in order to provide depth of focus. By restricting the selections, it was possible to draw on a range of offerings within an area, thereby illustrating the concepts with interrelated examples. This is not an indication of lesser importance ascribed to other groups, merely an attempt to provide analogous examples across a breadth of ideas.

Purposes for Using Multicultural Literature

In order for students to encounter high-quality literature with a range of perspectives, it has to be made available to them and highlighted in a way that tantalizes their interest. Teachers are in an excellent position to accomplish this task. However, that does not mean they are prepared. Teachers may not feel that they are sufficiently knowledgeable to select appropriate multicultural literature for their students. Overwhelmed with the already high demands of teaching, they may not have time for in-depth research required to locate and evaluate suitable selections. Teachers may decide it is better to avoid integrating multicultural literature with their curriculum rather than take the chance of including inappropriate choices. Therefore, this article seeks to do three things: provide information concerning the importance of including multicultural literature in the curriculum, present guidelines for selecting it, and offer high-quality examples.

Broader View of the World

A well-recognized goal of introducing multicultural literature into the classroom is to connect students to the world by providing a wider view. Literature can open doors to other cultures and introduce students to ideas and insights they would otherwise not have encountered. Rather than reading about cultures in a fact-filled textbook, students experience a culture through the eyes of other adolescents. They get to see people their age meeting challenges and solving problems. Unfamiliar aspects of other cultures—language, dress, beliefs—are less foreign when viewed through the lens of familiar issues. Fine fiction, according to Mazer (1993), has "the power to transform our understanding...[and] allow us to enter into another person's experience and to feel it as if it were our own" (p. viii).

Literature can serve as a bridge to awareness and understanding and help students make intercultural connections. Opening their eyes and their minds requires helping them discern the similarities among cultures while learning to appreciate the differences. Multicultural books that assist students in seeing the "commonalities across cultures...play an important role in helping students cross cultural borders" (Cai, 2002, p. 121). When students reading about diverse cultures discover similarities with their own, they begin to look beyond the differences and take a step toward appreciating the cultural connectedness of all humanity.

Adolescence is a time of questioning and searching as young people strive to comprehend who they are and how they fit in the world. Stover (2000) suggested a number of adolescent concerns that are common across cultural borders, including the need to define oneself outside the realm of family; come to terms with new visions of one's family as "less than perfect"; determine an individual set of moral, ethical, religious, or political principles; come to terms with developing sexuality and with the physiological changes brought on by puberty; develop positive relationships with peers; think about the future; and forge a niche in the larger society (p. 108).

Students reading about these issues across a variety of cultures are able to appreciate the commonalities as they see themselves mirrored within the similarities. In Yumoto's *The Friends* (1992), three middle school boys grapple with friendship, bravery, and ethics as they confront their tentative fascination with death. These youth struggle with intergenerational relationships, expectations regarding education, and pressure from peers. The story takes place in modern-day Japan, highlighting the universality of adolescent concerns. Yumoto's book speaks to all youth, regardless of culture. Readers can relate to the boys' efforts to face their fears and establish their developing identities as individuals.

Tangled Threads by Pegi Deitz Shea (2003) provides readers with a dual experience as they encounter Mai, a 13-year-old Hmong girl, in a Thailand refugee camp and follow her to a new life in the United States. Observing Mai and her grandmother before they immigrate equips readers to better understand the difficulties faced in their new surroundings. While illustrating the cultural differences faced by Mai and her family, Shea also focuses on the similarities challenging young teens. Peer pressure, moral dilemmas, and issues of loyalty to one's friends and family confront Mai as she adjusts to the differing standards in her new country.

Another perspective is offered by Francisco Jimenez in *The Circuit: Stories From the Life of a Migrant Child* (1997). Based on his own experiences and those of his family, Jimenez reveals the conditions of life for migrant families in the United States as he describes the constant moves to accommodate growing cycles that are critical to his family's survival. Attending school, we see in *Circuit*, is problematic for migrant children on several levels. Lack of steady attendance because of moving is compounded by the language barrier most migrant children face. In response to a question about school, Roberto replied,

> I remember being hit on the wrists with a twelve-inch ruler because I did not follow directions.... But how could I?.... [T]he teacher gave them all in English.... I always guessed what the teacher wanted me to do. And when she did not use the ruler on me, I knew I had guessed right. (p. 14)

Seeing the struggles Roberto and his siblings go through to get an education can open doors to understanding life differences and cultural inequities. Middle school students reading *The Circuit* are introduced to a culture within their own culture invisible or ignored by many.

Interrupting Prejudice and Misunderstanding

Crossing cultural borders involves understanding the similarities among cultures, while also appreciating the differences. It is this second point that is crucial to interrupting the inner boundary of prejudice and misunderstanding. Cai (2002) pointed out that "Ignorance and prejudice are two main stumbling blocks to mutual understanding and appreciation among ethnic groups. To remove these blocks we need more culturally specific books that give readers insights into cultures other than their own" (p. 25). However, Cai warned against the limitations of many books that "skim only superficial cultural differences" and "do not delve into entrenched bias and prejudice." He cautioned that such books "appear to offer an easy way to cross cultural barriers" (pp. 121–122). It is up to teachers to select appropriate readings and also to initiate discussions that stimulate student thought on issues of difference.

Bauman (1997) described how she uses literature to "help students explore the lives of people whose cultures are very different from theirs" (p. 104). Through questioning and discussion, Bauman urged her students to consider such issues as who is missing from their textbooks and how this might affect the self-esteem of those who are absent. She also indicated that frequently these readings "generate discussion about acts of prejudice or discrimination that students themselves have experienced in schools." She observes that "white students are often surprised to learn that incidents of intolerance are happening here and now to their own peers" (p. 105).

In *The Jacket*, Andrew Clements (2002) portrays a young boy's gradual realization of his own prejudice. When Phil, the middle school–aged protagonist, accuses a black schoolmate of stealing a jacket, it kindles Phil's reflection on prejudice. He speculates about his assumption that Daniel stole the jacket, asking himself, "What if Daniel had been a white kid? Would I have grabbed him like that?" (p. 36). He confronts his mother with his growing concern, "How come you never told me I was prejudiced?" (p. 37). Clements's story can unlock the silence surrounding discussion of prejudice and empower students and teachers to openly address issues commonly avoided.

Carvell (2002), influenced by her son's experiences, exposes the prejudice surrounding school mascots in *Who Will Tell My Brother?* Evan, following in his brother's footsteps, is determined to abolish his school's use of an Indian mascot. He meets stony opposition from the administration and outward hostility from other students. Written in free verse, Carvell's spare straightforward writing cuts directly to the heart.

> The word has gotten out.
> The word is spreading
> that I have done the unthinkable.
> I have questioned.
> I have questioned. I have questioned why we need
>   this mascot.
>
> They stare at me through the cold, hard eyes
> of those who feel threatened, whose pride
> whose tradition

> whose bigotry
> and narrow thought
> is threatened.
> I, too feel threatened. (p. 73)

By bringing the issue of offensive mascots to young students through the perspective of someone their own age, Carvell provides a vehicle for a stimulating discussion. Teachers interested in thoughtfully engaging their students will do well to add this book to their curriculum.

Another excellent young-adult book that inspires discussion on issues of prejudice and discrimination is *Crossing Jordan* by Adrian Fogelin (2000). In this story, Fogelin describes two young girls determined not to let their families' prejudice discourage their developing friendship.

> The For Sale sign on the house next door had hardly been up a week when Mama told us she'd heard that a black family had bought the old Faircloth place. Daddy brought his fist down on the table and the supper dishes jumped. "Place is gonna go downhill," he said.... "I'll just have to build me a fence." (p. 1)

Cass and Jemmie, with their mutual interest in competitive running and shared reading of *Jane Eyre*, slowly work on their families' antagonism. Through the girls' eyes, Fogelin exposes both subtle and explicit barriers impeding cross-racial friendships. Without resorting to an "all problems solved" happy ending, Fogelin still projects a hopeful future where families grow alongside one another in a healthful learning way.

Reflection of Self

Both of the above goals—exposing students to a broader view of the world and reducing prejudice and misunderstanding—are important objectives for teachers. Another major goal involves helping students see themselves in their reading. As Boyd stated, "In a profound sense, children look to story for self" (1997, p. 107). As a young reader, I encountered variations of my own culture. What must it be like for readers to find only images representing those unlike them? "Students need to be able to make connections between literature and their everyday lives. Children need to receive affirmation of themselves and their culture through literature" (Colby & Lyon, 2004, p. 24).

Not seeing one's self, or representations of one's culture, in literature can activate feelings of marginalization and cause students to question their place within society. Boyd (1997), describing her childhood reading experiences, reveals "As an African American female child, I never saw my face or the lives of my family, friends, and neighbors in the books I read" (p. 107). Nothing that she encountered in her reading included images of self. This lack of reflection affected her self-image and her feeling of belonging. Boyd recalled, "I realized that I was invisible, excluded, disaffirmed, spurned, discarded, scorned, and rejected in the white world of children's literature" (p. 107). What disastrous learning experiences her reading provided.

Boyd's destructive encounters with the invisibility of self in books should not be repeated. Children today have more options available. Increasingly, children's and young adult literature include selections by and about people of marginalized—or to use Cai's (2002) term—parallel cultures. Teachers can be an important source of information about available literature. The first step is recognizing the need for providing reading material that reflects students' cultural selves. Reporting on a study of prospective teachers' understandings of the importance of using multicultural literature, Colby and Lyon stated, "It was evident that many had not, until this point, considered the dilemma that children of color face in regards to having access to appropriate literature and an environment that acknowledges and celebrates diversity in the classroom" (2004, p. 24).

Colby and Lyon (2004) shared prospective teachers' comments after reading the article "African American children's literature that helps students find themselves" (Hefflin & Ralph, 2001).

> I didn't realize that there are children that feel like they have nothing to read and relate to...as a white child I never really thought about it because I already had books that I could relate to.... It seems obvious that readers want to identify with characters, but I never considered how all-white characters would affect African American students. (Colby & Lyon, p. 25)

These observations all share the same feature: not having given any thought to how students might feel who do not see themselves reflected in what they read. This study reveals the necessity of integrating multicultural literature into the classroom. These preservice teachers, one step away from guiding their own students, were first encountering the significance of how literature affects children's images of self and others and the importance of creating learning communities that celebrate diversity.

If multicultural literature were an integral part of education, preservice teachers would not be struggling to comprehend the necessity for infusing their teaching with a diversity of readings and images for their students: It would be an expected part of their curriculum. Students would not still be searching for reflections of their culture in what they read and see: they would enjoy and learn from the diverse range of inclusive offerings.

How will integrating multicultural literature with the curriculum better serve students? As a reiteration, Barta and Grindler (1996) presented Campbell and Wittenberg's (1980) six purposes:

1. It heightens respect for individuals. Children discover that all people have basic needs, feelings, and emotions.

2. It acknowledges contributions of minorities. Many cultures have made contributions to the world, and we should celebrate these accomplishments.

3. It brings children into contact with other cultures. Since children develop an awareness of differences among people at an early age, it is important that they be exposed to books that reflect a pluralistic society. This helps to eliminate

ethnocentrism and encourages respect and tolerance for others.

4. It enhances students' self-concept. Children realize that they have a cultural heritage of which they can be proud.

5. It helps children realize that society has developed a value system that validates some differences and minimizes others. This system is based on ignorance and misperception and its existence promotes inequality.

6. It encourages students to detect prejudice and to work toward its elimination. (p. 269)

Selecting Multicultural Literature

Once teachers embrace the idea of integrating multicultural literature with their teaching, the task of selecting appropriate material begins. There are a number of factors to think about when selecting multicultural books for students. Many of these are the same as with any book: developmental appropriateness, quality of writing, relevance of issues to students, general accuracy, believability of characters, and interest level of the story.

There are other important characteristics to consider when choosing books that focus on nonmainstream cultures. Guides and lists of criteria have been developed to assist teachers and others interested in selecting quality multicultural literature. After reviewing a range of helpful offerings (Agosto, n.d.; Cai, 2002; Higgins, 2002; Muse, 1997), I have synthesized them into the following broad categories:

• The accurate portrayal of the culture or cultures depicted in the book includes not only physical characteristics such as clothing and food, but relationships among people within the culture and with people of different cultures.

• There is diversity within the culture; characters are unique individuals, not stereotypical representatives.

• Dialogue is culturally authentic with characters using speech that accurately

represents their oral traditions. Non-English words are spelled and used correctly.

• Realistic social issues and problems are depicted frankly and accurately without oversimplification.

• Minority characters are shown as leaders within their community able to solve their own problems. Cultural minorities do not play a supporting or subservient role while whites are seen as possessing all the power.

Substantiating Cultural Authenticity

Cultural authenticity—the accuracy of the language, customs, values, and history of the culture—can be difficult, if not impossible, to determine if one is not familiar with the culture depicted. For instance, I do not know enough about the cultural differences among Native American peoples to determine if a writer is accurately depicting a specific group, or if there are inaccuracies that someone more knowledgeable would recognize. Therefore, it is important to have a means of substantiating a book's cultural authenticity.

Determining the author's credentials to write from the perspective of a culture is one way to ascertain a book's cultural authenticity. The question to ask is "What qualifies the author to write about this culture?" If the author is not a member of the culture being depicted, does the author have a background to qualify as an accepted representative? There is debate over whether only authors from a culture are qualified to write about that culture. This question is deceptively simple, with responses too complex and full of nuances to address here. As a general rule, a book written by an author with an emic—insider—perspective is likely to be culturally authentic; a book written from an etic—outsider—perspective may or may not be culturally authentic. Jacqueline Woodson, an award-winning African American writer, addressed this topic of people writing outside of their experiences, by stating,

My hope is that those who write about the tears and the laughter and the language in my grandmother's house have first sat down at the table with us and dipped the bread of their own experiences into our stew. (1998, p. 38)

When I am unsure of the cultural authenticity of a book, there are two important categories of valuable information that I search: (1) specific cultural awards, and (2) websites devoted to individual cultures.

When looking for appropriate books that feature a specific culture, a good place to look are the awards for books from that culture. If a book received an award or is on the list of honor books for the award, there is little doubt that it is culturally authentic. Following are major awards with a few award-winning examples specifically appropriate for middle school students.

- Coretta Scott King Award (African American)
  - *Bud, Not Buddy* by Christopher Paul Curtis (2000)
  - *Forged by Fire* by Sharon Draper (1998)
  - *Locomotion* by Jacqueline Woodson (2003)
- The Pura Belpré Award (Latino/Latina)
  - *Esperanza Rising* by Pam Muñoz Ryan (2002)
  - *Cuba 15* by Nancy Osa (2003)
- Tomás Rivera Award (Mexican American)
  - *My Land Sings: Stories From the Rio Grande* by Rudolfo Anaya (1999)
  - *Breaking Through* by Francisco Jimenez (2001)
- Sydney Taylor Award (Jewish)
  - *The Night Journey* by Kathryn Lasky (1981)
  - *Milkweed* by Jerry Spinelli (2003)
- Américas Book Award for Children's and Young Adult Literature (Latin America, the Caribbean, or Latinos in the United States)

  - *Before We Were Free* by Julia Alvarez (2003)
  - *The Color of My Words* by Lynn Joseph (2000)
- Mildred L. Batchelder Award (most outstanding children's book originally published in a foreign language and subsequently translated into English for publication in the United States)
  - *Run, Boy, Run* by Uri Orlev (2003)
  - *Samir and Yonatan* by Daniella Carmi (2002)

There are, of course, many fine and appropriate multicultural books that have not received awards. To track these down, I searched for websites focusing on outstanding books from a specific culture or from a variety of cultures. The following are sites that provide a wealth of resources.

www.asianamericanbooks.com/index .shtml (Asian American)

www.oyate.org (Native American)

www.isomedia.com/homes/jmele/joe .html (multicultural book reviews for K–12 educators)

www.ala.org/ala/yalsa/booklistsawards/ booklistsbook.htm (multicultural fiction)

As educators understand the importance of including multicultural literature in their curriculum and become confident in their ability to select appropriate high-quality writing, students will enjoy the benefits. Imaginary barriers dissolve as students see themselves reflected in a diversity of cultures and recognize similarities across invented boundaries. What was strange becomes familiar when viewed through age-mate perspectives. Doors open, eyes see, and minds grasp, as young adolescents encounter self within other—a kaleidoscope of opportunity.

References

Agosto, D.E. (n.d.). *Criteria for evaluating multicultural literature.* Retrieved February 1, 2006, from http://www.pages.drexel.edu/~dea22/multicultural.html

Alvarez, J. (2003). *Before we were free.* New York: Knopf Books for Young Readers.

Anaya, R. (1999). *My land sings: Stories from the Rio Grande.* New York: HarperTrophy.

Barta, J., & Grindler, M.C. (1996). Exploring bias using multicultural literature for children. *The Reading Teacher, 50,* 269–270.

Bauman, S. (1997). Between the lines: Literature as a tool for tolerance. In D. Muse (Ed.), *The New Press guide to multicultural resources for young readers* (pp. 104–106). New York: The New Press.

Boyd, C.D. (1997). I see myself in there: Experiencing self and others in multiethnic children's literature. In D. Muse (Ed.), *The New Press guide to multicultural resources for young readers* (pp. 106-114). New York: The New Press.

Cai, M. (2002). *Multicultural literature for children and young adults: Reflections on critical issues.* Westport, CT: Greenwood Press.

Campbell, P., & Wittenberg, J. (1980). How books influence children: What the research shows. *Interracial Books for Children Bulletin, 11*(6), 3–6.

Carmi, D. (2002). *Samir and Yonatan* (T. Lotan, Trans.). New York: Scholastic.

Carvell, M. (2002). *Who will tell my brother?* New York: Hyperion.

Clements, A. (2002). *The jacket.* New York: Simon & Schuster Books for Young Readers.

Colby, S.A., & Lyon, A.F. (2004). Heightening awareness about the importance of using multicultural literature. *Multicultural Education, 11*(3), 24–28.

Curtis, C.P. (2000). *Bud, not Buddy.* New York: Scholastic.

Draper, S. (1998). *Forged by fire.* New York: Simon Pulse.

Fogelin, A. (2000). *Crossing Jordan.* Atlanta, GA: Peachtree.

Ford, D.Y., Tyson, C.A., Howard, T.C., & Harris, J.J., III. (2000). Multicultural literature and gifted Black students: Promoting self-understanding, awareness, and pride. *The Roeper School, 22,* 235–240.

Hefflin, B.R., & Ralph, K.S. (2001). African American children's literature that helps students find themselves: Selection guidelines for grades K–3. *The Reading Teacher, 54,* 108–118.

Higgins, J.J. (2002, January). *Multicultural children's literature: Creating and applying an evaluation tool in response to the needs of urban educators.* New Horizons for Learning. Retrieved February 1, 2006, from http://www.newhorizons.org/strategies/multicultural/higgins.htm

Jimenez, F. (1997). *The circuit: Stories from the life of a migrant child.* Albuquerque: University of New Mexico Press.

Jimenez, F. (2001). *Breaking through.* Boston: Houghton Mifflin.

Joseph, L. (2000). *The color of my words.* New York: HarperTrophy.

Lasky, K. (1981). *The night journey.* New York: Puffin.

Mazer, A. (Ed.). (1993). *America Street: A multicultural anthology of stories.* New York: Persea.

Muse, D. (Ed.). (1997). *The New Press guide to multicultural resources for young readers.* New York: The New Press.

Orlev, U. (2003). *Run, boy, run* (H. Halkin, Trans.). Boston: Houghton Mifflin.

Osa, N. (2003). *Cuba 15.* New York: Delacorte Press.

Ryan, P.M. (2002). *Esperanza rising.* New York: Scholastic.

Salvner, G.M. (2001). Lessons and lives: Why young adult literature matters. *The ALAN Review, 28*(3), 9–13.

Shea, P.D. (2003). *Tangled threads: A Hmong girl's story.* New York: Clarion.

Spinelli, J. (2003). *Milkweed.* New York: Knopf.

Stover, L.T. (2000). Who am I? Who are you? Diversity and identity in the young adult novel. In V. Monseau & G. Salvner (Eds.), *Reading their world: The young adult novel in the classroom* (pp. 100–120). Portsmouth, NH: Boynton/Cook.

Woodson, J. (1998, January/February). Who can tell my story? *The Horn Book Magazine, 74,* 34–38.

Woodson, J. (2003). *Locomotion.* New York: Scholastic.

Yumoto, K. (1992). *The friends* (C. Hirano, Trans.). New York: Random House.

Zitlow, C.S., & Stover, L. (1998). Japanese and Japanese American youth in literature. *The ALAN Review.* Retrieved February 24, 2006, from http://scholar.lib.vt.edu/ejournals/ALAN/spring98/zitlow.html

A Road Map for Reading Specialists Entering Schools Without Exemplary Reading Programs: Seven Quick Lessons

Alfred W. Tatum

Several years ago, the National Commission on Teaching and America's Future (1996) referred to professional development as the missing link in achieving educational goals in the United States. More recently, U.S. President George W. Bush signed the No Child Left Behind Act (NCLBA) in January 2002. The law was drafted to change the culture of America's schools and improve student achievement across the country to ensure that students of all races, abilities, and ages receive a quality education. It was around the same time that the National Reading Panel (National Institute of Child Health and Human Development, 2000) determined from a small number of studies that inservice professional development produced significantly higher reading achievement. Also, improving the instructional practices of teachers is a major provision of the Reading Excellence Act (REA) of 1998 that targets children who are most in need of additional assistance.

With so much recent attention placed on improving teacher quality and reading achievement in low-performing schools and an emerging focus on using reading specialists to implement professional development experiences and reading programs (International Reading Association, 2000; Snow, Burns, & Griffin, 1998), knowledge about the functions and roles of reading specialists in this capacity is significant. Three recent publications about the roles of reading specialists—*What Do Reading Specialists Do? Results From a National Survey* (Bean, Cassidy, Grumet, Shelton, & Wallis, 2002), *The Role of the Reading Specialist: A Review of Research* (Quatroche, Bean, & Hamilton, 2001), and *Teaching All Children to Read: The Roles of the Reading Specialist: A Position Statement of the International Reading Association* (2000)—indicate that the responsibilities of reading specialists have expanded and are more complex than they were a decade ago. Reading specialists are now responsible for a range of activities that include, but are not limited to, providing instruction to struggling readers. In fact, some reading specialists spend the majority of their time providing professional development aimed at improving the quality of classroom instruction.

Bean, Swan, and Knaub (2003) found that reading specialists in schools with exemplary reading programs were involved in five broad roles: (1) resource to teachers, (2) school and community liaison, (3) coordinator of the reading program, (4) contributor to assessment, and (5) instructor. Although significant, knowledge about the role of reading specialists in schools with exemplary programs is insufficiently robust. However, there is little information about reading specialists entering and performing their roles in schools without exemplary reading programs. This is a major concern because it is highly probable that more reading

Preparing Reading Professionals (second edition), edited by Rita M. Bean, Natalie Heisey, and Cathy M. Roller. © 2010 by the International Reading Association. Reprinted from Tatum, A.W. (2004). A road map for reading specialists entering schools without exemplary reading programs: Seven quick lessons. *The Reading Teacher, 58*(1), 28–39. doi:10.1598/RT.58.1.3.

specialists will be assigned to schools without exemplary reading programs than assigned to schools with them.

A road map for reading specialists entering schools without exemplary reading programs is warranted. I hope to expand the profile of reading specialists generated by Bean et al. (2003) by sharing seven lessons from my experience as a reading specialist in a school with a chronic pattern of low literacy achievement, a school that initially did not have an exemplary reading program. I bring attention to how a cohesive system of professional development support was framed.

My description of reading specialists moves beyond the existing data in several ways. While most of the current research brings attention to reading specialists working with students in the primary grades, I focus on a reading specialist working with teachers of students in grades 4–8 in an urban school in the United States where more than 95% of the students were eligible for free or reduced-cost lunch. The description considers a broader conceptualization of the role of reading specialists working toward schoolwide reading achievement. It also moves beyond the traditional pull-out model or in-class model when the reading specialist collaborates with the classroom teacher. Focus is placed on the role of the reading specialist as a teacher leader in an environment characterized by a high percentage of students reading below grade level. Finally, I propose a direct link between the support of a reading specialist and improved reading achievement in the school.

The Context of the School

I was a reading specialist at Radnus Elementary (pseudonym), an urban K–8 elementary school with 450 students. All of the students were African American. The school suffered from a pattern of low achievement in both reading and mathematics. Ten years ago, 7% of the students were reading at or above national norms as reflected by data from the Iowa Test of Basic Skills (ITBS). By 1996, the percentage of students reading at or above national norms was 13%. Radnus was one of the lowest performing elementary schools in its large urban school district. At that time the school was placed on academic probation by its district's Office of Accountability.

The school was assigned a probation manager who served as a liaison with the Office of Accountability. A mentor principal joined the faculty, and the school was given external support from an educational organization that worked with staff to improve student achievement. By the 2001–2002 school year and after five years of additional discretionary funding for the external support partner, ITBS test data indicated that 18% of the students were reading at or above national norms. It was at this time that the school's principal sought help from a local university administrator who had extensive experience leading professional development efforts to improve students' reading achievement. To establish a plan of action for supporting the teachers, the university administrator conducted four half days of observation in the school. She observed that a large majority of the teachers relied on test preparation materials to raise students' standardized test scores. In most classrooms reading instruction consisted of filling in blanks in workbook pages, checking the pages by reading aloud orally, and round-robin oral reading.

The university administrator recommended implementing a schoolwide literacy framework that included daily read-alouds, guided reading instruction, independent reading, word study, and writing. This approach was largely derived from research on effective elementary teachers (Allington, 2002; Pressley, 1998; Wharton-McDonald et al., 1997). To move the implementation forward, two certified reading specialists with more than 25 combined years of experience in urban education were hired as part of a University Partnership Team (UPT). The reading specialists were supported by a university grant-funded project and the school's discretionary funds. Although the UPT worked collaboratively on schoolwide issues, I was hired to support eight teachers in grades 4–8 as they implemented the literacy framework, and I functioned primarily as a teacher leader.

After the teachers and I worked together for 19 months they were able to increase school-wide reading achievement. By the end of school year 2001–2002, 26% of the students were reading at or above national norms, up from 18%. ITBS data indicated gains in the percentage of students reading at or above grade level for all grades 4–8. The largest gains were from the seventh- and eighth-grade students where a more detailed case study of professional development was being conducted. At the beginning of school year 2001–2002, 22% of the seventh-grade students ($n = 28$) and 21% of the eighth-grade students ($n = 33$) were reading at or above national norms. By the end of the school year the percentages increased to 39% and 57%, respectively. ITBS standard scale scores indicated that students in grade 4 were close to achieving national average gains, while students in grades 7 and 8 surpassed national average gains. The gains of the students in grades 5 and 6 were not as large (see Table 1).

Negotiating a Situational Identity

I entered Radnus Elementary in the middle of school year 2000–2001. The principal introduced me during a staff meeting as an "expert" on reading who was going to get the school off "probation." For two weeks, I engaged in a process Angrosino and Mays de Perez (2000) referred to as "role making" to become familiar with the culture of the school and to determine how best to proceed with the teachers. This role making was critical to the development of my identity as a reading specialist because I did not "step into [a] fixed and fully defined position" (p. 683).

During the first six months, I had access to the teachers' classrooms and their teaching. I observed that the teachers were not implementing some of the recommended teaching practices, continuing instead to inundate students with test

---

Table 1
Gains and Losses Using Iowa Test of Basic Skills Standard Scores

The scale score was used because it is an equal-unit scale extending from the lowest achievement in kindergarten to the highest achievement in grade 12. Scale scores were developed so that progress can be followed over a period of years. They are used primarily for statistical analysis, such as obtaining and calculating gains.

Grade	Average Gains**
4	12 (14)
5	6 (13)
6	7 (12)*
7	25 (11)
8	33 (11)

*Multiple teacher changes.
**The number in parentheses is the approximate average growth from one grade to the next in reading in standard score units.

---

preparation materials. I met with teachers individually and in groups. I repeatedly expressed my consternation about their instructional practices during individual conferences and grade-level meetings. There was resistance. I was locked out of one teacher's classroom. Another teacher walked out of the classroom as I was modeling a lesson. The interactions of the first six months were tenuous, causing me to reflect on my ability to move the teachers toward change.

Being close to the students' failures created in me a desire to force teachers to change their instructional practices. Kohn (1999) referred to this as the "arrogance of top-down coercion" when those outside the classroom decide what the people in it are required to do. However, I determined that it was for the best to persuade teachers that the course of instruction I advocated was the one to take. Therefore, I had to find ways to negotiate my identity (Angrosino & Mays de Perez, 2000) with the teachers that would allow them to receive the support I could provide.

Aligning Function as Reading Specialist With School Context

I recorded notes of my efforts over the first six months in a weekly reflection log. My analysis led me to conclude that my support lacked a clear theoretical head. I had focused only on instruction to improve students' reading achievement. The teachers needed more support to implement the literacy framework. I assessed that the following steps were needed to align my role as reading specialist with the school context:

- Provide professional development support that is anatomically complete (see Figure 1).

- Discuss factors that include, but are not limited to, instructional practices that have the potential to improve students' reading achievement.

- Provide teachers with the physical supports and materials for instructing the students.

I expanded my role as reading specialist beyond the initial literacy framework to align my efforts with the needs of the teachers and students at Radnus Elementary. Lyons and Pinnell (2001) suggested the need for literacy programs with a cohesive system (i.e., an arrangement of things so intimately connected that they form a unified whole greater than the sum of their parts). Using the idea of a cohesive system, I examined three bodies of literature as

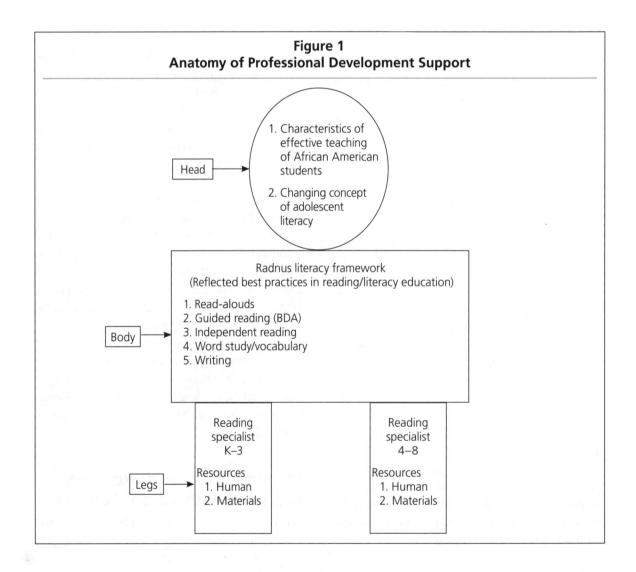

Figure 1
Anatomy of Professional Development Support

Head → 1. Characteristics of effective teaching of African American students

2. Changing concept of adolescent literacy

Body → Radnus literacy framework
(Reflected best practices in reading/literacy education)
1. Read-alouds
2. Guided reading (BDA)
3. Independent reading
4. Word study/vocabulary
5. Writing

Reading specialist K–3

Resources
1. Human
2. Materials

Reading specialist 4–8

Resources
1. Human
2. Materials

Legs →

being intimately connected and necessary to frame my role as reading specialist at Radnus Elementary. Understanding of the students' culture and literacy instruction specifically for adolescents were placed at the core of the enhanced supports (see Table 2).

There were several reasons for this broader framing. First, teachers of African American students from impoverished urban communities often have students with a wider array of developmental skills and cultural barriers than do other teachers who are not similarly situated (Louis & Miles, 1990). This problem is exacerbated when teachers responsible for these students have a limited concept of what it means for their students to be literate. A limited concept of pedagogical theories can also interfere with advancing the literacies of African American

students. A closer look at the "good teaching" of African American students (Foster, 1993; Irvine, 1991; Ladson-Billings, 1995; Lipman, 1995) has led to a distinctive educational philosophy and pedagogy considered effective for African American students.

Second, with regard to professional development for teachers, what little is invested is too often spent on training aimed at making conventional teachers a little better at what they conventionally do by making them more conscious of what they have been doing all along. There is a need to help teachers think differently about their work and work differently because of what they think (Schlechty, 1990).

Third, the concept of literacy for older children is changing. An emerging concept of literacy for older students moves beyond cognitive

Table 2
Three Bodies of Literature

Educating African American Students	Teacher Professional Development	Adolescent Literacy
Legitimate African American students' culture and make it a reference for learning.	Establish a strong conceptual basis when implementing the professional development support.	Recognize that the concept of adolescent literacy is changing.
Resist curriculum orientations that stifle or postpone academic growth.	Ground professional development support in teachers' own work and in research that is pertinent to the support.	Work to bridge the gap between adolescents' in-school literacies and out-of-school literacies.
Engage students in authentic discussions where they can analyze their realities in the context of the curriculum and discuss strategies for overcoming academic and societal barriers.	Make continuous learning a valued part of the professional development support.	Recognize that adolescents are developing a sense of self and that they draw on multiple literacies to define that self.
Guide students toward academic success and cultural competence.	Sustain the culture of the professional development support.	Provide explicit strategy instruction.
	Be context sensitive.	Structure supportive environments.
Address students' cognitive, affective, social, emotional, and developmental needs.	Systematically monitor the impact and involve teachers in the evaluation process.	Involve students in the assessment process and develop an assessment plan that pays attention to their cognitive and affective needs.
Require students to meet high academic standards.	Assure available resources and adequate support for teachers when their questions and concerns emerge.	
	Provide support that translates into visible changes in students' academic performance.	

approaches confined to in-school literacy materials for teaching students ways to handle text (Moje, Young, Readence, & Moore, 2000). It encompasses complex conceptions of literacy, and it is not limited to in-school literacy that is insufficient for a growing population of linguistically, culturally, and socioeconomically diverse students (Greenleaf, Schoenbach, Cziko, & Mueller, 2001; Hull & Schultz, 2002).

Several steps were taken to support the teachers' use of this broader frame. First, I sought ways to help the teachers reconceptualize their literacy instruction to address the needs of their students who were African American, poor, and living in an economically marginalized community. Second, I initiated an assessment profile of the students using multiple methods to identify students' strengths and weaknesses in reading. Third, I offered a core group of strategies to the teachers that they could use to build on students' strengths and address their needs. Fourth, I selected and offered curriculum materials and resources. In the following sections I explain how each goal was addressed.

Helping Teachers Reconceptualize Their Literacy Instruction

The attempt to get the teachers to reconceptualize their literacy instruction beyond their existing beliefs converged on a dialectic between the role of literacy instruction for African Americans historically and the present authority given to standardized tests to control literacy instruction. The reconceptualization focused on several dominant themes for the teachers that included getting them to (a) engage their students with authentic text and in authentic discussions where the students could analyze their realities in the context of the curriculum; (b) use meaningful literacy activities that address students' cognitive and affective domains, taking into account students' cultural characteristics; (c) acknowledge that skill development, increasing test scores, and nurturing students' cultural identity are fundamentally compatible; (d) make African American students' culture a reference for learning; and (e) resist curriculum orientations that stifle or postpone academic growth.

Developing a Comprehensive Assessment Profile

The University Partnership Team and the teachers entered school year 2001–2002 with a limited profile of the students' reading abilities. We were given a school progress report that indicated how well the students performed on the ITBS. There were no other assessments to provide a collection of evidence about students' strengths and weaknesses with reading. The test data were not useful for making instructional decisions. They only indicated that the teachers' practices, primarily aimed at increasing test scores, were marginally effective at best. The University Partnership Team decided that our assessment profile needed to be strengthened.

To ensure that students get the help they need, appropriate assessments should be used to identify the specific strategies and skills the students possess and their response to instructional practices. This is vital to responsive teaching, and even more so for students who struggle with reading. Also, an effective assessment plan is one that is ongoing, involves both informal and formal measures, and extends across several areas of reading. Therefore, there was a need to develop an assessment profile of students' strengths and weaknesses and the instruction they were receiving to respond to their needs.

Several types of assessments were used to identify students' strengths and weaknesses related to reading. The first assessment, completed in October 2001, was a decoding exercise using graded word lists from the Qualitative Reading Inventory–III. This assessment procedure was selected to gather a quick estimate of students' abilities to decode words in isolation. The results indicated that more than 70% of the students at each grade level were able to decode words at their grade level with 90% accuracy or better. However, the results also indicated that less than 70% were able to decode the words automatically (when they were flashed for one second). The results of this assessment were corroborated later with other forms of assessment to determine how students attempted to decode words in context that were unfamiliar to them.

Second, classrooms were observed for two months to identify patterns of literacy behaviors and instructional practices that could be shared with classroom teachers. Oral reading miscues, notes about students' engagement with the text, and students' responses to comprehension questions were recorded. Analysis of this data indicated that there was often a question–answer mismatch when students attempted to answer questions. In many cases, the students could not provide the rationale for their responses—they were passively engaged with the text. Many of the students struggled with the vocabulary in context although the teacher provided a definition.

Observation of the instructional practices revealed that students were not being held individually accountable for comprehension on a daily basis. Word study and vocabulary development were different in each classroom. Individual corrective feedback was sparse. Also, there was a mismatch between the type of questions the students were asked to answer in class and the type of questions generally found on standardized reading assessments.

In November 2001, the teachers were asked to consider the following steps to help gauge the students' needs more effectively: (1) Reduce the number of comprehension questions they had their students respond to during one lesson in hopes of getting students to invest more energy answering fewer questions. This strategy would also increase the time for explicit strategy instruction. (2) Require students to cite text-based evidence in writing for all of their responses to comprehension questions. This requirement would grant opportunities to assess students' responses more fully. (3) Reduce the number of vocabulary terms introduced during one lesson until students understood how to "map" the words.

To help the teachers gauge their students' progress and the usefulness of the recommended changes, the Gates–MacGinitie Reading Test (GMRT) was administered in January 2002 and hand scored to search for information about students' comprehension that might be useful for planning instruction. This gave the teachers a general idea of student reading achievement midway through the school year. The GMRT was selected because it provided teachers with data that extended beyond their classroom assessments. The teachers were asked to monitor and make notes about their students' behavior during the GMRT. They were also encouraged to gather students' reactions to the assessment after it was completed. Quantitative analysis indicated that 29% of the students did not complete the 48-item assessment and 19% of the students did not complete 10 or more of the items. The analysis of the data also indicated that there was no distinguishable difference in students' ability to correctly answer comprehension questions following expository and narrative text. Students had a higher number of incorrect responses on the second half of the assessment (items 25–48). Following a discussion of the results, we decided to continue to provide explicit strategy instruction using narrative and expository text, to nurture reading fluency, and to increase students' reading endurance by providing them with extended time for reading.

Developing an assessment profile that used both formal and informal measures was important because it allowed me to speak to the specific needs of the students and respond to the students' behaviors as they attempted to use the strategies they were taught. Developing an assessment profile this way also allowed the teachers to discuss the assessments with their students and gather information about the aspects of the process with which they had success or difficulty. More important, the ongoing assessment and discussion of the results with the teachers focused the instruction.

Offering a Core Group of Strategies

Fisher (2001) found that the identification of specific instructional strategies that teachers were expected to use was one of the components that led to significant increases in students' reading achievement. Graphic organizers and concept maps for vocabulary development were among the strategies. Using the assessment data, the teachers were asked to rally around a core group of strategies. They were asked to (a) teach students how to decode by analogy, (b) use semantic maps when introducing vocabulary, (c) teach question-and-answer relationships, and (d) use graphic organizers on a regular basis. Each of these approaches or strategies was modeled for the teachers during grade-level meetings and schoolwide staff development sessions.

To assist with the implementation of the strategies, teachers were given blank copies of semantic maps, transparencies of graphic organizers with directions for using them, and sample passages with questions they could use to introduce question-and-answer relationships. This allowed the teachers to focus on the strategies and eased their transition to the recommended approaches. They were also given information about the strategies and made aware of the potential outcomes the strategies would yield. This gave them the opportunity to monitor for observable differences in students' literacy behaviors. The teachers were encouraged throughout the year to continue with the core group of strategies, to engage in discussion about the strategies and students' responses to the instructional approaches, and to adapt the strategies to different curriculum materials.

Selecting and Offering Curriculum Materials and Resources

Having the autonomy to select curriculum materials to support the teachers at Radnus Elementary, I elected to use young adult (YA) literature. Being familiar with specific children's literature—novels written by African American authors and novels with African American characters—I presented the teachers with novels to consider. The goal was to increase students' engagement with the reading materials. It has been suggested that African American adolescents in low-level reading tracks, particularly those who live in poverty, need to read, write about, and discuss literature that is culturally relevant (Ladson-Billings, 1995). Teachers were presented with novels that could be mediated to help the students substantiate their existence. I wanted curriculum materials that would lead the teachers to

- Bridge the in-school and out-of-school literacy of their students,
- Use a culturally informed approach to nurture students' cultural competence,
- Use and discuss rich authentic literature,
- Provide wide opportunities for reading, and
- Rethink their curriculum orientations.

For example, *Slam* (Myers, 1996) was selected for one teacher because its contents provided opportunities to discuss making sound academic decisions and the consequences of inappropriate decisions with an African American teen at the center of the discussions. Other novels (see Figure 2) were selected if they could be mediated in similar ways to address students' adolescent and cultural identities. Most, but not all, of the titles were written by African American authors or had African American characters.

Although the curriculum materials were selected for the teachers and suggestions for using the novels were given, the teachers decided when to use the novels. They also determined the focus of the classroom discussions. I provided the teachers with feedback during postobservation conferences and grade-level meetings about ways to actively engage students in conversations about literature or ways to use literature to teach comprehension strategies. Over the course of the school year, some of the teachers developed rationale for their curriculum choices in relationship to the students' reactions and involvement with the materials.

By the end of the school year, the teachers were encouraged to select curriculum materials for the upcoming school year.

Sustaining the Momentum

During my time as reading specialist, the teachers were engaged in several professional development processes to sustain the momentum of the professional development support. Each teacher's classroom was visited an average of three times a month for the entire duration of the designated two-hour reading period to observe implementation of the literacy framework and to plan additional support. The professional development processes included 20-minute postobservation conferences usually held within 48 hours of a class visit, biweekly grade-level meetings, and monthly schoolwide staff development sessions. They were also given professional readings in the form of books, articles from professional journals, and handouts that moved beyond what could be discussed during face-to-face interactions (see Figure 3).

A major facet of sustaining the momentum of the professional development support was gathering teachers' perceptions about the aspects they found most useful for advancing their students' literacies. They found the following aspects useful: (a) a strong conceptual frame of the support provided by the reading specialist, (b) ongoing and specific feedback by the reading specialist, and (c) emphasis placed on culturally informed teaching.

Strong Conceptual Frame

Reading specialists must learn, as I had to learn, that support for teachers can be interrupted when those teachers do not have a strong conceptual grasp of the support provided by the reading specialist when it differs from previous attempts that failed to improve students' reading achievement. A strong conceptual basis in the planning and implementation of support for teachers is a key determinant for its effectiveness (Guskey, 2000; Hess, 1999; Joyce & Showers, 1988; Stallings, 1989). Modeling

Figure 2
Curriculum Materials Selected for Classroom Instruction

African American literature: Voices in tradition. (1998). New York: Holt Rinehart & Winston.

Babbitt, N. (1975). *Tuck everlasting.* Farrar Straus Giroux.

Clements, A. (1996). *Frindle.* New York: Aladdin.

Curtis, C.P. (1995). *The Watsons go to Birmingham—1963.* New York: Bantam Doubleday.

Gregory, D. (1990). *Nigger: An autobiography.* New York: Pocket Books.

Hamilton, V. (1990). *Cousins.* New York: Scholastic.

Johnson, A. (1998). *Heaven.* New York: Aladdin.

Kunjufu, J. (1987). *Lessons from history.* Chicago: African American Images.

Lowry, L. (1989). *Number the stars.* New York: Yearling.

Mead, A. (1998). *Junebug and the Reverend.* New York: Dell Yearling.

Myers, W.D. (1988). *Scorpions.* New York: HarperTrophy.

Myers, W.D. (1993). *Malcolm X: By any means necessary.* New York: Scholastic.

Myers, W.D. (1996). *Slam.* New York: Scholastic.

Naylor, P.R. (2000). *Shiloh.* New York: Aladdin

Neufeld, J. (1999). *Edgar Allan.* New York: Penguin.

Sachar, L. (1998). *Holes.* New York: Yearling.

Woodson, J. (1994). *I hadn't meant to tell you this.* New York: Laurel Leaf.

Wright, R. (1994). *Rites of passage.* New York: HarperTrophy.

Yep, L. (1995). *Hiroshima.* New York: Scholastic.

and remaining consistent helped the teachers at Radnus develop a strong conceptual background for the support provided. Providing information about anticipated changes in students' literacy behaviors reinforced this conceptual framework.

Ongoing and Specific Feedback

Teachers were provided with regular and specific support during postobservation conferences and grade-level meetings. Their concerns were addressed as they surfaced. Providing immediate feedback allowed me to sustain the momentum and manage dilemmas related to implementation and continuation of activities. Being welcomed as a support structure for

Figure 3
Professional Readings

Baker, M. (2002). Reading resistance in middle school: What can be done? *Journal of Adolescent & Adult Literacy*, *45*, 364–366.

Colvin, C., & Schlosser, L. (1998). Developing academic confidence to build literacy: What teachers can do. *Journal of Adolescent & Adult Literacy, 41*, 272–281.

Delpit, L. (1988). The silenced dialogue: Power and pedagogy in educating other peoples' children. *Harvard Educational Review, 58*, 280–298.

Foster, M., & Peele, T.B. (1999). Teaching black males: Lessons from the experts. In V. Polite & J. Davis (Eds.), *African American males in school and society: Practices & policies for effective education* (pp. 8–19). New York: Teachers College Press.

Fountas, I., & Pinnell, G.S. (1996). What is guided reading. In I. Fountas & G.S. Pinnell (Eds.), *Guided reading* (pp. 1–10). Portsmouth, NH: Heinemann.

Harvey, S., & Goudvis, A. (2000). Questioning. In S. Harvey & A. Goudvis, *Strategies that work: Teaching comprehension to enhance understanding* (pp. 81–94). York, ME: Stenhouse.

Harvey, S., & Goudvis, A. (2000). Strategy instruction and practice. In S. Harvey & A. Goudvis, *Strategies that work: Teaching comprehension to enhance understanding* (pp. 27–41). York, ME: Stenhouse.

Ivey, G., & Broaddus, K. (2001). "Just plain reading": A survey of what makes students want to read in middle school classrooms. *Reading Research Quarterly, 36*, 350–377.

Ladson-Billings, G. (1992). Reading between the lines and beyond the pages: A culturally relevant approach to literacy teaching. *Theory Into Practice, 31*, 312–320.

Ladson-Billings, G. (1994). *The dreamkeepers: Successful teachers of African American children*. San Francisco: Jossey-Bass.

Moore, D., Bean, T., Birdyshaw, D., & Rycik, J. (1999). Adolescent literacy: A position statement. *Journal of Adolescent & Adult Literacy, 43*, 97–111.

Rosenbaum, C. (2001). A word map for middle school: A tool for effective vocabulary instruction. *Journal of Adolescent & Adult Literacy, 45*, 44–49.

Samway, K.D., & Whang, G. (1996). *Literature study circles in a multicultural classroom*. Portland, ME: Stenhouse.

Tatum, A.W. (2000). Against marginalization and criminal curriculum standards for African American adolescents in low-level tracks: A retrospective of Baldwin's essay. *Journal of Adolescent & Adult Literacy, 43*, 570–572.

Tatum, A.W. (2000). Breaking down barriers that disenfranchise African American adolescents in low-level reading tracks. *Journal of Adolescent & Adult Literacy, 44*, 52–63.

Tatum, A.W. (2002). Professional development for teachers of African American adolescents. *Illinois Reading Council Journal, 30*, 42–52.

Tovani, C. (2000). *I read it, but I don't get it*. York, ME: Stenhouse.

Weir, C. (1998). Using embedded questions to jumpstart metacognition in middle school remedial readers. *Journal of Adolescent & Adult Literacy, 41*, 458–467.

Woodson, C.G. (2000). *The mis-education of the Negro*. Chicago: African American Images.

teachers or encountering their resistance can be factors that potentially influence whether the support provided by the reading specialist succeeds or fails to yield desired reading achievement outcomes.

Emphasis on Culturally Informed Teaching

The teachers found the emphasis on providing culturally informed teaching useful for helping them to advance their students' literacies.

Culturally informed teaching uses students' culture as a frame of reference to facilitate learning. Curriculum materials that reflected the students' culture were selected as the primary texts. In some instances, the curriculum materials reflected both the students' African American identities and their adolescent identities. This allowed the teachers to use literature to address concerns specific to their students. The materials also facilitated literature mediations that bridged the gap between the students' in-school and out-of-school literacies.

Learning the Lessons

With increasing demand for highly qualified reading specialists throughout the United States and the need to increase reading achievement in some of the nation's lowest performing schools, many reading specialists will begin their work in schools without exemplary reading programs. There are points of convergence for all reading specialists without regard to the presence of an exemplary reading program. Namely, specialists need to be a resource to teachers, work effectively with allied professionals and parents, have solid knowledge about instructional practices, have familiarity with multiple forms of assessment, provide diagnostic teaching, and be able to work with students. These were the lessons provided to us by reading specialists from schools with exemplary programs (Bean et al., 2003).

However, it is quite plausible that most reading specialists will not be found in such schools. The point of this article is to expand on the lessons provided by Bean et al. (2003) by sharing insights that emerged from my work as a reading specialist in a school that initially did not have an exemplary reading program. I end with seven quick lessons that were illuminated throughout the article.

Lesson 1: In the absence of exemplary reading programs reading specialists must be able to establish one. The process can be essentially messy and complex and require months to accomplish. Patience is key.

Lesson 2: A reading specialist who does not enter a fully "fixed" and defined role must be able to negotiate his or her identity.

Lesson 3: Being reflective is essential for reading specialists. This may lead to rethinking roles and functions and establishing new goals based on self-examination and continual professional development.

Lesson 4: There may be a need to align the role of the reading specialist with the school context. It will be necessary for many reading specialists to understand cultural and contextual forces that operate inside and outside of the schools in which they work. This might include moving toward an increased understanding of theories of pedagogy and curriculum orientations suitable for the students and teachers at a particular school.

Lesson 5: Being an effective reading specialist involves establishing measurable goals and planning instructional enhancements. In some cases, theoretical enhancements might be necessary for helping teachers reconceptualize the role of literacy instruction, developing a comprehensive assessment profile to identify students' strengths and weaknesses, offering teachers a core group of instructional strategies to teach students, and selecting appropriate curriculum materials and resources.

Lesson 6: Reading specialists should be able to sustain the momentum of their efforts to support teachers and students. This may require using various professional development processes and materials.

Lesson 7: Reading specialists should gather teachers' perceptions about the actions by the reading specialist that they find useful for helping them advance their students' literacies.

Final Thoughts

Being a reading specialist is dynamic and influenced by factors that cannot always be described in advance. A combination of synergistic factors determines how effective one is as a reading specialist. What works successfully in one environment may not be suitable in other environments. However, the emerging knowledge about the roles and functions of reading specialists is critical. The road map for reading specialists entering schools without exemplary reading programs described within this article and the associated lessons are part of the growing knowledge base useful for becoming an effective reading specialist. There are many lessons still to be learned. I hope these lessons will continue to come from reading specialists working across various contexts. Through these lessons, current and future reading specialists—and those who prepare reading specialists—can ask the right questions, make the appropriate decisions, and plan the necessary experiences that will ultimately lead to quality reading instruction and quality reading programs for all children.

References

Allington, R.L. (2002). What I've learned about effective reading instruction from a decade of studying exemplary classroom teachers. *Phi Delta Kappan, 83*, 740–747.

Angrosino, M., & Mays de Perez, K. (2000). Rethinking observation: From method to context. In N. Denzin & Y. Lincoln (Eds.), *Handbook of qualitative research* (2nd ed., pp. 673–702). Thousand Oaks, CA: Sage.

Bean, R., Cassidy, J., Grumet, J., Shelton, D., & Wallis, S. (2002). What do reading specialists do? Results from a national survey. *The Reading Teacher, 55*, 736–744.

Bean, R., Swan, A., & Knaub, R. (2003). Reading specialists in schools with exemplary reading programs: Functional, versatile, and prepared. *The Reading Teacher, 56*, 446–454.

Fisher, D. (2001). "We're moving on up": Creating a school-wide literacy effort in an urban high school. *Journal of Adolescent & Adult Literacy, 45*, 92–101.

Foster, M. (1993). Educating for competence in community and culture: Exploring the views of exemplary African American teachers. *Urban Education, 27*, 370–394.

Greenleaf, C.L., Schoenbach, R., Cziko, C., & Mueller, F. (2001). Apprenticing adolescent readers to academic literacy. *Harvard Educational Review, 71*, 79–129.

Guskey, T. (2000). *Evaluating professional development.* Thousand Oaks, CA: Corwin Press.

Hess, F. (1999). *Spinning wheels: The politics of urban school reform.* Washington, DC: Brookings Institution Press.

Hull, G., & Schultz, K. (2002). *School's out! Bridging out-of-school literacies with classroom practice.* New York: Teachers College Press.

International Reading Association. (2000). *Teaching all children to read: The role of the reading specialist.* Newark, DE: Author.

Irvine, J. (1991). *Black students and school failure: Policies, practices, and prescriptions.* Westport, CT: Praeger.

Joyce, B., & Showers, B. (1988). *Student achievement through staff development.* New York: Longman.

Kohn, A. (1999). *The schools our children deserve: Moving beyond traditional classrooms and tougher standards.* Boston: Houghton Mifflin.

Ladson-Billings, G. (1995). Toward a theory of culturally relevant pedagogy. *American Education Research Journal, 32*, 465–491.

Lipman, P. (1995). "Bringing out the best in them": The contribution of culturally relevant teachers in educational reform. *Theory Into Practice, 34*, 202–208.

Louis, K., & Miles, M. (1990). *Improving the urban high school: What works and why.* New York: Teachers College Press.

Lyons, C., & Pinnell, G. (2001). *Systems for change in literacy education: A guide to professional development.* Portsmouth, NH: Heinemann.

Moje, E., Young, J., Readence, J., & Moore, D. (2000). Reinventing adolescent literacy for new times: Perennial and millennial issues. *Journal of Adolescent & Adult Literacy, 43*, 400–410.

Myers, W.D. (1996). *Slam.* New York: Scholastic.

National Commission on Teaching and America's Future. (1996). *What matters most: Teaching for America's future.* New York: Author.

National Institute of Child Health and Human Development. (2000). *Report of the National Reading Panel: Teaching children to read: An evidence-based assessment of the scientific literature on reading and its implications for reading instruction* (NIH Publication No. 00-4769). Washington, DC: U.S. Government Printing Office.

Pressley, M. (1998). *Reading instruction that works: The case for balanced teaching.* New York: Guilford.

Quatroche, D., Bean, R., & Hamilton, R. (2001). The role of reading specialists: A review of research. *The Reading Teacher, 55*, 282–294.

Schlechty, P. (1990). *Schools for the 21st century.* San Francisco: Jossey-Bass.

Snow, C., Burns, M.S., & Griffin, P. (Eds.). (1998). *Preventing reading difficulties in young children.* Washington, DC: National Academy Press.

Stallings, J.A. (1989, March). *School achievement effects and staff development: What are some critical factors?* Paper presented at the annual meeting of the American Educational Research Association, San Francisco, CA.

Wharton-McDonald, R., Pressley, M., Rankin, J., Mistretta, J., Yokoi, L., & Ettenberger, S. (1997). Effective primary-grades literacy instruction = balanced literacy instruction. *The Reading Teacher, 50*, 518–521.

Code-Switching Pedagogies and African American Student Voices: Acceptance and Resistance

Kirsten Dara Hill

An ongoing phenomenon in the affluent Oak Valley School District [all names are pseudonyms] is the situation of working class African American students who cross the boundary from Detroit in the quest for educational parity. The desire for African American families to enroll their children is not necessarily based on the desire to integrate, but on awareness that resources follow the suburbs (Irvine, 1990). The transition is not easy, for in spite of derogatory messages conveyed about Detroit public schools, many transfer students are disconnected from the friends and communities they left behind. They are no longer minority majority students. Instead of being surrounded by peers and teachers who likely understand their speech patterns and cultural norms, they are more likely misunderstood and mislabeled.

Kiki and Monet were African American focal students in Mr. Lehrer's seventh-grade classroom during the 2004–2005 school year. They began their schooling in Detroit but transferred to Oak Valley during their upper elementary school years because their parents were dissatisfied with Detroit's schools. Hence, Oak Valley, an affluent suburb, was perceived as providing better educational opportunities than its urban neighbor, similar to Wells and Crain's (1997) notion of African Americans who perceive that better educational offerings are in the suburbs. However, many teachers at Barrington

Middle School were unprepared to effectively teach the precipitous influx of African American transfer students and assumed that their language differences correlated to minimal skills and abilities. Students faced teachers who were uncertain about providing access to standard writing conventions in a nonthreatening manner. This was because teacher preparation, historically, has prepared teachers for work in white, middle class settings (Cochran-Smith, 2000).

Mr. Lehrer was my key informant at Barrington and represents the culturally responsive teachers in the district. I was referred to Mr. Lehrer by a colleague who taught at Barrington. She expressed concerns about significant demographic changes and subsequent teacher discomfort. However, she professed that he viewed changing demography as an opportunity to tap into students' cultural and linguistic resources and employ what Ladson-Billings (1995) termed *culturally relevant teaching*.

Mr. Lehrer's classroom was an equitable space for all of his students to recognize that everyone speaks a deviation from Standard English. He acknowledged their voices in their writing. At the same time, students used their home language as a scaffold to standard school literacy, recommended by experts in the field (Adger, Christian, & Taylor, 1999; Bakhtin, 1986; Delpit & Dowdy, 2002; Wheeler & Swords, 2006), in a manner that Delpit (1995)

Preparing Reading Professionals (second edition), edited by Rita M. Bean, Natalie Heisey, and Cathy M. Roller. © 2010 by the International Reading Association. Reprinted from Hill, K.D. (2009). Code-switching pedagogies and African American student voices: Acceptance and resistance. *Journal of Adolescent & Adult Literacy*, 53(2), 120–131. doi:10.1598/JAAL.53.2.3.

and Delpit and Dowdy (2002) would term *nonthreatening*.

Purpose

In this study, I examine how Mr. Lehrer developed a respect for diversity in language use. Because Monet and Kiki actively voiced pride and confidence in their identity and use of African American Vernacular English (AAVE), this article chronicles their voices and writing as they acknowledged distinctions between home and school literacies. Mr. Lehrer's use of students' home languages to explore their unofficial world while providing access to Standard English is examined. Nonstandard writing conventions through Mr. Lehrer's enactment of poetry writing, informal literature responses, and writer's notebook, are demonstrated. Standard writing conventions are illustrated through a letter to future self, formal literature response, and district writing assessment.

AAVE

AAVE can be differentiated from other dialects of English. Therefore, its systematic grammatical and phonological features define AAVE as a variety of the English language (Rickford & Rickford, 2000). An example of a grammatical feature includes dropping the third-person singular *s*, as in *she do* for *she does*. Another grammatical feature includes the zero copula, or absence of *is* or *are*. Phonological features include *r*-lessness, such as *stow* for *store* and the absence of -g, as in *goin'* for *going* (Rickford & Rickford, 2000, p. 151). To that end, Rickford and Rickford contended that AAVE is a systematic and rule-governed language. AAVE is recognized as the "primary language of African American students," (Rickford, 1999, p. 1) which should be taken into account in "facilitating mastery of English language skills" (p. 1). Rickford and Rickford (2000) claimed that AAVE features can be detected in the speech patterns of working class speakers in urban areas. Moreover, many speakers of AAVE do not employ its features all the time, nor do all African Americans speak AAVE. AAVE speakers are typically made to feel that they are the only ones who speak a deviation from Standard English (Wolfram, 1999).

Code-Switching Pedagogies

Code-switching pedagogies call for employing students' home language to facilitate appropriate nonstandard and standard contexts for writing and speaking (Adger et al., 1999; Bakhtin, 1986; Delpit & Dowdy, 2002; Wheeler & Swords, 2006). Traditionally, teachers have regarded Standard English as correct while nonstandard features are deemed as errors that warrant correction. Carrie Secret, a noted teacher in Oakland, California, maintained a corrective approach until recognizing that students were more responsive upon being encouraged to translate the structure of AAVE in a first draft to Standard English for the final draft (Miner, 1997). Rather than regard AAVE features as incorrect, code-switching pedagogies require that teachers make a transition from the paradigm of correction to helping students use language patterns for appropriate settings (Baker, 2002; Wheeler & Swords, 2006). Teachers must be knowledgeable of AAVE features (Delpit, 1997) to model corresponding rule-governed aspects of AAVE and Standard English (Baker, 2002; Wheeler & Swords, 2006).

To illustrate, Wheeler and Swords (2006) pointed out the rule, owner + owned = possession, a rule-governed aspect of AAVE. In Standard English, the corresponding rule is owner's + owned = possession. The AAVE feature *friend house*, for instance, corresponds with the Standard English feature *friend's house*. Rather than assume that students do not understand possession, teachers must juxtapose grammatical differences side by side and help students determine the appropriate context for use (Wheeler & Swords, 2006). When writing a nonstandard narrative, for example, *friend house* would be acceptable. *Friend's house* would be appropriate for a formal essay or standardized test.

Code-switching pedagogies align with standards devised by the International Reading Association and National Council of Teachers of English (1996) and embed developing an understanding of, and respect for, diversity in language use, patterns, and dialects. Teachers in Michigan are required to implement standards from Grade Level Content Expectations (www.mich.gov) to inform instructional decisions. Nonstandard conventions are embedded in appropriating voice and a personal style by exhibiting individuality to enhance the written message.

In contrast, local and national standards posit that standard writing conventions embody standard grammar and usage. Fecho, Davis, and Moore's (2006) work with African American adolescents prompted researchers to question traditional grammar practices that were threatening in nature, because of conflicts surrounding what they knew about students' lives and perceptions that their use of AAVE was regarded as wrong. Researchers determined that explicit grammar instruction yielded minimal results, which prompted them to facilitate student analysis of mainstream and AAVE language features in a nonthreatening manner. Similarly, Baker (2002), a high school English teacher, prompted her students to study the features of how they speak with family and friends. Eventually, students became fascinated with what she terms *triangulation*, in which they compared home language features with academic and professional English.

Writers' Workshop

The workshop approach provides opportunities to enact the writing process, in which students participate in prewriting and drafting (Atwell & Newkirk, 1987; Calkins, 1994). Teacher and peer conferring supports students toward standard conventions in a final draft. Students are provided a scaffold from nonstandard to standard conventions of writing and speaking and supported in distinguishing between corresponding nonstandard and Standard English features (Baker, 2002; Wheeler & Swords, 2006).

In spite of teachers' intentions to provide code-switching pedagogies within the frame of the workshop approach, Fecho et al. (2006) revealed the potential for students to resist switching to the culture of power for any reason. Resistance is embedded in sensing their identity and home language have been compromised, as a result of code switching to standard word choices that do not accurately depict how they speak.

Methodology

Findings in this article are grounded in integrated and excerpt style (Emerson, Fretz, & Shaw, 1995). Data reduction was guided by salient themes that emerged through interpretation of units of analysis. Integrated units of analysis include in-the-moment field notes and student writing samples. Excerpted units of analysis include transcribed teacher and student interviews.

Research Site and Participants

Data were based on observations in a seventh-grade English classroom at Barrington Middle School in an affluent Detroit suburb. The class enrolled 29 students. Twenty-one students were European American, 5 were African American, 1 was Asian American, 1 was French, and 1 was Ethiopian. There were 15 girls and 14 boys. The participants were the most racially and ethnically diverse class of Mr. Lehrer's career. At the same time, the composition corresponded with a typical classroom at Barrington. I selected Monet and Kiki as focal students because they represented Detroit students entering Oak Valley for educational parity. In addition, they were selected because they desired to preserve their Detroit identity and were vocal about preserving their voices in their writing.

Data Collection and Analysis

The class was observed during one 46-minute period, three to five days per week over a five-month period from February to June 2005. The findings revealed in this article are situated in a broader dissertation and ethnographic case study, which emphasized the nature of literature-based instruction and writing practices in Mr. Lehrer's classroom. For the purpose of this article, data were gathered in an effort to demonstrate the nature of writing pedagogy that was conducive to code-switching pedagogies. Therefore, I focused on data which drew from Monet and Kiki's home language to support standard and nonstandard writing conventions.

From my field note analysis, I devised assertions that were guided by Mr. Lehrer's instructional decisions during the writing process. In addition, I paid attention to the manner in which Kiki and Monet responded to those decisions.

Teacher interview excerpts were analyzed and coded into theoretical memos. Salient themes were devised and coded into assertions. I made decisions about assertions and data reduction based on Mr. Lehrer's attentiveness to distinguishing between standard and nonstandard writing conventions and attention to language varieties. Student interview excerpts rendered salient themes that were coded into assertions. While analyzing interview data, I sought to identify what I perceived to be compelling responses regarding distinguishing between standard and nonstandard writing conventions.

Monet and Kiki's written artifacts were integrated to support assertions. Data reduction was determined by writing, which illustrated distinctions and transitions between standard and nonstandard writing conventions. To account for emic perspectives, writing conventions were interpreted in relation to corresponding rule-governed language features. Reference to and analysis of student writing samples that illustrate AAVE features, along with individual style and voice, are termed nonstandard. Integrated writing samples include illustrations of how Mr. Lehrer might have corrected, had he called for standard conventions. In addition, writing samples that focus on standard grammatical usage in the context of seventh-grade expectations are termed standard.

I approached the data with the following research questions: What is the nature of writing practices that facilitate standard and nonstandard writing conventions? How are these opportunities linked to student identity? How do focal students respond to these opportunities?

Nonstandard Writing Conventions

To establish a foundation for valuing nonstandard writing conventions, Mr. Lehrer reported in the following interview excerpt that he began the school year by reading aloud *Nightjohn* (Paulsen, 1993) to approve the notion of voice in the African American linguistic tradition and accurately depict the way a character speaks:

Mr. Lehrer: It comes from literature, in *Nightjohn*, the narrator Sarny has an uneducated way of telling the story with her terms. Right away they notice that and obviously I'm standing up there reading that and that must be some sort of stamp of approval.

Author: Right. You do give a stamp of approval, don't you?

Mr. Lehrer: You know, if you're a language artist, which is to say writer, you use languages in a natural way of conveying the way someone would speak.

Therefore, the stamp of approval and notion of language artist suggests that he sustained a comfort level for students to use nonstandard contexts for writing. Delineating features from literature provided a space for students to determine authentic use of voice, in a manner similar to Fecho et al. (2006) who facilitated critical analysis of AAVE features in literature with students.

During the onset of the study, students appropriated nonstandard conventions during poetry writing practices. According to integrated field notes, Mr. Lehrer modeled and listed actions that could become poems inspired by

Atwell (2002), including playing sports, styling hair, and playing music. He directed students to devise lists as a foundation for their own poem. Kiki's list included a death in the family and Monet's included a surprise party.

After designated time to construct lists, Mr. Lehrer displayed and read aloud poems written by students from Atwell's (2002) work and discussed features to model free-verse poetry. His students were attentive to word choices that conveyed personal experiences and voice.

Kiki employed nonstandard conventions to express sadness surrounding her cousin who died (see Figure 1):

> We were close friends also cousins did everything for one another...But now I got to live and make it somehow...I know I got to move on....

Kiki spoke strongly about preserving her voice in her writing, which is intimately connected with her family. Such writing opportunities allowed her to build on her cultural and linguistic strengths. Her use of "I got" illustrates the deletion of the word *have*, which Rickford and Rickford (2000) noted is a grammatical feature of AAVE. Her description of being friends and cousins has a rhythmic quality that displays her social world and fondness for rap music. Requiring standard conventions would have rendered the absence of Kiki's voice: "We were close friends and cousins and did everything for each other. Now I have got to live and make it somehow. I know I have got to move on....."

The following excerpts in Monet's poem about a surprise party for her uncle illustrate a strong sense of voice (see Figure 2):

> My uncle says "Where the kids at." She says "They busy."... She says "Whateva, but how did you do at the casino?

The examples that represent her relatives speaking naturally provide an accurate depiction of how they would speak. To write their voices in Standard English is an inaccurate depiction and diminishes who they are. Monet's appropriation of voices in her family is an example of acknowledging strength in cultural linguistic tradition. A phonological AAVE

**Figure 1
Kiki's Poem in Nonstandard Conventions**

The same with what she's been

Through.

Is her heart still to mine,

I want to cry sometimes.

I miss you

Leaving Elementary that's when she left me

We were close friends also cousins did everything for one

Another

Now she's gone and I'm lost without her here

Now

But I now I got to live and make it somehow

Now I'm sitting here thinking about her

And,

The days we used to share

It's driving me crazy I don't know what to do

And,

I want her here

I want to let her know that it's killing

Me

I know I got to move on and realize that she is gone.

feature can be detected in the presence of *r*-lessness (Rickford & Rickford, 2000), upon writing "whateva." In addition, a grammatical AAVE feature of the zero copula includes the absence of the verb *are* (Rickford & Rickford, 2000) upon writing "they busy." If standard conventions were required, it would have read, "My uncle says, 'Where are the kids?' My aunt says, 'They are busy.' She says, 'Whatever, but how did you do at the casino?'"

Students also employed nonstandard conventions during informal literature-based writing responses. Particularly salient were informal jottings about multicultural text set novels they were reading surrounding the theme prejudice. Monet identified prejudice in *Dragonwings* (Yep, 1981), in which written

**Figure 2
Monet's Poem in Nonstandard
Conventions**

We heard my uncle close his car door.

"When I say, 'Hey Jerry' And get him

down in the basement and ask,

'How'd you do at the casino last night?'

Everybody jump out and yell, 'surprise!!!'

My auntie, Kendal

wispers to us.

Knock, Knock, my uncle comes down stairs

my uncle says, "Where the kids At."

She says "They busy." He said,

"What is A two year old And a month

old 'busy' doing.

She says," Whateva, but how did you

do at the casino?"

Uncle tried to say good

but was left out about as fast as an alkaselter

when it drops into water

ideas were influenced by her peer-led discussion group (see Figure 3):

> The Chinese thought the white was bad and Moon Shadow Lee has killed people...Whites were mean to the Chinese and thought they were weird.

Because the assignment emphasized ideas conveyed by Monet's discussion group and not explicitly grammar, Monet's writing illustrates standard and nonstandard use of *was/were*. However, her use of AAVE features was not as prevalent as in her poem that invited her voice. A grammatical AAVE feature is detected in her use of "white was" (Rickford & Rickford, 2000). For a standard context, she would have jotted "whites were."

Writer's notebook was a daily enactment where students were required to write a half page daily. Students wrote about self-selected topics surrounding their daily experiences and social worlds. Integrated writing samples were not included in this article because Mr. Lehrer collected notebooks periodically and redistributed them very quickly, to ensure continued daily writing. However, the enactment is necessary to note, to illustrate an ongoing use of nonstandard writing conventions. Ongoing practice and integrated writing samples correspond with local and national standards to appropriate voice and style.

Monet and Kiki affirmed their awareness of writing nonstandard conventions during an interview:

Author: Monet, when you asked Mr. Lehrer if you could use your voice, he said of course you can, without being marked down.

Monet: Because I did spell words how I would say 'em, and, like *aight* (alright),

Kiki: *Y'all!*

Monet: Stuff like that, and y'all, because we don't talk like, yeah, you guys are, we don't talk like that, so it's just how I was raised and where I came from, they talk like that.

Kiki: It's not basically street talk.

Monet: It's how we were raised.

Author: And that's very important, that Mr. Lehrer sees that as important too, because that's your voice. If you read Maya Angelou, or even Mildred Taylor, there's so much of that rich language, even Joyce Hansen. It's really an important technique of writing.

Monet: Because he said it was important to write about us, and it would have been hard to write about me talking in someone else's voice.

My initial question to Monet was prompted by my observation during class when she asked Mr. Lehrer if she would be marked down for using her voice during a nonstandard writing opportunity. Given Mr. Lehrer's ongoing acceptance of students employing their voices, it appears odd that she would ask such a question. However, considering the broader context

Figure 3
Monet's Informal Literature-Based Writing Response

BIG QUESTIONS ABOUT THE BOOK

- **PREJUDICE:** How is prejudice part of the story?
  - ○ Gather examples from the story:
    - ▪ Who is showing prejudice and towards whom? *and towar...*
    - ▪ How is that prejudice wrong and not constructive?

Prejudice is a part of my story in many ways some ways are the Chinese thought the white was bad and moon Shadow Lee has killed people and Chinese people say white hurt them./whites were mmn to chinese and thought they were wierd.

of schooling that is typically not accepting of language varieties, Monet's question makes sense.

The following excerpt illustrates Kiki's voice, who exhibited contradictory emotions of not wanting to change her manner of speaking to fit in, but desired to be accepted by her peers:

Kiki: I've been going through a lot of ups and downs because people here say that oh my god, look at how ghetto she is.

Author: To you? Or you hear them saying it about you?

Kiki: It really doesn't matter, because like, I said, this is me. This year I started to fit in more with the white people because I start talking, like whew, and they start to say some of the stuff I say, like you would hear them say it, and it made me feel good, looking at them, that they might say like the words I use. Last year I was just so into getting into everybody but this year I think like who I want to be.

In this interview excerpt, Kiki voiced the importance of preserving her identity through her home language among her peers at Barrington. She spoke AAVE and was referring to her counterparts who spoke European American Vernacular English. Although both forms are deviations from Standard English, Kiki's reality was that the language she brought to school, as has been historically constructed by the dominant culture, was perceived by many of her teachers and peers as deficient.

Interview excerpts reveal that Monet and Kiki were openly aware of the distinctions between standard and nonstandard conventions of writing and speaking, along with the perception of their home language as street talk in the dominant culture and in school. Both girls grappled with their identity and knew that standard writing conventions were skills they needed. Similar to adolescents cited by Fecho et al. (2006) it meant accepting or rejecting Standard English and compromising their identity upon switching writing conventions to the culture of power.

Standard Writing Conventions

To facilitate standard conventions, Mr. Lehrer maintained an expectation of what he called the "errorless draft," which required students to respond to his written feedback in their final draft and to resubmit the attached rough draft so that he could detect that students responded to feedback. The expectation for writing standard conventions and appropriating skills in meaningful contexts reifies Delpit's (1995) assertion that intervention is needed to write in standard contexts. Scaffolding from students' home language to inform standard writing was an enactment of code-switching pedagogies (Baker, 2002; Bakhtin, 1986; Delpit, 1995; Wheeler & Swords, 2006). Whenever possible, he interacted with students to clarify feedback. Therefore, he actively sustained awareness of standard writing and skills in meaningful contexts, aligned with grammar and usage embedded in local and national standards.

During a formal interview, Mr. Lehrer acknowledged the importance of sustaining skills in meaningful contexts, as an integral facet of standard acquisition and usage:

Mr. Lehrer: Yeah, sure, because that's the basis of the class. I mean, really, this kind of class revolves around the idea that those skills exist...within the context of important language usage. So if you're using language in an important way, which is to say you're using it to express meaning.

Author: True, so, you put skills in meaningful contexts, not finding the subject and the predicate.

Mr. Lehrer: Even though occasionally I will do that if I really want to mention some things that they don't have, I think it's such a vacuum.

Author: So that would make you a little less approachable.

Mr. Lehrer: I think so, I think they know as the year goes on that I care about that stuff a lot. I really do. I demonstrate that when I get their papers and mark them up and when I talk to them about their writing, but it would have to be in a meaningful context.

This excerpt reveals that Mr. Lehrer's written comments were intended to provide skills in meaningful, nonthreatening contexts. He considered ongoing written feedback an impetus to talk to students about their writing in an effort for them to acquire standard conventions. Mr. Lehrer determined his enactment of providing skills instruction and linking Standard English with home language in the context of their writing was more effective than isolated grammar worksheets. In addition, he was more approachable to his students.

Providing written feedback for 137 students across all of Mr. Lehrer's class sections was time consuming and posed constraints for meeting each student personally to address his comments. However, each student was provided with at least written feedback and opportunities to confer with a peer. He expected them to assume responsibility and respond to written feedback until the draft was errorless.

The "Letter to Future Self" was a writing assignment that employed standard writing conventions. Students wrote a letter to their senior self graduating from high school. Student letters would be mailed to them near the end of their senior year of high school.

The guidelines dictated the letter genre. Each paragraph manifested topics that were appropriate to the student during their seventh-grade year, including physical appearance, things that have happened this school year, and hopes and dreams for the future. Rough drafts included Mr. Lehrer's feedback for students to apply to the final edited version.

Kiki wrote about her physical appearance (see Figure 4):

> Normally you see me wearing jeans, button-ups, skirts, and a lot of t-shirts. My hair is like a silky black with a tint of brown.

Figure 4
Kiki's Letter to Future Self

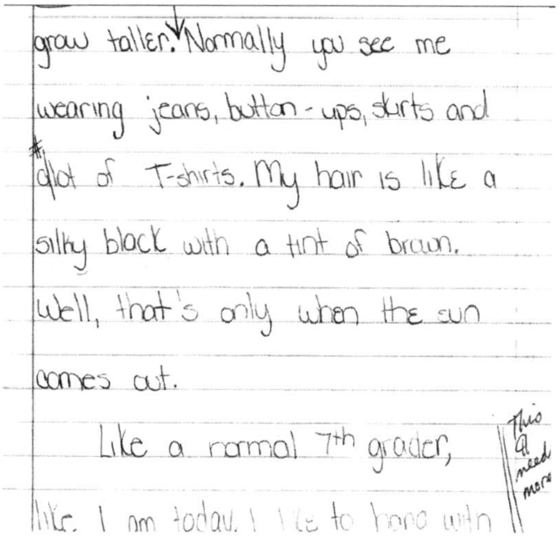
grow taller. Normally you see me wearing jeans, button-ups, skirts and alot of T-shirts. My hair is like a silky black with a tint of brown. Well, that's only when the sun comes out.

Like a normal 7th grader, like I am today. I like to hang with

This ¶ need more

Mr. Lehrer's feedback did not embody scaffolding toward Standard English, indicating Kiki's awareness of writing standard conventions for a standard context. In contrast with her poem, no AAVE features are detected in this sample. Comments indicated spelling clarification and including more detail in another paragraph. Kiki appropriated standard conventions in her writing under the directive to employ them. Her acceptance of Standard English is significant because she resisted Mr. Lehrer's feedback earlier in the study.

To illustrate, one month prior, Kiki was confrontational about preserving her nonstandard conventions in a formal essay paying tribute to her mother, similar to resistant students cited by Fecho et al. (2006). During that time, she was extremely vocal upon questioning Mr. Lehrer about his written feedback. According to integrated field notes, he suggested she write "My mother has taken care of me" instead of "My mother have taken care of me." Her use of "have" corresponds with what Rickford and Rickford (2000) suggested is a grammatical feature of AAVE. She reasoned that her voice would be compromised if she changed the wording. According to field note jottings, she bellowed,

> Mr. Lehrer, this is bold! You put down the way you wanted me to write, not the way I want to write it, in my own words!

Because Mr. Lehrer was conferring with another student, I intervened and informed her that she was writing in a standard context unlike her aforementioned poem. We discussed the importance of distinguishing between standard and nonstandard writing contexts, and that there are contexts where we give up a part of ourselves when we write for school. She seemed to understand more fully when I expressed that I give up a part of myself when I write for academic purposes. Hence, Kiki's letter illustrates that she used standard conventions on her own, which suggests her awareness of distinguishing between appropriate contexts for writing.

To express hopes and dreams for the future, Monet wrote the following (see Figure 5):

> My hopes and dreams for the future are to be a famous singer, and if that doesn't work I want to be a pediatrician. When I finish college, I want to make good money and be a very rich person.

Mr. Lehrer noted spelling errors and punctuation to help Monet prepare for her final draft. In contrast with her poem and reading response, Monet's draft does not indicate evidence of AAVE features. This illustrates her awareness of writing standard conventions for a standard context.

Upon completing *Dragonwings* (Yep, 1981), Monet wrote a final essay about prejudice in her book. The following illustrates her standard use of *was* and *were* (see Figure 6):

> The Chinese automatically thought that the white people were mean and that's racist. The white people were also racist to the Chinese people because they were mean to them....

Figure 5
Monet's Letter to Future Self

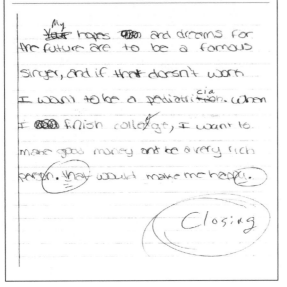

My hopes and dreams for the future are to be a famous singer, and if that doesn't work I want to be a pediatrician. When I finish college, I want to make good money and be a very rich person. That would make me happy.

Closing

Figure 6
Monet's Formal Essay

Dragonwings   May 24, 2008

In this book Dragonwings, there was racism. There was racism towards white people by the tang people (chinese people) and the white people had confrontations against each other. The chinese people automatically thought that the white people were mean and that's racist. The white people were also racist to the chinese people because they were mean to them and they showed that in many ways. As

Monet's writing reflects her response to Mr. Lehrer's feedback, in which he scaffolded the appropriate conventions for *was* and *were*. Her final draft does not indicate evidence of AAVE features. It was intended to be written in Standard English and presents a transition from her informal jottings one month prior.

Students took a district writing exam where they selected from three writing prompts and employed standard conventions. However, its impromptu nature allowed for students' editing marks. They drafted two writing samples and submitted the determined best draft to the district for scoring purposes. Kiki selected "Fitting in," a prompt that was personal in nature (see Figure 7):

> I'm still tryin to fit in with the school because really I'm still a girl from the ghetto.

Mr. Lehrer brought Kiki's writing test to my attention because he sensed that she responded sincerely to the writing prompt. In a formal setting, Kiki selected a topic that coincided with her experiences as an African American student in a suburban context. The majority of this unassisted writing sample indicates Kiki's awareness of standard conventions. For example, *I* consistently corresponds with *I'm*, in contrast to her use of *I* with the absence of *have* from her poem. However, her use of "tryin to fit in...I'm still a girl from the ghetto" presents an example of resisting the dominant discourse. She attempted to preserve a semblance of her voice in a context where preserving her sense of self compromised fitting in, a manner of resisting switching to the culture of power for any reason (Fecho et al., 2006). *Tryin* illustrates the absence of *-g*, a phonological AAVE feature (Rickford & Rickford, 2000).

Although Mr. Lehrer regarded Kiki's writing as a strong depiction of her experience, he submitted her other writing sample upon deciding it was more appropriate for outside readers. Therefore, Kiki's writing was acceptable to Mr. Lehrer, but for formal testing he sensed that her word choices, particularly *ghetto*, might displease the readers. He further reasoned the other draft would earn a higher score. Emically, standard language usage was acceptable for standardized testing purposes.

During an interview, Kiki and Monet described their awareness of writing Standard English and compromising their voice:

Author: So when you're in a classroom and when you're writing you know how to write formal and…

Monet: Right, I write formal.

Kiki: But it's different for me because when we moved over here my mother, my sister, my brother they were all changed, but it's hard for me.

Monet: I didn't change at all.

Kiki: Like my whole family changed when we moved over here.

Monet: I won't change my way of speaking. I would use better words, but I wouldn't try to change.

This excerpt illustrates not wanting to change who they were or how they spoke for anyone, similar to adolescents cited by Fecho et al. (2006), who resisted the culture of power for any reason. At the same time, they were aware of standard writing contexts in school. As former Detroit residents, they were deeply connected with their Detroit identity. They wanted to be understood and preserve their voices, not only for speaking purposes but also in writing for school contexts. However, writing samples and integrated field notes indicate that Kiki was more resistant to the culture of power than Monet, who was more accepting of code switching for appropriate contexts.

Conclusion

Mr. Lehrer facilitated a classroom community that nurtured students' awareness of language varieties from the onset of the school year. The ongoing use of code-switching pedagogies presented access to Standard English. Because they were presented with the same writing and revision opportunities, all students gained access to the dominant discourse, not just the African American students from Detroit. They drew from their home language to inform their voices in nonstandard writing contexts, and in

Figure 7
Kiki's District Writing Exam

I'm still tryin to fit in with the school Because really I'm still a girl from the ghetto. The struggle and hard times. I don't know if I will be fine. But I don't care what people say because this is me. My mother, sister and brother changed when we moved out here. But I'm still the same.

some instances they negotiated their voices in standard contexts. Monet and Kiki represented Detroit students who wrote successfully upon accessing their literate identity and culture of the home. At the same time, they were aware of standard writing contexts that required them to compromise themselves. Monet and Kiki were aware that different language forms were appropriate in different contexts.

Mr. Lehrer provided feedback to scaffold from home language to standard writing conventions within the frame of the workshop approach. Monet was responsive to feedback, but there were instances in which Kiki resisted compromising her voice. He simultaneously provided low-stakes opportunities to write in nonstandard contexts. Monet and Kiki's writing and interview excerpts illustrate their comfort level to write nonstandard conventions to convey their voices.

This occurred in a climate of uncertainty surrounding an unexpected influx of Detroit students. Mr. Lehrer's practices were enacted by few teachers, but his pedagogical decisions were embedded in state and national curriculum standards. Data suggest that students were empowered upon preserving their voice without the threat of correction while also employing home language as a foundation for standard conventions. Current conditions in the overall context of schooling minimize the linguistic aptitude students bring to the classroom.

Final Thoughts and Instructional Recommendations

The case of Mr. Lehrer presents an example of teaching emically at the local level in everyday practice within a larger structure that resists change (Erickson, 1986). For teachers in everyday practice, the following are recommendations for AAVE speakers and speakers of other varieties of English:

- Never tell students that home language features are wrong and Standard English features are right.

- Balance nonstandard and standard contexts for writing. Teachers must facilitate distinctions and support students as they negotiate appropriate contexts for employing language features.

- Inform student that everyone speaks nonstandard English. Delpit (1997) recommended exploring additional forms of English to compare and contrast varying ways and contexts in which people speak, including characters from different cultural groups on television or in literature.

- Instill motivation by exploring varying ways students express common ideas before emphasizing grammar rules (Baker, 2002). Once students are interested, teachers should make the transition to corresponding rules for academic and professional contexts.

- Provide written feedback during standard writing contexts and confer with students to scaffold from home language to Standard English features. Require students to submit the final draft with the initial draft to document changes.

- Model corresponding grammar features in home language and Standard English (Wheeler & Swords, 2006). Although not demonstrated by Mr. Lehrer, because of his preference to address conventions in the context of actual writing, this strategy supports applying rule-governed features to appropriate contexts. *Code-Switching: Teaching Standard English in Urban Classrooms* (Wheeler & Swords, 2006) is a unique teacher resource that illustrates corresponding AAVE and Standard English features. Although intended for elementary grades, the resource is applicable to middle school.

Ultimately, teachers must provide nonthreatening spaces for negotiating and applying nonstandard and Standard English and recognize that home language is linked to student identity (Delpit, 1995, 1997; Fecho et al., 2006). Standard English should be a choice, not an imposition (Baker, 2002). Teachers are responsible for providing awareness of language features and students will inevitably decide what they want to say in standard and nonstandard contexts.

References

Adger, C.T., Christian, D., & Taylor, O. (1999). *Making the connection. Language and academic achievement among African-American students.* Washington, DC: Center for Applied Linguistics.

Atwell, N. (2002). *Lessons that change writers.* Portsmouth, NH: Heinemann.

Atwell, N., & Newkirk, T. (1987). *Understanding writing: Ways of observing, learning, and teaching* (2nd ed.). Portsmouth, NH: Heinemann.

Baker, J. (2002). Triangualism. In L.D. Delpit & J.K. Dowdy (Eds.), *The skin that we speak. Thoughts and language and culture in the classroom* (pp. 49–62). New York: The New Press.

Bakhtin, M. (1986). *Speech genres and other late essays.* Austin: University of Texas Press.

Calkins, L.M. (1994). *The art of teaching writing* (New ed.). Portsmouth, NH: Heinemann.

Cochran-Smith, M. (2000). Blind vision: Unlearning racism in teacher education. *Harvard Educational Review, 70*(2), 157–190.

Delpit, L.D. (1995). *Other people's children: Cultural conflict in the classroom.* New York: The New Press.

Delpit, L.D. (1997). Ebonics and culturally responsive instruction. *Rethinking Schools Online, 12*(1). Retrieved June 1, 2008, from www.rethinkingschools.org/archive/12_01/ebdelpit.shtml

Delpit, L.D., & Dowdy, J.K. (2002). *The skin that we speak: Thoughts on language and culture in the classroom.* New York: The New Press.

Emerson, R.M., Fretz, R.I., & Shaw, L.L. (1995). *Writing ethnographic fieldnotes.* Chicago: The University of Chicago Press.

Erickson, F. (1986). *Teacher's practical ways of seeing and making sense.* East Lansing: Institute for Research on Teaching, Michigan State University.

Fecho, B., Davis, B., & Moore, R. (2006). Exploring race, language, and culture in critical literacy classrooms. In D.E. Alvermann, K.A. Hinchman, D.W. Moore, S.F. Phelps, & D.R. Waff (Eds.), *Reconceptualizing the literacies in adolescents' lives* (2nd ed., pp. 187–204). Mahwah, NJ: Erlbaum.

International Reading Association & National Council of Teachers of English. (1996). *Standards for the English language arts.* Newark, DE; Urbana, IL: Authors.

Irvine, J.J. (1990, April). *Black parents' perceptions of their children's desegregated school experiences.* Paper presented at the annual meeting of the American Educational Research Association, Boston, MA.

Ladson-Billings, G. (1995). Toward a theory of culturally relevant pedagogy. *American Educational Research Journal, 32*(3), 465–491.

Miner, B. (1997). Embracing Ebonics and teaching Standard English: An interview with Oakland teacher Carrie Secret. *Rethinking Schools Online, 12*(1). Retrieved June 1, 2008, from www.rethinkingschools.org/archive/12_01/ebsecret.shtml

Rickford, J.R. (1999). Language diversity and academic achievement in the education of African American students—An overview of the issues. In C.T. Adger, D. Christian, & O. Taylor (Eds.), *Making the connection: Language and academic achievement among African American students* (pp. 1–30). Washington, DC: Center for Applied Linguistics.

Rickford, J.R., & Rickford, R.J. (2000). *Spoken soul: The story of black English.* New York: Wiley.

Wells, A.S., & Crain, R.L. (1997). *Stepping over the color line. African-American students in white suburban schools.* New Haven, CT: Yale University Press.

Wheeler, R.S., & Swords, R. (2006). *Code-switching: Teaching Standard English in urban classrooms.* Urbana, IL: National Council of Teachers of English.

Wolfram, W. (1999). Repercussions from the Oakland Ebonics controversy—The critical role of dialect awareness programs. In C.T. Adger, D. Christian, & O. Taylor (Eds.), *Making the connection: Language and academic achievement among African American students* (pp. 61–80). Washington, DC: Center for Applied Linguistics.

Literature Cited

Paulsen, G. (1993). *Nightjohn*. New York: Bantam Doubleday Dell.

Yep, L. (1981). *Dragonwings*. New York: HarperTrophy.

Literate Environment

The Literate Environment Standard recognizes the need for integration of the information and skills identified in the first four standards to develop reading instruction that meets the needs of all learners. A literate environment comprises many instructional facets including physical, social, and motivational; reading professionals must know how to orchestrate these facets in ways that ensure effective instruction for all students. Standard 5 and its elements follow:

Standard 5. Literate Environment. Candidates create a literate environment that fosters reading and writing by integrating foundational knowledge, instructional practices, approaches and methods, curriculum materials, and the appropriate use of assessments. As a result, candidates

- **Element 5.1 Design the physical environment to optimize students' use of traditional print, digital, and online resources in reading and writing instruction.**

- **Element 5.2 Design a social environment that is low risk and includes choice, motivation, and scaffolded support to optimize students' opportunities for learning to read and write.**

- **Element 5.3 Use routines to support reading and writing instruction (e.g., time allocation, transitions from one activity to another, discussions, and peer feedback).**

- **Element 5.4 Use a variety of classroom configurations (i.e., whole class, small group, and individual) to differentiate instruction.**

Part 5 includes three journal articles that may be helpful in understanding the substance of the standard and its elements. These pieces are briefly described here.

The Casey (2008) article provides a useful instantiation of Standard 5 and all four of its elements. She describes a seventh grade teacher's use of learning clubs to motivate struggling students to engage in literacy events and foster literacy development. This teacher motivates the struggling students in this heterogeneous class toward success by balancing a strong awareness of content, context, discourse, and pedagogy. The findings suggest that learning clubs offer a useful framework for supporting adolescents who struggle with literacy and offer potential for work with all students across

Preparing Reading Professionals (second edition), edited by Rita M. Bean, Natalie Heisey, and Cathy M. Roller. © 2010 by the International Reading Association.

the content areas. In the article, Casey provides a description of learning clubs, which includes the physical and social environments, the use of routines and the way the teacher uses grouping configurations to differentiate instruction.

Woodward and Talbert-Johnson (2009) address issues related to providing adequate individual instruction, particularly for struggling readers. Classroom teachers and reading specialists have attempted to determine the most effective ways of working with struggling readers. Early intervention and quality instruction are the keys to assisting these struggling readers; however, determining how and where intervention-based instruction should occur is still a concern. The article describes a number of different approaches such as separate instruction, inclusion, and a combination of both. Struggling readers need extra time and specialized attention to achieve; however, educators and administrators continue to discuss whether this intervention should occur through separated instruction with small-group instruction, or whether students should be supported by specialists alongside classroom teachers in a whole-group setting. The article is useful in addressing all four of the elements of Standard 5.

Pflaum and Bishop (2004) focus specifically on motivating adolescent readers based on drawings and interviews with middle school students. This article presents the results of qualitative research into how middle school students experience school reading. Although the article contains information related to all four elements, it is particularly useful for understanding Element 5.2. Students from grades 4 through 8 from four different schools were asked individually to draw and then to talk about specific times of their choice when they were and were not engaged in learning. The combined method of drawing and talk encouraged deep reflection on the part of the students. The results indicated why students generally found independent, silent reading to be motivating and engaging and offered evidence that, for the most part, students disliked oral reading, not only because of qualms about audience but also because it hindered their comprehension.

Further Reading

Coppola, J., & Primas, E.V. (Eds.). (2009). *One classroom, many learners: Best literacy practices for today's multilingual classrooms.* Newark, DE: International Reading Association.

Guth, N.D., & Pettengill, S.S. (2005). *Leading a successful reading program: Administrators and reading specialists working together to make it happen.* Newark, DE: International Reading Association.

Kletzien, S.B., & Dreher, M.J. (2004). *Informational text in K–3 classrooms: Helping children read and write.* Newark, DE: International Reading Association.

McCormack, R.L., & Paratore, J.R. (Eds.). (2003). *After early intervention, then what? Teaching struggling readers in grades 3 and beyond.* Newark, DE: International Reading Association.

Parris, S.R., Fisher, D., & Headley, K. (Eds.). (2009). *Adolescent literacy, field tested: Effective solutions for every classroom.* Newark, DE: International Reading Association.

Richards, J.C., & Lassonde, C.A. (Eds.). (2009). *Literacy tutoring that works: A look at successful in-school, after-school, and summer programs.* Newark, DE: International Reading Association.

Questions for Reflection and Discussion

- How does Casey incorporate the elements of Standard 5 into learning clubs?

- Why is the social environment crucial for developing the motivation to read?

- Why are classroom routines important to learning to read? How can routines be established that also provide opportunities for student choice?

- How can classroom configurations contribute to individualizing instruction? In what ways do they help teachers establish a positive social environment?

Engaging the Disengaged: Using Learning Clubs to Motivate Struggling Adolescent Readers and Writers

Heather K. Casey

As Sharon's 19 seventh-grade students filter into class, a warm May breeze permeates room 212, which has housed books and students for nearly a hundred years (all teacher, student, and school names used are pseudonyms). The stubborn window in the corner, held up by a ruler and a stack of old textbooks, slams shut as the students open their books. "Alright," Sharon announces, "Let's begin." With that, the students reposition and reshuffle themselves until rows of desks have become five circles of learning, and the conversations around texts begin.

Frank Smith (1988) extends an invitation to the literacy club. Nancie Atwell (1998) invites students to the dining room table. Harvey Daniels (2002) organizes this as book clubs. All are interested in engaging students in active reading and writing events, recognizing that collaborative learning offers opportunities to work within students' abilities, engage learning, and provide access to literacy materials and events. In Sharon's class, 6 of the 19 students are eligible for basic skills literacy support. Often, it is during this group instruction time that these students would be pulled out for explicit instruction. According to Sharon, this is the time when these students need to be present the most. Sharon reflects on how her teaching has grown to place learning clubs as central.

> I had a kid who said to me finally, "I can't read." And I said, "But you waited this long to admit it to yourself?" And so I said, "Well, let's see what we can do." We started Readers' Workshop after school where they could come and bring books that they wanted to share. And we started out with sharing. And I've been a collector of children's books for years, so I have a lot of Steven Kellogg and Mercer Mayer, and I'd bring them, and they'd say, "Those are your favorite books?" I'd say, "Absolutely, look at the story." We'd talk about that, and they would come. We had it two or three times a week. They would come after school for an hour, and we'd sit and read, and they'd share what they had read. Bring your favorite book to share and tell us why, and this kind of stuff and for the first time I saw kids who couldn't or didn't read, reading. Next year, it was a main part of our class.

With this conversation, Sharon and I begin our work together. Sharon has been teaching language arts for 34 years in an inner-city school and is increasingly frustrated by her middle school students' lack of interest in literacy events. Sharon confirms what research suggests: Untangling the struggling adolescent learners' frustrations with reading and writing is a complex process of understanding ability, considering engagement, and providing access to appropriate materials (Biancarosa & Snow, 2004; Blum, Lipsett, & Yocom, 2002; Casey, 2007; Long & Gove, 2003/2004).

Conceptual Framework

The time I spend with teachers, my reading of research, and my reflections of my own work

Preparing Reading Professionals (second edition), edited by Rita M. Bean, Natalie Heisey, and Cathy M. Roller. © 2010 by the International Reading Association. Reprinted from Casey, H.K. (2008). Engaging the disengaged: Using learning clubs to motivate struggling adolescent readers and writers. *Journal of Adolescent & Adult Literacy, 52*(4), 284–294. doi:10.1598/JAAL.52.4.2.

are situated within a sociocultural framework. The appropriation of sociocultural theory to studies of classroom systems suggests that context is inclusive of the agents' shared communication, the physical tools and artifacts that mediate these exchanges, as well as the collective groups that form within these larger systems (Engeström, Miettinen, & Punamäki-Gital; 1999; Leont'ev, 1978; Vygotsky, 1978, 1934/1986). Activity is defined as the purposeful transformation of individuals, groups, and "social realities" based on the interactive relationship among all three (Davydov, 1999, p. 39). In this paradigm, teachers and students are positioned within multiple intellectual, cultural, economic, and spatial systems that situate these agents' construction of knowledge (Engeström et al., 1999; Leont'ev, 1978).

Learning clubs employ this paradigm because they evolve in response to the unique systems and agents (teachers and students) that are specific to the classroom and the larger school and community in which these agents learn and live. Sociocultural views of learning suggest adolescents' literacy development is related to the unique social communities that they inhabit. According to sociocultural theory, mapping adolescents' literacy development involves understanding the larger community in which the school is situated, recognizing the multiple social systems that exist within the classroom, and understanding the unique needs and interests of the individual students. Learning clubs, as described in this article, cannot be "plugged in" to curriculum but instead evolve in response to the literacy needs and interests of the individual adolescents and the unique social relationships that exist within the classroom community.

Learning clubs in this article are a grouping system teachers use to organize active learning events based on student-selected areas of interest. Literacy in a learning club is the tool for learning and shifts according to the area of study. Similar to literature circles and book clubs, teachers guide the process by deciding areas of inquiry available for students to select from, how groups will be structured, the nature of student involvement, and the formats available for response. The key difference is that the shared literacy event is not always tied to a piece of literature, thus broadening conceptions of text and offering possibilities for working across content areas. Central to the students' investigations are multiple texts that may include magazines, fiction, the Internet, videos, photographs, and conversations with "experts" (often teachers, parents, and members of the local community), among others, to guide their learning.

Observing the interactions that occur across these common learning episodes offers a portrait of how these clubs support middle school students' literacy development. Positioning the struggling adolescent learner within this paradigm offers an alternative lens that traditional remediation structures, either "pull-out" or "push-in," resist.

Accepting the Invitation: Joining the Literacy Club

Situating the Struggling Middle School Student

Adolescents who struggle with literacy typically bring a history of frustration and failure to their transactions with text (Alvermann, 2001; Ivey, 1999). According to popular resources for working with adolescents, in middle school this frustration is compounded by the expectation that children are no longer learning to read, but instead reading to learn (e.g., Beers, 2003; Biancarosa & Snow, 2004; Tovani, 2000). These students, often dismissed as lost, frequently are asked to engage in reading and writing activities across content areas that are frustrating. It is not uncommon for students to respond to this frustration with inappropriate outbursts or passive disengagement (Long, MacBlain, & MacBlain, 2007). Whether students are actively seeking ways out of the classroom or shutting down within, the achievement gap continues to widen (Fisher & Frey, 2007; Long et al., 2007).

Research in this area offers competing paradigms. There is support that suggests struggling middle school students meet with greater success when offered a range of motivating activities that encourage reading and writing (Boyd, 2002; Ivey, 1999). Curricular content and teacher instruction is designed to be responsive to individual students' needs and interests (Lewis, 2001). There is another body of research, however, that suggests middle school students who struggle with reading and writing need more explicit skill instruction. According to this work, students are motivated by the success that targeted instruction provides (Dole, Brown, & Trathen, 1996; Jacobsen et al., 2002).

Learning Clubs: Broadening Conceptions of Book Clubs and Literature Circles

Small-group reading experiences are commonly named "literature circles" in the K–12 classroom, situating reading as a socially discursive practice that is rooted in particular cultural contexts (Allen, Möller, & Stroup, 2003; Daniels, 2002). The terms *literature circles* and *book clubs* are often used interchangeably and share similar grouping procedures, though literature circles traditionally include more prescriptive roles than book clubs. In practice, both offer spaces for students to participate in facilitated conversations about common texts, which are generally, but not always, fiction. While effective teachers use this grouping system in multiple ways to suit the needs of the students, Daniels (2002) offers a framework that many, including Sharon, turn to when developing these clubs. Among the key pieces Daniels describes are student selection of text, temporary grouping systems, and regular, predictable meetings that are dialogue intensive. In a book club, the teacher becomes a facilitator of student communication and comprehension as the focus is the *process* of constructing and deconstructing text.

Classrooms are unique spaces because students and teachers form temporary communities based on their individual experiences outside of school as well as the shared learning events they participate in together during the school day (Engeström & Miettinen, 1999; Street, 2005; Wells & Claxton, 2002). Literature circles, or book clubs, are examples of smaller communities of learning that form within this larger classroom context. As students decode, describe, and react to a shared reading event, their individual identities and experiences shape conversations and the texts being considered while the conversations and texts shape the individual identities and experiences of the participants. As Claxton (2002) stated, "As we learn, we are also changing as learners" (p. 21). The activity—here the literature circle and within this article the learning club—unfolds as the participants do, as each experience is specific to the temporary community formed around the shared learning event.

As research predicts, students are engaged because they have the opportunity to make choices about their reading and their participation while sharing responsibility for learning with their peers and their teachers (Casey, 2007; Guthrie, 2004; McKool, 2007). Research described engaged readers as those who (a) are motivated by the material, (b) use multiple strategies to ensure comprehension, (c) are able to construct new knowledge as a result of the interaction with the text, and (d) draw on social interactions to mediate these literate processes (Guthrie, McGough, Bennett, & Rice, 1996). In Sharon's class, this is observed multiple times when the exchanges documented among small groups of students focus exclusively on the shared learning event and students are observed actively listening and responding to one another, often continuing the conversations as they move on to their next class.

I have named these temporary learning communities learning clubs in Sharon's classroom because she frequently invites students to form small groups based on a shared interest that invites students to use literacy to learn. The discursive dynamic that encourages active reading of literature and books can be used as a lens for actively engaging in learning that is not limited to sharing conversations around the bound word. Daniels (2002) described organizing groups around themes or shared areas of inquiry. As students begin working within these groups, the social dynamic that erupts across these collaborative experiences becomes the catalyst for learning (Johnston, 2004; King, 2001; Lewis, 2001).

Learning clubs have the potential to offer a paradigm for working with struggling middle school literacy learners that weaves together principles of motivation, engagement, and literacy development (Lewis, 2001). Small-group reading experiences have a long history of drawing on the social nature of learners to engage readers in text and deepen comprehension (Allen et al., 2003; Daniels, 2002; Guthrie, 2004). There are multiple opportunities to include struggling students within these systems while broadening what counts as text. The efficacy of these learning clubs in supporting struggling students' literacy development is explored in Sharon's classroom.

Room 212: Ms. Sharon Ailine

Situating Sharon

Mr. G., principal of Williams School, identifies Sharon as effective based on criteria rooted in research on effective teaching. This includes teachers' relationships with students, faculty, and parents; students' success on formal and informal assessment measures; and knowledge of pedagogy and content (e.g., Allington & Johnston, 2002; Morrow & Casey, 2003).

> She knows her subject very well. She's prepared when she walks in the classroom. She doesn't wing it. She doesn't shoot from the hip. I've been in that class numerous times. She doesn't raise her voice. The kids are always working. She does her traditional total class activities, then she has the kids in different groups. She's more of a facilitator.

In an era of increasing accountability, Mr. G. is impressed by Sharon's ability to navigate mounting external assessment pressures while continuing to motivate students.

Sharon has taught a variety of grades and subjects during her 34-year career. While Sharon maintains that her undergraduate work as an English major makes language arts a favorite subject to teach, her primary motivation for entering the field is the opportunity to positively impact students' lives.

Gathering Information

Data collected includes six 80-minute observations, two semi-structured interviews, a variety of informal conversations, and multiple documents, including lesson plans and photographs (Seidman, 1998). All observations and interviews were digitally recorded. The class I observed for six weeks was selected because, of the 19 students, 6 are identified as struggling with reading and writing. In this research, struggling students are defined as students eligible for basic skills literacy support. These are students who do not qualify for special education services but, because of low state test scores, grades, and teacher recommendation, are identified as in need of improvement. Old Gate School District does not have a formal basic skills program in the upper grades. Sharon identifies these 6 students based on poor performance on class reading and writing activities as well as their sixth-grade district test scores, which fall below 50% in reading and writing. Currently at Williams School the type and level of support for seventh-grade students who have reading and writing challenges, exempting those designated as special education, is largely determined by the classroom teacher.

This description of Sharon's work is part of a larger study of seventh-grade teachers identified as effective in supporting struggling middle school readers and writers. My work with Sharon revealed learning clubs to be a significant forum for supporting these students. This portion of the study is guided by the following three questions:

1. What structures does Sharon incorporate to frame small-group literacy events?

2. How does Sharon position struggling students within these groups?

3. How do these small-group literacy experiences inform the struggling middle school students' literacy development?

Why Are the Kids in Room 212 Learning to Read and Write?

The Big Picture: Snapshots of Sharon at Work

The clamor of construction outside Sharon's open windows competes with the clamor of seventh graders entering for the last period of the day. Sharon, a spirited woman with a memorable laugh, positions herself at the doorway, greeting entering students and pushing exiting students along to their next class. Frantic eighth graders looking for advice about fund raising and other extracurricular activities frequently interrupt casual conversations between Sharon and her students.

As Sharon moves to the podium in the front of the room, students know class is about to begin, and conversations quiet. Sharon invites student engagement by sparking curiosity about the day's lesson either through an interesting visual or questions such as, "I wonder how we might figure out this word?" Sharon's students are engaged because she privileges the learning processes over the products. These whole-class investigations then move to learning clubs, with Sharon moving from group to group, spending a significant amount of time guiding the struggling students. Each class generally concludes with another whole-class meeting, where together, Sharon and students reconstruct what they learned during the class period and look ahead to future work. This paradigm remained relatively consistent during our work together, and, according to Sharon, it is this consistency that the struggling students need.

Focusing In: What's Happening During Learning Club Meetings

Sharon's students use learning clubs for multiple learning events. It is not uncommon to find students grouped in homogeneous groups with specific roles to negotiate new vocabulary. In the following exchange, Luke and Wally—two of the struggling students—are working in their group to learn strategies for learning words. Sharon is helping students create a mental image of new vocabulary in an effort to increase comprehension.

Sharon: OK. So another way to remember this is a horizontal line creates right angles with a vertical line. Let's see if there's another way to say this, because this almost looks like you're making a blessing over the water or something. Dishka?

Dishka: Parallel. Parallel is two lines that don't meet.

Sharon: Two lines that don't meet. So then this line and this line....

Wally: No, no.

Luke: Gotta go this way. [holds hands parallel]

Sharon: Ah, Luke, what did you say?

Luke: They run together, like, like railroad tracks.

Sharon frequently uses this small-group forum to explicitly introduce and review reading and writing skills and strategies.

Sharon also employs this configuration when she uses heterogeneous groups when the students are reading *Roll of Thunder, Hear My Cry* (Taylor, 1976), a curricular requirement. The groups are organized according to learning interest, and the students are encouraged to choose from multiple processes to support comprehension. In the following exchange, Rakesh and Bill—two struggling students—are engaged with their group in sharing responses to the text.

Rakesh: I did a Venn diagram between me and Stacey and Cassie and Lily. I did Stacey and me so I would get to know him better because I got Stacey mixed up with a girl and a boy, so you know, um. The Venn diagram—Cassie and Lily have a lot in common. I did a Venn diagram about personal traits about them. Like Cassie I said she's a girl that is very confident. I wouldn't say that Lily has a lot of confidence. And for the other Venn diagram he has a whole lot of land and my parents only have a little bit of land.

Bill: Hey. I did mine. Originally I was going to do a poster and, to tell you the truth, I kind of ran out of time and I didn't have the pictures, I did do the paragraph, though, but. So instead I did a nice long chapter and I mean, I don't have to read it, if you guys want me to. [group murmurs yes] Alright, the next chapter in *Roll of Thunder*. [reading aloud from his response] "Come October we started talking about TJ. Little Man out of everyone was the most clueless about TJ. Was TJ going to be alright? And when was TJ going to—Not right now. School started out great. This new teacher, Mr. Crane, he's alright, he's a little mean though. I don't let it get to me. Jeremy still walks with a limp."

Desai: How did they save his leg?

Bill: You will have to read the next chapter.

Sharon maintains that students who struggle need to connect their conversation to a physical product. Sharon understands that students are motivated by choice and more engaged when directing their learning so she typically offers a "menu" for students to consider that allows the struggling students to link their learning to a forum that is accessible and interesting. Prior to each session, these students prepare a visual or written response to the reading. This is expected of all students, but according to Sharon it grew from her observations of the struggling students needing additional scaffolding to open up conversation. These products do not always fit the research definition of book clubs, but it does fit what Mr. G., the principal, calls "gut smarts" when describing Sharon. Sharon draws on strategies that will support the struggling students' movement toward a larger literacy objective. In reflecting on this particular group's work, Sharon comments,

> The reason why that group read *Roll of Thunder* is they had read an excerpt of this book in their basal text, and they made a good connection with it, and

so I said, "Would you like to know more about this problem?" and so we started to read it. And it was funny because Bill said something about, "Well I want to know about what happens next," and I said, "Well, that's called *Road to Memphis*" [Taylor, 1992].

> "There's another book?"
> And I said, "Oh, and there's a third one."
> "You have 'em?"
> I said, "Yeah we have 'em here somewhere." I said, "We'll find 'em."
> "Yeah, I want to read it, I want to read it."
> I said, "OK." I said, "We'll find it for you."

Sharon's careful reflection about how students respond to their work plays a significant role in her daily planning.

When students are working with shorter text, the reading and responding happens within the class session and the struggling students are more engaged. This is observed as this same group described above responds to the short poem "Feelings About Words" by Mary O'Neill (1994).

Bill: It talks about lots of different words.

Dishka: 'Cause there are so many words and there are different ways to use them and stuff.

Josh: Like how words look. Like the alphabet. It says some words are big, and, like, you say, umm, bulb, like a light bulb—

Bill: Where does it say some words are big? I missed that. [pause]

Desai: It says a few are small. It says some are thick.

Dishka: And some are thick. But does it say some are big?

Rebekah: Some words are slow.

Dishka: Which words are thick?

Josh: Glue, paste, and brick.

Dishka: It's like a metaphor.

In this group exchange, the students are engaged in a conversation that invites critical thinking instead of a presentation focused on decoding and describing. This remains consistent for the struggling students.

Understanding the Risk: Creating a Safe Space to Learn

Initially the struggling students resist participating in the learning clubs because they are dialogue intensive and require students to be active constructors of meaning as opposed to passive recipients of information. Sharon finds that many of her struggling students do not view themselves as readers and writers so they resist structures where reading and writing are primary. Sharon reflects on this after facilitating a book club meeting.

> These two groups interestingly enough didn't want to do any kind of literature circles. Feel much more comfortable doing chapter by chapter.... I don't know that it's necessarily because they feel it's easier. I think it's just the fact that it's more structured.

To alleviate this discomfort, Sharon devotes a large portion of class time, particularly in the beginning of the year, to constructing a safe learning environment.

> In order to have a conversation, you have to feel safe, and so that's the one thing that I try to create in the classroom is that everybody has an opinion and that every opinion is valid and that, even if you don't agree with that opinion, that your job then is to explain your opinion better and convince somebody not to put somebody down.... And so eventually what happens is more and more kids want to share because, no matter what is said, I never say they are wrong. And so then the dialogue starts so that, "Oh yeah, I wrote something, and it wasn't wrong, but maybe I didn't carry it far enough."

Once students are comfortable with these open exchanges, Sharon introduces literature circles. Initially, this is done through a class text to ensure understanding of how the roles work and gradually moves to students assuming more ownership of the structure and materials. The nature of these literature circles quickly shifts, however, as the roles offered by Daniels's (2002) work evolve and eventually dissolve in response to the students' interactions and reactions to text. Sharon then broadens this structure further to motivate learning events that require students to draw on their developing literacy to navigate learning that is sometimes, but not always, connected to written text.

Responsible Grouping Practices

A basic tenet of using book clubs in the classroom is that students will be able to comprehend the texts selected (Daniels, 2002). For struggling students who are often reading one or more grade levels below peers, this can become problematic if there are not appropriate resources. Even with appropriate resources, there is the additional problem of grouping by ability, which positions struggling readers with other struggling readers, and the cycle of frustration continues.

In room 212, Sharon guides her students' choices. Sharon mediates her knowledge about students' abilities, interests, and personalities with texts and concepts the students are interested in pursuing. Sharon is often frustrated by the current climate that limits this level of responsive teaching.

> We're not looking at individual kids any more. And I, as a classroom teacher, I teach individual kids. I don't teach a class: I teach a seventh grade that's made up of 19 kids and each kid has their own specific needs and yet they have to take a test where it's across the board because they're in seventh grade.

In this particular class, Sharon uses the group framework with a whole-class text initially and then moves to shorter selections that can be read in class. This allows Sharon to directly monitor student reading and scaffold the group process.

I observe this as the students engage in their final day of discussion around a short story read in the text. Jerry and Andrew—two struggling students—are disengaged until a concrete task is provided. Students are expected to discuss the character development in their group novels. Jerry and Andrew initially feign reading by flipping through pages and "busying" themselves with their notebooks. As Sharon comes around and hands each group a large piece of paper and a marker to create a character story board, however, they quickly become engaged in the reading and actively contribute to the task assigned. This careful scaffolding of the response to narrative text is characteristic of Sharon's work with the struggling students.

Responsive Management Structures

It is a lot of work to encourage struggling students to assume ownership of literacy events. Sharon strives to incorporate management systems that place the students in control of their work. This move toward independence involves careful scaffolding of written materials and instructional exchanges between Sharon and her students and the purposeful construction of groups. Sharon provides the groups with resource packets to support their reading. These packets include activities for completion as well as a variety of assessment products to select from. In addition, Sharon carefully selects the groups so the targeted students are working with strong readers who act as the "lead" and do a lot of the administrative tasks, collecting work, organizing assignments, and so on that teachers typically do.

> We talked about what the literature circle meant and what the responsibility was and how this would count. As a group you will get a grade, but then as individuals you will also get a grade, and you're working towards a final project so your discussions are really important so that you understand the story. And what I do is move from group to group.

Sharon recognizes that motivating the struggling readers and writers toward independence is more challenging. When given a lot of choice over their reading and writing events, these students frequently ask Sharon for further assistance.

Larry: How many things do I need to compare in the Venn diagram?

Sharon: Well, you're comparing yourself to Essie? How many did you come up with?

Larry: Ten.

Sharon: Well, ten is a good number then.

Sharon uses these small-group and individual exchanges to build independence by asking students focused questions designed to make them think about their reading and writing instead of simply telling them what to do.

Assessment

In Sharon's classroom, assessment is woven into instruction and is a catalyst for building students' independence. Students are invited to make decisions about the content of their work as well as the processes used to assess understanding. For example, students select different roles to assume during the meetings and choose from a menu of activities to demonstrate understanding and motivate conversation within groups. When the groups are meeting to discuss a series of informational articles, the students rotate the roles of discussion leader, vocabulary explainer, and researcher. These choices, however, are carefully mediated by Sharon as she maintains that students must cycle through each role at least once and produce a written description of how they enacted their roles.

Sharon also offers a menu of activities for students to choose from as a final response to their reading. These include the following:

- Create a final chapter.
- Develop a Venn diagram comparing yourself to another character.
- Develop a game around the plot of the novel.
- Create a multiple-choice test to administer to others.

Coupled with these final assessments is the opportunity for students to offer their own feedback on their learning and the learning of others. Sharon makes use of student checklists where the students describe how their group interacted, what they gained from the experience, and how negotiated challenges might inform future collaborative learning events. Sharon believes that making the struggling students part of the process motivates them to consider what is being learned and how they construct that learning. This is powerfully motivating for adolescents who feel marginalized by the larger literacy community.

Informing Practice

What Can We Learn?

Adolescents who struggle with literacy are often dismissed as lazy or lost—both descriptors doing little to empower these students to independently navigate text (Biancarosa & Snow, 2004; Ivey, 1999; Long et al., 2007). Sharon's work offers a different picture. These struggling students are engaged because their ideas about literature and literacy matter to Sharon, and in turn, to their peers around them. This engagement motivates these students to actively pursue literacy events because they want to become readers and writers. Sharon's comprehensive construction of learning clubs facilitates the struggling students' successes.

While the focus of this article is on struggling students, much of what is learned from observing Sharon's work and her reflections is inclusive of all students. Teachers considering adopting learning clubs as a part of their instruction across curricular areas should consider the following as it relates to their community of learners:

- Consider the topics available for students to investigate and how these are connected to their experiences and background and the larger community in which the school is situated.

- Offer a "topic talk" where students gain some insight into the areas open to investigate.

- Determine what types of texts students will use to navigate their learning and be sure multiple grade-level texts that reflect the multiple needs of students are available.

- Delineate the different roles that students within the small groups will assume to organize learning and facilitate conversation.

- Schedule class time for conversation and collaboration.

- Consider what artifacts you anticipate students will construct to demonstrate understanding.

- Coordinate assessment activities that link with the grouping objectives.

- Offer explicit examples and opportunity for students to see how these areas of inquiry connect to using literacy outside of the classroom space.

The learning clubs in Sharon's classroom are not recipes for success. Within these groups, relationships between peers are fostered, roles are outlined and described, and language becomes the vehicle for navigating conversations around literature, literacy, and learning. These clubs are successful because Sharon mediates the content of instruction with the context of the classroom community and the larger community situating the students' learning. This requires a careful balancing of pedagogy, content knowledge, and management of individual students' needs and identities. This is not something that can be neatly packaged and reproduced across classrooms but instead is organic and emerges within each setting according to the unique characteristics of the participants and the content being considered.

Where Do We Go From Here?

The use of multiple grouping configurations to support different kinds of learners and learning is well researched (Stein & Breed, 2004). Literature circles and book clubs offer successful paradigms for supporting students' engagement with fixed texts. The notion of learning clubs broadens this paradigm because these structures are focused learning events that extend beyond conversations around single texts. In Sharon's classroom, small groups move from discussing a particular poem to investigating patterns in words or events within the school or their community.

The learning club paradigm can move in multiple directions. It is possible that making use of cross-age groups with the struggling student as the director offers the opportunity to work on grade level while positioning these students, who are often marginalized, as powerful literacy participants. This is also a paradigm worthy of investigation across multiple content areas (Stein & Breed, 2004). Forming learning clubs in mathematics and science, for example, around a common concept or problem for investigation may be powerfully motivating and enable students to use literacy to learn (Guthrie, 2004).

Moving Beyond "The Text"

The 21st century finds students engaging in multimodal literacy events as part of their daily practice. These students move across virtual spaces, rapidly synthesizing multiple modes of fixed and moving text (Rowsell & Pahl, 2007). The literature circle/book club configuration has proven to engage students with texts. Moving into learning clubs may facilitate students' digital literacies, further broadening and enriching students' literacy independence. Sharon did not bring in much of students' outside literacy practices to support their work, but this is perhaps another possibility for supporting students' literacy independence. Recent research on digital video production suggests students are motivated by the technology to compose fixed and moving images that cross multiple genres and modes of communication (Ranker, 2008).

Conclusion

Sharon has been a part of students' literacy learning for 34 years. Sharon's ability to continue to help her students meet with success is a direct result of her interest in listening to her students, respecting who they are and what they know, and pairing this understanding with a strong awareness of content, pedagogy, and community. The learning clubs evolve in Sharon's class not because she read a single professional text and then reproduced it in her room, but because she is always reading and listening and learning and refuses to dismiss

the adolescent who struggles as lost. This is an important lesson to learn. The learning clubs are effective in this classroom because Sharon recognizes that their growth is situated within a distinct context. Learning clubs have the potential to motivate disengaged and frustrated adolescent readers and writers because they develop in response to the unique literacy needs and interests that exist in each classroom. Learning clubs have the potential to be a powerful vehicle for motivating engaged and interested learners across content areas to use literacy to build learning.

References

Allen, J., Möller, K., & Stroup, D. (2003). "Is this some kind of soap opera?": A tale of two readers across four literature discussion contexts. *Reading & Writing Quarterly*, *19*(3), 225–251. doi:10.1080/10573560308215

Allington, R.L., & Johnston, P.H. (2002). *Reading to learn: Lessons from exemplary fourth grade classrooms*. New York: Guilford.

Alvermann, D.E. (2001). Reading adolescents' reading identities: Looking back to see ahead. *Journal of Adolescent & Adult Literacy*, *44*(8), 676–690.

Atwell, N. (1998). *In the middle: New understandings about writing, reading, and learning* (2nd ed.). Portsmouth, NH: Boynton/Cook.

Beers, K. (2003). *When kids can't read, what teachers can do: A guide for teachers 6–12*. Portsmouth, NH: Heinemann.

Biancarosa, G., & Snow, C.E. (2004). *Reading next—a vision for action and research in middle and high school literacy: A report to Carnegie Corporation of New York*. Washington, DC: Alliance for Excellent Education.

Blum, H.T., Lipsett, L.R., & Yocom, D.J. (2002). Literature circles: A tool for self-determination in one middle school inclusive classroom. *Remedial and Special Education*, *23*(2), 99–108. doi:10.1177/074193250202300206

Boyd, F.B. (2002). Motivation to continue: Enhancing literacy learning for struggling readers and writers. *Reading & Writing Quarterly*, *18*(3), 257–277. doi:10.1080/07487630290061818

Casey, H.K. (2007). High stakes teaching in an era of high stakes testing. *The Journal of Curriculum and Instruction*, *1*(1), 14–30.

Claxton, G. (2002). Education for the learning age: A sociocultural approach to learning to learn. In G. Wells & G. Claxton (Eds.), *Learning for life in the 21st century: Sociocultural perspectives on the future of education* (pp. 21–33). Malden, MA: Blackwell.

Daniels, H. (2002). *Literature circles: Voice and choice in book clubs and reading groups* (2nd ed.). Portland, ME: Stenhouse.

Davydov, V.V. (1999). The content and unsolved problems of activity theory. In Y. Engeström, R. Miettinen, & R.L. Punamäki-Gital (Eds.), *Perspectives on activity theory* (pp. 39–52). Cambridge, U.K.: Cambridge University Press.

Dole, J.A., Brown, K.J., & Trathen, W. (1996). The effects of strategy instruction on the comprehension performance of at-risk students. *Reading Research Quarterly, 31*(1), 62–88. doi:10.1598/RRQ.31.1.4

Engeström, Y., & Miettinen, R. (1999). Introduction. In Y. Engeström, R. Miettinen, & R.L. Punamäki-Gital (Eds.), *Perspectives on activity theory* (pp. 1–18). New York: Cambridge University Press.

Engeström, Y., Miettinen, R., & Punamäki-Gital R.L. (Eds.). (1999). *Perspectives on activity theory.* New York: Cambridge University Press.

Fisher, D., & Frey, N. (2007). A tale of two middle schools: The differences in structure and instruction. *Journal of Adolescent & Adult Literacy, 51*(3), 204–211. doi:10.1598/JAAL.51.3.1

Guthrie, J.T. (2004). Teaching for literacy engagement. *Journal of Literacy Research, 36*(1), 1–29. doi:10.1207/s15548430jlr3601_2

Guthrie, J.T., McGough, K., Bennett, L., & Rice, M.E. (1996). Concept-oriented reading instruction: An integrated curriculum to develop motivations and strategies for reading. In L. Baker, P. Afflerbach, & D. Reinking (Eds.), *Developing engaged readers in school and home communities* (pp. 165–190). Mahwah, NJ: Erlbaum.

Ivey, G. (1999). Reflections on teaching struggling middle school readers. *Journal of Adolescent & Adult Literacy, 42*(5), 372–381.

Jacobsen, C., Bonds, M., Medders, K., Saenz, C., Stasch, K., & Sullivan, J. (2002). An intercession model for accelerated literacy. *Reading & Writing Quarterly, 18*(2), 151–173. doi:10.1080/10573560252808521

Johnston, P.H. (2004). *Choice words: How our language affects children's learning.* Portland, ME: Stenhouse.

King, C. (2001). "I like group reading because we can share ideas": The role of talk within the literature circle. *Reading, 35*(1), 32–36.

Leont'ev, A.N. (1978). *Activity, consciousness, and personality* (M. Hall, Trans). Englewood Cliffs, NJ: Prentice Hall.

Lewis, C. (2001). *Literary practices as social acts: Power, status, and cultural norms in the classroom.* Mahwah, NJ: Erlbaum.

Long, L., MacBlain, S., & MacBlain, M. (2007). Supporting students with dyslexia at the secondary level: An emotional model of literacy. *Journal of Adolescent & Adult Literacy, 51*(2), 124–134. doi:10.1598/JAAL.51.2.4

Long, T.W., & Gove, M.K. (2003/2004). How engagement strategies and literature circles promote critical response in a fourth-grade, urban classroom. *The Reading Teacher, 57*(4), 350–360.

McKool, S.S. (2007). Factors that influence the decision to read: An investigation of fifth grade students' out-of-school reading habits. *Reading Improvement, 44*(3), 111–131.

Morrow, L.M., & Casey, H.K. (2003). A comparison of exemplary characteristics in 1st and 4th grade teachers. *The California Reader, 36*(3), 5–17.

Ranker, J. (2008). Making meaning on the screen: Digital video production about the Dominican Republic. *Journal of Adolescent & Adult Literacy, 51*(5), 410–422. doi:10.1598/JAAL.51.5.4

Rowsell, J., & Pahl, K. (2007). Sedimented identities in texts: Instances of practice. *Reading Research Quarterly, 42*(3), 388–405. doi:10.1598/RRQ.42.3.3

Seidman, I. (1998). *Interviewing as qualitative research: A guide for researchers in education and the social sciences* (2nd ed.). New York: Teachers College Press.

Smith, F. (1988). *Joining the literacy club: Further essays into education.* Portsmouth, NH: Heinemann.

Stein, D., & Breed, P. (2004). Bridging the gap between fiction and nonfiction in the literature circle setting. *The Reading Teacher, 57*(6), 510–519.

Street, B. (Ed.). (2005). *Literacies across educational contexts: Mediating learning and teaching.* Philadelphia: Caslon.

Tovani, C. (2000). *I read it, but I don't get it: Comprehension strategies for adolescent readers.* Portland, ME: Stenhouse.

Vygotsky, L.S. (1978). *Mind in society: The development of higher psychological processes* (M. Cole, V. John-Steiner, S. Scribner, & E. Souberman, Eds. & Trans.). Cambridge, MA: Harvard University Press.

Vygotsky, L.S. (1986). *Thought and language* (A. Kozulin, Trans.). Cambridge, MA: MIT Press. (Original work published 1934)

Wells, G., & Claxton, G. (2002). Introduction: Sociocultural perspectives on the future of education. In G. Wells & G. Claxton (Eds.), *Learning for life in the 21st century* (pp. 1–17). Malden, MA: Blackwell.

Literature Cited

O'Neill, M. (1994). Feelings about words. In *Prentice Hall literature bronze* (p. 486). Englewood Cliffs, NJ: Prentice Hall.

Taylor, M.D. (1976). *Roll of thunder, hear my cry.* New York: Puffin.

Taylor, M.D. (1992). *Road to Memphis.* New York: Puffin.

Reading Intervention Models: Challenges of Classroom Support and Separated Instruction

Melissa M. Woodward and Carolyn Talbert-Johnson

In a recent literacy workshop for elementary educators, the researchers noted common concerns among classroom teachers and reading specialists when the presenter asked participants to identify factors that affect the quality of literacy instruction. There was silence for several seconds before several teachers responded in unison, "Time." The management of time in the classroom for language development activities, as well as how to differentiate instruction for the needs of readers at all levels, seemed to be of utmost concern for this group of teachers. The reality is that regardless of the quality of any program or teacher, there will always be students who need supplementary instruction designed to meet their specific needs.

Fortunately, education is not an isolated endeavor. Although some decisions regarding resources and reading programs are mandated by administrators or district leaders, the classroom teacher has the responsibility to make sure that the instructional needs of all students are met. This is a daunting task, as students are at varying skill levels in each subject area. For example, in a typical third-grade class, most students are able to comprehend grade-level material independently, while another group of students in the class may be reading one or more levels behind, and another group may need to be challenged because they can understand material three years ahead of the rest of the class. Valencia and Buly (2004) asserted that it is the teacher's responsibility to ensure that the individualized needs of struggling readers are addressed; however, classroom teachers are not expected to meet these needs alone. Research supports that some students will need expert, intensive intervention for sustained periods of time—possibly throughout their entire school careers—if they are to attain and maintain on-level reading proficiencies (Allington, 2004). Many schools provide some form of intervention support for at-risk students, including daily sessions with reading specialists through separated intervention or within the regular classroom.

Reading specialists have the responsibility of providing level-specific reading services to struggling readers. Bean (2004) suggested that reading specialists in today's schools are taking on additional roles. For example, many reading specialists are in an excellent position to assume the role of reading coach and mentor to classroom teachers in schools with many struggling readers. The goal of this article is to provide the advantages and disadvantages of separated instruction versus classroom support models as seen by teachers and researchers. We first provide the roles and responsibilities of reading specialists, determine the impact of the No Child Left Behind Act, identify possible

Preparing Reading Professionals (second edition), edited by Rita M. Bean, Natalie Heisey, and Cathy M. Roller. © 2010 by the International Reading Association. Reprinted from Woodward, M.M., & Talbert-Johnson, C. (2009). Reading intervention models: Challenges of classroom support and separated instruction. *The Reading Teacher, 63*(3), 190–200. doi:10.1598/RT.63.3.2.

models, and share feedback from teachers currently in classrooms.

Roles of an Elementary Reading Specialist

Reading specialists can play a critical role in the professional development of teachers (Dole, 2004), as they have extensive knowledge about the reading process and about high-quality reading instruction. It is evident that they have an important role to play in school leadership and instructional intervention in many schools (Bean, Cassidy, Grumet, Shelton, & Wallis, 2002; Quatroche, Bean, & Hamilton, 2001). It is not surprising that reading specialists have taken on the responsibility of providing quality instruction for all students. In the 1940s, reading specialists were referred to as "remedial" reading teachers and most recently as Title I reading teachers; however, reading specialists in today's schools have assumed additional roles (Bean, 2004). The International Reading Association expects reading specialists to be highly qualified literacy professionals who have prior experience as classroom teachers. Reading specialists are often responsible for supporting, supplementing, and extending quality classroom teaching. They also communicate effectively with key stakeholders (e.g., parents).

A reading specialist may be available in some schools to provide intervention for the groups that are developmentally reading below grade level, but how is this resource being used? Is it possible for classroom teachers to effectively use reading specialists to support instruction for all students in a class? What are the benefits of separated instruction for specific groups of students? Although most classrooms would benefit in some way from additional literacy support, the deciding factor for which students or which classrooms are assigned to a reading specialist often is determined by test results. It is not surprising that instructional groups change because of achievement test results; however, other reading performance factors are usually considered by the classroom teacher and reading specialist.

The Impact of No Child Left Behind on Reading Intervention

Every year thousands of students take standardized tests and state reading tests, and every year thousands of students fail them (Valencia & Buly, 2004). With the implementation of No Child Left Behind (NCLB), which mandates testing all children from grades 3 to 8 every year, these numbers will grow exponentially, and, unfortunately, alarming numbers of schools and students will be labeled as in need of improvement. The key provisions of NCLB include performance expectations in reading. Each state "must set annual targets that will lead to the goal of all students reaching proficiency in reading and mathematics by 2013–14" (U.S. Department of Education, 2006, p. 12). In the meantime, districts are expected to determine where improvement is needed in comprehensive instruction to address the five target areas identified by the National Reading Panel (National Institute of Child Health and Human Development, 2000): comprehension, fluency, vocabulary, phonemic awareness, and phonics.

According to recent reports from the Title I executive summary (U.S. Department of Education, 2006), there are concerns regarding intervention-based reading programs implemented in schools because there is little known about the effectiveness of these reading programs for struggling readers. As students are assessed by the state, and in the schools by teachers or reading specialists, there may be students identified who need additional intervention to overcome achievement gaps. Under the Response to Intervention process, to which many schools are now making the transition, "students who continue to struggle despite receiving initial intervention instruction will require more intense, targeted interventions" from reading specialists (Mesmer & Mesmer, 2008, p. 283). These students frequently continue to fall further behind because they do not possess the requisite skills to achieve (Dole, 2004).

To address this concern, schools are struggling to find solutions for improved performance in reading. For example, some schools have eliminated sustained silent reading in favor of more time for explicit instruction (Edmondson & Shannon, 2002), while other districts are buying special programs or mandating specific interventions. It is common to find teachers spending enormous amounts of time preparing students for these high-stakes tests (Olson, 2001).

The U.S. Department of Education (2006) identified at least 10 characteristics of effective reading intervention, including the following: small group size of three to six students who share the same reading difficulties, daily intervention for at least 30 minutes, intervention that addresses all five essential components of reading instruction, instruction that is explicit and direct but engaging and fast paced, feedback for students when errors are made, and many opportunities for students to respond to questions. Most important, intervention decisions are data driven. Therefore, ongoing assessment data determine the intensity and duration of the reading intervention, which is based on degree of reading risk. Although there are resources available to choose effective programs, there continues to be debate regarding how interventions should be implemented. There are proponents who believe that interventions should evolve in the classroom, with a reading specialist available to support all students during literacy instruction. The alternative would be to allow small groups of students to leave the classroom to work with a reading specialist for a block of time each day.

Approaches to Reading Intervention

Separated Intervention

There are several reasons why schools may prefer to implement separated (pull-out) reading intervention programs. First, they may want to target a specific group of students who may benefit from the individualized attention and quiet setting associated with this approach. Bean (2004) asserted that this approach may be beneficial when instruction is provided by a highly qualified teacher and instruction is tailored to address the individualized needs of students. Second, some reading intervention programs are designed for individualized instruction away from the classroom. Examples include Reading Recovery and Success for All (Allington, 2001). In addition, students receiving small-group, separated instruction may develop an increase in reading confidence by practicing specific skills and reading aloud with peers who share similar literacy development levels (Bean, 2004).

Unfortunately, separated instruction has been associated with a negative connotation since the 1930s and 1940s when students were sorted into ability groups and assigned to special reading teachers who would use instructionism-based approaches designed to drill until mastery is achieved (Bean, 2004; Johnson, 2004; Primeaux, 2000). According to Primeaux (2000), reading specialists are now trained to apply constructivist approaches that use students' current skill level as a starting point, requiring an ongoing cycle of authentic assessment, planning, and guided instruction using appropriate texts.

Additional concerns regarding separated instruction include the fact that children who experience reading difficulties are frequently separated from (pulled out of) their classrooms for level-specific reading instruction (Bean, 2004). Another concern is that separated instruction tends to lack integration with the regular classroom, which may result in a lack of communication between the teachers and reading specialists (Bean, 2004).

Classroom Support

Highly qualified teachers are needed to intervene effectively on the literacy skills of struggling readers (Dole, 2004). High-quality reading instruction is essential in every primary-grade classroom in schools with many struggling readers. This high-quality instruction is expected to minimize the number of students who will need intervention or supplementary instruction and will also minimize the number of students recommended for special education services.

One approach for involving reading specialists in the classroom is referred to as student-focused coaching, which is based on encouraging collaborative problem solving between classroom teachers and reading specialists to address an identified problem, such as a student's lack of progress in acquiring a specific academic skill (Hasbrouck & Denton, 2007). In this model, the grade-level teaching teams and reading specialists plan and collect data together to learn from observing student responses to interventions and instructional strategies developed collaboratively with teachers. Additional benefits of in-class reading intervention include less stigma and less negative attention for students who formerly left the classroom for reading services and the ability to maximize instructional time efficiently (Bean, 2004; Ziolkowska, 2007).

A school in Illinois implemented a similar collaboration-based program and improved student test scores on statewide tests using a building-wide support model named after the Anna School District. The Anna Plan involved taking strategies that were previously used only in Reading Recovery and Title I pull-out interventions and adapting strategies for use in primary-grade classrooms with flexible, daily guided reading groups:

> In the reading room, four small groups operate simultaneously, with each one being taught either by the classroom teacher or one of the reading specialists.... The four groups are fluid with students moving from one group to another as their needs dictate. (Miles, Stegle, Hubbs, Henk, & Mallette, 2004, p. 322)

In addition, students are assigned to groups based on Developmental Reading Assessment (DRA) levels, and leveled texts are used for instruction using an established reading plan for day 1 through day 5, including introduction of the text, comprehension minilessons, working with words, writing, and collaborative planning among reading specialists and teachers while another teacher conducts whole-group literacy activities.

The inclusion of reading specialists in the classroom presents special challenges, which may include conflicting philosophies and teaching styles. Overcrowded classrooms may also be a problem, as it limits areas needed for additional instruction. The dynamics of performing in a regular classroom may be too challenging and distracting for some students who have attention difficulties. In addition, collaborative planning, as described in the Anna Plan, between the classroom teacher and reading specialist may be limited.

Teacher Perspectives

In response to expectations for data-driven instructional decisions and accountability, school districts are looking for ways to use best practices to improve student achievement. The setting for this study was a suburban district in a Midwestern state with an enrollment of more than 10,000 students in grades K–12. Elementary students are identified for participation in the school reading intervention program using a matrix that looks at students' performance in the classroom based on teacher observations, scores from diagnostic or standardized tests, and DRA levels. Students who did not pass the third-grade achievement test in the fall or spring are also selected. Current policies require a parent or guardian to sign a permission form prior to beginning intervention with a specialist. A majority of reading specialists schedule selected students to meet daily in a small-group setting away from the regular classroom for 30 minutes of supplemental literacy instruction.

Methodology

Participants

The researchers designed and distributed a survey comprised of short answers and scaled responses to given statements (see Figure 1). A voluntary and anonymous sample of 50 classroom teachers was selected to allow for two teachers from each grade level at each of the five elementary buildings to provide feedback. Additional surveys were given to 14 elementary reading specialists in the district. Out of 64 total surveys distributed through the school

Sounds like Title I

Figure 1
Reading Intervention Survey

Current position: _____

Grade levels (circle one):
K   1   2   3   4   other

School building: _____

Total years of teaching experience: 1   2–5   6–10   11–20   21+

1. Classroom teachers only: How many below-average and/or at-risk readers are in your class this year?

    _____ out of _____ total students (for example: 5 out of 23)

    Reading specialists only: How many students do you work with at each grade level?

    K _____   1st _____   2nd _____   3rd _____   4th _____

2. At this time, which method do you prefer for your below-average and/or at-risk readers?
    ❏ Inclusion with a reading specialist in the classroom.
    ❏ Separated instruction (pull-out) or small-group intervention with a reading specialist.
    ❏ A combination of both approaches.

3. Is your preferred method currently used in your setting?   ❏ Yes   ❏ No

4. When you think of *pull-out reading instruction*, list two positive and two negative aspects of this form.

    Positive: Negative:
    _____   _____
    _____   _____

5. When you think of *inclusion for reading instruction*, list two positive and two negative aspects of this form.

    Positive: Negative:
    _____   _____
    _____   _____

6. Please indicate whether you strongly agree (SA), agree (A), feel undecided (U), disagree (D), or strongly disagree (SD) with these statements:

Students who are pulled out of the classroom miss instruction and/or time to work on assignments.	SA	A	U	D	SD
Reading lessons taught in intervention should match the ones that are being taught in the classroom.	SA	A	U	D	SD
Reading specialists and classroom teachers communicate effectively regarding the readers they work with.	SA	A	U	D	SD
The same students qualify for reading service year after year.	SA	A	U	D	SD
Parents often have concerns about allowing students to participate in intervention programs.	SA	A	U	D	SD
More state or federal funding of intervention programs will help at-risk readers.	SA	A	U	D	SD
30 minutes a day is enough time for students to work with a reading specialist.	SA	A	U	D	SD

7. Please list additional comments or questions you may have regarding this topic:

mail system, 47 were completed and returned, producing a 73% response rate. A majority of the respondents were veteran classroom teachers or reading specialists, with 70% reporting they have taught for at least six years. Of these respondents, 26% have more than 21 years of experience teaching.

The survey asked participants to respond to prompts including the following: (a) the number of below-average readers a teacher or reading specialist worked with, (b) an indication of reading intervention preferences, (c) an evaluation of whether the preferred intervention was used, (d) identification of at least two positive and two negative aspects of separated instruction versus classroom support, and (e) key issues regarding the separated versus classroom support interventions and student needs. A Likert 5-point scale from strongly agree to strongly disagree was used. Participants were also asked to list additional questions or comments.

Analysis of Results

According to the responses provided by the 12 reading specialists, the number of students a full-time reading specialist works with each day may range from 47 to 82, depending on the needs of the building, the number of reading specialists, and the number of classrooms serviced. The average number of students in a classroom was 25, and the number of below-average or at-risk readers in each classroom ranged from 2 to 10, as reported by the classroom teachers. A majority of classroom teachers, or 57%, would prefer to have a combination of classroom support and separated instruction interventions; however, only half of these teachers currently have the option. A majority of the reading specialists, or 58%, would also prefer a combination of intervention models.

Relevant to student outcomes, the classroom teachers and reading specialists both agreed that 30 minutes a day is not enough time for students to work with a reading specialist, although this is the amount of time allotted in most classroom schedules for reading intervention. This is important because it gives insight to quality of instruction and the efficiency of

the services provided. The teachers and reading specialists indicated that collaborative endeavors benefit all students, as having another adult in the classroom can assist student performance in reading.

Open-ended responses from the survey were coded and sorted according to the nature of the positive and negative aspects stated by classroom teachers and reading specialists. In regard to separated instruction, classroom teachers' responses for listing two positive aspects included small-group benefits, individualized attention, benefits of reading specialist instruction, impact on instruction for students remaining in the classroom, ability grouping, quietness, and daily reading consistency (see Table 1). However, negative aspects of separated instruction listed by classroom teachers included limited communication between the "regular" teacher and reading specialist, concerns related to scheduling and classroom routines, impact on student socialization as a result of peer labeling, and limited time for intervention students to read with the classroom teacher.

The positive and negative aspects listed by reading specialists regarding separated instruction were similar; however, reading specialists also noted attention to specific needs and materials available as positive aspects, as well as concerns for students as they travel to and from the classroom to the reading room (see Table 2). In addressing the positive factors of separated intervention, classroom teachers and reading specialists most frequently cited the benefits of individualized attention in a small-group setting, followed by a quieter or less distracting work area, and increased participation and opportunities for students to feel successful. The negative factors of separated intervention included the fact that students miss whole-group classroom instruction or activities with peers, the difficulties with scheduling, and the stigma associated with being labeled as a "reader" and leaving the classroom.

The comments by classroom teachers and reading specialists regarding the advantages and disadvantages of in-classroom support (see Tables 3 and 4) were focused on three areas:

[handwritten margin note: advantages & disadvantages of pull out interventions]

Table 1
Classroom Teachers' Survey Comments Regarding Separated Instruction

Positive Aspects Listed	Negative Aspects Listed
• *Small-group benefits*: Instruction without distractions from the class; taking time and not worrying about keeping up with other groups; students get small-group instruction and this allows them to feel comfortable to read; they are not as distracted by other stimuli in the classroom	• *Limited communication*: Communication between regular education teacher and reading teacher limited; sometimes we might not be at the same level because of time crunches and we do not see each other; overlapping titles of books
• *Individualized attention*: One-to-one ratio; ability to focus on students' individual needs	• *Scheduling and accessibility*: Scheduling can be difficult; higher readers miss out on an opportunity to meet with a reading specialist to challenge them; time lapse in between traveling from room to room; not all at risk get serviced
• *Reading specialist instruction*: More chance to actively participate; better opportunity for interaction in a small-group setting; students get a preview or reinforcement of what is being done in class; pinpoint strategies needed for improvement; they work with a specialist and get fabulous support and instruction; extra time spent on concepts; reading teacher is specialized; reports of how students progress; direct instruction	• *Socialization*: Removed from peers; other children want a turn to leave; being labeled as a "reader" by other students; some don't like being pulled out; self-esteem issues; child starts to realize they go to reading for a reason
• *Classroom benefits*: Allows the regular education teacher to do more difficult large-group lessons; smaller class size	• *Classroom schedules and routines*: Watching what to teach so kids don't have to catch up; missing whole-group instruction; missing class work; with 20–25% of the class gone, I don't introduce new material while they are gone
• *Ability grouping*: Homogeneous group moves at same speed; reading level improved; leveled groups	• *Limited reading with classroom teacher*: Difficult for classroom teacher to take reading grade for that 30 minutes; I see less of them to monitor progress
• *Quietness*: Quiet environment for students; less noise—easier to concentrate	
• *Daily reading sessions*: Regular schedule; chance to meet more times/on a daily basis; more classes can be served	

differentiating instruction, the physical learning environment, and potential for student improvement. Classroom teachers and reading specialists listed the following benefits of classroom support: (a) the opportunity for flexible grouping and peer reading models, (b) increased collaboration and communication between the reading specialist and classroom teacher, and (c) having the reading specialists available in the classroom as a resource for the classroom teacher as well as readers at all ability levels. The drawbacks to in-classroom support instruction cited by teachers and reading specialists included the following: (a) an increased number of distractions by noise and space limitations, (b) inadequate planning time or a general lack of interest in collaboration, and (c) fewer opportunities for providing one-on-one instruction or

remediation. The varied responses may possibly be attributed to the teaching styles, needs of students, or dynamics of the classroom.

As noted in Table 5, the scaled responses to the position statements were similar between classroom teachers and reading specialists, with the exception of the first statement. More than half of the classroom teachers agreed or strongly agreed that students who receive separated intervention miss classroom instruction or time to work on assignments, while more than half of the reading specialists disagreed or strongly disagreed with this statement.

Although the classroom teachers and reading specialists are aware of the positive and negative aspects of each form of intervention, the teachers are always willing to seek a variety of options and implement practices that will

Table 2
Reading Specialists' Survey Comments Regarding Separated Instruction

Positive Aspects Listed	Negative Aspects Listed
• *Attention to specific needs*: Give more attention to group; learn the child's specific needs better and can address them • *Less distractions*: At-risk readers are often more distractible—focus can be better • *More time learning*: No lost time changing classes; less waste of time • *Materials available*: Materials are easily accessible, which means more flexibility with materials on hand for impromptu lessons or something a reader needs • *Control*: I control the structure and behavioral expectations; more space if classroom teacher's room is small or poorly managed • *Instructional benefits*: Students receive a double dose of reading instruction; intense instruction geared at small group; reading specialist can plan own lessons for at-risk readers; very distracted students and very low-performing students can use alternative approaches • *Quietness*: Quiet atmosphere; quiet working environment • *Active participation*: They can feel successful; students more willing to open up in reading discussions; small group allows students more opportunity to ask questions and participate	• *Professional interaction limited*: No opportunity for modeling for the classroom teacher by the reading specialist; lack of communication between specialist and classroom teacher • *Limited number of students benefit*: No positive peer role models for readers; working with less students; limited, not flexible, grouping • *Transition time*: Travel time equals less work time; kids lose time in traveling to the reading room • *Potential for problems*: Materials forgotten in classroom; students moving in/out of the building without supervision (modular classrooms outside); some students tend to act out in front of a small peer group • *Student confidence*: Older students sometimes feel labeled or embarrassed; pulled away from classmates; some kids feel singled out • *Scheduling whole-group instruction*: Classroom teacher is limited to what can be done while the students are out; miss assignment work time and sometimes instruction

benefit the needs of all students. Teachers and reading specialists are visiting other reading programs or going to professional development events together to identify effective strategies that will benefit struggling readers. For instance, in one building, the principal redesigned building schedules to allow for uninterrupted blocks of literacy instruction, using the reading specialists as guided reading group models in the classroom. In another building at the third- and fourth-grade levels, classroom teachers are rotating students for specialist intervention based on need by using flexible grouping rather than keeping a static group from September to June. All buildings have implemented some form of before- or after-school intervention program, allowing for specialized instruction to prepare students for achievement tests or to provide skill reinforcement as needed.

Conclusions and Recommendations for Further Study

As educators, we constantly encounter students who struggle with reading. These students frequently fail standardized tests, and typically their needs cannot be met by the standard school curriculum. These struggling readers are instructionally needy. It is imperative that schools examine how reading instruction is implemented at each grade level. This may include having a reading specialist available at each grade level in each building, including one who works primarily with at-risk kindergarten students as a form of early intervention. A survey comment from a kindergarten teacher said, "Sometimes early intervention helps some children not need reading [intervention] in first *early intervention! (not focus on 3-5... even though that's where focus is because of standardized testing).

Table 3
Reading Specialists' Survey Comments Regarding In-Class Intervention

Positive Aspects Listed	Negative Aspects Listed
• *Collaboration and communication*: More time to collaborate with the classroom teacher by using a minute here or there; modeling for the classroom teacher by the reading specialist; teacher support	• *Potential for distractions*: Students distracted by other activities; at-risk students may not be as focused; confusion—loud—too many things going on in the classroom
• *More students work with reading specialist*: Affects entire classroom and teacher; more students are influenced; flexible grouping is more efficient; all students know reading specialist and grouping can be flexible based on skill being taught; allows peers with stronger abilities to be role models	• *Instructional changes*: Students don't get double dose of reading instruction; can miss specific needs of a student that small pull-out group may reveal; loss of intensive instruction needed by struggling readers; not enough remediation skill work; less 1:1 time with specialist; still servicing the same number of kids
• *Reading specialist participation*: Classroom teacher and reading specialist are on the same page; connection to class work; hearing other lesson(s) being taught; work on same skills, topics, etc. as classroom teacher; gives reading teacher perspective on how at-risk readers are doing compared to peers	• *Time*: Lose teaching time traveling from room to room and trading materials; being stopped in the hall by other teachers; need time to plan with teacher; not enough time in our reading service slots to do inclusion properly; students move much quicker than teachers!
• *Students stay in the classroom*: Student never leaves classroom; less travel time equals more instruction time; no student travel time lost	• *Limited space and materials*: Baggie book baskets not accessible; some teachers don't like to share their classroom; materials and space not readily available for reading teacher; some classrooms lack physical space for another group to be going on
	• *Teacher and specialist differences*: Some teaching styles don't match; classroom teacher and reading specialist may disagree on noise level/classroom management; teacher is not always ready to collaborate

and second grade," while another kindergarten teacher lamented that her students "do not receive enough intervention time because it is prioritized by fourth grade on down," because of the emphasis on statewide testing in the third and fourth grades.

Before trying a new approach to reading intervention in the classroom, it is important for a teacher or instructional team to reflect on responses to the following questions:

- What is the data telling us about our current methods? Are students who are receiving intervention services making progress as measured by formative and summative assessments?

- Can I make changes to my instructional routine to allow for more blocks of time for guided reading, and will a reading specialist be available to model effective guided reading lessons and strategies?

- As a grade level, or as a school, what are the best practices that we are currently using for effective reading instruction? Do we need to revisit these approaches or provide training for new staff members?

- often am I communicating with the reading specialist who works with my students? Does the reading specialist have additional resources that could be used to differentiate instruction for reading at all levels in my classroom?

By analyzing the feedback of district colleagues and sampling available research in the area of reading intervention, it is true that teachers can indeed teach children to read (Lose, 2007). There were no conclusive statements

Table 4
Classroom Teachers' Survey Comments Regarding In-Class Intervention

Positive Aspects Listed

- *Instructional consistency*: I can expand my teaching when necessary and not have to stop when they leave and come back to it when students return; can cover same skills at the same time; do what the rest of the class is doing; don't miss any instruction; follows my plans; aligning with your curriculum/current units is easier
- *Mixed-ability groups*: Higher-level readers can be role models; more opportunities for small-group discussion
- *Collaboration and mentoring*: Having another adult in the classroom who can help anyone or help me with guided reading groups would be great; extra expertise in the classroom; communication would be better between specialist and teacher
- *Instructional support for all readers*: Students can still be working on same types of activities but differentiated instruction is better with two teachers available; able to help other students as well as those identified; gives higher readers a chance to work with reading intervention teacher to enhance and challenge
- *Socialization*: Stay with peers; kids don't feel isolated; harder to identify the readers because they are being helped within the confines of the regular classroom; self-esteem

Negative Aspects Listed

- *More distractions and less space*: Not enough room or table space for all groups to work; some lessons would not lend themselves to needing extra help from the (reading) teacher; if there are too many students in a classroom, it is nice to separate at times for noise level and distractions that happen just because of the amount of kids in one area at the same time; students have to ignore two different voices for independent work; interruptions
- *Less small-group instruction*: Hard to work on specific needed skills with some lessons; distractions of classroom activities and environment; larger setting; perhaps they might miss out on more 1:1 instruction
- *Different levels and needs*: Various levels; may feel bad because they don't know what other kids know; more obvious to other students that reading lab children are struggling; those not needing intervention taking time from those needing intervention
- *Scheduling*: Needs to be scheduled during same time each day; scheduling will probably still be challenging; common planning?

---

regarding the most effective model based on the feedback from the district's teachers and reading specialists; however, it is vital that a combination of effective separated and supportive instructional strategies be employed to address the unique learning needs of all students.

It is important to note that the results of the survey are a reflection of each teacher's perceptions, shaped by years of experience and professionalism regarding how to deliver instruction appropriate to the differentiated literacy skills of each child. Determining which reading intervention approach is best depends on the needs of students, the facilities and qualified personnel available, and the willingness of classroom teachers and reading specialists to collaborate to maximize quality instructional time and resources to improve student achievement.

References

Allington, R.L. (2001). *What really matters for struggling readers: Designing research-based programs*. New York: Addison Wesley.

Allington, R.L. (2004). Setting the record straight. *Educational Leadership, 61*(6), 22–25.

Bean, R.M. (2004). *The reading specialist: Leadership for the classroom, school, and community*. New York: Guilford.

Bean, R.M., Cassidy, J., Grumet, J.E., Shelton, D.S., & Wallis, S.R. (2002). What do reading specialists do? Results from a national survey. *The Reading Teacher, 55*(8), 736–744.

Dole, J.A. (2004). The changing role of the reading specialist in school reform. *The Reading Teacher, 57*(5), 462–471. doi:10.1598/RT.57.5.6

Edmondson, J., & Shannon, P. (2002). The will of the people. *The Reading Teacher, 55*(5), 452–454.

Hasbrouck, J., & Denton, C.A. (2007). Student-focused coaching: A model for reading coaches. *The Reading Teacher, 60*(7), 690–693. doi:10.1598/RT.60.7.11

Johnson, G.M. (2004). Constructivist remediation: Correction in context. *International Journal of Special Education, 19*(1), 72–88.

Table 5
Classroom Teacher (CT) and Reading Specialist (RS) Statement Responses

	Strongly Agree	Agree	Undecided	Disagree	Strongly Disagree
Pulled-out students miss classroom instruction and/ or time to work on assignments.	CT 20% RS 8%	CT 40% RS 8%	CT 17% RS 8%	CT 20% RS 58%	CT 3% RS 16%
Intervention reading lessons should match the lessons taught in the classroom.	CT 14% RS 16%	CT 34% RS 25%	CT 14% RS 16%	CT 29% RS 25%	CT 9% RS 16%
Reading specialists and classroom teachers communicate effectively.	CT 51% RS 42%	CT 31% RS 50%	CT 11% RS 0%	CT 3% RS 8%	CT 3% RS 0%
The same students qualify for reading service every year.	CT 9% RS 0%	CT 29% RS 33%	CT 9% RS 16%	CT 37% RS 50%	CT 17% RS 0%
Parents have concerns about intervention programs.	CT 9% RS 16%	CT 29% RS 16%	CT 9% RS 8%	CT 37% RS 42%	CT 17% RS 16%
More funding is needed for reading intervention programs.	CT 40% RS 50%	CT 40% RS 25%	CT 17% RS 25%	CT 0% RS 0%	CT 3% RS 0%
30 minutes a day is enough time for students to work with a reading specialist.	CT 20% RS 8%	CT 23% RS 16%	CT 26% RS 25%	CT 26% RS 42%	CT 6% RS 8%

Lose, M. (2007). A child's response to intervention requires a responsive teacher of reading. *The Reading Teacher*, *61*(3), 276–279. doi:10.1598/RT.61.3.9

Mesmer, E.M., & Mesmer, H.A.E. (2008). Response to Intervention (RTI): What teachers of reading need to know. *The Reading Teacher*, *62*(4), 280–290. doi:10.1598/RT.62.4.1

Miles, P.A., Stegle, K.W., Hubbs, K.G., Henk, W.A., & Mallette, M.H. (2004). A whole-class support model for early literacy: The Anna Plan. *The Reading Teacher*, *58*(4), 318–327. doi:10.1598/RT.58.4.1

National Institute of Child Health and Human Development. (2000). *Report of the National Reading Panel. Teaching children to read: An evidence-based assessment of the scientific research literature on reading and its implications for reading instruction* (NIH Publication No. 00-4769). Washington, DC: U.S. Government Printing Office.

Olson, L. (2001). Overboard on testing. *Education Week*, *20*(17), 23–30.

Primeaux, J. (2000). Shifting perspectives on struggling readers. *Language Arts*, *77*(6), 537–542.

Quatroche, D.J., Bean, R.M., & Hamilton, R.L. (2001). The role of the reading specialist: A review of research. *The Reading Teacher*, *55*(3), 282–294.

U.S. Department of Education. (2006). *National assessment of Title I interim report: Executive summary.* Washington, DC: Institute of Education Sciences.

Valencia, S.W., & Buly, M.R. (2004). Behind test scores: What struggling readers *really* need. *The Reading Teacher*, *57*(6), 520–531.

Ziolkowska, R. (2007). Early intervention for students with reading and writing difficulties. *Reading Improvement*, *44*(2), 76–86.

Student Perceptions of Reading Engagement: Learning From the Learners

Susanna W. Pflaum and Penny A. Bishop

onstructivist educators are not surprised that "what is taught is not necessarily what is learned" (Pollard, Thiessen, & Filer, 1997, p. 5). What is learned is what students take from their experiences, not only as shown in tests and performances but also in terms of how students process their experiences. Students' experiences of reading in school are the building blocks for learning how to read and reading to learn. How students perceive reading in school has the potential of informing teachers about practice on many levels and in several content areas. "Teachers themselves need to know more about varieties of student experience if they are to educate a wide variety of students really well" (Erickson & Schultz, 1992, p. 471).

In this article we look at the ways middle school students in the United States perceive school reading experiences. The use of drawing with interview provided a way for us to reach students and examine their thinking about school and helped us gain deeper understanding of their perceptions of school—deeper than we would have by either drawings or interviews alone. The words and drawings of 20 Vermont middle school students illustrate the practices the students identified as important. The students identified times of reading engagement and times when not engaged; they voiced powerful and specific reactions to each.

We begin by looking at two drawings by Samantha shown in Figure 1. (All student and school names are pseudonyms.) Samantha is a 12-year-old sixth grader at Town School who has a history of school success. Both her drawings depicted experiences in social studies class. Her first drawing was in response to our request to draw about a time when she was deeply engaged in learning; the second was a time when she was detached. Samantha competently filled the papers with her clear images. In the first drawing Samantha is the girl on the right coming up behind the computer who asks, "Can I help?" She explained later that they were part of a group and were looking up information on the Internet to write reports and to prepare plays. The drawing depicts Samantha's desire to help the other girl find good information. The girls are on either side of the centered and substantial element, the computer.

As was typical in our work with these middle schoolers, the conversation between Samantha and one of the authors began with the drawings. When asked about her drawings, she explained her preference for collaborative reading experiences.

> Well, I feel that when I'm working in a group and not in the textbooks that I learn the most. 'Cause the textbooks. Some people they don't follow it. They put stuff in words and ways that you can't really understand it....

Preparing Reading Professionals (second edition), edited by Rita M. Bean, Natalie Heisey, and Cathy M. Roller. © 2010 by the International Reading Association. Reprinted from Pflaum, S.W., & Bishop, P.A. (2004). Student perceptions of reading engagement: Learning from the learners. *Journal of Adolescent & Adult Literacy, 48*(3), 202–213. doi:10.1598/JAAL.48.3.2.

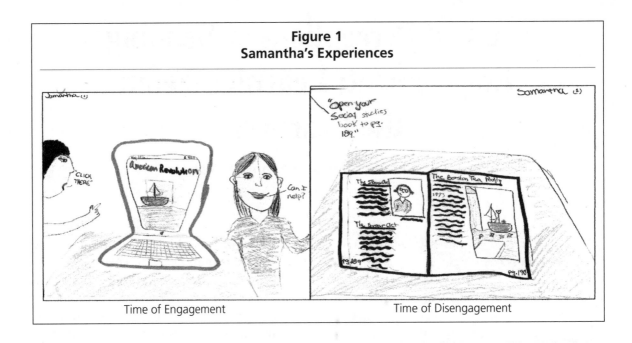

Figure 1
Samantha's Experiences

Time of Engagement | Time of Disengagement

Samantha's representation of textbook reading, the second drawing, was a time when she said everyone was on the same page. She shows the book through her eyes and includes the teacher's voice in the comment in the upper left.

Interviewer: OK, so why have you put this here? What is it about this activity that is negative for you?

Samantha: Well, when she says to open your books, we all have to open our books and just look at this and she asked someone to start reading and when you're reading...

Interviewer: Out loud?

Samantha: Out loud to the whole class. And you think, "Oh great, if I mess up I have to get every word right." And just when you're reading you're just thinking about yourself.... I think when you're researching by yourself and with your friends on the Internet, it's much more fun and this isn't my favorite thing to do.

Interviewer: So, it's not reading that causes you to feel this way, it's the cir-

cumstances of the reading? Like being on stage?

Samantha: Yeah. It's not just that, too. It's just they put it in a way that's hard to understand it and so when you're reading you're like, "Hey wait a minute. I don't really get this." But once you like see it on the Internet on different websites and when you read it in different books, you kind of get to know it better and.... When I'm just reading by myself I find that I can pay attention to the book easier and when I'm working with my friends on the Internet, I can talk to them and ask, "What sites have you seen?" But when you're doing this you can't ask any questions. And you can't...talk. You just have to listen to the reader. It's just not fun for me.

Interviewer: And that's quite different, too, from the other picture where everybody is...

Samantha: Like happy to be there and happy to help.

About the text, she also said,

> I kind of read it like if we're going to have a test the next day. I read it again by myself and I find that it works better by myself. And sometimes I get confused.... I end up going back and reading it again and kind of finding where this paragraph where I need to read is and looking for the information I need.

Samantha presented strong reactions to these two reading experiences. Her drawings were the source (the start) for the conversation that followed. They were the frame of reference as details and elaborations were added through talk. With the first drawing she showed and talked about how she was eager to talk to and question her peers. What she expressed served as an exemplar of engaged reading, as defined by Guthrie and Anderson (1999).

> Reading should be conceptualized as an engagement. Engaged readers not only have acquired reading skills, but use them for their own purposes in many contexts. They possess beliefs, desires, and interests that energize the hard work of becoming literate. From this perspective, motivation and social interactions are equal to cognitions as foundations for reading. (p. 17)

Samantha's example of not being engaged told us more about her perceptions of the school experience. The significance of the static book she pictured became meaningful as she talked about the practices involved. She was put off by being isolated and not interacting with others. She did not find the language of the text particularly accessible either; she was aware of the audience, and she read simply for the tests. Alvermann (2002) contrasted the literacy experiences of today's adolescents with the academic literacy of the classroom. She pointed out that school reading tends to privilege books over other media; by contrast, adolescents are interested in different media, particularly hypermedia. Much of Samantha's delight with the social context of group work and with the exploratory world of the Internet and her discouragement with the text reading illustrated such preferences.

In the remainder of this article, we examine other drawings and other comments. The first section describes the techniques we used to conduct the study. The next section focuses on students' experiences of read-alouds and silent, independent reading. We then turn to a discussion of oral reading, which many students identified as a practice associated with not being engaged. The final section includes comments and observations about other school reading practices and speculations on student perception and its potential for enhancing pedagogy for adolescent students.

The Study

We invited middle school students from four schools in different Vermont communities to talk and draw about their school experiences. Although the student group reflects the lack of ethnic and racial diversity of Vermont, we did obtain a group of 20 young adolescents, grades 4 through 8, who differed in other ways. Teachers nominated students they thought would be willing to meet with one of us; lists from different classes were combined and stratified for gender and academic achievement level as indicated by teachers. Five students were randomly selected from each school. We stratified the schools in terms of socioeconomic status (an important factor in Vermont schools), size, and geographic regions. The following school building classifications represented variation as well.

Town School was a middle-sized (N = 300 pupils), K–6 school located in the center of a town where the median income was about US$41,000. At this friendly, busy school, multiage classes were being eliminated for older students during the period of this study.

Village School was a very small, rural (N = 100) K–6 school with multiage classes and considerable teacher freedom in curricular decisions. The median income was about US$46,000.

Mountain School was a grades 6–8 school (N = 275) that had a traditional, departmentalized junior high school configuration. Families had lived in the town for many generations. The median income of about US$35,500 was the lowest of the towns in the study.

Main Street School was large (*N* = 1,112) with a smaller unit for grades 5 through 8. The middle school had a student-centered, interdisciplinary approach. The median income was US$73,000.

School and individual contextual data are clearly important and are provided here. In this study, because we sought student perceptions of their school lives, we do not refer to the labels and categories that make up the norms of school. In this way the students' experiences emerge without the interpretations that come with test scores or school reports. Ultimately, whether a student is a great reader or one who struggles, we felt their personal experiences of times of engagement and lack thereof would yield important information.

We met the students individually in private spaces in their schools during the school day. The drawing and interview sessions were each about an hour long. We tape-recorded and transcribed all interviews. The protocol was semistructured: We began by asking students to describe a typical day; they then drew a time when engaged in learning and talked about it, then drew and discussed a time when they were not engaged, and then talked about ideas for school reform. In second interviews, during the beginning of the next school year, we asked, "What are some of the different ways you read, in reading class and the other subjects? How have you learned more about reading?" The additional interview data enriched and confirmed our preliminary understandings of the students' perceptions of school reading.

In these interviews, the students revealed their prior successes and failures, their preferred ways of experiencing curriculum and pedagogy, and their thoughts about learning. In both interviews, they referred to recent and past events. The students talked about the classroom social structures. They were respectful of their teachers and schools; indeed, overall, these students seemed relatively pleased with their school lives. They talked about and depicted times when reading was central.

While surveys are effective for gathering data about learner attitudes, strategies, and preferences toward reading (e.g., Ivey & Broaddus, 2001), drawing is also a useful tool for exploring students' perceptions. Drawing has a history of being used as a form of intelligence testing in children (Goodenough, 1926) and as an indicator of the development of cognitive and drawing ability (Golomb, 1992). A few researchers have used drawing as a way to study students' perceptions of school experiences. Some have used drawing as a means for measuring student experience of school reform (e.g., Bebell, 2001; Chula, 1998; Haney, Russell, Gulek, & Fierros, 1998) or reactions to large-scale testing (Haney, Russell, & Jackson, 1997). Other authors studied perceptions of teachers (Weber & Mitchell, 1995). Among those who have used drawing, few have combined them with interview as Robert Coles (1990, 1995) did in his books about children's responses to crisis and compelling moral issues.

We felt the combination of the nonverbal drawing with talk in the interview provided methodological strengths. Although a few students expressed concern about their ability to draw, they were reassured by our explanations that we were interested in their thinking, not their artistry. The middle schoolers chose specific times for their drawings, and they connected those times to experiences over a longer period. The drawings focused the talk; in turn, the talk elaborated the meaning of the drawings. In this process, the drawings became objects from which the students gained perspective on their experiences. More important for applications to teaching, drawing maintained the students' experience as the focus; as a result, the students controlled the content of the interviews. The small sample size, combined with the ethnographic method, resulted in an in-depth and qualitative study of student perceptions of engagement. We mean to highlight the importance of different students' perceptions, not to generalize these experiences to other students.

Engaging Reading Experiences

Like the sixth graders in the Ivey and Broaddus (2001) report, the students spoke warmly about two kinds of reading: teacher read-alouds and silent, independent reading. These activities are common elements of classroom reading and appeared often in the interviews.

Although students did not draw about read-alouds, several spoke in passing of this practice as common in their school days. Charlie, a fifth grader at Town Elementary, in his typically unadorned and direct way, said, for example,

Charlie: My teacher reads to us and we listen.
Interviewer: This year?
Charlie: Yes. All years.

Several other students made similar comments.

At Mountain School, according to Cory, grade 7, "The whole team would meet…and we do like announcements and maybe Mr. H, it's usually him, he'd read a book or maybe a short story." Teachers at both Village and Town Elementary Schools were reading *Holes* (Sachar, 1998). Two girls voiced similar, favorable perspectives.

Linzzy: Yes. We all like it. We figure out all these things.
Stacey: It was really good.

Charlie, when asked whether he preferred read-alouds to silent reading, said, "Have her [the teacher] read it to the class. It's easier." Generally, these students seemed to appreciate when their teachers read to them.

Shelley, a high-achieving eighth grader at Mountain School (where more traditional approaches were used), however, had a more negative experience with a teacher reading expository material: "In geography and most of the days we just, like, our teachers will sit there and read out of the book or something and it's just really boring and it's hard to, like, concentrate on it because it's so boring." While read-alouds may support reading growth for younger students in regard to comprehension and vocabulary growth (Dreher, 2000), its value for older students needs further exploration. Ivey (2003) suggested an important link between read-alouds used as a model for reading and careful selection of interesting "informational text connected to your own curriculum standards" (pp. 812–813). Shelley would probably appreciate more contextualized reading.

Many students specified silent, independent reading as common in their school experiences. They showed the conditions of silent, independent reading that led to their perceptions of its being engaging. Nad's drawing revealed that his engagement was private, a time of being "lost" in the book—essentially disappearing into it. A strong reader but struggling with math, 11-year-old Nad (from tiny Village Elementary) told us he had moved several times prior to this school year but now, in this multiage class, was much happier. His drawing (Figure 2) expressed the quiet and security of this experience.

Nad explained, "I like…I just like…I always do good silent sustained reading. I'm always focused when I'm reading." Nad said he enjoyed the quiet atmosphere of the room at these times

**Figure 2
Reading Silently**

of Sustained Silent Reading (SSR). "Yeah...It's nice and quiet. I always like...I like.... Some people are still making noise 'cause they're like working on something maybe. And I always like to go to the quietest place in the school, well, as I can."

Others also said that silent reading supported their concentration. Although two grades ahead of Nad and at Mountain School, expressive Laurie found that independent reading helped her focus. "'Cause you can read what you want, that's what everybody is doing. You're not having to, like, concentrate from all the noise and stuff going on. It's just nicer." Another seventh grader at that school, Cory, said he liked the fact there were no assignments. "I think I like independent reading the most because I like not having to think of what I'm going to write down like in literature." And Amy, a serious student at Village Elementary, had a unique way of showing her preference for independent reading: "I love reading to my head."

Lance, a fifth grader at Town Elementary who was strong in reading but not in math, like Nad, also favored his time of independent reading, as shown in Figure 3. "OK, this is one of the first books I've read this year.... I chose this book because it's one of the better ones I've read. Because it was kind of short and I like short books. And it was suspenseful. It's a series book. I'm reading the eighth now." Here

he was referring to the events pictured. Lance has included his friend walking over to him with his book. Lance was permitted to read an entire series, and so connected deeply with the characters. The teacher allowed him to choose, one of the tenets of independent reading. For him, SSR allowed time and quiet for personal pleasure—and more practice in reading. This solitary experience of reading that Lance and others described is what many of us do as a matter of course; time in school for such reading is meant to entice more students into doing it.

Choice, pursuing personal preferences, quiet, and not having to write were conditions that led to these students' engagement in silent reading. When she was in the fourth grade, Linzzy showed that she was missing two of these conditions. A strong, confident student at Village School, Linzzy chafed because she felt she had no choice and because she had to complete repetitive writing assignments. In her second drawing, of a time when not engaged, Linzzy depicted herself at her desk with her book and other materials (see Figure 4). Two of the other nearby students had similar objects before them attesting to a common requirement. She represented herself as leaning over the book and her papers, saying, "Oh, man" in anticipation of a long period of silent reading.

> Well. I usually love to read but.... Our teachers will assign us books that we need to read, like, they'll ask us to read books. And I, like, sometimes I don't like the books they assign us to read. And that's when I get really bored because I'm reading books I don't like to read. But for, like, two or three hours, like well, like, two hours I'll be sitting.... And halfway through the book, they'll say, "Do a book report," and then at the end of the book, "I want you to do a book report."

Given the length of time in silent reading (probably not two hours as Linzzy said), one would want clear benefits. In speculating on the broader effects of various forms of silent, independent reading on achievement (summarizing quantitative studies), the National Reading Panel concluded,

> There are few beliefs more widely held than that teachers should encourage students to engage in

Figure 3
Independent Reading Time

voluntary reading and that if they did this successfully, better reading achievement would result. Unfortunately, research has not clearly demonstrated this relationship. In fact, the handful of experimental studies in which this idea has been tried raise serious questions about the efficacy of some of these procedures. (National Institute of Child Health and Human Development, 2000, p. 3-27)

What shall we make of this conundrum—on the one hand students who are engaged when reading silently and independently, preferably in books of their choice, and on the other a lack of evidence of positive impact on reading achievement? The answer, of course, may be that independent reading is a necessary motivator for engaged reading but still is not sufficient as a total reading program for many young adolescents. We looked further, hoping to find other reading experiences that would support reading achievement and found one mentioned often that is neither engaging nor likely to support growth—oral reading.

Oral Reading

Widely used since the beginning of formal education, round-robin sequential oral reading practices, of the sort Samantha describes at the start of this article, have been central to classroom pedagogy. In the words of the authors of the National Reading Panel report, however, these activities "have been criticized as boring, anxiety provoking, disruptive of fluency, and wasteful of instructional time, and their use has been found to have little or no relationship to gains in reading achievement" (National Institute of Child Health and Human Development, 2000, p. 3-11). Unfortunately, several young adolescents talked about just such experiences; in the process, they told us why oral reading was not helpful for them.

A student at Village Elementary, Amy, a reflective, intellectually curious sixth grader, talked about oral reading in social studies. Unlike Samantha, who did not appreciate oral reading of social studies, Amy said that she needed to learn to read orally better, but we noted some real ambivalence.

**Figure 4
Disengagement With Classwork**

We each read a paragraph, or a page, out loud. And it just helps, it helps me because I've read a lot in my head. I don't read out loud much. So this is really.... When I read out loud I kind of stutter and I kind of stumble over words and stuff.

While she believed oral reading was a skill she needed, she said she comprehended better in the silent mode.

Amy: Well, sometimes.... Well when I'm reading to myself, I can, like, remember. I can kind of, like, have a voice in my head that it's the voice that fits the book. But when I'm reading out loud I can't make the voice that fits what I'm reading. So I can't remember it. I'm just trying to think. I'm kind of making a picture because I'm reading faster and I get what's going on, so I get the picture like....

Interviewer: You can't do that when you are orally reading?

Amy: Well, no, it just doesn't go fast enough.

When reading to herself, Amy found "the voice that fits the book;" a strong reader, she was calling on strategies and making images, and she felt she needed to read fast enough to do that. Georgia, a 12-year-old at Main Street School, also needed the speed of silent reading:

> Because you can read at your own pace instead of having to either go too fast or too slow 'cause other people—like when you're in a group sometimes it will go really slow or it can go too fast where you can't understand everything that's going on.

Nad had thoughts about pace and oral reading.

> If I go at my own pace really the books seem better to me. Because some kids in my group they don't read with any expression. And they read really slowly even though I understand that they can't read as well but...I really, I like to just read alone.

In such situations, Laurie said,

> When other people are reading, I tend to read ahead and stuff.... A lot of the people in my class take it literally, are really slow readers and stuff. I don't know. I love to read and so I just like to read right ahead and then finish it.

Given the long history of professional advice against the practice of oral reading, it was surprising to hear from these students of its current use. Perhaps, if their teachers were to hear the students' voices, they would see that oral reading is an obstacle to comprehension, and they might modify their instruction to allow more silent and interactive reading experiences. There was one student, however, who favored some oral reading. Jacob, a seventh grader at Mountain School, said he liked, indeed needed, oral reading. "Just because I don't really like reading a lot and I can listen. So I can read and listen and do both." Jacob was a less successful reader who indicated he needed multiple senses to comprehend. If teachers were aware of students' perceptions, they could structure

differential instruction. Students like Jacob who don't like to read and need to hear as well as read might do that. Others might read silently.

Reading Strategies

Are the techniques of silent, independent reading; read-alouds; and oral reading (for students like Jacob) enough to help students meet the reading demands of secondary school? Research shows that students' comprehension is helped by certain combinations of reading strategies such as imaging, using mnemonic techniques, self-monitoring, using graphic organizers, asking and generating questions, learning story structure, summarizing, using prior knowledge, and, particularly, applying multiple strategies (National Institute of Child Health and Human Development, 2000). Pressley (2002) stressed the value of strategies such as predicting, questioning, imaging, seeking clarification, using prior knowledge, summarizing, and interpreting (p. 280). Teachers should model as they read, challenge (scaffold) students, help them apply the strategies, and talk explicitly about strategy use. Because middle school–age youngsters are asked to read text with increasing complexity, the question of the need for instruction in strategies for comprehending a variety of text types takes on some urgency.

We were mindful of Durkin's (1978/1979) observations that in middle-grade classes there was very little instruction in comprehension in contrast to time spent on assessment, but we thought that the focus on reading strategies and increased interest among local teachers since her study might have created a change in this regard. Pressley and Wharton-McDonald (1997) demonstrated little direct teaching of helpful strategies; still, we expected to find reference to strategy instruction in our data. When we reviewed the transcripts, however, there was only limited evidence of instruction in strategies. We did note above that Samantha reread and considered information needed for her reports and Amy made images to improve her comprehension; whether these girls used strategies as a result of instruction or self-teaching was not clear. We probed for information about strategy use and instruction with all the students and were struck by how little they perceived them as being taught. One exception was Laurie, who reported learning about character maps.

Laurie: I feel they're kind of stupid, and then that's the hero's journey thing. You write all the stuff that builds up to like the big climax, the big like frustration point in the story.

Interviewer: Looks like you haven't gotten to the climax.

Laurie: I guess not. I don't know. I'm so confused.

On the other hand, in response to the interviewer's queries—"But when you are trying to find out about Egypt, how do you know how to read to get information? And how do you know what's important information and what's not?" Lance responded:

Lance: Look in the index.

Interviewer: And how did you learn to look in the index?

Lance: I think it was from my mom.

The following exchange is from an interview with Charlie.

Interviewer: So how do you learn to read like a textbook? Do you have classes?

Charlie: Yeah. If we see a word and we don't know it, we ask the teacher, and the next time we see it, we remember what the teacher said.

The kinds of questions asked of students made a difference to their comprehension; some students were aware that certain questions guided them to greater understanding. Stacey, a serious student at Town School, described how she learned when she was talking about teacher-led reading groups.

Because the teacher asks us questions about the book. And we have to answer them. And we get more and more into it.... We have to write inferences and write why, like, why we wrote the inferences.

During our follow-up interviews, when talking about the conferences on her reading held in her new, fifth-grade class, Linzzy was more certain and specific about the role of questions that required her to construct answers from the literal meaning.

Linzzy: I don't know, she asks the kind of questions that don't really come out in the book. Like...not they've stated, "Treat was left by the monks under the bridge." Not, like, "How did Treat get there?" They just came out and said that. But the kind of questions that were kind of beneath the surface.

Interviewer: Beneath the surface?

Linzzy: Yeah.... You need to understand what you are reading and you need to figure things out to answer the questions.

Other students spoke of questions, too, but in ways that were reminiscent of Durkin's (1978/1979) observations of questions as assessment rather than as invitations to think more deeply. For example, Cory (Mountain School) said, "We have, like, readings and we have to answer questions," and Georgia (Main Street School) had this to say:

Georgia: We just basically we read to a certain chapter and then we have questions that we do. Sometimes we'll get a paper on it that might ask questions about the book.

Interviewer: Do you talk about it?

Georgia: Yep. We have discussions about it, and some people can ask questions about what's going on in the book and things like that.

Some students felt that grouping for reading was an important part of their school reading experiences. Shelley said she liked small groups because "you can talk." She said, "And sometimes we have, like, paired reading. Well, like, if it's not, like, a silent work time we get to pick a partner we want to read with and we get to read the same book."

Several students mentioned literature groups, for example, a fifth grader from Town School named Wildflower.

Wildflower: The whole group is reading the same book and we all have different jobs.

Interviewer: What's your job?

Wildflower: My job right now is Passage Master. I find passages in the book that I like and I want to discuss with the group.

Paula, an eighth grader, reported on a literature group experience at Main Street School.

> Actually I'm in a larger group that Mr. A is teaching...but usually you just, like, talk about what's going on and what you've read, like, that night or, like, some problems in that chapter or something like setting, characters and stuff.

Another eighth grader at Main Street, an advanced student, Anthony, said students chose their literature class.

> Like currently the one I'm in, Mr. H. is doing it, it's not one book. We're reading a lot of short stories. He titled it the Twilight Zone and kind of.... We're working with human strengths and lack of human strengths.

Anthony made it clear that the literature study was conceptually organized. Though present in their school experiences, literature groups were not portrayed in student drawings as times of engagement or lack thereof.

What can we make of these perceptions of the relative frequency of techniques such as read-alouds; independent, silent reading; answering questions; oral reading; and literature groups compared with the absence of much representation of direct teaching of reading strategies? Even though read-alouds and silent reading are engaging, they are probably not sufficient for middle school students. The solution lies in balance. We concur with Pressley's (2002) notion that young adolescents need experience with independent, silent, free choice reading and also with the explicit teaching of skills and, especially, the combination of strategies taught in ways that help students practice their use.

The recent report issued by the RAND Corporation (Snow et al., 2002) called attention to this issue:

> Research has shown that many children who read at the third grade level in grade 3 will not automatically become proficient comprehenders in later grades. Therefore, teachers must teach comprehension explicitly, beginning in the primary grades and continuing through high school. (p. 10)

This major research review and interpretation highlighted the need for strategy instruction to be taught explicitly, especially for poor comprehenders.

In shaping reading instruction for middle-grade students that is engaging and also enhances critical comprehension, knowing about student perception is important. Teachers who know how individual students perceive and understand classroom events could adapt to their needs. If Laurie's teacher knew that she thought character maps were unhelpful, even stupid, he or she would be in a much stronger position for redesigning instruction to show Laurie more about how these techniques could deepen knowledge of characters and character development. If Nad's teacher understood the importance of a quiet environment to Nad's reading engagement, he might turn more of his attention to matters of classroom climate. If the teachers who use oral reading were to hear their students' complaints that it hinders, not helps, comprehension, they might use those perceptions as important indicators.

More generally, class discussion and sharing of perceptions, especially using drawing, could provide opportunities for learning. Reflections on how students gather information from reading would be opportunities for learning from one another. If students saw

Samantha's picture and heard her talk about the value of reading material off the Internet for her reports and plays, they might consider how one decides what information to use. If her peers heard about Amy's voice in her head, they might discuss aspects of metacognition and reading. Linzzy's talk of questions that led her to consider the meaning beneath the surface could be a chance to compare questions. If classrooms were open to talk about how new ideas and experiences were perceived, students could learn from one another, teachers could design strategy instruction that meets student needs, and confusion and misunderstanding could be avoided.

Given the traditional power relationships between teachers and students, however, it would be incorrect to imply that it would be easy to move into open sharing of student perceptions. Students hide their thoughts, of course, as Jackson (1960/1990) pointed out, and as many others have noted. Cook-Sather (2002), a strong advocate of listening to students, cautioned that it is essential to react to what we hear from students; otherwise there is a reversion to the same old power relationships. As a result, it is necessary to be deliberate and intentional when encouraging student perceptions. We are mindful that such interaction is delicate.

Though this is an initial exploration, we intend to follow up to find whether the use of drawing is a technique for teachers to use in initiating helpful talk with their students. We expect that, as was the case for our 20 students, as students draw their own experiences and as they talk with peers and teachers about those pictures, their drawings will become increasingly important to them and to others. As objects that tell stories that are neither right nor wrong, the drawings stimulate reflection about process. The drawings and the talk around them foster reactions in which the uniqueness of each student's perceptions is honored. The material of the drawings and talk provides educators with valuable information that is useful to fit reading instruction to student needs.

References

Alvermann, D. (2002). Effective literacy instruction. *Journal of Literacy Research, 34*, 189–208.

Bebell, D.J. (2001, April). *1,000 words: What can we learn from middle school students' classroom drawings?* Paper presented at the annual meeting of the New England Educational Research Organization, Portsmouth, NH.

Chula, M. (1998, April). *Adolescents' drawings: A view of their worlds.* Paper presented at the annual meeting of the American Educational Research Association, San Diego, CA.

Coles, R. (1990). *The spiritual life of children.* Boston: Houghton Mifflin.

Coles, R. (1995). *Listening to children: A moral journey with Robert Coles.* Video produced by Social Media Productions in cooperation with the Center for Documentary Studies at Duke University. Distributed by PBS Home Video.

Cook-Sather, A. (2002). Authorizing students' perspectives: Toward trust, dialogue, and change in education. *Educational Research, 31*, 3–14.

Dreher, M.J. (2000). Fostering reading for learning. In L. Baker, M.J. Dreher, & J.T. Guthrie, (Eds.), *Engaging young readers: Promoting achievement and motivation* (pp. 68–93). New York: Guilford.

Durkin, D. (1978/1979). What classroom observations reveal about reading comprehension. *Reading Research Quarterly, 15*, 481–533.

Erickson, F., & Schultz, J. (1992). *Handbook of research on curriculum.* New York: MacMillan.

Golomb, C. (1992). *The child's creation of a pictorial world.* Berkeley: University of California Press.

Goodenough, F. (1926). *The measurement of intelligence by drawing.* New York: New World Books.

Guthrie, J.T., & Anderson, E. (1999). Engagement in reading: Processes of motivated, strategic, knowledgeable, social readers. In J.T. Guthrie & D.E. Alvermann (Eds.), *Engaged reading: Processes, practices and policy implications* (pp. 17–45). New York: Teachers College Press.

Haney, W., Russell, M., Gulek, C., & Fierros, E. (1998). Drawing on education: Using student drawings to promote middle school improvement. *Schools in the Middle, 7*(3), 38–43.

Haney, W., Russell, M., & Jackson, L. (1997). *Drawing on education: Using drawings to study and change education and schooling* [Research proposal]. Unpublished manuscript, Center for the Study of Testing, Evaluation, and Educational Policy at Boston College, Chestnut Hill, MA.

Ivey, G. (2003). "The teacher makes it more explainable" and other reasons to read aloud in the intermediate grades. *The Reading Teacher, 56*, 812–814.

Ivey, G., & Broaddus, K. (2001). "Just plain reading": A survey of what makes students want to read in middle school classrooms. *Reading Research Quarterly, 36*, 350–377. doi: 10.1598/RRQ.36.4.2

Jackson, P. (1990). *Life in classrooms.* New York: Teachers College Press. (Original work published 1960)

National Institute of Child Health and Human Development. (2000). *Report of the National Reading Panel. Teaching children to read: An evidence-based assessment of the scientific research literature on reading and its implications for reading instruction: Reports of the subgroups.* (NIH Publication No. 00-4769). Washington, DC: U.S. Government Printing Office.

Pollard, A., Thiessen, D., & Filer, A. (Eds.). (1997). *Children and their curriculum: The perspectives of primary and elementary school children.* London: Falmer.

Pressley, M. (2002). *Reading instruction that works: The case for balanced teaching* (2nd ed.). New York: Guilford.

Pressley, M., & Wharton-McDonald, R. (1997). Skilled comprehension and its development through instruction. *School Psychology Review, 26,* 448–466.

Sachar, L. (1998). *Holes.* New York: Farrar Straus Giroux.

Snow, C.E., Alvermann, D., Dole, J., Garcia, G.E., Gaskins, I., Graesser, A., et al. (2002). *Reading for understanding: Toward an R&D program in reading comprehension.* Santa Monica, CA: RAND Corporation.

Weber, S., & Mitchell, C. (1995). *"That's funny, you don't look like a teacher": Interrogating images and identity in popular culture.* London: Falmer.

Professional Learning and Leadership

The Professional Learning and Leadership Standard is based on a commitment to lifelong learning by all reading professionals. Educators learn in many different ways (e.g., individual learning through various activities such as reading, pursuing advanced degrees, or attendance at professional meetings). At the same time, such learning is often collaborative and occurs in the workplace through activities such as grade-level meetings, academic team meetings, workshops, and study groups. One of the underlying assumptions of this standard is that quality teaching is not something learned and then repeated as a routine, but rather such teaching is a constantly evolving activity that requires continuous reflection and revision. Standard 6 and its elements follow:

> **Standard 6. Professional Learning and Leadership. Candidates recognize the importance of, demonstrate, and facilitate professional learning and leadership as a career-long effort and responsibility. As a result, candidates**
>
> • **Element 6.1 Demonstrate foundational knowledge of adult learning theories and related research about organizational change, professional development, and school culture.**
>
> • **Element 6.2 Display positive dispositions related to their own reading and writing and the teaching of reading and writing, and pursue the development of individual professional knowledge and behaviors.**
>
> • **Element 6.3 Participate in, design, facilitate, lead, and evaluate effective and differentiated professional development programs.**
>
> • **Element 6.4 Understand and influence local, state, or national policy decisions.**

Part 6 includes four journal articles and two news briefs that may be helpful in understanding the substance of the standard and its elements. These pieces are briefly described here.

Risko and colleagues (2008) provide a review and critique of empirical investigations on teacher preparation for reading instruction. Several important findings about effective university practices include the need for explicit explanations and examples, demonstrations, and opportunities for guided practice in practicum settings with pupils. Cobb (2005) discusses the importance of a team approach to literacy leadership, indicating that when schools become collegial communities of practice, teaching and learning will be engaging, motivating, and invigorating. Both of these articles provide important information about adult learning, especially adults preparing to be reading professionals or those working in school settings (Elements 6.1, 6.3).

Blamey, Meyer, and Walpole (2008) discuss the results of a national survey of practicing middle school and high school coaches and indicate that such professionals need to have "research-based knowledge of literacy strategies, content area literacy instruction, and effective adult learning techniques" (pp. 367–368). This article provides important information about the individual competence needed by reading professionals that is important to those designing certification or preparation programs for reading specialists/literacy coaches (Elements 6.1, 6.2, 6.3).

L'Allier, Elish-Piper, and Bean (2009) describe seven research-based principles for those serving as literacy coaches; the article includes supporting evidence and examples for those reading professionals serving as reading specialists or literacy coaches in schools. This article addressees Elements 6.2 and 6.3, identifying important information about the knowledge, skills, and dispositions needed by reading professionals and the importance of coaching as an approach to professional development.

The final two news briefs, which speak specifically to Element 6.4, come from the Literacy Coaching Clearinghouse (www.literacycoachingonline.org) supported by International Reading Association/National Council of Teachers of English. The first news brief by Mangin (July 24, 2009) addresses the factors that influence districts to employ literacy coaches; the second by Bean and Isler (July 26, 2008) discusses questions that local school boards may have about literacy coaching and its effectiveness as a means of improving teacher practices and student learning. When professionals have an understanding of the issues underlying decisions made by local, state, or national agencies, they are be better prepared to influence those decisions.

The pieces in this section give substance to the concept of professionalism. They include those that describe research in the field, especially related to preparing classroom teachers of reading, and those that emphasize application of research findings to lifelong learning of reading professionals.

Further Reading

Blachowicz, C.L.Z., Buhle, R., Ogle, D., Frost, S., Correa, A., & Kinner, J.D. (2010). Hit the ground running: Ten ideas for preparing and supporting urban literacy coaches. *The Reading Teacher, 63*(5), 348–359.

Dole, J.A. (2004). The changing role of the reading specialist in school reform. *The Reading Teacher, 57*(5), 462–471. doi:10.1598/RT.57.5.6

International Reading Association. (2006). *Standards for middle and high school literacy coaches.* Newark, DE: Author.

Kinnucan-Welsch, K., Rosemary, C.A., & Grogan, P.R. (2006). Accountability by design in literacy professional development. *The Reading Teacher, 59*(5), 426–435. doi:10.1598/RT.59.5.2

Thibodeau, G.M. (2008). A content literacy collaborative study group: High school teachers take charge of their professional learning. *Journal of Adolescent & Adult Literacy, 52*(1), 54–64. doi:10.1598/JAAL.52.1.6

Questions for Reflection and Discussion

• What are the key ideas about preparing teachers that can be gleaned from the Risko et al. synthesis of research about teacher preparation? How can these ideas enhance the knowledge, skills, and dispositions of beginning teachers?

• What attributes of effective professional development are identified in the articles presented for this standard? In what ways can schools use these attributes to build an effective professional development program for their faculty?

• After reading the articles about literacy coaches and coaching in this section, what qualifications do you believe are essential for those preparing for such a position? What should be included in any program designed to prepare literacy coaches?

• If asked to build a job description for a literacy coaching position, what would it include as part of the coaching role? What expectations would be identified for the coach? How would the coach be expected to distribute his or her time?

A Critical Analysis of Research on Reading Teacher Education

Victoria J. Risko, Cathy M. Roller, Carrice Cummins, Rita M. Bean, Cathy Collins Block, Patricia L. Anders, and James Flood

The effectiveness of teacher preparation for reading instruction has been a focus of literacy researchers during the last decade and a half. This work has been conducted in the context of a larger literature investigating the effectiveness of teacher preparation in general. Our understanding of how prospective teachers learn to teach has increased during the last 30 years (Feiman-Nemser, 1990; Wilson, Floden, & Ferrini-Mundy, 2001), but findings are contradictory (Wideen, Mayer-Smith, & Moon, 1998) or insufficient for providing explanatory power about features of effective teacher education programs, especially when their effectiveness is measured by pupil gains in the classrooms where prospective teachers teach. The purpose of this review is to examine and synthesize the extant research, focusing specifically on college students enrolled in university- or college-based teacher education programs preparing future K–12 classroom teachers to teach reading.

Conceptualizing the Review

Seminal reviews of the general "learning to teach" research have been conducted, including those by Carter (1990), Grant and Secada (1990), Sleeter (2001), and Wideen et al. (1998). These reviews, particularly Wideen et al. (1998), helped us to frame our review around the broad goals of identifying the characteristics and understandings of a field's research and analyzing these understandings. To focus our review further, we examined the literature reviews of reading teacher education that have been reported within the last decade: Darling-Hammond (1999), Anders, Hoffman, and Duffy (2000), Hoffman and Pearson (2000), National Institute of Child Health and Human Development (NICHD; 2000), Pearson (2001), Roskos, Vukelich, and Risko (2001), Clift and Brady (2005), and Pang and Kamil (2006).

These literature reviews vary in the types of research included and how the reviewers judged their contributions and usefulness. There is general agreement among these reviewers that limited research is available to guide teacher education programmatic design or specific course development. We describe briefly these reviews and their methodologies.

The National Reading Panel report (NICHD, 2000) restricted studies examined to experimental or quasi-experimental studies and located only 11 such studies. They found these studies encouraging, in that most of them indicated that teacher education does affect prospective teachers' learning, but they concluded that there were too few studies to draw conclusions about the content of teacher preparation. They also noted that none of the 11 studies provided measures of student achievement.

The literature reviews by the others listed above included studies representing a broader range of research methodologies and were generally more positive about teacher preparation for reading instruction. Darling-Hammond (1999) correlated certification and reading

Preparing Reading Professionals (second edition), edited by Rita M. Bean, Natalie Heisey, and Cathy M. Roller. © 2010 by the International Reading Association. Reprinted from Risko, V.J., Roller, C.M., Cummins, C., Bean, R.M., Block, C.C., Anders, P.L., et al. (2008). A critical analysis of research on reading teacher education. *Reading Research Quarterly, 43*(3), 252–288. doi:10.1598/RRQ.43.3.3.

achievement using National Assessment of Educational Process reading scores and concluded that pupils taught by certified teachers had higher reading achievement scores than those taught by teachers who were not certified. Pearson (2001), citing the Darling-Hammond study and other correlational work, arrived at a similar conclusion. Hoffman and Pearson (2000) argued that the field has advanced by shifting its focus from technical training-oriented programs to more robust preparation-oriented programs based on a view of teaching as a complex domain. A review by Anders and colleagues (2000) noted that the literature showed positive teacher outcomes related to attitude and to the expressed value of teacher preparation. Roskos and colleagues' (2001) review focused on prospective teachers' reflection practices. They concluded that, although researchers have established detailed descriptions of prospective teachers' reflective thinking and of procedures for evaluating it, researchers have offered limited guidance for advancing reflective thinking. Finally, Pang and Kamil (2006) concluded that the qualitative studies they reviewed provided in-depth descriptions of how researchers examined reflective teaching and instructional decision making. They also advocated for mixed-method studies to build on this descriptive work.

Clift and Brady (2005), members of the American Educational Research Association panel on research and teacher education, analyzed research published between 1995 and 2001 that focused on the impact of methods courses (i.e., those courses that prepare teachers to teach) and teaching experiences in K–12 classrooms on teacher learning. A small part of their review examined studies of reading and English language arts methods courses. They noted an overall positive trend in prospective teachers' development in methods courses. They also concluded that prospective teachers often resist content taught in methods courses and field experiences; benefit from structured and sustained interactions with students in field placements; and benefit from mentoring and supervised teaching experiences, including mentoring from peer coaches.

These reviews indicated that a close, comprehensive analysis of current reading teacher education research was needed. As appointed members of the Teacher Education Task Force of the International Reading Association (IRA), the author team for this review included faculty researchers from six universities and IRA's Director of Research and Policy. We came to this project with the belief that reading teacher educators need a comprehensive understanding of the current research of reading teacher education so as to be able to explain its benefits and limitations and to inform and improve future research.

We began our work by delineating specific objectives: (a) to identify criteria (and quality indicators) for selecting high-quality research, (b) to conduct a comprehensive search and analysis of empirical research meeting these criteria, (c) to analyze the theoretical arguments and practical questions guiding research studies and their relative contributions to a teacher education research agenda, and (d) to identify the questions and designs that hold promise for guiding future research recommendations.

Inclusiveness of Review Criteria

Multiple theoretical perspectives have influenced teacher education research, and these are represented in the studies we reviewed. Authors of this review were committed to being inclusive of research studies that represent different theoretical stances and related paradigms and to representing their contributions to building understandings of how prospective teachers learn to teach reading. We assumed that we would find that the theoretical arguments grounding the studies in our review would lie in the grand theories of learning: behaviorism, cognitivism, constructivism, socioculturalism, and critical theory. We were well acquainted with these theories and recognized that the distinctions between them are often blurred. For example, as Windschitl (2002) noted, researchers often fail to distinguish cognitive constructivism from social constructivism. Nonetheless, we were curious as to the theories researchers linked to their work.

One perspective assumes a body of well-specified knowledge that teachers need to learn to be effective; we have labeled this a positivist/behavioral theoretical perspective. Researchers who align their research with this theory typically set up conditions and didactic forms of instruction to impart or transmit this knowledge to learners. Learning to teach is viewed as an additive process—a process where knowledge and teaching behaviors are hypothesized and documented as being acquired within teacher education courses or activities and then applied in supervised teaching situations. This theory dominated the teacher effectiveness research of the 1970s and 1980s (e.g., Rosenshine, 1979) and was linked to training studies and competency-based teacher education programs of the 1970s (Ryan, 1975) and to teaching effectiveness and process product studies of the 1980s (Duffy, 1981; Hoffman, 1986). Consistent with a positivist/behavioral paradigm were expectations for prospective teachers to master specific observable teacher behaviors and competencies that, in some studies, correlated with pupil achievement scores. Numerous lists of skills and knowledge areas were developed and taught. Prospective teachers were taught in didactic settings where outcomes are specified and measured and contexts for learning are carefully controlled. One outcome of this work resulted in preparing teachers to follow direct instruction teaching cycles (i.e., teach–assess–reteach with contingent reinforcement; Rosenshine, 1979; Stallings & Kaskowitz, 1974). These positivist/behavioral explanations of teaching and learning are well embedded in educational practice and continue to influence teacher education research.

A second theory influencing teacher education research is cognitive. Bartlett (1932) and Piaget (1932) described memory as schemata, and the importance of learners' prior knowledge was foregrounded. For teacher educators, this meant drawing attention to the study of how prospective teachers learned professional and practical knowledge and how prior beliefs and experience may affect such learning and decision making (Carter, 1990; Lanier, 1982; Zumwalt, 1982). Additionally, cognitive researches are interested in establishing what prospective teachers need to know, conditions where particular forms of knowledge may be required, and how reflective processes can deepen knowledge and flexible applications while teaching (Fenstermacher, 1994).

Constructivist learning theory as it applies to teacher education research had its roots in the study of how prospective teachers transform their professional knowledge as they make connections to prior knowledge and construct meanings of classrooms and learning while guided by others, including teacher educators and the children in their classrooms (Shulman, 1986). Constructivists focus on teacher education as a learning problem and document conditions that may contribute to changes in teachers' use of multiple knowledge sources to solve problems (Wilson et al., 2001). Building on this orientation, constructivist researchers in the 1990s considered more specifically how prospective teachers acquire knowledge within problem-solving, inquiry, and collaborative dialogic learning activities designed to help them generate connections between theory, their own beliefs, prior knowledge, and practice. The constructivist orientation, in particular, is grounded in assumptions that knowledge acquisition requires intentionality of the learner (e.g., teachers' own inquiry, teachers' problem solving; Gardner, 1989; Murray, 1996); it represents shifts away from transmission models of teaching. Researchers also are interested in how knowledge is developed and shared with peers and others and in conditions enabling this social construction of changed knowledge, perceptions, and beliefs.

Sociocultural theory describes learning as not simply what happens in the brain of an individual but what happens to the individual in relation to a social context and the multiple forms of interactions with others (e.g., Bakhtin, 1981; Scribner & Cole, 1981; Wertsch, 2002). This theory has had an impact on teacher education because it helps educators to better understand the possibilities for teaching culturally and linguistically diverse students (Grant & Secada, 1990; Nieto, 1999; Sleeter, 2001). This perspective prioritizes helping prospective teachers understand their own cultural practices and those of others, the impact of cultural experiences on teaching and learning, and the value of implementing culturally supportive reading instruction (e.g., Ellsworth, 1989).

As education literacy scholars explore constructivist and sociocultural theories of teaching reading, questions related to power relationships and social justice emerge; hence, critical theories have become a source of exploration and explanation for teacher education. Siegel and Fernandez (2000) noted that critical theory and its related approaches address questions about the "inequalities and injustices that persist in schools and society...and how literacy instruction may become a site for contesting the status quo" (p. 140). Hence, this theory draws attention to the importance of teachers attending to issues of social justice and the ways that teachers, other educators, and policymakers are responsible for equitable learning conditions in schools and classrooms.

We made every effort to be fair and inclusive of others' perspectives in our review and to report on the relative contributions of the theories informing the work of our researchers. We recognized that our contributions to this review were influenced by our individual theories, and we attempted to maintain objectivity by acknowledging these with one another by coming together at least six times to discuss our analytical notes and interpretations and to gather evidence from studies that contributed to our interpretations, by collaborating in joint inquiry, and by developing shared and negotiated understandings of the papers. As we examined each study, we considered how theoretical assumptions guided research questions, design, methodology, and interpretations, and we shared the theoretical perspectives of the researchers as contributing elements of the work. We then engaged in our own discourse to generate a collaborative interpretive analysis

and critique. This collaboration enabled us to understand the researchers' perspectives and one another's preconceptions and expectations. This discussion often took us back to the studies to seek details that confirmed our hunches and interpretations or to raise questions, with the continuing goal of representing accurately the perspectives of the researchers. We agreed with Wideen and colleagues (1998), however, that our histories, experiences, and perspectives were influential on the meaning that we made of these individual reports and the sense that we constructed across the reports.[1]

The author team was also inclusive of research methodologies. We designed our methodology—including our coding instruments—in ways that would honor diverse methodologies, and we consulted with a range of scholars throughout the design process.[2]

Finally, as we approached this task, we recognized the limitations of teacher education research in general—and more specifically the research focusing on preparing future classroom teachers for reading instruction—are well documented in the previous reviews. Sparse funding has historically limited efforts to build cross-programmatic research collaborations, longitudinal studies, and comprehensive research databases or to establish empirical evidence on teaching practices and pupil achievement that can be associated with specific methods of teacher preparation. Research studies tend to be small in scale, typically conducted at the local level to examine teaching and learning in one or two college courses.

Method for Literature Review

This review examines high-quality, published studies identified by criteria we established. We evaluated each study's methodology in relation to the questions addressed and the adequacy and quality of the methodology for addressing the stated questions. We adhered to the "logics in use" concept (i.e., methodological paradigms and research designs must conform to the questions under study) provided by Kaplan (1964) and discussed by Howe and Eisenhart (1990).

Selection of Empirical Studies for Review

The selection process involved several steps. First, we identified four parameters for studies to be eligible for inclusion:

1. Must have been published empirical and peer-reviewed studies, representing different methodological paradigms

2. Must have been published between 1990 and 2006

3. Must have been focused on the preparation of precertification teachers for K–12 classroom reading instruction

4. Must have been conducted in the United States

Critiques and calls for teacher education reform by the Carnegie Task Force on Teaching as a Profession (1986) and Goodlad (1990) laid the foundation for several seminal papers on teacher education and the development of professional knowledge (e.g., Carter, 1990; Feiman-Nemser, 1990; Kagan, 1992). Noting the increased attention to teacher education research initiated around 1990, we selected 1990 as the starting date for our review. We conducted a series of electronic searches of several databases (ERIC, InfoTrac, ISI Web, PsycINFO) using terms associated with preparing teachers for reading instruction.[3] Next, we completed manual searches of annual conference yearbooks published by the National Reading Conference (NRC), the College Reading Association (CRA), and the American Reading Forum (ARF); the inclusion of empirical papers from annual conference publications was based on knowledge that all papers published had received two rounds of blind peer review for inclusion on the program and for publication. And, finally, we did manual searches of recent journals whose articles would not yet be included in databases.

Our search yielded over 400 abstracts that focused on precertification K–12 teachers. We eliminated theoretical papers, book chapters, unpublished papers, and dissertations because of the absence of the peer review process. We also eliminated articles from international sources because we were not able to assemble what we considered to be a critical mass based on replicable search mechanisms. A total of 233 studies met our basic criteria for inclusion in this review. Of the total 233, 79 came from electronic searches, 53 from NRC, 24 from ARF, 40 from CRA, 8 from the manual journal search, and 29 from bibliographies of other reviews (e.g., Clift & Brady, 2005; Pang & Kamil, 2006) Our fourth selection criterion—research conducted only in the United States—was added after we inspected the 233 papers more closely. Of these, only three reported on research conducted outside the United States. Even with an additional search of all electronic databases available to us and a manual and online search of international journals available to us through our respective universities, we were unable to identify any additional international teacher education studies. We decided to eliminate the three papers we were able to access and limit our review to U.S.-only studies. We judged three studies to be an insufficient number for a critical mass that would allow us to represent fairly the work of teacher educator researchers outside the United States.

Screening for Quality

First, we established seven criteria (associated with three superordinate categories) to assess the quality of the studies. These three categories and the seven criteria are displayed in Table 1. The criteria were influenced by those applied by others (Cochran-Smith & Zeichner, 2005; NICHD, 2000) and identified in the Education Sciences Reform Act (Eisenhart & Towne, 2003). The three categories, which we call standards, were drawn from Guba and Lincoln (1994) and Hatch and Wisniewski (1995), as well as advice from our personal communication with expert research methodologists.

Table 1
Criteria to Assess the Quality of the Studies

Standard	Quality Criteria
Standard 1: Provides a clear argument that links theory and research and demonstrates a coherent chain of reasoning. Explicates theoretical and previous research in a way that builds the formulation of the question(s).	1.1 Explicates theory and previous research in a way that builds the formulation of the question. Poses a question/purpose/objective that can be investigated empirically. 1.2 Explicitly links findings to previous theory and research or argument for study.
Standard 2: Applies rigorous, systematic, and objective methodology to obtain reliable and valid knowledge relevant to education activities and programs.	2.1 Ensures that methods are presented in sufficient detail and clarity to clearly visualize procedures (another person could actually collect the same data). Data collection should be described so that readers can replicate the procedures in a quantitative study and follow the trail of data analysis in a qualitative study. For a qualitative study, researcher should report some of the following: the number of observations, interviews, or documents analyzed; if interviews and observations are taped and/or transcribed; the duration of the observations; the diversity of material analyzed; and the degree of investigator's involvement in the data collection and analysis. 2.2 Relies on measurements or observational methods that provide reliability, credibility, and trustworthiness. For qualitative studies, several aspects of the data collection and analysis should be provided, such as: Were multiple sources of information used to corroborate findings? Was more than one investigator involved in collecting and analyzing data? Was one reseracher checking to represent participants' viewpoints? What kind of sampling occurred (e.g., purposive sampling, unusual cases, typical cases, sampling convenience, critical cases)? How were data classified? 2.3 Describes participants.
Standard 3: Present finding and make claims that are appropriate to and supported by the methods that have been employed. (2 of 3 conditions must be met)	3.1 Findings are consistent with intention of question/purpose. 3.2 Findings are legitimate or consistent for data collected.

Coding of Studies for Inclusion in Review

Next came the coding of the 233 papers, and only papers that met all seven criteria were included in this review. The articles were assigned an overall score of 3 (meets all criteria), 2 (meets between two and six criteria), or 1 (meets one or zero criteria). Eleven independent raters located at four sites were taught to apply the criteria to each paper.[4] To establish reliability, each rater applied the coding criteria on the same 10 articles and, after discussion, raters modified their coding until a concurrence rate of 90% was reached for each article. The coders then scored a second set of 10 articles. Inter-rater reliability on this second set was 92% overall. Thereafter, at least two reviewers at each site read each article and scored on the seven criteria. In every case, the two reviewers of each article resolved disagreements and assigned the final score. Ninety-one articles received a score of 3.

To test for inter-rater reliability of coding over the course of the project, a 10% sample of the articles was distributed to the four review sites for scoring. Agreement among reviewers for each of the seven criteria ranged from 79% to 100%, with an average of 90%. The average discrepancy in the total score on the seven criteria was 0.5. The agreement on the overall scores was 86%.

Because standard 2—adequacy of methodology—had a lower rate of agreement than the other criteria, the team decided to conduct a second coding. The author team working in pairs reanalyzed all articles with a score of 3, plus all articles with a 2 that met at least four of the seven criteria. Each member of the pair independently generated a summary of the research papers assigned to the pair so as to facilitate discussion between the partners and with the larger group. During this process, 11 papers originally rated as a 3 were downgraded to a 2, and two papers originally rated as a 2 were upgraded to a 3. Eighty-two studies comprised the final corpus. Inter-rater agreement on the final scoring across pairs was 94%, with all disagreements resolved through discussion and reference to the two summaries generated for each research paper.

Finally, we used the summaries to code for descriptive information and patterns we were observing in our discussions. One pattern that we coded at this level—explicitness—will be discussed in detail in our findings section of this paper. We also coded what we called "effect strength." To do this we examined for each reported effect the number of participants demonstrating it. We coded as "strong" any effect that held for 75% of the subjects, we coded as "differential" any effect that held for between 50% and 74% of the subjects and as "weak" any effect that held for between 10% and 50% of participants. When effects held for 10% or less, we coded the study as "no effect." Explicitness was scored from 0–5, based upon

how many of the following elements were included in the instruction: explicit explanation, examples, modeling, guided practice, and independent practice.

Two authors conducted the third coding. They worked together on a randomly selected subset of articles until they reached 90% agreement. In addition, they coded one or two studies from each of the seven content categories (discussed below; depending on the total number of studies in the category and whether the researchers achieved 90% agreement) to make sure that there were no anomalies related to article content. Once the coders reached the 90% agreement rate, each researcher coded the remaining articles.

Method for Data Analysis

Because most of the studies in our final pool were qualitative, we applied an inductive paradigmatic analysis process (Polkinghorne, 1995) to analyze the final set of 82 studies. Initially, our analytic task involved identifying and producing categories by classifying details, events, and situations represented in each study and forming networks of concepts out of the data. This analysis produced seven broad content topics: university pedagogy (23%), theoretical orientation (21%), struggling readers (or students experiencing reading difficulties; 17%), content area reading (14%), diversity (12%), reflection (8%), and assessment (6%). Next, we refined our analysis by identifying primary conceptual foci of the studies (i.e., primary research question supported by the authors' argumentation and literature review and addressed with the data analysis). This action reduced our categories to four: research on prospective teachers' beliefs, research on prospective teachers' knowledge and reflection, research on prospective teachers' pedagogy, and research on teacher education programs. This latter category, different from all others in our set, represented those studies that had a primary research focus on the impact of a program (multiple courses and experiences) on teacher preparation (e.g., how prospective teachers valued a sequence of field experiences offered in a program).

The four categories are grounded in our analysis of the studies and derived from our interpretations of the researchers' intentions. Nevertheless, we realize that there may be other ways to organize these data sets for analysis and reporting.

The author team read and reread the studies and developed detailed synopses of each that included the explicit coherence of logic between the theoretical and conceptual arguments, data collection and analysis procedures, results, and implications. Next, we read, reread, and discussed one another's synopses. The discussions often took us back to the papers to check for accuracy and to draw on one another's perspectives for deriving hypotheses, interpretations, and conclusions. Our analytic work enabled us to make connections between the studies by identifying "successive layers of inferential glue" (Miles & Huberman, 1984, p. 238) to derive and confirm conceptual networks guiding the research collection. Through our discussions we generated extensive notes, which we called interpretive comments, to represent our agreed-upon patterns within studies and our collaborative interpretations and critiques. After completing our analyses, we implemented another inductive paradigmatic analysis to identify patterns across the entire corpus of studies, referred to as our macroanalysis (as compared to the more microanalysis of each study within categories). This analysis resulted in a coding matrix that recorded patterns and instances of occurrence across the studies as a whole. We then generated written descriptions of this material.

Limitations

Our review has several limitations. First, as we describe above, our review is limited to those studies conducted within the United States. The decision to exclude all others was made deliberately because of the difficulties we experienced with access and because we would need to restrict the review to those studies written in English. Only three studies were identified in our multiple search attempts, including our manual searches of all international journals available in our respective libraries or online and published in English.

However, we believe that the questions, issues, and findings of this study speak to reading teacher educators and researchers across countries. The methodology of this study might be useful for other researchers who investigate the scope and results of reading teacher education research in their countries. We believe such a review is needed to expand on the work here. While there are similarities across international programs, there are also differences in how prospective teachers are recruited, in the ways in which they are prepared, and in how they are evaluated in terms of their initial performance. We expect, too, that theoretical frameworks may be similar and different.

Second, we organized our review around four conceptual categories: beliefs, knowledge, pedagogy, and program research. These represent the researchers' primary questions—the intentions for their work—and are grounded in our analysis. We acknowledge, however, that there may be other ways to report on and synthesize these studies.

Third, our review is limited to research focusing on prospective teachers, those who are enrolled as undergraduates or graduate students in programs of education that prepare them for initial certification as classroom teachers. Almost all of the prospective teachers in the studies we reviewed were seeking certification in elementary education (which in the United States could prepare teachers for K–4 classrooms, K–8 classrooms, or some combination of these grades).

Findings

We began this review with questions about the defining characteristics (e.g., who were the prospective teachers involved in this research, where and how was research conducted) of our selected studies. Next, we studied the questions of the researchers as we induced categories representing the studies' conceptual foci.

We wanted to understand each study and its relative contribution to this body of work. And once we developed a sense of the studies within categories, we initiated our next inductive analysis to derive patterns representing the set as a whole. We report our findings to represent the questions we posed. First, we present the descriptive and demographic characteristics of the studies. Second, we organize the studies by the four primary conceptual foci that we described earlier, and discuss interpretive patterns we derived. We conclude our discussion of each set of studies with a brief discussion of contributions and concerns. Third, we discuss patterns derived from our macroanalysis of the entire corpus of studies and across conceptual themes.

Our reporting of findings is much like what Wideen et al. (1998) described as a collage—or bricolage (coming from the term *bricoleur* used by Denzin and Lincoln [1994] as someone who has multiple and divergent viewpoints)—conceptually drawing together multiple perspectives by the categories we generated. As our collage developed, however, we could not identify a historical continuity or a way to foreground the historical aspects of this work. In our macroanalysis, we do identify a few historical trends, but for the most part this body of work lacked historical integrity; researchers did not treat their work as building on what came before. We discuss this latter point later in this paper. We did, however, identify high convergence among researchers' goals, questions, and findings, which we believe brings a degree of credibility to the collection as a whole.

Descriptive Characteristics of Studies

With our initial goal to identify defining characteristics, we coded each study for its setting, length, and theoretical orientation; the researchers' role and population characteristics; and the journal type. We use these descriptive data to explain, as much as possible, the context for the studies we reviewed. Our ability to discuss context for this set of studies is limited to the information researchers provided; for the most part, researchers situated their studies in a course or two that they taught or supervised and were silent about how the larger teacher education program may have influenced the work under study. The exception is found in the six studies that examined programmatic features.

Settings for these studies can be described in several ways. First, there is the question about program certification goals. Sixty-two (76%) of the studies were located within a program preparing teachers for elementary and upper grades teaching certification, 11 (13%) were located in secondary certification programs, 4 (5%) were located within programs preparing teachers for early childhood and early grades certification (typically in the United States preparing teachers to teach children from 18 months to age 7), 4 (5%) were located within special education teaching certification programs, and 1 (1%) was located within a K–12 certification program. Because there were so few studies in any category other than elementary education, we could not sort our studies by certification areas for further analysis. However, we do discuss specific patterns associated with the secondary certification studies.

Second, we sorted studies by location within undergraduate versus graduate programs. In the United States, prospective teachers can earn their initial licensure either as undergraduates or as graduates enrolled in master's degree programs with added certification requirements. In the studies, 74 (90%) involved undergraduate students, 5 (6%) involved graduate students, and 3 (4%) had both undergraduate and graduate students enrolled in initial certification programs. With the preponderance of the studies occurring at the undergraduate level, we could not analyze our studies according to undergraduate or graduate placement; there were too few of the latter to be representative.

A third setting characteristic is the type of course or experience where data were collected. The top five settings were methods courses, in which prospective teaches learn about methods of teaching reading (41%), methods courses with practicum (27%), practica with a single student (10%), student teaching (9%), and lab settings organized for data collection (7%).

Fifty-three percent of the studies occurred during one semester, with 7% occurring in a time period less than a semester; 9% occurred during two semesters or one year, 4% occurred over three semesters, 2% occurred during two years or four semesters, and 6% were conducted for more than two years or four semesters. Type of study was coded to identify if researchers described learning or teaching across the time period for groups or cases (11%), performance on prestudy assessments compared to poststudy assessments (43%), performance on single assessments only (37%), and applied experimental or quasi-experimental methods (10%).

Seventy-three percent of the researchers represented a cognitive or constructivist orientation (i.e., 27% and 46% for cognitive and constructivist, respectively) and considered impact of prior knowledge and situated events in the teacher education program on learning to teach. Interpretive work, providing narrative descriptions of teacher education instruction, and prospective teachers' participation in learning or teaching events characterizes the work of this group. Twenty-two percent of the studies represented a sociocultural perspective, including 5% with a critical theory orientation. Researchers in this category drew attention to the importance of learning about multicultural and social inequities issues and the use of this information on cultural responsive pedagogy, with a slight trend toward increased appearance of these studies within the last five years. Five percent adopted a positivist/behavioral perspective.

The following characteristics come from the coding for our remaining descriptive categories. Forty-three percent of the researchers did not specify their role in the investigation, with 31% indicating they were course instructors (observer-participants), and 19% indicating a team of both observer-participants and independent researchers. The research studies were published in refereed research journals (57%) and refereed proceedings (43%; 29% of the 150 papers taken from conference proceedings met our criteria for inclusion in the review).

Papers selected from the refereed research journals were located in literacy journals (43%), teacher education journals (40%), special education journals (4%), and other journals (13%). Regarding population characteristics of the studies, 41% of the researchers did not report gender and 64% and 70%, respectively, did not report race or ethnicity. When reported, two thirds of participants were white females.

In summary, research represented in our review was situated mostly in elementary education teacher certification programs with undergraduate students and in reading methods courses with little to no information reported about the programmatic context of these courses. Typically, study duration was not longer than one semester and researchers were also the course instructors with little additional information provided about their histories or beliefs. A constructivist theoretical framework guided almost half of the studies. When reported, prospective teachers were primarily white females of traditional undergraduate age.

We compared these findings to descriptive characteristics of the studies that were eliminated by our quality indices to determine if our sample was representative of the larger pool. We noted the same trends on all variables—75% of these studies occurred in elementary teacher education programs, 85% studied undergraduate populations, 42% occurred in a methods course, 56% during one semester, 3% involved mixed methods, and 45% oriented by a constructivist framework (with others framed respectively by cognitive [33%], sociocultural [13%], and critical theory [3%] orientations). We concluded that our set of studies was representative of the larger set of studies and did not privilege particular theoretical constructs, populations, situations, or duration.

Findings From Research on Beliefs

Once we established the characteristics of our studies, our analysis led us to the heart of our review: We wanted to understand the questions pursued by these researchers and what they learned from their work. In this first section on findings, we discuss 23 (28%) of our 82 studies that addressed prospective teachers' beliefs about the reading process and reading instruction. These studies are summarized in Table 2. Later in the Pedagogy section, we discuss studies examining two additional belief questions: prospective teachers' beliefs about the capabilities of students and their beliefs about their competence as teachers.

Researchers in this category did not include explicit definitions of beliefs and attitudes. Their understandings of teacher beliefs, generally implied in their research questions, however, aligned with definitions commonly found in the teacher belief literature. Such definitions represent beliefs as "any simple proposition, conscious or unconscious, inferred from what a person says or does" (Rokeach, 1972, p. 113)

that can be embedded in an "I believe" statement, and attitudes were treated as an "organization of beliefs" (Rokeach, 1972, p. 113) or more generalized statements of beliefs (e.g., I like to read).

As reported in Table 2, these researchers drew on cognitive (43%), sociocultural (30%), and constructivist (26%) theories to rationalize their study design. From a cognitive perspective, researchers aimed to delineate specific beliefs prospective teachers held about the reading process or reading instruction. Beliefs about cultural differences and their relationship to learning were examined from a sociocultural perspective, while goals to mediate beliefs through guided learning events and peer support were examined from constructivist perspectives.

Table 2
Summaries of Studies—Beliefs

Author(s), Year	Theoretical Orientation	Research Focus	Participants and Setting	Data Sources	Data Analysis
Bean, 1997	Sociocultural	PSTs' vocabulary and comprehension teaching strategies	$N = 27$ (17 F, 10 M; 6 API, 21 C) Content area methods course	Interviews	Constant comparative analysis
Bean & Zulich, 1990	Sociocultural	PSTs' beliefs about content area reading	$N = 3$ (2 C, 1 API) Content area methods course	Dialogue journals	Analytic induction of patterns
Bean & Zulich, 1992	Sociocultural	PSTs' beliefs about content area reading and use in practica	$N = 3$ (ages 39, 42, 88) Content area methods course	Dialogue journals	Constant comparative analysis
Draper, Barksdale-Ladd, & Radencich, 2000	Cognitive	PSTs' beliefs about reading and writing and about reading habits	$N = 24$ Intermediate-grade literacy and language arts methods course	Semistructured interviews	Constant comparative analysis
Dynak & Smith, 1994	Cognitive	PSTs' use of comprehension strategies for summarizing	$N = 132$ Content area methods course	Article summaries and question responses	Repeated measures analysis of variance
Fazio, 2000	Cognitive	PSTs' beliefs about comprehension and metacognitive instruction	$N = 28$ (26 F, 2 M, ages 20–52) Language arts methods course	Dialogue journals, surveys, reflective essays	Constant comparative analysis

(continued)

Table 2 (Continued)
Summaries of Studies—Beliefs

Author(s), Year	Theoretical Orientation	Research Focus	Participants and Setting	Data Sources	Data Analysis
Fazio, 2003	Cognitive	PSTs' beliefs about comprehension and metacognitive instruction; use in year 1 teaching	$N = 1$ (F, C) Language arts methods class in rural middle school	Interviews, observations, course and teaching artifacts, surveys	Constant comparative analysis
Fox, 1994	Constructivist	PSTs' beliefs about literacy instruction	$N = 2$ Teaching literature methods	Semistructured interviews, observations, artifacts, reflective log	Constant comparative analysis; cross-case analysis
Konopak, Readence, & Wilson, 1994	Sociocultural	PSTs' beliefs about content area reading instruction	$N = 58$ (65% F, 35% M); $N = 46$ inservice teachers (70% F, 30% M) Content area methods course	Belief statements, lesson plans	Chi-square
Linek, Sampson, Raine, Klakamp, & Smith, 2006	Constructivist	PSTs' beliefs about reading instruction and possible factors associated with changes	$N = 11$ (F, C) Three methods and practica	Pre-, , mid-, and postquestionnaires field notes, lesson plans and reflections, interviews	Constant comparative analysis; triangulation of data sources
Lonberger, 1992	Cognitive	PSTs' belief systems and instructional choices	$N = 37$ Reading methods course	Pre- and postquestionnaires	Frequency data
Many, Howard, & Hoge, 1998	Constructivist	PSTs' views of themselves as readers	$N = 19$ (15 F, 4 M) Language arts methods course with practica	Interviews, reflections and response logs, surveys, essays	Constant comparative analysis with triangulation
Matanzo & Harris, 1999	Cognitive	PSTs' increased metacognitive awareness after metacognitive instruction	$N = 62$ Reading methods course	Pretest observations, reflections	Interpretative analysis
Moller & Hug, 2006	Constructivist	PSTs' perceptions of connections between science and literacy	$N = 8$ Reading, math, science, and technology methods courses; professional development school	Lesson plans, reflections, field notes, audiotaped lessons	Qualitative—Iterative analysis
Nourie & Lenski, 1998	Sociocultural	PSTs' willingness to learn literacy strategies for content area reading	$N = 90$ and 113 (2 groups) Content area methods course	Pre- and postattitude surveys	Frequency data

(continued)

Table 2 (Continued)
Summaries of Studies—Beliefs

Author(s), Year	Theoretical Orientation	Research Focus	Participants and Setting	Data Sources	Data Analysis
O'Brien & Stewart, 1990	Cognitive	PSTs' attitudes toward content area methods instruction	N = 245 PSTs and 5 teachers Content area methods course	Precourse statements, surveys, learning logs, interviews	Constant comparative analysis
Raine, Levingston, Linek, Sampson, & Linder, 2003	Constructivist	PSTs' beliefs, practices, and change processes at various levels of course work	N = 22 PSTs Internship reading course	Pre- and postquestionnaires	Constant comparative analysis
Stevens, 2002	Sociocultural	PSTs' understandings of adolescent literacy	N = 24 Content area methods course	Audiotapes, field notes, online discussions	Constant comparative analysis
Sturtevant & Spor, 1990	Cognitive	PSTs' use of strategies taught	N = 23 (11 F, 12 M, ages 22–40) Student teaching course	Questionnaires	Quantitative—Tabulation of frequency use
Theurer, 2002	Constructivist	PSTs' changing beliefs as revealed by analyzing own miscues	N = 1 PST (F) Reading methods course	Audio recordings of text readings; retrospective miscue analysis during interview	Qualitative—Identification of patterns, descriptive analysis
Wham, 1993	Cognitive	PSTs' beliefs in relation to course experiences over three semesters, including student teaching	N = 35 PSTs Reading methods courses, Student teaching	Multiple administrations of the TORP (DeFord, 1979) over three semesters	Quantitative comparisons of TORP scores over time; descriptive data on cooperating teachers
Wolf, Carey, & Mieras, 1996a	Cognitive	PSTs' connections between course instruction on artistic interpretation and classroom practice with children	N = 43 PSTs Children's literature course	Case study reports, field notes, artistic renderings	Case study analysis
Zulich, Bean, & Herrick, 1992	Sociocultural	PSTs' stages of teacher development	N = 8 postbaccalaureate students Three courses (introduction, content area, student teaching seminar)	Dialogue journals	Category analysis

Note. PST = prospective teacher; F = female, M = male; A = Asian, AA = African American, API = Asian/Pacific Islander, C = Caucasian, L = Latino, PA = Palestine American, NR = not reported.

Theoretical Stance. In five belief studies, primarily occurring in the early 1990s, researchers examined prospective teachers' beliefs about reading and reading instruction. These researchers adopted a neutral stance and did not intervene explicitly to change beliefs. Their goals were to identify prospective teachers' beliefs either prior to or before and after completing a reading methods course.

Lonberger (1992), Wham (1993), and Konopak, Readance, and Wilson (1994) administered Likert-scale questionnaires to identify alignment of beliefs with explanations of reading (e.g., Goodman, 1967; Rumelhart, 1985) as text-based, interactive, or schema-based. They determined whether prospective teachers' beliefs aligned with their choice of instructional procedures, which were also described on the questionnaires. All three reported a tendency toward an interactive perspective and Lonberger and Wham both reported increased alignment between orientation and instructional beliefs for prospective teachers completing a reading methods course. The Lonberger study typifies the research direction of these researchers. Prospective teachers ($n = 37$) at the beginning and end of the course defined reading as an interactive process, but initially responses about how children learn to read and how the prospective teachers would teach children to read reflected a text-based orientation. At the end of the course and after prospective teachers participated in multiple discussions about factors affecting the reading process, schema-based definitions almost doubled, text-based definitions were nonexistent, and 84% of the prospective teachers chose instructional scenarios consistent with their theoretical orientation. The hypothesis derived by these researchers is that beliefs were mediated through the course readings and class discussions.

Researchers in two other studies reported mixed findings. Fox (1994) documented very different patterns of two prospective teachers' orientation to instructional theory. One prospective teacher reported alignment with reader response theory (Rosenblatt, 1978) and instruction; the other prospective teacher rejected alignment for both. Raine, Levingston, Linek, Sampson, and Linder (2003) documented prospective teachers' belief statements—while not changing in orientation—expanded in breadth, depth, and became more specific.

A notable change in approach to the theoretical orientations research occurred in more recent studies. Influenced by socioconstructivist paradigms that emphasize some form of intervention, such as teacher guided learning activities (e.g., Vygotsky, 1978), researchers abandoned neutrality. Instead, they reported on instructional conditions designed to change or broaden prospective teachers' beliefs about reading. In each study, researchers implemented specific actions to institute some form of guided instruction to mediate beliefs. For example, Theurer (2002) had a prospective teacher examine her own oral reading miscues while reading unfamiliar texts. During the conference about these oral miscues, Theurer shared and modeled her interpretations of the miscues and drew specific connections to course readings about the reading process. Fazio (2000, 2003) and Matanzo and Harris (1999) demonstrated and guided applications of text reading strategies with the course textbook. Wolf, Carey, and Mieras (1996a) had prospective teachers apply reader response teaching strategies during read-aloud sessions with children after they had modeled and practiced these in their college classes. Stevens (2002) held collaborative discussions with her college students in which she demonstrated her personal applications of content area reading strategies while she investigated whether her college students were beginning to discuss similar applications of content area reading strategies. Linek, Sampson, Raine, Klakamp, and Smith (2006) used prospective teachers' lesson reflections to initiate discussions and identify teaching experiences precipitating belief changes. All studies involved the college instructor in demonstrations and shared learning activities with guided practice in the application of targeted course content and in using the content to enhance their own reading or with children. Drawing on multiple data sets (i.e., interviews, observations, surveys, journal writings), all studies reported belief shifts in expected directions.

Beliefs Resistant to Change. The studies in content area reading, involving secondary (i.e., middle school and high school) prospective teachers, add another dimension to the belief literature. Researchers examined beliefs about reading instruction that support disciplinary learning. Reporting mixed reactions to this instruction (Bean & Zulich, 1990, 1992; Dynak & Smith, 1994; Nourie & Lenski, 1998; O'Brien & Stewart, 1990; Sturtevant & Spor, 1990; Zulich, Bean, & Herrick, 1992), some researchers identified factors such as history with reading strategies, the structure of disciplinary knowledge, and instructional expectations (Bean, 1997; Dynak & Smith, 1994; Zulich et al., 1992) as contributors to negative attitudes about content area reading instruction.

The following studies illustrate the range of beliefs observed by these researchers. O'Brien and Stewart (1990) administered surveys to 250 prospective teachers and reported negative attitudes that held constant across the semester. These prospective teachers believed that content area reading strategies were impractical, that the strategies were common sense, and that content area reading instruction was "incompatible" with their view of teaching. A few students with positive views believed the strategies would have helped their own comprehension.

In contrast, Nourie and Lenski (1998) surveyed two different groups of prospective teachers ($n = 90$ and 113, respectively) and reported that prospective teachers who enjoyed their content area reading course work also had a positive attitude toward reading and were readers themselves; the exception was those with grade point averages below 2.5 on a 4.0 scale. Several studies also reported mixed findings and provided information about contextual influences, including that cooperating teachers knew little or nothing about content area reading strategies (Sturtevant & Spor, 1990); that prospective teachers' personal biographies were related to the subculture of their discipline, the courses they had taken, and the apprenticeship norms of school-based field placements (Zulich et al., 1992); and that prospective teachers began

to value strategies (e.g., summarization) that improved their own reading comprehension. However, even with increased appreciation, they had difficulty knowing how to use them (Dynak & Smith, 1994).

The Bean (1997) study provided additional insights about conditions associated with the differing outcomes researchers report. He followed prospective teachers from a content area literacy class to a practicum or student teaching. All but two prospective teachers continued to use content area reading strategies. The expected reaction of the cooperating teachers—beliefs about the structure, the discipline, and personal or situational characteristics (e.g., identity, need to maintain classroom control)—were among the factors that influenced use. Bean's findings support a shifting emphasis in the pedagogy of secondary reading, from a perspective favoring generalizable principles for strategy selection to those specific to disciplinary knowledge structures. Among the factors for further investigation is how to encourage and structure cross-disciplinary teaching to support integrating literacy with content knowledge, such as in science, as noted by Moller and Hug (2006) who observed that their case study prospective teachers ($n = 4$) benefited from participating in the integrated teaching of these two college instructors.

Readers as Reading Teachers. In two studies (Draper, Barksdale-Ladd, & Radencich, 2000; Many, Howard, & Hoge, 1998), researchers investigated their assumptions that good readers and those who find reading pleasurable will be good teachers of reading. Findings indicated, however, that attitudes toward reading and writing were not consistently linked in predictable directions.

Interpretive Commentary

Teacher education researchers have investigated the impact of beliefs on teaching for decades, arguing that beliefs are "highly resistant to change" (Block & Hazelip, 1995, p. 27) and serve as filters that can inhibit taking on new perspectives when those perspectives are in conflict with those already developed (Pajares, 1992). The prevailing concern is that conflicting perspectives will inhibit learning and the examination of misconceptions. Despite efforts to either change or broaden perspectives, researchers have not established explicit links between expressed beliefs and practice, factors that may contribute to established beliefs, or reliable measures for exposing individuals' beliefs (Kane, Sandretto, & Heath, 2002).

Several researchers (Fazio, 2000, 2003; Matanzo & Harris, 1999; Stevens, 2002; Theurer, 2002; Wolf et al., 1996a) demonstrated quite specifically that instructional and situated events can be catalysts for changes in beliefs. They clearly refute the argument that beliefs are intractable. Two important issues to carry forward for additional study are the suggestions that beliefs are affected by situated events and that it is important to help prospective teachers make explicit their beliefs and events as objects of study (e.g., Theurer's procedure for eliciting beliefs through retrospective miscue analysis or with interviews). Prospective teachers' tacit beliefs may go unrecognized and intrude on learning in ways that are difficult to identify. Acting out these beliefs can have a profound effect on building awareness of rationales for holding on to some beliefs but discarding others (Johnston, 1996). Further, it brings clarity to beliefs that prospective teachers may hold as "ideal" but not workable when applied (Samuelowicz & Bain, 2001).

In addition, 11 investigations examined beliefs about content area reading instruction of prospective teachers. They call attention to a theoretical shift in the conceptualization of content area literacy courses away from generalizable principles of instruction and toward specific principles related to the way knowledge is structured within disciplines. A positive finding of several studies is that content area literacy seems to be gaining acceptance by prospective teachers. Yet there is much work to be done that addresses the questions posed by Bean (1997) and Moller and Hug (2006) that relate to the culture of the university and a need for structures to support cross-disciplinary teaching so that prospective teachers can experience firsthand the effects of interdisciplinary teaching.

The troubling characteristics of these studies, though, are similar to those found in the teacher belief research in general (Kane et al., 2002; Wideen et al., 1998). Too often the belief construct is viewed as a static and stable entity. Or beliefs are treated as a tightly formed construct lacking complexity. Researchers often do not distinguish those beliefs more amenable to change from those more deeply rooted. What is needed is a careful and comprehensive examination of beliefs as a dynamic that is affected by multiple situated and cultural histories and events, and beliefs are examined during the activity of the events rather than retrospectively.

These studies pay little attention to cultural influences (e.g., the culture of the college classroom, prospective teachers' history as students), with the exception of the Moller and Hug (2006) study, and fail to apply cultural and situated lenses. The studies are characterized by a linear view rather than one that is multiplicative and that allows for beliefs to be both constant (e.g., spiritual views) and difficult to change and also be ever changing entities influenced by ongoing action. We are concerned, too, that researchers neglect their own roles in the culture of events (e.g., class discussions, professor in the authority role who assigns grades) affecting beliefs. It is quite possible, even probable, that professors' beliefs (though unintentionally) shape student conversations and their data analysis. Thus, the role of the researcher/teacher educator as the person of authority must be examined explicitly.

In addition, we agree with Kane and colleagues (2002), who argue that exposing beliefs is like "telling half a story." Rather, it is important to examine beliefs in action (Argyris, Putnam, & Smith, 1985). Such an approach would assess both expressed beliefs and beliefs-in-use and the congruence between the two. Several researchers in the belief set are moving the field in that direction, including Bean (1997), Fazio (2003), Matanzo and

Harris (1999), and Stevens (2002) who reveal both expressed beliefs and examine how they are influencing actions in methods courses and teaching in classrooms. Additional studies are needed that examine the nuances of belief changes, teasing out specifically situational factors influencing beliefs and developing tools that can capture beliefs in the happening.

Findings From Research on Knowledge and Reflective Reasoning

In this section, we report on 17 knowledge and reflective reasoning studies, representing 21% of the selected studies. These studies are summarized within Table 3. We included reflection research in this category because of its primary goal to provide spaces, activities, and opportunities for helping future teachers to think about and evaluate what they are learning about teaching practice. For example, Foote and Linder (2000) drew on sociocultural theory to argue for building prospective teachers' knowledge of family literacy, while Leland, Harste, and Youssef (1997) explained their work from a critical theory perspective to support their emphasis on social justice issues. On the whole, 29% of the researchers referenced cognitive theory, 47% drew on constructivist theory, and 2% of researchers supported their work with sociocultural or critical theories.

Table 3
Summaries of Studies—Knowledge and Reflective Reasoning

Author(s), Year	Theoretical Orientation	Research Focus	Participants and Setting	Data Sources	Data Analysis
Alderman, Klein, Seeley, & Sanders, 1993	Cognitive	PSTs' responses to metacognitive strategy instruction	*N* = 44 PSTs Educational psychology course	Learning logs, course grades	Identification of patterns, descriptive analysis
Briggs, Tully, & Stiefer, 1998	Constructivist	Reading education professors' use of informal assessment	*N* = 41 reading education professors Teacher education programs in five states	Surveys	Response frequency tabulation
Foegen, Espin, Allinder, & Markell, 2001	Constructivist	PSTs' beliefs about curriculum-based measurement	*N* = 45 PSTs (41 F, 4 M) Special education introduction course	Questionnaires	Repeated measures analysis of variance
Foote & Linder, 2000	Sociocultural	PSTs' and mentors' awareness of family literacy	*N* = 23 PSTs and 23 mentor teachers Professional development school	Questionnaires, interviews, lesson plans, reflection journals, portfolios	Constant comparative analysis
Harlin & Lipa, 1995	Constructivist	PSTs' analyses of sample portfolio documents in relation to course work	*N* = 25 PSTs Two teacher education reading methods	Case summaries, questionnaires	Descriptive analysis, response frequency tabulation
Kasten & Padak, 1997	Constructivist	PSTs' reflection statements during first classroom experience	*N* = 29 PSTs Final literacy course prior to student teaching	Lesson reflections, end-of-course reflection	Inductive analysis

(continued)

Table 3 (Continued)
Summaries of Studies—Knowledge and Reflective Reasoning

Author(s), Year	Theoretical Orientation	Research Focus	Participants and Setting	Data Sources	Data Analysis
Leland, Harste, & Youssef, 1997	Critical theory	PSTs' developing reflections on equity and justice	N = 16 PSTs Four-semester course work and student teaching	Journals entries from each field experience	Evaluative analysis
Mather, Bos, & Babur, 2001	Cognitive	PSTs' knowledge of early literacy instruction	N = 293 PSTs (mostly F, 131 inservice teachers) Student teaching, K–3 classrooms	Perception surveys, knowledge assessments	Mixed design analysis of variance
McMahon, 1997	Constructivist	PSTs' developing thoughts, as represented through language	N = 2 PSTs (1 F, 1 M) Elementary methods and practicum	Double-entry journals, lesson plans, notes of discussions, portfolios, field notes	Case study inductive analysis
Mottley & Telfer, 1997	Cognitive	PSTs' knowledge of storytelling and its effects on literacy development	N = 106 PSTs (91% F, 8% M; 75% C, 11% AA, 14% NR) Reading methods course	Storytelling questionnaire	Response frequency tabulation
O'Sullivan & Jiang, 2002	Cognitive	The efficacy of the RICA examination	N = 106 PSTs Teacher education program	Standardized test scores	Logistic regression
Risko, Roskos, & Vukelich, 1999	Constructivist	PSTs' reflections on course content and teaching	N = 36 PSTs (29 F, 7 M) Literacy methods course	Double-entry reflection journals	Open, analytic induction; selective coding
Risko, Roskos, & Vukelich, 2002	Constructivist	PSTs' mental strategies for reflecting on course content	N = 30 PSTs (23 F, 7 M) Literacy methods course at three universities	Double-entry reflection journals	Open, analytic induction; selective coding
Sadoski, Norton, Rodriguez, Nichols, & Gerla, 1998	Critical theory	PSTs' and inservice teachers' knowledge of literature	N = 22 PSTs, 11 inservice teachers (30 F, 3 M) Children's literature course	Knowledge and literary analysis survey booklets	Correlational analysis
Shefelbine & Shiel, 1990	Cognitive	PSTs' knowledge of reading instruction	N = 39 PSTs (mostly F) Reading methods course	Written scenarios describing instruction	Descriptive analysis of categories derived inductively
Traynelis-Yurek & Strong, 2000	Cognitive	PSTs' ability to administer an informal reading inventory	N = 169 PSTs Teacher preparation courses at three institutions	Informal reading inventories	One-sample t-tests
Truscott & Walker, 1998	Constructivist	PSTs' portfolio artifacts representing reflective thinking	N = 63 PSTs Reading methods course	Artifacts, questionnaires	Tabulation and description of frequency data

Note. PST = prospective teacher; F = female, M = male; A = Asian, AA = African American, API = Asian/Pacific Islander, C = Caucasian, L = Latino, PA = Palestine American, NR = not reported.

Topical Knowledge. Calderhead (1996) distinguished teacher knowledge from beliefs by defining knowledge as "factual propositions and the understandings that inform skills action" (p. 715). Teacher knowledge has been categorized in different ways (Kane et al., 2002), with numerous researchers investigating subject knowledge (Grossman, 1992; Ormrod & Cole, 1996) and craft or pedagogical knowledge (e.g., Calderhead, 1996) and assuming that a strong content focus in course work will improve teaching. This relationship, however, is yet to be established (Floden, 1997; Floden & Meniketti, 2005).

Researchers in our studies approached their work with a narrow view of knowledge and did not address the question of what prospective teachers need to know to be effective reading teachers. Instead, these researchers assessed (with no attempts to teach) a wide array of topics they viewed as important. The results provide a disparate set of findings that are not linked to one another or to any indicators verifying importance of this knowledge for improving teaching.

In seven of the nine studies within this category, researchers conducted a one-time testing of topical knowledge and, in all cases, reported that prospective teachers were inadequately prepared in those areas. Assessment instruments were researcher developed, validity and reliability of these instruments were not reported, and in most studies the assessments were conducted independent of knowledge about the students' academic history. No researchers attempted to relate findings to the contexts of students' programs or course work. Taken together, findings indicated that prospective teachers had difficulty (a) defining literary terms and performing comprehension tasks related to short stories and poems (Sadoski, Norton, Rodriguez, Nichols, & Gerla, 1998), (b) defining metalinguistic terminology (Mather, Bos, & Babur, 2001), (c) understanding family–school partnerships for supporting literacy development (Foote & Linder, 2000), and (d) telling stories (Mottley & Telfer, 1997).

Researchers also reported that (a) one-time practice with an informal reading inventory is not sufficient (Traynelis-Yurek & Strong, 2000), (b) prospective teachers reported benefiting more from videos based on anecdotal evidence than from a video presentation emphasizing statistical concepts (Foegen, Espin, Allinder, & Markell, 2001), and (c) prospective teachers preferred work samples (over norm-referenced group tests) for an assessment task but were less discriminating about reliability and usefulness of other assessment forms (Harlin & Lipa, 1995).

One study that assessed metalinguistic (phonology, phonemic awareness, and morphology) knowledge illustrates the direction of this set of studies. Mather and colleagues (2001) assessed the perceptions and knowledge of 293 prospective teachers and 131 inservice teachers and found that neither group obtained high scores. The researchers concluded that recent advances in understandings of these metalinguistic areas did not have substantial impact on teacher preparation.

Two exceptions to the one-time testing investigations were those of Shefelbine and Shiel (1990) and Alderman, Klein, Seeley, and Sanders (1993), who traced knowledge acquisition across a semester. Both groups of researchers concluded that learning was associated with explicit representations of content to be learned. Shefelbine and Shiel taught their 39 prospective teachers to conceptualize the reading process as a hierarchical arrangement of multiple skills associated with word identification, decoding, and comprehension. They reported a significant difference by the end of the course in knowledge of those components that are more easily observed, such as fluency, over more inclusive and more abstract components, such as word identification and use of background knowledge.

Alderman and colleagues (1993) analyzed 44 prospective teachers' learning logs for use of text reading strategies taught in a reading methods course. Prospective teachers who used the strategies taught to them were the most successful in the class. They concluded that all prospective teachers could benefit from strategy instruction to enhance their learning of course content.

Two additional studies related to the knowledge topic. The first focused on prospective teachers' access to assessment content in which teacher education programs from five states were analyzed (Briggs, Tully, & Stiefer, 1998). The researchers concluded that these programs preferred informal assessments to more formal ones. The second examined California's use of a knowledge test for admission into teacher education programs (O'Sullivan & Jiang, 2002). Researchers concluded that the California Reading Instruction Competence Assessment (RICA) was redundant to other forms of assessment already in place.

Reflective Reasoning. Seven studies investigated reflective practice as a tool for enhancing knowledge and reasoning about course content and pedagogy. The major finding from these investigations pointed to the need for explicit guidance and focused instructional support to deepen reflective thinking. Pedagogical thinking remained at the technical, subjective, and factual levels with little change across a semester in the absence of models or demonstrations (McMahon, 1997; Risko, Roskos, & Vukelich, 1999, 2002; Truscott & Walker, 1998).

In two studies, researchers reported positive shifts in reflective thinking, and these shifts were associated with a form of guided practice. Kasten and Padak (1997) provided questions (e.g., "What did the children learn?" or "What would you do differently next time?") to guide journal writing about field experiences and found that for some prospective teachers this prompt led to a deepening awareness of multiple factors affecting reading performance and instruction.

The most robust impact on reflection was reported by Leland and colleagues (1997). Their goal was to foster knowledge of social inequities and how teachers can affect positive change. Working with a cohort of interns across three semesters, they "primed" class discussions and journal writings with explicit attention to inequities observed in school settings and described in course readings and with change actions teachers can implement. The researchers learned that (a) increases in critical reflection by the interns paralleled the ever widening and explicit focus on critical literacy taught in the course, and (b) the examples of critical literacy found in the journal entries paralleled the amount of time and emphasis on critical literacy issues that the researchers taught in the class. This study alone found that reflective power is deepened. The change occurred only after three semesters of focused and explicit guidance.

Interpretive Commentary

This set of studies had two parts. First, the studies on topical and assessment knowledge do not advance our understanding of what prospective teachers should know when they leave their programs; on the whole, this set of studies is disappointing. Second, the findings from the reflection studies mirror those reported by many researchers, specifically by Roskos and colleagues (2001) in their critical analysis of reflection research that was published between 1985 and 2000. Two primary issues regarding the reflection studies are the impact of guided or unguided directives on reflective thinking and increasing depth of thinking over time. The finding that reflection deepens with guidance distinguishes the outcomes. Explicit attention combined with explicit guidance can evoke critical analysis. The coupling of reflection work with specific content (i.e., what to think about during reflection) is another important finding of this study. Additionally, researchers found that questions can guide more complete reflective writings and that reflective work, when situated within teaching activities, leads to more thoughtful consideration of decisions and dilemmas.

Not addressed by these researchers is how individuals' dispositions and goals for reflection may affect approach and outcome. We believe, also, that McMahon's (1997) finding that different levels of thinking can occur simultaneously is important because it suggests that reflection characteristics may be specific to perceived need and situations. For example, some problems might be solved with technical reasoning, while others require critical analysis, and still others require procedural knowledge. Applying levels to identify sequentially developing reasoning abilities may undervalue lower order levels.

Findings From Research on Pedagogy

Guiding prospective teachers' knowledge development for application to their teaching is the primary focus of 36 (44%) of the 82 studies. And in most of the pedagogy studies summarized in Table 4, prolonged engagement with pupils in field placements is viewed as the catalyst for reconstructing prior beliefs and

Table 4
Summaries of Studies—Pedagogy

Author(s), Year	Theoretical Orientation	Research Focus	Participants and Setting	Data Sources	Data Analysis
Abrego, Rubin, & Sutterby, 2006	Sociocultural	PSTs' attitudes toward parental involvement	*N* = 127 PSTs (85% L) University–elementary partnership	Weekly reflections, end-of-course surveys, field notes	Pattern analysis, triangulation
Anderson, Caswell, & Hayes, 1994	Constructivist	PSTs' responses to feedback from supervisors	*N* = 34 PSTs (30 F, 4 M) Reading methods course with practica	Dialogue journals, observations, field notes, surveys, reflections	Freelisting coding
Boling, 2003	Constructivist	Professors' responses to the use of technology	*N* = 5 teacher educators Two research methodology courses	E-mails, conversation notes, audiotaped interviews	Constant comparative analysis
Clark & Medina, 2000	Constructivist	PSTs' understandings of literacy and pedagogy	*N* = 60 PSTs, master's students Secondary content area course	Student writings, audiotaped group discussions, e-mails, interviews, observation, field notes	Constant comparative analysis
Dowhower, 1990	Constructivist	PSTs' analyses of classroom reading instruction observed in field placements	*N* = 155 PSTs Reading methods course	Responses to questions requiring analysis of reading methods	Inductive coding, constant comparative analysis
Fecho, Commeyras, Bauer, & Font, 2000	Critical theory	PSTs' understandings of teacher's classroom authority	*N* = 3 professors Reading methods courses	Observations, conferences, interviews, reading responses, assignments	Constant comparative analysis
Hinchman & Lalik, 2000	Critical theory	Teacher educators' critical inquiry related to their teaching	*N* = 2 teacher educators/student teacher mentors (F), 24 current and former education students Teacher education program	E-mail logs, student interviews	Constant comparative analysis

(continued)

Table 4 (Continued)
Summaries of Studies—Pedagogy

Author(s), Year	Theoretical Orientation	Research Focus	Participants and Setting	Data Sources	Data Analysis
Hughes, Packard, & Pearson, 2000	Constructivist	PSTs' perceptions of media in their education experiences	*N* = 15 PSTs, post-baccalaureate students (14 C, 1 L) Literacy methods course	Paper assignments, interviews, videotaped work sessions, surveys	Constant comparative analysis
Kaste, 2001	Constructivist	PSTs' practices in promoting literacy in content area instruction	*N* = 2 PSTs (2 F; 1 AA, 1 C) Course field-based experiences	Field notes, videotaped observations, audiotaped debriefing session, lesson plans, artifacts, field journals	Naturalistic procedures, constant comparative analysis
Kidd, Sanchez, & Thorp, 2000	Constructivist	PSTs' ability to facilitate culturally responsive language and literacy learning	*N* = 11 PSTs Intersession project in field-based, literacy methods course	Questionnaires	Qualitative—Inductive coding, descriptive analysis
Kidd, Sanchez, & Thorp, 2002	Sociocultural	PSTs' responses to family stories	*N* = 14 PSTs (13 F, 1 M; 8 W, 2 AA, 1 A, 1 PA) Early literacy course	Pre- and post-questionnaires, reflections	Descriptive analysis
Klesius, Searls, & Zielonka, 1990	Cognitive	PSTs' responses to various delivery modes	*N* = 74 PSTs Reading methods course	Observations, videotaped lessons	Repeated measures analysis of variance
L'Allier, 2005	Constructivist	PSTs' reflections on instructor's practices	*N* = 85 PSTs Three reading methods courses	Reflective responses, lesson reflections	Descriptive category analysis
Lalik & Niles, 1990	Cognitive	PSTs' responses to collaborative planning task	*N* = 26 PSTs Student teaching in elementary and junior high	Planning item evaluations, lesson plans	Data reduction procedures
Lazar, 2001	Sociocultural	PSTs' reactions related to culturally responsive teaching	*N* = 13 PSTs (12 F, 1 M) Literacy course and practicum	Surveys, open-ended questions, written memos, field notes, reflections	Triangulation of data, inductive coding, descriptive analysis
Levin, 1995	Cognitive	PSTs' understandings of case study reports with and without discussion	*N* = 24 PSTs (21 F, 3 M), 8 student teachers, 8 experienced teachers Reading methods course	Case studies, video- and audiotaped case study discussions	Quantitative—descriptive analysis, analysis of variance, constant comparative analysis
Maheady, B. Mallette, & Harper, 1996	Positivist/ Behavioral	PSTs' responses to peer coaching intervention	*N* = 3 PSTs (F; 1 AA, 1 C, 1 L) Field placement in urban school, exceptional learner methods plus field placement	Number of strategies used, number of literature books used, curriculum-based measurement scores	Multiple baseline experimental design, visual inspection of data across subjects

(continued)

Table 4 (Continued)
Summaries of Studies—Pedagogy

Author(s), Year	Theoretical Orientation	Research Focus	Participants and Setting	Data Sources	Data Analysis
B. Mallette, Maheady, & Harper, 1999	Positivist/ Behavioral	PSTs' use of peer coaching; satisfaction, and impact on pupils	N = 6 PSTs Introduction to exceptional learner methods course	Audiotaped debriefing sessions, videos of instructional and peer-coaching strategies; tutored pupils' reading scores	Multiple baseline experiment, Pearson correlation; analysis of pupil data; descriptive analysis of satisfaction data
M.H. Mallette, Kile, Smith, McKinney, & Readence, 2000	Cognitive	PSTs' beliefs about students reading difficulties	N = 6 PSTs (F) Reading diagnostic course plus practicum	Student diagnostic reports, field notes	Descriptive coding, cross-case analysis
Massey, 1990	Sociocultural	PSTs' applications of pedagogical knowledge during tutoring field placement	N = 24 PSTs (F, 21 C, 2 AA, 1 L) Three 140-hour internships, field placement	Informal reading assessments, lesson plans, observations, field notes, interviews	Content analysis, data triangulation
Massey, 2006	Cognitive	PSTs' use of preparation content in first year of teaching	N = 1 first-year teacher Title I elementary school with 78% minority population	Interviews, field notes, telephone transcripts, e-mails, lesson plans, class observations	Constant comparative analysis, triangulation
Mora & Grisham, 2001	Constructivist	PSTs' attitudes toward revised literacy courses	N = 25 PSTs Literacy methods course plus experiences at professional development school	Observation, case studies, program and course evaluations, focus group interviews	Inductive coding and pattern analysis, constant comparative analysis
D.N. Morgan, Timmons, & Shaheen, 2006	Positivist/ Behavioral	PSTs' perceptions and/or implementations of field-based tutoring experiences	N = 45 PSTs (44 F, 1 M) Field placement in K–3 partnership school	Tutoring notes, tutoring reflections, field notes, interviews	Qualitative— Constant comparative analysis
R.L. Morgan, Gustafson, Hudson, & Salzberg, 1992	Constructivist	PSTs' responses to peer coaching	N = 5 PSTs, 2 peer coaches, 26 elementary pupils Special education course and field placements	Observations, documentation of effective and ineffective teaching behaviors	Multiple baseline experimental design, visual inspection of graphs by subject over time
Nierstheimer, Hopkins, Dillon, & Schmitt, 2000	Constructivist	PSTs' knowledge and beliefs about struggling	N = 67 PSTs (60 F, 7 M) Reading methods course	Questionnaires, videotaped lessons, interviews, audiotaped discussions, observations field notes	Within and cross-case analysis, data triangulation
Risko, 1992	Constructivist	PSTs' use of videocases in representing teaching and learning and their beliefs about knowledge acquisition	N = 16 PSTs, 14 inservice teachers Undergraduate literacy difficulties course; graduate language and literacy methods course and practica	Pre- and postcase scenario analysis, student-generated analysis critique	Constant comparative analysis, cross-protocol analysis

(continued)

Table 4 (Continued)
Summaries of Studies—Pedagogy

Author(s), Year	Theoretical Orientation	Research Focus	Participants and Setting	Data Sources	Data Analysis
Risko, Peter, & McAllister, 1996	Constructivist	PSTs' use of literacy instruction knowledge in teaching diverse learners	*N* = 3 PSTs (2 C F, 1 AA M) Literacy difficulties course and field placement	Interviews, pre- and postassessments, journals, dialogue transcripts, lesson plans, case reports	Constant comparative analysis, cross-case pattern analysis
Roberts & Hsu, 2000	Positivist/ Behavioral	PSTs' use of technology to create instructional materials	*N* = 130 PSTs Reading/language arts methods course	Writing prompts, questionnaire responses	Descriptions; frequency data
Roskos & Walker, 1993	Constructivist	PSTs' selections of information to construct pedagogical knowledge	*N* = 122 PSTs (108 F, 14 M) Reading diagnostic courses	Pre- and post-problem reader response data	Analytic induction, constant comparative analysis
Roskos & Walker, 1994	Constructivist	PSTs' pedagogical concepts as reflected in instructional choices & reasoning	*N* = 18 PSTs Reading diagnosis course	Pre- and postresponses to the case studies	Quantitative— Analytic induction
Wolf, Ballentine, & Hill, 2000	Sociocultural	PSTs' reflections on data collected about their focus children	*N* = 3 PSTs (2 F,1 M, 3 C) Literacy/social studies methods course and practica	Autobiographies, field notes, analytical papers, interviews	Analytic categorization
Wolf, Carey, & Mieras, 1996b	Cognitive	PSTs' use of case studies to support students' responses to literature	*N* = 43 PSTs (37 F, 6 M); Children's literature course and practica	Field notes, reflections	Coding induction, constant comparative analysis
Wolf, Hill, & Ballentine, 1999	Sociocultural	PSTs' demonstrations and implications of "fissured ground"	*N* = 8 PSTs (mostly F), 9 children Children's literature course and field placement	Field notes, final papers	Analytic categorization
Worthy & Patterson, 2001	Constructivist	PSTs' reflections on tutoring in low-income schools	*N* = 71 PSTs (67 F, 4 M; 47% C, 33% L, 10% AA) Reading methods course and tutoring practica	Pre- and post-written reflections, group session notes, oral reflections	Constant comparative analysis
Xu, 2000a	Sociocultural	PSTs' explorations of diversity while working with diverse students	*N* = 20 PSTs Reading methods course	Biographies, charts, case reports, strategy sheets, observations, field notes, lesson plans, reflections	Inductive coding of patterns, triangulation of data sets

(continued)

Table 4 (Continued)
Summaries of Studies—Pedagogy

Author(s), Year	Theoretical Orientation	Research Focus	Participants and Setting	Data Sources	Data Analysis
Xu, 2000b	Constructivist	PSTs' under-standings and integration of cultural back-grounds and their students' cultural backgrounds in instruction	N = 3 PSTs (F) Second semester education block	Autobiographies, case studies biog-raphies, cultural analysis, lesson plans, reflections	Inductive coding, constant com-parative analysis

Note. PST = prospective teacher; F = female, M = male; A = Asian, AA = African American, API = Asian/Pacific Islander, C = Caucasian, L = Latino, PA = Palestine American, NR = not reported.

refining pedagogical knowledge. Researchers in this group investigated the dynamic inter-play of knowledge, teaching, and beliefs while implementing instruction aimed at enhancing all three. For the most part, this effort led to positive outcomes. Thus, one striking differ-ence between the studies discussed previously in the knowledge area and those reported here is researchers' attention to multiple and complex factors that are possibly acting synergistically to influence knowledge development, specifically knowledge about teaching. Among the multiple factors addressed in these studies are prospective teachers' beliefs about the capabilities of pupils and about their own teaching competence—two areas that we identified earlier in this paper as important to the belief research. In 47% of the studies focusing on pedagogy, researchers draw on constructivist theory to guide their research, with 19% grounding their work in sociocultural theory and 17% in constructivist theory. Five percent, 4%, and 2% of the studies are influ-enced by cognitive, positivist/behavioral, and critical theory, respectively.

Researchers apply four tools—pupil data collection, case-based methodologies, personal writing, and explicit and structured teaching formats—to enhance prospective teachers' practical knowledge and pedagogy. And while researchers don't study explicitly their own teaching methods, with the exception of Fecho, Commeyras, Bauer, and Font (2000) and

Hinchman and Lalik (2000), they explain how their instructional routines create conditions for the usefulness of these instructional tools and conjecture that these conditions are important to enable teacher learning. Studies using each of these tools will be discussed with examples.

Pupil Data Collection. In six studies, researchers (Lazar, 2001; M.H. Mallette, Kile, Smith, McKinney, & Readence, 2000; Mora & Grisham, 2001; Wolf, Ballentine, & Hill, 2000; Wolf, Carey, & Mieras, 1996b; Wolf, Hill, & Ballentine, 1999) taught prospective teachers to analyze pupil data from informal assess-ments (e.g., oral reading or written records, lit-erary responses, artistic impressions, field notes) and demonstrated the interpretation and use of these data for teaching. Mora and Grisham (2001) reported on 21 prospective teachers; the other five studies reported on smaller groups of prospective teachers chosen either randomly or as a purposive sample from a larger group. Researchers evaluated multiple data sources collected across a semester that included observational data, interviews, ana-lytical papers, prospective teachers' field notes, and assessment reports. All researchers report-ed positive changes in prospective teachers' assessment knowledge, beliefs about the capa-bilities of struggling readers and linguistically diverse students, and confidence in their own ability to teach these students.

M.H. Mallette et al. (2000) described course conditions that contributed to positive changes of six prospective teachers. These conditions included opportunities for prospective teachers to foster personal relationships with their students, the positive and carefully managed support provided by the supervising teacher, specific feedback on interpretations of data and field notes, and the college professor who helps prospective teachers be more explicit about their changing viewpoints and reasons for these changes. These same conditions were described by the other researchers in this group as facilitative of the changes they observed at their respective sites.

Additional contributions of these studies include the charting of the ups and downs of prospective teachers' knowledge development (e.g., Wolf and her colleagues). Explaining their findings, Wolf et al. (1996b, 1999, 2000) and Lazar (2001) indicated that prospective teachers' knowledge increased in ways that aided their ability to identify school inequities and instructional methods that capitalized on children's interests and capabilities. Lazar, however, learned that increased understandings about school inequities in urban settings may have been insufficient for promoting prospective teachers' confidence in addressing the inequities. Mora and Grisham (2001) also found that prospective teachers increased their knowledge of linguistic features of different languages and expressed a need for additional professional development in teaching methods (associated with identified areas where they felt less knowledgeable).

Case-Based Methodologies. Applying problem-solving and constructivist perspectives to their own instruction within reading methods courses, researchers in this group asked prospective teachers to analyze teaching problems embedded within written or multimedia cases representing classroom reading instruction. Findings indicated that videos and hypermedia materials can (a) enrich prospective teachers' learning, engagement, and analysis of assessment and teaching events (Boling,

2003; Hughes, Packard, & Pearson, 2000; Risko, 1992; Risko, Peter, & McAllister, 1996); (b) aid retention of course information (Klesius, Searls, & Zielonka, 1990); and (c) enhance understandings of procedural knowledge. In addition, Roberts and Hsu (2000), examining influences of technology on the learning of 130 prospective teachers, reported that technology prompts enhanced creation of teaching materials (when compared to written prompts). Exploring the question of what prospective teachers learn from multimedia cases, Risko (1992) documented an increase in the number of case issues identified, the number and complexity of rationale statements generated to support these choices, and an increase in the number of perspectives (taken from course readings or case teachers) referenced to support the prospective teachers' conclusions on problem-solving tasks.

Similarly, Roskos and Walker (1993) found decreased reliance on subjective reasoning, the use of generalities to solve the case issues, and an increase in objective reasoning and procedural recommendations. In a subsequent study where they reanalyzed their data set, Roskos and Walker (1994) again found that procedural knowledge increased, but predicting consequences of teaching decisions did not deepen substantially across this one semester of teaching. Risko and colleagues (1996) identified two course features essential for facilitating change in ability to plan and implement instruction: (1) explicit references to course and case content and (2) guidance with explicit feedback during lesson planning and debriefing after teaching.

Levin (1995) reported on the added advantage of discussing cases (in addition to reading and writing about them). Her conclusion seemed to support the evidence from all researchers described above who reported increased engagement with course content when discussing relevant teaching cases. Relevant to the potential importance of class discussions on learning are the recommendations of Fecho et al. (2000) and Hinchman and Lalik (2000), who examined their own participation as authority figures during class discussions.

Both concluded that teaching for democratic learning requires self study and practices in which teacher educators examine their own language (in class and in e-mail communications), observe class participation, and listen carefully to their students' responses.

Personal Writing. Four studies use prospective teachers' personal writing as tools for preparing them to teach culturally and linguistically diverse students. Different forms of narratives and reflective writings (autobiographies, biographies, family stories) had positive effects on beliefs and knowledge about cultural differences in all four investigations (Clark & Medina, 2000; Kidd, Sanchez, & Thorp, 2002; Xu, 2000a, 2000b), but one of the four found limited impact on applications to teaching (Xu, 2000a, 2000b). In a fifth study in which narratives were not used, Kaste (2001), serving as an independent observer, reported on two prospective teachers' applications of Au's (1998) cultural teaching framework and concluded that they, too, had difficulty applying cultural pedagogical knowledge to their own teachings.

An example of positive changes in beliefs and knowledge is illustrated with the Clark and Medina (2000) investigation. They asked 60 prospective teachers to read and discuss book-length autobiographical literacy narratives (e.g., Luis J. Rodriguez's Always Running) and to then write narratives about their own literacy and language development. They documented three changes in the prospective teachers: seeing literacy as influenced by "social situations and interactions," adopting more multicultural perspectives, and understanding the importance of their pupils' stories for teaching. Clark and Medina concluded that the use of narratives enabled prospective teachers to make connections with individuals whose culture was different from their own, and the narratives helped to "disrupt" previously held stereotypes.

Despite increased knowledge about culturally and linguistically diverse students, researchers documented its limited effect on pedagogical knowledge. About half of 14 prospective teachers writing family stories did not see the value of these stories for teaching (Kidd et al., 2002); others within Xu's (2000a, 2000b) studies (n = 20 and 3, respectively) implemented at least some aspects of culturally relevant instruction, but they had difficulty accommodating for pupils' home language, building relationships with the community, and selecting relevant instructional materials.

Explicit and Structured Teaching Formats.
Two groups of studies focused on aspects of preparing teachers for reading instruction. One group points to difficulties associated with learning in field placements. Dowhower (1990) examined perceptions of early field experiences held by 155 prospective teachers and expressed concern about negative models on prospective teachers' developing pedagogical knowledge. Both Lalik and Niles (1990) (n = 26) and Kidd, Sanchez, and Thorp (2000) (n = 13) examined collaborative planning tasks and found that prospective teachers discussed a variety of activities and engaged in higher order thinking processes that were viewed by the participants as a positive influence on their learning; in both studies, however, prospective teachers found collaboration useful but difficult. And Anderson, Caswell, and Hayes (1994), examining the benefits and drawbacks related to observations by a professor and a peer during an early field experience for 34 prospective teachers, found that they felt more comfortable with and believed they benefited from the peer observation. The authors concluded that peer coaching should be considered as a viable method for providing additional feedback to prospective teachers.

In the second group, nine studies focused on the use of the college instructor's guided teaching formats to prepare prospective teachers for their field placements. Eight of these studies addressed instruction for struggling readers. In all eight studies (Abrego, Rubin, & Sutterby, 2006; Maheady, B. Mallette, & Harper, 1996; B. Mallette, Maheady, & Harper, 1999; Massey, 1990; D.N. Morgan, Timmons, & Shaheen, 2006; R.L. Morgan, Gustafson, Hudson, & Salzberg, 1992; Nierstheimer, Hopkins, Dillon,

& Schmitt, 2000; Worthy & Patterson, 2001), researchers demonstrated positive outcomes on multiple assessments, including teaching observations, transcripts, lesson plans, and assessment and teaching reports. Features of these studies contributing to positive outcomes were (a) demonstration of teaching strategies within methods courses, including use of videotape models (Nierstheimer et al., 2000); (b) adherence to a structured format for lesson planning and teaching that provided explicit attention to reading skills and strategies; and (c) an instructor's careful guidance and specific feedback while teaching. All but Massey (1990), D.N. Morgan et al. (2006), and Abrego et al. (2006) also included both peer and instructor feedback during teaching.

We describe in detail four studies from this set. In a one-semester study with 71 prospective teachers, Worthy and Patterson (2001) provided a tutoring lesson plan with explicit attention to read-alouds, fluency, guided text reading, writing, and word study components to use as a guide for planning lessons. Both peer and instructor feedback sessions followed observations. At the end of the semester, they reported gains in pedagogical knowledge and positive belief shifts for at least half of their prospective teachers. When their beliefs changed in a positive direction, prospective teachers displayed confidence in their ability to teach struggling readers, exhibited a more caring attitude, and changed their deficit views to recognition of their students' unique capabilities. Worthy and Patterson identified that tutoring one student and the personal, caring relationships established between the tutors and students contributed to change. They also reported that belief changes were not uniform across all prospective teachers and at least half held to their belief that the home was responsible for reading difficulties.

Similarly, B. Mallette and colleagues (1999) collected data on six prospective teachers enrolled in a one-semester special education course with accompanying practicum. They focused on effects of peer coaching in addition to the use of structured lesson plans, and they

carefully supervised teaching of prospective teachers. They taught their prospective teachers to implement direct instructional strategies (for partner reading, story retellings, paragraph shrinking, and oral reading fluency), following the Peabody Peer-Assisted Learning Strategies (PALS) model (Fuchs, Mathes, & Fuchs, 1994), and to collect daily assessment data on pupil learning in a special education placement. The lesson plan for instruction included modeling, contingent reinforcement, error-correction strategies, and provision of specific feedback. Additionally, prospective teachers were prepared to provide reciprocal coaching and feedback to their peers. Applying a multiple baseline design, they found that increased knowledge of PALS procedures corresponded with increases in pupils' overall reading comprehension and that tutors with a higher rate of implementation accuracy had pupils who showed an increase in percentage of correct reading comprehension responses; this performance, however, did not remain after instruction ended. Pupils' performance reported on oral fluency measures during the PALS instruction was mixed with no clear pattern identified for a relationship between PALS teaching and pupil performance. In addition, B. Mallette and her colleagues found that preparation in reciprocal peer coaching improved the prospective teachers' abilities to provide explicit feedback to one another on specified teaching routines.

Massey's (1990) study occurred across three semesters. During two semesters, she examined application of content and teaching strategies (assessment, comprehension, fluency, letter and word identification) within a field placement where 24 prospective teachers tutored one child each semester and then one year later during their student teaching semester. Massey reported that all prospective teachers made gains in their use of some strategies while tutoring one student, with the greatest improvement in use of assessment tools, teaching word identification and comprehension strategies, and awareness of pupils' attitudes toward reading. Her analysis of data collected on the 57 pupils who were tutored by the prospective teachers over two semesters revealed variability, with some increases in their performance. She reported an increase in interest and confidence for 15 pupils and increased scores on achievement tests for 23.

When Massey followed these prospective teachers from the practicum to their student teaching classroom setting, she found that 21 of the 24 (88%) used methods they had learned in the tutoring setting for individualizing instruction in their classrooms. Massey noted, too, that classroom settings were supportive (e.g., expectations of cooperating teachers, curricula guidelines) of such applications and thus did not inhibit potential transfer of instruction from the tutorial setting. D.N. Morgan et al. (2006) reported similar findings for 39 of their 45 prospective teachers when interviewed during student teaching. However, Massey (2006) reported on the difficulties a first-year teacher had in using the knowledge and skills taught in her preparation program within a high-stakes testing environment that held teaching expectations (e.g., test preparation instruction, adhering to prescribed curriculum) that were different from her student teaching experiences. The lack of congruence between this experience and her teacher preparation program was viewed as inhibiting her ability to apply what she had learned.

Researchers traced pupil performance when tutored by prospective teachers in four studies (Maheady et al., 1996; B. Mallette et al., 1999; Massey, 1990; R.L. Morgan et al., 1992). They reported positive tendencies but overall mixed results. All expressed caution about the use of these data to form conclusions about teaching performance.

In a final study, L'Allier (2005) reported that prospective teachers (*n* = 85) tended to use those teaching practices that were both demonstrated in university classrooms and given guided practice in a field placement when compared to ones described in textbook readings only—or even those that were described in their textbook and demonstrated in class. If this finding holds in additional studies, it raises questions about selection of such strategies for practice (e.g., are there those that can be more universally applied, what criteria are used for selection).

Interpretive Commentary

The studies addressed two major issues confronting teacher educators for decades. One issue is the deficit beliefs prospective teachers hold about culturally and linguistically diverse students and students who are identified as struggling readers. The second is the belief that they, as future classroom teachers, are not responsible for the instruction of these students.

Two positive trends characterize the findings of these studies. First, beliefs about capabilities sometimes change from deficit views to positive ones, and prospective teachers increasingly accept responsibility for teaching these students. While researchers report differential performance of prospective teachers, overall trends point in a positive direction for this line of research. Second, along with changes in beliefs, researchers observed increases in knowledge of assessment tools and ability to interpret pupil data (e.g., Mora & Grisham, 2001), knowledge of principles guiding culturally responsive pedagogy (e.g., Xu, 2000a, 2000b), and pedagogical knowledge (e.g., Worthy & Patterson, 2001).

Several researchers (Nierstheimer et al., 2000; Worthy & Patterson, 2001) argued that prolonged engagement in field settings is a necessary condition for changing beliefs and expectations for several reasons: (a) prospective teachers have sufficient time to form personal relationships with their students and learn about their capabilities as readers and writers, and (b) with prolonged engagement, prospective teachers observe positive effects of teaching on pupil learning, indicating to them that instruction can make a positive difference. Implementing instructional strategies that are made explicit and tracing pupils' learning when using these strategies seemed to help prospective teachers appreciate their power as teachers and the positive impact of their teaching on struggling readers. As reported by the content area reading researchers, teaching placements congruent with their preparation program were advantageous.

Four studies (Maheady et al., 1996; B. Mallette et al., 1999; Massey, 1990; R.L. Morgan et al., 1992) demonstrated the difficulty of identifying the impact of instruction on pupils' reading performances within short-term interventions. One of our author team's criticisms about this aspect of the studies is the researchers' lack of attention to the larger classroom and school context and the other forms of instruction provided for these pupils that likely affected pupil performance in addition to the instruction provided by the prospective teachers for a few hours per week.

As with the other research topics in our investigation, the strength of the findings we report in this section are limited by the small set of studies represented in the pool—all research was conducted in the researchers' own classrooms, two thirds occurred in one course, and all the studies were conducted in one semester. Yet we believe the research with structured and guided teaching formats in particular is one of the more mature areas. To affect teachers' expectations and instruction, researchers immersed prospective teachers in guided instruction with individual struggling readers, a direction that produced positive results for both teachers and pupils. Findings across studies point to the positive benefits of guided tutoring and the study of case students, often accompanied with explicit feedback and peer collaboration for building knowledge, changing beliefs, and developing teaching strategies. Further, Massey (1990) and D.N. Morgan et al. (2006) provided some support for the claim that pedagogical knowledge that is developed when teaching one student can transfer to classroom instruction.

In these studies, we found a particular emphasis on knowledge required for teaching or on teacher practical knowledge, as described by Clandinin and Connelly (1987, 1991). Such knowledge is affected by past experiences, present contexts, and visions of future applications. It is assumed that with repeated and guided practice, technical aspects of teaching become automatic. And in the studies we reviewed, that outcome of increased skill and adherence to pedagogical goals set for the prospective teachers was documented across sites. We do not know, however, what knowledge about teaching was constructed during this instruction. For example, were they learning a technical view of teaching over one that emphasizes decision making and problem solving and that allows for different and situated applications of the pedagogical knowledge they were developing? Further research is needed to examine the long-term effects of these learning conditions, addressing specifically, for example, if an emphasis on procedural knowledge (how to teach reading) without (sufficient) attention to flexible and situated use of this knowledge inhibits long-term teaching gains. As Leinhardt (1990) indicated, craft knowledge can include deep knowledge that is situation specific and "fragmentary, superstitious, and often [with] inaccurate opinions" (p. 18). Longitudinal studies would be helpful for examining teaching across situations and conditions.

These researchers maximized the benefits of qualitative and multiple baseline designs by carefully tracing changes in beliefs, knowledge, and teaching over time and by situating these changes within the study of conditions affecting change. In contrast to large-group comparison studies, case methodology and detailed analysis of individual performance enabled these researchers to reveal quite specifically individual and idiosyncratic differences in response to treatments. For example, researchers such as Worthy and Patterson (2001) and Morgan et al. (1992) reported that belief changes (away from deficit views) was not uniform for all of their prospective teachers even when they had successful teaching experiences in the practicum. And Fox (1994) described how two prospective teachers involved in the same demonstrations of literature-based instruction had very different responses by the end of the course, with one rejecting reader-response theory and the other adopting it. We believe, overall, that researchers could go further in explaining how individual difference variables within situated conditions are synergistic; thus, triangulating multiple data points, with the use of continuous interviews or tools evaluating conceptualization such as those developed by Roskos and Walker (1994), could specify further the trajectory of individual development. This careful look at individual differences is long overdue according to Korthagen and Wubbels (1995), but the researchers in this group have begun the work that is necessary to achieve that outcome.

Findings From Programmatic Research

Two types of studies fell into this programmatic group (see Table 5), those that examined the processes involved in changing programs or described program features (Keehn et al., 2003; Vagle, Dillon, Davison-Jenkins, LaDuca, & Olson, 2006) and those that followed graduates into teaching (Grisham, 2000; Hoffman et

Table 5
Summaries of Studies—Programmatic

Author(s), Year	Theoretical Orientation	Research Focus	Participants and Setting	Data Sources	Data Analysis
Grisham, 2000	Constructivist	PSTs' belief systems and instructional practices in relation to constructivist literacy course work	N = 12 PSTs (all F, 11 C, 1 A) Literacy methods course and teaching classrooms in years 2–3	Interviews, videotaped observations, written artifacts, reflective logs	Case study, cross-case analysis
Hoffman, Roller, Maloch, Sailors, Duffy, & Beretvas, 2005	Constructivist	PSTs' responses to knowledge and beliefs guiding their preparation programs	N = 101 beginning teachers, individuals Teaching school sites	One-day classroom observational data	Analysis of longitudinal data, quasi-experimental
Keehn, Martinez, Harmon, Hedrick, Steinmetz, & Perez, 2003	Constructivist	Teacher educators' redesign of preparation program	N = 5 reading faculty, 30 inservice teachers Preparation program	Pre- and post-course syllabi, surveys, interviews, observations, meeting minutes	Inductive coding across multiple data sets, constant comparative analysis
Maloch, Flint, Eldridge, Harmon, Loven, Fine, et al., 2003	Constructivist	PSTs' knowledge, beliefs, practices, and student engagement in their second and third year of teaching	N = 101 PSTs (mostly F; 40 reading specialists, 28 education graduates, 33 graduates other programs) Teacher education programs	Structured, audiotaped telephone interviews	Inductive categories generated from interview data, constant comparison analysis
Sailors, Keehn, Martinez, & Harmon, 2005	Constructivist	PSTs' field experiences and the value placed on these experiences	Study 1: N = 73 first-year teachers (96% F, 3% M) Elementary/middle schools, urban and suburban	Study 1: Telephone interviews (two per participant)	Inductive method, constant comparative analysis
			Study 2: N = 8 faculty members Preparation programs	Study 2: 36 course syllabi, faculty questionnaires	
Vagle, Dillon, Davison-Jenkins, LaDuca, & Olson, 2006	Social Constructivist	PSTs' content knowledge, practices, and dispositions	N = 23 university faculty, 3 graduate students Four higher education institutions in Minnesota	Faculty interviews, student work, end-of-year reports, pre- and postsyllabi	Interpretative case study

Note. PST = prospective teacher; F = female, M = male; A = Asian, AA = African American, API = Asian/Pacific Islander, C = Caucasian, L = Latino, PA = Palestine American, NR = not reported.

al., 2005; Maloch et al., 2003; Sailors, Keehn, Martinez, & Harmon, 2005).

Vagle and colleagues (2006) reported on a three-year professional development project to strengthen literacy teacher preparation at four institutions of higher education and described the benefits of a collaborative process that resulted in new curricula, assessments, and clinical experiences for K–12 prospective teachers. They were able to develop a literacy conceptual framework and four class assignments that formed the basis of curriculum planning at all four institutions. Similarly, Keehn and colleagues' (2003) collaboration to study their program's alignment with features of excellence identified by the International Reading Association's National Commission for Excellence in Elementary Teacher Preparation for Reading (the Commission) produced specific program changes (i.e., increase of four field-based courses and hours required for fieldwork in reading instruction).

The remaining four studies followed graduates from preparation programs into teaching. Grisham (2000), implementing case methodology, followed a group of 12 individuals over a three-year period as they participated in a graduate program for precertification teachers during their first years of teaching. She examined participants' beliefs about and practice in reading/language arts and documented growth in professional and practical knowledge that held during their preparation and field experiences. She attributed this finding to the cohesiveness of content focus across their program. Indicators of personal knowledge revealed the most changes during field experiences and when the participants had their own classrooms (changing from whole language more toward skills-based instruction), and it appeared that the context of the teaching situation made the difference. The increasing pressure for accountability in teaching may also have influenced teachers' beliefs and practices. Sailors and colleagues (2005) reported on the early field experiences offered to those prospective teachers and the value of those experiences to the teachers. Former teacher education students described their perceived importance of carefully structured, supervised field experiences that are closely linked to university course work.

The remaining two studies reported on teachers from eight different excellent programs (as determined by the Commission) as their graduates moved into teaching. Maloch and colleagues (2003) followed 101 prospective teachers through their first year of teaching. Results indicated that graduates with a reading major tended to speak in clear, thoughtful ways about their instruction; sustained a focus on assessing and meeting their students' needs; and were more likely to report seeking support for the development of their own learning than were comparison teachers from the general teacher preparation and programs with reading methods embedded in the program but no special emphasis. Hoffman and colleagues (2005) reported on second and third year data from eight sites of recognized excellence. Graduates of the excellent programs were more effective than teachers in comparison groups at creating and engaging their students with a high-quality literacy environment (as determined by analyses of classroom observation data).

Interpretive Commentary

This group of studies includes descriptive analyses of changes in teacher education programs and descriptions of particular features. It is the second group of studies, those that follow prospective teachers from preparation programs into teaching and over a three-year period, that provides a description of how programmatic efforts may influence later teacher performance. This group of studies tackled difficulties of following graduates of particular programs into the complex environments of schools. While these studies were successful in following graduates over an extended period, there were significant drops in the numbers of teachers participating in the second and third years of the study. Teachers moved to different schools or left the profession. In addition, the researchers were not able to collect reliable achievement data on the school children taught by these teachers.

We need a variety of approaches to study the longer term effects of preparation programs. The work could be supplemented by studies that start in school districts so that valid and reliable achievement data can be connected to teachers and then traced back to various preparation programs. In addition, it would be useful to have more intense study of what is happening to beginning teachers as they encounter various environments in their school assignments. How does professional development provided by schools interface with knowledge and skills learned in preparation programs? What happens when there are mismatches between preparation programs and school-based programs? Each of these questions is important to answer if we are to understand how prospective teachers become the teachers they ultimately become.

Findings From Macroanalysis

In this section we discuss patterns derived from our inductive paradigmatic analysis of all 82 studies. We report on four patterns: (1) changes in beliefs and pedagogical knowledge, (2) conditions associated with these changes, (3) use of explicit teaching conditions, and (4) instructional tools commonly used by the teacher educator researchers.

First, many studies report that changes in beliefs (Fazio, 2000, 2003; Linek et al., 2006; Lonberger, 1992; Matanzo & Harris, 1999; Theurer, 2002; Wolf et al., 1996a) and changes in pedagogical knowledge (Alderman et al., 1993; Boling, 2003; Clark & Medina, 2000; Hughes et al., 2000; Kidd et al., 2002; Klesius et al., 1990; Levin, 1995; Risko, 1992; Risko et al., 1996; Roskos & Walker, 1993, 1994; Shefelbine & Shiel, 1990; Xu, 2000a, 2000b) occurred. Several studies report that changes of beliefs and knowledge occur while prospective teachers are collecting pupil data (Lazar, 2001; M.H. Mallette et al., 2000; Mora & Grisham, 2001; Wolf et al., 1996b; Wolf et al., 1999; Wolf et al., 2000) or are engaging teaching

activities in the field placements (Abrego et al., 2006; Maheady et al., 1996; B. Mallette et al., 1999; Massey, 1990; D.N. Morgan et al., 2006; R.L. Morgan et al., 1992; Nierstheimer et al., 2000; Worthy & Patterson, 2001). This finding is important given the convergence of evidence across sites and populations. In addition, there was some evidence that knowledge and beliefs are most strongly affected in the context of methods courses and that maintaining these may be difficult later on during student teaching when conditions are less supportive (e.g., classroom organization didn't facilitate use of strategies learned in the methods course [Bean, 1997; Massey, 1990; D.N. Morgan et al., 2006]). Tempering the reports of positive change is the reminder that almost all of these studies report on short-term interventions (typically one semester) by the instructors who taught the courses in which learning and changes are reported. These limitations raise questions about the long-term durability of beliefs and knowledge and a need for independent evaluations of prospective teacher performance and replications of studies.

Second, there is evidence that the impact of the teacher education program is stronger when researchers report using a "learning and doing" approach to teaching in the teacher education program. For example, Fazio (2000, 2003) demonstrated text comprehension strategies in his college classes and then assisted his prospective teachers' applications of these while reading their own college textbooks. He then surveyed his students during the course to determine if they continued to use these strategies and why. These prospective teachers reported that they found the strategies helpful for their own learning and believed they would benefit their future students. Others, such as the researchers in the Pedagogy set, demonstrated assessment and teaching procedures in the college classroom and assisted and monitored prospective teachers' use of these in the field settings. And while the researchers did not examine directly their own instruction, there was a consistent emphasis on instruction that engages prospective teachers' application of knowledge while learning. We noticed across studies that teacher educators were implementing a pedagogy built around explicit teaching that includes explicit explanations, use of examples, modeling, focused feedback, practice within the university classroom, and frequent practice with pupils in field settings. Researchers consistently used language such as "intense," "structured," "carefully supervised," "modeling," "focused feedback," and "intensive practice" to describe how they structured and supervised teaching and learning.

Our third coding, described earlier in our methodology section, helped us trace this perceived pattern more specifically by generating codes for explicitness of teaching and for effect strength. We did this coding to capture what we thought might be a relevant explanation for the strength of the patterns we detected within the pedagogical studies. We preface this discussion by acknowledging that our data and analyses are not at the level that permits drawing strong conclusions. The designs of the reviewed studies were predominantly qualitative, and our coding of effect strength, while logical and reliable, certainly does not have the precision and validity of calculated effect sizes (weighted for sample size and adjusted for independence when single studies contribute more than one effect) from experimental and quasi-experimental studies. Many of the studies reviewed here were not designed to answer causal questions, and our secondary analysis is also correlational.

For the purposes of this coding, we defined explicitness to include five elements—explicit explanation, use of examples, modeling, practice within the university classroom, and practice with pupils in field settings. In no sense do we confine explicitness to rigid definitions of "direct instruction" associated with competency-based education methods or those employing teach–reteach cycles with contingent reinforcement (Cruickshank, 1970; Rosenshine, 1979). After coding each of the intervention studies for the five elements, we assigned an explicitness score by counting the number of elements of explicitness reported. We then did cross-tabulations to explore the nature of the relationship between explicitness and effect strength.

There is evidence of a strong relationship between explicitness and effect strength. As the reported number of elements of explicitness increased, the strength of the effect also increased (Pearson chi-square test of significance = 87.2, $p < .000$). Again, we caution that these data are correlational and based on studies not designed to address questions of causality. However, the relationship between explicitness and effect strength has the potential for explanatory power and should be a focus for future research. This potential relationship is also consistent with more general findings related to explicit teaching and learning within guided teaching formats (Pearson & Gallagher, 1983).

We also looked at the relationship of explicitness and effect strength within our seven topic areas described previously. The relationship of explicitness and effect strength was strong across all topics except assessment (where there was only one intervention study). For struggling readers where all the studies produced strong effects and were explicit, no studies in that group contained less then three elements of explicitness. Furthermore, two of the topic areas (i.e., struggling readers and reflection) seem to function as anchor points at opposite ends of the continuum for the explicitness effect. In several of the reflection studies (McMahon, 1997; Risko et al., 1999, 2002; Truscott & Walker, 1998), teacher educators were purposefully not explicit in their teaching of reflection. They provided very little guidance on how to reflect because of theoretical understandings that suggested that guiding reflection would impose the teacher educator's thought processes on prospective teachers and would not generate genuine reflection. When Leland and colleagues (1997) decided to provide more guidance by specifically addressing critical literacy in the university classroom and by providing feedback about critical literacy, they were successful in increasing the amount of critical reflections. In the struggling readers studies, the instruction provided by teacher educators was highly explicit and was evaluated as strong by both the researchers and the prospective teachers. Perhaps the care and attention teacher educators devote to guided teaching settings would be similarly effective in other settings.

This hypothesis raises the question of how explicit teacher educators should be and how intense instruction must be to produce learning in prospective teachers. For example, the studies reviewed in the Reflective Reasoning set were remarkably ineffective in influencing sophisticated, multileveled thinking about instruction. One plausible explanation for this failure is the aforementioned lack of guidance and explicitness, but another may be intensity—teaching prospective teachers to reflect may require much more time and effort on the part of teacher educators. The explicitness, intensity, and positive changes in the struggling readers studies suggest that prospective teachers learn well when teacher educators provide them with intense support that includes explicit teaching and a lot of time and structure. Teacher educators believe that effective tutoring of struggling readers is a complex activity that requires a very high level of structured support. Accordingly, several researchers (Abrego et al., 2006; Maheady et al., 1996; B. Mallette et al., 1999; Massey, 1990; D.N. Morgan et al., 2006; R.L. Morgan et al., 1992; Nierstheimer et al., 2000; Worthy & Patterson, 2001) provided structured lesson planning, specified instructional routines to implement, and well-specified self-reporting requirements. They observed prospective teachers and provided feedback both orally and in writing, and they often included collaboration with a partner, a team, or both. All reported positive changes in lesson plan development and instruction in the field placement. Yet to be determined, however, are operational and functional definitions of our "explicit" and "intensity" constructs.

We had additional questions about explicit instruction. The complexity, intensity, and difficulty of the task may determine how much of each element must be present to achieve specific learning goals. It is also highly probable that there are differences among prospective

teachers' responses to the elements of explicitness and the intensity of their use. And as we discussed earlier, we must examine the knowledge that prospective teachers are constructing while learning in these structured and explicated guided learning environments; are they concluding that teaching is merely technical (i.e., learning routines that are applied systematically) or that teaching draws on multiple resources for problem solving?

A fourth pattern derived from our analysis of the whole set of studies relates to instructional tools commonly used by teacher educators. In addition to preparing their prospective teachers to collect and report on pupil data and engaging them in supervising teaching assignments as we described above, researchers describe a favorable influence of several other tools. Examining personal uses of reading strategies (e.g., Fazio, 2000, 2003; Matanzo & Harris, 1999; Theurer, 2002), writing narratives about personal literacy development (Clark & Medina, 2000; Xu, 2000a, 2000b), or writing the family histories of their pupils (Kidd et al., 2002) seemed to be useful tools for helping prospective teachers become explicit about their beliefs, which is a necessary prelude for authentic self-reflection that can evoke positive changes such as a movement away from deficit views of their students. Collaboration with other prospective teachers and peer coaching (e.g., B. Mallette et al., 1999) were also tools identified to influence the development of beliefs and pedagogical knowledge. Researchers described above who advocated for carefully structured teaching experiences in which prospective teachers are guided to content from the methods courses to their teaching (e.g., Nierstheimer et al., 2000; Worthy & Patterson, 2001) also advocated for the power of personal relationships between prospective teachers and their students to support acquiring positive beliefs about the students (e.g., these students can learn to read) and their own teaching abilities (e.g., I can teach struggling readers). And in the studies that included tutoring (Abrego et al., 2006; Maheady et al., 1996; B. Mallette et al., 1999; Massey, 1990; D.N. Morgan et al., 2006; R.L. Morgan et al., 1992;

Niersheimer et al., 2000; Worthy & Patterson, 2001) and working with pupils to collect and analyze reading assessment data (Lazar, 2001; M.H. Mallette et al., 2000; Mora & Grisham, 2001; Wolf et al., 1996b; Wolf et al., 1999; Wolf et al., 2000), researchers hypothesized that collecting data over a prolonged period was important. Furthermore, instructor's feedback related to that data might also be an important tool to support learning. For example, M.H. Mallette and her colleagues (2000) and Wolf and her colleagues (1996b, 1999, 2000) reported that teacher educators reacted to and made comments in learning logs, field notes, and dialogue journals that prospective teachers kept after interacting with students.

Taken as a whole, the patterns we derived require further scrutiny and provide a catalyst for future research. They do not represent prescriptions for best practices, but they are fertile for growing and directing new questions that might guide future investigations. We have raised questions throughout this report in our interpretive summaries that might be useful for directing this future work. Questions about the situatedness of the findings we describe must be kept front and center. A series of studies that attempt to replicate those clustered around our identified patterns are needed to more closely examine multiple situated factors, such as program, participant, and instructional characteristics, that affect the reported outcomes.

Critique of the Research

The research we reviewed focused on preparing prospective teachers to teach reading to children and adolescents. Because of the specific content focus of this review, it distinguishes itself from reviews that examine what is often referred to as general teacher education research (e.g., Cochran-Smith & Zeichner, 2005) or multicultural teacher education research (Grant & Secada, 1990; Sleeter, 2001). In the following sections, we critique the design and quality of this research and, when possible, draw comparisons and contrasts between our review and reviews of others, including the Clift and

Brady (2005) review of English language arts teacher education studies that had goals similar to ours. We describe both the contributions of this research and our concerns.

A Content Focus

Carter (1990), Grant and Secada (1990), Sleeter (2001), and Wideen et al. (1998) concluded that teacher education research is fragmented and scattered in focus. Clift and Brady (2005) reviewed research across disciplinary areas, and thus, only a small portion of their review focused specifically on teaching English language arts. In contrast, our review had a primary organizing feature—reading teacher education research—from its inception. Having such a focus enabled us to search for and identify broad themes and networks of conceptual relationships that define this body of work. The merits of delimiting the parameters of our review to a particular content area enabled us to reveal quite explicitly the conceptual networks in play, theories underlying researchers' objects of study, and data supporting researchers' conclusions. Taking care to identify the particulars of each study, we were able to draw comparisons across studies, a process advocated by Guba and Lincoln (1994) and Wideen et al. (1998) for comparing interpretive studies or those influenced by postmodern methodologies. We believe this review serves to identify areas of congruence across studies and conditions within that might enable teacher education researchers to implement replication studies, where interventions described by one set of researchers are repeated with new participants at different sites. Such a movement would address the issue of replication within post-positivist/behavioral paradigms (Guba & Lincoln, 1994).

When compared with the Clift and Brady (2005) review, we can identify several points of convergence. First, seven studies that were included in their review were also included in ours. Second, in both reviews, clusters of studies have common findings. Conclusions from both reviews indicated that prospective teachers' pedagogical knowledge was enhanced within structured teaching formats and sustained interactions with students and that application of pedagogical knowledge is enhanced with mentoring that includes feedback on teaching and peer coaching. An additional finding reported by Clift and Brady—that prospective teachers resist information taught in methods courses—was not a universal finding in the studies we reviewed. It was, however, a finding discussed by researchers investigating secondary education majors and their preparation for teaching content area reading in secondary schools. As we discussed earlier, researchers in that area identified factors contributing to mixed reactions to that preparation and point to new directions undertaken by adolescent literacy researchers.

Quality Controls

The empirical work we reviewed is similar in design to the research reviewed by Wideen et al. (1998), Sleeter (2001), and Clift and Brady (2005). Studies in our review were mostly qualitative (conducted in researchers' teacher education classes with samples of convenience), employed self-report methodologies, and typically occurred during one semester. Researchers employed paradigmatic analytical procedures to identify common elements and derive patterns and themes across their data sets (e.g., belief statements, journal writing, and lesson plans; teaching performance; interviews or notes taken during teaching debriefing sessions). Four studies, also one semester in length, compared performance of groups or individuals using experimental and quasi-experimental designs, including single-subject research designs. Only six studies examined programmatic effects on teacher development. Design features, such as samples of convenience and self-report methodologies, are limitations of this body of research.

Because this work is situated primarily within a qualitative research paradigm, one of the most compelling issues for our critique is the control for internal quality that assures trustworthiness and authenticity of data collection and reporting (Guba & Lincoln, 1994).

As we described in our methodology section, our initial coding procedures provided a screen of internal quality by examining whether researchers provided a clear audit trail, documenting data collection and data analysis procedures, and sufficient representativeness of data to support claims and conclusions. For experimental and quasi-experimental studies, inclusion criteria required adherence to internal and external validity requirements; interpretive studies, including case studies, required sufficient description of events and contexts and multiple data points to provide credible explanatory power.

Although all 82 studies in our final pool met our criteria, we still found variability in level of detail of reporting and analysis. Many studies would have benefited from more detailed and complete descriptions of data collection procedures, data analysis and coding procedures, and how patterns were derived from the data analysis. In 48% of the studies, researchers provided insufficient information (e.g., gender, ethnicity, race, school history) about the participants and included little information about themselves as the teacher educators/researchers.

Our best examples of applying strong controls for internal quality are in the guided teaching and struggling readers studies. Researchers (Maheady et al., 1996; B. Mallette et al., 1999; Massey, 1990; Nierstheimer et al., 2000; Worthy & Patterson, 2001) described course conditions (e.g., structured lesson plans, guides for peer coaching) and methods for following and supporting participants during their teaching (e.g., forms of feedback on lesson planning, procedures for holding debriefing sessions), and they reported and cross-referenced multiple data sets (e.g., journal writing, lessons plans, transcript data from debriefing sessions) to support their claims. Their descriptions were sufficiently detailed to convey what prospective teachers did, feedback they received, and how they responded to this feedback. In addition, they provided clear explanations of analytical categories (e.g., effective vs. ineffective teaching procedures) used to interpret their data, they provided sufficient examples or quotes from transcripts to document patterns, and they reported disconfirming evidence to illustrate participants' individual differences and raise questions for future investigations.

Eleven percent of the researchers drew on data that described learning events and prospective teachers' actions and reactions to events to produce stories or case studies. These case studies were situated within the context of the course happenings and were bounded by a beginning and ending event. To develop their case studies, researchers inferred possible relationships between the multiple events of the course and prospective teachers' actions. They described multiple forms of data (e.g., interviews, teaching observations, lesson planning) and multiple data points in their attempts to describe a dynamic interplay of several factors occurring simultaneously within a series of successive incidents and to explain how these incidents might have negatively or positively affected participants' development, which were represented as typical cases and sometimes contrasted with atypical cases.

Most notably, we recognize the work of M.H. Mallette and colleagues (2000), who systematically traced changes of six participants (one represented a negative case) in stance and pedagogy across multiple measures and experiences to document individual and idiosyncratic meanings of struggling readers, conditions contributing to construction of new knowledge, and how selectivity of goals influenced meaningful changes in learning. Also, the work of Wolf and colleagues (1999), who conducted within and across case analyses to trace learning over time, produced a rich description of phases of learning (referred to as fissured ground) that includes conceptual and emotional disequilibrium prior to changes that are transformative. Having noted the careful work of these researchers, however, we must also acknowledge that these studies are situated in particular events and places; replication is needed to test how similar goals and events would develop and affect learning in other settings.

Historical Continuity Issues

Another issue considered in our critique is the degree to which researchers considered and built upon previous research. We found variability in this factor. Some researchers carefully referenced previous and relevant research in their target areas and explained how their work built on and extended previous work (e.g., Kasten & Padak, 1997; Xu, 2000a, 2000b). Others seldom referenced the work of their literacy colleagues and instead drew on studies frequently associated with a research domain. For example, reflection researchers often drew on Schön's (1987, 1991) rationale for teaching as a reflective activity but neglected to establish the historical continuity that comes from a study of reflection research. Roskos and colleagues (2001) reported a similar neglect of establishing historical continuity in the teacher reflection research they reviewed.

Some researchers brought depth to their work through a series of carefully designed studies that built on one another and, in the end, provided power for drawing conclusions. For example, Bean and his colleagues (Bean, 1997; Bean & Zulich, 1990, 1992; Zulich et al., 1992) designed four studies with different populations to explicate a coherent representation of how beliefs about disciplinary knowledge impact beliefs and choice of content area reading strategies. Similarly, Wolf and her colleagues (Wolf et al., 1996a, 1996b; Wolf et al., 1999; Wolf et al., 2000), across four studies, tested their intervention (e.g., child-study projects) on changing beliefs of different groups of prospective teachers. Across these studies, we saw agreement on the importance of teacher–student interactions and the use of pupil data to build positive perceptions of culturally diverse students. Similarly, Roskos and Walker's (1994) second level of analysis of data reported in an earlier study of theirs (1993) revealed prospective teachers' difficulty in understanding complex relationships among teaching decisions, and in the process these researchers rendered valuable the use of conceptual mapping for revealing thought processes.

Researchers in our pool of studies defied the snark syndrome as described by Byrne (1993) and considered by several reviewers of teacher education research. The snark syndrome refers to concepts and beliefs that have gained privileged status only from their repeated use in the literature. As posited by Wideen et al. (1998), these notions often have not been tested widely, if at all, and references to them can be inaccurate. For example, researchers widely claim that prospective teachers hold on to deficit beliefs about students whose culture is different from their own or that beliefs are difficult to change. Researchers tested this claim in the diversity category (Clark & Medina, 2000; Kidd et al., 2002; Wolf et al., 1999; Wolf et al., 2000; Xu, 2000a, 2000b) and in the struggling reader category (Nierstheimer et al., 2000; Worthy & Patterson, 2001). They provided evidence that stereotypical beliefs can be disrupted and changed and that with tutoring experience prospective teachers' confidence in teaching struggling readers can be enhanced. Similarly, McMahon (1997) questioned the long-standing belief that reflective thinking occurs in levels and that lower order levels are prerequisite for higher order ones. Her data supported her counterargument that several levels of reflection can and do occur simultaneously.

We noted earlier that it was difficult to historically trace how studies were conceptualized or how earlier studies may have influenced later ones. The overall questions motivating the work—questions about beliefs, knowledge, pedagogy, and impact of programs—remained fairly stable across the 16 years. We do note, however, at least a few changes in assumptions and approach to the teaching methods of these teacher educators. For example, in the beliefs and reflection research, we found that researchers moved away from neutrality and "hands off" approaches to implement those that demonstrated alternate viewpoints or that guided learning through elaborated instructional events (e.g., multiple readings and focused discussions on social issues coupled with journal writings and field observations [Leland et al., 1997]). And as we previously noted, secondary students in

more recent studies seemed to appreciate content area reading instruction, especially when it was favorable to the structure of the discipline under study and personal applications were made apparent.

Other Concerns

We identified additional concerns. First, researchers in these studies did not attend to their participants' individual differences (e.g., their history, their culture, their goals) in ways that would reveal possible synergistic relationships between personal characteristics and the learning conditions. Roskos and colleagues (2001) similarly reported an inattention to individual differences in their review of teacher reflection research. As with the teacher reflection studies, researchers in this review who reported variable response to their interventions provided little attention to how personal attributes (such as how individuals approach assignments [e.g., Korthagen & Wubbels, 1995]), personal interests, identities, or goals may interact with course assignments or teaching experiences. Researchers applying case study methodologies, such as M.H. Mallette and her colleagues (2000), were the most helpful in their attempt to juxtapose personal stances with learning conditions and with school cultural features to explain idiosyncratic and common features of learning changes.

Similar to the findings reported by Roskos and colleagues (2001) and Wideen et al. (1998), few researchers in our review questioned programmatic features that may influence or inhibit prospective teachers' development. Few considered the impact of others involved in teacher education, such as mentor teachers (or those certified teachers who are supervising prospective teachers) during student teaching or liberal arts professors. Even when content area researchers attributed differences in learning and attitude to their academic majors, none examined the specific content of those courses or the influence of the academic professors in these disciplines. One exception was the research reported by Grisham (2000), who examined effects of programmatic contexts on prospective teachers' beliefs and practices.

The researchers we reviewed did not problematize the issue of time, such as what is expected from one semester's work. Some took for granted that the one semester provided insufficient time for learning or for changing beliefs or teaching performance. For example, researchers in the diversity strand hypothesized that changes in teaching diverse learners required more time; however, as we reported above, many researchers in our review described changes in learning, beliefs, and teaching within one semester. We believe that time alone is not the determining factor in producing changes; instead, it is quite plausible that time coupled with other variables, such as explicit instruction or intensity of support for learning, must be considered and that multiple combinations of factors affect learning and change.

Weaknesses found in our studies, and also cited by Wideen et al. (1998), are a lack of disclosure by researchers about their role in data collection and analysis (and how this role may have affected outcomes or was attended to with specific controls) and a lack of researchers' self-reflections on their own teaching practices. In addition, researchers who were also course instructors did not report how they assigned grades independent of prospective teachers' performance on research tasks and if participant change was attributed to end-of-course grades. Although it was evident that our researchers did control for personal biases, manipulation of data (e.g., drawing on independent raters, completing member checks, establishing inter-rater agreements), and in some cases how grades were assigned, studies could have been strengthened by explicit attention to these issues. The second concern expressed by Wideen et al.—self reflection—was addressed by several of our researchers, such as Fecho and colleagues (2000), who examined their struggle with their authority in the college classroom, and Hinchman and Lalik (2000), who studied the controlling nature of their discourse and participation in class discussions.

Some Concluding Thoughts

Grant and Secada (1990) argued, "we need programs of research that acknowledge what is lacking but that also provide a vision and hope for what might be done" (p. 420). Wideen et al. (1998) also discussed this issue of vision. They concluded that research (and research reviews) can be judged as valuable if it (a) provides new hypotheses, conceptual frameworks that push thinking forward, and directions for researchers and (b) contributes to improving the lives of those being researched. We believe the studies we reviewed do provide conceptualizations of teaching and direction for future work. Our studies as a whole underscore that learning to teach is much more complex than providing propositional knowledge. The studies help us to unravel components of instruction (e.g., teaching tools, forms of explicit instruction, use of pupil data collection measures) that support learning, conditions that change firmly held beliefs (e.g., one-to-one teaching experiences), how personal stances and approaches to teaching affect practices, and assessment tools (e.g., Roskos and Walker's [1994] use of concept mapping) that make visible thinking and learning in process. Further, several researchers (e.g., Risko, 1992; Wolf et al., 1999; Wolf et al., 2000) portray learning to teach as a process that includes forward and backward movements, disequilibrium replaced by equilibrium and vice versa; it is a process that requires careful support to help prospective teachers apply what they are learning within new contexts. With further investigations and refinement of questions, it is possible that the long-term outcomes of this research will positively affect both teacher educators and prospective teachers.

Recommendations

We offer the following recommendations for future research.

First, *build on the research we have.* Throughout this review, we described convergence of research questions and findings across multiple researchers that hold promise for generating hypotheses for guiding future research. We believe, however, that researchers' designs of future studies must attend closely to the quality controls (e.g., complete descriptions of data collection and analysis procedures) and other concerns (e.g., role of education and discipline instructors, durability of change over time) we discussed previously. Future research that is systematic and intentional in maintaining quality controls could address claims of the researchers we discussed throughout this paper (e.g., guided practice enhances pedagogy, disciplinary structures align differentially with content area reading strategies) and questions we raised (e.g., what strategies or teaching practices are most optimal for guided practice?) to build on the current knowledge base. We recommend that the empirical work be located in both specific courses and at the program level and within multisite designs. Such an approach would provide both a broad and an up-close analysis of the directions proposed in this review and would be well suited to examining learning and teaching as situated—variable and complex. A series of well-designed studies across sites, which clearly build on the history of the work under study, is needed to systematically trace situated factors that affect findings.

This future work should account for multiple layers of events and settings by taking an ecological approach, as suggested by Wideen et al. (1998), that allows for a simultaneous study of a range of issues (e.g., impact and culture of disciplinary courses and knowledge, forms of explicit instruction), participants' involvement—from college administrators to classroom teachers serving as mentors—and settings, and participants' histories and cultural influences (e.g., professors' beliefs, prospective teachers' out-of-school lives). Embedded in this multidimensional work is a need for ethnographic and case study research to study potential qualitative differences across conditions and to provide a rich body of data to support interpretations and hypotheses derived from the work. Willard Waller (1961), a sociologist who studied teaching, pursued the question "What does teaching do to teachers?" Instead,

by taking an ecological stance to guide future work, we could address the question "What does teacher education do to [and for] teachers?"

In our set of studies, we noticed a slight trend favoring deeper learning and changes in beliefs and teaching when the learning was situated within methods courses or methods courses combined with field placements, as compared to situations in which learning occurred only through field placements or student teaching alone. This finding counters typical claims by teacher educators that the student teaching semester is the most important for integrating and extending knowledge that has been developed previously. The finding by Bean (1997) that some conditions during student teaching are not favorable to advance knowledge and, instead, may be counterproductive is an important area to pursue with the hope of identifying conditions that may have a differential impact. And, given the finding that the studies in our set occurred mostly with upper level teacher education students enrolled in their last two years of the program and in methods courses or field experiences, there is a need to examine in similar ways the impact of early teacher education experiences (e.g., foundation courses, early fieldwork).

We also recommend design studies for placing a fine-tuned microscope on educational events within methods courses and other such courses because these studies can capture learning in action and the dynamic events influencing learning within methods courses and student teaching seminars. With design studies, researchers would make visible their conjectures about prospective teachers learning under specific instructional conditions and the specific variables in play that may be affecting learning and changing beliefs. Linking small-scale studies, such as design studies across sites, is one way to accomplish the "strategic investment" of efforts described by Wilson and colleagues (2001), with robust results as a potential outcome.

Second, *expand and deepen the research agenda*. Several issues identified in our review require further study, such as the issues of "learning and doing" and intensity and explicitness of instruction (as examined in our third coding). Each requires a systematic unpacking of the variables involved in such instruction, conditions contributing and inhibiting learning and engagement, and responses given particular situations. While we find it quite probable that these explicit demonstrations and guidance can influence beliefs and pedagogical knowledge development, our earlier questions about what prospective teachers learned from such guided practice formats requires additional study. For example, are prospective teachers learning to implement particular strategies in a way that enhances their ability to teach with independence or does the form of guidance they receive suggest to them a mechanistic approach to teaching (i.e., routinized and one way to solve the problem)? And within such guided formats, when do prospective teachers learn to adapt these practices or adopt new ones that may be necessary in novel situations? Are there different forms of apprenticeship models that could be compared and contrasted for relative contributions to teacher development. Similarly, in addition to or instead of demonstrations and guided models of teaching, we need to explore alternate models, such as inquiry models, that might also provide engaged learning and positive and different outcomes. We need to study the discourse of guided instructional models and examine characteristics of these instructional conversations. And we need to carefully study the knowledge prospective teachers are constructing when engaged in these different methods to enhance their learning. Little attention was given to multimedia and technology-rich environments that could support deeper learning while drawing on the multiple literacies that prospective teachers use in their everyday lives and also preparing them to teach within multiple literacy learning spaces. This seems to be a serious omission in the current research.

We need to conduct multiple longitudinal studies that follow prospective teachers across their course work to student teaching and independent teaching in their own classrooms. A few studies in our review (e.g., Grisham, 2000; Hoffman et al., 2005) report on positive learning outcomes in these settings, especially as related to pedagogical knowledge. Yet we know little about the durability of this knowledge, especially when confronted with obstacles such as those described by Massey (2006).

Perhaps as Adorno (1998) feared, content and professional knowledge are irrelevant. At the least, they seemed to be irrelevant to the researchers we reviewed. Other than the research directed toward building pedagogical knowledge, we have no hints from this body of work on the forms of knowledge that are important for teacher development and effectiveness, and no investigations that attempted to uncover forms of knowledge that can be transformative, as described by Britzman (2003) and others. For example, if we expect future teachers to refute inequities of schooling and instructional routines or to teach deep understandings of disciplinary knowledge, what knowledge is instrumental for achieving those goals? And with the need for research of knowledge is the concomitant need for researchers to develop assessment tools that are reliable and authentic.

A crucial need for future research is in the area of diversity. A series of studies that focuses specifically on preparing teachers to teach culturally and linguistically diverse students and to confront inequitable schooling conditions that can inhibit literacy development is needed. Researchers who pursue this line of inquiry might consider deeper and more inclusive definitions of diversity. Such a definition would include immigrants, migrants, class, and the histories of teachers who challenge normative assumptions. Our current set of studies provides several stepping off points that lay some foundational directions for increasing knowledge and sensitivity to cultural diversity (e.g., use of narratives, community-based field experiences that are guided and purposeful). The effect of these starting points on building pedagogical knowledge is underexplored. A drawing together of researchers across theoretical paradigms (e.g., sociolinguists, critical race theorists, bidialectical, bilingual, biliteracy theorists) is needed to approach this issue much more comprehensively and to drive the future of this work.

Third, *deepen and broaden theoretical paradigms guiding future research and draw on multiple research methodologies to capture layers of factors affecting teacher development.* As we noted at the beginning of this article, the studies could have benefited from more detailed discussion of the theories guiding their work. For example, researchers who describe their work as following constructivist paradigms provide no clues about the particular premises (e.g., failing to distinguish cognitive constructivism from social constructivism, as discussed by Windschitl, 2002). Yet even with more explicit explanations, the theoretical frames guiding this body of research failed to capture the complexity of multiple layers of situated practices embodied within the course and programmatic structures. A careful study of the multiple instructional practices adopted by teacher education researchers and theory as an object to be critiqued (see Dressman [2007] for a more complete discussion) is necessary to challenge and refute or elaborate on existing theories in ways that extend current conceptions of teacher development and the situated practices of teacher education. One suggestion is to draw on activity theory (Cole, 1996; Engeström, 1999) to represent and study the dynamic interplay of features of instructional and organizational arrangements, histories and goals of teacher educators and prospective teachers, and personal understandings as they are developing within the activity of teacher education. Teacher education could then be studied as a dialogic activity (Bakhtin, 1981) that is influenced by one's history, present activities, and future goals. Additionally, researchers should draw on multiple methods for data collection and analysis (e.g., detailed case studies within design studies, discourse analyses within college classrooms) that would allow for more complex designs to study the complex environments associated with teacher education.

In her ethnographic study of learning to teach in high school, Britzman (2003) reminds us of the importance of investigating the theories that prospective teachers grasp and retain to guide their thinking. We need to understand the images of theory that prospective teachers form and those they dismiss—and the reasons for these choices. Questions about personal theories that we envision are similar to those pursued by Clandinin and Connelly (1987), who described teachers' personal practical knowledge as practical knowledge informed by both personal beliefs and growing knowledge about others' beliefs. Taking the cue from Britzman and Clandinin and Connelly, the construct of teacher beliefs becomes more nuanced and inclusive of multiple ways of knowing and believing.

Fourth, *mechanisms are needed to form research collaboratives that can shape the public and policy discourse on teacher education.* We approached our review with a sense of urgency at wanting to respond to many voices (e.g., policymakers questioning the value of teacher education, our own need for an understanding of the research) that are competing for our attention. We were not surprised to learn that most research about reading teacher education is conducted by individuals within specific programs and that there are few large-scale studies. Thus, generalizations across institutions and programs are difficult to make. For too long, teacher education research has been marginalized (with few national funding programs and inattention at national literacy meetings). Yet collaborative work, for which grand-scale funding is needed, is crucial to advancing knowledge in this field. Such work can provide insights based on data rather than take-it-for-granted notions (e.g., judging prospective teacher performance with high stakes tests, use of pupil achievement scores to judge teacher quality) that may be distracting teacher education researchers from work that is more central to identifying the impact of teacher education on differences that really matter for teachers and the students they teach.

Notes

[1] As teacher educators and researchers, we are deeply committed to advancing knowledge about teaching and learning and teachers' professional development. We have each

spent our professional careers as reading teacher educator scholars. Our graduate studies focused on reading processes and our professional appointments have involved us in reading teacher education for a combined total of over 200 years. Initially, each of us was prepared for traditional positivist/behavioral research but have, over the years, broadened our respective research perspectives to include descriptive, qualitative, and critical research methodologies. We have each conducted research and provided instruction on topics including characteristics of readers, professional development, teacher reflection, teacher education, and reading/literacy processes. We have all taught school in communities characterized as multicultural and diverse in terms of socioeconomic status, ethnicity, and geography (urban and rural). Some of us have taught and conducted research with Native American teachers, children and youth, and each of us have taught African American, Latino, and Anglo teachers and youth. We are Caucasian and middle class but to describe us as homogeneous would be a mistake. We each bring the breadth and depth of our experience to this comprehensive review.

[2] We asked for advice from Judith Green (personal communication, December 18, 2003; October 9, 2004), with regard to research perspectives associated with interactional sociolinguistics; John Guthrie (personal communication, December 1, 2003), for research perspectives associated with mixed-method designs including testing of predictors of performance; Donna Alvermann (personal communication, December 5, 2003), for research associated with narrative approaches, feminist theories, and power relationships; and Janice Almasi (personal communication, July 24, 2003), for qualitative and interpretive analyses of descriptive research.

[3] Database: ERIC; Query: (de=((student teachers) or (preservice teachers) or (preservice teacher education) or (student teacher supervisors) or (student teaching) or (teacher interns) or (teacher supervision) or (reading teachers) or (beginning teachers)) and de=((evaluation methods) or (student surveys) or (attitude measures) or (measures individuals) or opinions or questionnaires or (teacher response) or attitudes or (student teacher attitudes) or (teacher behavior) or beliefs or (educational attitudes) or (teacher attitudes) or (follow-up studies) or (outcomes of education) or (program effectiveness) or (educational benefits) or (educational indicators) or (attitude change) or (behavior change) or (questioning techniques) or (educational change) or influences) and PT=((reports research) or (reports evaluative)) and DE=(reading or (reading instruction))) or (DE=(preservice teacher education) and DE=(reading or (reading instruction)) and PT=((reports research) or (reports evaluative)))

[4] Sheri R. Parris and Kelly Morton Reid at Texas Christian University; Greg Turner, Julie Ankrum, Aimee Morewood, and Sara Helfrich-Thomas at University of Pittsburgh; Julie Justice and Patrick Tiedemann at Vanderbilt University; Jennifer Cromley, Caroline Mark, and Alison Nathan at the District of Columbia site.

We dedicate this paper to the memory of our colleague Dr. James Flood, who was a member of our research team and an exemplary teacher educator. We learned from his vision about teacher preparation and appreciated his wit and "can do" expressions of support. We acknowledge the contributions that Dr. Flood made to this work and to our ongoing efforts to prepare quality reading teachers. We thank the IRA Board of Directors, who appointed a task force to study teacher education research. And we thank Erin Cushing and Kathy Baughman for the electronic searches of multiple databases and Becky Fetterolf for the copy editing. Also, we thank the anonymous reviewers and the RRQ editors for their careful reading of our manuscript and their constructive suggestions for revisions.

Note From the RRQ Editors:

Research reported in this article was conducted by a group constituted by the International Reading Association, which is also the publisher of this journal. The review of the article by the journal was conducted using standard review procedures with no special consideration given to the sponsor of the research.

References

Abrego, M.H., Rubin, R., & Sutterby, J.A. (2006). They call me "maestra": Preservice teachers' interactions with parents in a reading tutoring program. *Action in Teacher Education*, *28*(1), 3–12.

Adorno, T.W. (1998). *Critical models: Interventions and catchwords* (Henry W. Pickford, Trans.). New York: Columbia University Press.

Alderman, M.K., Klein, R., Seeley, S.K., & Sanders, M. (1993). Metacognitive self-portraits: Preservice teachers as learners. *Reading Research and Instruction*, *32*(2), 38–54.

Anders, P.L., Hoffman, J.V., & Duffy, G.G. (2000). Teaching teachers to teach reading: Paradigm shifts, persistent problems, and challenges. In M.L. Kamil, P.B. Mosenthal, P.D. Pearson, & R. Barr (Eds.), *Handbook of reading research* (Vol. 3, pp. 719–742). Mahwah, NJ: Erlbaum.

Anderson, N., Caswell, I., & Hayes, M. (1994). Using peer coaching to provide additional feedback to preservice teachers of reading in an early field experience. *Yearbook of the College Reading Association*, *16*, 211–221.

Argyris, C., Putnam, R., & Smith, D.M. (1985). *Action science*. San Francisco: Jossey-Bass.

Au, K.H. (1998). Social constructivism and the school literacy learning of students of diverse backgrounds. *Journal of Literacy Research*, *30*(2), 297–319.

Bakhtin, M. (1981). *The dialogic imagination: Four essays* (M. Holquist, Ed.; C. Emerson & M. Holquist, Trans.). Austin: University of Texas Press.

Bartlett, F.C. (1932). *Remembering: A study in experimental and social psychology*. Cambridge, England: Cambridge University Press.

Bean, T.W. (1997). Preservice teachers' selection and use of content area literacy strategies. *Journal of Educational Research*, *90*(3), 154–163.

Bean, T.W., & Zulich, J. (1990). Teaching students to learn from text: Preservice content teachers' changing view of their role through the window of their student–professor dialogue journals. *National Reading Conference Yearbook*, *39*, 171–178.

Bean, T.W., & Zulich, J. (1992). A case study of three preservice teachers' beliefs about content area reading through the window of student–professor dialogue journals. *National Reading Conference Yearbook, 41*, 463–474.

Block, J.H., & Hazelip, K. (1995). Teachers' beliefs and belief systems. In L.W. Anderson (Ed.), *International encyclopedia of teaching and teacher education* (2nd ed., pp. 25–28). New York: Pergamon.

Boling, E.C. (2003). The transformation of instruction through technology: Promoting inclusive learning communities in teacher education courses. *Action in Teacher Education, 24*(4), 64–73.

Briggs, C., Tully, B., & Stiefer, T. (1998). Direct informed assessment: Frequency of use in preservice teacher education programs within a five-state region. *Action in Teacher Education, 20*(3), 30–38.

Britzman, D.P. (2003). *Practice makes practice: A critical study of learning to teach.* Albany: State University of New York Press.

Byrne, E. (1993). *Woman and science: The snark syndrome.* London: Falmer.

Calderhead, J. (1996). Teachers: Beliefs and knowledge. In D.C. Berliner & R.C. Calfee (Eds.), *Handbook of educational psychology* (pp. 709–725). New York: Macmillan.

Carnegie Task Force on Teaching as a Profession. (1986). *A nation prepared: Teachers for the 21st century.* New York: Carnegie Forum on Education and the Economy.

Carter, K. (1990). Teachers' knowledge and learning to teach. In W.R. Houston, M. Haberman, J.P. Sikula (Eds.), *Handbook of research on teacher education* (pp. 291–310). New York: Macmillan.

Clandinin, D.J., & Connelly, F.M. (1987). Teachers' personal knowledge: What counts as "personal" in studies of the personal. *Journal of Curriculum Studies, 19*(6), 487–500.

Clandinin, D.J., & Connelly, F.M. (1991). Narrative and story in practice and research. In D.A. Schön (Ed.), *The reflective turn: Case studies in and on educational practice* (pp. 258–281). New York: Teachers College Press.

Clark, C., & Medina, C. (2000). How reading and writing literacy narratives affect preservice teachers' understandings of literacy, pedagogy, and multiculturalism. *Journal of Teacher Education, 51*(1), 63–76.

Clift, R.T., & Brady, P. (2005). Research on methods courses and field experiences. In M. Cochran-Smith & K.M. Zeichner (Eds.), *Studying teacher education: The report of the AERA panel on research and teacher education* (pp. 309–424). Mahwah, NJ: Erlbaum.

Cole, M. (1996). *Cultural psychology: A once and future discipline.* Cambridge, MA: Harvard University Press.

Cruickshank, D.R. (1970) *Blueprints for teacher education: A review of phase II proposals for the USOE comprehensive elementary teacher education program.* Washington, DC: U.S. Department of Health, Education, and Welfare. (ERIC Document Reproduction Service No. ED045581)

Darling-Hammond, L. (1999). Educating teachers: The academy's greatest failure or its most important future? *Academe, 85*(1), 26–33.

DeFord, D.E. (1979). *The DeFord Theoretical Orientation to Reading Profile* (TORP; Rep. No. CS 207 936). Bloomington: Indiana University.

Denzin, N.K., & Lincoln, Y.S. (Eds.). (1994). *Handbook of qualitative research.* Thousand Oaks, CA: Sage.

Dowhower, S. (1990). Students' perceptions of early field experiences in reading. *Yearbook of the American Reading Forum, 10*, 163–179.

Draper, M.C., Barksdale-Ladd, M.A., & Radencich, M.C. (2000). Reading and writing habits of preservice teachers. *Reading Horizons, 40*(3), 185–203.

Dressman, M. (2007). Theoretically framed: Argument and desire in the production of general knowledge about literacy. *Reading Research Quarterly, 42*(3), 332–363.

Duffy, G.G. (1981). Teacher effectiveness research: Implications for the reading profession. In M. Kamil (Ed.), *Directions in reading: Research and instruction.* (30th yearbook of the National Reading Conference, pp. 113–136). Washington, DC: National Reading Conference.

Dynak, J., & Smith, M.J. (1994). Summarization: Preservice teachers' abilities and instructional views. In C.J. Kinzer and D.J. Leu (Eds.), *Multidimensional aspects of literacy research, theory, and practice.* 43rd yearbook of National Reading Conference Yearbook (387–393). Chicago: National Reading Conference.

Eisenhart, M., & Towne, L. (2003). Contestation and change in national policy on "scientifically based" education research. *Educational Researcher, 32*(7), 31–38.

Ellsworth, E. (1989). Why doesn't this feel empowering? Working through the repressive myths of critical pedagogy. *Harvard Educational Review, 59*(3), 297–324.

Engeström, Y. (1999). Activity theory and individual and social transformation. In Y. Engeström, R. Miettinen, & R.-L. Punamäki (Eds.), *Perspectives on activity theory* (pp. 19–38). New York: Cambridge University Press.

Fazio, M. (2000). Constructive comprehension and metacognitive strategy instruction in a field-based teacher education program. *Yearbook of the College Reading Association, 22*, 177–190.

Fazio, M. (2003). Constructive comprehension and metacognitive strategy reading instruction in a field-based teacher education program: Effecting change in preservice and inservice teachers—participant one. *Yearbook of the College Reading Association, 25*, 23–45.

Fecho, B., Commeyras, M., Bauer, E.B., & Font, G. (2000). In rehearsal: Complicating authority in undergraduate critical-inquiry classrooms. *Journal of Literacy Research, 32*(4), 471–504.

Feiman-Nemser, S. (1990). Teacher preparation: Structural and conceptual alternatives. In W.R. Houston, M. Huberman, & J. Sikula (Eds.), *Handbook of research on teacher education* (pp. 212–233). New York: Macmillan.

Fenstermacher, G.D. (1994). The knower and the known: The nature of knowledge in research on teaching. *Review of Research in Education, 20*, 3–56.

Floden, R.E. (1997). Reforms that call for more than you understand. In N.C. Burbules & D.T. Hansen (Eds.), *Teaching and its predicaments* (pp. 11–28). Boulder, CO: Westview.

Floden, R., & Meniketti, M. (2005). Research on the effects of coursework in the arts and sciences and in the foundations of education. In M. Cochran-Smith & K.M. Zeichner (Eds.), *Studying teacher education: The report of the AERA panel on research and teacher education* (pp. 261–308). Mahwah, NJ: Erlbaum.

Foegen, A., Espin, C.A., Allinder, R.M., & Markell, M.A. (2001). Translating research into practice: Preservice teachers' beliefs about curriculum-based measurement. *Journal of Special Education, 34*(4), 226–236.

Foote, M.M., & Linder, P.E. (2000). What they know and believe about family literacy: Preservice and mentor teachers respond and reflect. *Yearbook of the College Reading Association, 22,* 159–176.

Fox, D.L. (1994). What is literature? Two preservice teachers' conceptions of literature and of the teaching of literature. *National Reading Conference Yearbook, 43,* 394–406.

Fuchs, D., Mathes, P., & Fuchs, L.S. (1994). *Handbook on Peabody Classwide Peer Tutoring.* Nashville: Peabody/Vanderbilt University.

Gardner, W. (1989). Preface. In M.C. Reynolds (Ed.), *Knowledge base for the beginning teacher* (pp. ix–xii). New York: Pergamon.

Goodlad, J.I. (1990). *Teachers for our nation's schools.* San Francisco: Jossey-Bass.

Goodman, K. (1967). Reading: A psycholinguistic guessing game. *Journal of the Reading Specialist, 6,* 126–135.

Grant, C., & Secada, W. (1990). Preparing teachers for diversity. In W.R. Houston, M. Haberman, & J. Sikula (Eds.), *Handbook of research on teacher education* (pp. 403–422). New York: Macmillan.

Grisham, D.L. (2000). Connecting theoretical conceptions of reading to practice: A longitudinal study of elementary school teachers. *Reading Psychology, 21*(2), 145–170.

Grossman, P.L. (1992) Why models matter: An alternate view on professional growth in teaching. *Review of Educational Research, 62*(2), 171–179.

Guba, E., & Lincoln, Y.S. (1994). Competing paradigms in qualitative research. In N.K. Denzin & Y.S. Lincoln (Eds.), *Handbook of qualitative research* (pp. 105–118). Thousand Oaks, CA: Sage.

Harlin, R.P., & Lipa, S.E. (1995). How teachers' literacy coursework and experiences affect their perceptions and utilization of portfolio documents. *Reading Research and Instruction, 35*(1), 1–18.

Hatch, J.A., & Wisniewski, R. (Eds.). (1995). *Life history and narrative.* London: Falmer Press.

Hinchman, K.A., & Lalik, R. (2000). Power-knowledge formations in literacy teacher education: Exploring the perspectives of two teacher educators. Journal of *Educational Research, 93*(3), 182–191.

Hoffman, J.V. (1986). Process-product research on effective teaching: A primer for a paradigm. In J.V. Hoffman (Ed.), *Effective teaching of reading: Research and practice* (pp. 39–52). Newark, DE: International Reading Association.

Hoffman, J.V, & Pearson, P.D. (2000). Reading teacher education in the next millennium: What your grandmother's teacher didn't know that your granddaughter's teacher should. *Reading Research Quarterly, 35*(1), 28–44.

Hoffman, J.V., Roller, C., Maloch, B., Sailors, M., Duffy, G., & Beretvas, S.N. (2005). Teachers' preparation to teach reading and their experiences and practices in the first three years of teaching. *The Elementary School Journal, 105*(3), 267–287.

Howe, K., & Eisenhart, M. (1990). Standards in qualitative (and quantitative) research: A prolegomenon. *Educational Researcher, 19*(4), 2–9.

Hughes, J.E., Packard, B.W.-L., & Pearson, P.D. (2000). Preservice teachers' perceptions of using hypermedia and video to examine the nature of literacy instruction. *Journal of Literacy Research, 32*(4), 599–629.

Johnston, S. (1996). What can we learn about teaching from our best university teachers? *Teaching in Higher Education, 1*(2), 213–225.

Kagan, D.M. (1992). Professional growth among preservice teachers and beginning teachers. *Review of Educational Research, 62*(2), 129–169.

Kane, R., Sandretto, S., & Heath, C. (2002). Telling half the story: A critical review of research on the teaching beliefs and practices of university academics. *Review of Educational Research, 72*(2), 177–228.

Kaplan, A. (1964). *The conduct of inquiry: Methodology for behavioral science.* San Francisco: Chandler Publishing Company.

Kaste, J.A. (2001). Examining two preservice teachers' practices for promoting culturally responsive literacy in the middle grades. *National Reading Conference Yearbook, 50,* 311–322.

Kasten, C.K., & Padak, N.D. (1997). Nurturing preservice teachers' reflection on literacy. *National Reading Conference Yearbook, 46,* 335–346.

Keehn, S., Martinez, M., Harmon, J., Hedrick, W., Steinmetz, L., & Perez, B. (2003). Teacher preparation in reading: A case study of change in one university-based undergraduate program. *National Reading Conference Yearbook, 52,* 230–244.

Kidd, J.K., Sanchez, S.Y., & Thorp, E.K. (2000). Integrating language and literacy through projects: An applied internship experience. *Yearbook of the College Reading Association, 22,* 206–225.

Kidd, J.K., Sanchez, S.Y., & Thorp, E.K. (2002). A focus on family stories: Enhancing pre-service teachers' cultural awareness. *National Reading Conference Yearbook, 51,* 242–252.

Klesius, J.P., Searls, E.F., & Zielonka, P. (1990). A comparison of two methods of direct instruction of preservice teachers. *Journal of Teacher Education, 41*(4), 34–44.

Konopak, B.C., Readence, J.E., & Wilson, E.K. (1994). Preservice and inservice secondary teachers' orientations toward content area reading. *Journal of Educational Research, 87*(4), 220–227.

Korthagen, F.A.J., & Wubbels, T. (1995). Characteristics of reflective practitioners: Towards an operationalization of the concept of reflection. *Teachers and Teaching: Theory and Practice, 1*(1), 51–72.

Lalik, R.V., & Niles, J.A. (1990). Collaborative planning by two groups of student teachers. *The Elementary School Journal, 90*(3), 319–336.

Lanier, J. (1982). Teacher education: Needed research and practice for the preparation of teacher professionals. In D. Corrigan, D.J. Palmer, & P.A. Alexander (Ed.), *The future of teacher education: Needed research and practice* (pp. 13–36). College Station: College of Education, Texas A&M University.

L'Allier, S. (2005). Using the reflections of preservice teachers to help teacher educators improve their own practice. In P.E. Linder, M.B. Sampson, J.R. Dugan, & B. Brancato (Eds.), *Building bridges* (27th yearbook of the College Reading Association, pp. 80–93). Commerce: Texas A&M University.

Lazar, A. (2001). Preparing white preservice teachers for urban classrooms: Growth in a Philadelphia-based literacy practicum. *National Reading Conference Yearbook, 50,* 367–381.

Leinhardt, G. (1990). Capturing craft knowledge in teaching. *Educational Researcher, 19*(2), 18–25.

Leland, C.H., Harste, J.C., & Youssef, O. (1997). Teacher education and critical literacy. *National Reading Conference Yearbook, 46,* 385–396.

Levin, B.B. (1995). Using the case method in teacher education: The role of discussion and experience in teachers' thinking about cases. *Teaching and Teacher Education, 11*(1), 63–79.

Linek, W.M., Sampson, M.B., Raine, I.L., Klakamp, K., & Smith, B. (2006). Development of literacy beliefs and practices: Preservice teachers with reading specializations in a field-based program. *Reading Horizons, 46*(3), 183–213.

Lonberger, R.B. (1992). The belief systems and instructional choices of preservice teachers. *Yearbook of the College Reading Association, 14,* 71–78.

Maheady, L., Mallette, B., & Harper, G.F. (1996). The pair tutoring program: An early field-based experience to prepare general educators to work with students with special learning needs. *Teacher Education and Special Education, 19*(4), 277–297.

Mallette, B., Maheady, L., & Harper, G.F. (1999). The effects of reciprocal peer coaching on preservice general educators' instruction of students with special learning needs. *Teacher Education and Special Education, 22*(4), 201–216.

Mallette, M.H., Kile, R.S., Smith, M.M., McKinney, M., & Readence, J.E. (2000). Constructing meaning about literacy difficulties: Preservice teachers beginning to think about pedagogy. *Teaching and Teacher Education, 16*(5–6), 593–612.

Maloch, B., Flint, A.S., Eldridge, D., Harmon, J., Loven, R., Fine, J., et al. (2003). Understandings, beliefs, and reported decision making of first-year teachers from different reading teacher preparation programs. *The Elementary School Journal, 103*(5), 431–457.

Many, J.E., Howard, F.M., & Hoge, P. (1998). Personal literacy and literature-based instruction: Exploring preservice teachers' views of themselves as readers. *National Reading Conference Yearbook, 47,* 496–507.

Massey, D.D. (1990). Preservice teachers as tutors: Influences of tutoring on whole-class literacy instruction. *National Reading Conference Yearbook, 52,* 259–271.

Massey, D.D. (2006). "You teach for me; I've had it!" A first-year teacher's cry for help. *Action in Teacher Education, 28*(3), 73–85.

Matanzo, J.B., & Harris, D.L. (1999). Encouraging metacognitive awareness in preservice literacy courses. *Yearbook of the College Reading Association, 21,* 201–225.

Mather, N., Bos, C., & Babur, N. (2001). Perceptions and knowledge of preservice and inservice teachers about early literacy instruction. *Journal of Learning Disabilities, 34*(5), 472–482.

McMahon, S.I. (1997). Using documented written and oral dialogue to understand and challenge preservice teachers' reflections. *Teaching and Teacher Education, 13*(2), 199–213.

Miles, M.B., & Huberman, A.M. (1984). *Qualitative data analysis: A sourcebook of new methods.* Newbury Park, CA: Sage.

Moller, K.J., & Hug, B. (2006). Connections across literacy and science instruction in early childhood education: Interweaving disciplines in preservice teacher. In J.V. Hoffman, D.L. Schallert, C.M. Fairbanks, J. Worthy, & B. Maloch (Eds.), *55th yearbook of the National Reading Conference* (pp. 195–211). Oak Creek, WI: National Reading Conference.

Mora, J.K., & Grisham, D.L. (2001). !What deliches tortillas!: Preparing teachers for literacy instruction in linguistically diverse classrooms. *Teacher Education Quarterly, 28*(4), 51–70.

Morgan, D.N., Timmons, B., & Shaheen, M. (2006). Tutoring: A personal and professional space for preservice teachers to learn about literacy instruction. In J.V. Hoffman, D.L. Schallert, C.M. Fairbanks, J. Worthy, & B. Maloch (Eds.), *55th yearbook of the National Reading Conference* (pp. 212–223). Oak Creek, WI: National Reading Conference.

Morgan, R.L., Gustafson, K.J., Hudson, P.J., & Salzberg, C.L. (1992). Peer coaching in a preservice special education program. *Teacher Education and Special Education, 15*(4), 249–258.

Mottley, R., & Telfer, R. (1997). Storytelling to promote emergent literacy: Prospective teachers' storytelling experiences and expectations. *Yearbook of the American Reading Forum, 17,* 127–149.

Murray, F.B. (Ed.). (1996). *The teacher educator's handbook: Building a knowledge base for the preparation of teachers.* Washington, DC: American Association of Colleges for Teacher Education.

National Institute of Child Health and Human Development. (2000). Report of the National Reading Panel. *Teaching children to read: An evidence-based assessment of the scientific research literature on reading and its implications for reading instruction* (NIH Publication No. 00-4769). Washington, DC: U.S. Government Printing Office.

Niersheimer, S.L., Hopkins, C.J., Dillon, D.R., & Schmitt, M.C. (2000). Preservice teachers' shifting beliefs about struggling literacy learners. *Reading Research and Instruction, 40*(1), 1–16.

Nieto, S. (1999). *The light in their eyes: Creating multicultural learning communities.* New York: Teachers College Press.

Nourie, B.L., & Lenski, S.D. (1998). The (in)effectiveness of content area literacy instruction for secondary preservice teachers. *Clearing House, 71*(6), 372–374.

O'Brien, D.G., & Stewart, R.A. (1990). Preservice teachers' perspectives on why every teacher is not a teacher of reading: A qualitative analysis. *Journal of Reading Behavior, 22*(2), 101–129.

Ormrod, J.E., & Cole, D.B. (1996). Teaching content knowledge and pedagogical content knowledge: A model from geographic education. *Journal of Teacher Education, 47*(1), 37–42.

O'Sullivan, S., & Jiang, Y.H. (2002). Determining the efficacy of the California Reading Instruction Competence Assessment (RICA). *Teacher Education Quarterly, 29*(3), 61–72.

Pajares, M.F. (1992). Teachers' beliefs and educational research: Cleaning up a messy construct. *Review of Educational Research, 62*(3), 307–332.

Pang, E., & Kamil, M.L. (2006). Blending experimental and descriptive research: The case of educating reading teachers. In R. Subotnik & H. Walberg (Eds.), *Scientific basis of educational productivity* (pp. 45–84). Greenwich, CT: Information Age Publishing.

Pearson, P.D. (2001). Learning to teach reading: The status of the knowledge base. In C.M. Roller (Ed.), *Learning to teach reading: Setting the research agenda* (pp. 4–19). Newark, DE: International Reading Association.

Pearson, P.D., & Gallagher, M. (1983). The instruction of reading comprehension. *Contemporary Educational Psychology, 8*(3), 317–344.

Piaget, J. (1932). *The moral judgment of the child.* New York: Free Press.

Polkinghorne, D.E. (1995). Narrative configuration in qualitative analysis. In J.A. Hatch & R. Wisniewski (Eds.), *Life history and narrative* (pp. 5–23). London: Falmer.

Raine, I.L., Levingston, C., Linek, W.M., Sampson, M.B., & Linder, P.E. (2003). A view of the literacy beliefs and growth processes of undergraduate preservice teachers with a concentration in reading: Interns, paraprofessionals, and interns serving as teachers of record. *Yearbook of the College Reading Association, 25*, 224–238.

Risko, V.J. (1992). Developing problem solving environments to prepare teachers for instruction of diverse learners. *Yearbook of the American Reading Forum, 12*, 1–13.

Risko, V.J., Peter, J.A., & McAllister, D. (1996). Conceptual changes: Preservice teachers' pathways to providing literacy instruction. *Yearbook of the College Reading Association, 18*, 104–119.

Risko, V.J., Roskos, K., & Vukelich, C. (1999). Making connections: Preservice teachers' reflection processes and strategies. *National Reading Conference Yearbook, 48*, 412–422.

Risko, V.J., Roskos, K., & Vukelich, C. (2002). Prospective teachers' reflection: Strategies, qualities, and perceptions in learning to teach reading. *Reading Research and Instruction, 41*(2), 149–176.

Roberts, S.K., & Hsu, Y.-S. (2000). The tools of teacher education: Preservice teachers' use of technology to create instructional materials. *Journal of Technology and Teacher Education, 8*(2), 133–152.

Rokeach, M. (1972). *Beliefs, attitudes, and values: A theory of organization and change.* San Francisco: Jossey-Bass.

Rosenblatt, L.M. (1978). *The reader, the text, the poem: The transactional theory of the literary work.* Carbondale: Southern Illinois University Press.

Rosenshine, B. (1979). Content, time, and direct instruction. In P.L. Peterson & H.J. Walberg (Eds.), *Research on teaching: Concepts, findings, and implications* (pp. 38–71). Berkeley, CA: McCutchan.

Roskos, K., Vukelich, C., & Risko, V.J. (2001). Reflection and learning to teach reading: A critical review of literacy and general teacher education studies. *Journal of Literacy Research, 33*(4), 595–635.

Roskos, K., & Walker, B. (1993). Preservice teachers' epistemology in the teaching of problem readers. *National Reading Conference Yearbook, 42*, 325–334.

Roskos, K., & Walker, B. (1994). An analysis of preservice teachers' pedagogical concepts in the teaching of problem readers. *National Reading Conference Yearbook, 43*, 418–428.

Rumelhart, D.E. (1985). Toward an interactive model of reading. In H. Singer & R.B. Ruddell (Eds.), *Theoretical models and processes of reading* (3rd ed., pp. 722–750). Newark, DE: International Reading Association.

Ryan, K. (Ed.). (1975). *Teacher education, 74th Yearbook of the National Society for the Study of Education.* Chicago: University of Chicago Press.

Sadoski, M., Norton, D.E., Rodriguez, M., Nichols, W.D., & Gerla, J.P. (1998). Preservice and inservice reading teachers' knowledge of literary concepts and literary analysis. *Reading Psychology, 19*(3), 267–286.

Sailors, M., Keehn, S., Martinez, M., & Harmon, J. (2005). Early field experiences offered to and valued by preservice teachers at sites of excellence in reading teacher education programs. *Teacher Education and Practice, 18*(4), 458–470.

Samuelowicz, K., & Bain, J.D. (2001). Revisiting academics' beliefs about teaching and learning. *Higher Education, 41*(3), 299–325.

Schön, D.A. (1987). *Educating the reflective practitioner: Toward a new design for teaching and learning in the professions.* San Francisco: Jossey-Bass.

Schön, D.A. (1991). *The reflective practitioner: How professionals think in action.* New York: Basic Books.

Scribner, S., & Cole, M. (1981). *The psychology of literacy.* Cambridge, MA: Harvard University Press.

Shefelbine, J., & Shiel, G. (1990). Preservice teachers' schemata for a diagnostic framework in reading. *Reading Research and Instruction, 30*(1), 30–43.

Shulman, L. (1986). Those who understand: Knowledge growth in teaching. *Educational Researcher, 15*(2), 4–14.

Siegel, M., & Fernandez, S.L. (2000). Critical approaches. In M.L. Kamil, P.B. Mosenthal, P.D. Pearson, & R. Barr (Eds.), *Handbook of reading research* (Vol. 3, pp. 141–151). Mahwah, NJ: Erlbaum.

Sleeter, C. (2001). Epistemological diversity in research on preservice teacher preparation for historically underserved children. In W. Secada (Ed.), *Review of research in education* (Vol. 25, pp. 209–250). Washington, DC: American Educational Research Association.

Stallings, J., & Kaskowitz, D. (1974). *Follow-through classroom observation evaluation 1972–1973. Project URU-7370.* Stanford, CA: Stanford Research Institute.

Stevens, L.P. (2002). Making the road by walking: The transition from content area literacy to adolescent literacy. *Reading Research and Instruction, 41*(3), 267–278.

Sturtevant, E.G., & Spor, M.W. (1990). Student teacher use of content reading strategies. *Yearbook of the College Reading Association, 12*, 25–30.

Theurer, J.L. (2002). The power of retrospective miscue analysis: One preservice teacher's journey as she reconsiders the reading process. *Reading Matrix: An International Online Journal, 2*(1).

Traynelis-Yurek, E., & Strong, M.W. (2000). Preservice teachers' ability to determine miscues and comprehension response errors of elementary students. *Journal of Reading Education, 26*(1), 15–22.

Truscott, D.M., & Walker, B.J. (1998). The influence of portfolio selection on reflective thinking. *Yearbook of the College Reading Association, 20,* 291–303.

Vagle, M.D., Dillon, D.R., Davison-Jenkins, J., LaDuca, B., & Olson, V. (2006). Redesigning literacy preservice education at four institutions: A three-year collaborative project. In J.V. Hoffman, D.L. Schallert, C.M. Fairbanks, J. Worthy, & B. Maloch (Eds.), *55th yearbook of the National Reading Conference* (pp. 324–340). Oak Creek, WI: National Reading Conference.

Vygotsky, L.S. (1978). *Mind in society: The development of higher psychological processes.* (M. Cole, V. John-Steiner, S. Scribner, & E. Souberman, Eds. & Trans.). Cambridge, MA: Harvard University Press.

Waller, W. (1961). *The sociology of teaching.* New York: Russell & Russell.

Wertsch, J.V. (2002). *Voices of collective remembering.* Cambridge, England: Cambridge University Press.

Wham, M.A. (1993). The relationship between undergraduate course work and beliefs about reading instruction. *Journal of Research and Development in Education, 27*(1), 9–17.

Wideen, M., Mayer-Smith, J., & Moon, B. (1998). A critical analysis of the research on learning to teach: Making the case for an ecological perspective on inquiry. *Review of Educational Research, 68*(2), 130–178.

Wilson, S.M., Floden, R.E., & Ferrini-Mundy, J. (2001). *Teacher preparation research: Current knowledge, gaps, and recommendations.* Seattle: Center for the Study of Teaching and Policy, University of Washington.

Windschitl, M. (2002). Framing constructivism in practice as the negotiation of dilemmas: An analysis of the conceptual, pedagogical, cultural, and political challenges facing teachers. *Review of Educational Research, 72,* 131–175.

Wolf, S.A., Ballentine, D., & Hill, L.A. (2000). "Only connect!": Cross-cultural connections in the reading lives of preservice teachers and children. *Journal of Literacy Research, 32*(4), 533–569.

Wolf, S.A., Carey, A.A., & Mieras, E.L. (1996a). The art of literary interpretation: Preservice teachers learning about the arts in language arts. *National Reading Conference Yearbook, 45,* 447–460.

Wolf, S.A., Carey, A.A., & Mieras, E.L. (1996b). "What is this literachurch stuff anyway?": Preservice teachers' growth in understanding children's literary response. *Reading Research Quarterly, 31*(2), 130–157.

Wolf, S.A., Hill, L.A., & Ballentine, D. (1999). Teaching on fissured ground: Preparing preservice teachers for culturally conscious pedagogy. *National Reading Conference Yearbook, 48,* 423–436.

Worthy, J., & Patterson, E. (2001). "I can't wait to see Carlos!": Preservice teachers, situated learning, and personal relationships with students. *Journal of Literacy Research, 33*(2), 303–344.

Xu, S.H. (2000a). Preservice teachers in a literacy methods course consider issues of diversity. *Journal of Literacy Research, 32*(4), 505–531.

Xu, S.H. (2000b). Preservice teachers integrate understandings of diversity into literacy instruction: An adaptation of the ABC's Model. *Journal of Teacher Education, 51*(2), 135–142.

Zulich, J., Bean, T.W., & Herrick, J. (1992). Charting stages of preservice teacher development and reflection in a multicultural community through dialogue journal analysis. *Teaching and Teacher Education, 8*(4), 345–360.

Zumwalt, K. (1982). Research on teaching: Policy implications for teacher education. In A. Leiberman & M. McLaughlin (Eds.), *Policy making an education: 81st yearbook of NSSE* (pp. 215–248). Chicago: University of Chicago Press.

Literacy Teams: Sharing Leadership to Improve Student Learning

Charlene Cobb

As the United States enters year 3 of the No Child Left Behind Act (2002), the U.S. Department of Education clearly states the expectations for schools. They are embodied in the following components: accountability, commitment, sharing, and leadership. The intent is for schools to focus on reading and bring about improved reading performance for all students (National Institute for Literacy, 2002). Discussions on these federal initiatives, whether in faculty meetings or in school hallways, are never dull. Whatever side of the argument you choose, there is no denying that literacy instruction in U.S. schools is changing. Initiatives are not concentrating on what and how teachers are teaching; administrators and teachers are being asked to explain what and how students are learning.

Accountability, through annual testing, drives schools and districts to focus on improving test scores. Districts seek the best programs to teach reading and the most effective professional development providers for their teachers' inservice. Publishers of test preparation materials are geared to provide schools with whatever is needed to improve student scores. This need to look outward for solutions is typical. Someone out there has developed a better program; we just have to find it, so that all of our students make adequate yearly progress. But, rather than looking outside for answers, schools could look within and find that they have many of the solutions already. Schools need to widen their vision beyond accountability and also

take commitment, sharing, and leadership into perspective.

The Role of Principal as Leader

The American Heritage Dictionary (2000) defines a *leader* as "one that leads or guides" and *leadership* as "guidance," "direction," and the "capacity or ability to lead." Traditionally, the principal is the leader of a school. For the better part of the last century, this leadership role largely meant managing the school. Management encompassed a wide range of tasks, including but not limited to developing schedules, maintaining budgets, meeting with parents and other community groups, and evaluating certified and noncertified staff. In a well-managed school, principals worked in their offices and teachers worked in their classrooms. More recently, there has been a call for principals to serve as instructional leaders in their schools, taking time that was previously spent on managerial tasks to become more involved with the instructional program. Ready or not, principals are being asked to take on the role of change agent in their schools.

Any one person who could provide knowledge and guidance in all areas of the curriculum and still have time to manage a building full of teachers and students would have to be Superman or Wonder Woman. And yet the role of principal as instructional leader has become a widely accepted, somewhat understood, and all too often impractical one.

Preparing Reading Professionals (second edition), edited by Rita M. Bean, Natalie Heisey, and Cathy M. Roller. © 2010 by the International Reading Association. Reprinted from Cobb, C. (2005). Literacy teams: Sharing leadership to improve student learning. *The Reading Teacher, 58*(5), 472–474. doi:10.1598/RT.58.5.7.

Changing the Vision of Leadership

Booth and Rowsell (2002) provided three facets for the role of principal as literacy leader. The principal can act as instructional leader and supporter of teachers' needs, but shared leadership is the facet that leads to significant changes in teacher and student performance. Building a system of shared leadership in a school means giving more than lip service to the idea of teachers and administrators sharing responsibilities for student learning. It begins with commitment from every staff member—from the principal to the custodian—that learning is what is valued, and that every effort will be made to keep learning at the center of school activities. Fullan (2002) outlined some characteristics of leaders: They have a moral purpose and work to make a difference with other leaders in a school. They are knowledgeable about the change process and realize that change will create resistance, but they have the tools at hand to help others address concerns and commit to it. They establish and improve relationships with teachers who support change, as well as those teachers who resist it. Leaders recognize that teachers who share information through the social process of engaged discourse achieve personal and professional growth. They provide stability through coherence. Efforts of improvement are targeted, specific, and focused on student learning. With these characteristics in mind, let's envision a shared literacy leadership team.

What Does the Team Look Like?

There is no one model of a literacy leadership team. However, essential members would be the principal, the reading specialist or literacy coach, a primary-level teacher, an intermediate-level teacher, and any resource teachers (bilingual or special education) who work with students across multiple grade levels. The team doesn't require a teacher from each grade level, but it does require an understanding that information must be shared. Each member of the literacy leadership team is responsible for communicating with the other teachers in the building.

A starting point for developing roles and responsibilities is the International Reading Association's *Standards for Reading Professionals* (Professional Standards and Ethics Committee, International Reading Association, 2003). They offer a range of categories, including reading specialists/literacy coaches, classroom teachers, and administrators. For some reading specialists, applying these standards might mean revising their role as the special teacher who takes students down the hall to that of the teacher and learner who works closely with other teachers and students. Principals are vital to the literacy leadership team. They play a critical role in organizing and facilitating shared leadership.

How Does the Team Sound?

The sounds of a literacy leadership team can be heard through the "voice" of a firm definition of literacy instruction and learning, one established through a guaranteed and viable curriculum. This definition puts learning at the front of all conversations. Faculty meetings move from committee reports and discussion of field trips to in-depth discussions of curriculum issues, analysis of data, and goal setting for improvement. There is consistency (not to be confused with conformity) in the language of instruction. The expectation is that all students can and will learn. There is no room for preconceived ideas about learners on the basis of ethnicity, socioeconomic status, or other factors outside of a teacher's control.

The literacy leadership team must be the voice of reason and support and take a positive perspective on change. Difficult issues must be discussed at the table, not in the parking lot. Discussions must not only honor each teacher's level of professional knowledge but also motivate all teachers to study, practice, and refine their craft of teaching literacy.

How Does the Team Act?

The actions of a principal who is literacy leader will always speak louder than words. School walkthroughs (Ginsberg & Murphy, 2002) are a good example of that. The purpose of these unscheduled visits to classrooms is not to evaluate teacher performance but to observe student learning. A walkthrough is a short visit, usually no more than five minutes, and a principal might simply observe levels of student engagement or listen in as students hold a small-group discussion. Because the focus is always on student learning, not teacher performance, walk-throughs can establish a sense of shared responsibility for student learning between administrators and teachers. Feedback is an essential component of walk-throughs and can be in the form of a quick e-mail, or a sticky note left in the teacher's mailbox. Feedback should be specific and constructive, such as "Thanks for letting me see your student discussions in action. They are great thinkers!" or "You have an interesting way of posing questions to students. Would you consider sharing this at our next staff meeting?" Walk-throughs require that principals create risk-free environments where teachers are not afraid to be seen doing a lesson that isn't picture perfect.

Reading specialists can serve as leaders by planning and teaching cooperatively. They can also "substitute" in teachers' classrooms, enabling those teachers to leave and observe other teachers. In addition, reading specialists and other literacy leadership team members might form study groups (Lambert, 2002) around a specific topic or text. Literacy leadership team members can help locate professional reading materials to support the study group as well as facilitate discussions or train others as facilitators. Study groups can meet before school, during lunch, or after school. Meetings can even be held electronically in a chat room on a website.

Schools that develop a framework for shared literacy leadership become collegial communities of instructional practice where learning is the shared responsibility of all members. These are schools where teaching and learning are engaging, motivating, and invigorating. They are the schools that every teacher and student deserves.

References

The American Heritage Dictionary (4th ed.). (2000). Boston: Houghton Mifflin.

Booth, D., & Rowsell, J. (2002). *The literacy principal: Leading, supporting and assessing reading and writing initiatives*. Markham, ON: Pembroke.

Fullan, M. (2002). The change leader. *Educational Leadership*, 59(8), 16–20.

Ginsberg, M.B., & Murphy, D. (2002). How walkthroughs open doors. *Educational Leadership*, 59(8), 34–36.

Lambert, L. (2002). A framework for shared leadership. *Educational Leadership*, 59(8), 37–40.

National Institute for Literacy. (2002). *The Reading Leadership Academy Guidebook*. Washington, DC: U.S. Department of Education.

No Child Left Behind Act of 2001, Pub. L., No 107-110, 115 Stat. 1425 (2002). Retrieved September 1, 2004, from http://www.ed.gov/policy/elsec/leg/esea02/index.html

Professional Standards and Ethics Committee, International Reading Association. (2003). *Standards for reading professionals—Revised 2003*. Newark, DE: International Reading Association. Retrieved September 1, 2004, from http://www.reading.org/advocacy/standards/standards03_revised

Middle and High School Literacy Coaches: A National Survey

Katrin L. Blamey, Carla Kay Meyer, and Sharon Walpole

This study examines the actual and potential roles of secondary literacy coaches outlined in the *Standards for Middle and High School Literacy Coaches* (International Reading Association, 2006). Because the standards themselves are new, we wondered if acting secondary coaches in the United States met the qualifications and participated in the activities described in the standards. In addition, we wanted to know what secondary literacy coaches identified as their own professional learning needs within the context of the standards. Beyond the standards, we wondered what personal qualities these coaches considered essential and how secondary coaches could be supported through professional development.

Standards for Middle and High School Literacy Coaches

In an unprecedented partnership, the International Reading Association (IRA), the National Council of Teachers of English, the National Council of Teachers of Mathematics, the National Science Teachers Association, and the National Council for the Social Studies created standards for middle and high school literacy coaches. The standards require secondary literacy coaches to assume the following roles: (a) collaborators, (b) job-embedded coaches, (c) evaluators of literacy needs, and (d) instructional strategists in English language arts, mathematics, science, and social studies (IRA, 2006).

The standards categorize the first three roles—collaborators, coaches, and evaluators—as leadership roles within the middle or high school setting. As a collaborator, a literacy coach must work effectively with a school's literacy team while establishing productive relationships with the school's staff. The coaching role involves mentoring teachers on an individual, team, or building level, providing professional development to improve literacy strategies being implemented. Moreover, an effective coach observes and provides nonevaluative feedback of teachers' implementation of reading and writing strategies. Finally, as an effective evaluator of literacy needs, a coach must assist schools in the selection, use, and interpretation of assessments to make informed decisions about the literacy needs of students.

The standards that align with leadership skills address more generic standards that apply to literacy coaching as a whole; the content area standards address the unique challenge that middle and high school coaches face. Secondary coaches must understand how and why content area learning in English, mathematics, science, and social studies interacts with literacy strategies (IRA, 2006). According to the standards (IRA, 2006), secondary coaches need a breadth of content knowledge that enables them to provide appropriate support to content teachers and to improve academic literacy in each core subject area.

Preparing Reading Professionals (second edition), edited by Rita M. Bean, Natalie Heisey, and Cathy M. Roller. © 2010 by the International Reading Association. Reprinted from Blamey, K.L., Meyer, C.K., & Walpole, S. (2008). Middle and high school literacy coaches: A national survey. *Journal of Adolescent & Adult Literacy, 52*(4), 310–323. doi:10.1598/JAAL.52.4.4

Research on Literacy Coaching

Research on literacy coaching at the elementary level indicates that effective coaches fulfill multiple roles (Shanklin, 2006; Toll, 2005; Walpole & McKenna, 2004). As professional developers, coaches provide training one-on-one or to groups of teachers on a variety of topics including assessment, curriculum, literacy strategies, and research-based practices (Toll, 2005; Walpole & McKenna, 2004). Informing their professional development, coaches serve as assessors, making careful choices about appropriate assessments, helping administer assessments, and using the data to inform classroom practice (Walpole & McKenna, 2004). To encourage application of ideas from professional development, coaches function as observers and modelers. Coaches observe teachers using literacy strategies and offer informative, confidential feedback to facilitate teachers' reflective practice and improvement (Toll, 2005; Walpole & McKenna, 2004). As modelers, coaches model literacy strategies and research-based practices in the classroom as the teacher observes (Walpole & McKenna, 2004).

Effective literacy coaches may also go beyond the role of on-site professional developers. As planners, coaches work with teachers to develop comprehensive lesson plans and ways to differentiate instruction to meet the specific needs of individual students (Walpole & McKenna, 2007). Planning also may involve working closely with principals to consider the specific literacy needs of their schools (Shanklin, 2006; Taylor, Moxley, Chanter, & Boulware, 2007). Part of school-level planning requires coaches to be curriculum experts, initially helping to choose appropriate resources for a school and then knowing how to use them effectively (Walpole & McKenna, 2004). Additionally, coaches may also manage shared resources, including book rooms and professional libraries (Walpole & McKenna, 2004).

While fulfilling each of these roles, successful coaches also forge collaborative, trusting relationships with key stakeholders such as teachers, principals, and superintendents (Toll, 2006). When working with teachers, successful coaches know how to maneuver between colleague and expert, walking a delicate line between the two. Coaches are often asked to serve as a liaison between district and state-level administration, communicating policy, data, and implementation progress clearly (Sturtevant, 2003; Toll, 2006). Therefore, coaches must draw from an arsenal of personal attributes, including good communication skills, a sense of humor, and trustworthiness.

Although certain roles of coaching at the elementary and secondary levels overlap, others do not. Several researchers have argued that coaching in the secondary setting is completely different than coaching in the elementary setting (Riddle-Buly, Coskie, Robinson, & Egawa, 2006; Snow, Ippolito, & Schwartz, 2006). For example, coaches at the secondary level often struggle to justify their existence to secondary teachers who may or may not believe that reading and writing can build knowledge in their content area (Schen, Rao, & Dobles, 2005). Furthermore, secondary coaches must have a thorough understanding of adolescents and secondary school culture (Sturtevant, 2003). In addition, while elementary coaches help teachers begin initial reading instruction, secondary coaches have the unique responsibility of helping teachers instruct students who may be far behind where they should be in reading development (Riddle-Buly et al., 2006).

Unfortunately, research on literacy coaching at the secondary level is extremely limited. More research is needed on the actual roles and duties of secondary literacy coaches to assess the extent to which coaches at the secondary setting are fulfilling the roles described for them in the standards, evaluate the impact of literacy coaches on teacher and student performance, inform the work of professional developers who prepare coaches, and advise principals who work closely with coaches. A first step in research on coaching effectiveness is to document what literacy coaches do at the secondary level. To our knowledge, only one other survey has addressed the gap in the current research literature available on the roles literacy coaches fulfill in secondary settings (Roller, 2006). However, this study was not focused exclusively on secondary coaches; only 24% of participants worked at the secondary level compared with 76% at the elementary level. Therefore, it was our aim in this study to describe the actual roles performed by middle and secondary literacy coaches exclusively to assess the appropriateness of the standards and to contribute to the knowledge base surrounding secondary literacy coaching.

The Current Study

Given the complexity of the standards for secondary coaches, we wondered whether current coaches are prepared to fulfill activities as collaborators, coaches, and evaluators that the standards outline. Moreover, with the emphasis the standards place on secondary coaches as "skillful instructional strategists" (IRA, 2006, p. 5) in the areas of English language arts, mathematics, science, *and* social studies, we wondered whether coaches currently working in the field felt qualified to coach teachers of multiple content areas. Therefore, we sought a sample of current coaches in the United States and explored their educational background, their teaching experience, their specific coaching preparation, and their roles and responsibilities, using language taken specifically from the standards. In addition, we asked the coaches to share insights about their own professional development needs and to provide advice for those considering a career in middle and high school coaching.

Method

The study employed a web-based national survey of practicing middle school and high school coaches to collect information about their qualifications and roles. Survey items were tested in a small pilot study in the fall of 2006 and then collected in a three-week period in January of 2007.

Researchers

It is important to say a few words about who we are as researchers, as our frame of reference shapes how we conducted this research. The first author is an early childhood literacy coach. The second author spent several years as a secondary literacy coach in an urban setting. The third author was also a coach and now serves as a researcher designing and providing professional development for literacy coaches working in elementary school reform initiatives. Collectively, our experiences as literacy coaches and working with literacy coaches have placed us in a position to consider the multifaceted roles of the secondary literacy coaches who are the subjects of this research.

Sample

Using a data retrieval firm, we located potential participants currently working in middle and high schools in the United States. Given that the role of literacy coach is relatively new, we had to consider different descriptors that might be used by coaches. We purchased a potential sample ($n = 8,561$) of individuals who listed their jobs as literacy coordinator, literacy/reading coach, reading specialist, or reading teacher. Potential participants were forwarded an e-mail that included a letter describing the project and a link to an online survey. Participant rights were protected in that no survey responses could be linked to any personal contact information.

Given the exploratory nature of this study and the difficulty we had in identifying a sample of individuals who classify themselves as middle or high school coach, no rewards were offered for participation; we assumed that our sample, identified only through an online service, would include many individuals who were not actually literacy coaches—including those who were athletic coaches.

For this reason, it is more appropriate to gauge response rate based on those who actually opened the survey; they were able to first see its purpose and then decide whether they had received the e-mail in error. Of the 443 potential participants who viewed the online survey, 147 (33%) coaches completed the survey. Given that the nature of the survey was anonymous, demographic data on participants in our study, other than the educational background questions asked in the survey itself, is unavailable.

Survey Design

The 25-item online survey comprised forced-choice and open-ended questions (see Figure 1). In all cases, the forced-choice items were derived directly from the language of the standards (IRA, 2006). Respondents were asked to indicate which responsibilities among multiple choices outlined by the standards (IRA, 2006) they had participated in as a coach in the most recent academic year. For example, one forced-choice question asked participants: "In which activities have you participated to prepare for your role as a literacy/reading coach? (Check all that apply.)" Several choices were given from which participants could choose multiple

---

Figure 1
Online Survey

Educational background
1. Check all that apply:
    ❏ I have a bachelor's degree in something other than education.
    ❏ I have a bachelor's degree in early childhood education.
    ❏ I have a bachelor's degree in elementary education.
    ❏ I have a bachelor's degree in math education.
    ❏ I have a bachelor's degree in science education.
    ❏ I have a bachelor's degree in social studies education.
    ❏ I have a bachelor's degree in English/language arts education.
    ❏ I have a bachelor's degree in special education.
    ❏ I have a bachelor's degree in music, art, or physical education.
    ❏ I have a teaching certificate for the state in which I teach.
    ❏ I have a master's degree with an emphasis in literacy.
    ❏ I have a master's degree with an emphasis in something other than literacy.
    ❏ I have a reading specialist certificate.
    ❏ I have a master's degree in education emphasizing something other than literacy.
    ❏ I have a PhD or EdD.

Teaching Experience
2. For how many years have you been a coach?
3. Do you coach full-time (e.g., it is your only job) or part-time (e.g., you also teach students every day)?
4. How many years of classroom teaching experience do you have?
5. If you are a reading specialist, how many years have you worked as a reading specialist (e.g., teaching struggling readers daily)?
6. How many years of teaching experience do you have at the middle or high school levels as a classroom teacher?
7. If you have middle or high school classroom experience, which content areas have you taught? (Check all that apply.)
    ❏ English/language arts
    ❏ Foreign language
    ❏ Math
    ❏ Science
    ❏ Social studies
    ❏ Other, please specify

(continued)

Figure 1 (Continued)
Online Survey

8. In which building level(s) do you serve as a literacy/reading coach?
   ❑ Middle school
   ❑ High school
   ❑ Both
9. How has your role been defined by your district?
10. How has your role been defined by your principal(s)?
11. What do you consider your primary role or responsibility?
12. Approximately how many teachers do you work with each school year?

Coaching Preparation

13. In which activities have you participated to prepare for your role as a literacy/reading coach? (Check all that apply.)
   ❑ Graduate-level course(s)
   ❑ National conferences
   ❑ State-level professional development
   ❑ District-level professional development
   ❑ Professional reading
   ❑ Study groups
   ❑ Work with literacy coach mentor
   ❑ Other, please specify
   ❑ None of the above
14. Out of the above activities, which 3 activities do you feel have helped you develop the most as a literacy/reading coach?
15. What advice would you give future designers of professional development for literacy/reading coaches?

Roles and Responsibilities

16. As a **collaborator**, check all the activities that you have participated in during the most recent school year.
   ❑ Assisted the principal in developing a literacy team.
   ❑ Collaborated to conduct an initial schoolwide literacy assessment.
   ❑ Facilitated small- and large-group discussions with teachers about students' skills.
   ❑ Communicated the findings of the initial schoolwide literacy assessment to staff and other stake holders.
   ❑ Developed and implemented a literacy improvement plan.
   ❑ Helped align curriculum to state and district requirements.
   ❑ Conducted ongoing evaluations of literacy improvement action plan (or school improvement plan).
   ❑ Managed time and/or resources in support of literacy instruction.
   ❑ Showcased effective strategies employed by content area teachers.
   ❑ Listened and responded to the needs of students.
   ❑ Listened and responded to the needs of staff.
   ❑ Listened and responded to the needs of parents.
   ❑ Understood and respected issues of confidentiality.
   ❑ Responded promptly to requests for assistance from teachers.
   ❑ Facilitated discussions on issues in adolescent literacy.
   ❑ Demonstrated positive expectations for students' learning.
   ❑ Applied concepts of adult learning and motivation to the design of professional development.
   ❑ Encouraged the reading specialist to serve as resource for the content area teachers.
   ❑ Kept administrators informed and involved in literacy efforts.

(continued)

Figure 1 (Continued)
Online Survey

- ❑ Remained current with professional literature on the latest research.
- ❑ Examined best practices.
- ❑ Examined curriculum materials.
- ❑ Met regularly (at least once a month) with other coaches in the school or district.
- ❑ Attended professional seminars, conventions, and other training in order to receive instruction on research-based literacy strategies.
- ❑ Attended professional seminars, conventions, and other training in order to receive instruction on how to work effectively with adult learners.

17. Out of the above activities, rank the top 3 activities with which you believe you need the most support in terms of your future professional learning.

18. As a **coach**, check all the activities you have participated in during the most recent school year.
- ❑ Worked with teachers individually, providing support on a full range of reading, writing, and communication strategies.
- ❑ Worked with teachers in collaborative teams, providing support on a full range of reading, writing, and communication strategies.
- ❑ Worked with teachers in departments, providing support on a full range of reading, writing, and communication strategies.
- ❑ Assisted teachers in the analysis and selection of content area texts and instructional materials that meet the diverse needs of students.
- ❑ Assisted teachers in developing instruction designed to improve students' abilities to read and understand content area text and spur students' interest in more complex text.
- ❑ Provided content area teachers with professional development related to metacognitive reading strategies.
- ❑ Facilitated professional development related to instructional strategies for literacy that content area teachers could adopt and adapt for their classrooms.
- ❑ Explored with content area teachers cross-cultural communication patterns in speaking and writing and their relationship with literacy skills in English.
- ❑ Developed a repertoire of reading strategies to share with and model for content area teachers.
- ❑ Helped determine which reading strategies are best to use with the content being taught.
- ❑ Assisted teachers with improving writing instruction, student writing, and appropriateness of writing instruction and assignments.
- ❑ Facilitated professional development related to strategies to help students analyze and evaluate Internet sources.
- ❑ Linked teachers to current evidence-based research to help make research more tangible and applicable.
- ❑ Observed and provided feedback to teachers on instruction-related literacy development and content area knowledge.
- ❑ Ensured teacher observations are nonthreatening (used as a tool to spark discussion).
- ❑ Regularly conducted observations of content area classes to collect informal data on strategy implementation and student engagement.
- ❑ Before and after observations, engaged in reflective dialogue with teachers.
- ❑ Demonstrated instructional strategies.
- ❑ Provided ongoing support to teachers as they try strategies out themselves.

19. Out of the above activities, rank the top 3 activities with which you believe you need the most support in terms of your future professional learning.

20. As an **evaluator**, check all the activities that you have participated in during the most recent school year.
- ❑ Led faculty in the selection and use of a range of assessment tools in order to make sound decisions about the students' literacy needs.
- ❑ Developed a comprehensive assessment program that uses both informal and formal measures of achievement.

(continued)

Figure 1 (Continued)
Online Survey

❑ Set schedules for administering and analyzing both formative and summative assessments.

❑ Aided in the design and/or implementation of formative assessments to determine the effectiveness of a strategy.

❑ Helped teachers standardize the scoring of writing and other literacy measures.

❑ Reviewed current research and trends in assessment methodologies.

❑ Conducted regular meetings with content area teachers to examine student work and monitor progress.

❑ Introduced content area teachers to ways to observe adolescent's literacy skills.

❑ Introduced content area teachers to ways to observe ELL's language development progress.

❑ Helped teachers analyze trends in content area achievement tests.

❑ Helped teachers use the analysis of various assessment results to determine which strategies will support higher achievement.

21. Out of the above activities, rank the top 3 activities with which you believe you need the most support in terms of your future professional learning.

22. Check all that you feel competent in:
   ❑ Developing and implementing instructional strategies to improve academic literacy in English/language arts.
   ❑ Developing and implementing instructional strategies to improve academic literacy in mathematics.
   ❑ Developing and implementing instructional strategies to improve academic literacy in science.
   ❑ Developing and implementing instructional strategies to improve academic literacy in social studies.

23. In which area do you feel the need for greatest improvement?
   ❑ Developing and implementing instructional strategies to improve academic literacy in English/language arts.
   ❑ Developing and implementing instructional strategies to improve academic literacy in mathematics.
   ❑ Developing and implementing instructional strategies to improve academic literacy in science.
   ❑ Developing and implementing instructional strategies to improve academic literacy in social studies.

Professional Dispositions

24. What are the 3 most important personal attributes you believe a middle/high school literacy/reading coach should have in order to be successful?

25. What advice would you give future middle/high school literacy/reading coaches?

responses. Open-ended prompts asked current coaches to reflect on advice they would give to future coaches and designers of professional development for secondary literacy coaches. For example, one open-ended question asked participants: "What do you consider your primary role or responsibility?" The survey included open-ended questions about coaches' educational backgrounds and teaching experiences, coaching preparation, roles and responsibilities as collaborators, coaches, and evaluators, and finally, open-ended questions on their professional dispositions.

Analysis

Descriptive data were computed for educational background and for appropriate items involving teaching experience, coaching preparation, and roles and responsibilities. Qualitative data analysis involved multiple steps. First, two authors grouped open-ended questions together based on concept. Once the questions were grouped, individual responses to the questions were broken into idea units, which were coded using an inductive process of comparing and contrasting. When uncertainty in coding occurred, the two authors would discuss the codes and data until a consensus was reached. Codes were then grouped, named, and defined. A codebook was created to organize the codes into categories. For example, several codes—analyst, collaborator, differentiated supporter—emerged from analysis of the data and were organized into the "Roles" category. Other codes such as optimist and learner fell under the "Personal Attributes" category. The two authors then returned to the data to review the idea units within each category to check the internal validity of the coding. As an additional check, the third author—who had not been a part of the initial coding—recoded the data using the codebook. Any discrepancies between the initial coding and recoding were resolved through discussion and group consensus. Remaining categories were collapsed to represent the recoded data, and the codebook was rewritten to reflect the changes.

Results

Our results begin with descriptive data on the educational background, teaching experience, and preparation of the coaches. We then provide frequency data on the roles and responsibilities of coaches as collaborators, coaches, and evaluators, followed by coaches' reports on areas in which they need more support. Finally, we share themes in the coaches' reports about the personal attributes they consider essential for coaching and the advice that they give to future coaches.

Qualification and Background of Coaches

According to the standards, literacy coaches at the secondary level are expected to have either a master's degree with an emphasis in reading or a reading certification endorsement (IRA, 2006). To understand the qualifications of our participants, we asked them to report their educational background, number of years of teaching experience, and any reading specialist or reading certification endorsements they held. (The requirements for reading certification endorsements vary by state but generally involve teaching experience, additional graduate course work, and successful completion of a state assessment.) In addition, we asked the participants to differentiate which content areas they had taught at the secondary level and the amount of time they had done so. Table 1 presents frequency data on participants' educational background. Note that respondents could report multiple degrees. Almost all (94%) respondents reported undergraduate degrees in three areas: English education, elementary education, or areas outside education. Seventy-six percent were certified in their states, 48% reported reading specialist certification, and 40% reported a master's degree in literacy.

Participants also described their current work: 37% of the respondents coached in a middle school, 46% coached in a high school, and 17% served in both a middle and a high school. Coaches reported a mean of 19 years of classroom teaching experience, with a range of 2 to 40; 15 of those years, on average, were at the middle or high school level. When we queried the coaches about the content areas in which they had taught, we allowed for multiple responses. Therefore, our percentages, if added together, yield more than 100%. Eighty-five percent had taught English/Language Arts, 8% had taught foreign language, 18% had taught math, 11% had taught science, 23% had taught social studies, 53% also indicated teaching experience in areas other than these. Those who were reading specialists reported 13 years in that job. The mean number of years reported in coaching was 8.

Coaching Preparation

The standards maintain that literacy coaches undertake measures to strengthen their own professional knowledge (IRA, 2006). These measures may include participating in one of seven activities outlined by the standards and listed in Table 2.

Table 2 provides frequency data on the specific preparation that participants underwent prior to becoming and while serving as a literacy coach. The final column of data identifies the activities that these coaches reported as most helpful to their development. Of the seven activities specified in the standards, coaches reported participation in an average of 54%. Graduate-level coursework, district-level professional development, and professional readings were included in coaching preparation of most of the respondents.

Role Definition

To understand the extent to which secondary literacy coaches are actually being asked by their principals to fulfill the roles and responsibilities outlined by the standards, we asked coaches to report on how their role has been defined by both their district and their principal. Participants provided open-ended information to this prompt. Frequency data show that 90 responses, or 74%, indicate that the role remains undefined. Eighteen responses, or 15%, indicate that the district, with no input from the coach, defined the coaching role through a top-down construction. Finally, we noted 13 responses, or 11%, that indicate the role was defined through a collaborative process between the district and the coach.

Table 1
Educational Background

Education	Number (N = 147)	Percentage
BA/BS English education	51	35
BA/BS elementary education	45	31
BA/BS outside education	41	28
BA/BS social studies education	8	6
BA/BS early childhood	6	4
BA/BS special education	6	4
BA/BS music, art, or physical education	4	3
BA/BS science education	2	1
BA/BS math education	0	0
State teaching certificate	109	76
Reading specialist certificate	69	48
Master's degree in literacy	58	40
Master's degree in education area	44	31
Master's degree in an area outside education	27	19
Doctoral degree	7	5

Note. The numbers reported are not mutually exclusive.

Table 2
Coaching Preparation

Activity	Number (N = 147)	Percentage	One of the Three Most Helpful
District-level professional development	107	74	26%
Graduate-level coursework	102	71	41%
Professional reading	100	69	32%
State-level professional development	84	58	19%
National conferences	73	51	24%
Study groups	46	32	13%
Work with mentor	37	26	17%
Other	34	24	21%
None of the above	6	4	0%

Note. Items are listed in order of occurrence.

Roles and Responsibilities

The standards outline specific activities undertaken by coaches within three broad roles: collaborators, coaches, and evaluators. We report on each of the roles separately in the order in which it is included in the standards. Participants provided frequency data on their activities as collaborators, as coaches, and as evaluators. For these items, participants were asked whether they had engaged in any of these activities in the past year; all respondents reported multiple activities. The final column in each table indicates those activities for which the coaches reported that they need more support; in this case, they were limited to three responses.

Collaborator. Table 3 provides frequency data on the specific activities that these coaches engaged in to fulfill their role as collaborator. The standards identified 24 activities characterized as evidence of collaboration. On average, respondents reported participation in 62% of those activities. A large percentage (> 80%) reported evidence of specific aspects of collaboration: They respected confidentiality, demonstrated positive expectations for students, examined best practices and curriculum

Table 3
Activities as Collaborator

Activity	Number (N = 147)	Percentage	Needs Most Support
Respected confidentiality	124	87	2%
Examined best practices	123	86	8%
Examined curriculum materials	123	86	0%
Responded to student needs	122	85	10%
Responded to staff needs	120	84	5%
Demonstrated positive expectations for students	118	83	1%
Responded to teacher requests	116	81	1%
Remained current with professional literature	108	76	9%
Attended professional development	108	76	10%
Communicated schoolwide literacy assessment data	107	75	0%
Managed time/resources	98	69	2%
Kept administrators informed	97	68	5%
Responded to parent needs	86	60	3%
Facilitated discussions on adolescent literacy	79	55	3%
Showcased content area strategies	76	53	2%
Aligned curriculum to state/local requirements	75	52	5%
Implemented schoolwide literacy improvement plan	65	45	7%
Applied concepts of adult learning to professional development	64	45	0%
Conducted schoolwide literacy assessment	58	41	1%
Conducted evaluations of action plans	59	41	1%
Developed literacy team	56	39	3%
Met regularly with other coaches	55	38	8%
Encouraged reading specialist to serve as resource	53	37	2%
Attended professional development on adult learning	45	31	1%

Note. Items are listed in order of occurrence.

materials, and listened to and responded to students and staff.

Coach. Table 4 provides frequency data on the specific activities that these coaches engaged in to fulfill their role as coach. The standards included 19 activities in the role of coach; participants, on average, reported engaging in 46% percent of those in the past year. There was generally less consensus among our participants in activities described as coaching; no activity was used by more than 80% of the participants. There was a group of low-incidence activities, and they clustered around observation of instruction and providing feedback, assisting teachers with technology, and collecting data on strategy implementation.

Evaluator. Table 5 provides frequency data on the specific activities that these coaches engaged in to fulfill their role as evaluator. There were 11 activities in this area; participants, on average, reported engaging in 27% percent of them in the past year; not one activity in this area was reported by even half of the coaches. Fewer than 25% of the coaches worked specifically with selecting a range of assessment tools or developing a comprehensive assessment program. Likewise, few engaged with teachers in analysis of student achievement on content area tests or review of student work for progress monitoring.

Personal Attributes. The standards indicate that ideal secondary literacy coaches are skilled listeners, problem solvers, and relationship builders. Participants provided advice, in the

| | Table 4 | | |
| | Activities as Coach | | |
Activity	Number (N = 147)	Percentage	Needs Most Support
Worked with teachers individually	103	72	0%
Assisted teachers in instruction of content area texts	94	66	0%
Worked with teaching teams	89	62	3%
Demonstrated instructional strategies	87	61	3%
Provided ongoing support to teachers	86	60	10%
Worked with departments	81	57	1%
Developed repertoire of reading strategies	82	57	11%
Helped determine content-specific reading strategies	79	55	6%
Facilitated professional development in instructional strategies	73	51	4%
Assisted teachers to improve writing instruction	70	49	3%
Provided professional development in metacognitive strategies	69	48	1%
Helped select content area texts	61	43	1%
Observed and provided feedback to teachers	50	35	7%
Linked teachers to evidence-based research	49	34	0%
Ensured teacher observations nonthreatening	46	32	3%
Facilitated reflective dialogue	38	27	3%
Explored cross-cultural communication patterns	37	26	3%
Assisted teachers using Internet sources	25	17	1%
Regularly conducted observations of strategy implementation and student engagement	23	16	0%

Note. Items are listed in order of occurrence.

Table 5
Activities as Evaluator

Activity	Number (N = 147)	Percentage	Needs Most Support
Reviewed assessment research	69	48	10%
Helped teachers standardize scoring of writing	47	33	4%
Helped teachers determine which strategies support achievement	45	31	8%
Introduced teachers to ways to observe adolescent literacy skills	42	29	3%
Aided in implementation of formative assessments	40	28	6%
Set schedules for administering/analyzing formative and summative assessments	38	27	3%
Led faculty to select range of assessments	35	24	2%
Developed comprehensive assessment program	33	23	4%
Helped teachers analyze trends in content area achievement tests	38	22	3%
Examined student work with teachers	23	16	11%
Introduced ways to observe English-language learners' language development	20	14	6%

Note. Items are listed in order of occurrence.

form of open-ended comments, about the personal attributes they viewed as most important to the success of a middle or high school literacy coach.

According to our coaches, the model secondary literacy coach is first and foremost an optimistic person. When confronted with challenges, he or she draws from a personal arsenal of patience, resilience, and flexibility to persevere. As one participant stated,

> Coaching is a difficult position, and in some instances you get a lot of resistance...the math teacher doesn't necessarily think [he or she is] nor want[s] to be a 'reading' teacher. You have to find a way to 'sell' it to them—to make them buy into the idea that we are ALL responsible for the students' literacy.

For many participants, having an optimistic outlook enabled them to continue their efforts despite classroom teachers' reluctance to adopt literacy strategies.

In addition to optimism, participants discussed the need for coaches to be expert communicators and collaborators. A coach must be able to communicate with teachers effectively, a task which includes listening to individual needs and presenting ideas and suggestions for improvement. Related to communication skills, the coach must be able to collaborate. Participants stressed the importance of collaboration as a means of empowering teachers to incorporate literacy strategies into their own instruction: "Be more of a mentor—coaches aren't the 'fix-it' people. They should work WITH the teachers to develop what will work in the teacher's classroom."

Lastly, the model secondary literacy coach is both an expert and a learner. The coach comes to the job possessing strong background knowledge in literacy development and both content and content-specific literacy instruction; the coach draws from this extensive personal knowledge when problem-solving with teachers. For example, one participant explained,

> If you (as a coach) can recommend a specific book, strategy, etc., to a teacher and show the teacher how it would fit in with the content they are required to teach, then the teacher is much more likely to

incorporate literacy strategies into their regular teaching.

Along with expertise in literacy instruction, the secondary coach continues to pursue his or her own learning. The coach is committed to learning new concepts and ideas relevant to literacy and content area instruction, actively pursuing venues for developing knowledge.

While personal attributes such as optimism, communication skills, and commitment to learning are necessary for coaching success, they are not sufficient. Participants indicated several areas that require strategic planning.

Advice for Future Coaches

Along with personal attributes that would be helpful to possess, participants offered advice about enacting the role of secondary literacy coach. Consistently, participants urged future coaches to make conscious decisions about how they presented themselves to teachers. Based on their experiences, participants agreed on the importance of presenting oneself as a credible teacher. The credible teacher instructs students and teachers, establishing trust by fostering relationships. Moreover, background knowledge and expertise in literacy instruction lend credibility to this work.

In addition to being a credible teacher, current coaches recommended providing differentiated support to teachers based on need, rather than creating a one-size-fits-all professional development program. According to our participants, a coach who provides differentiated support plans and implements professional development, using effective techniques for adult learning to meet individual teachers' needs. One coach suggested, "Find what content teachers are doing. Then adjust strategies to tailor to that teacher. Sometimes the best way to lead is to find out where everyone is going."

Part of knowing how to support teachers comes from analyzing classroom- and school-level data. Participants report that an effective coach assesses the needs of the school, teachers, and students by examining test data. The coach collects and uses school- and student-level data

to inform decisions about professional development and instruction. One coach commented, "I also analyze testing data for reading and prepare analysis of in-house and state testing data." Notably, while participants described the importance of being able to analyze and use data, they also indicated that analyzing data is the area in which they need the most support.

Finally, participants advise future coaches to be strategic leaders. They stress the importance of defining and advocating for a specific role from the very first day on the job. Many of the participants described performing jobs that had not been defined by their principal or their district; this lack of job clarity made it hard for the coaches to devote their time to supporting teachers, for they were often used in other capacities unrelated to literacy.

Advice for Designers of Professional Development

Going beyond the standards, we asked participants to provide advice to designers of professional development. The advice most often given by participants involved providing opportunities for collaborative professional development. Participants discussed the importance of having time to network with other literacy coaches, commenting on the necessity of common time to plan and discuss new research-based concepts. As one coach stated, "Have your reading coaches meet regularly to share and formulate strategies that work." Related to the concept of collaborative professional development, participants stressed the importance of professional development that is ongoing. The antithesis of the one-workshop approach, ongoing professional development includes "extensive follow-up throughout the year." Having opportunities to meet together regularly to share ideas, to discuss what works and what does not, and to commiserate on the challenges of the job helped participants immeasurably.

Participants also described the need for professional development focusing specifically on strengthening coaches' research-based knowledge of literacy strategies, content area literacy instruction, and effective adult learning techniques. Coaches discussed the need for professional development to introduce them to new literacy strategies, "stay current with the research and provide [coaches] with well-researched strategies." In addition, coaches need knowledge of content literacy strategies. Participants urged designers of professional development to "recognize that teaching secondary students is a lot different than teaching young, developing readers." Similarly, when working with teachers, coaches needed to know and use strategies that would motivate and engage adult learners: "PD [professional development] needs to address all the myriad issues of getting adults to adapt and change their professional practice. Understanding group dynamics is crucial, as is working with adult learners."

Lastly, participants suggested that professional developers also focus on practical knowledge. Practical knowledge included not only techniques in time management and organization for the coaches but also concrete, easily transferable teaching ideas that the coaches could model for their teachers. As one participant advised, "balance theory with practical application in a classroom setting." Participants stressed the need for professional development that modeled classroom techniques: "Make it [professional development] hands on. Provide realistic experiences and applications."

Discussion

Recently, literacy coaching was deemed a hot topic for literacy research (Cassidy & Cassidy, 2008). Legislation such as Reading First, Early Reading First, and Reading Next has provided the necessary funding to bring literacy coaches to struggling schools. Standards such as those at the heart of this study have been set to guide coaches' work (IRA, 2006). Research has begun to study the effectiveness of literacy coaching on school reform efforts (Shanklin, 2006). Moreover, organizations such as the Literacy Coaching Clearinghouse have formed

to disseminate resources and generate national focus on the impact of literacy coaching. Yet questions remain regarding who coaches are, what they do, and whether they are effective.

While research has begun to investigate elementary literacy coaching, far less is known about coaching at the secondary level. Therefore, the purpose of this study was to explore what some coaches at the secondary level are doing, what they would like help doing, and what they think future coaches should know. The experiences of our participants may have implications for coaches, school administrators working closely with coaches, providers of professional development for coaches, and policymakers. However, we realize that our sample was small and is not generalizable to all middle school and high school coaches.

A key finding supports prior research (Riddle-Buly et al., 2006; Snow et al., 2006), which has argued that literacy coaching at the secondary level is distinct from coaching at the elementary level. Secondary coaches serve larger numbers of teachers (because high schools are generally much larger than elementary schools) who serve more diverse groups of students (because achievement gaps widen over time) than elementary coaches. Moreover, participants discussed a challenge of convincing teachers specialized in the content areas that providing reading and writing support to secondary students was worthwhile. Given the unique nature of coaching at the secondary level, future coaches and designers of professional development should be cautious when drawing from research focused exclusively on elementary coaches.

Despite the standards (IRA, 2006), participants report that their roles and responsibilities remain relatively ambiguous at the school- and district-level. As a result, many secondary coaches expend a great deal of energy trying to create an identity. Because of the vague nature of the role, a range of preparedness exists among the current coaches. School administrators could facilitate the work of coaches by providing concrete expectations and discussing how they see the work of coaches as supporting professional development efforts. Moreover, policymakers could develop clearer descriptions for coaches so that all stakeholders know what to expect when a literacy coach begins work.

The most salient finding in our survey was the frequency at which coaches performed the three leadership roles targeted in the standards. Coaches reported participating in a wide variety of activities in the area of collaboration; however, they participated in fewer coaching activities and even fewer evaluation activities. The standards emphasize coaches' roles in schoolwide data analysis. A coach should know how to choose appropriate assessments, administer assessments, analyze assessment data, interpret results, and use results to differentiate classroom instruction and plan appropriate professional development for teachers (IRA, 2006). Yet participants consistently indicated data evaluation as an activity they did not participate in frequently and felt they could benefit from professional development opportunities. This finding is important given the federal emphasis placed on using student achievement data to monitor student progress and a school's adequate yearly progress and should inform designers of professional development. Future coaches will need to feel more comfortable in the role of data analyst; beyond professional development, university education programs training preservice coaches could build in more emphasis on evaluation.

When asked what advice they would give designers of professional development, participants were very clear about what they needed to learn and effective modes for their learning. In order for secondary coaches to fulfill the needs of secondary teachers, professional development must address strategies for infusing literacy into content areas. Participants indicated a high level of comfort with incorporating literacy strategies into the English language arts classroom but were far less confident about appropriate literacy strategies for mathematics, social studies, and science. In addition, participants need professional development on effective adult learning techniques for use in their own work with teachers. In terms of how they learn best, participants stressed the importance of comprehensive, ongoing inservice support and flexible graduate programs. Participants recommended that coaches seek opportunities to learn through traditional educational settings, national and state conferences, and state- and district-level professional development. Additionally, mentors and coaching networks provide much needed ongoing support. For our participants, every opportunity to learn seemed to improve their ability to coach.

Lessons learned from coaches currently in the field provide important insight for coaches and those working with coaches. However, the current study was exploratory in nature and limited by its reliance on self-report data. Future research could expand understandings of the roles of secondary literacy coaches found in this study through triangulation of self-report data, observation, and participant interviews. Important questions remain regarding the appropriateness of the coaching model for the secondary setting and the balance between literacy and content expertise a secondary coach should possess. However, participants from our survey testify to the potential promise of secondary coaching and the need to pursue future research on coaching.

References

Cassidy, J., & Cassidy, D. (2008). What's hot for 2008. *Reading Today, 25*(4), 1, 10–11.

International Reading Association. (2006). *Standards for middle and high school literacy coaches.* Newark, DE: Author.

Riddle-Buly, M.R., Coskie, T., Robinson, L., & Egawa, K. (2006). Literacy coaching: Coming out of the corner. *Voices From the Middle, 13*(4), 24–28.

Roller, C. (2006). *Reading and literacy coaches report on hiring requirements and duties survey.* Newark, DE: International Reading Association.

Schen, M., Rao, S., & Dobles, R. (2005). *Coaches in the high school classroom: Studies in implementing high school reform.* Providence, RI: Annenberg Institute for School Reform at Brown University.

Shanklin, N.L. (2006). *What are the characteristics of effective literacy coaching?* Denver, CO: Literacy Coaching Clearinghouse.

Snow, C., Ippolito, J., & Schwartz, R. (2006). What we know and what we need to know about literacy coaches in middle and high schools: A research synthesis and proposed research agenda. In *Standards for middle and high school literacy coaches* (pp. 35–49). Newark, DE: International Reading Association.

Sturtevant, E. (2003). *The literacy coach: A key to improving teaching and learning in secondary schools.* Washington, DC: Alliance for Excellent Education.

Taylor, R.T., Moxley, D.E., Chanter, C., & Boulware, D. (2007). Three techniques for successful literacy coaching. *Principal Leadership, 7*(6), 22–25.

Toll, C. (2005). *The literacy coach's survival guide: Essential questions and practical answers.* Newark, DE: International Reading Association.

Toll, C. (2006). *Literacy coach's desk reference: The processes and perspectives for effective coaching.* Urbana, IL: National Council of Teachers of English.

Walpole, S., & McKenna, M.C. (2004). *The literacy coach's handbook: A guide to research-based practice.* New York: Guilford.

Walpole, S., & McKenna, M.C. (2007). *Differentiated reading instruction: Strategies for the primary grades.* New York: Guilford.

What Matters for Elementary Literacy Coaching? Guiding Principles for Instructional Improvement and Student Achievement

Susan L'Allier, Laurie Elish-Piper and Rita M. Bean

Amanda Davis (all names are pseudonyms), the literacy coach at Washburn Elementary, arrives at school and checks her e-mail. She responds to a message from her principal about an upcoming staff meeting, and she replies to a third-grade teacher who wants to meet with her. Amanda then reviews her daily calendar. She will be modeling a guided reading lesson in a first-grade classroom, holding a preobservation conference with a second-grade teacher, and meeting with the kindergarten teachers to discuss their students' phonemic awareness assessment scores. Amanda also plans to prepare for an upcoming book study group. Although Amanda has clear plans for her day, she often finds herself faced with unexpected situations, requests, and emergencies. For example, she may be asked to assess a newly enrolled student, or she may find herself researching information about a reading strategy to respond to an inquiry from a grade-level team. At times, Amanda feels overwhelmed and wonders how she can best spend her time so that she is able to support teachers and students in her school.

Whether a reading professional is spending all of her time coaching, dividing time between coaching and working with students, or considering adding coaching to her work as a reading specialist, the tasks that fall to this individual can be daunting. Questions remain about literacy coaching such as, What types of knowledge and preparation does a literacy coach need to be successful in the position? How much time should the literacy coach devote to working directly with teachers as compared with completing other coaching activities? What can a literacy coach do to build collaborative relationships with teachers? Which literacy coaching activities help teachers enhance their instruction and students improve their learning? These types of questions suggest that further guidance is needed regarding the qualifications, activities, and roles of literacy coaches. In this article, we provide such guidance in the form of seven research-based principles for literacy coaching.

Background

Literacy coaching provides job-embedded, ongoing professional development for teachers (International Reading Association [IRA], 2004). This approach to professional development is rooted in cognitive coaching, peer coaching, and mentoring (Costa & Garmston, 1994; Showers, 1984; Toll, 2005, 2006). To date, the available research related to literacy coaching has focused mainly on roles, responsibilities, and relationships (e.g., Bean et al., 2007; Bean, Swan, & Knaub, 2003; Bean &

Preparing Reading Professionals (second edition), edited by Rita M. Bean, Natalie Heisey, and Cathy M. Roller. © 2010 by the International Reading Association. Reprinted from L'Allier, S., Elish-Piper, L., & Bean, R.M. (2010). What Matters for Elementary Literacy Coaching? Guiding Principles for Instructional Improvement and Student Achievement. *The Reading Teacher, 63*(7), 544–554.

Zigmond, 2007; Deussen, Coskie, Robinson, & Autio, 2007; Dole, 2004; Poglinco et al., 2003; Rainville & Jones, 2008). Some research has examined the relationship between literacy coaching and teacher knowledge, beliefs, and practices (Blachowicz, Obrochta, & Fogelberg, 2005; Gibson, 2006; Neufeld & Roper, 2003). Yet other research has investigated the effects of literacy coaching on student achievement in reading (Bean et al., 2008; Biancarosa, Bryk, & Dexter, 2008; Elish-Piper & L'Allier, 2007; L'Allier & Elish-Piper, 2006, 2009).

We synthesized the findings from our studies (Bean et al., 2007; Bean et al., 2008; Bean et al., 2003; Bean & Zigmond, 2007; Elish-Piper & L'Allier, 2007; L'Allier & Elish-Piper, 2006, 2009) and the related literature to develop seven guiding principles that literacy coaches can use to focus their work on the improvement of literacy teaching and learning in the elementary grades. In addition, a vignette is provided to illustrate each guiding principle in action. We developed the vignettes based on our several years of work with literacy coaches during professional development and research activities.

Guiding Principles for Literacy Coaching

Principle 1: Coaching Requires Specialized Knowledge

The major responsibilities of literacy coaches involve helping classroom teachers improve their instruction through job-embedded, ongoing professional development. These professional development activities may include providing large-group presentations about literacy education, facilitating small teacher-study groups and grade-level team meetings, and supporting individual teachers as they work to develop their instructional and assessment skills (IRA, 2004). All of these activities revolve around knowledge of literacy processes, acquisition, assessment, and instruction; therefore, it is essential that literacy coaches bring a strong knowledge base about the various aspects of literacy education to their coaching (Frost & Bean, 2006). Coaches also need to

know how to work effectively with teachers; this requires an understanding of adult learning principles which suggest that adults are most open to learning when they are involved in planning instruction, when experience is the basis for learning, when learning has immediate job-related relevance, and when learning is problem-centered (Flaherty, 2005; Knowles, 1984).

How do coaches develop this expansive knowledge base? Successful classroom teaching experiences must form the foundation of any coach's knowledge base. In addition, their active participation in ongoing professional development builds on the knowledge and skills gained during their initial certification programs. Furthermore, a graduate degree that leads to advanced certification helps them gain in-depth knowledge of literacy and provides opportunities for them to learn about how to work with teachers to improve their practice. Taken together, these experiences enable coaches to meet IRA's (2004) criteria.

Sometimes schools must hire literacy coaches quickly to meet grant requirements or to address district mandates (Frost & Bean, 2006). In other instances, principals want to appoint one of their exemplary teachers as the literacy coach. In such cases, does it really matter if a coach has advanced preparation in reading?

What Can Be Learned From the Research?
Yes, advanced preparation for coaches does matter! L'Allier and Elish-Piper (2006) conducted a study in a diverse, low-income school district that had received a Reading First grant (hereafter referred to as the Valley District Study). The study's participants included 5 literacy coaches, 65 kindergarten through grade 3 classroom teachers, and 1,596 students. The researchers collected students' fall and spring test scores as well as weekly literacy coaching logs that used a structured protocol. Analysis of the data indicated that the highest average student reading gains occurred in classrooms supported by a literacy coach who held a Reading Teacher endorsement (24 credit hours of course

work in reading); conversely, the lowest average student gains occurred in classrooms supported by a literacy coach who had neither an advanced degree in reading nor a Reading Teacher endorsement.

In a second study conducted by Elish-Piper and L'Allier (2007), the participants included 12 literacy coaches, 121 kindergarten through grade 3 classroom teachers, and 3,029 students (hereafter referred to as the Metropolitan District Study). The Metropolitan District Study was also conducted in a diverse, low-income school district that had received a Reading First grant.

Teachers in both districts used a core textbook, guided reading instruction, and literacy centers/stations within the framework of an uninterrupted 90-minute reading block. As in the Valley District Study, weekly coaching logs and students' fall and spring test scores were collected. Analysis of the data using hierarchical linear modeling (HLM) suggested that significant reading achievement gains were made by students of teachers who received support from a literacy coach who had either a Reading Teacher endorsement or Reading Specialist certificate (32 credit hours of course work in reading).

While the specific requirements for a master's degree, reading endorsement, or reading certificate may vary from state to state, completion of advanced preparation in literacy education indicates that the coach has acquired a solid knowledge base through an articulated set of courses so that her understanding of literacy is both broad and deep. In summary, the results from these two studies indicate that advanced preparation does make a difference for literacy coaching effectiveness related to student reading performance.

The Guiding Principle in Action. Amanda Davis, who was introduced at the beginning of this article, is a case in point. She recently earned her master's degree in reading, which enabled her to meet the qualifications for a Reading Teacher endorsement. She finds that she relies on her knowledge on a daily basis in her work as a literacy coach in a large urban district. Her previous experience as an elementary teacher is very helpful in her work with teachers, but she realizes that literacy coaching also requires specialized knowledge across multiple grade levels and at the student, classroom, and school levels. She developed much of that knowledge while completing her master's degree, and she continues to update her knowledge base by reading professional journals and books and by attending conferences. In addition, her graduate course work and ongoing professional development have enabled her to enhance her expertise with assessment, data analysis, Response to Intervention (RTI), and other new initiatives that are essential for her literacy coaching work. When asked about what has contributed to her success as a literacy coach, Amanda responded, "Having the Reading Teacher endorsement and using the in-depth knowledge from my graduate program are key pieces of my literacy coaching success."

Principle 2: Time Working With Teachers Is the Focus of Coaching

To provide ongoing, job-embedded professional development for teachers, coaches spend time with teachers engaged in activities such as observing, modeling, conferencing, co-teaching, and leading book study groups (Casey, 2006; Froelich & Puig, 2010; IRA, 2004). However, many coaches also spend a great deal of time on other activities such as organizing book rooms, administering assessments, and participating in district-level meetings (Bean et al., 2007; Bean & Zigmond, 2007; Knight, 2006; Roller, 2006). In fact, a study of 190 coaches working in school districts funded by Reading First grants (Deussen et al., 2007) indicated that, on average, coaches spent only 28% of their time working with teachers. Using time allocation to categorize the main focus of their coaching, four categories of coaches emerged: teacher-oriented, student-oriented, data-oriented, and managerial. Only one third were classified as teacher-oriented coaches—coaches who spent between 41% and 52% of their time interacting with teachers. In light of the varied ways that coaches spend their time, it seems important to ask, do students benefit when coaches' schedules include a high percentage of time working with teachers?

What Can Be Learned From the Research?
Yes, students do benefit when coaches work with teachers! Results from the Valley District Study (L'Allier & Elish-Piper, 2006) indicated that the highest average student reading gains occurred in classrooms supported by a literacy coach who engaged in the most interactions with teachers; conversely, the lowest average student gains occurred in classrooms supported by a literacy coach who spent the lowest percentage of time with teachers.

In a study of literacy coaching in schools that received Reading First grants, 20 literacy coaches each participated in five in-depth retrospective interviews during which they described exactly what they had been doing during the previous 24-hour period (Bean et al., 2008). The researchers divided the schools where the literacy coaches worked into two groups based on the median amount of time coaches spent working with teachers engaged in group and individual coaching. The researchers found significant differences between the two groups of schools; that is, schools in which coaches spent more time working directly with teachers (i.e., high coaching schools) had a greater percentage of students scoring at the proficient level in first and second grade. Furthermore, in high coaching schools, a lower percentage of first- and second-grade students scored in the at-risk range on standardized assessments. The results of these studies indicate that students benefit when literacy coaches' time is spent working directly with teachers to help them improve their practice.

The Guiding Principle in Action. Let's listen in as Selena Rodriguez, a literacy coach at Lincoln Elementary School located in a suburban school district, meets with her principal, Marilyn Tobart, to discuss her goal of increasing her coaching time with teachers. Marilyn begins their discussion by saying, "I love the way you've organized the book room and compiled all of the assessment data."

Selena replies, "Yes, I'm pleased with my work in both areas, but they did take a lot of time—reducing the time I spent with teachers. Next year's schedule offers more opportunities for working with teachers; there are different designated times for the primary and intermediate literacy blocks as well as common planning times for each grade level. If someone could catalog and organize new guided reading materials and help me input the assessment data, I could spend more time helping teachers with guided reading and assisting them in designing data-driven instruction."

After further discussion, Marilyn responds, "I can schedule time for one of our teaching assistants to input the assessment data. I also know a retired teacher who wants to volunteer in our school; the book room activities might be perfect for her." Selena leaves the meeting confident that there is a plan in place to help her meet her goal of spending at least 50% of her coaching time with teachers.

Principle 3: Collaborative Relationships Are Essential for Coaching
Although a shared focus on student achievement can provide the foundation for collaborative relationships between coaches and teachers, coaches must build on that foundation by establishing trust, maintaining confidentiality, and communicating effectively with teachers. Coaches establish trust by openly respecting teachers' professional expertise (Knight, 2009) and following through on the commitments they make to teachers. As coaches engage in activities such as making classroom observations and conferencing with teachers about those observations, they must maintain confidentiality by not discussing those activities with other teachers or the principal (Rainville & Jones, 2008). And when coaches focus their discussions on how to address the needs of students—rather than

on the strengths or weaknesses of a teacher's instruction (McCombs & Marsh, 2009)—they clearly communicate their intention to be a collaborator with the teacher, not an evaluator (Casey, 2006; Toll, 2005).

What Can Be Learned From the Research?

Insights about building collaborative relationships can be gained from listening to teachers who work with literacy coaches (L'Allier & Elish-Piper, 2009; Vanderberg & Stephens, 2009). Vanderberg and Stephens interviewed 35 teachers, each of whom had worked with a literacy coach for three years. In terms of building trust, interview data indicated that teachers felt coaches respected their abilities to select strategies based on their students' needs. Teachers also noted that their coach was "more like a facilitator of their learning rather than a dictator" (p. 3). The coaches' willingness to answer questions and to offer suggestions, not absolute solutions, was cited as an example of this facilitative communication style.

In another study involving 6 literacy coaches and 19 of the teachers with whom they worked, findings from structured interviews indicated that teachers consistently cited trust and confidentiality as two essential elements of effective literacy coaching (L'Allier & Elish-Piper, 2009). One teacher we interviewed in that study explained, "I know my literacy coach is there to help me and not to judge me. She is professional, and she will keep my questions, no matter how silly I think they may be, private."

Additional insights about building collaborative relationships can be gained from the research about coaches' use of language. Perkins (1998) found that, when compared with novice coaches, experienced coaches' conversations with teachers included more paraphrasing of teacher concerns and comments, more open-ended questions, and more respect for teachers' opinions, indicating that experienced coaches used their language to build collaborative relationships with teachers. Rainville and Jones (2008) concluded that a coach's language is often indicative of the relationship between the coach and the teacher. Thus, they suggest that

professional development for coaches include opportunities to analyze the language used by other coaches as well as to reflect on their own use of coaching language through role-playing activities. Such activities will highlight the important role that language plays in the development of collaborative relationships.

The Guiding Principle in Action. Selena Rodriguez believes that trust is the foundation for all of her coaching work; therefore, she uses a three-pronged approach to build trusting relationships with the teachers in her school. First, she contacts teachers who are new to the building before the start of the school year to introduce herself, to explain what her role is, and to offer help in setting up their classroom libraries. Selena also works hard to establish and maintain trusting relationships with all teachers by clarifying through her words and actions that she is not part of the evaluation process and that her primary goal is to be a person with whom teachers can think and solve problems. She often prefaces conferences with teachers by saying, "Remember, I'm here to be a sounding board and a resource. What we discuss will stay here." Finally, by actively participating in grade-level meetings and attending local conferences and workshops with groups of teachers, Selena positions herself as a colearner with the teachers in her school.

Selena also knows that the way she says something can be as important as what she says. For example, she recently met with Jasmine, a teacher who came to Selena for ideas to improve her guided reading instruction. Selena started the conversation by saying, "So, Jasmine, tell me about your guided reading groups." By using an open-ended prompt, Selena invited Jasmine to share her ideas without creating a tense or negative situation. Jasmine replied, "I think I've grouped the students well, and I'm finding interesting materials that are appropriate for each group. However, I'm really concerned that I'm not providing enough instruction." Selena responded, "Let's talk about what you are doing now and then discuss some ideas you might want to add to ensure that your instruction supports students' learning. Or I can come in to watch you teach a group to get a better idea of what you are doing. Which would be most helpful to you?" By using this type of response, Selena gives the teacher choices while also emphasizing the importance of working together to help Jasmine reach her goal of improving guided reading instruction.

Principle 4: Coaching That Supports Student Reading Achievement Focuses on a Set of Core Activities

Literacy coaches juggle dozens of different activities in a typical week as they work to support teachers (Walpole & Blamey, 2008). For example, Geraldine Martin, a literacy coach in an urban school, facilitates grade-level meetings, coplans lessons, coteaches in classrooms, facilitates professional book clubs, and delivers monthly professional development workshops for teachers. With so many activities that can be done to support teachers, Geraldine wonders which coaching activities she should prioritize—especially because she wants to focus on activities that support student reading achievement.

What Can Be Learned From the Research?

Findings from the HLM analyses of the Metropolitan District Study (Elish-Piper & L'Allier, 2007) suggested that when literacy coaches administer and discuss student assessments with teachers, observe teachers' instruction and offer supportive feedback, conference with teachers about their instruction and students, and model instruction in classrooms, student achievement in reading increases significantly more than in comparable classrooms where these coaching activities are not provided. What is it about these literacy coaching activities that supports student achievement gains?

When a literacy coach administers assessments and shares results with a classroom teacher, she is able to explain results, offer suggestions for grouping, and help develop plans to differentiate instruction. When a literacy coach

observes a teacher's instruction and offers supportive feedback, the teacher is able to enhance and fine-tune her implementation of best practices. When a literacy coach conferences with a teacher, she is able to discuss that teacher's instruction, curriculum, and students in an in-depth manner. Finally, when a literacy coach models instruction in a classroom, that teacher is able to see best practices in action with her own students, which provides a foundation to support the teacher with implementing such instruction in the future. By engaging in these activities, a literacy coach is able to provide support that is tailored to each individual teacher's students, needs, and goals (Kise, 2006).

The Guiding Principle in Action. Let's visit Geraldine Martin, the literacy coach at a large urban elementary school, to see what this principle looks like in her coaching work. Geraldine's belief that assessment should drive instruction (Bernhardt, 2008) is apparent in her recent work with Tyson Davis, a third-grade teacher. At his request, she completed a Developmental Reading Assessment (DRA) for several of the struggling readers in his classroom.

Geraldine shared the results of the DRA with Tyson, and they discussed how Tyson is currently teaching these students. Tyson explained, "I do guided reading with these kids, but I'm not sure they are getting the comprehension instruction they need." Geraldine suggested, "Why don't I come in to observe these students during guided reading? I would then have a better idea about how we can work together to improve their comprehension." Tyson agreed, and Geraldine observed in his classroom the next morning. Later that day, Tyson and Geraldine met to confer about her observations, his questions, and their next steps. When Geraldine asked if he thought the think-aloud approach might help these students, Tyson responded, "I've tried it a few times, but I don't really feel confident using think-alouds." Geraldine asked, "Would you like me to model a guided reading lesson with a think-aloud for comprehension instruction tomorrow?" Tyson agreed, and Geraldine modeled the think-aloud strategy while Tyson observed. By focusing her coaching on the activities of administering and discussing assessments, observing, conferencing, and modeling, Geraldine was able to stay on target with her coaching goals—supporting teachers and promoting student reading achievement gains.

Principle 5: Coaching Must Be Both Intentional and Opportunistic

Effective coaches recognize that intentionality is critical to their successes. In each situation, the coach must have a plan for working with teachers that is deliberate but flexible. For example, a coach working with a novice teacher may decide that modeling is a good first step followed by coteaching and, finally, observing the teacher in action. That same coach may select a different route with an experienced teacher who is hesitant about coaching support. The coach might, for instance, facilitate discussions at grade-level meetings that include the sharing of instructional ideas by all members. The key is that coaches have road maps that guide their work, and they understand the need to modify and readjust, if necessary.

At the same time, effective and efficient coaches take advantage of opportunities. They are available and accessible. They chat with teachers in the hallways, stop in classrooms, and visit the teachers' lounge to say "hello" or to talk briefly with teachers. They have an open-door policy not only for classroom teachers but also for others such as librarians, special educators, and administrators. Most of these encounters are short and spontaneous. They often lead to more intense interactions that can then become intentional.

What Can Be Learned From the Research?

In an interview study of 20 coaches who worked in districts that received Reading First grants, Bean and colleagues (2008) concluded that these coaches had an in-depth understanding of why and how they were working with teachers. Several examples from the interviews illustrated this notion of intentional coaching. In one instance where the coach felt that the teacher would benefit from extended support to implement the literacy framework, the coach worked with that teacher during the entire 90-minute reading block, 3 days a week for 3 weeks. In another instance, the coach provided an experienced third-grade teacher with some supplemental resources for her struggling readers, reviewed their use, and then suggested that the two of them meet at the end of the week to discuss whether the materials were helpful. From past experience, the coach knew that this teacher would be more likely to raise questions and identify possible next steps (e.g., coplanning and modeling) if she first had the opportunity to actually use new strategies or materials with her students.

Eighteen of the 20 coaches also reported opportunistic or on-the-fly coaching. For example, teachers would stop the coaches in the hallways or catch them in the office in the morning. Sometimes, opportunistic coaching occurred when coach and teacher happened to be sitting next to each other at a school meeting. Several coaches noted that these encounters opened the door to intentional coaching.

The Guiding Principle in Action. Geraldine Martin, in building her schedule for the upcoming week, reserved three 30-minute periods in the morning where she could work with a new second-grade teacher who was experiencing difficulty with guided reading. She had planned with this teacher yesterday, and they had decided how their work would proceed during the three lessons. Geraldine also scheduled a meeting with two kindergarten teachers who, while walking into school with her that morning, had voiced their concerns about the effectiveness of their instruction for several of their students who were English-language learners. Geraldine suggested that they meet to talk about their concerns in more depth.

After scheduling several activities for the upcoming week, Geraldine walked down the hall to coteach a phonics lesson in a first-grade classroom. On the way, Sam, the special education teacher, stopped her to talk about a new student. Specifically, he wanted to know what some of the assessment scores in the student's folder meant. Geraldine took a few minutes to answer Sam's question and indicated her willingness to review the entire folder with him at another time. She then continued down the hallway to the first-grade classroom. It is evident that Geraldine is intentional about her coaching, and also, that by being accessible and receptive, she often has on-the-fly opportunities to coach.

Principle 6: Coaches Must Be Literacy Leaders in the School

Literacy coaches are frequently involved in three practices that are considered essential for successful literacy leadership: setting goals or directions in a school, developing people, and redesigning the organization to facilitate accomplishment of goals (Leithwood, Louis, Anderson, & Wahlstrom, 2004). Many coaches, along with teachers, are involved in setting the direction for the school in the area of literacy. Further, in their role as a developer of people, coaches support teachers' professional growth by working collaboratively with teachers to help them achieve the school's literacy goals, by facilitating study groups about literacy topics, and by working with individual teachers. Through these activities, literacy coaches promote collegiality and teacher leadership in the school.

Coaches also contribute to redesigning the organization in various ways; they can work with principals to create literacy blocks that enable teachers to effectively implement the school's literacy framework and to develop a plan for using paraprofessionals to support small-group, differentiated instruction. Moreover, these coaches often serve as the communication hub for the school—they share information about local, state, and federal literacy initiatives with teachers and administrators, and serve as a link to parents and the community. They also serve as advocates for the school, highlighting its accomplishments to the community (Bean et al., 2008; Quatroche & Wepner, 2008).

What Can Be Learned From the Research?

In-depth interviews of 20 coaches in schools that received Reading First grants (Bean et al., 2008) revealed that these coaches often took leadership roles. Many chaired committees that made decisions about goals for the reading program or the selection of materials; others were involved in writing proposals for funding. Most worked collaboratively with specialized personnel and teachers to make decisions about how to provide effective instruction for all students. All had responsibilities for developing people through facilitating grade-level meetings, providing professional development, and coaching individual teachers. By working closely with the principal, the coaches also had a voice in making decisions about how to modify the organizational structure to facilitate reading instruction.

Coaches in the Bean and colleagues (2008) study were involved in developing and scheduling learning labs for students as an additional period for reading instruction and changing schedules so that teachers at a specific grade level could meet together. As summarized in Leithwood and colleagues (2004), administrators cannot do the job alone; they need the contributions of others, including literacy coaches, to help them conceptualize, implement, and evaluate their literacy programs.

The Guiding Principle in Action. As Ben Jackman, a literacy coach in a rural elementary school, reviewed the reading test scores of the fifth-grade students, he noted that many of these students were having difficulty with reading comprehension. He also observed differences between their comprehension of narrative text as compared with informational text. Given that the teachers had identified improvement in reading comprehension as one of the key goals for the school year, Ben knew they would want to address these results. Although he had talked informally with individual fifth-grade teachers about teaching comprehension, Ben felt that teachers needed to see the data across classrooms and to begin thinking as a group about reasons for the lack of improvement. This could be an important professional development experience for these teachers.

After the meeting, Ben began to think about the teachers' suggestion that more time be allocated in the reading block for meeting with small groups and for discussions that called for higher levels of thinking. Ben had promised the teachers that he would model such a discussion for them. In addition, he would work with the principal to identify possible modifications to the current schedule that would allow time for meeting with small groups and then discuss those options with the teachers. By helping teachers focus on one of the school's reading goals and by setting into action a series of steps that would build teacher knowledge and modify the schedule to allow for small-group work, Ben certainly demonstrated his role as a literacy leader.

Principle 7: Coaching Evolves Over Time

Some coaches who accept a coaching position do so with a great deal of teaching and collaborative experience; they enjoy working with adults and have excellent leadership and interpersonal skills in addition to having in-depth knowledge about literacy and instruction. On the other hand, some new coaches begin their role with little experience in working with other adults, even though they may be experienced teachers. Moreover, there may be little structure or direction for them, given the newness of the position. These coaches, faced with an uncertain agenda and some tentativeness about their role, may have a more difficult journey as they learn on the job. But both sets of coaches continue to learn, develop positive relationships with teachers, and modify what they do as they evolve as literacy coaches.

What Can Be Learned From the Research?

In a study of coaches from districts in Pennsylvania that received Reading First grants

(Bean & Zigmond, 2007), the 30 coaches who completed logs in the first year of Reading First funding and then again in the third year changed significantly in how they allocated their time. There were significant decreases over those years in the percentage of time they allocated to assessing students, entering and analyzing data, and attending professional development sessions. On the other hand, there were significant increases in time spent conferring with teachers, observing in classrooms, and coteaching. The coaches also spent significantly more time providing professional development to groups of teachers in their schools.

Although coaches spent significantly less time planning and organizing, there was a significant increase in the time allocated to administrative tasks, such as scheduling and providing materials for testing, distributing and organizing instructional resources, and copying materials needed by teachers. This increase in administrative duties seemed to be a reflection of the demands of the Reading First grant with its reporting expectations as well as the fact that school leadership often relied on coaches to handle various administrative responsibilities. Overall, however, coaches seemed to allocate more time to working directly to support teachers during the third year than in the first year on the job.

The Guiding Principle in Action. Ben Jackman was looking forward to another busy day of coaching. He had structured his day so that he could be in each third-grade teacher's classroom for 30 minutes. The teacher would be conducting a guided reading group; the reading teacher would also be in the classroom, working with a small group; and Ben's responsibility, as agreed upon by the teachers, would be to observe the teachers' guided reading groups and monitor the students working independently so that he could talk with the teachers about what they thought went well, their concerns, and possible next steps.

The plan to schedule these classroom visits and follow-up conversations with the third-grade team was made by the teachers and Ben after they had reviewed the progress monitoring data last week. In 15 minutes, they had planned and organized the activities. What a difference a year makes! Ben thought back to his initial attempts last year as a new coach. Even after looking at test data, teachers seemed hesitant about his suggestion that he visit their classrooms to get a sense of how the students were doing. It seemed as though it took several months before teachers were willing to trust that he was there to support their efforts. And even then, he reflected, it was not until he had worked closely and successfully with Molly O'Day, the lead teacher in third grade, that the other members of the team seemed to become more comfortable with him. Finally, he was easily able to schedule individual and group coaching activities because the teachers saw them as opportunities to discuss students' needs and the instructional practices that would address those needs. Coaching was so much more effective and rewarding now, he thought.

Discussion and Conclusions

The number of literacy coaches in elementary schools is increasing, and this offers great promise in terms of improving teacher practice and student reading achievement. To fulfill this promise, literacy coaches and administrators who hire them can benefit from guidance regarding the qualifications, activities, and roles of literacy coaches. The guiding principles in this article offer research-based suggestions for literacy coaching.

First and foremost, literacy coaches must have specialized knowledge that goes beyond just knowing how to teach reading well; they must also understand how to work effectively with adults. Additionally, literacy coaches need to spend at least half of their time working directly with teachers because when literacy coaches are working directly with teachers, they are more likely to produce positive growth in teacher practice and in student learning. Furthermore, literacy coaches must develop productive working relationships with the teachers they coach. Such relationships are the foundation for all coaching work; therefore, building trust, maintaining confidentiality, and communicating effectively with teachers must be primary considerations for literacy coaches.

In addition, literacy coaches must prioritize the activities they implement so that they focus on research-based practices associated with student achievement gains. Namely, coaches are more likely to produce student reading achievement gains in the classrooms where they coach when they focus on conferencing with teachers, administering and discussing assessments with teachers, observing classroom instruction and offering supportive feedback, and modeling instruction in classrooms. Literacy coaches also need to balance intentional coaching with opportunistic coaching to make the best use of their time and to support teachers in meaningful and relevant ways. Additionally, literacy coaches must view themselves and be viewed by others in their schools as literacy leaders who set goals and directions for the literacy program, support teachers and other school personnel in providing high quality literacy instruction for all students, and redesigning the school organization to meet literacy goals. Finally, because literacy coaching evolves over time; educators must be patient and mindful of the goals of coaching while providing time for new literacy coaches to lay the foundation for their coaching work.

As the coaching stories about Amanda, Selena, Geraldine, and Ben illustrate, literacy coaching is a complex process. We believe these seven research-based guidelines will help literacy coaches make decisions and enact practices that will have the greatest impact on classroom instruction and student reading achievement.

References

Bean, R.M., Belcastro, B., Draper, J., Jackson, V., Jenkins, K., Vandermolen, J., et al. (2008). *Literacy coaching in Reading First schools: The blind men and the elephant.* Paper presented at the National Reading Conference, Orlando, FL.

Bean, R.M., Jenkins, K., Belcastro, B., Wilson, R., Turner, G., & Zigmond, N. (2007, December). *What reading coaches do and why they do it: A diary study.* Paper presented at the National Reading Conference, Austin, TX.

Bean, R.M., Swan, A.L., & Knaub, R. (2003). Reading specialists in schools with exemplary reading programs: Functional, versatile, and prepared. *The Reading Teacher, 56*(5), 446–455.

Bean, R.M., & Zigmond, N. (2007, March). *The work of coaches in Reading First schools and their roles in professional development.* Presentation at American Educational Research Association Conference, Chicago, IL.

Bernhardt, V.L. (2008). *Data, data everywhere: Bringing all the data together for continuous school improvement.* Larchmont, NY: Eye on Education.

Biancarosa, G., Bryk, A., & Dexter, E. (2008, April). *Assessing the value-added effects of Literacy Collaborative professional development on student learning.* Paper presented at the meeting of the American Educational Research Association, New York, NY.

Blachowicz, C.L.Z., Obrochta, C., & Fogelberg, E. (2005). Literacy coaching for change. *Educational Leadership, 62*(6), 55–58.

Casey, K. (2006). *Literacy coaching: The essentials.* Portsmouth, NH: Heinemann.

Costa, A.L., & Garmston, R.J. (1994). *Cognitive coaching: A foundation for Renaissance Schools.* Norwood, MA: Christopher-Gordon.

Deussen, T., Coskie, T., Robinson, L., & Autio, E. (2007). *"Coach" can mean many things: Five categories of literacy coaches in Reading First* (Issues & Answers Report, REL 2007-No. 005). Washington, DC: U.S. Department of Education, Institute of Education Sciences, National Center for Education Evaluation and Regional Assistance, Regional Educational Laboratory Northwest. Retrieved July 5, 2007, from ies.ed.gov/ncee/edlabs/regions/northwest/pdf/REL_2007005.pdf

Dole, J.A. (2004). The changing role of the reading specialist in school reform. *The Reading Teacher, 57*(5), 462–471. doi:10.1598/RT.57.5.6

Elish-Piper, L.A., & L'Allier, S.K. (2007, December). *Does literacy coaching make a difference? The effects of literacy coaching on reading achievement in grades K–3 in a Reading First district.* Paper presented at the annual conference of the National Reading Conference, Austin, TX.

Flaherty, J. (2005). *Coaching: Evoking excellence in others* (2nd ed.). Burlington, MA: Elsevier Butterworth-Heinemann.

Froelich, K.S., & Puig, E.A. (2010). *The literacy leadership team: Sustaining and expanding success.* Boston: Pearson/Allyn & Bacon.

Frost, S., & Bean, R. (2006, September). *Qualifications for literacy coaches: Achieving the gold standard.* Retrieved March 20, 2009, from www.literacycoachingonline.org/briefs/LiteracyCoaching.pdf

Gibson, S.A. (2006). Lesson observation and feedback: The practice of an expert reading coach. *Reading Research and Instruction, 45*(4), 295–318.

International Reading Association. (2004). *The role and qualifications of the reading coach in the United States. A position statement of the International Reading Association.* Newark, DE: International Reading Association.

Kise, J.A.G. (2006). *Differentiated coaching: A framework for helping teachers change.* Thousand Oaks, CA: Corwin.

Knight, J. (2006). Instructional coaching: Eight factors for realizing better classroom teaching through support, feedback and intensive, individualized professional learning. *School Administrator, 63*(4), 36–40.

Knight, J. (2009). What can we do about teacher resistance? *Phi Delta Kappan, 90*(7), 508–513.

Knowles, M.S. (1984). *Andragogy in action: Applying modern principles of adult learning.* San Francisco: Jossey Bass.

L'Allier, S.K., & Elish-Piper, L. (2006, December). *An initial examination of the effects of literacy coaching on student achievement in reading in grades K–3.* Paper presented at the annual conference of the National Reading Conference, Los Angeles, CA.

L'Allier, S.K., & Elish-Piper, L. (2009, May). *Literacy coaching in three school districts: Examining the effects of literacy coaching on student reading achievement.* Paper presented at the annual conference of the International Reading Association, Minneapolis, MN.

Leithwood, K., Louis, K.S., Anderson, S., & Wahlstrom, K. (2004). *Review of research: How leadership influences student learning.* Minneapolis: Center for Applied Research and Educational Improvement (University of Minnesota); Toronto: Ontario Institute for Studies in Education at the University of Toronto.

McCombs, J.S., & Marsh, J.A. (2009). Lessons for boosting the effectiveness of reading coaches. *Phi Delta Kappan, 90*(7), 501–507.

Neufeld, B., & Roper, D. (2003). *Coaching: A strategy for developing institutional capacity—Promises and practicalities.* Washington, DC: Aspen Institute Program on Education; Providence, RI: Annenberg Institute for School Reform. Retrieved June 28, 2007, from www.annenberginstitute.org/pdf/Coaching.pdf

Perkins, S.J. (1998). On becoming a peer coach: Practices, identities, and beliefs of inexperienced coaches. *Journal of Curriculum and Supervision, 13*(3), 235–254.

Poglinco, S.M., Bach, A.J., Hovde, K., Rosenblum, S., Saunders, M., & Supovitz, J.A. (2003). *The heart of the matter: The coaching model in America's choice schools.* Philadelphia: University of Pennsylvania Consortium for Policy Research in Education.

Quatroche, D.J., & Wepner, S.B. (2008). Developing reading specialists as leaders: New directions for program development. *Literacy Research and Instruction, 47*(2), 99–115. doi:10.1080/19388070701878816

Rainville, K.N., & Jones, S. (2008). Situated identities: Power and positioning in the work of a literacy coach. *The Reading Teacher, 61*(6), 440–448. doi:10.1598/RT.61.6.1

Roller, C.M. (2006). *Reading and literacy coaches: Report on hiring requirements and duties survey.* Newark, DE: International Reading Association.

Showers, B. (1984). *Peer coaching: A strategy for facilitating transfer of training.* Eugene, OR: Center for Educational Policy and Management.

Toll, C.A. (2005). *The literacy coach's survival guide: Essential questions and practical answers.* Newark, DE: International Reading Association.

Toll, C.A. (2006). *The literacy coach's desk reference: Processes and perspectives for effective coaching.* Urbana, IL: National Council of Teachers of English.

Vanderberg, M., & Stephens, D. (2009, January). *What teachers say they changed because of their coach and how they think their coach helped them.* Retrieved March 31, 2009, from www.literacycoachingonline.org/briefs/what_teachers_say_about_coaching_1.2.09.pdf

Walpole, S., & Blamey, K.L. (2008). Elementary literacy coaches: The reality of dual roles. *The Reading Teacher, 62*(3), 222–231. doi:10.1598/RT.62.3.4

To Have or Not to Have? Factors That Influence District Decisions About Literacy Coaches

Melinda Mangin

Across the nation, from large urban centers to small rural districts, many schools have turned to literacy coaching as a means to improve teaching and learning. While much has been written about the advantages of having a literacy coach on staff (Moran, 2007; Toll, 2005; Walpole & McKenna, 2004) and there has been some research on school-level coaching practices (Mangin & Stoelinga, 2008) little attention has been paid to the factors that influence the decision to have a literacy coach.

To better understand the decision-making process, I spent three years learning from district-level administrators in 20 Midwestern school districts that were considering hiring, and in some cases, already had hired, literacy coaches as part of their instructional improvement strategy (Mangin, 2009). These 20, demographically diverse districts were part of the same regional district, which actively advocated for literacy coach roles and provided free professional development on literacy coaching to any interested district. All 20 districts took advantage of this training opportunity, sending teachers, principals, reading specialists, department chairs, and other educators to learn about literacy coaching. Not all districts, however, decided to add a literacy coach to their staff. My on-going conversations, surveys, and annual interviews with district administrators in the 20 districts provided insights into the factors that influenced districts' decisions about literacy coaches.

Factors That Positively Influenced District Decisions About Literacy Coaches

Districts' interest in literacy coaches was positively influenced by three factors: state and national reform contexts; student performance data; and existing roles and programs.

Pressure to Improve as a Result of State and National Reform Contexts

At the national level, these pressures included compliance with standardized testing regulations, yearly progress measures, and teachers' subject area qualifications. At the state level, accountability pressures included compliance with new curriculum standards, school improvement frameworks, accreditation regulations, new graduation requirements, and increased focus on student performance. These pressures led districts to consider literacy coach roles as a way to facilitate compliance with national and state mandates and to raise student achievement.

Identified Need for Coaching Due to Low Student Performance Data

Low student performance on standardized assessments was another factor that caused districts to consider literacy coaches. One assistant superintendent explained that low achievement had galvanized her district to develop coach roles: "When you have half your kids not making it, gosh that's a wakeup call." Districts realized that disaggregated test scores revealed areas of weakness that could be addressed with the support of a literacy coach. The literacy coach could work with teachers to identify students' needs and target areas for instructional improvement for the end goal of improving student performance.

Exposure to Coaching Through Existing Roles and Programs

Literacy coaches were more likely to be added to a school or district if teachers had been exposed to coaching practices as a result of other roles and programs in their schools: cognitive coaches, curriculum coaches, or restructuring coaches. Similarly, where reading specialists performed coaching functions or schools had successfully implemented professional learning communities characterized by collaboration and dialog, the teachers were more receptive to coaching. As a result, these districts were more likely to add a literacy coach to their staff.

Factors That Negatively Influenced District Decisions About Literacy Coaches

Districts' interest in literacy coaches was negatively influenced by three factors: limited finances; satisfactory student performance data; and existing roles and programs.

Limited Finances for New Initiatives

All 20 districts reported that the state's economic situation had resulted in budget shortfalls and spending cutbacks which decreased funding and made it difficult to introduce new initiatives. Half of the districts reported that the lack of funds prevented them from adding literacy coaches to their staffs. As one administrator explained, "We haven't been in the position of adding new programs or new services." Faced with limited resources, all of the districts had to make choices about the kinds of reforms they could implement, prompting half the districts to reject literacy coaching as a feasible improvement strategy.

Satisfactory Student Performance

In a quarter of the districts, aggregated test score data served as a disincentive for the implementation of literacy coach roles. In these districts, satisfactory test scores made it difficult for district leaders to make a case for coaching—there was no apparent need to improve instruction. An administrator in one such district explained the following:

> We perform pretty well and the reason we do is because we have pretty affluent children. So when you have 90% or 95% of your kids at the elementary level passing the reading [test], it's pretty difficult to say we need to improve. Now, we're not scoring that well across the board…But we haven't done a very good job of putting that data in front of teachers.

Thus, aggregated test scores projected satisfactory student performance, reducing the perceived need for literacy coaching.

Reluctance to Eliminate Existing Roles and Programs

In half the districts, long-standing roles such as reading specialist and para-professional were described as hindering district efforts to hire literacy coaches. Teachers had come to rely on reading specialists and para-professionals to work with under-performing students. In many cases, reading specialists and para-professionals were deeply institutionalized members of the school and local communities. Administrators were reluctant to eliminate the positions and the idea of assigning coaching responsibilities to these existing roles was not easily translated into practice. As one administrator explained, "They don't want to give up their kids. They don't feel confident enough that they can coach others."

How Districts Capitalized on Facilitating Factors and Reduced Constraints

Districts that capitalized on the factors that facilitated literacy coach roles and deemphasized the constraining factors were more likely to implement literacy coach initiatives. On the contrary, districts that focused on the constraining factors failed to implement literacy coach roles despite the supports they received from the regional district. In addition, districts that chose to have literacy coaches:

- *Prioritized student learning.* National and state mandates that focused on improving student achievement served as an impetus to direct improvement efforts toward increasing student learning. Districts recognized the need to do things differently, examine long-standing practices, and question their assumptions about how to best improve teaching and learning.

- *Pledged to help all students.* Districts rejected the notion that aggregated test scores were an adequate measure of individual student performance and actively sought to identify areas for improvement. Using disaggregated student performance data allowed districts to better understand their instructional strengths and weaknesses. Data were viewed as a formative source of information that could provide insights into areas for improvement, not as a tool for casting blame. As such, all students were the target of instructional improvement efforts.

- *Recognized the collective responsibility for improvement.* In a departure from traditional student support services where select teachers (such as reading specialists) were responsible for underperforming students, all teachers were viewed as sharing responsibility for all students. Teachers could no longer subscribe to a "fix the kid" mentality and send low achievers out of the classroom for instruction. Classroom teachers had to take responsibility for helping all students learn.

- *Prioritized teacher learning.* Recognition that all teachers would need to take responsibility for all students led districts to more actively support teachers' learning. Districts worked to strengthen opportunities for content-area professional development and put structures in place that would facilitate school-embedded professional development. Building teachers' instructional capacity was understood as a key component to increasing student learning.

- *Promoted coaching practices as a means to improvement.* Districts worked to promote coaching practices and to provide teachers with on-going learning opportunities by taking advantage of in-house expertise and building teachers' understanding of literacy coaching. By providing teachers with time to observe and model in each other's classrooms and to engage in critical conversation about instructional practices, districts worked to strengthen teachers' comfort with coaching and their receptivity to literacy coach roles.

- *Reallocated finances to reflect new priorities.* Districts demonstrated a willingness to shift resources to focus on new priorities. In particular, districts with growing populations of under-achieving students examined the capacity of existing reading specialist and para-professional roles to service large numbers of students. Following Elmore's contention that "(T)he money is there. The problem is that it's already spent on other things" (p. 27), these districts worked to reallocate resources toward the twin priorities of teacher and student learning. In almost all cases, this included shifting resources away from, and sometimes eliminating, other programs and initiatives.

Conclusion

While it may be important to focus on facilitating factors, the factors that constrain literacy coach implementation should not be trivialized or ignored. Financial constraints are very real and can seriously limit school improvement efforts. Likewise, reading specialists and para-professional roles should not be discarded lightly, particularly given the heavy investments many schools and districts make in developing these roles. At the same time, districts should carefully attend to improvement indicators from disaggregated student performance data. Doing so can help districts focus on real needs and pose difficult questions about how resources are being used, how they might be optimized, and what kinds of changes might need to occur. Ultimately, however, districts that commit to literacy coaching will need to build and emphasize the facilitative factors described here.

References

Elmore, R. F. (2002). *Bridging the gap between standards and achievement: Report on the imperative for professional development in education.* Washington, DC: Albert Shanker Institute.

Mangin, M. M. (2009, under review). Literacy coach role implementation: How district context influences reform. *Educational Administration Quarterly.*

Mangin, M. M., & Stoelinga, S. R. (Eds.). (2008) *Effective Teacher Leadership: Using Research to Inform and Reform.* New York: Teachers College Press.

Moran, M. C. (2007). *Differentiated literacy coaching: Scaffolding for student and teacher success.* Alexandria, VA: Association for Supervision and Curriculum Development.

Toll, C. A. (2005). *The literacy coach's survival guide: Essential questions and practical answers.* Newark, DE: International Reading Association

Walpole, S., & McKenna, M.C. (2004). *The literacy coach's handbook: A guide to research-based practice.* New York: Guilford.

The School Board Wants to Know:
Why Literacy Coaching?

Rita M. Bean and William Isler

School board members, teachers, university faculty, school district administrators, and even literacy coaches themselves often have questions about literacy coaching. These questions generally focus on several major issues: What should literacy coaches do? What qualifications should they possess? Is the cost worth it? A key question often revolves around what evidence there is to support the presence of coaches in schools.

The two questions related to cost and cost-benefit are ones that school board members often ask when faced with a proposal to support literacy coaching in schools. When asked for such funding, they often ask, "Why don't teachers have the knowledge they need to teach their students; didn't universities and colleges do their job of preparing teachers?" "Why aren't coaches working with students rather than with teachers?" "Why money for literacy coaching; we need support for the band or athletics, or...?" "What do I tell my constituents when they ask about the cost?"

As a member of the Pittsburgh Public School Board, Mr. Isler has heard these and other questions. He recognizes the need to inform school boards and the citizenry about what coaching is and how it can serve as a means for improving student achievement. The purpose of this brief is to provide information for school boards and administrators to help them understand literacy coaching. We address three major questions: What is literacy coaching? Why is there a need for coaching in the schools? What evidence do we have that it works? We conclude by discussing three key points that are essential if a coaching plan is to be implemented in a school.

What Is Literacy Coaching?

Literacy coaching is defined most often as a job-embedded approach to professional development (Shanklin, 2006). Such professional development is based on what teachers need to know in order to teach their students, is literacy-focused, and provides on-going support that may include classroom observations and feedback to teachers. There is evidence that this type of professional development (AERA, 2005; Joyce & Showers, 2002) is more effective than the more traditional one-day or short-term workshops often seen in schools. In the one day format, teachers may come together once for a large workshop on a specific topic, i.e., small group reading instruction. In the short term format, districts may schedule meetings during which consultants provide an overview of a new curricular framework or reading program. These consultants who oversee these meetings may make follow-up visits to schools to respond to teacher questions.

However, one day or even multi-day workshops often do not provide the support teachers need to help them think more reflectively about how they can improve instruction to better meet the needs of students in their classrooms. Literacy Coaches provide this long-term support. They can co-plan, co-teach, model, or observe and provide feedback to support teacher learning; they can lead study groups or hold large group workshops.

Preparing Reading Professionals (second edition), edited by Rita M. Bean, Natalie Heisey, and Cathy M. Roller. © 2010 by the International Reading Association. Reprinted from Bean, R., & Isler, W. (2008, July 26). *The school board wants to know: Why literacy coaching?* Retrieved from www.literacycoachingonline.org/briefs/SchoolBoardBrief.pdf

In other words, Literacy Coaches can help teachers achieve their short-term goals of learning how to implement a specific program or instructional strategy and their long-term goals of becoming more effective literacy teachers.

Literacy coaches are professionals who know their content area, have classroom experience, possess excellent interpersonal and communication skills, and know how to work effectively with adults (Frost & Bean, 2006; International Reading Association, 2004). Literacy coaches are often selected from within the school, have a strong literacy background, and are known to be effective teachers; they also have great credibility with their peers. They work in a non-evaluative, non-judgmental manner to provide support to teachers who are attempting to try new approaches to teaching or to differentiate instruction so that the needs of all students are met. Coaches are there to work cooperatively and collaboratively with teachers to solve problems that teachers may face. Coaches help teachers with such goals as how to (a) meet the needs of students who can't read the content textbook, (b) create more active engagement in the classroom, and (c) differentiate reading instruction in a specific classroom, given the identified needs and abilities of students. They are there to help teachers at all levels (Pre-K through grade 12) become better at their craft and to improve student learning.

But Why Literacy Coaching?

Shouldn't teachers have the skills and competencies they need upon graduation from teacher preparation programs? The job of Colleges of Education is to provide schools with effective first year teachers. These teachers though are novices and, like other professionals, need on-going professional development to move from novice to expert. The initial years of teaching provide the basis for the development of that expertise—expertise that cannot possibly be learned in the several years of coursework and field experiences provided in any teacher preparation program. Coaching for these novice teachers is money well spent. With coaching feedback, these young teachers become experts more quickly.

Coaches also provide on-going professional development for experienced teachers and help them increase their knowledge base about how to teach reading (PreK-12), and about differentiating instruction within the classroom.

Increasing Teachers' Understanding of How to Teach Reading

In the last twenty years and particularly in the last decade, there has been an increase in knowledge about how to teach reading. This new knowledge has created a need for ongoing learning by teachers. For example, research at the adolescent level has helped us understand that teachers in the various disciplines can be more effective if they know how to help students read their textbook effectively and know how to create classrooms in which instruction is not just lecture-based, but draws on various collaborative, social activities, and builds on prior knowledge of students (Biancarosa & Snow, 2004; Conley, 2008; Sturdevant, et al., 2006). At the elementary level, the field has come to understand that one-size does not fit all (National Reading Panel Report, 2000) and that teachers need to understand their students as readers and teach to those needs.

Increasing Teachers' Knowledge of How to Differentiate Instruction

Schools today are more heterogeneous than ever and all stakeholders are increasingly more cognizant of the responsibility to educate every one of the students in the school, e.g., students from diverse racial, ethnic and socio-economic backgrounds, English Language learners, and students who range in abilities from the gifted to those identified as special-needs. Response to intervention guidelines (RTI) require schools to initiate practices that provide for differentiated instruction in classrooms. There is ample research which demonstrates ways to meet the needs of all students and teachers need to learn these new ways to address the multiple demands of the students they meet each day.

Does Literacy Coaching "Work"?

As some say, "this is the million dollar question." There are several ways to answer this question: we can ask teachers (self-report), we can look at teacher and classroom practices, and finally, we can try to relate achievement improvement directly to coaching in the school. Obviously, the gold standard would be relating coaching to student achievement, and that is the hope of many researchers studying this approach to professional development. However, this is complex, given the many other factors that may be contributing to student achievement, e.g., new reading programs, increases in time allotted to reading instruction in schools, more use of data to modify instruction, small class size, etc., and it will take researchers some time to answer this question of coaching and its influence on student achievement.

At the same time, we do have evidence that gives us much hope in terms of the power of coaching. First, teachers do report that coaching is valuable and helps them to do their job better (Bean, et al., 2008; Brown, et al, 2007; Neufeld & Roper, 2006). Such findings exist at the elementary and secondary levels. For example, in the Pennsylvania High School Coaching Initiative (PAHSCI), English and math teachers who participated in the program reported benefits from their participation in the project (Brown, et al., 2007), including increased levels of student engagement and improved teaching.

We also have evidence that teachers who have been coached are changing their practices in positive ways (Bean, et al, 2008). These include such practices as increasing the numbers of high-level thinking questions being asked, more active engagement of students, and increased ability to make adaptations in academic materials and skills.

Key Points

In sum, what are the key points for administrators and school board members if they decide that literacy coaching is a worthwhile investment and decide to implement such a program in their schools? We believe the following three points are essential.

- Collaboration. A literacy coaching program must be developed collaboratively. Administrators should consult with key teachers, union representatives, and school board members, to discuss and come to a consensus about key issues such as the qualifications and roles of coaches. Building job descriptions that help all understand the role is critical.

- Support. Various types of support are essential. Principals must help coaches by designing school schedules that provide them with the time to work with teachers; they must serve as "cheerleaders" for coaches to help them establish good working relationships with teachers. Moreover, coaches within a district need opportunities to network and continue to learn their craft. And there is a need for fiscal support, so that the coaches have the resources needed to accomplish their goals.

- On-going evaluation and assessment. When a district commits to a coaching program, it needs also to commit to an on-going evaluation effort that is both formative and summative. Formative data, which includes providing feedback to coaches about how to improve their performance, is essential. Summative data, which addresses questions about changes in teacher practices and student achievement, will help the school district make future decisions about how to make the literacy coaching program as effective as possible.

References

American Educational Research Association. (2005). *Research points: Teaching teachers: Professional development to improve students' achievement* [Brochure, *3*(1)]. Washington, D.C.: Author.

Bean, R. M., Belcastro, B., Hathaway, J., Risko, V., Rosemary, C. & Roskos, K. (2008). *A review of the research on instructional coaching.* Paper presented at the American Educational Research Association Conference, New York.

Bean, R. M., Turner, G., Draper, J., Heisey, N., & Zigmond, N. (2008, March). *Coaching and its contribution* to reading achievement in Reading First schools. Paper presented at American Educational Research Conference, New York.

Biancarosa, G., & Snow, C. (2004). *Reading next—A vision for action and research in middle and high school literacy: A report from Carnegie Corporation of New York.* Washington, DC: Alliance for Excellent Education.

Brown, D., Reumann-Moore, R., Hugh, R., Christman, J. B., Riffer, M., duPlessis, P., Maluk, H.P. (2007). *Making a difference: Year two reports of the Pennsylvania high school coaching initiatives.* Philadelphia: Research for Action.

Conley, M. W. (2008, Spring). Cognitive strategy instruction for adolescents: What we know about the promise, what we don't know about the potential. *Harvard Educational Review, 78*(1), 84-106.

Frost, S. & Bean, R. M. (2006, September). *Qualifications for literacy coaches: Achieving the gold standard.* Retrieved June 29, 2008, from www.literacycoaching online.org

International Reading Association. (2004). *The role and qualifications of the reading coach in the United States: A position statement of the International Reading Association* [Brochure]. Newark, DE: Author.

Joyce, B. & Showers, B. (2002). *Student achievement through staff development.* Alexandria, VA: Association for Supervision and Curriculum Development.

National Reading Panel. (2000). *Teaching children to read: An evidence-based assessment of the scientific research literature on reading and its implications for reading instruction.* Rockville, MD: National Institute of Child Health and Human Development.

Neufeld, B., & Roper, D. (2006). *Summary of the report: Instructional improvement in the Boston Public Schools: 1996–2006.* Available at www.renniecenter .org/research_docs/Summary-Instruction.pdf

Shanklin, N. (2006, September). *What are the characteristics of effective literacy coaching?* Retrieved June 29, 2008, from http://www.literacycoachingonline.org

Sturtevant, E., Boyd, F. B., Brozo,W. G., Hinchman, K.A., Moore,D.W., & Alvermann, D.E. (2006). *Principled practices for adolescent literacy: A framework for instruction and policy.* Mahwah, N.J.: Lawrence Erlbaum Associates.